ROUTLEDGE HANDBOOK OF THE FUTURE OF WARFARE

This handbook provides a comprehensive, problem-driven and dynamic overview of the future of warfare.

The volatilities and uncertainties of the global security environment raise timely and important questions about the future of humanity's oldest occupation: war. This volume addresses these questions through a collection of cutting-edge contributions by leading scholars in the field. Its overall focus is prognostic rather than futuristic, highlighting discernible trends, key developments and themes without downplaying the lessons from the past. By making the past meet the present in order to envision the future, the handbook offers a diversified outlook on the future of warfare, which will be indispensable for researchers, students and military practitioners alike. The volume is divided into six thematic sections. Section I draws out general trends in the phenomenon of war and sketches the most significant developments, from the past to the present and into the future. Section II looks at the areas and domains which actively shape the future of warfare. Section III engages with the main theories and conceptions of warfare, capturing those attributes of contemporary conflicts which will most likely persist and determine the dynamics and directions of their transformations. The fourth section addresses differentiation and complexity in the domain of warfare, pointing to those factors which will exert a strong impact on the structure and properties of that domain. Section V focuses on technology as the principal trigger of changes and alterations in the essence of warfare. The final section draws on the general trends identified in Section I and sheds light on how those trends have manifested in specific local contexts. This section zooms in on particular geographies which are seen and anticipated as hotbeds where future warfare will most likely assume its shape and reveal its true colours.

This book will be of great interest to students of strategic studies, defence studies, war and technology, and International Relations.

Artur Gruszczak is a Professor of Social Sciences and Chair of National Security at Jagiellonian University in Krakow, Poland. He is the author/editor of three books, including *Technology, Ethics and the Protocols of Modern War*, co-edited with Pawel Frankowski (Routledge 2018).

Sebastian Kaempf is a Senior Lecturer in Peace and Conflict Studies at the School of Political Science and International Studies at the University of Queensland, Australia. He is the author of *Saving Soldiers or Civilians* (Cambridge University Press 2018).

ROUTLEDGE HANDBOOK OF THE FUTURE OF WARFARE

Edited by
Artur Gruszczak and Sebastian Kaempf

LONDON AND NEW YORK

Cover image: Getty Images © Aleksandra Malysheva

First published 2024
by Routledge
4 Park Square, Milton Park, Abingdon, Oxon OX14 4RN

and by Routledge
605 Third Avenue, New York, NY 10158

Routledge is an imprint of the Taylor & Francis Group, an informa business

© 2024 selection and editorial matter, Artur Gruszczak and Sebastian Kaempf;
individual chapters, the contributors

British Library Cataloguing-in-Publication Data
A catalogue record for this book is available from the British Library

Library of Congress Cataloging-in-Publication Data
Names: Gruszczak, Artur, 1965– editor. | Kaempf, Sebastian, editor.
Title: Routledge handbook of the future of warfare / edited by
Artur Gruszczak and Sebastian Kaempf.
Description: Abingdon, Oxon; New York, NY: Routledge, 2024. |
Includes bibliographical references and index.
Identifiers: LCCN 2023011055 (print) | LCCN 2023011056 (ebook) |
ISBN 9781032288901 (hardback) | ISBN 9781032288994 (paperback) |
ISBN 9781003299011 (ebook)
Subjects: LCSH: War—Forecasting. | Military art and science—Forecasting. |
Military art and science—Technological innovations. | Security,
Internatonal.
Classification: LCC U21.2 .R673 2024 (print) | LCC U21.2 (ebook) |
DDC 355.02—dc23/eng/20230627
LC record available at https://lccn.loc.gov/2023011055
LC ebook record available at https://lccn.loc.gov/2023011056

ISBN: 978-1-032-28890-1 (hbk)
ISBN: 978-1-032-28899-4 (pbk)
ISBN: 978-1-003-29901-1 (ebk)

DOI: 10.4324/9781003299011

Typeset in Times New Roman
by codeMantra

CONTENTS

FIGURES

TABLES

CONTRIBUTORS

Rubén Arcos is a Senior Lecturer in Communication Sciences at University Rey Juan Carlos. He serves as the Vice-Chair of the Intelligence Studies Section at the International Studies Association (ISA). His research is focused on intelligence services and intelligence analysis, foreign disinformation, and hybrid threats. He has been appointed national member for the NATO Science & Technology Organization's exploratory group SAS-ET-FG 'Prediction and Intelligence Analysis'.

Ivan Arreguín-Toft is a Research Associate in the International Security Program at Harvard's Kennedy School of Government, Harvard University, and a US Army military intelligence veteran. He is the author of *How the Weak Win Wars: A Theory of Asymmetric Conflict* (Cambridge University Press 2005) and is currently working to complete an empirical inquiry into the utility of barbarism: the deliberate harm of noncombatants as a strategy in war or military occupation. His most recent publications focus on asymmetric conflict dynamics in emerging technologies (AI, autonomous weapons) and great power competition.

Jonathan Luke Austin is an Assistant Professor of International Relations at the University of Copenhagen and Director of the Centre for Advanced Security Theory. He also currently leads 'The Future of Humanitarian Design' (with Javier Fernandez Contreras and Anna Leander) research project, as well as a wider agenda on International Political Design. More broadly, his work explores the global dynamics of political violence, the design of emerging technologies and the material-aesthetics of political phenomena.

Alex J. Bellamy is a Professor of Peace and Conflict Studies and Director of the Asia-Pacific Centre for the Responsibility to Protect at the University of Queensland, Australia. A Fellow of the Academy of Social Sciences in Australia, he has been a consultant to the United Nations and Visiting Fellow at the University of Oxford. His most recent books are *Syria Betrayed: War, Atrocities, and the Failure of International Diplomacy* (Columbia 2022) and *Warmonger: Vladimir Putin's Imperial Wars* (Agenda 2023).

Dani Belo is an Assistant Professor of International Relations at Webster University in St. Louis, MO, USA. His research focuses on grey-zone conflicts, non-state actors in hybrid warfare, transatlantic security, grand strategy of middle powers, the evolution of NATO–Russia relations, ethnic conflicts and nationalism in the post-Soviet region. Dani also served as an analyst for the Government of Canada. His research on unconventional conflicts was featured at the US Army Judge Advocate General's Legal Center and School, the Royal Military College of Canada, University of Pennsylvania Law School Center for Ethics and the Rule of Law, Columbia University Harriman Institute, the Global Centre for Pluralism (Ottawa) and the European Commission.

Lauren J. Borja is a Fellow at the Center for Global Security Research (CGSR) at Lawrence Livermore National Laboratory. Her research focuses on high-energy laser directed energy weapons. She was a 2019–2020 Stanton Nuclear Security postdoctoral fellow at the Center for International Security and Cooperation at Stanford University and a Simons postdoctoral fellow at the University of British Columbia's School of Public Policy and Global Affairs from 2017 to 2019. In 2016, she received her PhD from the University of California, Berkeley in Physical Chemistry.

Antoine Bousquet is an Associate Professor at the Swedish Defence University, Stockholm. His principal research focus is on the relation of science, technology and war. He is the author of *The Eye of War* (2018) and *The Scientific Way of Warfare* (2009). He has contributed an array of peer-reviewed articles and book chapters on subjects that include Cold War computing, the revolution in military affairs, jihadist networks, complexity theory, violent aesthetics and the conceptualization of war. He is currently writing a research monograph on the advent of nuclear weapons as an event in thought.

David Carment is a Professor of International Affairs at Carleton University. He is also a series editor for Palgrave's Canada and International Affairs, editor of *Canadian Foreign Policy Journal* and Fellow of the Canadian Global Affairs Institute. David's research focuses on Canadian foreign policy, mediation and negotiation, fragile states and diaspora politics. He is the author, editor or co-editor of 21 books and has authored or co-authored over 90 peer-reviewed journal articles and book chapters. His most recent books focus on diaspora cooperation, corruption in Canada, branding Canadian foreign policy and state fragility. In 2017, Carment was a visiting scholar at the World Institute for Development Economics Research, Finland, and in 2015 a Fellow at the Centre for Global Cooperation Research, Germany.

Helena Salim de Castro is a PhD student in International Relations. Her research interests include gender studies, criminality and drug policy. She is an Associate Researcher at the Defence and International Security Study Group (GEDES) and the Centre for Transnational Security Studies (NETS). She has published an article in the *Oxford Research Encyclopedia of Politics* titled 'The Drug Policy in the Americas from a Gender Perspective'. Her recent publications have appeared in journals such as *Conjuntura Austral: Journal of the Global South* and *Monções*.

Lindsay Clark is a Lecturer in International Relations at the University of Sussex. Lindsay's interests are in the politics of gender in warfare, feminist International Relations, creative methodologies and science and technology studies. She has published a monograph, *Gender and Drone Warfare: A Hauntological Approach* with Routledge, and articles in journals including the *Feminist Journal of International Politics* and *Security Dialogue*.

Christopher Coker is the Director of LSE IDEAS, the foreign policy think tank of the LSE. He is also Professor Emeritus in International Relations Department, LSE. He is the author of 20 other books including *Why War?* (Hurst 2021); *The Rise of the Civilisational State* (Polity, 2017); *Rebooting Clausewitz* (Hurst 2016) and *Barbarous Philosophers: Reflections on the Nature of War* (Hurst, 2010).

Marek Czajkowski is a Professor in the Department of National Security of the Jagiellonian University in Kraków. His research focuses on international security, including human activities in outer space in the security context, the military aspect of international relations and Russia's security policy and strategy. The most recent book, published in 2020, is *Outer Space in the National Security Strategy of the USA*.

James Der Derian is the Michael Hintze Chair of International Security and Director of the Centre of International Security Studies at the University of Sydney. He writes books and makes documentaries on war, peace, media and technology, including *After 9/11* (2003), *Virtuous War: Mapping the Military-Industrial-Media-Entertainment Network* (2009), *Critical Practices in International Theory* (2009), *Human Terrain: War Becomes Academic* (2010), *Project Z: The Final Global Event* (2015) and *Quantum International Relations: A Human Science for World Politics* (co-edited with Alexander Wendt, 2022). He is currently working on a book and documentary film, *Project Q: War, Peace and Quantum Mechanics*.

Angélica Durán-Martínez is an Associate Professor of Political Science at the University of Massachusetts-Lowell. She is the author of the award-winning book *The Politics of Drug Violence: Criminals, Cops, and Politicians in Colombia and Mexico* (Oxford University Press 2018). Her research focuses on organized crime, political and criminal violence, and the state in Latin America. Her research appears in numerous book chapters and journals including *Comparative Political Studies*, *Journal of Conflict Resolution*, *Journal of Peace Research*, *Latin American Politics and Society*, *Comparative Political Studies* and *Crime, Law and Social Change*.

Enrico Fels is the Managing Director of the Center for Advanced Security, Strategic and Integration Studies (CASSIS) at Bonn University. His research interests include traditional and non-traditional security studies, international political economics and the strategic consequences of a rising Asia. He has frequently published about current and future strategic matters and authored as well as co-edited several books including *Shifting Power in Asia-Pacific? The Rise of China, Sino-US Competition and Regional Middle Power Allegiance* (Springer 2018). Dr Fels was a Visiting Fellow at the Australian National University and held visiting lectureships at the University of Tokyo (Tōdai) and the Andrássy University Budapest.

Anastasia Filippidou is a Senior Lecturer and Programme Director of the MSc Counterterrorism at the Cranfield Forensic Institute, Cranfield University. Her research and publications focus on terrorism, intelligence and conflict resolution. Some of her recent publications have appeared in journals such as *Terrorism and Political Violence, Behavioural Sciences of Terrorism and Political Aggression*. She is the author/editor of *Deterrence: Concepts and Approaches for Current and Emerging Threats* (2020). She has professionally engaged with a variety of governmental departments in the United Kingdom and abroad, including the Ministry of Defence, NATO, law enforcement and security forces in Lebanon, Palestine, Uruguay, Morocco and Pakistan.

Artur Gruszczak is a Professor of Social Sciences, holding the Chair in National Security at the Faculty of International and Political Studies, Jagiellonian University in Kraków. He is an expert at the Centre International de Formation Européenne in Nice. His current research interests include the evolution of warfare, intelligence cooperation and security protocolarization. He is the author of *Intelligence Security in the European Union. Building a Strategic Intelligence Community* (Palgrave Macmillan 2016) and co-editor of *Technology, Ethics and the Protocols of Modern War* (Routledge 2018).

Beatrice Heuser holds the Chair in International Relations at the University of Glasgow. Her research interests turn around war and strategy, and her major publications include *The Evolution of Strategy* (CUP 2010) and *War: A Genealogy of Western Ideas and Practices* (OUP 2022). She has also published more specifically on nuclear strategy and on patterns of insurgencies and counterinsurgency, and on culture (national mentalities) and strategy. Professor Heuser is currently seconded to the General Staff College of the Bundeswehr in Hamburg as Director of Strategy.

Iveta Hlouchova is a Professor in the School of International Relations at the University of New York in Prague (UNYP) where she also works as a research manager, overseeing institutional research. Her research focuses on security policy and strategy development, (counter)insurgency, (counter)terrorism, NATO and privatization of security. She is the author of numerous articles and a monograph titled *Czech Approach toward Counterinsurgency.* She has extensive experience working in civil-military environments.

Daniela Irrera is an Associate Professor of International Relations at the University of Catania and Professor of Political Violence and Terrorism at the OSCE Academy in Bishkek. Her research focuses on non-state actors' influence on global politics, both positive (civil society movements, NGOs) and negative (organized crime groups, terrorists). She is the co-editor of the Springer Book Series on Non-state Actors in International Relations. She has published in *Global Crime, Perspectives in European Politics and Society, European Security, European Foreign Affairs Review.*

Joachim Isacsson is a Swedish Colonel embedded at the UK MOD Development, Concepts and Doctrine Centre where he co-leads the Futures team and the Global Strategic Trends programme, which provides an analysis of characteristics of plausible future worlds 30 years from now to support forward looking strategy and policy development.

Sebastian Kaempf is a Senior Lecturer in Peace and Conflict Studies at the University of Queensland. His research and teaching interests include international security, ethics and the laws of war, and information technology relating to global politics and violent conflict. He has published a book with Cambridge University Press in 2018 titled *Saving Soldiers or Civilians? Casualty-aversion versus Civilian Protection in Asymmetric Conflicts.* Some of his recent publications have appeared in *EJIR, Social Identities* and *Australian Journal of International Affairs.*

Mary Kaldor is a Professor Emeritus of Global Governance and Director of the Conflict and Civicness Research Group within PeaceRep at the London School of Economics. She has pioneered the concepts of new wars and global civil society. Her elaboration of the real-world implementation of human security has directly influenced European and national governments. She is the author of many books and articles including *New and Old Wars: Organised Violence in a Global Era* (3rd edition, 2012), *International Law and New Wars* (with Christine Chinkin, 2017) and *Global Security Cultures* (2018).

Łukasz Kamieński is an Associate Professor at the Faculty of International and Political Studies at the Jagiellonian University in Kraków. His research concentrates on military technology and military transformation, the history and the future of war, and biotechnology and military human enhancement. He is an author of *Shooting Up. A Short History of Drugs and War* (OUP 2016). His publications appeared in journals such as *Armed Forces and Society*, *Journal of Military Ethics* and *Perspectives on Politics*.

Vicky Karyoti is a Post-doctoral Researcher at the Swedish Institute of International Affairs. Her research focuses on the impact of new military technologies on defence cooperation. Other research interests include international security, military sociology and ethics of militarized AI. She has contributed to edited volumes with Routledge such as *European Strategic Autonomy and Small States' Security*, as well as publishing in the French Air and Space Force's journal *Vortex*.

David Kilcullen is a Professor of International and Political Studies at UNSW Canberra, Professor of Practice in Global Security at Arizona State University and CEO of the analysis firm Cordillera Applications Group. Professor Kilcullen is a theorist and practitioner of guerrilla and unconventional warfare, counterinsurgency and counterterrorism, with operational experience over 25 years with the Australian and US governments as a light infantry officer, intelligence analyst, policy adviser and diplomat. He served in Iraq as senior counterinsurgency advisor to Multinational Force Iraq, then as senior counterterrorism advisor to Secretary of State Condoleezza Rice, deploying to Afghanistan, Pakistan, Somalia, Libya and Colombia. He is the author of seven books and numerous scholarly papers on terrorism, insurgency, urbanization and future warfare, and was awarded the 2015 Walkley Award for his reporting on the rise of Islamic State. He heads the Future Operations Research Group at UNSW Canberra, and teaches contemporary strategy, special operations, urban warfare, military innovation and adaptation. He has led several concept-design projects for US and allied governments on risk prediction, resilience and counterterrorism. He works with advanced research agencies in the United States, Canada, and the United Kingdom on technology, artificial intelligence and future conflict.

Elke Krahmann is a Professor of International Relations at the University of Kiel, Germany. She has published widely on the privatization of security, global governance and international norms in journals such as *Security Dialogue*, *European Journal of International Relations*, *International Affairs*, and *Cooperation and Conflict*. Her book *States, Citizens and the Privatization of Security* (CUP 2010) was awarded the Ernst-Otto Czempiel Prize for best monograph in Peace and Conflict Studies.

Mark Lacy is a Senior Lecturer in the Department of Politics, Philosophy and Religion at Lancaster University. He has published in *Review of International Studies*, *Millennium*, *Alternatives* and *Contributions to Indian Sociology*. He is lead editor of *Routledge Studies in Conflict, Security and Technology* and author of *Theorising Future Conflict: War Out to 2049* (Routledge 2024) and a chapter on design and security in the textbook edited by Kyle Grayson and Xavier Guillaume, *Security Studies: Critical Perspectives* (OUP 2023). Mark's research interests focus on the changing character of war, the military design movement, science fiction and international politics, the work of Paul Virilio.

Andrew N. Liaropoulos is an Assistant Professor in the University of Piraeus, Department of International and European Studies, Greece. He earned his Master's degree in Intelligence and Strategic Studies at Aberystwyth University and his Doctorate Diploma at Swansea University. His research interests include international security, intelligence reform, strategy, European security, foreign policy analysis, cybersecurity and information warfare. Dr Liaropoulos is also a Senior

Analyst in the Research Institute for European and American Studies (RIEAS) and a member of the editorial board of the *Journal of Information Warfare* (JIW).

Tanner Mirrlees is the Director of Communication and Digital Media Studies at Ontario Tech University. Some of Tanner's current research interests include the globalization of the US and China's digital media and cultural industries and new technology, militainment and the future of warfare. Tanner is the author of *Global Entertainment Media: Between Cultural Imperialism and Cultural Globalization* (Routledge) and *Hearts and Mines: The US Empire's Culture Industry* (UBC Press), and the co-editor of *Media Imperialism: Continuity and Change* (Rowman & Littlefield) and a special issue of *Democratic Communiqué* entitled 'Media, Technology, and the Culture of Militarism'.

Valerie Morkevičius is an Associate Professor in Political Science at Colgate University. Her work focuses on the intersection between strategy and ethics, and the applicability of traditional just war thinking to contemporary challenges. She is the author of *Realist Ethics: Just War Traditions as Power Politics* (CUP 2018). She has published in journals such as *Ethics and International Affairs*, *Journal of Military Ethics* and *International Studies Quarterly*. Her most recent research explores the ethical implications of disinformation and artificial intelligence.

Rain Ottis is a Professor of Cyber Operations and the Head of the Centre for Digital Forensics and Cyber Security in Tallinn University of Technology. Previously he has served at the NATO Cooperative Cyber Defence Centre of Excellence and the Estonian Defence Forces. His research interests include cyber conflict, national cyber security and cyber security exercises.

Iavor Rangelov is a Research Fellow at LSE IDEAS, London School of Economics and Political Science. His research interests include human rights, human security, justice and civic activism. He is the author of *Nationalism and the Rule of Law: Lessons from the Balkans and Beyond* (CUP 2014) and has published in journals such as *Journal of Human Rights, Conflict, Security & Development*, *London Review of International Law* and *Global Policy*. He is co-founder of the Civic Ecosystems Initiative.

Vladimir Rauta is a Lecturer in Politics and International Relations at the University of Reading, United Kingdom, and one of the editors of the forthcoming *Routledge Handbook of Proxy Wars*.

Neil C. Renic is a Researcher at the Centre for Military Studies at the University of Copenhagen. He is also a Fellow at the Institute for Peace Research and Security Policy at the University of Hamburg. His current work focuses on the changing character and regulation of armed conflict, and emerging military technologies such as armed drones and autonomous weapons. He is the author of *Asymmetric Killing: Risk Avoidance, Just War, and the Warrior Ethos* (OUP 2020). Neil's work has also featured in journals such as the *European Journal of International Relations*, *Ethics and International Affairs*, *International Relations*, *Survival* and the *Journal of Military Ethics*.

Sebastiaan Rietjens is a full Professor of Intelligence & Security at the Netherlands Defence Academy and holds the special Chair of Intelligence in War & Conflict at Leiden University. His main research focus is on intelligence during military operations, peacekeeping intelligence, warning for hybrid threats and future developments that confront intelligence organizations. Sebastiaan is a member of the editorial boards of *Armed Forces and Society* and the *International Journal* *of Intelligence & Counterintelligence*, board member of the Netherlands Intelligence Studies Association (NISA) and editor of several volumes including the *Routledge Handbook of Research Methods in Military Studies* (Routledge 2014).

Stuart Rollo is a Postdoctoral Research Fellow at the Centre for International Security Studies at the University of Sydney, currently working on the centre's Quantum Meta-Ethics project. His research focuses on geopolitics, imperial history and the US-China relationship. He writes regularly on international affairs, politics and cultural issues in global media. His latest book is *Terminus: Westward Expansion, China, and the End of American Empire.*

Lauren Sanders is a Senior Research Fellow with the University of Queensland's Law and Future of War project. Lauren's research and teaching interests include international criminal law, international humanitarian law and counterterrorism law. She is the editor of the University of Queensland's Law and Future of War podcast and publishes on the application of the law to emerging and disruptive military technologies with journals such as the *Journal of Conflict and Security Law*. She has extensive experience as a military legal officer and legal practitioner in applying international law to the use and development of new technologies.

Olivier Schmitt is a Professor (with special responsibilities) at the Center for War Studies, University of Southern Denmark. His research interests include multinational military operations, military power, European security and the transformation of armed forces. He is the author *of Allies that Count. Junior Partners in Coalition Warfare* (Georgetown UP 2018), and of *French Defence Policy since the End of the Cold War* (Routledge 2020, with Alice Pannier).

Elke Schwarz is a Reader in Political Theory at Queen Mary University, London. Her research focuses on the intersection of ethics of war and ethics of technology with an emphasis on unmanned and autonomous/intelligent military technologies and their impact on the politics of contemporary warfare. She is the author of *Death Machines: The Ethics of Violent Technologies* (Manchester University Press). Her work has also been published in a range of philosophical and security focused journals, including *Philosophy Today, Security Dialogue, Critical Studies on Terrorism* and the *Journal of International Political Theory* among others.

Paweł Ścigaj is an Assistant Professor at the Faculty of International and Political Studies at the Jagiellonian University in Kraków. His research and teaching interests include political violence, dehumanization and rehumanization, intergroup relations and intergroup hostility. He has published on political psychology and political theory.

David Snetselaar is a PhD candidate in Conflict Studies at the Netherlands Defence Academy and at Utrecht University. He is writing his dissertation on the perception of hybrid threats that has emerged in Europe over the past two decades and the concrete responses this has triggered in various policy areas. These policy areas include international research and innovation, telecommunication networks and transportation infrastructure. David's research has been published in *European Security* (2022), *NATO Review* (2022) and the edited volume *Space of War, War of Spaces* (2020).

Samuel Alves Soares is an Associate Professor at San Tiago Graduate Program in International Relations at São Paulo State University. Former president of the Brazilian Defence Studies

Association, Samuel's research and teaching interests include the use of force and forms of violence, futures studies and international relations theory. He has published, among others, the book *Controls and Autonomy: the Armed Forces and the Brazilian Political System* and articles on his research topics. He has done post-doctoral studies at Georgetown University. In addition, he is a researcher at the National Council for Research and Development (Brazil).

Giuseppe Spatafora is a PhD candidate in International Relations at the University of Oxford. His research and policy interests include the international dimensions of civil wars, proxy wars, military interventions and alliances. Giuseppe served as the Vice-President of the Oxford University Strategic Studies Group and is an alumnus of the SWAMOS workshop at Cornell.

David P. Succi Junior is a Postdoctoral Researcher at the Institute of Public Policies and International Relations (IPPRI) of the São Paulo State University (UNESP). His research interests include critical security studies, violence and legitimacy, civil-military relations and future studies in International Relations. He is an Associated Researcher at the Defense and International Security Study Group (GEDES) and the Group for Elaboration of Scenarios and Future Studies (GECEF). His recent publications have appeared in journals such as *Armed Forces and Society* and *Studies in Conflict and Terrorism*.

Olaf Theiler is a Historian and Political Scientist working for the German Armed Forces. He has lectured for the University of Arts in Berlin and the Bundeswehr Academy for Information and Communication and was a national expert in NATO-HQ Brussels. His current profession is long-term future analysis and strategic foresight. Dr Theiler has published on NATO, transatlantic relations, German security policy and strategic foresight.

Amelie Theussen is an Associate Professor at the Royal Danish Defense College. Her interdisciplinary research focuses on the effects of changes to war and warfare on international legal and political norms regulating the use of force. Additionally, she writes about German and Danish defence and security policy, and Arctic and Baltic Sea security. Amelie also designs and conducts award winning simulation games and exercises for universities and military institutions. Her work has been published among others with Brookings and Chatham House, Routledge, Palgrave and in *International Politics* and the *British Journal of Educational Technology*.

Sanne Cornelia J. Verschuren is a Marie Sklodowska-Curie Postdoctoral Fellow with the Center for International Studies at Sciences Po, funded by the European Union (grant agreement number 101027421). In September 2023, she will start as an Assistant Professor of International Security at the Frederick S. Pardee School of Global Studies, Boston University. Her research focuses on the development of military technology, states' understanding of core strategic concepts and the intersection between nuclear and conventional capabilities.

Thomas Waldman is a Senior Lecturer in Security Studies at Loughborough University. His most recent book published by Bristol University Press is titled *Vicarious Warfare: American Military Strategy and the Illusion of War on the Cheap*. Tom has published widely on war, strategy, statebuilding and the research-policy nexus in journals such as *International Affairs, Survival, Contemporary Security Policy, Defence Studies, Parameters, Civil Wars, Journal of Statebuilding and Intervention,* and *Conflict, Security and Development*. He is a member of the editorial board of the journal *Contemporary Security Studies* and the Palgrave book series 'Studies in Contemporary Warfare'.

Austin Wyatt is an Associate Researcher at RAND Australia. His research focuses on military transformation, remote and autonomous systems, military applications of AI, and regional security. Austin's publications include a number of academic research articles in journals such as *Defence Studies*, *Australian Journal of International Affairs* and *Journal of Indo-Pacific Affairs*, as well as a book entitled *Exploring the Disruptive Implications of Lethal Autonomous Weapons Systems in Southeast Asia*.

INTRODUCTION

Gazing into the Future of Warfare

Artur Gruszczak and Sebastian Kaempf

The future of warfare has become one of the most hotly debated topics amongst academics, militaries, and policy makers alike. Previously held assumptions about war's nature, logic, and shape are being questioned with a new urgency. In part, this has been triggered by the (subjectively felt *and* objectively verified) proliferation and intensification of violence over the past one and a half decades. Yet, there is also a clear sense that warfare is currently undergoing an accelerated transformation, morphing and diversifying into wider and perhaps novel forms, from hybrid, compound, mosaic, unrestricted, three-block, to surrogate, vicarious, postmodern and chaoplexic. At the same time, recent innovations in military technology and weapon systems, aimed at rendering the use of kinetic force more effective, have also been found to be limited in the context of seemingly ever more protracted local wars or against the emergence of new types of actors and warfighting methods. Adding to these uncertainties, the transformation of information technology and global communication networks has begun to further accelerate and colour the conduct of war. The Syrian civil war, the Taliban takeover in Afghanistan, the failure of allied operations in Iraq and Russia's military invasion of Ukraine, to name just a few, have provoked debates over the utility of high technologies and the effectiveness of psychological warfare, communication and morale. Concurrently, the volatilities and uncertainties of the global security environment raise timely and important questions about the future of humanity's oldest occupation: war. What have been the most pertinent trends and developments in warfare? How are they interfering with politics, society, culture and technology? And what can they tell us about the future of warfare? Discussing these questions is the objective of this Handbook.

Addressing the complexities of contemporary and future warfare

Contemporary security studies have significantly expanded since the beginning of the 21st century, encompassing today a much wider range of fields which are oftentimes linked together on an interdisciplinary basis. Military science and theories of warfare have been enriched by novel methodologies and new directions in the study of warfare determined by ethical, environmental, cultural, psychological and technological factors. The broadening of the knowledge about the causes, nature and logics of war has contributed to the growing interest in the future of warfare stimulated by theoretical debates, practical needs and anticipatory models. Strategic foresight,

DOI: 10.4324/9781003299011-1

military tunnelling and agnostic solutions are just a few concepts which recently have acquired a new meaning and application to the study of warfare. They illustrate accelerating trends in the research and applications of current forms and features of warfare, which to a considerable extent aim to satisfy the growing interest in the military aspects of security. Politicians, managers, military commanders, journalists, scholars and students have expressed their eagerness in studying and elaborating on the transformation of contemporary warfare and its implications for the future. This Handbook is a direct response to that interest and provides a comprehensive, problem-driven and dynamic gaze into the future of warfare, which builds on predominant trends and highlights potentially far-reaching implications.

Analysing the essence of warfare and gazing into its future is a challenging task. It requires a comprehensive take on the nature of war and insights into varieties of warfare that manifest themselves in ever changing security environments and contexts. And yet, the imposing legacy of the study of the art of war with its historically grounded insights into armed conflicts of the past cannot be brushed aside. Debates on power politics and relevant military potentials put the emphasis on competition and rivalry in the international arena. The probability of a wide-range and full-scale confrontation between regional or global powers (or pretenders to such status) has never been eliminated. The memory of great wars and their devastating consequences raise the problem of risks and threats to peace, stability and people's well-being. Social, cultural and economic factors add up to the sources of turmoil, unrest and violence. The inspiration coming from indigenous, grass-root elements is often lurking behind local rebellions, organised crime and terrorism. Tensions and cleavages in societies or local communities undermine political regimes and question the legitimacy of state authorities. Armed violence is too often chosen as the means of last resort, and military might ultimately seems to be the only effective way to attain strategic goals.

In this context, reflections on the use of force and the nature of warfare need to address both the causes of war and the patterns, methods, tools and intensity of warfare. The causes of war can be located at various levels of social and political organisation of contemporary states and societies. The essence of warfare can be captured in the complex connectivities that exist between ideas, actors, structures and instruments which seek to justify and drive armed violence. Bellicosity has been determined by violent intergroup conflicts, as well as opportunities created by human innovation, technological progress and production capacities (industrialisation). And many of the effects of technological leverage have been augmented by a strong belief in the decisive role of the application of military technologies in warfare. It is these constellations, for instance, that have underpinned the Revolution in Military Affairs (RMA) – and later net-centric warfare – as a fundamental concept stimulating the transformation of military systems and modern warfare in the late 20th century (at least for Western militaries). The RMA was propagated as a paradigm shift in military organisation, strategic culture and political strategy essential for acquiring foreknowledge of the possible directions of the transformation of warfare in the future. And yet, the proactive and anticipatory aspects of the RMA brought about some unexpected consequences. Technological predominance was counterbalanced by extremist behaviour of organised rebels who turned the asymmetry of warfare to their advantage. Relatively simple, not to say primitive, methods of unrestricted violence applied by irregular forces or organised mobs proved effective enough to counter the armed forces of states and force them to give up in the long run. The cases of Somalia, Iraq and Afghanistan questioned the belief in the absolute dominance of high-tech military systems in warfare and signified a bifurcation of pathways to the future of warfare. Irrespective of the widening gap between sophisticated high-tech military systems and primitive methods and tools of armed

2

violence, the processual logic of the evolution of warfare entailed the emergence and proliferation of unconventional forms of military confrontation, which in turn has questioned much of our traditional understanding of war and peace.

Already in the 1990s, Christopher Coker contemplated irony as a feature of the post-Cold War era in which war and peace overlap, where the main objective was not to win, but to contain and manage the fighting, where militaries were not fully conscious of the true change in the nature of war, and where the victorious side often felt worse off than the defeated enemy (Coker 1998). More recently developed concepts such as 'nonwar wars' (McFate 2019), 'liminal warfare' (Kilcullen 2019) or 'unpeace' (Kello 2017) added a certain amount of scepticism to traditional ways of thinking about war and peace, the conventional security paradigm and warfare itself. These kinds of provocative propositions about the nature of warfare raise important questions as to the evolution of contemporary forms of warfare and the extent to which they will shape states' policies, social dynamics and individual behaviours. They posit that the trends which can be noticed at present should not be disregarded, even if they could be bucked or reversed in the future. Recently, Frans Osinga convincingly discussed the paradoxes of the study of contemporary wars, calling for warfare to be put back into the societal discourse in order to "regain the frame of reference so that we can understand this tragic phenomenon in all its facets […]" (Osinga 2021, p. 31). Such a ramification needs to encompass war as a predominantly human construct which has shaped our destiny. In times to come, war will be recurrently explored as part of our human condition and warfare will be appraised as an expression of organisational and technological progress geared towards the maximum efficient use of violence.

The rationale behind studying the future of warfare

We began our work on this handbook in late 2021 in an uncertain yet apparently predictable security environment. We were aware of the worsening of the international security situation, evidenced by the findings of leading think tanks, such as the International Institute of Security Studies (IISS 2022), the Stockholm Peace Research Institute (SIPRI 2022) or the Centre for Strategic and International Studies (CSIS 2022). The intensification of regional and local conflicts (especially in Syria, Ukraine, Yemen, Afghanistan, Myanmar, in the Sahel region, the Horn of Africa and the Asia-Pacific), the growing defence expenditures and increasing competition over advanced military technologies, as well as the nuclear programmes by North Korea and Iran were already key developments that robbed many security experts of their sleep. On a geostrategic level, the revisionist policies of China and Russia concerning the global security system and balance of power extended much beyond the defiant posture of rogue states, such as Iran and North Korea. And the worldwide campaign against the COVID-19 pandemic further exposed the weaknesses and vulnerabilities of today's global security environment.

We also felt a growing concern over the weaponisation of 'new' domains of warfare, such as cyber space, artificial intelligence, quantum sciences and a renewed weaponisation of outer space. These activities in many ways seem to bolster the capabilities of not only great powers, but also middle countries. What is more, non-state military actors have also shown increasing signs of becoming involved in these same mechanisms of weaponisation, exploiting states' weaknesses and shortcomings, or acting as proxies, willing to avail themselves of the state-driven outsourcing of some forms of warfare. Added to this, the widespread production and circulation of information via social media and wireless communications have generated new vulnerabilities and opportunities for propaganda and mis/dis-information in warfare.

This disquieting account of the state of international security and the questions it raised about the future of warfare then gained an additional urgency due to the largely unexpected Russian military aggression against Ukraine in February 2022. Despite the growing tensions between the two states following the 2014 Russian-sponsored secession of two Ukrainian eastern provinces and the annexation of Crimea, the probability of a full-scale invasion of Ukraine took most experts by surprise. Some projections, as Robert A Johnson wrote,

> [...] Dismissed as absurd by contemporaries, proved accurate in time. Selection, exaggeration, absurdity, contemporary fears and preferences, misunderstanding, and misplaced long-range forecasts were the characteristics of predicting future war in the past, and all these traits still dominate the present.
>
> (Johnson 2014, p. 66)

It is this broader context that re-energised today's debates about the future of warfare with a new urgency. And our Handbook is a direct response to this urgency, seeking to facilitate fresh and thoughtful insights into what current trends and developments mean for the future of warfare. And yet, gazing into the future of warfare is difficult. It requires an analytical journey across various generations of war, faring through today's turbulent violent landscapes and detecting signs of what might lie ahead in the years to come. At the same time, we must remain cautious not to belittle the classical theories of warfare and the relevance of the art of war. In many ways, the complexity and intricacy of the nature of war have not changed much over millennia. Similarly, the role of technology, information, organisation and morale remains as important today as it has been in recent and ancient pasts. And yet, contemporary warfighting and its future applications display a clear tendency to the widening of tactics, methods and tools (weapons) which exert a growing impact on political, economic and social systems. Even though the major ongoing military conflicts, such as the Russo-Ukrainian war and the Syrian civil war, can be perceived as 'blasts from the past', they prove that today's warfare is unfolding in an increasingly complex environment saturated with advanced technologies, massive information flows, as well as widespread surveillance and intelligence activities. These factors will most likely determine the planning and conduct of military operations in the future. However, moral, cultural and irrational aspects of warfare, manifested by friction, the infamous 'fog of war', contingencies and aggressiveness, are unlikely to disappear. Apart from that, the economy of warfare will depend on trade-offs between a nation's prosperity and sacrifice for the military build-up. Under the conditions of asymmetry between the sides of a military conflict, an effective warfare may be conceived as an art to make use of cheap technologies for reaching high-value targets.

Contemporary warfare therefore needs to be seen in a broad and varied context. First, it encompasses traditional forms of warfighting, engaging state and non-state armed groups in the four classical military domains: land, sea, air and space. Second, it stretches these classical domains out by applying modern technologies and weapons, such as unmanned vehicles, satellite telecommunications, electronic surveillance and AI-driven battlefield systems. Third, it increases the relevance of the human factor in beginning and escalating hostilities. Human emotions, fear and stress have been accompanying war activities for long (see Milevski 2020). Feelings of despair, vengeance and hatred used to modify human cognition and behaviour in war (see Zilincik 2022). War propaganda, disinformation and 'active measures' in the cognitive domain can sustainably determine the public attitudes towards warfare and be decisive regarding the termination of hostilities. Widespread and fast circulation of (dis)information via conventional broadcasting and electronic networks, especially Internet-based social media, may give a boost for warmongers or guarantee acquiescence to a protracted use of military force.

The shapes of wars to come, and their accompanying forms of warfare, are likely to reflect the complexity of human civilisation and the simplicity of human nature. They will encompass high technologies empowering infrastructure systems, dense networks of command, control and communication, as well as human-to-human and human-to-machine connectivities. Concurrently, they will epitomise primal instincts of humans, motivating both biological security needs (see Jaffe 2010) and predatory desires to conquering territories and reigning over the vanquished adversaries. Proclivity for savage and dehumanising treatment of the enemy seems to illustrate the dark side of the human nature. The contrast between technological achievements and primitive ways and means already has loomed large in asymmetric forms of warfare. Effectiveness of crude and brutal methods of violence, organised or not, may be a strong incentive for adversaries to engage in widespread and ferocious hostilities in the future, despite the terrible human toll and bloodshed.

State of the field

The *Routledge Handbook of the Future of Warfare* is the first comprehensive publication to provide some guidance to the debates and deliberations on the directions, trends and forms of warfare in the foreseeable future.

There are some handbooks that take up the issue of warfare either in general terms, making a general reference to war as an overarching phenomenon, or highlighting some of the relevant topics in war studies, such as technology, ethics and law. The first category may be illustrated by *The Oxford Handbook of* War (Boyer & Lindley-French 2012) and *The Ashgate Research Companion to Modern Warfare* (Kassimeris & Buckley 2010). The second one includes *The Routledge Handbook of War, Law and Technology* (Gow et al. 2019), *The Routledge Handbook of Ethics and War. Just War Theory in the Twenty-First Century* (Allhoff, Evans & Henschke 2013) and *The Handbook of Fifth-Generation Warfare (5GW)* (Abbott 2010). Some books on general security matters, such as *The Routledge Handbook of Security Studies* (Cavelty & Balzacq 2017) or *The Routledge Handbook of New Security Studies* (Burgess 2010) can be mentioned as well. While these existing handbooks are evidence of the need for and general interest in questions on the future of warfare, they are limited in two particular ways. First, given the speed at which changes in warfare are occurring, many of them are dated. Second, a number of them have narrowly focused on very pertinent but particular themes, such as technology or ethics/law. By contrast, our handbook engages with the most recent trends and state of research and in a thematically comprehensive manner.

As far as the evolution of war and the future of warfare are concerned, there are some valuable monographic books which present a specific individual vision of 'future war' based on historical, philosophical, ethical and technological premises. Examples of such books are: *The Future of War: The Re-Enchantment of War in the Twenty-First Century* (Coker 2004); *Future War* (Coker 2015); *Future War: Preparing for the New Global Battlefield* (Latiff 2017); *The Future of War: A History* (Freedman 2017); *Future War and the Defence of Europe* (Allen, Hodges & Lindley-French 2021); *The Future of US Warfare* (Romaniuk & Grice 2017); *The Future of War. Power, Technology and American World Dominance in the Twenty-first Century* (Friedman 1998). Recently, an inspiring and insightful volume framing military thought on the conduct of war in the 21st century was published by Routledge. *The Conduct of War in the 21st Century. Kinetic, Connected and Synthetic* (Johnson, Kitzen & Sweijs 2021) depicts how military actions have been carried out since the beginning of the present century and contains many useful hints on thinking about defence policy and warfare in the future.

Some books explore the technological imperatives of the development of new autonomous weapon systems driven by artificial intelligence and equipped with high-tech sensors and shooters. Impressive examples are: *Research Handbook on Remote Warfare* (Ohlin 2019); *Genius Weapons. Artificial Intelligence, Autonomous Weaponry, and the Future of Warfare* (Del Monte 2018); *Army of None. Autonomous Weapons and the Future of War* (Scharre 2019); and *I, Warbot: The Dawn of Artificially Intelligent Conflict* (Payne 2021).

The topic of the future of warfare has also been explored by teams of analysts and experts affiliated with research centres. In 2014, the Emirates Center for Strategic Studies and Research published a book titled *The Future of Warfare in the Twenty First Century* (Emirates Center for Strategic Studies and Research 2014). It is a collection of nine research papers written by prominent international experts and researchers. Most recently, researchers participating in the RAND Corporations's AIR FORCE's Strategy and Doctrine Program launched *The Future of Warfare* series (RAND 2020). It focused on US strategic dilemmas examining the key trends that will shape the conflicts in the 2020s. It was dedicated to the US military although global trends were pinpointed and discussed as well.

What has been lacking in the field of military science and security studies has been a collection of newly written, up-to-date and cutting-edge contributions by leading scholars in the field. This Handbook seeks to fill this gap by not only documenting recent developments in research and scholarship, but also by identifying trends and stimulating reflections on warfare now and into the future.

Overview and core themes

The Handbook offers a comprehensive collection of thought-provoking chapters on key topics of contemporary research and debate about the future of warfare. They range from the principal features of the evolution of war to the more specific aspects of future warfare determined by a wide set of variables and themes. While insights into the complex nature of contemporary warfare are future-oriented, their predictive values are principally limited to the foreseeable future; hence, they are prognostic rather than futuristic. In other words, the chapters do not contain visions or fantasies about the shape of warfare to come. Instead, they highlight discernible trends, key developments and themes. At the same time, they do not downplay the lessons from the past. As Hanzi Freinacht (2020) stated: "The purpose of writing and studying history is to shape the future". Each chapter in this Handbook therefore exhibits the relevance of current events, processes and circumstances which create opportunities for the employment of future forms of violence. As a collection, the chapters are intended to make the past meet the present and then help navigate the journey into the future.

For us as Handbook editors, it was important to place the emphasis on diversity and equity in terms of contributors, approaches and themes. Admittedly, this was not an easy task, given the nature of the field of international security in general and studies of warfare in particular, which to this day tends to be dominated by white and privileged male academics based – mostly – at English-speaking universities. Regarding contributors, we have deliberately sought out up and coming early career scholars alongside senior and established academics. Nearly 50% of our chapters are written by a female (co)author. Many contributors are non-English mother tongue speakers and, in general terms, are spread all over the globe. Moreover, the Handbook does not follow one particular theoretical or epistemological approach, but encourages engagement from its contributors from a variety of perspectives and approaches. It is, at least more than any other publication in this field, a truly global engagement with the future of warfare.

The Handbook is divided into six sections. Section I ('Approaching Future Wars') draws out general trends occurring to the phenomenon of war. Written by some of the most eminent 'big picture' thinkers, this section sketches the most significant developments in war, from the past to the present and into the future. Sections II–VI then engage with the most pertinent and specific themes regarding the future of war. Section II ('Systemic Variables of the Future of Warfare') offers a glance at the areas and domains which actively shape the future of warfare. Section III ('Concepts and Theories of Future Warfare') engages with the main theories and conceptions of warfare, capturing those attributes of contemporary conflicts which most likely will persist and determine the dynamics and directions of their transformations. The fourth section ('Structural Complexity') addresses differentiation and complexity of the domain of warfare, pointing to those factors which will exert a strong impact on the structure and properties of that domain. Section V ('Technoscience') focuses on technology as the principal trigger of changes and alterations in the essence of warfare. The final section ('Harbingers of Future Warfare') draws on the general trends identified in Section I and sheds light on how those general trends have been manifesting themselves in specific local contexts. This section zooms in on some unique constellations and characteristics of violence which are currently emerging and that might therefore signal particular features of warfare which will most likely assume its shape and reveal their true colours.

References

Abbott, D H (ed) 2010, *The Handbook of Fifth-Generation Warfare (5GW)*, Nimble Books, Ann Arbor, MI.

Allen, J A, Hodges, F B & Lindley-French, J 2021, *Future War and the Defence of Europe*, Oxford University Press, Oxford.

Allhoff, F, Evans, N G & Henschke A (eds) 2013, *The Routledge Handbook of Ethics and War. Just War Theory in the Twenty-First Century*, Routledge, London & New York.

Boyer Y & Lindley-French J (eds) 2012, *The Oxford Handbook of War*, Oxford University Press, Oxford.

Burgess J P (ed) 2010, *The Routledge Handbook of New Security Studies*, Routledge, London & New York.

Cavelty, M D & Balzacq, T (eds) 2017, *The Routledge Handbook of Security Studies*, 2nd edn, Routledge, London & New York.

Coker, C 1998, 'Post-Modern War', *RUSI Journal*, vol. 143, no. 3, pp. 7–14.

Coker, C 2004, *The Future of War: The Re-Enchantment of War in the Twenty-First Century*, Blackwell Publishing, Malden, MA & Oxford.

Coker, C 2015, *Future War*, Polity, Cambridge & Malden, MA.

CSIS 2022, *Global Security Forum 2021. Softening Sharp Divides: Foreign Policy in an Era of Domestic Division*, Center for Strategic & International Studies, Washington, DC.

Del Monte, L A 2018, *Genius Weapons. Artificial Intelligence, Autonomous Weaponry, and the Future of Warfare*, Prometheus Books, Amherst, NY.

Emirates Center for Strategic Studies and Research 2014, *The Future of Warfare in the Twenty First Century*, Emirates Center for Strategic Studies and Research, Abu Dhabi.

Freedman, L 2017, *The Future of War: A History*, Public Affairs, New York.

Freinacht, H 2020, 'Introduction Chapter to the Next Hanzi Book: The 6 Hidden Patterns of History', *Metamoderna*, 20 August, <https://metamoderna.org/introduction-chapter-to-the-next-hanzi-book-the-6-hidden-patterns-of-history/> (accessed 16 September 2022).

Friedman G & M 1998, *The Future of War. Power, Technology and American World Dominance in the Twenty-first Century*, St. Martin's Griffin, New York.

Gow, J, Dijxhoorn, E, Kerr R & Verdirame, G (eds) 2019, *The Routledge Handbook of War*, Routledge, London & New York.

IISS 2022, *The Military Balance 2022*, The International Institute for Strategic Studies, London / Routledge, Abingdon.

Jaffe, M D 2010, *The Primal Instinct. How Biological Security Motivates Behavior, Promotes Morality, Determines Authority, and Explains Our Search for a God*, Rowman & Littlefield, Boulder, CO.

Johnson, R A 2014, 'Predicting Future War', *Parameters*, vol. 44, no. 1, pp. 65–76.

Johnson, R, Kitzen, M & Sweijs, T (eds) 2021, *The Conduct of War in the 21st Century. Kinetic, Connected and Synthetic*, Routledge, London & New York.

Kassimeris G & Buckley J (eds) 2010, *The Ashgate Research Companion to Modern Warfare*, Ashgate, Farnham & Burlington, VT.

Kello, L 2017, *The Virtual Weapon and International Order*, Yale University Press, New Haven, CT.

Kilcullen, D 2019, 'The Evolution of Unconventional Warfare', *Scandinavian Journal of Military Studies*, vol. 2, no. 1, pp. 61–71, https://doi.org/10.31374/sjms.35.

Latiff, R H 2017, *Future War: Preparing for the New Global Battlefield*, Alfred A Knopf, New York.

McFate, S 2019, *The New Rules of War: Victory in the Age of Durable Disorder*, William Morrow, New York.

Milevski, L 2020, 'Battle and its Emotional Effect in War Termination', *Comparative Strategy*, vol. 39, no. 6, pp. 535–48, https://doi.org/10.1080/01495933.2020.1826844.

Ohlin, J D (ed) 2019, *Research Handbook on Remote Warfare*, Edward Elgar, Cheltenham & Northampton, MA.

Osinga, F 2021, 'Strategic Underperformance. The West and Three Decades of War', in R Johnson, M Kitzen & T Sweijs (eds), *The Conduct of War in the 21st Century. Kinetic, Connected and Synthetic*, Routledge, London & New York, pp. 17–41.

Payne, K 2021, *I, Warbot: The Dawn of Artificially Intelligent Conflict*, Hurst, London.

RAND 2020, *The Future of Warfare Boxed Set*, RAND Corporation, Santa Monica, CA, https://doi.org/10.7249/RR2849.

Romaniuk, S N & Grice, F 2017, *The Future of US Warfare*, Routledge, London & New York.

Scharre, P 2019, *Army of None: Autonomous Weapons and the Future of War*, W.W. Norton, New York.

SIPRI 2022, *SIPRI Yearbook 2022. Armaments, Disarmament and International Security*, SIPRI, Stockholm / Oxford University Press, Oxford.

Zilincik, S 2022, 'The Role of Emotions in Military Strategy', *Texas National Security Review*, vol. 5, no. 2, pp. 11–25, http://dx.doi.org/10.26153/tsw/24029.

PART I

Approaching Future Wars

1

STRATEGIC FORESIGHT AND FUTURE WAR

A Discussion of Methodologies

Beatrice Heuser, Joachim Isacsson and Olaf Theiler

Introduction

This chapter, which stands alongside that of Mark Lacy to introduce this volume, discusses methodologies to serve the practical need to reflect on future potentialities. Due to all the complex drivers of change and the unpredictability of the human nature, we cannot predict events in the future with any kind of precision. Despite the efforts of generations of social scientists to claim otherwise, the consensus is growing again that forecasting – actual predictions of future developments – is very limited in verisimilitude, and for issues of war and peace or macro-economics will at best give some indications for the very short term. In its place, a tool-set has been developed that is referred to as foresight, generally flagging multiple possible developments and their consequences. Defence ministries around the world therefore employ specialists of 'strategic foresight' whose work is to be factored into decisions with long-term consequences.

Strategy and the futures dilemma

The future of war and the shape wars might take in the future are at the heart of military planning. This turns on making decisions about force structures, defence procurement, and many other choices, usually with a limited budget, necessitating prioritisation. This process of prioritising and choosing between options has been described as strategy making, ranging from the strategy for a particular concept to the drawing up of strategic concepts to guide policy making for several years.

Every decision is about the future. And far-reaching and consequential decisions have to be made by governments, commercial enterprises, institutions, and individuals alike. Not making a decision, postponing a decision, in itself amounts to a decision. All decisions are based on assumptions about what the future might bring, and how one's decision could have a positive impact on the future, deflecting unfavourable developments, encouraging or bringing about desirable developments. The valid critiques of oracles, astrology or 'scientific' forms of naïf positivism aside, decisions have to be based on some reasoned reflection regarding possibilities, developments, and outcomes.

To understand and work with the future presents a very specific challenge: the future has not yet happened. Therefore, the evidence for arguments about what the future might look like will inevitably be very different from facts-based traditional academic research, and always be open for questioning, particularly the further ahead you try you look: Why should I believe this? Which

 DOI: 10.4324/9781003299011-3

risks do I take by having my policies informed by this? What if we are getting it wrong? Our inability to predict it with any precision makes especially long-term future analysis easy to disregard because the present is a 'safer place' for analysis and the 'urgent' always trumps the 'important'.

All this comes back to how we humans think about the future, especially the more distant one, where our default image tends to be an extension of the present – 'more of the same'. This is mixed up with images and scenarios we pick up from all kinds of sources – especially those that are repeated over and over. Our ideas about the future are deeply intertwined with our understanding of the present, including our own individual hopes and fears, but also the strategic context in which we and our countries exist – our history, our experiences, our culture. This means that linear thinking, groupthink, and personal biases will always present major challenges to any objective future analysis and forward-looking strategy development.

To summarise, strategic foresight and forward-looking strategy and policy development need to find ways to deal with the following challenges:

- The deafening noise of the present in politics;
- The limits to the human cognitive ability to think about and anticipate the future.

These include:

- Confirmation bias: when we're scanning the horizon for trends and weak signals, we tend to pick up and remember the ones that confirm our pre-existing ideas about how the world works, and its trajectory;
- Our proclivity to use analytical shortcuts rather than to analyse each situation in all its detail (Buffet & Heuser 1998);
- Linear thinking – the tendency to project existing trends into the future, without consideration for ruptures or discontinuities;
- The plausibility trap: we tend to disregard developments that are considered implausible in our own times, until they become inevitable.
- The disinclination to contemplate events or actions of small likelihood.

'Futurists' do not claim they can predict the future, simply because of the unpredictability of human nature and the complexity of life. But we prepare better for the possibilities of the future. For that purpose, we need to enhance our understanding of the forces and the factors that drive change – and their implications when it comes to security and potentials for conflict and war. That is what strategic foresight is about – considering a multitude of possible futures and identifying key uncertainties in the context of strategy development within defence. In the end, this can also be defined as 'management of the unknown' or 'uncertainty management'. The ultimate purpose of any future analysis is always to relate the future back to the present and ask what we need to do today to prepare for the future, to put ourselves in a better place by adapting to change – and even to influence and shape the future into something we want it to be. In defence policy making, this is very much about understanding a future operating environment and character of future conflicts – and then ask how we best prepare to meet future security challenges. Any long-term strategy that does not take long-term change into account will fail to meet its objectives and fall apart, as the only thing we do know about the future is that it will not be linear, i.e. it will not simply be 'more of the same'.

The tools of strategic foresight

'Futures' or 'strategic foresight' are umbrella terms for a wide range of techniques and methodologies designed to think about possible futures – from Philip Tetlock's super forecasting tournaments (Schoemaker & Tetlock 2016, pp. 73–8) to the more sweeping, long-term global trends projects that analyse potential future world orders. It is an academic discipline, based on scientific methods, but primarily in the domain of practitioners, strategy developers, and policy planners.

There is a wealth of literature and schools of thoughts about methods for futures and strategic foresight analysis, which we have no space to cover in this brief review of methodologies. The key to how you approach your analysis is always its purpose and the needs of your stakeholders or customers. This requires you to understand the motivation and aims of those you are trying to inform and what you are trying to change – this includes the ecology of an organisation's thinking and strategy making. For the results of the analysis to be useful, it will need to be put into a context in which the implications of the analysis can be seen and used. There needs to be a strong and clear link between futures thinking and futures application, which is a broader strategic planning process issue. A vital part of the process is engagement with stakeholders to get them to understand and integrate the outcome of foresight analysis, without allowing the analysis to become guided by wishful thinking and already established policy objectives. This requires an organisational culture that allows for challenge and that understands what futures analysis can and cannot do.

The time-horizon that frames analysis is crucially important since it makes a real difference whether it is short-term *prediction* ('*forecasting*') or long-term *foresight* that is required. The former looks for signals, trends and their projections into the near future. Short-term predictions mostly fail to hit the mark when they are related to 'game changing' or 'disruptive' new technologies. They generally fail to account for the long timeframes for mature technology-development, the normally slow military adaptation as well as acquisition, and the time needed for their integration into new military doctrines that normally improve through trial and error, and then for application and testing in training before they can be practiced with reasonable chances of success. Therefore, the normal form of progress in the military realm is evolutionary and not revolutionary – although the latter exists, it is a much rarer occurrence in military history than most people would think (Heuser 2022, pp. 34–65).

The longer the stretch of time, the bigger the influence of other trends and events on projections. Therefore, any timeframe beyond two years excludes itself practically from any kind of forecast or prediction simply because the intervening variables become overwhelmingly influential. Thus, for longer term analysis, the focus changes from prediction to imagination, from forecast to foresight, from a single future projection to multiple future possibilities. In the latter context, *scenario building* is a useful way to emphasis the spread of potential futures or – differently phrased: better to manage uncertainty.

Given the complexity of futures analysis, when looking at the toolbox, it is important to understand that various methods complement and support each other. After defining the lead question and its context, *trend analysis* aims to understand the character of change – speed and magnitude, the drivers behind it, the actors involved. Identifying these are necessary steps to develop scenarios and games. These can complement a *trend process* with alternative developments, which in turn help to gain a better understanding of different dimensions of uncertainty and, therefore, is laying the foundations for assumptions, strategy, and policy options. The outcome of the analysis also tends to generate new tasks which are likely to require a combination of tools to fulfil them.

Any analysis will include data/evidence collection and processing used to support various insights and conclusions. This process is becoming increasingly computerised using algorithms, which allow an extensive scan of digital data with a high degree of precision and intelligent modelling of the data in a limited amount of time. This has become almost a science of its own with major resources spent on this by major military powers. The Intelligence Advanced Research Projects Activity (IARPA)'s Mercury project is an example of a US Intelligence project using computational techniques to forecast political violence. The project examines whether automated analysis applied to secret intelligence sources can deliver forecasts with higher accuracy and faster lead-time compared to open-source databases. In established futures teams, data and evidence collection is an ongoing activity often called *trend management* or *horizon scanning*. The importance of documentation of the evidence, and its accessibility for those working with it, cannot be underestimated, especially since the act of translating this analysis into policy advice or strategy still has to be undertaken by human intelligence.

At the beginning of most future analysis processes stands a *trend analysis*. A trend might be defined as a movement or development over time that is identified either by quantitative or qualitative means. Such a trend, identified from past to the present, can be projected into the future. Since no trend is an absolute singular process, over time other trends will be influencing its future development by either strengthening, weakening, completely breaking or just transforming its trajectory. There is no single future development even in trend analysis, but instead, one can imagine multiple futures. Most important, therefore, is the interrelation of trends, the necessary undertaking to understand the relationships and cross-influences of important trends. The instrument to further this kind of understanding the complexity of trends is the *'cross-impact analysis'*, often supported by IT systems and algorithms but basically to be done by human analysts and their subjective judgement. With this method, it is possible to identify drivers, the trends that are pushing other trends, and passive trends that depend on being pushed by others. For example, digitalisation is currently among the former, transformations in the labour market among the latter. The consistency-analysis of trends is designed to help identify clusters of trends that are mutually supporting.

A *system* approach to trend analysis can be used to gain a better understanding of how trends interact with each other and create second- and third-order effects – starting the trend analysis more broadly to identify drivers of change – and focusing on drivers of stress and tensions. Actor analysis is key to this as the system does not live its own life but is driven by actors with a wide range of ambitions and shaping power. *Scenario analysis* complement trend analysis by providing alternative developments. Both forms of trend analysis can be the starting point for scenario analysis, especially the consistency analysis. Here, the identified trend clusters can be used as key factors describing a vision of a world to come. Namely, drivers of change or of stress and tensions in a chosen time frame, context, theme or even geography can, therefore, be developed into a narrative, a 'future story' or conflict scenario.

Scenario analysis is not only to be done as a continuation of trend analysis, but an instrument on its own. For the purposes of strategic foresight, scenarios can be defined as hypothetical pictures or visualisations of potential futures. They are a kind of qualitative or verbal descriptions of a future situation including the path leading to that future. They help to better focus the thinking about future are visualising existing expectations as much as clarifying major uncertainties and critical decision points. The latter have to be identified by specific methods like *'road mapping'* or *'back tracking'*, both looking into different steps and prerequisite events or actions, only, the one starting from today's situation, the other looking back from a future point of view. Scenarios also help in workshops and conferences to open the minds of participants to future thinking and encourage to think out of the box. They can be constructed in different ways, either by simple construction of a narrative about a potential future or by using complex methodologies starting with '*impact uncertainty matrixes*' or lists of potentially important factors related to the issue in question, identifying the key factors shaping the different possibilities of a future world. While the first mentioned method is simply a question of creativity and results in a highly subjective future story, the latter methods lead to a more complex multi-scenario process. Here, the necessary greater efforts are compensated by a more structured outcome, covering multiple potential outcomes that allow for further steps of strategy building or exercising in order to be best prepared for whatever the future might offer.

Games

There are at least three important purposes of games relaing to foresight, with growing complexity needed to fulfil the tasks: opening the mind to future thinking, educating about possible future and future possibilities, and testing specific scenarios or strategies related to future developments. While a variety of simple games like Trend Quartets or Quiz Games can be used for starting points of workshops, raising the mental preparation for future thinking as much as the motivation to engage, more complex games are needed to either educate a specific audience about future developments or even to test assumptions and strategies related to policy or warfighting. The time and effort that goes into the preparation of and playing of such games varies according to their complexity and the number of players. Properly done, they can provide invaluable contributions to preparing for the multiple futures we face and the challenges as much as the chances related to them.

Especially in defence, gaming ('wargaming') is a well-established tool and has recently become an increasingly used method to further examine human behaviour, perceptions and implications of strategic decision-making in certain contexts. The UK Ministry of Defence Wargaming Handbook describes a wargame as a scenario-based warfare model in which the outcome and sequence of events affect, and are affected by, the decisions made by the players. Simulation and modelling are elements of a wargame but not a wargame in itself. Gaming can be seen as a method of exploring alternative futures that builds on the principle of simulations. The core value comes back to better understanding perceptions and testing assumptions by exploring why future conflicts might turn out in particular ways and for mapping these possible pathways. Wargaming based on future scenarios can be a way to translate foresight results into military planning.

Matrix games combine focused discussions with iterative play to identify emerging themes. The players that play different actors in a chosen context try to achieve/protect their strategic objectives, which gives an idea of perceptions about how far and with which tools certain actors are ready to use. Matrix games focus on consequences and consequence management and are not meant to solve a problem but rather to identify its boundaries, to test and challenge extant policies and strategies against potential futures where identification of gaps and potential opportunities for exploitation are particularly important.

Advanced computerised Artificial Intelligence (AI)-supported wargames games simulate a certain strategic decision-making environment that builds on the decision of the players where the game delivers a result of the decision that takes the player to the next step until a certain future dependent on the choices made has been achieved, exploring trade-offs resulting from strategic decisions. AI-based tools will in the future enable an instant transformation of situation assessments into decision-making at the tactical or operational levels, offering the commanding officer a range of reasonable options including additional information about related risks and opportunities. This might further enhance the speed and effectiveness of warfighting in an environment of high uncertainty.

Difficulties and risks

The analysts' *proximity to politics* can be a blessing and a curse. On the one hand, research or analysis units within the ministries or at subordinate authorities know the processes and subjects on which the political leadership is currently focusing. These units can thus directly and immediately adapt the subjects and methodology of their work accordingly and also present their results in a language appropriate to the current discourse. Therefore, while external advice is often only partly used or sometimes even fully ignored by policy makers (Fichtner & Smoltczyk 2013), advice is much harder to ignore if the advice comes out of the system itself. On the other hand, these units within governments are more aware of political pressures than any external political consulting agency (Theiler 2019, pp. 33–8).

Confirmation biases present another problem, as is the aversion to considering extremely unwelcome possibilities. As the American nuclear strategist Herman Kahn rightly commented, there are scenarios and possible developments too horrible to contemplate, but this does not free us of the need to 'think the unthinkable' through, lest their actual occurrence has even worse consequences than if they are *not* prepared for in some form (Kahn 1962). Further dangers stem from developing 'blind spots', unintentionally eclipsing factors and developments in certain areas from the overall analysis, even though they may become very influential. For futurists, therefore, it becomes crucial to be aware of cultural, social or political biases.

In contrast to other types of political consulting, strategic foresight does not present ready-made results, but rather offers a procedure for the joint development of results drawing both on academics and practitioners. This means, however, that the quality of the results depends on the organisation and *communication skills* of the method experts as well as on the *expertise* and commitment of those participating in the project, and on navigating between overcomplexity and oversimplification.

Creativity is a crucial attribute for futurists, not one generally encouraged in bureaucracies. This means that the performance of the staff ultimately depends on skilful recruitment and the protection of spaces where thinking out of the box is valued.

Interdisciplinary work is very important, but again is more difficult to foster with within governmental structures than outside. An interdisciplinary composition of staff from the very beginning is thus a rare 'luxury'. Another way to bring in a diversity of inputs would be to 'import' knowledge and expertise from specialised companies or different academic sources, but the integration of these inputs into a governmental decision-making process requires careful management.

Two aspects of *bureaucratic politics* present a great obstacle for Strategic Foresight. What is even more difficult to achieve than inter-disciplinarity is inter-ministerial cooperation, which is indispensable for a whole-of-government-approach. This type of cooperation becomes necessary in government action whenever the complexity of a task requires the cooperation of several ministries and other government institutions. In states with coalition governments, this becomes especially cumbersome due to conflicting priorities of key decision-makers. While smooth cooperation is often inhibited by bureaucratic politics and differences in organisational culture between government departments, cases demanding an all-of-government approach are increasingly frequent.

Finally, results need to be translated into the language appropriate in the specific bureaucratic or political environment it wants to inform. Method-oriented strategic foresight offers the significant advantage of making many decision-makers part of the process even before its implementation, at least at the operational and middle management levels.

The greatest challenge is to persuade governments and gain the backing of parliamentarians and the larger public to devote considerable parts of these resources to preventing or mitigating something bad that has not yet happened. We generally give credence to forecasts of a thunderstorm when the skies are clear, and we stock fuel in the summer for the coming winter. But already when it comes to seizing the opportunity of buying cheap building sites in floodplains, or founding a town at the foot of a volcano, short-term thinking often outweighs prudent planning. As Lord Ricketts, a very senior British civil servant who served as Chair of the Joint Intelligence Committee and who co-ordinated the 2010 British National Security Review as the Prime Minister's National Security Adviser has summed up his experience: "Modern political leaders suffer acutely from the tyranny of the immediate. […] Keeping your job depends on dealing with the immediate crisis, not planning for something which may or may not happen in months or years" (Ricketts 2021, p. 127). Or during a politician's time in office, one might add. A risk might be identified, and yet crucial resources might not be spent on it, particularly in times of austerity. Ricketts rightly argues that strategy making is all about making 'hard choices' and prioritising, as governments (at least in democracies) never have the resources to fund everything that would be good to have to meet a National Risk Register (which in the UK by now identifies over 100 risks). Even with the best support by strategic foresight teams, it is hard indeed to make what retrospectively turns out to have been the right strategic choices.

Managing uncertainty

One of the core functions of futures analysis is to support decision-makers working and dealing with uncertainty and connected risks and opportunities. Critical uncertainties and risks/opportunities relate to a nation or organisation's strategic objectives, strengths, and vulnerabilities and will form parts of mitigation/resilience strategies, choices to provide agility/adaptability, and opportunities to be exploited. They are also likely to be areas that require further analysis and understanding. The introduction to the UK's Defence Concepts and Doctrine Centre's Global Trends 6 provides an example of a visualisation of how uncertainty can be explored. Here 16 uncertainties are identified as focus areas for further research (UK Government 2020).

All the methods in the toolbox will identify uncertainties and depend on assumptions. An essential part in this is to try to understand the weakness in an analysis and to identify questions that could not be answered, yet where the answer could change the result. That allows the contextualisation (using the questions as a guide) of uncertainty when making decisions and a better understanding of potential consequences and risks. Uncertainty is often contextualised in terms of statistics based on surveys that move from the qualitative to the quantitative – something that often appeals to decision-makers as it allows them to 'bound' the uncertainty. However, surveys, even the *Delphi* surveys that ask experts for their predictions based on hunches rather than evidence furnished, are still a collection of perceptions. Indeed, it has been argued that expert forecasts about the future are at times 'next to worthless' (Gardner 2011). This might be due to the experts' thinking being overloaded by recent and current knowledge that tends to create an overconfidence about future developments. Therefore, participants as much as their knowledge need to be carefully managed by futurists in order to achieve the necessary intellectual openness for potential futures. By contrast, expert and stakeholder interviews/engagements are vital when selecting critical uncertainties that should influence policy/strategy as they are direct part of their management.

A key to understanding the relevance of the uncertainties is their assessed impact and probability. It is therefore important to define what kind of impact you are studying and criteria for its measurement. Although high-probability and high-impact events naturally tend to gain high priority, the futures problem comes back to the unpredictability and the fact that assessments of probability will never be precise and can lead to false security/assumptions built on biased perceptions – the so-called 'probability trap'. Outliers, completely unexpected events ('black swans' or 'wildcards', defined as low-probability events with high impact) are important to consider as they may constitute major surprises. Scenarios and games can be used to explore further aspects of uncertainties and how they may evolve in certain contexts, help identifying decision points, indicators or weak-signals – but are also likely to reveal new uncertainties in turn.

Part of management of uncertainty is to challenge current assumptions and policies using a 'what if?' approach where questions such as what if this less plausible and unwelcome development happens anyway. This is also a good way of testing potential strategic surprises and shocks. Examples of such testing questions could be: what if strategies/capacities we expect to work do not; what if developments we expect to continue do not; or if events we do not expect to happen do? The Japanese attack on the US Navy anchoring in Pearl Harbour in December 1941 is an example of such a very unwelcome strategic surprise. This resulted from the American misperception that the sanctions cutting off Japan from energy would force Japan to negotiate and abandon its aggression towards China – and that Japan would never go to war against the powerful USA.

The past and the future

The Pearl Harbour example already shows that there is a role for historical research in imagining the future. There are several ways in which awareness of the past is useful for thinking about possible future developments: three are those of precedent, analogy, and evidence for trends. We are not talking about the popular debate about how history does or does not repeat itself, how it stutters, how it always happens twice, once as a tragedy once as a farce, and so on. Two things can be said authoritatively, however: first, that no two situations are entirely identical. The second, however, is that not identical, but similar configurations can be found in history, sometimes with similar consequences and outcomes. Testing developments in gaming (see above) has its limits, as entire societies cannot be put into laboratory experiments in which, all *ceteris paribus,* one can change one variable to test causalities. Only the study of the past can identify similar *patterns* – configurations with similar outcomes – which might suggest some degree of causality, and that in the future, again, similar configurations might produce similar results, if crucial variables follow the same constellation.

There are thus close links between foresight and history – having a historical sensibility or at least involving historians who can help us look back in order to look forward is greatly helpful to the understanding of various contexts of patterns of change. History also helps us overcome limits of our own imagination by injecting evidence of past developments that jar with 'intuitive' expectations of what would happen in particular crises. Also, it helps take the long view – the *longue durée* – as some trends *do* endure, and it helps critical thinking in decision-making, to stress test assumptions, not reinforce them.

To repeat, there are historical trends – trends that have begun in the past and that can plausibly be expected to continue into the future, unless a game changer event or development cuts them short or deflects them. This is of course the basis of trend analyses which, as we have noted, must always take into account mutually obstructing or mutually reinforcing trends, plus the wildcards that can change them.

The commemoration of past wars and anticipatory intelligence

Fourthly, historical precedents can play a role in the present and future in yet another way: not in terms of what happened, but how the past is evoked. It may be the *conscious* way in which societies relate to the past, usually with a considerable degree of distortion, that gives observers some idea of the possibilities for their political developments in the near future. Different ways of commemorating past wars are indicators of the short- and medium-future foreign political intentions of a government, and of the degree of support it might have among its population for foreign aggression.

Even similar societies can differ fundamentally in their attitudes to war and peace. This becomes apparent from studying the self-perception of nations, their narratives of the past and especially 'lessons' they have drawn from past experiences of wars. The recollection, invocation and remembrance of past conflicts in which a society (or its – real or imagined – forebears) has been involved plays a crucial role in the crystallisation or re-affirmation of its identity and solidarity. Past wars and other conflicts are often invoked as 'mythical'[1] models for action in a current or future political context (Heuser & Buffet 1998; Deruelle 2023). They can be evoked to keep alive or revive hostilities, and where they led to defeats and to the cession of territory to the victors, to fuel revanchism (Connerton 2001). Also in other ways they can be indicators of an expansionist or otherwise aggressive foreign policy agenda, as bases for territorial claims or claims to overlordship, or dominant status beyond one's state frontiers.

By contrast, the way in which a society reflects upon its own past can also be indicators of a pacific disposition of a culture, stressing peace, and reconciliation (Ashplant et al. 2002). State-funded places of memory, together with regular or 'round anniversary'-based public commemorations of wars, are indicators of political agendas and intentions of governments. The treatment of wars in literature and feature films builds on popular perceptions which an expansionist, aggressive government may be able to manipulate further in support of its own agenda. Such indicators can be marshalled to the needs of 'anticipatory intelligence' in US administration parlance (US Administration 2019). Jeannie Johnson and Marilyn Maines, leading practitioners of this form of cultural anthropological research, use the term 'mapping cultural topography' to identify these and other cultural habits and traits of societies, and their potential political implications (Johnson & Maines 2018, p. 32). They will not allow firm predictions, but can identify potentials. All this can well be demonstrated by the Russian government's use of history in the psychological buildup to the invasion of Ukraine, 2014–2022 (Aunoble 2023).

Last not least, contemplating the past helps us to shed the blinkers of our own ways of thinking, and to open our mind to different ideas held in other cultures. Our very ancestors thought differently from us about so many crucial things, so why believe that other cultures today think like us?.

Conclusions

This kind of anticipatory intelligence based on the mapping of a polity's 'cultural topography' needs to be complemented by the many other tools of intelligence. Here as elsewhere, no claim is made that one methodology of forecasting, or for a longer time ahead, developing strategic foresight will be able to fulfil all needs. Much to the contrary, a holistic approach needs to take into account the interplay of macro-trends and factors such as technological developments, the economy, availability and spread of resources, demography, climate change, ideologies, all factors that are in constant movement. Each of these dimensions is of course worth exploring, but to gain an overall vision of what the future of warfare might hold in store, we have to bring together the explorations in the following chapters concerning the impact of new technologies, of the terrains, of actors, and tactics. None of these *on their own* will allow helpful conceptualisations of potential future developments. Jointly, they can prompt us to think through challenges and possible answers.

It will always be tempting to take all kinds of shortcuts to predicting the future, such as projecting single trends or making bold predictions about the consequences of technological innovation, instead of trying to understand the complex interrelationship of multiple trends. It will be tempting to look for the most probable or even favourable future rather than taking wild cards or black swans into account. Ad-hockery tends to offer short-term benefits for decision-makers with a limited period in office. Nevertheless, to prepare for the future as well as possible, there is no way around the detailed engagement with complexity, with multiple and disagreeable future scenarios. When long-term policy or strategy making is required, strategic foresight offers the tools to get the best and most robust results, even though there is no way of approaching perfection.

Using data, a variety of analytical techniques but more importantly facilitating conversations about these assumptions and what might make them vulnerable is part of that. In the context of war and defence planning, strategic foresight is an integral part of future force- and forward-looking concept development – which ultimately aims at finding effective ways to deter and thus prevent, and/or prevail in future wars. Strategic foresight should not be confused with intelligence analysis, which is of predictive threat-based character aiming at supporting current force readiness and posture, and capability acquisition. Nevertheless, we can build on this kind of knowledge as a starting point. In the Anthropocene, the Future is in large part what mankind has made of it, but humanity continues to have an influence on it, for better or worse. It is for us to decide what form our influence will take.

Note

1 'Myth' is taken here to mean particular interpretations of an historical or legendary experience, advocating a policy for the present that is inspired by real or legendary precedent. See Heuser & Buffet 1998, p. ix, and individual case studies in the same volume.

References

Ashplant, T G, Dawson, G & Roger, M (eds) 2002, *The Politics of War Memory and Commemoration*, Routledge, London.
Aunoble, É 2023, 'La Guerre entre la Russie et l'Ukraine: unie Fatalité historique? (2022), in Deruelle (ed.) 2023, pp. 21–39.
Connerton, P 1989, *How Societies Remember*, Cambridge University Press, Cambridge.
Deruelle, B (ed.) 2023, *Quand l'Histoire sert à faire la guerre*, Leméac, Montréal.
Fichtner, U & Smoltczyk, A 2013, 'Mein Gott, Liegen Wir Richtig', *Der Spiegel*, 20 September, pp. 64–8.
Gardner, D 2011, *Future Babble: Why Expert Predictions are Next to Worthless*, Dutton, New York.
Hallam, E & Hockley, J 2001, *Death, Memory and Material Culture*, Berg, Oxford.
Heuser, B 2022, *War: A Genealogy of Western Ideas and Practices*, Oxford University Press, Oxford.
Heuser, B & Buffet, C 1998, 'Introduction: Of Myths and Men', in C Buffet & B Heuser (eds), *Haunted by History: Myths in International Relations*, Berghahn Books, Providence, RI & Oxford, pp. vii–x.
Johnson, J & Maines, M 2018, 'The Cultural Topography Analytic Framework', in J Johnson, K Kartchner & M Maines (eds), *Crossing Nuclear Thresholds: Leveraging Sociocultural Insights into Nuclear Decision-making*, Palgrave Macmillan, London, pp. 29–60.
Kahn, H 1962, *Thinking about the Unthinkable*, Horizon Press, New York.
Ricketts, P 2021, *Hard Choices: The Making and Unmaking of Global Britain*, Atlantic Books, London.
Schoemaker, P & Tetlock, P 2016, 'Superforecasting: How to Upgrade your Company's Judgment,' *Harvard Business Review*, vol. 94, no. 5, pp. 73–8.
Theiler, O 2019, 'Because Today Will Tomorrow Have Been Yesterday – Future Analysis as an Instrument of Strategy Consulting', in G Hellmann & D Jacobi (eds), *The German White Paper 2016 and the Challenge of Crafting Security Strategies*, Aspen-Institute Germany, Berlin & Goethe-University, Frankfurt a. M., pp. 33–8.
UK Government 2020, *National Risk Register*, <https://www.gov.uk/government/publications/global-strategic-trends#:~:text=Global%20Strategic%20Trends%20%20%E2%80%93%20The%20Future%20Starts%20Today%20(6th%20Edition), adapt%20to%20the%20evolving%20future> (accessed 25 August 2022).
US Administration 2019, 'Anticipatory Intelligence', in *The National Intelligence Strategy of the USA*, <https://knowww.eu/nodes/5c7cde51aee7869aa9b3f00e> (accessed 28 June 2022).

2

PREDICTING THE FUTURE OF WAR IN THE 21ST CENTURY

A Future War Studies?

Mark Lacy

Introduction

In modernity, the state and its military become increasingly focused on the future 'threat horizon,' on the risks and dangers that might pose 'existential threats' to a society – and the new tactics, technologies and domains that will require investment and innovation in response to future insecurities and vulnerabilities. These concerns about the uncertainty and insecurity of the future result in a variety of 'horizon scanning' and 'scenario planning' techniques.

But in a time of geopolitical and technological change and transformation, there does seem to be a greater awareness of the limits of our 'futures thinking' and horizon scanning (Freedman 2018). On one level, there might be a greater a sense of uncertainty on the multiple (and multiplying) possible geopolitical, technological, economic, political and social futures ahead of us. As the science fiction writer Kim Stanley Robinson puts it: "The future is radically unknowable: it could hold anything from an age of peaceful prosperity to a horrific mass-extinction event. The sheer breadth of possibility is disorienting and even stunning" (Robinson 2018). There is also the impression (from the perspective of the academic world) that this uncertainty about the multiplication of futures – the emerging technologies, the range of different 'actors' (from satellites used in war through to 'cyberpunk' hackers operating in the 'grey zones' of international politics) through to the different emerging terrains or domains (from space to cyberspace and down into the networks of undersea cables) – is producing an interest in new ways of seeing what 'black swans' or 'wild-card events' might be on the horizon or, in light of what might be viewed as the continual production of strategic and tactical mistakes by the most 'advanced' states, to develop new approaches to security and war.

This chapter begins with an overview of key areas driving this contemporary concern with 'the future': geopolitical uncertainty and the technological acceleration. This overview is followed by a discussion on emerging trends in 'futures' work that may or may not reveal something significant about how states and militaries are responding to threats and geopolitical uncertainties and challenges. Indeed, the essay suggests that more work needs to be done in a 'future war studies' on understanding and evaluating how liberal states are developing new organisational techniques, networks and infrastructures to prepare for future wars and security challenges – a task that presents a researcher outside of the military with a variety of intellectual and 'practical' research challenges.

DOI: 10.4324/9781003299011-4

But at the same time, an emerging future war studies also needs to try to understand the 'strategic cultures' of states outside the liberal world, the thinking on international conflict in a multipolar world where the liberal way of war might be confronted with rival techniques and tactics of future war (and ideas or 'imaginaries' on war and geopolitical competition, conflict and power).

The black swans of modernity and war

States develop organisations and bureaucracies specifically focused on the future of war, security and international politics. For example, in the United Kingdom, the Development, Concepts and Doctrine Centre (DCDC) produces reports and research on all aspects on the future of security and war, attempting to see what challenges might be on the horizon. The Defence, Science and Technology Laboratory (DSTL) in the United Kingdom does the work of developing the technical capability to deal with future threats while at the same time developing its own techniques and 'future threat programmes' for seeing what dangers we might be ignoring (or not even imagining as a possibility).

Before the time of lockdowns, I attended a workshop organised by DSTL and the Ministry of Defence and, posted on the wall as part of the promotional material for the event, was a poster that included an image of a *black swan*. This was very likely a reference to *The Black Swan: The Impact of the Highly Improbable* by Nassim Nicholas Taleb (2010), a book that became hugely influential since its publication, part of a series of books on the problems faced by organisations dealing with complex and disruptive events magnified by interconnectedness and technology, events that people should see on the horizon but often fail to. Taleb explores the reasons for the failure to see the black swan and explores what can be done on both an individual or organisational level to build what he describes as *antifragility* (Taleb 2013). For Taleb, you might not be able to avoid some of the catastrophic events and strategic surprises that you will be 'hit with' but you might be able to build a society or organisation that can 'weather the storm' more effectivity. Building 'resilience' or antifragility are the buzzwords in a time when strategic shocks are viewed as inevitable and unavoidable – and might be increasing in frequency and severity in a time of geopolitical and technological change.

What will all these dangers (and opportunities) in acceleration, entanglement and disruption in technology and geopolitics mean for the future of war? And how do we begin to open up thinking and discussion on the uncertainty on the future of war and international politics in a time of technological acceleration? Along with all the provocative and wide-ranging explorations of technology and the future (Basar, Coupland & Obrist 2015; Harari 2017; Azhar 2022), there are a growing number of books that begin to think about how war will change in this time of technological acceleration, books such as Christopher Coker's *Future War* (Coker 2015) and Mick Ryan's *War Transformed: The Future of Twenty First Century Great Power Competition and Conflict* (Ryan 2022). There are also books that go beyond the ethical and the strategic issues to open up questions about the limits and problems of thinking about the future, exploring innovative techniques to think about the future of security and war. For example, in *To Boldly Go: Leadership, Strategy, and Conflict in the 21st Century and Beyond* (Klug & Leonard 2021), various military academics and strategists begin to explore how Science Fiction can be used by the military to help understand the future of war; there is a similar project in *Strategy Strikes Back: How Star Wars Explains Modern Military Conflict* (Brooks et al. 2018).

To be sure, there is nothing particularly unusual about this interest in the future of war and international politics. But what is striking about the current interest on the future of war and international politics is the sense of unease and uncertainty on the range of possible world orders and future events. In the following sections, I am going to outline two broad areas/drivers of concern that fuel the contemporary anxiety on the future of war and world (dis)order: geopolitical uncertainty and technological acceleration. This will be followed by an overview on questions that are emerging over contemporary responses to the future of war.

Geopolitical uncertainty

After 9/11 one of the important strategic debates in the United States was on how the world's only superpower should use its military power in a situation where there were no clear 'peer competitors' and where threats emerged in parts of the world where the United States was able to use a variety of emerging tactics and technologies, the production of what the political geographer Derek Gregory (2011) described as 'the everywhere war.' Realist thinkers in international politics, like Stephen Walt & John Mearsheimer, argued that there were serious dangers with this position of geopolitical primacy (Walt 2005); without any counterbalancing forces, the danger of a unipolar world was that there were no limits to power, no limits on the temptation to fight unnecessary wars, wars that could prove to be strategic mistakes. The question for the realist is indicated in the title of Walt's (2005) book *Taming American Power: The Global Response to U.S. Primacy*.

For some commentators, the danger now lies in the 'Thucydides trap' where the tensions posed by great power transformation could result in military conflict, conflict that could be driven by the strategic anxiety and paranoia generated by the emergence of a military and economic rival that could attempt to shape and dominate international politics (Allison 2018). The anxiety in strategic debates often focuses on how far the liberal world would go in defending its interests (and what those interests are in a tense, multipolar world). Books such as *Ghost Fleet: A Novel of the Next World War* by Peter W Singer & August Cole (2015) used fiction to explore what future war with China might look like: Cole described the use of futuristic fiction to explore the future of war as FICINT (fiction coupled with intelligence thinking) (Cole 2019).

With the invasion of Ukraine in 2022, any optimism about the emerging multipolar world faded with the realisation that – for all the liberal optimism offered by commentators like Steven Pinker – war might be as central to the 21st century as it was to the previous century. While conflict between nuclear states might not take place, shifting balances of power mean that states with an unresolved territorial desires or grievances would begin to exploit the time of geopolitical transformation and uncertainty, to test the diplomatic and military 'waters'. There might also be wars before new waves of technological and tactical innovation created new defensive possibilities, the type of tactics and technologies that created problems for Russia in Ukraine (Boot 2022).

Simply put, optimism about globalisation, interconnectedness and what is known as 'deterrence by entanglement' gave way to anxiety about a world where war had not disappeared from the international condition; there are many possibilities for the future of war, possibilities that range from interstate war involving states like Russia and China through to war with global terrorist networks (networks enhanced by the 'democraticisation of technology'), wars generated by ecological damage and economic disorder and inequality – and the continual possibility that liberal states might embark on future 'unnecessary wars'. The threat horizon remains filled with reasons for geopolitical pessimism.

In the 2020s, the future of war and international politics looks messier and more dangerous than anything found in liberal (where the liberal 'end of history' looked like the only 'rational' game in town, a position that has become unsettled by the apparent effectiveness of authoritarian superpowers like China) or realist positions (where the most dangerous actors are always states). The geopolitical anxiety is of a future of radical uncertainty congested and accelerated with emerging tactics, technologies, domains, terrains and actors in international politics, a future that makes the 'realist' depiction of the 'international system' appear like the simplification many of its critics always argued it was (Der Derian 2009). As the French sociologist and philosopher Bruno Latour put it in a discussion of climate change and ecological futures:

> The geopolitical strategists who pride themselves on belonging to the "realist school" will have to modify somewhat the *reality* that their battle plans will have to face. Formerly, it was possible to say that humans were "on earth" or "in nature," that they found themselves in "the modern period" and that that they were "humans" more or less "responsible" for their action...But how can we say where we are if the place "on" or "in" which we are located begins to react to our actions, turns against us, encloses us, dominates us, demands something of us and carries us along its path?
>
> (Latour 2018, p. 41)

Technological acceleration

Modernity introduces new technologies, new ways of communicating and new forms of mobility/movement: innovations that transform all parts of the world, innovations that transform all aspects of life, economy, politics and war. As the French philosopher Paul Virilio put it, history progresses at the speed of its weapons systems (Virilio 2006, p. 90). War (and society) is transformed by the new technologies (such as trains and rail networks) that enable you to move greater numbers of troops across a territory, by the possibility of hypersonic weapons, by the systems to make decisions faster than your enemies (and now to possibly use AI to analyse data and assist decision-making or even make decisions), to use a 'smart phone' to report the movement of tanks and troops near your village.

Virilio argued that war was a key driver of technological acceleration and innovation: much vital research and development would take place in 'closed systems' that required all the capacities of the state to access funding, expertise and resources in the development of the latest weaponry. While much military innovation still emerges from the closed system of the state in the 21st century, much of our current technological innovation emerges in the 'open' systems where individuals and groups can innovate in the digital or robotic – and where you do not have to have the resources of the state to be technologically creative (and possibly destructive). As Audrey Kurth Cronin (2020) argues in *Power to The People*: *How Open Technological Innovation is Arming Tomorrow's Terrorists*, managing this time of 'open innovation' in technology is one of the key geopolitical challenges of our time – when individuals and groups are able to enhance their capabilities in cybercrime, cyberwar and drone war (and the crimes of the future which we cannot currently see or imagine).

Indeed, many have commented that the war in Ukraine illustrated how a centralised, bureaucratic state and military confronted the challenge posed by a 'networked,' 'decentralised' military using smart phones and drones to attack a more 'conventional' military (Friedman 2022; Tett 2022). The hierarchies of economic and military power where the richest and most advanced have the advantage might be disrupted in ways that are difficult for us to imagine. What would the invasion of Iraq look like in the 2020s or 2030s (or 2060s)? Are we entering the age of 'defensive dominance' where only the most irresponsible state would risk intervening in a state or city viewed (by some strategic thinkers) as economically or technologically inferior – but able to produce deadly and congested battlespaces with no easy 'technical fix,' filled with new 'machinic black swans'?

Will advanced states be confronted with a variety of actors that are not easily deterred but have constantly evolving tactics and technologies of creative destruction? For some commentators, the fundamental problem is the pace of change in technology (driven by Moore's law and the various other laws outlined in Azhar's *Exponential*). What will a smart phone be able to do in 2049? How will drones or robots be used? How will AI transform war (Lee & Qiufan 2021)? Will we even by using terms such as 'smart phone,' 'drone'/'robot' or 'AI' by 2049 (the year of the *Blade Runner* sequel *and* the year that China aims to match or overtake US military power)? What techniques can we use to see what is on the horizon?

And how will technologies transform the terrains and actors in war and international politics? Our technological acceleration and machine-based civilisation on earth depend on satellite technology but the pace of our technological change is making near/outer space a potentially vital zone of military and economic competition (Deudney 2020). There might be emerging domains such as the digital 'innerspace' of the 'metaverse' or virtual reality (the type of scenarios depicted in *Ready Player One* or *The Peripheral*) that become important spaces of (in)security. What will cities look like in coming decades when the range of urban futures ranges from the utopian/dystopian 'smart cities' through to high tech or low tech 'feral cities' – and possibly complex hybrids of the smart and the feral in a climate emergency (Powell 2020)? And what technologies will be available for militaries that have to operate in the possible multiplication and intensification of differently 'congested' future urban battlespaces (King 2021)?

There might be terrains or domains we are not even thinking about – or able to imagine. It might be that it is the 'human being' that is subject to the most radical transformations in the coming decades, transformed through a mix of pharmaceutical and machinic modification (Bickford 2020). Simply put, we live in a time when any serious discussions of the future of war soon begin to feel like science fiction. How should we begin to think about the future without Cole's 'FICINT' becoming either too cautious and conservative or too fictional and fantastical?

Weirdos from William Gibson Novels!

The focus and interest on the future, as I have suggested, has long been part of government and military concern – for states that have the resources to focus on 'horizon' scanning. After 9/11 there was a particularly urgent focus on the future in the liberal world, a concern with 'black swans,' low probability but high impact 'wild cards' exemplified by an event organised by Francis Fukuyama and others that became an edited book, *Blindside*: *How to Anticipate Forcing Events and Wild Cards in Global Politics* (Fukuyama 2007).

Part of what drove this interest in wild card events and black swans was a concern that the tools and techniques to prepare for the future might be lacking - or out of date - in a world of dangerous connectivity and technological acceleration: indeed, I carried out a brief project for DSTL and the Economic and Social Research Council (ESRC) that set out to see what the implications of Taleb's work might be for government (and especially on the implications of the emerging work in academia influenced by *The Black Swan*). Underpinning this interest in the future was a concern with what 9/11 revealed both about new threats and vulnerabilities but also the problems of decision-making and foreign/domestic policy; and how, in particular, policy makers might have downplayed some of the scenarios and problems that confronted the United States and its allies in Iraq and Afghanistan.

The concern with risk and the future was then heightened by the financial crisis in 2008, another event that raised the issue of how policymakers and economic organisations failed to see the risks that should have been taken more seriously. Then in the times that followed the financial crisis, the implications of technological, geopolitical and ecological change became far clearer (albeit possibly in a way that felt more unsettling, disruptive and uncertain); political disruption in liberal states, pandemics and lockdowns, conflict moving beyond the 'grey zone' into war in Ukraine, a growing sense of what the climate emergency might become.

But it is difficult to assess to whether this concern and anxiety about the future and global disorder has resulted in new ideas and approaches in government. On one side of the debate, there are commentators such as Dominic Cummings, the controversial British political 'strategist' and once chief advisor to then Prime Minister Boris Johnson. In a widely publicised comment, Cummings made this provocative statement in 2020 on his 'blog,' a blog that often focused on the limits of government thinking and planning on future threats and challenges:

> We need some true wild cards, artists, people who never went to university and fought their way out of an appalling hell hole, weirdos from William Gibson novels like that girl hired by Bigend as a brand 'diviner' who feels sick at the sight of Tommy Hilfiger or that Chinese-Cuban free runner from a crime family hired by the KGB. If you want to figure out what characters around Putin might do, or how international criminal gangs might exploit holes in our border security, you don't want more Oxbridge English graduates who chat about Lacan at dinner parties with TV producers and spread fake news about fake news.
>
> (Cummings 2020)

In other words, complex times will require people who can think differently, who can think and act disruptively in 'slow' and traditional bureaucracies that are out of time with the pace of change in geopolitics and technology, who can think outside of the boxes created by the bureaucratic elites. In a sense what he is suggesting resonates with the position taken by Taleb in books like *The Black Swan* and *Antifragility*. Taleb seems to take the view that social scientists or arts graduates often lack useful intellectual or methodological skills (the graduates who Cummings says chat about Lacan), the technical knowledge that students of STEM subjects (or people who work 'in the trenches') have; and many organisations suffer from what Taleb (2010) refers to as 'tunnelling', the 'group think' that emerges when a limited view on an issue becomes dominant (a limited view that could come as much from a science perspective as it could from a social science one).

Cummings is suggesting that government needs to dismantle a culture of tunnelling that he seems to be suggesting is dominated by students from the arts and social sciences. Government needs the wild cards, those who have the technical knowledge or the 'real world' experience to think outside the traditional bureaucratic box. To be sure, Cummings might be rather 'colourful' in his vision of civil servants working for government being like characters from William Gibson novels but his point resonates with the general direction of this essay so far: we are living in a time of dramatic technological, geopolitical and ecological change, confronted with the possibility of worlds and realities like the ones imagined by Gibson in books like *The Peripheral*. In *The Peripheral* the world has been devasted by the waves of different catastrophic events – what Gibson calls The Jackpot – that have ended modernity as we know it (Gibson 2015, p. 320).

Cummings does not specifically mention the Ministry of Defence, DSTL or DCDC; it might be the case that he is focusing on the Home Office or the departments tasked with polices he was specifically interested in. But the examples he points to – including the reference to Putin – leave his proposal rather broad; he might well be talking about the parts of the state tasked with dealing with security and war. At the same time, it might also be the case that he simply did not know enough about all the initiatives going on across government. Or it might be the case that he did know - and was not impressed: in some comments, he suggests that part of the problem is an underfunded

MOD – and a military that is not focusing (or allowed to focus) on the tactics and technologies that are needed in the 21st century. But it certainly seems to be the case that there are people in government working on the type of radical and disruptive geopolitical and technological futures that he sees as so important, questions on the pace of change, complexity and security. For example, organisations such as DSTL encourage a combination of graduates from the social sciences and STEM subjects to explore future threats. While there might not be the 'wild cards' who did not go to university (and even this is debatable – there may well be strategists who work in this area who have taken other routes), there certainly appears (from the outside) to be an openness to think outside the box, a recognition that new ideas and approaches are needed across government. For example, what was known as the Future Threat Programme in DSTL produced a short futuristic film about the way government employees could be targeted or manipulated in a world of smart devices, opening up questions about new tactics of espionage and manipulation in times of geopolitical and technological acceleration and uncertainty. I have certainly seen initiatives where there were projects that involved talking to a broad range of academics/researchers (among many other groups) about future threats and black swans that policymakers in government might need new thinking on.

But just because there are initiatives to think creatively, outside the box, it does not mean that these attempts are impactful or significant: this might be the point Cummings is making. But putting this question over Cummings's provocative statement to one side, there does seem to be an interest in new approaches to future threats and future wars in militaries around the world (or certainly around the liberal world). For example, what is often described as the 'military design movement' has brought together a broad range of disciplines and intellectual approaches (some of which would resonate with the interests of Cummings) to challenge the traditional techniques of military planning and strategic thinking (Danielson 2020; Beaulieu-Brossard 2021; Stanczak, Talbott & Zweibelson 2021). For the military designer, strategic planning and thinking can often be too narrow in its approach to the geopolitical and technological change on the horizon.

In the military design world, techniques have been developed using the tools that are often used in design projects outside the military to create the space for new ideas and approaches. Role-playing games like *Dungeons and Dragons* have inspired the creation of games to explore future scenarios, games that are less about trying to 'predict' the future (although new insights might result from the process) but more about getting participants to see the limits of the way they approach problems, the limits of their 'sensemaking' on future threats (Archipelago of Design 2020).

Central to the military design project is the idea that future conflicts will be unlike anything confronted in the past. To be sure, it might still be important to teach the history of warfare and the 'key thinkers' like Sun Tzu and Clausewitz – but the future is likely to involve radical new tactics, technologies and terrains or domains of warfighting and international conflict. While you might not be able to predict the strategic surprises that future militaries will confront, you might be able to produce the type of military personnel who are able to think creatively and critically about the problems they will have to respond to. As Nolan Peterson puts it:

> Throughout history, US military-industrial dominance has permitted the luxury of warmup periods in its wars to arrive at a coherent strategic vision and develop workable tactics to achieve victory. Famously, US military forces honed their combat acumen on the North African front in World War II before embarking on the liberation of Europe. […] However, against a near-peer adversary such as Russia or China, US military forces will have less time to hone their tactics and find their confidence in battle. The next war may be over before America's armed forces learn how to fight it.
>
> (Peterson 2021)

Members of the military design movement might possibly be in agreement with Cummings on the need for 'wild cards' in traditional and often conservative institutions; and it does appear to be the case that we there are lots of attempts at expanding (or creatively disrupting) how military organisations prepare for the future. But what remains unclear (from the university world) is how significant these attempts are.

Regardless of whether Cummings is making his provocative statement from lack of knowledge or if he is pointing to a need to do more to make politicians and policymakers more engaged and knowledgeable about the work being done at DSTL or by the military design movement, it is clear that more research needs to be done on the 'state of play' on the new trends in this area: a 'future war studies' needs to take stock of the new attempts to prepare for war and insecurity in this time of technological and geopolitical acceleration. In particular, these questions might be a useful point of departure to see how this area on the future of war and security is developing:

One. How do key players working on future war and security challenges see the current effectiveness of the techniques and organisations tasked with preparing for future challenges? What are the problems with the way things currently being developed? What needs to be done to improve work on future challenges? Or is the distinctiveness of 21st Century problems of geopolitical and technological uncertainty and acceleration being overstated or 'hyped up'?

Two. How significant and important are initiatives such as the 'military design movement' or some of the other creative attempts to respond to future challenges (such as the use of Science Fiction/FICINT by militaries)? Do these developments exist on the margins of government and military organisations or are we seeing a significant and influential new 'turn' in futures work?

Three. Is there sufficient collaboration between those strategic thinkers who focus on geopolitical change (often from a social science background) and more technical planners focused on technological acceleration (often from a STEM background)? Do those with a STEM education think differently about future trends and threats in technology and geopolitics compared to those with a humanities or social science background?

Fourth. From an international perspective, what are the techniques and approaches that appear to be useful and innovative? What differences do we see across NATO members? Are there important differences between, for example, the French approach to future war thinking and U.S. approaches? Is there sufficient international collaboration and dialogue on 'future war studies'?

Fifth. Is the fundamental problem still one of 'tunnelling'? In other words, we might have new insightful and creative techniques but the challenge is still a problem of politicians and policymakers failing to understand the strategic challenges and uncertainties on the horizon? Are there initiatives that need to be developed to connect the 'futures worlds' with those working in government on often more 'immediate' issues and challenges?

A future war studies?

So we live in a time of intense anxiety and uncertainty about the future of war and international politics. For some, the years between 2001 and 2021 were another 'Twenty Years Crisis' culminating in the withdrawal of the United States military from Afghanistan, signalling for some (possibly Vladimir Putin) the confirmation of a multipolar post-American age in international politics, the end of the end of history. For others, a crisis of inequality, climate emergency and the damaging impact of a new digital age on politics, society and economy is producing chaos that will not be managed by a technical or strategic and foreign policy 'fix': geopolitical change and transformation is one element in the global disorder to come.

The focus of this essay has been on liberal states and the future of war and international politics. But in a multipolar world with emerging Great Powers, it might be the case that the future character of war will be increasingly shaped by states outside of the liberal world. In this sense, attempting to understand how 'authoritarian' states understand the future of war – and are preparing for future wars – might be an essential part of a future war studies. To be sure, it might be the case that in the international politics of the 21st-century authoritarian states are no better or worse than liberal states when it comes to waging unnecessary wars or making strategic mistakes. It might be the case that authoritarian states become masters in the arts of what Kilcullen (2020) terms 'liminal war,' activities in the 'grey zones' of international politics where we – as Mark Galeotti concludes in *The Weaponisation of Everything: A Field Guide to the New Way of War* – we learn to love the permanent 'bloodless' war of grey, hybrid times (Galeotti 2022, p. 207): The invasion of Ukraine might be a momentary lapse of authoritarian reason that serves as a warning for others.

But it might be the case that authoritarian states are profoundly limited (out of a mix of bureaucratic fear, hubris and centralisation) when it comes to evaluating and understanding their military, economic and technological power – possibly overestimating their own capacities and underestimating the capabilities of others in a time of technological acceleration. Equally, it might be the case that we enter a time of creativity and innovation in the development of 'unrestricted warfare' that it might be increasingly difficult for liberal states to counter or match. Either way, a future war studies needs to attempt to research the 'strategic cultures' (Johnson 2018) of the states (and other actors) that might shape the future of war in 21st-century international politics, to evaluate the decision-making conditions that might create the possibility of aggressive tactics and actions in times of geopolitical, technological and ecological disruption – and also the possibility of catastrophic miscalculations and errors of judgement, catastrophic strategies that pushes 'deterrence by entanglement' to its limits.

References

Allison, G 2018, *Destined for War: Can America and China Escape Thucydides' Trap?* Scribe, London.

Archipelago of Design 2022, *How Might Wargaming Tear Down Barriers To Innovative Thinking in Defence and Security Cultures*, 13 July, <https://www.youtube.com/watch?v=5A-WiOluxY4> (accessed 26 October 2022).

Azhar, A 2022, *Exponential: Order and Chaos in an Age of Accelerating Technology*, Penguin, London.

Basar, S, Coupland, D & Obrist, H 2015, *The Age of Earthquakes: A Guide to the Extreme Present*, Penguin, London.

Beaulieu-Brossard, P 2021, 'Encountering Nomads in Israel Defense Forces and Beyond,' P Ish-Shalom (ed), *Concepts at Work: On the Linguistic Infrastructure of World Politics*, University of Michigan Press, Ann Arbor, MI, pp. 91–117.

Bickford, A 2020, *Chemical Heroes: Pharmacological Supersoldiers in the US Military*, Duke University Press, Durham, NC.

Boot, M 2022, 'Russia Learns the Perils of Aggression in an Age of Defensive Dominance,' *The Washington Post*, 4 May, <https://www.washingtonpost.com/opinions/2022/05/04/russia-ukraine-aggression-in-age-defensive-dominance/> (accessed 25 October 2022).

Brooks, M, Amble, J, Cavanaugh, M L & Gates, J 2018, *Strategy Strikes Back: How Star Wars Explains Modern Military Conflict*, Potomac Books, Lincoln, NE.

Coker, C 2015, *Future War*, Polity, Cambridge.

Cole, A 2019, '"FICINT" Envisioning The Future of War Through Fiction and Intelligence', *War Room*, 22 May, <https://warroom.armywarcollege.edu/special-series/indo-pacific-region/ficint-envisioning-future-war-through-fiction-intelligence-indo-pacific-series/> (accessed 25 October 2022).

Cronin, A K 2020, *Power to The People: How Open Technological Innovation is Arming Tomorrow's Terrorists*, Oxford University Press, Oxford.

Cummings, D 2020, '"Two Hands Are a Lot" – We're Hiring Data Scientists, Project Managers, Policy Experts, Assorted Weirdos…', *Dominic Cummings Blog*, 2 January, <https://dominiccummings.com/> (accessed 25 October 2022).

Danielson, A 2020, 'Knowledge in and of Military Operations: Enriching the Reflexive Gaze in Critical Research on the Military', *Critical Military Studies*, vol. 8, no. 4, pp. 1–19, https://doi.org/10.1080/23337486.2020.1835341.

Der Derian, J 2009, *Virtuous War*, Routledge, London.

Deudney, D 2020, *Dark Skies: Space Expansionism, Planetary Geopolitics, and the Ends of Humanity*, Oxford University Press, Oxford.

Freedman, L 2018, *The Future of War: A History*, Penguin, London.

Friedman, T 2022, 'Free Advice for Putin: 'Make Peace, You Fool', *The New York Times*, 13 April, <https://www.nytimes.com/2022/04/13/opinion/putin-ukraine-war-strategy.html> (accessed 25 October 2022).

Fukuyama, F 2007, *Blindside: How to Anticipate Forcing Events and Wild Cards in Global Politics*, Brookings Institution, Washington, DC.

Galeotti, M 2022, *The Weaponisation of Everything: A Field Guide to the New Way of War*, Yale University Press, New Haven, CT.

Gibson, W 2015, *The Peripheral*, Penguin, London.

Gregory, D 2011, 'The Everywhere War', *The Geographical Journal*, vol. 177, no. 3, pp. 238–50, https://doi.org/10.1111/j.1475-4959.2011.00426.x.

Harari, Y N 2017, *Homo Deus: A Brief History of Tomorrow*, Harper, London.

Johnson, J 2018, *The Marines, Counter-Insurgency and Strategic Culture*, Georgetown University Press, Washington, DC.

Kilcullen, D 2020, *The Dragon and the Snakes: How the Rest Learned to Fight the West*, Hurst & Co, London.

King, A 2021, *Urban Warfare in the 21st Century*, Polity, Cambridge.

Klug, J & Leonard, S 2021, *To Boldly Go: Leadership, Strategy, and Conflict in the 21st Century and Beyond*, Casemate Publishers, Oxford.

Latour, B 2018, *Down To Earth: Politics in the New Climatic Regime*, Polity, Cambridge.

Lee, K & Qiufan, C 2021, *AI 2041: Ten Visions for Our Future*, WH Allen, London.

Mearsheimer, J 2021, 'The Inevitable Rivalry: America, China, and the Tragedy of Great Power Politics', *Foreign Affairs*, November/December, <https://www.foreignaffairs.com/articles/china/2021-10-19/inevitable-rivalry-cold-war> (accessed 27 October 2022).

Peterson, N 2021, 'Inside Project Galahad: How the 75th Ranger Regiment Used 'Creative Destruction' to Prepare for the Modern Battlefield,' *Coffee or Die Magazine*, 6 January, <https://www.coffeeordie.com/project-galahad> (accessed 25 October 2022).

Powell, J 2020, *The 2084 Report: A History of Global Warming from the Future*, Hodder & Stoughton, London.

Robinson, K S 2018, 'Empty Half the Earth of its Humans. It's the Only Way to Save the Planet', *The Guardian*, 20 March, <https://www.theguardian.com/cities/2018/mar/20/save-the-planet-half-earth-kim-stanley-robinson > (accessed 26 October 2022).

Ryan, M 2022, *War Transformed: The Future of Twenty First Century Great Power Competition and Conflict*, Naval Institute Press, Annapolis, MD.

Singer, P W & Cole, A 2015, *Ghost Fleet: A Novel of the Next World War*, Houghton Mifflin Harcourt, London.

Stanczak, J, Talbott, P & Zweibelson, B 2021, 'Designing at the Cutting Edge of Battle: The 75th Ranger Regiment's Project Galahad', *Special Operations Journal*, vol. 7, no. 1, pp. 1–16.

Taleb, N T 2010, *The Black Swan: The Impact of the Highly Improbable*, Penguin, London.

Taleb, N T 2013, *Anti-Fragile: Things That Gain from Disorder*, Penguin, London.

Tett, G 2022, 'Inside Ukraine's Open-Source War', *Financial Times*, 22 July, <https://www.ft.com/content/297d3300-1a65-4793-982b-1ba2372241a3> (accessed 25 October 2022).

Virilio, P 2006, *Speed and Politics*, trans. M Polizzotti, Semiotext(e), Los Angeles, CA.

Walt, S 2005, *Taming American Power: The Global Response to U.S. Primacy*, W.W. Norton, New York.

Weber, C 2005, *Imagining America at War*, Routledge, London.

3

THINKING ABOUT
THE FUTURE OF WAR

Christopher Coker

Introduction

When we talk about the future of anything these days, we tend to think largely about technology, though experts disagree on how it shapes or will reshape our lives. Silicon Valley geeks and techno-futurists tell us that we are on the cusp of an era of technological change unprecedented in history. Others think that this is all overblown, and that we will largely be tweaking the present. Whoever will be proved right, it is worth remembering that we are a unique species. We are not the only animals to use tools, but we are the only animals to use technology. Through its use, we continue to reframe the boundaries of who we are and what we may yet achieve.

Futurists as a group tend to make bold claims. In his book, *The Inevitable: Understanding the twelve technological forces that will shape our future* Kevin Kelly makes three predictions:

1 Most technologies that will dominate life have not yet been invented.
2 The technologies we are already using will only continue to be useful through constant up-grades. We will be constantly catching up with the future.
3 The cycle of obsolescence is accelerating all the time (Kelly 2016).

These propositions may well be true, but they also beg many questions. If I look back, I can say that two technologies have shaped war in my own lifetime: nuclear weapons which were invented eight years before I was born and the Internet which first appeared 30 years ago. But I have also lived through a very sluggish period of innovation. Commercial aircraft fly no faster than they did in the 1960s; we have not gone back to the moon since 1972. And we still deploy diesel powered submarines. Even drones were first used in war back in 1971. Amazingly, B-52 are still flying and will continue to do so until 2030.

And will the cycle of obsolescence really accelerate? We should always be alert, writes David Edgerton, "to the complex interaction of the old and the new and the dangers of naïve futurism" (Edgerton 2006, p. 153). That is the moral of *Superiority* (1951), a short story by the veteran sci-fi writer Arthur C Clarke. In his imagined future, the most advanced technological power eventually loses a war because, in constantly updating its systems, it introduces them before they become fully operational, while its enemy continues to add to its arsenal of older but usable weapons. In

  DOI: 10.4324/9781003299011-5

the end numbers tell. What triumphs in the end is what David Edgerton calls 'the shock of the old'. Clarke's short story was once required reading for students enrolled on the industrial design course at the Massachusetts Institute of Technology (MIT). Technology, nevertheless, has an unstoppable propulsive force – if something can be built it will be even if it leaves you vulnerable. The most famous example is the *Dreadnought*, a super battleship first launched by the British in 1906 which rendered all other battleships obsolete, including their own. In the event, they kept ahead of the competition, but only just.

Thinking about technology

We really must be careful, nonetheless, not to overemphasise the pace of technological change. A recent report for the European Parliament, *Innovative technologies shaping the 2040 battlefield* (EPRS 2021), suggests that whenever thinking about how technology will shape the future, we should adopt an *agnostic* approach. Futurists tend to measure trends and their implications and then offer persuasive suppositions about what comes next. But the future is rarely the end of a trend line. And no one technology should be privileged over another as we cannot know its historical impact which is most likely in fact to stem from its being combined with others. And the introduction of any technology usually depends on the trade-offs that a society is willing to make to attain different ends. That is why an approach grounded in 'technology-agnostic solutions' is more likely to foster resilience and adaptability (EPRS 2021, p. 53)

So, how do we think *agnostically*? The best approach is to employ four methodological filters.

Lexical

One is language. What do we mean by the words, 'invention' or 'new', 'radical' or 'revolutionary' which we use all the time? They are not, as you might think at first fixed, transparent terms but shifting and highly charged ideas historically. When we claim something is new, do we mean that it is 'original' or 'recent', or 'modern'?

A striking example is the US Navy's electro-magnetic rail gun which can fire projectiles at speeds far exceeding those of missiles. First tested in 2014, the rounds destroy their target with the force of their impact rather than detonating an explosive warhead. Long a staple of science fiction, energy weapons may be the future of war, but the electro-magnetic rail gun has a history, quite a long one; it is merely the latest development of the catapult, and it was first patented by a French scientist nearly a century ago (Coghlan 2014, p. 24). Sometimes the 'new' has not been noticed, or its potential understood. But for that matter, what do we mean by 'potential'? The rail gun is a case in point: it can manage a few shots per hour as compared with some existing guns that can fire 20 rounds per minute.

It is the long haul that decides the impact of weapons systems for most usually go through a series of stages of adoption, diffusion, improvement, recycling and even hybridisation. Often, we make the mistake of focussing on innovation rather than use. Many of the inventions that have shaped war are re-inventions: the flamethrower, a Byzantine innovation of the 9th century; the submarine which first appeared in the Napoleonic wars and the fusion-fused hand grenade, first invented in 1861 but not used effectively until 1914 (Black 2013, p. 8). Society, writes David Gelernter, "replaces a thing when it finds something better, not when it finds something newer" (Gelernter 2012, p. 46). The rail gun may be a good example. In *Ghost Fleet*, Peter Singer's futuristic novel about a future Sino-American war, it turns the tide for the US. In the real world, it may well represent a technological dead-end.

Ontological

Another question is what impact positive or negative does the 'new' have on us ontologically? Ontology is a grand word which means essentially the study of being. To write of ontology is to write of our humanity, what make us the distinctive species that we are. We are not, for example, the only species to use tools but we are the only one to use technology and our relationship with the latter is often life-defining. Technology can shape our lives in ways that are so familiar that we no longer recognise how it does so. A weapons-system for example can change the way its users think about war. Every technology for that reason has a social history. Take the machine gun which changed the way the Western powers conceived war in the late 19th century. It was seen to be the product of industrialisation, a process restricted at that time entirely to the West. It was seen to embody such modern principles as productivity and efficiency – more output for less input. It also followed that the machine gun could be used to make people who didn't have it to 'see reason', to see that resistance was futile. If they continued to resist, they were clearly being 'unreasonable' (Ellis 1976, p. 21).

But changes can also result not only from an attitude of mind (as in the case of the machine gun); they can also be produced by changes in the brain itself (Greenfield 2011). Drones, the weapon of choice in the War on Terror, have a social history too. It was once feared that drone pilots would find themselves living in a sanitised environment where they would be cut off from the consequences of their own actions. Some neuroscientists expressed concern that an online screen life would encourage them to regard war as a computer game. Most of them, after all, came from a generation that spent an average of 80 hours a week on online gaming. The fear was what psychologists call 'dissociation' or 'moral de-skilling'. It was feared that they would log off emotionally (the brain protects us from information overload by shutting down reflection). It was also thought that the hours they spent looking at screens would weaken the 'deep processing' that underpins inductive analysis, critical thinking, and most important of all, empathy, the ability to imagine someone else's pain.

This did not come to pass. Drone pilots today suffer from high instances of post-traumatic stress, which is why the USAF has a shortfall of people wanting to sign up. Unlike the players of video games like *Soldier of Anarchy* and *First Battalion* most do not regard the battlespace as just a 'kill box'. Even so, it is likely that the new technologies with which we be interfacing more and more will make us not only more machine-readable but by default more machine friendly. The danger is not that computers begin to think for us, but that we begin to think like them. The real threat is that one day the artificial intelligence we are creating may turn out to be our own (Carr 2015, p. 29).

Imaginative

The future is imagined long before it is realised. Until the 19th century, western societies had no real tool for anticipating future events except history on the understanding as the book of *Ecclesiastes* puts it, there is nothing new under the sun. But at the turn of the 20th century, we invented a new literary genre: science fiction. And science fiction writers introduced us to a novel idea – that the most important event in our lives might not be something that happened in the past but something that we might eventually encounter in the future.

Today science fiction is now prescribed reading in the military. The novel *Ender's Game* has been on the syllabus of the Marine Corps University at Quantico for some time. It is also on the USN's Professional Leadership Program along with *Starship Troopers*. Our reliance on science fiction is growing all the time. In Germany, *Project Cassandra*, a recent collaboration between the military and the Literature Department at the University of Tübingen asks professors to imagine the future of war; are not they well equipped precisely because the fictional world they write about is a world of the imagination? (Oltermann 2021). In France, the Defence Innovation Agency has set up a team of science fiction writers to propose scenarios that might not occur to most military planners. In the US the Pentagon went to Hollywood after 9/11 to ask sci-fi writers what was likely to be the next terrorist atrocity (the sci-fi writer Han Song (*2066: Red Star over America*) had predicted the World Trade Center attack the previous year).

There is a good reason for this: writers and film producers have a more fertile imagination than most of us. It is after all, their stock in trade. Let me provide two particularly striking examples. The first attack on an iconic building was staged in a 1909 movie: it showed anarchists flying four biplanes into the dome of St Paul's Cathedral in what was then the world's most globalised city. It is easy to marvel at the film's prescience, but it also shows how wretchedly predictable 9/11 was. Even more remarkable, a striking technological breakthrough – the atomic bomb – was not imagined until a novelist got there first. The prospect of an atomic war was first predicted by H G Wells in 1914 in his book *The World Set Free*. It first occurred to a scientist 19 years later, on the morning of 12 September 1933, when Leo Szillard was crossing Southampton Row in London. On that day he glimpsed the shape of things to come: the possibility of creating a nuclear chain reaction which, in turn, could be utilised to build a bomb. Had he experienced his epiphany ten years earlier, the Second World War might well have been fought by both sides with nuclear weapons.

H G Wells, remember, was a scientist by training; his graphic visions of the future were grounded in what he knew to be scientifically possible; that is why he got the future right more than most. He even imagined submarine-launched ballistic missiles (he called them 'air torpedoes') Wells was an excellent storyteller which is why his early since fiction works have never been out of print; even so, his grasp of the future sometimes failed him. His novel *War in the Air* (1908) has Zeppelins, not aircraft, bombing New York. Wells may have got the details wrong, nevertheless he was extraordinarily perceptive in realising how total 20th-century war would be, and where its logic would ultimately lead. The problem is that most works of science fiction are based on what Karl Popper called 'promissory materialism'; they depend, in other words on promissory notes for discoveries not yet made, and technologies not yet invented. In 2021, the US 'won' a war with China in a wargame by using technologies that were not yet in production, such as sixth-generation fighters.

Historical

The fourth methodological approach is the oldest: the study of history. We may live forwards (we apparently think about the future several times every hour) but we still *think* backwards. And we are better equipped to do so than our ancestors thanks to the professional study of history which dates back only to the mid-19th century. This is to be welcomed; the past may not be the best guide to the future, but it is the only we have got.

But will we continue to rely on historians much longer? The technologies that made possible the so-called Revolution in Military Affairs (RMA) in the 1990s, claimed one American general, had 'abolished history' and Clausewitz with it (Buley 2007, p. 123). Many will be heartened by that news! Many scientists believe that Artificial Intelligence (AI) and quantum computing will replace history altogether a higher order of analysis. The German army has already begun outsourcing to algorithms in a programme called 'Preview–Prediction–Visualisation–Early Warning'. It is meant to support the work of human analysts, not to replace them but these are early days, and the prospect of redundancy looms. In the market, traders have long been replaced by algorithms. Will historians be rendered redundant too?

For the moment, at least history still offers us the best methodology for thinking about the future because it establishes a plot line that we can recognise that we are living through right now. What I think we can identify over the last 7,000 years or more is an *evolutionary trajectory*. A Natural Science Foundation report entitled *Converging Technologies for Improving Human Performance* (2003) argued that improving human performance is the way in which we will continue to exploit possibilities that so far have been unrealised (Rocco & Bainbridge 2003). Is that not exactly what we have been doing for the past 7,000 years? 'History shows' is a term open to misuse but what military history shows (not without many reverses along the way) is a trajectory from the simple to the complex, from the general to the specific (specialisation), and from the instinctual to the intellectual.

Physical

We have gone from the muscular power required to use a bow with twice the range of a spear, to the chemical power of guns which trumped archery, to machine guns which trumped every hand-held gun. The aim has always been to reduce the physical input of the soldier. It took 20 years to train a longbowman at Agincourt. It took 37 different steps to fire a musket in the 17th century. It took 15 minutes to learn how to fire a machine gun. We went from bashing others over the head with stones and rocks to using catapults and slings, and later guns and guided missiles. Today we hack into enemy computers.

Cerebral

War continues to demand what Mark Pagel calls, a "more domesticated set of abilities" – i.e., more cerebral (Pagel 2012, p. 28). For we have also augmented our mental performance using our brains, as well as our muscles. The Greeks were the first to introduce ballistics and geometry into war, and we have never looked back. In terms of mental ability, there is an internal logic. Today's 'analytical warrior' is in the process of replacing the stereotypes of old. Mental agility, communication skills and multitasking are all important assets in today's military.

Whereas the physical and cerebral increase in performance began several thousand years ago, the *human–machine interface* is very recent. Only since the invention of the computer, have we been interfacing with machines as we have begun to do already. In turn, this has led to an undergoing ontological shift in the way we look at the world and ourselves. Academia has not lost its love for the prefix 'post' despite the death of post-modernism and post-structuralism. Professors tell us is that we are about to enter a radically different age to which we have given the term *post-human*.

The challenge of artificial intelligence (AI)

Central to that condition is our relationship with machines that may one day think for us. What we do know is that one day we will be sharing life with an intelligence that thinks differently from us. Until that time we will be interfacing with machines in radically new ways.

As computer power increases exponentially, we will have to keep in step. If we are not to surrender our power altogether to computers – whether they ever attain consciousness or not – we will have to *interface* with them in completely new ways. This, in turn, will require us to adopt new technologies. For the moment, we use a keyboard that creates a binary world of 'it' and 'us.'

To be able to interface effectively, we would have to back-engineer the brain to make it computer compatible. That means brain implants. This is where we enter the realm of William Gibson's novel *Neuromancer*. Gibson's novel was ahead of the game in its vision of collapsing altogether the distinction between the machine and the organic.

The future of war or so we tell ourselves will be determined above all by Artificial Intelligence (AI). AI is merely the latest manifestation of a long-term trend but of course it is likely to be the real game changer even if experts disagree about exactly how it will shape or reshape our future. The pass has probably already been sold. In December 2021, the UN Convention on Conventional Weapons failed to reach agreement on banning 'killer robots' or even controlling their introduction into the theatre of war. Even when rules are put in place, they tend to be non-binding. Science has become an end in itself; we must simply proceed at full speed and deal with the fall-out, however fatal, retrospectively – if we can.

But let us not get carried away. Let us apply the four filters I have employed to see how AI might or might not – change the character of war, and possibly even its nature.

Lexical

Frequently, we engage in loose thinking because we do not define terms strictly enough. AI is a good case in point: the concept has no universally agreed definition. There is huge difference between Artificial Narrow Intelligence (ANI) which includes systems that are able to perform autonomously a narrow range of tasks; Artificial General Intelligence (AGI) which refers to systems that are able to perform autonomously a range of tasks by learning, understanding and functioning, the way humans advance; and Artificial Superintelligence (ASI) which encompasses systems that will exceed human performance in ways that at present we cannot really imagine. The last is still largely the subject of science fiction.

AGI was first imagined by Isadore Gudak who forecast that there would be an 'intelligence explosion' when a system came to understand its own design and had the wherewithal to enhance itself again and again in a feedback cycle (Grayling 2022, p. 76). The question is not how soon artificial intelligence will surpass human problem-solving skills; the question is how soon after that they will be able to potentially 'bootstrap' themselves to unrecognisable levels of superintelligence in a matter of weeks or even days. But let's not lose touch with reality. Even in the case of AGI, a recent study by RAND suggests that it is unlikely to make a significant difference to war fighting for the next 20 years (EPRS 2021, p. 23).

It is also important to nail down what we mean by the word 'autonomy' when we read about the production of ever more sophisticated Autonomous Weapons Systems. Usually, we mean a system which can repair itself, maintain itself, improve over time (learn from its environment) and reproduce (the biggest challenge of all)? Until recently machines could accomplish one of these tasks. Commercial aircraft run on autopilot most of the time; human pilots are often there to reassure the passengers. Communications systems can repair but not reproduce themselves. A computer virus can reproduce but not learn how to improve its performance.

What scientists can agree is that systems will become consciously autonomous through 'emergence'. After all, that is how we ourselves develop in childhood. A child observing the world around it, develops emotional intelligence by the age of three (thanks to parental bonding) and social intelligence by the age of five (thanks to building up a network of friends). This is how computer experts believe machines will acquire cognitive abilities (artificial life). Consciousness may or may not follow. For there are many computer scientists who think that it will not. Just because a machine may behave as though it is thinking does not mean that it really is. Some scientists argue that no non-biological life form will ever evolve volitional intelligence (the wish to will anything other than its program). And others believe that no machine will ever be able to *imagine* things could be different than they are. History is a story of change precisely because for thousands of years we have imagined a better future. Freud called one of his last books *Civilisation and its Discontents*. Hunter-gatherer societies live perfectly contented lives because they find themselves trapped in an eternal present. Once you throw civilisation into the mix, humans tend to find themselves permanently discontented; they always want more for themselves and sometimes others. In other words, there are many reasons to challenge the popular idea that artificial intelligence will ever be fully autonomous (i.e. self-conscious). But until we can agree on what the terms mean, we won't make much progress with our predictions.

Ontological

Will AI change our ontological status? Probably not much, at least not to begin with. Much of the growing optimism about the prospect of human-like artificial intelligence is based on a fundamentally flawed conception of what human intelligence really is. It is true that machines can replicate some aspects of humanity with a method called 'Inverse Reinforcement Learning'. They can infer what a human being is trying to do and outstrip him/her in performance. But most of the time they cannot always grasp what would be the right thing to do because they have no system of values.

Even the AI systems we now use have been found to freeze systemic biases into code. This is a problem with courts in the US where judges increasingly use algorithms for sentencing criminals. An investigation by Pro Publica showed that black defendants in criminal cases were sentenced at twice the rate of white defendants for comparable offences (Grayling 2022, p. 69). Judges are encouraged to apply longer sentences to black offenders on the statistical grounds that there are more black people in jail than white. It is not that algorithms are not intelligent. The problem is that they do not understand abstract concepts such as fairness. And one reason for that is that they lack emotional intelligence. Empathy is built into us both biologically and culturally. Biologically, mirror neurons enable us to imagine another's pain, which is why regrettably, we are the only species that likes to torture its own kind. Cats do not torture mice; they cannot imagine their distress; they simply play with them until they get bored. Psychopaths are very different; they have too much imagination. They can imagine the pain of others.

Social intelligence like emotional intelligence is learned from interacting with others. That seems to be true of every other biological life-form, too. And it may also be true of machines. Their greatest limitation is that they cannot deal with *abductive reasoning*. For us, deductive and inductive reasoning is a given. In deductive reading, we prove things with necessity (i.e. logical contradictions cannot be true); with inductive reasoning, we make general claims from particular instances. But abductive reasoning is equally important. It allows for guesswork, speculation, intuition; all three make it possible for us to rely on common sense to make informed judgements with the limited evidence available. It is what helps keep us not only ahead of the game but also within it. At present, nobody has the slightest idea how to program abductive reasoning into a machine; apparently, no one is even working on it (Larson 2021). Until they do humans are likely to remain key players.

Perhaps, it is time in fact to start thinking of machines as collaborators, or members of the same team. They will probably not replace us, but they will increasingly assist us. This is already happening. All poker professionals now employ AI to train and create 'game theory optimal' (GTO) strategies. Another example is the game of chess. It is true that since 2005 computers have been able to beat a chess Grand Master, but a new program CENTAUR has given chess players access to every game ever played. As a result, the number of Grand Masters has doubled in recent years. Garry Kasparov, who lost that famous 2005 game to IBM Deep Blue, went onto develop *Advanced Chess,* a programme which allows a human being and a machine to work together. Whenever they do so, they tend to beat a computer working on its own every time. In other words, humans and machines work more effectively when they work together rather than when they work alone. Remember too, that as machines communicate with us more often so they will begin to develop social skills. A soldier wouldn't want to be told by a nurse-bot on the battlefield that statistically he has zero chance of surviving it to a field hospital. He will want to be told: 'Just hang in there: You'll make it!' Even if he and his friends suspect that he will not.

Imaginative

Novels are not the only way in which we imagine the future. Movies play an even more important role. The *Terminator* movies have lodged themselves firmly in the popular imagination for a reason. We know that robotics is the future of war in one form or another, which is why we will continue to remain fearful. The UN 'Campaign to Stop Killer Robots' is a catchy slogan after all, not least because it combines two of the most potent nightmares of science fiction – a powerful weapon, allied to a non-human intelligence which might find it difficult to appreciate the value of human life, let alone the significance of its loss.

It is the exponential increase in computer power that has led science fiction writers to predict that one day machines will wake up. Scientists call it the 'Singularity'. A desktop PC can do around 10^9 calculations per second. The largest computer in the US at Lawrence Livermore National Lab can do 10^{15} (or 1,000 trillion). Within a few years, this level of processing power will be built into our desktops. By the early 2030s, computers will be operating up to 10^{29} (100 octillion) (Cooper 2019). At that point, will we have arrived at the Singularity, the day the machines begin to think for themselves?

Not everyone however is convinced that this will happen. John Rennie, the former editor of *Scientific American*, calls these claims an example of 'slippery futurism' because they border on the unfalsifiable (Edwards & Brooks 2018, p. 228). As the theoretical physicist Wolfgang Pauli said of any claim that is un-falsifiable, it is not only not right, it is 'not even wrong'. Unfortunately, the Singularity has become a quasi-religious discourse which has its own followers and creeds, its own orthodoxies and priests, and its own eschatological framework: the promise that one day the machines will wake up and begin to have their own thoughts. Whether this happens or not, is not the point; the point about any Singularity is that you cannot describe it and you cannot see past it which is why there cannot be any understanding of what will happen to us after the event.

Historical

AI is going to change the experience of war quite significantly but will it, as the Pentagon's first report on AI (2019) claimed also change the *nature* of war? Many military men predict that it will. Let me quote a memorandum by Gen Barry McCaffrey in October 2007: "We have already made a hundred-year war fighting leap-ahead with MQ-1 Predator MQ-9 Reaper and Global Hawk – they fundamentally change the nature of war" (Doyle 2013, p. 11). The inescapable point of reference here is Clausewitz who tells us that while the character of war is in constant flux, its nature is not.

And the nature of war until now is what it was in Thucydides' day who called it *to anthropon* – the human thing.

War, claims Martin van Creveld, will never change its nature as long as it remains a purely human experience, governed by the same sentiments, passions and emotions which have persuaded us to kill each other with a good conscience, and often to sacrifice our own lives for family or a cause. (1) When the chips are down war is primarily an affair of the heart; it is fuelled by such illogical factors as honour, duty, and loyalty which are very human and quite independent of the technology or weapons we use; (2) technology will never change the function of war which is to win; this is what human beings aim for; machines do not have ambitions, only programs and they find it remarkably difficult to deceive us; they can't think strategically; (3) technology is linear. It involves cause and effect, repetitiveness, specialisation and efficiency. War is non-linear which is why it is still the most unpredictable of all human activities (Van Creveld 1991, pp. 314–15). These are all compelling arguments, but then van Creveld was writing back in 1991. Much has changed since then including the prospect that one day we might devolve responsibility for decision-making to machines.

A more pressing question, perhaps, is whether we will be able to develop in the next 10–20 years a weapons system that, though not conscious in our sense of the word, is fully able to take decisions without reference to human operators. More importantly, of course, why would we wish to? One reason is purely practical. In an age of hypersonic missiles, speed is at a premium – machines can think faster than we can and react faster still. But another reason is cultural. It is the recognition to quote one biologist that simply being human is the weakest point in the kill chain. When it comes to making life or death decisions, machines may be more reliable. Besides though some of us may be good at thinking, many of us are not always very thoughtful. We are ruled by the passions of the moment. We often act out of character much to our own surprise. We frequently disobey our own rules. We are often confronted with a very human choice between what we may think in a particular situation it is lawful to do and what is the right thing to do. The choice can be the difference between a right judgement call and a war crime.

That is why many roboticists believe that autonomy will offer us a *moral upgrade* – the latest historical upgrade in human performance – one that will compensate for the fact that we are the weakest link in the kill chain. A machine would not be moved to take revenge for the loss of another machine. It would not dehumanise its enemies using racial or ethnic filters. It would not act badly because it was inexperienced or poorly trained. It would not derive any pleasure from killing. Machines would not be nicer, more compassionate, or more reasonable, let alone more humane. They would just be better at goal fulfilment. You could not scare them into running away, or bribe them to behave better, or appeal to their better nature. You would not be able to reason them out of anything. They would not be open to arguments of any kind. For some of us this is what makes them so frightening.

Conclusion

AI is only one of the inventions that will reshape war as well as our understanding of it. At present we have AI-enabled weapons but not AI weapons, but for how much longer? We are careering into the unknown, at a faster pace than at any other time in history. We are using cyberspace for offensive operations; we are talking of building bases on the Moon; in 20 years' time robots may be doing most of the fighting. Nevertheless, the technologies we introduce into war may take much longer to make a significant impact. Agnosticism should be the order of the day.

References

Black, J 2013, *War and Technology*, Indiana University Press, Bloomington, IN.

Buley, B 2007, *The New American Way of War: Military Culture and the Political Utility of Force*, Routledge, London.

Carr, N 2015, *The Glass Cage: Where Automation Is Taking Us*, Bodley Head, London.

Coghlan, T 2014, 'The US Unveils a 5,400mph Electro-Gun', *The Times*, 10 April.

Cooper, K 2019, *The Contact Paradox*, Bloomsbury, London.

Doyle, J 2013, 'Rise of the Robots? Western Unmanned Air Operations in Iraq and Afghanistan, 2001 to 2010', *Air Power Review*, vol. 16, no. 2, pp. 10–31.

Edgerton, D 2006, *The Shock of the Old: Technology and Global History Since 1900*, Profile Books, London.

Edwards, R & Brooks, M 2018, *Science(ish): The Peculiar Science Behind the Movies*, Atlantic Books, London.

Ellis, J 1976, *The Social History of the Machine Gun*, Pimlico, London.

EPRS 2021, *Innovative Technologies Shaping the 2040 Battlefield*, European Parliament, Strasbourg.

Gelernter, D 2012, 'Recursive Structure', in J Brockman (ed), *This Will Make You Smarter*, Random House, New York, pp. 246–9.

Grayling, A C 2022, *For the Good of the World*, One World, London.

Greenfield, S 2011, *You and Me: The Neuroscience of Identity*, Notting Hill Editions, London.

Kelly, K 2016, *The Inevitable: Understanding the 12 Technological Forces That Will Shape Our Future*, Viking, New York.

Kissinger, H A 1957, *Nuclear Weapons and Foreign Policy*, Harper & Brothers, New York.

Larson, E 2021, *The Myth of AI*, Harvard University Press, Cambridge, MA.

Millburn, C N 2002, 'Nanotech in the Age of Post-Human Engineering: Science Fiction as Science? *Configurations*, vol. 10, no. 2, pp. 261–95.

Oltermann, P 2021, 'At First, I Thought This Is Crazy: The Real-Life Plans to Use Novels to Predict the Next War', *The Guardian*, 26 June.

Pagel, M 2012, *Wired for Culture: The Natural History of Human Cooperation*, Allen Lane, London.

Parrinder, P 1979, *Science Fiction: A Critical Guide*, Longman, London.

Parris, M 2009, 'In the Fog Remember This: Victory Is Impossible', *The Times*, 4 July.

Radick, G 2014, 'Consciously Digital', *Times Literary Supplement*, 20 June.

Rocco, M & Bainbridge, W 2003, *Converging Technologies for Improving Human Performance*, The National Science Foundation, Washington, DC.

Sterling, B 2010, 'Atemporality for the Creative Artist', *Wired*, 25 February, <https://www.wired.com/2010/02/atemporality-for-the-creative-artist> (accessed 28 October 2022).

Van Creveld, M 1991, *Technology and War: From 2000 B.C. to the Present*, The Free Press, New York.

4

HUMAN SECURITY IN FUTURE MILITARY OPERATIONS

Mary Kaldor and Iavor Rangelov

Introduction

'Human security' is in the air. The concept has established itself within the development community for some time. But in recent years, there has been a growing interest in the topic within the defence community. The new Strategic Concept of the North Atlantic Treaty Organization (NATO), the outcome of the June 2022 Summit in Madrid, 'emphasises' the need to 'integrate' human security, along with climate change and the Women, Peace and Security agenda, 'across all our core tasks' (NATO 2022, p. 1). And several NATO members – notably the UK, which in 2021 adopted a Joined Service Publication (JSP) on incorporating human security in Defence – are 'mainstreaming' human security throughout the armed forces (UK Ministry of Defence 2021).

Human security is usually defined as the security of *individuals* and the communities in which they live, in the context of multiple economic, environmental, health, and physical threats. It is generally contrasted with national security, which is about the defence of borders from the threat of foreign attack. In other words, human security is an alternative to war. Were it to be adopted universally, it would mean the end of organised collective violence between two groups. Were it to be adopted by some states and not others, it could mean a dampening down of conflicts and a defensive non-escalatory response to acts of aggression, genocide, or massive violations of human rights.

The first use of the term was in the 1994 Human Development Report of the United Nations Development Programme (UNDP), where the emphasis was on economic and social development as a way of preventing war; this understanding remains the main approach to human security in United Nations (UN) circles. Indeed, for most proponents of the concept, the implementation of human security involves a much greater emphasis on addressing a range of non-military insecurities – development, health, or the environment. Nevertheless, there is a role for the military, among other instruments, in minimising the harm to individual human beings from different forms of political and criminal violence, what is called within NATO Allied Command Transformation 'MC2HS', or the Military Contribution to Human Security.

This chapter is an attempt to elucidate what human security currently means in military operations and what it could mean in the future. It starts by tracing the trajectory of the growing interest in human security within NATO and in the specific case of the UK, drawing on recent

DOI: 10.4324/9781003299011-6

developments and insights from a series of exchanges we had with people in the defence community.[1] It then considers what human security in future military operations might mean in practice – the core human security roles of the military, the principles of human security in military operations, and the relevant legal regime. Finally, it briefly outlines the implications of the adoption of human security for military budgets and new technologies.

The turn to human security among the military

For both NATO and the UK, human security is understood as an umbrella concept that encompasses Building Integrity (anti-corruption), Protection of Civilians, Cultural Property Protection, Children and Armed Conflict, Conflict-related Sexual and Gender-based Violence, Human Trafficking, and Women, Peace and Security. A human security unit was established inside NATO by the Secretary General in 2019. A similar initiative was taken by the then Minister of Defence, Gavin Williamson, in the UK Ministry of Defence.

Subsequently, these plans have speeded up with a new directive being developed in NATO's Supreme Headquarters Allied Powers Europe (SHAPE) and a new Joint Service Publication in the UK. There is an emphasis on integrating human security in training and in technological development, and, in the UK case, the introduction of human security advisors in all operational units.

This new emphasis on human security is the consequence of several overlapping factors. The first factor has been the actual experience of out of area operations, particularly but not only Afghanistan. According to one British officer we spoke with, it can be traced back to the Responsibility Protect/Libya and the experience in Basra in 2008–2009 where the commanding officer, General Andy Salmon, adopted an explicitly human security agenda, and it arrived in the UK via the Women, Peace and Security agenda. Another reference point for British officers is Helmand, which is seen as an innovation in adopting a human security approach that was ultimately undermined by the ways in which British forces were attacked; it was a 'tripartite approach' involving the Ministry of Defence (MoD), the Foreign and Commonwealth Office (FCO) and the Department for International Development (DFID) but the sustained attacks meant that the MoD became preeminent. Other examples are Mali, the Royal Navy operations in the Caribbean for humanitarian relief and in the Mediterranean for migrants, as well as the British-led European anti-piracy mission in the Gulf. In addition, the experiences of Kosovo and Iraq were important in drawing attention to the issue of cultural heritage.

The NATO role in Afghanistan has been particularly salient. As one British officer put it:

> There is real appetite for understanding the human environment better – a different way of analysing the human environment that is conflict sensitive. It took a long time to understand the local dynamics in Afghanistan, the multiple reasons for fighting … the human environment. We tend to think about the adversary as a group. But sometimes it is about the structural factors that produce conflict . . . Framing through the adversary is not always the most useful analytical lens. There needs to be a Human Security approach in understanding and engaging.[2]

Particularly important was the growing emphasis on protection of civilians – something that gained traction because air strikes and night raids were undermining the legitimacy of the international presence in Afghanistan. A comprehensive Protection of Civilians policy was adopted in July

2016. As one study points out, "Not only was NATO receiving significant international backlash over highly publicised incidents of civilian harm but commanders began to identify civilian harm as fuelling the growing insurgency" (Holt 2021, p. 5).

A second factor was the evolution of the European Security and Defence Policy. In the early 2000s, a series of reports on European security capabilities were presented to Javier Solana, then High Representative for Common Foreign and Security Policy, by the Study Group on European Security Capabilities, later renamed the Human Security Study Group.[3] The Study Group proposed a human security doctrine for the European Union (EU) as a distinctive way of doing security. According to this version, human security is what individuals enjoy in rights-based, law-governed societies. It is assumed that the state will protect individuals from existential threats and that emergency services – including ambulances, firefighters, and police – are part of state provision. In a global context, human security is about extending individual rights beyond domestic borders and about developing a capacity at a regional or global level to provide emergency services that can be deployed in situations where states either lack capacity or are themselves the source of existential threats. The Study Group proposed a human security force composed of both civilians and military and based on a set of principles, which are very different from the principles that apply to the military in a classic war-fighting role. These proposals were echoed in the State of the Union address by Ursula von der Leyen in 2021:

> The European Union is a unique security provider. There will be missions where NATO or the UN will not be present, but where the EU should be. On the ground, our soldiers work side-by-side with police officers, lawyers and doctors, with humanitarian workers and human rights defenders, with teachers and engineers. We can combine military and civilian, along with diplomacy and development – and we have a long history in building and protecting peace.
>
> (Leyen 2021)

It can be argued that the European pillar of NATO has been enhanced partly as a consequence of the Trump years, when the US was less present, but more importantly under the impetus of the war in Ukraine and the impending membership of Sweden and Finland. The New Force Model proposed in the 2022 Strategic Concept will increase the number of ready forces available to NATO and these are likely to be European (Biscop 2022).

A third factor is the growing influence of NGOs, and a much greater readiness for working together with civilians, including other government agencies, international organisations as well as industry and academia. We were told that NATO cooperates with the International Red Cross on cyber security issues and does a two-week human security course with the UN. At SHAPE, we were recommended to talk with a range of NGOs including the Stimson Centre, which has played a pioneering role in protection of civilians; Civilians in Conflict, the NGO that collects data on civilian casualties; PAX for Peace in the Netherlands, which has long spearheaded demands for human security; and the Center for Cultural Heritage and Armed Conflict.

And the final, and perhaps counterintuitive, factor is the war in Ukraine. One might have expected that the war in Ukraine would encourage a return to a more traditional emphasis on war-fighting. A senior NATO official told us that Ukraine has been 'a wake-up call' – while traditional NATO planning was based on the assumption of a World-War-II-type conflict with millions of civilian casualties, nowadays that is seen as completely unacceptable. This may explain both the emphasis on conventional and defensive forms of deterrence in the new Strategic Concept as well as human security. It is not just concern about minimising loss of life and preventing escalation; a very important issue is legitimacy. As one of our UK interviewees put it, Russia is focused on delivering human insecurity – brutality towards civilians, destruction of cultural heritage, sexual violence, looting. Conforming with International Humanitarian Law (IHL) is hugely important for legitimacy, something they stress in contingency training for Ukrainian soldiers.

What is not clear as yet is whether the umbrella approach to human security actually involves a paradigm shift in how military operations are conducted. There are tensions between the various topics included under the heading of human security. Some fear that the emphasis on gender and climate change waters down the significance of human security, while some of those who focus on the Women, Peace, and Security agenda do not talk about human security because of concerns that this new concept detracts from a focus on gender issues. More importantly perhaps, it is not clear whether the new emphasis on human security merely means taking IHL and the various components of the umbrella terms very seriously when conducting military operations – something that is, of course, a positive development – or whether it portends more far-reaching change in how the military operate.

Almost everyone interviewed for this chapter were enthusiastic proponents of human security. Indeed, an interviewee who was chosen because she was not part of the human security institutional framework, responded to our questions about whether ordinary soldiers were affected by these efforts, by saying that it is absolutely the case and it is in fact 'all over everything'. Yet several of our interlocutors expressed frustration about the difficulty of changing mindsets. They felt that the shift to human security has not yet materialised in a heartfelt manner; it has not yet reached a 'tipping point'.

So what might human security in future military operations mean?

Future military contributions to human security: roles, principles, legality

Evidently, implementing human security requires a range of non-military capabilities – humanitarian responders, health workers, engineers, firefighters, police, and so on and the mix depends on the type of contingency – natural disasters, famines, or war, for example. The military contribution to human security is focused on meeting large-scale physical threats to individuals and their communities; these might include military invasions, genocide, or massive violations of human rights. The aim of any military operation has to be defensive and non-escalatory. In other words, it is about defending people from organised violence without at the same time provoking further violence; something which is very difficult for soldiers to undertake. It is about the legal use of force, but this is not the same as war-fighting. In this section, we discuss the specific roles in which the military might be used for human security in the future, the principles that should guide such operations, and the relevant legal framework.

Roles

There are two main roles in which the military may be required in order to implement human security. One is defence of people against the crime of aggression, as in Ukraine, and the other is the contribution to international peace-keeping and crisis management.

Defence against aggression is different from engaging in military competition along geopolitical lines. Rather than matching capabilities of potential aggressors, the idea is to be able to demonstrate effective defence, to show that aggression cannot succeed, without at the same time being perceived as a potential threat to other states.

During the 1980s, there was much concern about the offensive posture of NATO and the dangers of weapons of mass destruction. At that time, proposals were put forward for what was known as defensive deterrence (Boserup & Neild 1990), i.e., deterring foreign attacks through a credible conventional defensive posture rather than through the threat of nuclear or conventional retaliation. It was the idea behind Gorbachev's notion of 'reasonable sufficiency'. Proposals for area defence or in-depth defence were put forward that would have meant drawing down nuclear weapons as well as conventional offensive capabilities, such as bombers or massed tanks (though evidently some are needed for defensive purposes). It is worth asking whether Putin would have invaded Ukraine had he realised that Ukraine would put up such an effective conventional defence.

In terms of crisis management and peace-keeping, that is to say intervention in intractable conflicts, the aim is to end such wars by dampening down conflict and reducing the incentives for violence rather than through victory or a single top-down peace agreement. Central to this goal is the establishment of legitimate and inclusive political authority and a rule of law (SGESC 2004; HSSG 2007; HSSG 2016). Human security interventions are always civilian led and involve a combination of civilian and military actors. The tasks of the (external) military in these circumstances could include: protecting civilians from attack and creating a safe environment in which a legitimate political authority can be established; monitoring and upholding local peace agreements and cease-fires as part of multi-level peace building involving civil society, especially women; establishing humanitarian space through corridors and safe havens that allow for the delivery of humanitarian assistance; and arresting war criminals. A similar approach was adopted by the British in Northern Ireland or the EU-led anti-piracy mission in the Gulf of Aden, which combined the arrest of pirates with non-military measures such as the introduction of fishing licenses on the coast of Somalia.

This is very different from counter-insurgency and counter-terror where the goal is victory over an enemy. In Afghanistan, for example, the goal was the destruction of the Taliban, al Qaeda and later ISIS Khorasan, rather than the security of Afghans. This meant continuing attacks (air strikes and night raids) that provoked and strengthened the insurgency as well as allying with corrupt commanders who undermined the legitimacy of the Afghan government. It also marginalised the civilian leadership of the international intervention, notably the UN Special Representative (Rangelov & Theros 2019; Kaldor 2021).

Principles

How such operations are conducted is as important as why. The practice of the military in protecting civilians must conform to human security principles. Human security is about human rights rather than war. It is about saving all lives including the lives of enemies. It is about law-based security rather than war-based security; in other words, it is more like policing than war-fighting. One way to think about it is as an inversion of the law of armed conflict. Under IHL, the killing of civilians is sometimes permitted if it is necessary to achieve a military objective and the harm is proportionate to what would be achieved by victory. For human security, it is the other way round. The killing of enemies is permitted if it is necessary to protect civilians or save lives.

The principles for conducting military operations within a human security framework include:

- *Minimising all loss of life*. Military operations are carried out in ways that seek to minimise all casualties, civilians as well as combatants – including enemy combatants.
- *Stability rather than victory*. The aim of the military contribution to human security is to help stabilise crises by reducing the incentives for violence and protecting civilians rather than pursuing military victory.

- *Defensive rather than offensive.* Military operations have a defensive focus and employ defensive rather than offensive capabilities across the spectrum of conventional and cyber systems and weapons, including Artificial Intelligence (AI)-enabled capabilities.
- *Civilian control.* Military operations are civilian led and aligned with civilian priorities.

Legality

If human security entails a law-based rather than a war-based approach to security, the question is what law? The answer depends on the concept of human security that is adopted. Different understandings of human security unfold across the spectrum of international law relating to a diverse set of issues, shaping how international law constructs its subjects, identifies its sources, and creates obligations for states and non-state actors, as well as informing forward-looking proposals how it may do so in the future (Oberleitner 2022). Thus the 'broad' UNDP version of human security invites consideration of the frameworks for promoting social, economic, and cultural rights and countering structural inequality under international law (Estrada-Tanck 2022) or specific bodies of law such as international food law (Steier, Kang & Ramdas 2022) or global health law (Forman 2022).

The 'narrow' Canadian version of human security informs the Responsibility to Protect (R2P) concept developed by the International Commission on Intervention and State Sovereignty (ICISS 2001) and formally adopted by the UN General Assembly in 2005. R2P seeks to address the perceived need for a 'humanitarian exception' to the prohibition on the use of force under the UN Charter, which provides only for a 'self-defence' exception. It spells out the responsibility of the international community to intervene, including by using military force as a last resort, in cases of mass human rights violations such as ethnic cleansing and genocide. The UN Security Council authorised the NATO intervention in Libya in 2011 with an R2P mandate with Security Council Resolution 1973 adopted on 17 March 2011.

From a human security perspective, R2P is too state-centric and top-down. It enhances the power of the permanent members of the Security Council, which means that in cases like Syria, it becomes irrelevant. Moreover, as its implementation in Libya demonstrates, it relies on warfighting methods (air strikes) that contradict its humanitarian objectives, prioritise force protection over civilian protection, and blur the boundaries between humanitarian intervention and regime change. Human security requires a shift in focus from the responsibility of states to intervene with military means to the rights of human beings to be protected. A shift from the Responsibility to Protect to a Right to be Protected under international law means that

> Human security might necessitate the use of force in situations of humanitarian emergency, but under much tighter rules of engagement, which are aimed at minimizing all loss of life, with a defensive focus on individuals on the ground and involving, where possible, the arrest rather than killing of those responsible for human rights violations as well as enhanced accountability.
>
> (Chinkin & Kaldor 2017, p. 539)

Human security requires a similar shift in military operations carried out in self-defence. Human security is the inverse of IHL, which permits the killing of civilians when militarily necessary, subject to the principles of distinction and proportionality. The principle of military necessity permits combatants to carry out necessary attacks to achieve a legitimate military objective, even if these attacks will result in foreseen civilian casualties. Its application is based on the rules of distinction (requiring combatants to distinguish between civilians and civilian objects, on the one hand, and combatants and military objectives, on the other) and proportionality (demanding that when estimating the civilian deaths or injuries caused by an attack on a legitimate military target, the harm caused cannot be excessive (disproportionate) to the anticipated military advantage to be obtained by the attack).

For IHL, the objective of military operations is to defeat the enemy and that determines when the killing of civilians is permissible in pursuit of that objective (the military necessity, distinction and proportionality principles). For human security, the objective of military operations is to protect individuals and communities and that determines when the killing of combatants is permissible in pursuit of that objective (when it is necessary to protect civilians or save lives). The rules of engagement from a human security perspective are the inverse of IHL because of this shift in the means and ends of military operations. Or to put it another way, the rules of engagement are much tighter than for IHL and are complemented by International Human Rights Law, International Criminal Law, and the so-called 'human security treaties'.[4]

Human security implications for military spending and new/emerging technologies

Most of the human security literature starts from the presumption that military spending should be reduced and the funding released should be used to address a range of non-military existential threats such as extreme poverty, pandemics, or climate change. Indeed, this was the thrust of the original UNDP concept of human security. The idea that reducing expenditure on the arms race and increasing expenditure on development would increase overall security had already been expressed in a series of expert reports and commissions such as the Brandt Commission.

Evidently, human security does require increased expenditure on such issues as health, the environment, education, or livelihoods. But, as we make clear in this chapter, there is a role for military forces in protecting people from foreign attack, as well as from other forms of political violence. It is not immediately evident that this would mean a reduction in military spending.

The two main functions of military forces are defence against external attack and a contribution to peace-keeping, or more particularly, protection of civilians in crisis situations. In the case of defence against external attack, we have argued that deterrence consists of effective defence rather than retaliation. This would require increased expenditure on personnel and precision systems including cyber security rather than nuclear weapons and complex offensive systems. A human security approach to crisis management prioritises the civilian elements – development and legitimate governance. Nevertheless, it may also require an increased peace-keeping and crisis-management role, involving the protection of civilians, the protection of humanitarian space, mediation and monitoring of ceasefires. Expenditure on UN peace-keeping in 2021 was $6.8 billion, a tiny proportion of the total $3 trillion global expenditures, though this does not include peace-keeping expenditures by other international organisations, such as the EU or the AU (Brzoska, Omitoogun & Sköns 2022).

A shift from national to human security among the big military spenders, the US, Russia and China, would involve big reductions in military spending, though additional costs would be required for destruction and recycling of military equipment, for reintegration of military personnel and for the conversion of defence industries. The big falls in military spending after the end of the Cold War did lead to a big rise in mercenaries and private security companies as well as an increase in the private sales of surplus weapons. There was also persistent pressure from industry to restart military production. Likewise, there is also a human security case for reductions among big military spenders in the so-called Global South, where military spending is artificially high as a consequence of purchases of expensive systems often linked to corruption (indeed, human security might be a useful way to reframe Security Sector Reform programmes). For those countries where military spending is around the global average of 2% of GDP, there is a need for more detailed analysis of what a shift to human security might mean in financial terms.

The key point is that the shift from national to human security is not just about a shift from military spending to other types of social spending. There needs to be a change in the content of military spending and without further research, it is not clear whether this would be cheaper or more expensive.

The military applications of new and emerging technologies have potentially far-reaching consequences for human security in future military operations, which also require further investigation. Several clusters of emerging technologies are expected to mature and become deployable in the battlefield in the next two to three decades. They include the uses of AI in information warfare, cyber operations, weapons systems, and Command, Control, Communications, Computers, Intelligence, Surveillance, and Reconnaissance (C4ISR); advanced robotics and autonomous systems including unmanned vehicles operating without human supervision or control; quantum technology applications for C4ISR and both offensive and defensive cyber capabilities/operations; technologies that deliver novel kinetic and non-kinetic effects including hypersonic weapons systems and Directed Energy Weapons (DEW) (e.g., high-energy lasers); satellites and space-based technologies including anti-satellite (ASAT) capabilities; and biotechnologies such as physical or cognitive Human Enhancement Technology (HET) and synthetic biology (e.g., weaponisation of biological pathogens and advanced delivery systems) (EPRS 2021; Favaro, Renic & Kühn 2022).

Although a nascent arms race involving major powers – the Unites States, Russia, and China – may already be underway in areas such as AI and hypersonic weapons, there is much debate and uncertainty about the future adoption and impact of emerging technologies in military operations. It is possible to anticipate some of the human security implications of specific technologies based on their technical characteristics and possible uses. However, much more significant but difficult to forecast is their cumulative impact. How new technologies interact with each other, with legacy systems (conventional and nuclear) and with changes in the broader environment in which military operations are justified, planned, and carried out, will determine their overall impact on human security.

A recent study forecasting the future impact of 12 emerging technologies on international stability and human security concludes that taken together, the net impact of all 12 technologies is negative. With respect to human security, the authors find that only one of the technologies they study – quantum technology for C4IRS – is likely to strengthen humanitarian principles. They describe the combined effect of emerging technologies as 'negative multiplicity', highlighting 'the predominantly negative, concurrent, and in some cases similar, first- and second-order effects that emerging technologies are expected to have on international stability and human security' (Favaro, Renic & Kühn 2022, p. 49).

The implications of specific technologies for human security will depend on how they are used in practice. For example, DEWs can be used in offensive operations against human and material targets, but they also have significant defensive potential for countering rockets, artillery, mortars, hypersonic weapons or drones. Similarly, quantum technology can be used offensively (e.g., for decrypting data secured by public key encryption) but also defensively (e.g., using quantum-resilient algorithms to develop encryption that can withstand even quantum computers).

The use of AI for information warfare is expected to blur the distinction between combatants and civilians and to exploit exiting social biases and stereotypes, thereby increasing the vulnerability of protected persons, whereas the use of AI for cyber operations raises concerns about distinguishing between military and non-military objects and about accountability and attribution (Favaro, Renic & Kühn 2022, pp. 40–1). For the International Committee of the Red Cross (ICRC), there are two other areas where the use of AI and machine learning by conflict parties raises particularly serious concerns. One is the increasing autonomy in physical robotic systems, including weapons, and the other is the impact of 'decision support' or 'automated decision-making' systems on the nature of decision-making in armed conflict – especially decisions for selecting and attacking targets (ICRC 2020).

The impact of AI-enabled systems and weapons on human security in future military operations will depend on how these capabilities are developed and deployed in practice. There is broad consensus about the need to regulate the military applications of AI and machine learning with a view to ensuring 'human-centricity', however what that means in practice can be interpreted differently and may result in the emergence of different kinds of AI principles and rules.

The UK Ministry of Defence, for example, takes a human impact-based approach, which stresses the need to assess and consider the full range of effects of AI-enabled systems on humans, both positive and negative, across the entire system lifecycle: 'The choice to develop and deploy AI systems is an ethical one, which must be taken with human implications in mind' (UK Ministry of Defence 2022, p. 9). The ICRC advocates a human control-based approach that emphasises preserving human control over tasks and human judgment in decisions, especially decisions that pose risks to human life: "This starts with consideration of the obligations and responsibilities of humans and what is required to ensure that the use of these technologies is compatible with international law, as well as societal and ethical values" (ICRC 2020, p. 471).

As a law-based model of security, human security depends on the ability to enforce international law, investigate and document violations, and hold perpetrators to account including through criminal prosecution (Rangelov, Theros & Kandić 2018, pp. 144–6). The three guiding principles for the use of AI adopted by the French Ministry of Defence – compliance with international law, maintaining significant human control, and ensuring permanent command responsibility (ICRC 2020, p. 474) – are critical for human security in any military operation involving AI-enabled systems and weapons.

Conclusion

What we are learning from the current experience in Ukraine, and indeed from the interventions in Iraq and Afghanistan, is that wars are very difficult to win nowadays. They either risk escalation and the real possibility of human extinction, or they became intractable low-level conflicts, as in Syria or DRC – characterised by forced displacement, sexual violence, the spread of transnational crime, or the destruction of cultural heritage and human capital – that reproduce themselves. The rise of AI, cyber and information warfare, may contribute both to escalation and to intractability.

In analysing future warfare, one possibility is extrapolation from the present – more intractable conflicts, as well as the reappearance of inter-state conflicts as in Ukraine or perhaps Taiwan. This is a bleak scenario that could even mean human extinction. But there are openings that could potentially redirect this trajectory and make war less likely. In this chapter, we have explored the practical potential of applying a human security approach to future military operations, and the steps that are already being taken within NATO and a number of individual national militaries.

The aim of such an approach would be to prevent future wars of aggression through effective non-threatening defensive deterrence, to protect people from political and criminal violence, and to contribute to the dampening down of intractable conflicts along with other, non-military instruments and actors. If this were to happen, we might be able to envisage the phasing out of warfare in the future.

Notes

1 This includes 12 interviews and exploratory conversations with officials from NATO and the UK Ministry of Defence and British Army officers. The data gathered in these exchanges has been anonymised upon request of our interlocutors.
2 See *supra* note 1.
3 The Human Security Study Group was reconvened in 2015–2016 to feed into the consultation for the EU Global Strategy 2016 (European Union 2016). See the Barcelona, Madrid, and Berlin Reports of the Study Group (SGESC 2004; HSSG 2007; HSSG 2016). On the evolution and impact of human security thinking in Europe, see Rangelov 2022.
4 They are labelled 'human security treaties' because their development was driven by advocates of human security among states, international institutions, and most importantly NGOs. They include the Ottawa Convention, the Convention on Cluster Munitions, the Rome Statute establishing the International Criminal Court, the Optional Protocol to the Convention on the Rights of the Child on involvement of children in armed conflict, and the Arms Trade Treaty. See Daft 2022.

References

Biscop, S 2022, 'The New Force Model: NATO's European Army?', *Trans European Policy Studies Association*, 9 September, <www.tepsa.eu/the-new-force-model-natos-european-army-sven-biscop-egmont-belgium> (accessed 18 October 2022).

Boserup, A & Neild, R 1990, *The Foundations of Defensive Defence*, Palgrave Macmillan, London.

Brzoska, M, Omitoogun, W & Sköns, E 2022, *The Human Security Case for Rebalancing Military Expenditure,* SIPRI, Stockholm.

Chinkin, C & Kaldor, M 2017, *International Law and New Wars*, Cambridge University Press, Cambridge.

Daft, S 2022, 'Human Security and International Law: Why? How?', in G Oberleitner (ed), *Research Handbook on International Law and Human Security*, Edward Elgar, Cheltenham, pp. 25–38.

EPRS 2021, 'Innovative Technologies Shaping the 2040 Battlefield', *European Parliamentary Research Service, European Parliament*, <https://www.europarl.europa.eu/thinktank/en/document/EPRS_STU(2021)690038> (accessed 15 October 2022)

Estrada-Tanck, D 2022, 'Human Security: Countering Structural Inequality and Fostering Resilience Under International Law', in G Oberleitner (ed), *Research Handbook on International Law and Human Security*, Edward Elgar, Cheltenham, pp. 305–19.

European Union 2016, *Shared Vision, Common Action: A Stronger Europe – A Global Strategy for the European Union's Foreign and Security Policy*, Brussels, June.

Favaro, M, Renic, N & Kühn, U 2022, *Negative Multiplicity: Forecasting the Future Impact of Emerging Technologies on International Stability and Human Security*, IFSH Report #010, Institute for Peace Research and Security Policy, University of Hamburg, <https://ifsh.de/file/publication/Research_Report/010/Research_Report_010.pdf> (accessed 25 October 2022).

Forman, L 2022, 'Global Health Law: WHO, COVID-19, and Human Security', in G Oberleitner (ed), *Research Handbook on International Law and Human Security*, Edward Elgar, Cheltenham, pp. 339–54.

Holt, V K 2021, 'Origins, Progress, and Unfinished Business: NATO's Protection of Civilians Policy', *Stimson Centre*, 18 March.

HSSG 2007, *A European Way of Security*, The Madrid Report of the Human Security Study Group presented to EU High Representative for Common Foreign and Security Policy Javier Solana, Madrid, 8 November.

HSSG 2016, *From Hybrid Peace to Human Security: Rethinking EU Approaches to Conflict*, The Berlin Report of the Human Security Study Group presented to the High Representative of the Union for Foreign Affairs and Security Policy Federica Mogherini, Brussels, 24 February.

ICISS 2001, *The Responsibility to Protect: Report of the International Commission on Intervention and State Sovereignty*, International Development Research Centre, Ottawa.

ICRC 2020, 'Artificial Intelligence and Machine Learning in Armed Conflict: A Human-Centred Approach', *International Review of the Red Cross*, vol. 102, no. 913, pp. 463–79, https://doi.org/10.1017/S1816383120000454.

Kaldor, M 2021, 'The Main Lesson from Afghanistan is that the War on Terror Does Not Work', *Guardian*, 24 August.

Leyen, U von der 2021, *State of the Union 2021*, Speech by the President of the European Commission, <https://ec.europa.eu/commission/presscorner/detail/en/SPEECH_21_4701> (accessed 14 August 2022).

NATO 2022, *NATO Strategic Concept 2022*, adopted by Heads of State and Government at the Summit in Madrid, 29 June.

Oberleitner, G 2022, 'Introduction', in G Oberleitner (ed), *Research Handbook on International Law and Human Security*, Edward Elgar, Cheltenham, pp. 1–23.

Rangelov, I 2022, 'Human Security in Europe: The European Union and Beyond', in G Oberleitner (ed.), *Research Handbook on International Law and Human Security*, Edward Elgar, Cheltenham, pp. 356–71.

Rangelov, I, Theros, M & Kandić, N 2018, 'EU Approaches to Justice in Conflict and Transition', in M Kaldor, I Rangelov & S Selchow (eds), *EU Global Strategy and Human Security: Rethinking Approaches to Conflict*, Routledge, London, pp. 142–57.

Rangelov, I & Theros, M 2019, 'Political Functions of Impunity in the War on Terror: Evidence from Afghanistan', *Journal of Human Rights*, vol. 18, no. 4, pp. 403–18, https://doi.org/10.1080/14754835.2019.1629889.

SGESC 2004, *A Human Security Doctrine for Europe*, The Barcelona Report of the Study Group on Europe's Security Capabilities presented to EU High Representative for Common Foreign and Security Policy Javier Solana, Barcelona, 15 September.

Steier, G, Kang, M & Ramdas, S 2022, 'Food Security and the Right to Food: Pillars of Humanity Arising from Food and Agriculture Law', in G Oberleitner (ed), *Research Handbook on International Law and Human Security*, Edward Elgar, Cheltenham, pp. 320–38.

UK Ministry of Defence 2021, 'JSP 985: Human Security in Defence', *MoD Joint Service Publication*, 1 December.

UK Ministry of Defence 2022, 'Ambitious, Safe, Responsible: Our Approach to the Delivery of AI-enabled Capability in Defence', *MOD Policy Paper*, 15 June.

5

GREAT POWERS AND WAR IN THE 21ST CENTURY

Blast from the Past

Vicky Karyoti, Olivier Schmitt and Amelie Theussen

Introduction

Major wars are characterized by three attributes:

> All the great powers in the system are involved; the wars are all-out conflicts fought at the highest level of intensity (that is, full military mobilization); and they contain a strong possibility that one or more of the contending great powers could be eliminated as sovereign states.
>
> (Copeland 2001, p. 3)

These events are quite rare in the international system, although not impossible, but while wars between great powers are infrequent, it does not mean that great powers have not been at war. Indeed, we can get a glimpse at future warfare by looking at past practices, in this case by looking at wars as waged by great powers since the 1991 Gulf War.

Forecasting future warfare is fraught with difficulties, as Chapters 1 and 2 of this handbook explain. Hironaka (2019) has also detailed the methodological challenges of predicting future warfare by looking at the single data points that are past military operations. Nevertheless, we believe there is value in taking stock of warfare as waged by great powers since the end of the Cold War for two main reasons. The first one is a degree of path dependency: to wage specific wars, great powers have developed weapons systems and their associated doctrine and practices, which have a degree of stickiness. Of course, we do not imply that past practices determine future conduct. However, looking at the past provides the necessary context to analyse future defence reform efforts. Second, looking at great powers is important because of their normative effect on other states: great powers practices establish what kind of weapons systems or military practices are desirable, contributing to a form of global military isomorphism (Farrell 2005).

Therefore, while being cautious about the risks of over-generalization, looking at great power warfare can still yield interesting insights to identify continuities and ruptures in future military operations.

In this chapter, we look at military operations as conducted by the United States and Russia since the 1991 Gulf War. We focus on these two states because the United States has been the

DOI: 10.4324/9781003299011-7

world's sole superpower since 1991, while Russia has been a 'recovering great power' defining itself against Western military practices and, with the 2022 invasion of Ukraine, being involved in the largest military campaign in Europe since World War II. We exclude China from the analysis because of the absence of Chinese involvements in major combat operations since 1991, although our analysis might be helpful to assess Chinese military power. We discuss four key themes in turn: the importance of technology in war, the importance of strategic culture in shaping war-making, the issue of the normative environment and, finally, the challenge of war preparation and war adaptation.

Your technology does not solve everything

The history of warfare has shown time and time again that for an effective and successful campaign, resources matter, whether material or human. Material resources such as technology have always been central to warfare, and are a focal point for strategic analysts.

Modern warfare has been characterized by an increase in complexity, and a focus on intelligence and data collection, analysis, and sharing amongst allies. The Gulf War and the widespread use of new technologies by Western forces, kickstarted a discourse around Revolutions in Military Affairs (RMAs): developments in military technologies so profound and effective that would change the character of warfare (Pretorius 2008). But what these new technologies in the last three decades since the Gulf War promised above all was connectivity and information. The 'revolution' was followed by doctrinal changes in both the United States and Russia, as new technologies were amalgamated into official doctrines. In the United States, the key word was 'transformation', as seen through speeches and interviews from numerous US military and political officials, especially after the Gulf War and during the planning of the operations 'Enduring Freedom' and 'Iraqi Freedom', characterized by the speed by which they were decided, planned, and carried out. That initial speed gave rise to a litany of beliefs that network-centric warfare (NCW), defined as "the integrated technological system of intelligence, unified forces command and fire control" (Revaitis 2020, p. 6), with its simultaneous operations by numerous different forces, working jointly and with a never-before seen integration of air, land, and sea units, would be the new revolution in military affairs which would provide that much-desired simple and quick battlefield victory. NCW became the doctrinal buzzword of the day.

In terms of doctrinal change, an influential innovation was effects-based operations (EBO), or "operations conceived and planned in a systems framework that considers the full range of direct, indirect, and cascading effects – effects that may, with different degrees of probability, be achieved by the application of military, diplomatic, psychological, and economic instruments" (Davis 2001, p. xiii). The thinking behind EBO was engaging and affecting the enemy as an integrated system, thereby increasing effectiveness and maximizing capabilities. It was an effort against the standardization of battleplans and the traditional warfare models.

These doctrinal developments did not bring about the results they promised; battlefield circumstances and real-life operations did not neatly correspond to what the creators and advocates of NCW and EBO envisioned, thereby forcing the need for doctrinal adjustment. The operations in Iraq and Afghanistan brought to the forefront the concept of Counterinsurgency (COIN), or in other words the idea that "civil actions can be taken to increase support for a central government and thereby decrease support for an internal rebellion" (Mason 2021, p. 19). The goal of the COIN doctrine is to strengthen the legitimacy of the local government and protect the population of insurgent activities, a doctrine which was used rather unsuccessfully in Iraq and Afghanistan.

With the advent of a changing global security environment, and a shift of the gravity of US's interests away from Europe towards Asia – especially China as a military and economic competitor – the United States turned its eye towards the creation of a new concept for warfare, what eventually was coined the 'Third Offset' (Work 2015). Starting as a strategic concept in 2014 to reassure US's European allies, while updating its capabilities with new, innovative technologies to offset China's edge in military capabilities, the concept lacked a clear vision and subsequently failed. Locked in a labyrinth of bureaucratic checkpoints, budget negotiations, unclear objectives, and Silicon Valley start-ups, the 'Third Offset' made big promises built on new, emerging technologies based on AI and advanced drones. Drones and AI in particular follow the natural steps of network-centric warfare, with their focus on data collection and processing. At the same time, global power competition has changed vastly in the past decades, allowing technological competition to become a 'first mover' game, in which whoever is first at developing and exploiting a technological edge first is promised increased returns for their dollar.

Are these technologies revolutionizing warfare? Political and military leaders have been convinced that access to such capabilities will ensure victory in the battlefield, but lessons from the past three decades tell us that it is hardly the case. The term RMA has now fallen out of fashion, while more and more practitioners and scholars realize that the Gulf War experience was a fluke; no single technology or platform has changed the nature of warfare to the extent of achieving that decisive victory it claimed to ensure, as in the "irrelevance of advanced military technology amid an insurgency in Iraq" (Pretorius 2008, p. 3).

Parallel to the promises of new technologies, the new doctrines also failed to capitalize on what the new technologies offered. In the cases of NCW, EBO, and the 'Third Offset' the fault lied within the alleged overreliance and exaggeration of the role assigned to technology (Carvin 2022). The experiences from USA's recent campaigns in Iraq and Afghanistan showed that improvements on weapons platforms cannot by themselves win battles, and certainly not wars. For many authors, the culprit is the 'new wars': the changed character of warfare which now has a strong emphasis on urban environments, the use of civilian population for concealment and other guerrilla tactics, the 'grey zone' within which warfare takes place, temporally, geographically, and legally (Kaldor 2012). For others, the problem is less about the environment and more about the institutions: militaries tend to stick to what has worked, what seems to be promising without taking big risks in terms of organizational change, and an overall organizational inertia.

Russia also seems to be fraught with problems of stickiness and resistance to change. At least in terms of their military, which is characterized by a culture of conservativism. As will be shown in the section regarding strategic culture, Russia is averse to reform and emulation; it refuses to adopt 'externally imported' concepts and doctrines, as they are seen to not match with Russia's unique position in the international security environment, and its domestic structures and cultures. This 'stubbornness' seemed to be changing during 2014–2015, as – according to Gerasimov – Russia should be learning from its experiences, especially from Syria, and modernize its forces.

Politically, because of Russia's efforts to level the field with its rivals, it has been focusing on the importance of the same technologies and weapon platforms while recognizing the contribution of other means of warfare, which embrace the human and cultural element. According to Galeotti, the mixing of conventional military means with non-military means in warfare is hardly novel, as the 'new wars' scholars claim. It simply means "the combining of battlefield combat, covert subversion, disinformation, cyberattacks and anything else one side or the other can throw in the mix" (Galeotti 2022, p. 10). The 2014 campaign against Ukraine was heavily characterized by a focus on information and narratives: Russia strategically used non-state actors and the utilization of social media to spread their own narrative to mobilize support, collect information, and disseminate propaganda. In Crimea in 2014, Russia 'weaponized everything', so why has the 2022 campaign in Ukraine proven to be so difficult?

The 2022 campaign in Ukraine demonstrated that Russian high-tech posturing is simply not enough to provide a decisive battlefield victory, even when coupled with ages-long doctrine development. The international system witnessed the complexity of battlefield operations and high strategy for what it is: a messy amalgamation of material, human capacity for resilience, global economic ripple effects, and geopolitics. It also showcased that warfare does not exist in a nebulous sum of armaments, soldiers, and technological marvels, but it is heavily influenced by non-material elements, and will likely continue to do so in the future.

Strategic culture and its importance in war

The main point of the previous section is that technology is not all there is. Both superpowers enjoyed technological superiority and a host of seemingly well-thought doctrines to go along with them, but these two elements do not exist in a vacuum, but rather function in a more or less cohesive political and strategic environment, or strategic culture.

The two superpowers have different strategic cultures. According to Covington (2016), US strategic culture is based on US exceptionalism, whereas Russia's is based on Russian uniqueness. These two conceptualizations, while at a first glance similar, are built on different assumptions and ideas: American exceptionalism is based on innovative thinking, forward-looking, leading-the-world mindsets, while Russian uniqueness is based on the view that Russia's position in the geostrategic environment is unique and precarious, too different for foreign concepts to describe and apply to its case. These different conceptualizations of strategic culture lend themselves to a vast set of divergent rules, procedures, attitudes, beliefs, and preferences. US's extroversion contrasts Russia's introversion in the ways each power thinks about its military posture, duties and responsibilities, threats, and attitude towards change. For many authors, strategic culture at its broadest sense is influenced by domestic cultures and national ways of war. According to Adamsky (2018), Russian strategic culture presents a continuity rather than change; while it can be innovative, it largely fosters an environment of conservativism and traditionalism. Russia's rejection of the post-Cold War international environment, and its deeply embedded belief that it is a system specifically designed and maintained to function against Russian interests, is reflected in the Russian armed forces, which seem to have an aversion towards 'reform', preferring instead a more conservative and autocratic attitude which favours centralization of power and rejection of emulation.

The USA, on the contrary, has been influenced by a strong technologically driven spirit, a spirit of innovation within a military environment which was not able to translate tactical advantages into favourable strategic and political outcomes. That disconnect can be attributed to a detachment between those tactical advantages and strategic goals. The conclusion from the cases of the United States and Russia is that the two main elements – technology and strategic thinking – are not by themselves or even both enough to ensure the achievement of political goals, but what is necessary is the connection between them. Both the *what*, and the *how* have to correspond to each other, to achieve each state's strategic and political objectives.

What this means for the future is that simply over-relying on certain elements of high strategy and politics will likely result in – often – catastrophic failures. Such lessons are to be taken with great care not just for superpowers, but for any actor in the international system with enough considerations for the future of warfare.

The normative environment

While the above has shown that technology does not provide the silver bullet for winning wars it is made out to be, information technology has had a fundamental effect on armed conflict over the last three decades. In the past, states were able to dominate the battle of the narrative. War was perceived, in a Clausewitzian fashion, as a duel, a polarized contest between two sides. A warring party only had to keep in mind two audiences when designing and distributing its narratives – one's own side, and the enemy's side. However, this has changed (Simpson 2012). Today, the power to create, shape, and distribute narratives lies in the hands of many, ranging from the traditional state-actors over non-state actors such as armed groups and broadcasting and communications companies to individuals on social media. Two fundamental changes made the globalization of the production of narratives and their audiences possible: first, at the end of the Cold War, the emergence of 24-hour news reporting through global news media produced what became known as the 'CNN effect': global, televised news able to affect foreign-policy decision-making. The second development was the emergence of social media, allowing individuals to share news, videos, and pictures with a global audience. Together with shifts in global power distribution and evolving constraints on the legal restraints of warfare, which bound the possibilities of narration and provide normative resources for assessing competing claims, this has impacted the way the United States and Russia have fought their recent wars.

With the end of the Cold War and collapse of the Soviet Union, the United States was the sole remaining superpower. It had achieved quick victory in the First Gulf War, the information revolution strengthened its power, and it did not have to worry about major power rivals. By 1994, Russia had joined NATO's Partnership for Peace and set up a rather ambitious cooperation with the alliance. Throughout the 1990s, the idea on both sides was an integration of Russia into the West's normative sphere on the basis of shared interests and values. Despite its unipolar moment, the United States experienced two challenges in the 1990s that were to set the stage for further developments: on the one hand, the Black Hawk Down incident in Mogadishu in 1993 showed how powerful information technologies had become, directly affecting security policy decisions of the world's only superpower. On the other hand, the 1999 NATO bombing of Yugoslavia during the Kosovo War led to a deterioration of the relationship between Russia and NATO. Classified as humanitarian intervention, the NATO operation did not have the UN Security Council's authorization – and resulted in a weakening of the legal norms of intervention that constrain the use of armed force.

In the aftermath of the terror attacks on September 11, US policy further attempted to erode existing legal constraints on armed conflict, arguing that international humanitarian law did not apply to so-called *enemy combatants*, reserving for itself the right to anticipatory self-defence, "even if uncertainty remains as to the time and place of the enemy's attack" (Bush 2002, p. 15), and once more intervening without Security Council's authorization, this time in Iraq in 2003. On the other hand, the United States started to include information superiority (or dominance) as a key enabler for *full spectrum dominance* in the Pentagon's *Joint Vision 2020* from 2000. *Information operations* became seen as so important to battlefield success that the US Army released a 314-page manual on the topic in 2003 and 'information war' became incorporated into the core of military strategy. The summary of the 2018 National Defence Strategy reconfirms the importance of information superiority (Mattis 2018). Yet, where the United States is relying on high-tech capabilities and sensors for its information dominance, Russia relies on a state-sponsored army of internet trolls and hackers, spreading disinformation, stealing (and leaking) information, and thereby attempt to influence policies and even elections. In 2014, the (dis-)information and intelligence campaigns that accompanied Russia's use of force in Ukraine were crucial to the success of the military operation (Theussen & Jakobsen 2021). The Russian version of information war provides the country with relatively low-cost means to manage crisis indirectly through attempting to affect public opinion, and thus political will and decision-making.

In this information war, the weakening legal constraints become normative arguments for the legitimacy of the use of armed force. Instead of constraining armed conflict and allowing an assessment of competing claims, the legal normative framework is routinely used as rhetoric tool to justify the use of force. This has given rise to the idea of *lawfare* – "the strategy of using—or misusing—law as a substitute for traditional military means to achieve a warfighting objective" (Dunlap Jr. 2008) explored in Chapter ten of this volume. Here Russia can exploit Western disagreements about the legal constraints on the use of force, such as the limits of self-defence, importance of Security Council's authorizations, and limits of humanitarian intervention and the responsibility to protect.

The war between Russia and Ukraine that started in February 2022 is a good example of these dynamics: open-source data and information operations have become a key aspect of operational success for Ukraine, while both sides accuse each other of war crimes and genocide in attempts delegitimize the opponents' actions. Yet, controlling the narrative is easier for an authoritarian state; until now Russia is able to control the narrative about its war in Ukraine towards its own population and even towards some states. The United States on the other hand has had a hard time controlling the narrative in its wars in Afghanistan, Iraq, and even against the Islamic State – all of which have been mired with civilian casualty scandals.

Today Russia and China are able to attack US information technology and dreams of achieving information dominance are fleeting. War games show that the United States might lose a confrontation with its competitors if the technology-focused thinking enshrined in concepts such as information superiority or dominance continues. Instead, information advantage, the concept in the 2018 National Defence Strategy itself, should be understood much more broadly to acknowledge the highly contested nature of the information space and encompass technical systems, cognitive processes, and perceptual/psychological effects. On the other hand Russia, "[f]or at least the past 25 years, [...] has broken its information war theory into information-technical and information-psychological categories" and employs them in an integrated design (Thomas 2019, p. 8–14). Information warfare is here to stay; and might well result in international law becoming little more than a catalogue of arguments to choose from to legitimize one's use of armed force.

Adapting under fire: adjusting to the realities of war

It is commonplace among critics of the military profession to say that armies tend to prepare to fight the last war. Yet, a multitude of scholarly work points to the contrary, namely that military organizations do change, investing time and resources in trying to stay relevant for an evolving strategic environment (Grissom 2006). Nevertheless, the challenge of figuring out what the next war will be like is particularly daunting, and it is common for military organizations to be forced to adjust their practices, doctrines, and sometimes equipment while fighting. By its very nature, war creates enormous pressures on military organizations: people are killed, and equipment destroyed, through the application of violence, and being confronted to an intelligent, adapting enemy requires the armed forces to constantly adjust their own practices in order to maintain their edge and their superiority.

Both the United States and Russia have been waging war since 1991, albeit with different patterns. The United States led a successful multinational conventional campaign during the Gulf

War, before waging coercive campaigns through air power in the Balkans in the 1990s, pivoting to a mixture of raiding, counter-insurgency operations, and conventional operations in Iraq and Afghanistan during the 2000s and part of the 2010s, and finally waging a 'surrogate warfare' (Krieg & Rickli 2019) combining support to local forces and airpower in Libya, Syria, and Iraq. Of course, these experiences are quite different from the large-scale combat operations that the US military is also preparing for against Russia and China, and reconciling these two contradictory impulses has been a challenge. The pattern is different for Moscow, which conducted gruesome counterinsurgency campaigns in Chechnya while managing the consequences of the collapse of the USSR during the 1990s, conducted limited military interventions in its near-abroad (notably Georgia and Ukraine) and upped the ante with an 'out-of-area' military intervention in Syria in 2015 and a large-scale combat operation in Ukraine in 2022. The learning experiences of the two countries can be compared alongside several dimensions: experiences of coalition warfare, perceptions of the utility of force in counter-insurgency settings and implementation of joint operations.

The first defining feature of the post-Cold War US military experience is the importance of coalition warfare, either in an ad hoc or a formal setting. Coalition warfare is incredibly difficult, since commanders must reconcile the diverging political preferences of the various participating countries while coordinating military organizations that have diverse cultures, technologies and practices. The first major coalition operation was obviously the 1991 Gulf War, during which the United States assembled a military coalition of nominally 35 countries, although the brunt of the fighting was conducted by the US forces, and to a much lesser degree the United Kingdom, France, Saudi Arabia, Syria, and Egypt. Because of their overwhelming control of the operational planning process, and through the flexibility afforded by the ad hoc nature of the coalition, the United States managed to integrate both the political red lines and the military contributions of the other participating states relatively smoothly. The 1999 Kosovo air campaign against Serbian forces was more challenging in that regard: it was the first major combat operation conducted by the North Atlantic Treaty Organisation (NATO), and Washington felt that the planning process was cumbersome and overburdened by political considerations. This experience goes a long way in explaining the US' decision not to initially involve NATO when, two years later, military planners were contemplating the invasion of Afghanistan in retaliation for the 9/11 attacks. It was only in 2003 that NATO got involved in the Afghan war, at a time when the United States was focusing on the invasion and occupation of Iraq. During this war, Washington decided once again to rely on a limited number of allies for the invasion phase, but nevertheless wanted to reap the political benefits of showcasing the alleged political support for the invasion, considering how divisive it was in the United States and worldwide. The result was an odd mix of countries nominally participating in the stabilization of Iraq, but which had little military utility on the ground, and very few countries (namely the United States and the United Kingdom) involved in actual fighting operations. To a degree, the same situation happened in Afghanistan, although the number of countries actually fighting was higher, illustrating the cohesive effect of NATO (Schmitt 2018). Embroiled in the withdrawal from Iraq and the intensification of the combat operations in Afghanistan, the United States adopted a so-called "leadership from behind" approach during the 2011 intervention in Libya but was a driving force in leading the air campaign against the Islamic State. Since the end of the Cold War, the United States has thus acquired considerable experience in managing coalition operations, either in a formal setting such as NATO or in an ad hoc setting. These military campaigns have created deep professional links between military officers of allied countries, have permitted to establish common planning procedures, and facilitated interoperability through the adoption of common technical standards. Of course, the challenges of coalition warfare remain, but the US military is better equipped to deal with them, an experience that is likely to transfer to future operations. In contrast, Russia (let alone China) has no experience of coalition operations, apart from some joint exercises with central Asian countries. While it is a theoretical possibility that Moscow may conduct coalition operations in the future (for example with countries belonging to the Collective Security Treaty Organization – CSTO), this lack of experience will likely hinder their military effectiveness in a way that the United States and their partners have predominantly learnt to overcome.

A second potential comparison between the US and the Russian experience of war has to do with the use of violence in counter-insurgency settings. The United States has been engaged in intense counter-insurgency operations between 2004 and 2014 in Iraq and Afghanistan. The shift towards counterinsurgency has somehow become mythologized, centred around the narrative of a few officers working with General David Petraeus and writing the new doctrinal document FM 3–24 adopted in 2006. This allegedly helped shift the dynamics of the campaign in Iraq, although the application in Afghanistan was less successful. The story is more complicated than this leader-centric account, and research has demonstrated that specific units in Iraq were already autonomously adopting counterinsurgency practices well before the publication of FM 3–24, but an important trend for Western armed forces has been the difficult adaptation to the operational environment in Iraq and Afghanistan through a shift in military practices. Yet, this shift led to the adoption of the so-called 'population-centric' version of counterinsurgency: the central idea is to create good enough security and living conditions for the local population, which should deny the insurgents local support and gradually cut them from their base. This approach involves, on the military side, restraint in the use of force (which is also consistent with international humanitarian law) and, on the political side, a good cooperation with the local and national authorities. However, researchers have questioned the soundness of this approach. First, 'restraint' in the use of force and good governance would not be sufficient: military force and the co-optation of local elites would be more effective (Hazelton 2021). Second, the cooperation with the local and national authorities is hindered by the fact that external intervention structurally disrupts the patronage networks on which these elites rely to maintain power, and which may be the cause of the insurgency in the first place: the counterinsurgents are then caught into an unsolvable dilemma of being forced to rely on local elites that have no incentive to change their practices but thus keep fuelling the insurgency. This helps explain why recent counterinsurgency operations led by Western states such as the campaigns in Iraq and Afghanistan or the French campaign in the Sahel (2013–2022) can be classified as failures: Western military organizations are thus now wary of engaging in such operations. In contrast, the Russian experience of counterinsurgency has been marked by the gruesome campaigns in Chechnya in the 1990s, which seemed to have cemented among the Russian military the notion that violence has a value of its own. Russia is thus conducting an 'authoritarian counterinsurgency', based on the reinforcement of local 'strongmen' (Kadyrov in Chechnya, Assad in Syria) and the use of violence against civilians if it helps achieving pacification. Between 2011 and 2018, the civil war in Syria has caused the death of 222,000 civilians, of which 92% (or 204,240) have been caused by the Assad regime or Syria. In contrast, the US-led war in Afghanistan and Iraq has led between 2001 and 2018 to the death of 244,000 civilians, of which 12.8% (31,000) have been caused by the United States or their allies. In other terms, Russia and the Syrian regime have created in seven years and in one territory six times more civilian casualties than the United States and their allies in 17 years and on a multiplicity of territories. It is likely that Moscow considers that its intervention in Syria is a success and will have incentives to 'export' this model of authoritarian counterinsurgency to other places, for example to reinforce authoritarian regimes in Africa. In contrast, the Western appetite for population-centric counterinsurgencies is likely to be limited in the coming decade.

The third dimension of comparison deals with the implementation of so-called 'joint operations' which, in military parlance, designates the synergy and integration between two or more services (army, navy, air force, cyber force, etc.) to maximize military effectiveness. While joint operations emerged in the US military doctrine in the 1980s, the promises of the so-called "Revolution in Military Affairs" identified by Andrew Marshall and his colleagues accelerated the trend towards better inter-service coordination. As discussed above, the idea behind the RMA (and derived concepts such as Network-Centric Warfare) was that military organizations should transform into combined arms system of systems linking together intelligence, surveillance and reconnaissance capabilities (ISR), command and control (C2) systems, and precision standoff fires. While the full promises of NCW were never realized, the US armed forces have nevertheless clearly made progress towards jointness, precision strikes and compression of the so-called 'kill chain' (which designates the time between the detection and the destruction of an enemy's capability). This integration was possible thanks to the actual battlefield testing of key command and control and communication systems over the past three decades, and the next step towards further integration is the current development of so-called 'multi-domain operations'. The idea of the RMA originated from soviet military thinking, and the Russian armed forces have made steps towards integrating the key concepts and weapon systems necessary to implement what is known in Russian military parlance as a 'reconnaissance-strike complex'. Yet, the 2008 invasion of Georgia highlighted shortcomings in the key capabilities necessary to pursue that kind of warfare: ISR, precision-guided munitions, C2, and the ability to coordinate the different services. The 2015 campaign in Syria demonstrated improvements in all these domains, which led analysts to conclude that the reform of the Russian armed forces initiated after the Georgian campaign was at least partially successful. Yet, the 2022 invasion of Ukraine has once again demonstrated shortcomings in key capabilities, notably army-air force cooperation, targeting and ISR. While true joint operations are challenging, the military organizations able to implement them are likely to have an edge on the future battlefield.

Conclusion

Looking at warfare as waged by great powers for the past 30 years gives some indications of what it may look like in the future. None of these insights is particularly new: technology is not a silver bullet, strategic practices are shaped by cultural factors, allies can tip the strategic balance in one's favour, etc. But these aspects take a specific and contextual shape that explains the differences in US and Russian war-making in the past thirty years and are relevant to understand future warfare. In particular, it will be important to observe China's military development in comparison with the practices of other great powers in order to properly assess the balance of power in the emerging international system.

While past practices do not determine future conduct, as was outlined in the introduction to this chapter, the weapons systems, doctrines and practices developed by the great powers do have a degree of stickiness that creates tendencies for path dependency. This chapter's analysis of the last three decades of wars fought by the United States and Russia indicates three dimensions that will guide great power war and future warfare.

First, while the development of new technology is crucially important for military power, technological supremacy alone does not win wars. A technological arms race is already underway, in the fields of artificial intelligence and hypersonics, but if doctrine and practices are not adapted to technological progress and – even more important – if the disconnect between technological, tactical advantage and strategic and political goals persists, technology will not win wars in the future either.

Second, great powers and their behaviour have normative effects. As the global order moves towards increasing multipolarity, the battle over the information space and convincing narratives will increase further. The past has shown that it is difficult to control the narrative, especially for democratic powers, and past disregard for international law sets dangerous precedents, which have the potential to reduce international law to a set of arguments to legitimize one's own actions.

Finally, the patterns of the US' and Russia's wars in the last three decades have resulted in a Western preference for coalition warfare but distaste for COIN operations, while Russia has had little experience with the former but much more success with the latter. The patterns also point to joint (or multi-domain) operations as the important warfighting concept of the future. Whoever gets this right might well have a battlefield advantage in the wars to come.

References

Adamsky, D D 2018, 'From Moscow with Coercion: Russian Deterrence Theory and Strategic Culture', *Journal of Strategic Studies*, vol. 41, no. 1–2, pp. 33–60, https://doi.org/10.1080/01402390.2017.1347872)

Bush, G W 2002, 'The National Security Strategy of the United States of America', *The White House*, <https://2009-2017.state.gov/documents/organization/63562.pdf> (accessed 18 December 2022).

Carvin, S 2022, 'How Not to War', *International Affairs*, vol. 98, no. 5, pp. 1695–716, https://doi.org/10.1093/ia/iiac189.

Copeland, D 2001, *The Origins of Major War*, Cornell University Press, Ithaca, NY.

Covington, S R 2016, *The Culture of Strategic Thought Behind Russia's Modern Approaches to Warfare*, Belfer Centre for Science and International Affairs, Cambridge, MA, <https://www.belfercenter.org/sites/default/files/legacy/files/Culture%20of%20Strategic%20Thought%203.pdf> (accessed 18 December 2022).

Davis, P K 2001, *Effects-Based Operations: A Grand Challenge for the Analytical Community*, RAND, Santa Monica, CA.

Dunlap Jr., C J 2008, 'Lawfare Today: A Perspective', *Yale Journal of International Affairs*, Winter, pp. 146–54, <https://drive.google.com/file/d/17RP_wpkUjXyrPVuHUfvPYsJ3Ig7MnyHA/view (accessed 18 December 2022).

Farrell, T 2005, 'World Culture and Military Power', *Security Studies*, vol. 14, no. 2, pp. 448–88, https://doi.org/10.1080/09636410500323187.

Galeotti, M 2022, *The Weaponization of Everything*, Yale University Press, New Haven, CT.

Gray, C S 1999, *Modern Strategy*, Oxford University Press, Oxford.

Grissom, T 2006, 'The Future of Military Innovation Studies', *Journal of Strategic Studies*, vol. 29, no. 5, pp. 905–34, https://doi.org/10.1080/01402390600901067.

Hazelton, J 2021, *Bullets Not Ballots. Success in Counterinsurgency* Warfare, Cornell University Press, Ithaca, NY.

Hironaka, A 2019, *Tokens of Power. Rethinking War*, Cambridge University Press, Cambridge.

Kaldor, M 2012, *New and Old Wars*, 3rd ed, Polity Press, Cambridge – Malden, MA.

Krieg, A & Rickly, J-M 2019, *Surrogate Warfare. The Transformation of War in the Twenty-First Century*, Georgetown University Press, Washington, DC.

Mason, C M 2021, 'COIN Doctrine Is Wrong', *Parameters*, vol. 51, no. 2, pp. 19–34, <https://press.army-warcollege.edu/cgi/viewcontent.cgi?article=3065&context=parameters> (accessed 18 December 2022).

Mattis, J 2018, 'Summary of the 2018 National Defense Strategy of the United States of America', *Department of Defence*, <https://dod.defense.gov/Portals/1/Documents/pubs/2018-National-Defense-Strategy-Summary.pdf> (accessed 18 December 2022).

Pretorius, J 2008, 'The Technological Culture of War', *Bulletin of Science, Technology & Society*, vol. 28, no. 4, pp. 299–305, https://doi.org/10.1177/0270467608319592.

Revaitis, A 2020, 'Russian Perception of its Network-Centric Warfare Capabilities in Syria', *Journal on Baltic Security*, vol. 6, no. 1, pp. 33–50, <https://journalonbalticsecurity.com/journal/JOBS/article/16/file/pdf> (accessed 18 December 2022).

Schmitt, O 2018, *Allies that Count. Junior Partners in Coalition Warfare*, Georgetown University Press, Washington, DC.

Simpson, E 2012, *War from the Ground Up: Twenty-First Century Combat as Politics*, Hurst, London.

Sondhaus, L 2006, *Strategic Culture and Ways of War*, Routledge, New York.

Theussen, A & Jakobsen, P V 2021, 'In the Shadows: The Challenge of Russian and Chinese Gray Zone Conflict for the West', in S Rynning, O Schmitt & A Theussen (eds), *War Time: Temporality and the Decline of Western Military Power*, Brookings Institution Press, Washington, DC/Chatham House, London, pp. 161–83.

Thomas, T L 2019, *Russian Military Thought: Concepts and Elements*, Mitre Product MP190451V1, MITRE, McLean, VA, <https://www.mitre.org/sites/default/files/2021-11/prs-19-1004-russian-military-thought-concepts-elements.pdf> (accessed 18 December 2022).

Work, R O 2015, 'The Third U.S. Offset Strategy and its Implications for Partner and Allies', *US Department of Defence*, January, <http://www.defense.gov/News/Speeches/Speech-View/Article/606641/the-third-us-offset-strategy-and-its-implications-for-partners-and-allies> (accessed 18 December 2022).

6

THE ECOLOGY OF VIOLENCE

Jonathan Luke Austin

Introduction

In 2022, the High Representative of the EU for Foreign Affairs and Security Policy, Josep Borrell Fontelles gave a controversial speech in which he declared that:

> Yes, Europe is a garden. We have built a garden… [But] the rest of the world… is not exactly a garden. Most of the rest of the world is a jungle, and the jungle could invade the garden. The gardeners should take care of it, but they will not protect the garden by building walls. A nice small garden surrounded by high walls in order to prevent the jungle from coming in is not going to be a solution. Because the jungle has a strong growth capacity, and the wall will never be high enough in order to protect the garden.
>
> (EEAS Press Team 2022)

Borrell's speech was attacked for its seeming attachment to racist civilizational stereotypes that centre a Western European and North American metropole (the 'garden') in need of protection from the 'jungle' of 'most of the rest of the world.' Such rhetoric also echoes – however – a long intellectual history, still present within Political Science and International Relations, that has made similar claims. This ranges from long-standing controversy surrounding Huntington's (1997) clash of civilizations thesis, towards Robert Kagan's (2018) more recent claim that the 'jungle grows back' and, as such, neo-imperial action by the United States and its allies is a necessary part of maintaining the liberal international order. Setting aside the controversy surrounding remarks like these, they attest to the strength of a particular 'ecological' vision of world politics. Particularly when referencing violence, war, or conflict, frequent appeal is made to biological, natural, and cognate metaphors across history. These metaphors render political violence a systemic phenomenon ('the jungle has a strong growth capacity') embedded in natural processes. They have also proliferated, more recently, given the rise of environmentally-linked security concerns that render the planet itself a source of potential conflict and violence (Chandler, Cudworth & Hobden 2018).

In this chapter, I address the politics and implications of such 'ecological' understandings of (political) violence in three ways. First, I stress that while the rhetoric of Borrell or Kagan is

 DOI: 10.4324/9781003299011-8

disquieting, it tends to remain rhetoric. Here, analogies between political violence, conflict, or war and natural phenomena are essentially metaphorical. Although the consequences of such rhetoric can be severe, it must be distinguished from what I will refer to as 'ecological ontologies' of violence. Ecological ontologies of political violence can be traced to a mix of complexity, systems, and cybernetic theory, cross-fertilized with the insights of post-structuralist and post-modern philosophy (Coyne 2008). In general, such approaches are relational ontologies that foreground a post-humanist, distributed, and complexity-orientated understanding of social life. These ecological ontologies have – importantly – grown in influence both for the academic study of violence but also within military, security, and other agencies whose operational doctrines are now directly influenced by natural concepts in order to foreground warfare's rhizomatic, symbiotic, fluid, embodied, and environmentally fluctuating qualities (Bousquet 2018; Öberg 2018; Austin 2019c, 2020a; Grove 2019).

Second, I discuss the ethico-political questions that are raised when such ecological ontologies are deployed. In theory, ecological *ontologies* are normatively neutral, and should be sharply distinguished from the risk of civilizational, racist, and neo-imperialist tropes that are frequently associated with the use of ecological *metaphors*. Nonetheless, these ontologies do risk presenting social life in a 'naturalized' form that raises multiple ethico-political questions. This includes the question of attributing responsibility for the use of political violence, the risk of a further naturalization of the use of literally posthuman forms of warfare (autonomous weapons systems, etc.), and – ultimately – the return to a naturalized cosmology of violence that sees the presence of violence as integral to (post)human society. The third focus of this discussion seeks to address these concerns. It does so by stepping outside the realm of political violence to see how ecological ontologies/approaches have been deployed within the field of public health to *prevent* harm. My goal there is to stress how similar methods of intervening-in/against political violence can be imagined within the scope of ecological ontologies, but that doing so requires a sustained shift away from a contemporary preoccupation with legal and ideational approaches to violence prevention. My final focus here is thus on teasing out an agenda for what such a future – in line with the goals of this handbook – of violence prevention might look like. A future, to put it simply, of designing-*against* ecologies of violence.

Metaphor or ontology?

Political violence has a long history of being spoken about through natural metaphors. Indeed, one might argue that earlier explanations for the persistence of organized violence in human society embraced a naturalistic view in which for evolutionary, theological, or other reasons, such violence was an inevitable part of the circle of life (Keeley 1996; Collins 2008). Slowly, such cosmologies of violence as a natural phenomenon – akin to the winds and tides – declined as an ethico-political imperative to avoid the ravages of total war took hold in the 20th century. Nonetheless, the metaphorical appeal to natural, ecological, or cognate concepts continues. Israel, for instance, speaks of its military activities in occupied Palestine as 'mowing the grass' (Inbar & Shamir 2014). The United States developed a 'Human Terrain' system in Iraq, with the hope of better capturing the 'hearts and minds' of Iraqis, implicitly equating physical, natural, and human 'terrains' or 'landscapes' to be conquered (Zehfuss 2012). More generally, violence, conflict, and war have been suffused with bodily metaphors of health and disease: with enemies described as cancerous cells and those to be protected as bodies (Wilcox 2015). Such metaphors are important, as in any sphere of social life. Metaphorical reasoning allows for the production of concepts that help us make sense of the complexity of the world and – therefore – to act within it more or less 'effectively' (Chilton 1996).

Nonetheless, as many have noted, these use of naturalistic metaphors to explain violence, conflict, and war is frequently a depoliticizing move (Bell 2012). By taking phenomena fundamentally connected to human society and its political disjunctures, but reading them through ecological metaphors, we seem to take them away from the sphere of political debate and contestation. Such a depoliticizing tendency has been especially evident in security politics after the Cold War, for example, as well as in the rise of concepts like 'resilience' within peace-building discourse (Neocleous 2011, 2022; Duffield 2019). When Borrell describes Europe as a garden, and the rest of the world as a jungle, he appears (despite his denials[1]) to endorse a naturalized status quo in which Europe's intervention elsewhere in the world is not a political move but simply a pragmatic response that addresses the dynamics of a 'naturalized' international order. It is important to stress, however, that when these processes are left at a metaphorical level, critique of such depoliticization remains possible. We can critique a military commander for using such metaphors during a counter-insurgency campaign, as critiques of US doctrine in Iraq, or any other case, make clear. Equally, we can critique a politician who declares their enemy to be a subhuman, cancerous, plague on the nation. And Borrell's remarks were indeed met with immediate – and harsh – critique. Put simply, while metaphors can work to depoliticize, the possibility of re-politicization remains open at this discursive-rhetorical level.

But what occurs when the use of natural or ecological terminology is meant ontologically, rather than metaphorically? Increasingly, ecological or natural terms are not deployed analogically, but with the goal of expressing a distinct ontological understanding of social reality. For example, in Jairus Grove's *Savage Ecology*, he defines an ecological approach to politics as involving a:

Form of analysis characterized by inhuman encounters and deep relational processes across geographical scales rather than a form of political thinking that relies on discreteness, causality, and an exceptional notion of human agency

(Grove 2019, p. 10)

He stresses that this is *not* "a metaphor for analysing the world" but, instead, something that emerges from "empirical scrutiny" (Grove 2019, p. 14). Such ecological ontological thinking can be traced to numerous social theoretical traditions, but especially those inspired by Gilles Deleuze and Félix Guattari, as well as earlier work within complex systems, chaos, and cybernetic theory, and which have coalesced today into work around assemblage theory, actor-network theory, new materialism, and cognate work.[2] The precepts of such ecological social theory are diverse. But, broadly speaking, they share some common assumptions. First, ecological ontologies are – ultimately – relational understandings of social life that deny any object (human or non-human) possesses an autonomous 'essence' that exists outside its relational ties to other objects. In this view, social phenomena are produced through entangled relations between objects, which can be assembled, reassembled, or disassembled in an infinite number of ways (Best et al. 2013). Second, ecological ontologies generally follow a 'symmetry' principle in which agency can be attributed to non-human actors, including technologies, tools, landscapes, atmospheres, etc. These non-human entities possess agency because their presence or absence within ecological relations fundamentally changes the nature of social reality (Sayes 2014). Third, because of this symmetry principle, agency is also seen as a 'distributed effect' in which no single actor can possess autonomous agency in the world: their capacity to act is, instead, reliant on the agency of other human and non-human things. In this reading, actions taken by specific individuals, groups, or objects cannot be said to have *entirely* originated within those objects. Instead, the potential for these actions to occur relied upon agency distributed across other persons, objects, and things.

Ecological-relational ontologies have a long history of being deployed to study social and political events. However, their use in the academic study of (political) violence is relatively nascent. The accounts that exist are generally preoccupied with the 'posthuman' understanding of violence that emerges from ecological ontologies, in large part because this aspect of such ontologies is most disruptive for our typically humanist understanding of the mechanics of violence. For example, Austin (2016, 2019b) describes how the practice of torture emerges through a globalized set of relations that bind individual human perpetrators into a historically sedimented set of techniques of violence that are materialized in both banal and everyday (chairs, whips) and more high-technological (internet platforms, etc.) material infrastructures. At the broader level of 'war' itself, Bousquet, Grove and Shah (2020, p. 104) describe how "war is both a thing and a process, a unity and an assembly, an event and an ecology of relations." In this, their focus – alongside others – is on the distributed agentic drivers of war and violence (De Landa 1991; Der Derian 2009). Naturally, much attention has also been focused on how an ecological ontology can unpack the emergence of, and potential effects of, autonomous weapons systems. Especially notably, this literature focuses on how the rise of the drone is radically changing the nature of warfare, both from the perspective of those who perpetrate violence and the communities who fall under the gaze of the drone by drawing – in particular – on the focus on 'affect' within ecological ontologies (Walters 2014; Chamayou 2015; Austin 2020b; Malaviya 2020).

Practice and purpose

The status of ecological ontologies for exploring political violence is not an academic question. Indeed, academic research in this area has followed work within military science and practice. Weizmann discussed this development in 2006 when exploring how the Israeli Defence Forces (IDF) drew on post-modern social theory to re-think military action, deploying concepts such as inverse geometry, swarming, emergence, connectivity, and beyond to augment their capacity to (violently) control Palestinian space. As he notes, this represents a paradoxical situation in which concepts from "the humanities, [which are] often believed to be the best lasting weapon with which to combat imperialism... [have] been adopted as imperialism's own weapon" (Weizman 2007, p. 15). Indeed, a sustained 'military design' movement has developed across the world, predicated on deploying variants of ecological ontologies to augment military capacity (Öberg 2018). These developments are relatively unsurprising given a long lineage of military thinking preoccupied with the logistics of organizing large-scale operations, which lead to an interest in cybernetics and complex systems theory from an early stage (Lawson 2011; Bousquet, Grove & Shah 2017; Bousquet 2018). The 'reality' of the deployment of ecological ontologies of violence *in practice* is important because it moves us away from the realm of pure intellectual reflection. All ontological claims are contestable, but their impact becomes acutely felt when they are taken to be 'real' by those who deploy them in practice and for specific purposes. In her classical *Sex and Death in the Rational World of Defence Intellectuals* – for instance – Carol Cohn described how US defence professionals were immersed in a (linguistic) world that legitimized a rationalist ontology of conflict, risking nuclear catastrophe. As she put it:

> Those of us who find US nuclear policy desperately misguided... faced a serious quandary. If we refuse to learn the language [of a rationalist ontology], we are virtually guaranteed that our voices will remain outside the 'politically relevant' spectrum of opinion. Yet, if we do

learn and speak it, we not only severely limit what we can say but we also invite the transformation, the militarization, of our own thinking.

(Cohn 1987, p. 716)

When taken as 'reality' and put 'into practice' ontologies have real effects that limit our capacity
to think differently. Thus, when Grove (2019) describes ecological ontologies as not simply one
contestable ontology among another but as an observable truth that "accretes from reality," he is
simultaneously referencing the way this ontology aligns with what we see in the world analyti-
cally *and* its deployment by violence workers of all kinds *in practice*. This unusually practically-
embedded 'reality' of ecological ontologies is important because it raises several serious ethical
and political implications that are – in many ways – more acute than those that emerge from the
simple use of contestable ecological metaphors seen above.

First, ethical questions of adjudicating responsibility emerge especially strongly via ecological ontologies. While natural metaphors depoliticize, natural ontologies radically diffuse questions of responsibility for violence. This is true at multiple scales. At the macro-level, ecological
theories appear to make it difficult to adjudicate 'why' a war began, as its dynamics would be
rooted in complex emergent relations without a linear causal path to trace (De Landa 1991;
Bousquet, Grove & Shah 2020). In and of itself, this may not be entirely problematical: even
within more traditional ontologies of social life, adjudicating responsibility for macro-level
events is exceptionally difficult. The challenge – however – is that the solution to this indeterminacy has often rested on addressing 'conduct' in situations of conflict or war, and assuming
the capacity of individuals – whether political leaders or soldiers – to be held accountable for
their actions once an 'event' has occurred (Sikkink 2011). An ecological perspective – taken to
its logical conclusion – however, also undermines our capacity to see individual beings as fully
agentic actors in control of their conduct: whether violent or not. Principles of distributed agency
equally imply that the presence of material objects or technologies, the affective conditions of
the environments in which our actions occur, and so on, all dilute the autonomous capacity of
human beings. In this regard, ecological ontologies radicalize the older 'banality of evil' thesis
by extending its focus on the ideationally, bureaucratically, and/or culturally produced 'thought-
lessness' underlying mass violence towards a focus on how material infrastructures and affective
atmospheres make thinking *against* violence frequently impossible (c.f. Haraway 2016; Arendt
1963). Under this reading – to put it simply – we can locate 'responsibility' for violence neither
at an individual nor structural level of social reality. Instead, violence becomes a 'subjectless'
thing (Austin 2020a).

Second, if ecological ontologies are embraced as reflecting social reality, they also seem likely
to contribute to the rise of *literally* post-humanist modes of violence. Debates over the place of
autonomous weapons systems in warfare, for instance, are usually situated in a dichotomy that
compares their affordances, capacities, and effects to those of human beings engaging in acts of
violence. There is the capacity to claim, for instance, that emerging technologies might comply
more closely with international human rights and humanitarian law than human beings are capable
of, or vice versa (Müller 2016). But if ecological perspectives stress that war always-already-has-
been posthuman, and human violence is inextricably shaped by material, environmental, atmospheric, etc. conditions, then this comparison dissolves. Indeed, if violence is accepted to already
be driven by our ecological entanglement with non-human agency, then different justifications
for deploying more advanced technologies can be developed. For example, the post-humanist
sensibilities of ecological ontologies would imply that the capacity of human beings to act 'ethically' or in compliance with international law can be augmented through their further enmeshing

with material-technological infrastructures. In this reading, an ethical *imperative* to deploy novel technological modes of warfare might emerge through the practical acceptance of ecological ontologies as reflecting social reality.

Third, the above factors, alongside others, combine to – in essence – take us back in time to older 'natural' cosmologies of violence. For example, Bousquet, Shah, and Grove (Bousquet, Grove & Shah 2020, pp. 103, 112) describe how though the 'radical empiricism' through which they engage the study of violence risks "downplaying its abominable destructive consequences," they are ultimately forced to "insist on the inherently generative powers of war – its intimate affinity to the pre-personal flux of becoming." In their view, this is necessary because ecological ontologies describe "the world as it is, not as we wish it were" (Bousquet, Grove & Shah 2020). Indeed, though ecological ontologies tend to stress the indeterminacy, flux, and non-linear nature of social reality – thus appearing to be the *opposite* of a 'naturalizing' framework – their focus on intense relational complexity and distributed agency can often make it as difficult to imagine a world without violence as it was in earlier theological or evolutionary perspectives on its place in human society. It was, in part, for this reason that distinct ontological and epistemological perspectives on war, violence, and conflict came to prominence in the 20th century. The rise of human rights discourse and humanitarian law, for instance, stems directly from theories of normativity and contestation that more radically embrace the capacity for human beings to make change in and/on the world (Sikkink 2011). By contrast, within ecological ontologies, violence risks becoming seen as being a 'viscous plasma' that encompasses such a vast proportion of human (and non-human) history that escaping the hold of its relational entanglements appears impossible (Austin 2023).

Symbiosis, balance, and prevention

The dilemmas posed by the practical deployment of ecological ontologies – described above – are above all ethical and political. In this, they pose serious questions for those who would seek a more 'critical' perspective on (political) violence. Grove, for instance, stresses that an ecological approach goes against the view that "being critical is synonymous with being normative." He stresses that we cannot 'will' an ecological ontology of violence out of existence. At the same time, Grove notes that "we can struggle to intervene in those arrangements that are disgusting to our sense of good but any intervention that is not allied with the world.... will likely fail" (Grove 2014, p. 369). This point was also made by Manuel De Landa in his seminal *War in the age of intelligent machines*. In his discussion of the present and possible future uses of machines, robots, and other technologies in political violence, De Landa noted that an ecological ontology allows for such technologies to have multiple purposes. On the one hand, "technology may be used to allow robots to become responsive to the world" and so to "get humans out of the decision-making loop" (De Landa 1991, p. 123). On the other hand, ecological perspectives might also offer new ways of allowing "machines to become responsive to the needs of their users" and so to "bring humans back to the centre of the loop" (De Landa 1991, p. 123).

In these remarks from De Landa and Grove, we see how a more subtle reading of ecological ontologies of violence does not require falling-back upon the three troubling implications raised about as *fait acompli*. It is possible to imagine re-assembling the relational entanglements described by these ontologies such that they would serve progressive – even emancipatory – rather than violent ends. Indeed, much earlier work in cybernetics, complexity-theory, and post-humanist thought sought to imagine just such a move towards 'liberation technologies' of different kinds (Haraway 1987; Diamond 2010; Pickering 2010). Indeed, it is crucially important to stress that while ecological ontologies do 'decentre' the human subject from social analysis to some degree, they are not intended to 'efface' that subject and its potentiality (Pickering 1993). At a theoretical level, it is not impossible for ecological ontologies to describe a world allied *against* the ravages of violence. Neither Grove nor De Landa, however, offer guidance for the kinds of interventions that might be possible within the violent ecologies of modernity. Moreover, de Landa (1991, p. 123) stresses that the great difficulty in imagining such interventions relates to the embedding of violence and war within longstanding historical processes. As violence, war, and conflict have evolved throughout history, a series of inertias or path-dependencies have been embedded in its ecologies (Keeley 1996). The ultimate challenge is therefore to disrupt these historical sedimented intertias for the purposes of preventing political violence.

How – then – can we imagine alternative modes of intervening against political violence that are 'allied with the world'? In my view, getting there requires that we, first, redirect our gaze away from the extreme forms of war, conflict, and violence that are usually imagined when this question is raised. The basic precepts of ecological approaches are accepted within many of what are presumed to be more prosaic, applied, or technical sciences that seek to study and intervene in what *appear* to be less political and/or dramatic phenomena. Consider public health. In that field, an 'ecological approach' is prominent which works to integrate "material, biological, social, and cultural aspects of public health" to develop more effective interventions (Bronfenbrenner 1979; Lang & Rayner 2012). The field accepts the 'complex and multi-layered connections' that affect public health outcomes, implicitly accepting many of the more esoteric philosophical concepts of ecological ontologies (Lang & Rayner 2012, p. 3). Its success as a programme can also be linked to models of preventive medicine, which do not see disease as a property 'possessed' by an individual human, but as a phenomenon distributed across social ecologies (Rose 1985; Austin 2023).

These ecological approaches to public health are interesting because they have been especially effective in tackling medical issues caused by 'population level' problems such as – say – smoking. Recognizing that a significant degree of disease and illness is caused by factors 'outside' the individual body (or mind), public health has focused on how ecological factors drive a propensity towards harmful behaviours such as smoking. This included, for instance, a focus on the tactics of big tobacco corporations to market their products towards young people and socio-economically disadvantaged groups. It also included a focus on the aesthetic crafting of the material object of the cigarette: packaging, filters, etc., as well as the use of advertising. Beyond this, public health has explored the connection of smoking to popular cultural tropes, as well as historical connections to heroism and war (not least World War II), alongside a focus on how the built environment and architectural schemas – such as allowing indoor smoking – increase the numbers of individuals addicted to tobacco (Milov 2019; Wailoo 2021). By recognizing these ecological drivers of smoking (and its related medical issues), public health approaches sought to develop 'symmetrical' interventions that would work to adjust such drivers. This has included advocating for adjusting the material-architectural environment (through the prohibition of smoking in public spaces), intervening in the aesthetics of cigarettes (packaging restrictions, advertising restrictions, etc.), as well as more obvious consciousness-raising campaigns. This 'holistic' approach to public health essentially seeks to balance-out our ecological entanglement with drivers of smoking by introducing 'counter-balancing' interventions.

The analogy to public health and smoking above is especially relevant to the question of political violence. On the one hand, tobacco companies can be seen as similar in their awareness, and exploitation, of ecological factors to military, security, and other agents and their embrace of ecological ontologies. Indeed, at a wider level, corporations have long known how material, aesthetic, affective, and other ecological factors can drive our behaviour (Lee, Broderick & Chamberlain 2007). On the other hand, the awareness of medical professionals of the need to counter-balance those initiatives with interventions that operate at the same ecological level is *not* mirrored – to a large degree – in those seeking to counter political violence. Instead, most modes of intervening-against political violence remain preoccupied with legalistic tools (human rights law, prosecutions, etc.) and normative processes of socialization. While such efforts are very important at a certain in-tersubjective ecological level, and as such must always be maintained, they do not counter-balance our entanglement with material, affective, aesthetic, and other distributed drivers of violence. In consequence, I wish to suggest that what is required to bridge this gap is a focus on a distinct eco-logical term: symbiosis (c.f. Austin 2019a). As Michelle Serres (1995, p. 195) once wrote:

> Objectively, we have to continue living with cancer, with germs, with evil and even vio-lence. It's better to find a symbiotic equilibrium, even fairly primitive, than to reopen a war that is always lost... If we were to implacably clean up all the germs, as Puritanism would have us do, they would soon become resistant to our techniques of elimination and require new armaments. Instead, why not culture them in curdled milk, which sometimes results in delicious cheeses?

To reach such a symbiotic relationship, which can convert violence into something positive, requires a rebalanced focus within violence prevention efforts on introducing material, technological, affec-tive, and aesthetic objects that work to alter the 'balance of distributed agency' across the ecologies we live in. Precisely what these might look like is – as yet – unknown, though important precedents have been set by criminologists and those working within forensic architecture (Weizman 2017; Celermajer 2018; Austin 2020a). To reach more concrete proposals for such a symbiotic rebalanc-ing of the future ecologies of violence requires – however – that a more sustained focus is put on averting our gaze from the violent reality of our contemporary social ecologies and towards a speculative – even utopian – set of alternative possibilities (Stengers 2013; Haraway 2016).

The future ecologies of violence

Understanding political violence, war, and conflict from within the frame of ecological ontologies can be disquieting. While natural metaphors have long been used to frame the global experience of violence and – in particular and as we saw in the introduction – to discursively legitimatize ex-clusionary, hierarchical, racialized, and neo-imperial logics of domination, such metaphors remain open to contestation at a political level. By contrast, ecological ontologies appear to more firmly anchor the spectre of violence within reality at a level of complexity, entanglement, and non-linearity, that escape can appear impossible. This is especially true in the contemporary moment where renewed geopolitical posturing, alongside the rise of emerging technologies that promise a quite literally post-human future of violence, seems to have crystalized the real-world conse-quences of such an ontology. Equally, the embrace of these ontologies by practitioners of violence themselves – transnationally – can turn the above into a self-fulfilling prophecy. Even if such an ontology is not, in fact, an accurate representation of social reality, the belief that it is true among those who hold the power to wage violence and shape its morphologies globally will enact its precepts, risks, and potentials in any case. In sum, what is disquieting is the risk of a return to naturalizing violence in society.

Countering these risks, and their attendant dilemmas, requires creativity. At its base, an ecologi-cal ontology can be applied to many different social phenomena and, in other spheres, has been deployed for progressive political ends. In this discussion, I have thus advocated that an ecological ontology of violence might be inverted to design *against* political violence, if we can avert our gaze from the spectacle of contemporary political violence and, instead, learn from other social fields that have developed symbiotic ecological tools for intervening in social reality. Getting there will be a long-term and complicated affair. But taking up this challenge is important, given the very theme of this handbook. Ecological ontologies hold the potential within them both to make the future of warfare more terrible than previously imagined, as well as seemingly inescapable, whilst also containing a hidden capacity to create different future in which the ravages of war and violence are placed back under human control, to some degree. Which path is taken over the next decades will depend on the work of analysts, practitioners, and civil society alike.

Notes

1 Borrell claims his remarks were purely metaphorical and referenced a need to protect the liberal international order from the predations of power politics. See Borrell 2022.
2 For summaries see Coyne 2008; Abrahamsen & Williams 2009; Bennett et al. 2010; Pickering 2010; Bousquet & Curtis 2011; Austin 2016; DeLanda 2016.

References

Abrahamsen, R & Williams, M C 2009, 'Security Beyond the State: Global Security Assemblages in International Politics', *International Political Sociology*, vol. 3, no. 1, pp. 1–17, https://doi.org/10.1111/j.1749-5687.2008.00060.x.
Arendt, H 1963, *Eichmann in Jerusalem*, The Viking Press, New York.
Austin, J L 2016, 'Torture and the Material-Semiotic Networks of Violence Across Borders', *International Political Sociology,* vol. 10 no. 1, pp. 3–21, https://doi.org/10.1093/ips/olv001.
Austin, J L 2019a, 'A Parasitic Critique for International Relations', *International Political Sociology,* vol. 13, no. 2, pp. 215–31, https://doi.org/10.1093/ips/oly032.
Austin, J L 2019b, 'Posthumanism and Perpetrators', in S C Knittel & Z J Goldberg (eds), *The Routledge International Handbook of Perpetrator Studies*, Routledge, London, pp. 169–80.
Austin, J L 2020a, 'The Poetry of Moans and Sighs: Designs for and Against Violence', *Frame: Journal of Literary Studies,* vol. 33, no. 2, pp. 13–31.
Austin, J L 2020b, 'The Departed Militant: A Portrait of Joy, Violence and Political Evil', *Security Dialogue,* vol. 51, no. 6, pp. 537–56, https://doi.org/10.1177/0967010620901906.
Austin, J L 2023, 'The Plasma of Violence: Towards a Preventive Medicine for Political Evil', *Review of International Studies*, vol. 49, no. 1, pp. 105–24, https://doi.org/10.1017/S0260210522000316.
Bell, C 2012, 'War and the Allegory of Medical Intervention: Why Metaphors Matter', *International Political Sociology,* vol. 6, no. 3, pp. 325–8, https://doi.org/10.1111/j.1749-5687.2012.00166_5.x.
Bennett, J, Pheng Cheah, M & Grosz, E 2010, *New Materialisms: Ontology, Agency, and Politics*, Duke University Press, Durham, NC.
Best, J et al. 2013, 'IPS Forum Contributions: Actor-Network Theory and International Relationality', *International Political Sociology*, vol. 7, no. 3, pp. 332–49.
Borrell, J 2022, 'On Metaphors and Geo-Politics', *European External Action Service*, 18 October, <https://www.eeas.europa.eu/eeas/metaphors-and-geo-politics_en> (accessed 20 December 2022).
Bousquet, A 2018, *The Eye of War*, University of Minnesota Press, Minneapolis, MN.
Bousquet, A & Curtis, S 2011, 'Beyond Models and Metaphors: Complexity Theory, Systems Thinking and International Relations', *Cambridge Review of International Affairs,* vol. 24, no. 1, pp. 43–62, https://doi.org/10.1080/09557571.2011.558054.
Bousquet, A, Grove, J & Shah, N 2017, 'Becoming Weapon: An Open Call to Arms', *Critical Studies on Security*, vol. 5, no. 1, pp. 1–8, https://doi.org/10.1080/21624887.2017.1343010.
Bousquet, A, Grove, J & Shah, N 2020, 'Becoming War: Towards a Martial Empiricism', *Security Dialogue*, vol. 51, no. 2–3, pp. 99–118, https://doi.org/10.1177/0967010619895660.
Bronfenbrenner, U 1979, *The Ecology of Human Development: Experiments by Nature and Design*, Harvard University Press, Cambridge, MA.
Celermajer, D 2018, *The Prevention of Torture: An Ecological Approach*, Cambridge University Press, Cambridge.

Chamayou, G 2015, *A Theory of the Drone*, Penguin, London.

Chandler, D, Cudworth, E & Hobden, S 2018, 'Anthropocene, Capitalocene and Liberal Cosmopolitan IR', *Millennium: Journal of International Studies*, vol. 46, no. 2, pp. 190–208, https://doi.
org/10.1177/0305829817715247.

Chilton, P 1996, *Security Metaphors: Cold War Discourse from Containment to Common House*, Peter Lang,
New York, Bern & Frankfurt a. M.

Cohn, C 1987, 'Sex and Death in the Rational World of Defense Intellectuals', *Signs,* vol. 12, no. 4,
pp. 687–718.

Collins, R 2008, *Violence: A Micro-Sociological Theory*, Princeton University Press, Princeton, NJ & Oxford.

Coyne, R 2008, 'The Net Effect: Design, the Rhizome, and Complex Philosophy', *Futures*, vol. 40, no. 6,
pp. 552–61, https://doi.org/10.1016/j.futures.2007.11.003.

De Landa, M 1991, *War in the Age of Intelligent Machines*, Zone Books, Princeton, NJ.

De Landa, M 2016, *Assemblage Theory*, Edinburgh University Press, Edinburgh.

Der Derian, J 2009, *Virtuous War: Mapping the Military-Industrial-Media-Entertainment Network*, Routledge,
New York.

Diamond, L 2010, 'Liberation Technology', *Journal of Democracy*, vol. 21, no. 3, pp. 69–83.

Duffield, M 2019, 'Post-Humanitarianism: Governing Precarity through Adaptive Design', *Journal of
Humanitarian Affairs*, vol. 1, no. 1, pp. 15–27, http://dx.doi.org/10.7227/JHA.003.

EEAS Press Team 2022, 'European Diplomatic Academy: Opening remarks by High Representative Josep
Borrell at the inauguration of the pilot programme,' *European Union External Action Service* <https://
www.eeas.europa.eu/eeas/european-diplomatic-academy-opening-remarks-high-representative-josep-
borrell-inauguration_en (accessed 17 May 2023).

Grove, J 2014, 'Ecology as Critical Security Method', *Critical Studies on Security*, vol. 2, no. 3, pp. 366–9,
https://doi.org/10.1080/21624887.2014.982402.

Grove, J 2019, *Savage Ecology: War and Geopolitics at the End of the World*, Duke University Press, Durham
NC & London.

Haraway, D 1987, 'A Manifesto for Cyborgs: Science, Technology, and Socialist Feminism in the 1980s',
Australian Feminist Studies, vol. 2, no. 4, pp. 1–42.

Haraway, D 2016, *Staying with the Trouble*, Duke University Press, Durham NC & London.

Huntington, S P 1997, *The Clash of Civilizations and the Remaking of World Order*, Penguin Books India,
New Delhi.

Inbar, E & Shamir, E 2014, 'Mowing the Grass': Israel's Strategy for Protracted Intractable Conflict', *Journal
of Strategic Studies*, vol. 37, no. 1, pp. 65–90, https://doi.org/10.1080/01402390.2013.830972.

Kagan, R 2018, *The Jungle Grows Back: America and Our Imperiled World*, Albert A Knopf, New York.

Keeley, L 1996, *War Before Civilization: The Myth of the Peaceful Savage*, Oxford University Press, Oxford.

Lang, T & Rayner, G 2012, 'Ecological Public Health: The 21st Century's Big Idea? An Essay by Tim Lang
and Geof Rayner', *BMJ*, vol. 345, pp. 17–20, https://doi.org/10.1136/bmj.e5466.

Lawson, S 2011, 'Cold War Military Systems Science and the Emergence of a Nonlinear View of War in the
US Military', *Cold War History*, vol. 11, no. 3, pp. 421–40, https://doi.org/10.1080/14682745.2010.494
302.

Lee, N, Broderick, A & Chamberlain, L 2007, 'What Is 'Neuromarketing'? A Discussion and Agenda for
Future Research', *International Journal of Psychophysiology*, vol. 63, no. 2, pp. 199–204, https://doi.
org/10.1016/j.ijpsycho.2006.03.007.

Malaviya, S 2020, 'Digitising the Virtual: Movement and Relations in Drone Warfare', *Millennium*, vol. 49,
no. 1, pp. 80–104, https://doi.org/10.1177/0305829820971694.

Milov, S 2019, *The Cigarette: A Political History*, Harvard University Press, Cambridge, MA.

Müller, V C 2016, 'Autonomous Killer Robots Are Probably Good News', in E Di Nucci & F Santoni de
Sio (eds), *Drones and Responsibility. Legal, Philosophical, and Sociotechnical Perspectives on Remotely
Controlled Weapons*, Routledge, London & New York, pp. 67–81.

Neocleous, M 2011, 'The Police of Civilization: The War on Terror as Civilizing Offensive', *International
Political Sociology*, vol. 5, no. 2, pp. 144–59, https://doi.org/10.1111/j.1749-5687.2011.00126.x.

Neocleous, M 2022, *The Politics of Immunity: Security and the Policing of Bodies*, Verso Books, London.

Öberg, D 2018, 'Warfare as Design: Transgressive Creativity and Reductive Operational Planning', *Security
Dialogue*, vol. 49, no. 6, pp. 493–509, https://doi.org/10.1177/0967010618795787.

Pickering, A 1993, 'The Mangle of Practice: Agency and Emergence in the Sociology of Science', *American
Journal of Sociology*, vol. 99, no. 3, pp. 559–89, https://doi.org/10.1086/230316.

Pickering, A 2010, *The Cybernetic Brain: Sketches of Another Future*, University of Chicago Press, Chicago, IL.

Rose, G 1985, 'Sick Individuals and Sick Populations', *International Journal of Epidemiology*, vol. 30, no. 3, pp. 427–32, https://doi.org/10.1093/ije/30.3.427.

Sayes, E 2014, 'Actor-Network Theory and Methodology: Just What Does It Mean to Say That Nonhumans Have Agency?', *Social Studies of Science*, vol. 44, no. 1, pp. 134–49, https://doi.org/10.1177/0306312713511867.

Serres, M & Latour, B 1995, *Conversations on Science, Culture, and Time*, transl. by R Lapidus, University of Michigan Press, Ann Arbor, MI.

Sikkink, K 2011, *The Justice Cascade: How Human Rights Prosecutions Are Changing World Politics*, W. W. Norton, New York.

Stengers, I 2013, 'Introductory Notes on an Ecology of Practices', *Cultural Studies Review*, vol. 11, no. 1, pp. 183–96, https://doi.org/10.5130/csr.v11i1.3459.

Wailoo, K 2021, *Pushing Cool: Big Tobacco, Racial Marketing, and the Untold Story of the Menthol Cigarette*, University of Chicago Press, Chicago, IL.

Walters, W 2014, 'Drone Strikes, Dingpolitik and Beyond: Furthering the Debate on Materiality and Security', *Security Dialogue*, vol. 45, no. 2, pp. 101–18, https://doi.org/10.1177/0967010613519162.

Weizman, E 2007, 'Walking Through Walls', *Transversal Texts*, <https://transversal.at/transversal/0507/weizman/en> (accessed 20 December 2022).

Weizman, E 2017, *Forensic Architecture: Violence at the Threshold of Detectability*, MIT Press, Cambridge, MA.

Wilcox, L 2015, *Bodies of Violence: Theorizing Embodied Subjects in International Relations*, Oxford University Press, Oxford.

Zehfuss, M 2012, 'Culturally Sensitive War? The Human Terrain System and the Seduction of Ethics', *Security Dialogue*, vol. 43, no. 2, pp. 175–90, https://doi.org/10.1177/0967010612438431.

7

MILITAINMENT FOR FUTURE WARFARE

Tanner Mirrlees

Introduction: militainment, made in China, Russia, and the United States

Over the past decade, two authoritarian states – Xi Jinping's one-party China and Vladimir Putin's petro-nationalist Russia – have been using entertainment to build popular support for wars, past and future. To celebrate its 100th anniversary, the Chinese Communist Party (CCP) funneled $200 million through its Publicity Department toward *The Battle at Lake Changjin* (2021): This war movie tells the story of a heroic People's Army joining North Korea to battle villainous American forces (Andersen 2021). In the same year that the CCP's Korean War movie became China's highest grossing worldwide blockbuster of all time, Russia released *Solntsepyok* (2021), a future war movie in which the Russian military invades Ukraine to protect the Russian-backed separatist Luhansk People's Republic against Ukrainians, who are vilified as genocidal Nazis. Released on the state-aligned NTV broadcaster and streaming platforms, this movie primed Russians for Putin's invasion of Ukraine, before it happened (Dolgopolov 2022). Non-state actors have also been turning entertainment into war propaganda: Daesh modified versions of *Grand Theft Auto IV* and *Call of Duty* and then used these games for recruiting and training combatants to fight its Western enemies (Kang 2014).

China, Russia and Daesh's weaponization of entertainment for war is obvious and commonly chided. What is less frequently recognized is how the United States (US), a liberal democratic country, is the globe's most significant center for "militainment". While many countries around in the world create and sell their own national militainment (or, military-themed entertainment that is frequently made by media corporations with assistance from military publicity offices), from World War I forward, the United States has been militainment's global trailblazer. Today, the US Department of Defense (DoD) presides over the world's most powerful military and Hollywood runs the most profitable movie industry. Together, they often co-produce militainment that transforms complex and controversial acts of state violence into spectacles for global mass consumption. In *The Suicide Squad* (2021), a DC franchise movie made by Warner Bros with assistant from the DoD's entertainment liaison office, Harley Quinn organizes criminal anti-heroes to overthrow a South American government that threatens US security in the region. Released in time for Memorial Day and also made with DoD backing, *Top Gun: Maverick* (2022) scripts Pete "Maverick" Mitchell training the best-of-the-best fighter pilots to fly Boeing F-18 Super Hornets in a daredevil

DOI: 10.4324/9781003299011-9

missile attack on another country's uranium enrichment facility. This was the highest grossing movie at the North American box office in 2022.

Even though the DoD and media-entertainment corporations are different types of organizations (the former is primarily concerned with defense and security in world politics and the latter pursues profit in world markets), DoD publicity agencies routinely work with the world's most talented image-makers and storytellers to make sure the military will look great on screen and off. This United States's "military-entertainment complex" produces and sells militainment for markets that ultimately puts US military personnel and the wars they fight before the world in a positive light, attracts and recruits new enlistees, raises the morale of soldiers and civilians, and shows off advanced weapons technologies (Der Derian 2009; Stahl 2009; Mirrlees 2016, 2019, 2021; Stahl et al. 2022). While the United States is militainment's global vanguard, China, Russia, and many more countries – some US allies and others not – are ratcheting up efforts to weld entertainment to new and emerging ways of war. But as the United States is the oldest example of a security state that enlists entertainment into its imagination of future warfare and the most paradigmatic case of how a military creates and deploys entertainment to prepare for and fight these wars, the United States is the focus of this chapter.

To show how the DoD uses militainment for imagining (and waging) future warfare, the chapter's first section contextualizes the US superpower's military-corporate futurism industry, the DoD's hegemonic genre of dystopian futurism, and the DoD's new partnership with science fiction (sci-fi) writers. Drawing from past and present examples, the second section identifies eight salient ways that the DoD uses militainment to sustain its dystopian future warfare imaginary. Militainment helps the DoD: (1) imagine future threats to national security; (2) imagine future enemies; (3) imagine how future warfare will be fought; (4) imagine futuristic weapons systems and R&D projects; (5) imagine future soldier identities; (6) enlist personnel for future warfare; (7) train the imagination of personnel in preparation for future warfare; and (8) move the civilian imagination towards future warfare. For the near and foreseeable future, the likely outcome of the US military-entertainment complex's militainment will be more conflict and war, both real and imagined.

Hegemonic futurism: industry, defense, and dystopian sci-fi

From the post-WWII era to our time, futurists have served universities, corporations and militaries. In general, futurists are researchers, consultants, and strategists who forecast futures with the goal of preparing society for what may come (Van Creveld 2020). In the United States, futurism has always intertwined with the country's growth and maintenance as a superpower, or Empire. Following World War II, RAND and SRI International researched and developed future scenarios that helped the United States achieve national and global security goals vis-à-vis the Soviet Union, its competitor for the planet's future. From the late 1960s forward, futurism grew into a big business and today its coteries of think-tanks and consultancies produce and sell commercialized futurism. Call it Futurism Inc. The booming industry's main clients are military agencies and corporations who, being interested in maintaining their social power, are pleased to pay for imaginaries of a future world that look much like today, and tend not to consult the radical imagination for a better tomorrow (Eschrich 2017). Due to market constraints and incentives, many futurists are inclined to accept the status quo: that warfare and capitalism will go on, *ad infinitum*. This brand of futurism is most often at work in the interest of militaries who seek strategies to secure nations against future threats and corporations competing for profit in future markets. It is biased to hard realist foreign policy ("there is no alternative to conflict and war in an anarchic international system of self-interested states") and neoliberal ideology ("there is no alternative to capitalism"). Hegemonic futurism ensures that the futurists who imagine a truly different and better world beyond military and corporate priorities will be excluded from real scenario planning.

In the first decade of the 21st century, the DoD was a key driver of this hegemonic futurism. Following the terrorist attacks of 9/11 and in a context of "changing concepts of warfare in the early 21st century, with its new emphasis on 'asymmetric' warfare, terrorism and insurgency across the global 'battlespace' rather than conventional wars between states" (Carr 2010, p. 17), the DoD was producing strategic future doctrines, blueprints, and templates that were "extremely pessimistic" and "spectacularly bleak" (Carr 2010, pp. 16, 19). In the DoD's dystopian discourse of future warfare, the national security of the United States and its allies are permanently threatened by "rogue states, weapons of mass destruction and terrorism", as well as by "resurgent nationalism, conflicts over dwindling resources, migration, disease, organized crime, abrupt climate change and the emergence of 'failed cities' where social disorder is rife" (Carr 2010, p. 13). The DoD's dystopian futurism makes possible and far off security threats to America and the world seem real and ever-present. Bolstered by this genre, the DoD wins vast "budgets to populate the future with robot armies, super soldiers and airborne drones that 'see' inside buildings and kill their occupants", provides the US security state with "a justification for endless global war against enemies that may never exist", and lays "the foundations for a militarized and weaponized future" even as it shapes "the wars and conflicts of the present (Carr 2010, p. 31).

Since World War II, the DoD has conscripted sci-fi writers to help it imagine and get ready for future warfare, and while many sci-fi authors have willingly cooperated with it, others used the sci-fi genre to protest war (Deadman 2016). But over the past ten years or so, the DoD has ramped up its efforts to marshal the minds of sci-fi writers and even trained its own personnel to read, interpret and write sci-fi with the goal of augmenting its capacity to prepare for, fight and win future wars (Liptak 2020). Sci-fi is today key to the military-entertainment complex and the most sought after militainment form: all kinds of military strategists and creative professionals are interested in the genre.

Take, for example, how in 2013, Steven Grundman, a defense consultant and senior fellow with the Forward Defence practice of the Atlantic Council's Scowcroft Center for Strategy and Security, organized the Art of Future Warfare Project (AFWP) to explore how fiction, art, and entertainment media could serve the military. In attendance at the symposium kick-off were Grundman, futurist August Cole, sci-fi writer David Brin, and *Call of Duty: Black Ops II* writer Dave Anthony, who received funding from the Atlantic Council to publish a military science fiction anthology called *War Stories From the Future* (Art of Future Warfare Project 2015). Similarly, in 2016, the US Marine Corps Warfighting Laboratory organized a Science Fiction Futures Workshop which catalyzed the creation of *Marine Corps Security Environment Forecast Futures: 2030–2045*, an anthology of science fiction stories about the future of global conflict and war (Atherton 2017). In the anthology's forward, US Marine Corps Commanding General Julian Dale Alford described how as the Marine Corps prepares "for the challenges of the world we think we know today, we must leave room for imagination and creative anticipation" and explained how "we take the broad worlds" crafted for the anthology to "offer possible tactical and operational level vignettes of the distant future through the medium of science fiction" (US Marine Corps 2016, p. i).

In that same year, NATO's Allied Command Transformation (ACT) funded a group of sci-fi writers to pen future war stories based on the doctrines stored in the Allied Command Transformation's library of futures (e.g., Strategic Foresight Analysis, Framework for Future Alliance Operations, Technology Trends Survey and Long-Term Aspects of requirements). In the foreword to the resulting *Visions of Warfare 2036*, U.S. Air Force Lieutenant General Jeffrey Lofgren described this anthology of future war stories as inciting "inventive thinking and discussion about future possibilities" that the "Alliance military and others can leverage to imagine and contemplate how

NATO will undertake operations in the coming decades" (Allied Command Transformation 2016, p. 9). Lauding this volume's many "insights", Lofgren declared this creative militainment project to have "literally taken on the challenge levied by Sergey Brin, one of the founders of Google, who said, 'If what we are doing is not seen by some people as science fiction, it's probably not transformative enough'" (Allied Command Transformation 2016, p. 10).

Evidently, sci-fi is important to the DoD, and yet, it is just one example of how entangled militainment is with future warfare. Whether incubated from within the military-entertainment complex, produced by media companies without any military oversight, or made by the military's own creative media makers, militainment is immensely useful to the DoD. In the next section, I identify eight salient ways that the DoD uses militainment to sustain its dystopian future warfare imaginary.

The DoD's uses of militainment for future warfare

Future threats

Future warfare requires the permanent specter of threats. Sans threat, the DoD has no rationale for securing the nation (and its "interest") and loses its justification for massive defense budgets and global build-up. Whereas Cold War futurists focused on the Soviet Union's threat to America, 21st-century military futurists imagine both non-state and state threats, and look to militainment to fuel their threat imaginary. After 9/11, the DoD commissioned some Hollywood screenwriters, like *Die Hard*'s Steven E. de Souza, to imagine future threat scenarios. Years later, *Call of Duty*'s writer Dave Anthony was praised by the Atlantic Council for "imagining new types of threats" to the United States and world, and strengthening its "work on emerging challenges, disruptive technologies, and security and defense strategy" (Drennan 2014). Some militainment threat scenarios are plausible: based on John Carlin's *A Farewell to Arms* (an essay about a cyber-attack scenario called *The Day After*) (Carlin 1997), *Live Free or Die Hard* (2007) represents a cyber strike on the United States's transportation, telecommunications, financial, and public utility computer systems: "Its depiction of cyberwarfare is actually very realistic," said Siim Alatalu, of the NATO Cooperative Cyber Defence Centre of Excellence (Maack 2019). Other militainment threat scenarios are improbable, even ridiculous. Assisted by the DoD's entertainment liaison office, *Transformers* (2007) and *Transformers: Revenge of the Fallen* (2009) narrate American teenagers, troops and friendly robots disguised as GM vehicles teaming up to defeat evil alien robots (Mirrlees 2016). Relatedly, some of the "most successful commercial video wargame franchises have employed the imagined future threat environments and strategic responses to them outlined in DoD reports as the basis for game scenarios" (Lenoir & Caldwell 2018, p. 43). In most cases, militainment's future threats are rogue states and terrorists, sometimes even other worldly monsters. Never are they social system-level threats to human security, such as global capitalism, climate change, or healthcare, education, and welfare deprivation.

Future enemies

Future warfare relies upon real and possible future enemies for the US DoD to fight, and militainment imagines these when extrapolating from present-day inter-state tensions. In the best-selling first-person shooter game *Call of Duty 4: Modern Warfare* (2007), civilians play as US soldiers fighting an ultranationalist Russia, which invades Virginia and Maryland, obliterates much of Camp David and the Pentagon, and starts World War III, leading to nuclear catastrophe. In Tom Clancy's novel *Ghost Recon* (2001), Russian ultranationalists invade Georgia (seven years before that really happened), and an elite US Army force defends US allies in the Baltic region and then eventually defeats the Russians in a climactic battle at the Kremlin, in the Red Square. In *Homefront* (2011), the year is 2027, the US financial system has collapsed, and Kim Jong-un has unified North and South Korea into the Greater Korean Republic (GKR), a military superpower that destroys the United States's cyber-network with an orbital nuclear strike, conquers Hawaii and invades the American Midwest. In *Red Dawn* (2012), a Hollywood remake of the Reagan-era Cold War flick by the same name (written by John Milius, a *Homefront* consultant), Kim Jong-un's North Korea is again the enemy: beleaguered by a weakened NATO and a strengthened Russia, North Korea invades the United States, and an Iraq war vet and group of teenager football players use guerrilla warfare tactics to oust the occupier. China is cast as America's future enemy in *Battlefield 4: China Rising* (2013). In *Call of Duty: Ghosts* (2013), the year is 2027, and "the Federation of Americas" (a coalition of South American states with their capital in Caracas, Venezuela), invades the United States. *Battlefield's Combat Mission: Shock Force* (2007) simulated a US-led NATO war against Syria, seven years before the United States actually tried to oust Bashar al-Assad. Militainment's future imaginary of enemies taps into state discourses of a righteous American Self and vile anti-American Other, often casting the United States as war's victim, not its instigator. In any case, it scripts a world where diplomacy is not an option and peace is fanciful.

Future ways of fighting

Future warfare imagines new ways of fighting, and projects them into a future where the military's potential has come to fruition. Established in the mid-1990s, the DoD's Revolution in Military Affairs (RMA) doctrine extols the integration of information and communication technologies (ICTs) with soldiers and weapons systems as a catalyst for Network Centric Warfare (NCW), and digital militainment products such as *SOCOM: U.S. Navy Seals* and *Medal of Honour* simulate various future scenarios that idealize the NCW doctrines. Perhaps most significant to the military's imagination of how future wars may be fought is the FICINT (Fiction Intelligence) genre, novels that are said to blend "fiction and intelligence" and offer "strategic foresight" into "alternative futures contexts for strategic decision-making to anticipate threats, risks and opportunities and identify ways to manage those potentials" (Sullivan 2020). In *Ghost Fleet* (2015), a FICINT novel by military futurists Peter Singer and August Cole, the United States and a post-Communist China wage cyber-naval warfare supported by electromagnetic railguns, aerial vehicles (UAVs), and weaponized satellites. In *Burn-In: A Novel of the Real Robotic Revolution* (2020), their follow up FICINT novel, the United States has become a techno-capitalist dystopia of total automation where AI, Big Data, robots, drones, and ubiquitous surveillance stoke social unrest and strife. The fictional heroine, Lara Keegan, a former Marine turned FBI agent partners with a police robot called TAMS (Tactical Autonomous Mobility System) to bring down a neo-Luddite terrorist network of jihadists, neo-Nazis, neo-Marxists, and environmentalists revolting to overthrow the society. Militainment also launches future ways of war in outer space: *Call of Duty: Infinite Warfare* imagines full-on space combat between the hybrid plane/spaceship systems. Robot war is moreover on militainment's horizon: Joe Haldeman's *Forever Peace* imagines a future where soldiers use robot surrogates ("soldierboys" and "flyboys") that are physically and mentally integrated through brain-computer interfaces and battle Latin American "rebel" countries and "the Ngumi," an African-led insurgency. ICTs, AI, and robots could be designed for a future of non-violence and peace, but militainment fetters these wonders to warfighting and tells the world that every new and emerging means must be readied for the ends of war.

Future weapons

Future warfare necessitates the research and development (R&D) of future weapons. As Dwight D. Eisenhower's science advisor James Killian said in 1956: "If there are to be yet unimagined weapons affecting the balance of military power tomorrow, we want to have the men and the means to imagine them first." Established by Eisenhower in 1958 a year after the Soviet launch of the Sputnik, the Defence Advanced Research Projects Agency (DARPA) unites military agencies, universities and corporations to imagine "breakthrough technologies and capabilities for national security" and transform "revolutionary concepts and even seeming impossibilities into practical [weapons] capabilities" (DARPA 2022). While future warfare preparedness underwrites billions on projects that try to actualize wild concepts into well-designed weapons, DARPA's techno-fantasies conversely draw from fictional works. From advanced submarines to the Internet, many military inventions first appeared in fiction, and today, Hollywood-scripted weapons sometimes inspire military-led R&D projects (Weinberger 2006, 2017). The *Star Wars*, *Star Trek*, and *Gundam* series represent laser guns; since the 1950s, the US Office of Naval Research has undertaken R&D on a laser weapon prototype, and its latest Layered Laser Defence (LLD) system is capable of shooting down drones and destroying speedboats. *Wanted* (2009) depicts self-guided bullets chasing their targets, and DARPA's Extreme Accuracy Tasked Ordnance program (EXACTO) and Sandia National Laboratories have subsequently tinkered with "smart bullets". In *Top Gun: Maverick* (2022), Maverick tests the SR-72 Darkstar, a fictional super-sonic aircraft whose real offshoot – the SR-71 Blackbird – is being made by Lockheed Martin's "Skunkworks". Fiction also prefigured the military's weaponization of the biosphere: *Sparrowhawk* (1990), *Minority Report* (2002) and *Avatar* (2009) depict the integration of spiders, bees, and beetles into remotely controllable cybernetic systems (Stahl 2014) while video games such as *Call of Duty: Black Ops II* (2012) and *Call of Duty: Advanced Warfare* (2014) let us crawl the battlefield as "Ziggy" the spider drone and soar over the battlefield as a "fly drone", respectively. And while the military has long forced animals (from mounted cavalry to homing pigeons) to fight, its cyborgian insects are straight out of science fiction (Stahl 2014). While giving us a glimpse of imagined weapons, militainment greases the wheels of R&D programs and projects that aim to shuttle tech fantasy into reality. New technologies can improve the quality of life on earth for billions, but militainment supplants techno-invention for the social good with machine making for future warfare and death.

Future soldiers

Future warfare relies upon future soldiers, and the military imagines these with help from fiction. In the late 1970s, the US Army tried to cultivate super-soldiers by way of paranormally inflected New Age literature (Ronson 2004). As part of the Army's "Stargate Project", US military personnel were imagined as "Jedi warriors" who, with invisibility cloaks, would teleport through walls, read the future, and kill their enemies (and goats) by staring at them to death (Ronson 2004). Goats notwithstanding, the US Army's *Future Soldier 2030* initiative aims "to identify capabilities a Soldier might carry into battle", "stir imaginations", and "start a dialogue about how best to equip the Soldier" of the future (US Army 2009, p. 2). Declaring that "augmented and virtual environments will be ubiquitous and will support almost every facet of warfare including communications, data visualization, system control, and training", *Future Soldier 2030* aims to provide soldiers with a "tremendous edge in combat" (US Army 2009, p. 3). This initiative seeks to *equip* soldiers with "behavioral, neural and physiological sensors" for "augmented capabilities" and a "powered exoskeleton" for "interact[ing] with robotics, software systems and hardware platforms"

(US Army 2009, p. 3). Hollywood has helped the DoD bring these future soldiers to life on screen when scripting all kinds of heroes battling evil in suits and exoskeletons. In *Aliens* (1986), Ripley (Sigourney Weaver) wears an exoskeleton called the "Power Loader" to defeat the Alien Queen. In *The Matrix* trilogy (1999, 2003), humans plug in to Armored Personnel Units (APU) to battle squid-like machines bent on wiping out humans. The suits worn by Tony Stark, the hero of the *Iron Man* franchise (2008, 2010, 2013), inspired various cyborgian future soldier prototypes. *Elysium* (2013), *Edge of Tomorrow* (2014) and *Pacific Rim* (2013, 2018) all feature exoskeletons that augment ordinary soldiers into super-powered fighters (Tucker 2017) while video games such as *Call of Duty: Advanced Warfare*, *Halo*, *Crysis*, and *Black Ops III* make weaponized suits playable. Inspired by *Future Soldier 2030*, *Ghost Recon: Future Soldier* (2012) invites players to step into "the shoes of a Special Forces soldier in a near future scenario". Beyond imagining soldiers for future war and enlisting viewers-players to identify with these roles, militainment also dovetails with a raft of real cyborg-soldier R&D projects by Lockheed Martin (e.g., the Tactical Assault Light Operator Suit and the Fortis exoskeleton) and Raytheon (XOS 2). Augmented humans need not be militarized or put to work for future warfare, but militainment points toward a future where cyborg-soldiers are the norm.

Future recruitment

A country permanently at war requires a permanent recruitment campaign, and in the absence of conscription, future warfare will always require future citizens to voluntarily enlist. As such, much militainment is designed to "hail" and "recruit" civilians into the real military. Hollywood has long collaborated on DoD recruitment campaigns, and enabled military public affairs officers to shape the scripts of thousands of films and TV to gain access to real bases, battleships, and fighter jets (Jenkins & Secker 2021; Stahl et al. 2022). The DoD assisted the production of *Top Gun* (1986) and Air Force recruiters set up booths at the film's nationwide premiere, and repeated the arrangement for the film's reprise *Top Gun: Maverick* (2022). "Whether they want to aim high or fly Navy, we just want them to come join us. We want them to be excited about military service", said Major General Edward Thomas, head of Air Force Recruiting Service (Baldor 2022). Perhaps cognizant of how *Top Gun*'s toxic masculinity risked alienating prospective women recruits, the Air Force militarized "girl power" when assisting Marvel Studios' *Captain Marvel* (2019) and screening a 30-second recruitment ad called "Origin Story" as a trailer before the super-heroine movie. Yet the DoD's greatest century militainment recruitment tool is *America's Army*. Developed by MOVES at the Naval Postgraduate School and managed by the US Military Academy at West Point, *America's Army* was funded by the military, and launched for Windows PC on Independence Day, 2002. Just in-time for the Bush Administration's Global War on Terror, it targeted prospective recruits at malls, sports events and amusement parks. After 20 years of service, *America's Army* was deoperationalized in 2022: the real Army's latest recruitment media is YouTube, Twitch, and TikTok (Kelly 2021; Morris 2022). Hollywood and social media militainment's recruitment function make future warfare seem inevitable.

Future training

Future warfare requires the continuous training of military personnel and militainment plays a role in this process. Ever since the publication of Ernest Dunlop Swinton's *The Defence of Duffer's Drift* (1904), a story about a soldier who has six dreams of trying but failing to defend a river crossing during the Boer War, works of fiction have been of interest to future war trainers and educators. In 2020, the US Army Cyber Institute at West Point and Arizona State University's "Threatcasting Lab" (Arizona State University 2022) published a 71-page graphic novel titled *Invisible Force: Information Warfare and the Future of Conflict* (Army Cyber Institute at West Point 2020). The twelfth edition to the US Army's "science fiction prototypes" program of military pedagogy, this graphic novel aimed to teach strategists to imagine the future of warfare and train military personnel to think creatively about their roles in future wars. The Modern War Institute (MWI) at West Point also embraces comic books as "one of the most important but least respected means of education" about warfare. MWI fellow Max Brooks (2017, 2019), the author of *World War Z*, a 2006 zombie apocalyptic horror novel turned into a Hollywood film starring Brad Pitt, blogs for the MWI and posts lists of must-read comic books for military training and professional development. Meanwhile, the US Naval Institute's *Proceedings* magazine publishes science fiction stories, as does the Marine Corps University Brute Krulak Centre for Innovation and Creativity and the Air Force's Air University Blue Horizons fellows' program (Singer & Cole 2015). The Army, Navy, Air Force, and Marines also use computer modeling and simulation systems (and interactive games) to train military personnel for the future (Halter 2006). Following the Gulf War (1990–91), the Institute for Defense Analyses Simulation Center frequently used SIMNET, a networked multi-user combat simulation system envisaged by DARPA's Jack Thorpe as a way to use war history to prepare for war's futures (Lenori & Caldwell 2018, p. 54). Since 2006, the US Army Simulation and Training Technology Centre (STTC) and the ICT-USC (2022) have managed *UrbanSim*, a training application operationalized between 2003 and 2011 to train soldiers to combat the Iraq insurgency. By enabling military personnel to play-train-perform in a variety of battle scenarios, war simulation games help the US military prepare for victory in future wars. Here, militainment's prognosis is a future of permanent training for a nation forever at war.

Future propaganda

All wars, including future wars, marshal a media propaganda campaign to convince civilians that their nations' wars are mostly right and good, or sometimes necessary to combat outside evils. In this regard, the challenge of winning or manufacturing the public's consent to future wars weighs heavily on the DoD, whose media-cultural workers are tasked with persuading people to passively or actively support these wars. Today militainment primes the public to imagine war as inevitably and inexorably part of the United States's whole way of life. Given that propaganda can be said to be "the deliberate, systematic attempt to shape perceptions, manipulate cognitions, and direct behavior to achieve a response that furthers the desired intent of the propagandist" (Jowett & O'Donnell 2015, p. 7), the DoD's militainment for future wars fits the mold. As the DoD and entertainment industries have been collaborating since the early 20th century, militainment for future war is a *systematic* process: audio-visual and interactive entertainment do not reflect the world "as it is" but aim to shape and possibly even change perceptions and cognitions of DoD personnel, policies, practices and technologies, now and for the future. And while militainment for future warfare is not propaganda of the kind found in authoritarian countries, where the state directly owns or controls the media system and uses it to control the public mind, it is propaganda no less, and sometimes far less obvious to the people targeted and potentially manipulated by it because it is packaged as commercial entertainment, not military propaganda. Moving forward, as competition and conflict between the United States, China and Russia intensifies, militainment will become ever more integral to these country's propaganda campaigns.

Conclusion: the future of warfare, through entertainment

This chapter has demonstrated how significant militainment is to the DoD's dystopian future warfare imaginary and to its new and emerging threat calculus, enemy construction, warfighting doctrines, weapons R&D, soldier prototypes, enlistment campaigns, training regimen and propaganda. For the near future, the US military-entertainment complex will produce and circulate militainment whose fictional imagining of future wars serve the DoD and security state's present-day strategic geopolitical and economic exigencies while portending and preparing for real dystopian futures of boundless and endless wars between America and a wide range of state and non-state actors. In the short term, militainment will be essential to the future of American warfare and routinely made and mobilized by US planners to elicit public support for the US military's global conflicts, increases in defense outlays, and articulation of patriotism to military outlooks and actions. As it travels the globe, this militainment will serve the US security state crucially as a form of "soft power" for its "hard power" and work to persuade the world to support the US military's unrivaled global presence and the violence of its many interventions.

Yet, the globalization of American militainment may inspire or agitate other countries to make anti-American militainment. Having recognized the potency of the US military-entertainment complex to get non-American publics to wholly identify with or grudgingly accept the United States's dystopian future warfare imaginary as their own, the military and media elites of non-US countries may build up or reinforce their existing military-entertainment complexes and deploy homegrown militainment against the United States. Thus, American militainment may have a "boomerang effect" that destabilizes the United States's global military hegemony. As a consequence of the countries once targeted by American militainment becoming national militainment powers in their own right, the prospect of more inter-state conflict and war will increase and the chance for world peace will diminish.

In every case, the future of warfare will be fought through entertainment media. Future warfare is not inevitable but probable absent the victory of movements advancing alternative future imaginaries that free humanity from the necessities of global capitalism and its war-prone inter-state system. The world desperately needs futurists to answer global humanity's biggest question: what types of future social systems must we imagine and invent to ensure the lasting survival of all species, on earth? Whether made-in-America or in China or Russia, militainment has no creative answers. Everywhere, it is a weapon that harms and hurts the radical imagination of all those who dare to dream of qualitatively different and better futures (Wager 1999; Wright 2010; Robinson 2021).

References

Allied Command Transformation 2016, *Visions of Warfare: 2036*, Allied Command Transformation, Norfolk, VA, <https://www.act.nato.int/images/stories/events/2012/fc_ipr/visions-of-warfare-2036.pdf> (accessed 22 November 2022).

Andersen, R 2021, 'Beijing's Movie War Propaganda--and Washington's', *FAIR*, 31 December, <https://fair.org/home/beijings-movie-war-propaganda-and-washingtons/> (accessed 22 November 2022).

Arizona State University 2022, *Threatcasting Lab*, <https://threatcasting.asu.edu/> (accessed 22 November 2022).

Army Cyber Institute at West Point 2020, *Invisible Force: Information Warfare and the Future of Conflict*, <https://threatcasting.asu.edu/sites/default/files/2020-06/Invisible_Force_%5BWEB%5D_0.pdf> (accessed 22 November).

Art of Future Warfare Project 2015, 'War Stories from the Future', *Atlantic Council*, <https://www.atlantic-council.org/in-depth-research-reports/books/war-stories-from-the-future/> (accessed 22 November 2022).

Atherton, K 2017, 'Marines Solicit Science Fiction stories to Imagine the Future of Conflict', *USNI News*, 17 October, <https://news.usni.org/2017/10/17/marines-solicit-science-fiction-stories-imagine-future-conflicts> (accessed 22 November 2022).

Baldor, L 2022, 'As Recruiters Struggle, Air Force Seeks Lift from "Top Gun"', *ABC News*, 20 July, <https://abcnews.go.com/Entertainment/wireStory/recruiters-struggle-air-force-seeks-lift-top-gun-87138460> (accessed 22 November 2022).

Brooks, M 2017, 'War Books, Special Edition: Max Brooks on Reading Comics to Understand War', *Modern War Institute at West Point*, 25 September, <https://mwi.usma.edu/war-books-special-edition-reading-comics-understand-war-max-brooks/> (accessed 22 November 2022).

Brooks, M 2019, 'War Books, Special Edition: Max Brooks on Reading Comics to Understand War, Part 2', *Modern War Institute at West Point*, 6 March, <https://mwi.usma.edu/war-books-special-edition-max-brooks-reading-comics-understand-war-part-2/> (accessed 22 November 2022).

Carlin, J 1997, 'A Farewell to Arms', *Wired*, 1 May, <https://www.wired.com/1997/05/netizen-2/> (accessed 22 November 2022).

Carr, M 2010, 'Slouching Towards Dystopia: The New Military Futurism', *Race & Class*, vol. 51, no. 3, pp. 13–32, https://doi.org/10.1177/030639680935416.

DARPA 2022, *Defense Advanced Research Projects Agency Homepage*, <https://www.darpa.mil/> (accessed 22 November 2022).

Deadman, S 2016, *May the Armed Forces Be with You: The Relationship Between Science Fiction and the United States Military*, McFarland & Company, Inc, Jefferson, NC, <https://books.google.ca/books?id=CyD3DAAAQBAJ&printsec=frontcover&source=gbs_ge_summary_r&cad=0#v=onepage&q&f=false> (accessed 22 November).

Der Derian, J 2009, *Virtuous War: Mapping the Military-Industrial-Media-Entertainment-Network*, Routledge, New York.

Dolgopolov, G 2022, 'How Solntsepyok, a Brutal 2021 Propaganda Film, Primed Russians for war with Ukraine', *The Conversation*, 5 July, <https://theconversation.com/how-solntsepyok-a-brutal-2021-propaganda-film-primed-russians-for-war-with-ukraine-185701> (accessed 22 November 2022).

Drennan, J, 2014 'Call of Duty: Star Video Game Director Takes Unusual Think Tank Job', Foreign Policy, September 22, available at https://foreignpolicy.com/2014/09/22/call-of-duty-star-video-game-director-takes-unusual-think-tank-job/ (accessed on 14 May 2023).

Eschrich, J 2017, 'The Futurism Industry's Blind Spot', *Slate*, 20 September, <https://slate.com/technology/2017/09/futurists-rarely-imagine-a-tomorrow-without-capitalism.html> (accessed 22 November 2022).

Halter, E 2006, *From Sun Tau to Xbox: War and Video Games*, Thunder Mouth Press, New York.

ICT-USC 2022, 'UrbanSim', *Institute for Creative Technologies at the University of Southern California*, <https://ict.usc.edu/research/projects/urbansim/> (accessed 22 November 2022).

Jenkins, T & Secker, T 2021, *Superheroes, Movies, and the State: How the U.S. Government Shapes Cinematic Universes*, University Press of Kansas, Lawrence, KS.

Kang, J C 2014, 'ISIS's Call of Duty', *The New Yorker*, 18 September, <https://www.newyorker.com/tech/annals-of-technology/isis-video-game> (accessed 22 November 2022).

Kelly, M 2021, 'The Army Is in Hot Water Over TikTok Recruiting Activity', *The Verge*, 14 December, <https://www.theverge.com/2021/12/14/22834405/tiktok-army-marco-rubio-ban-report-government-personal-devices> (accessed 22 November 2022).

Jowett, G S & O'Donnell, V J 2015, *Propaganda & Persuasion*, 6th edn, Sage Publications, Thousand Oaks, CA.

Lenoir, T & Caldwell, L 2018, *The Military-Entertainment Complex*, Harvard University Press, Cambridge, MA.

Liptak, A 2020, 'The U.S. Military Is Turning to Science Fiction to Shape the Future of War', *OneZero*, 29 July, <https://onezero.medium.com/the-u-s-military-is-turning-to-science-fiction-to-shape-the-future-of-war-1b40d11eb6b4> (accessed 22 November 2022).

Maack, M M 2019, 'Die Hard 4 is the Perfect Description of Real Cyberwarfare', *TNW*, 2 April, <https://thenextweb.com/news/nato-strategist-die-hard-4-is-the-perfect-way-to-describe-real-cyberwarfare> (accessed 22 November 2022).

Mirrlees, T 2016, *Hearts and Mines: The US Empire's Culture Industry*, UBC Press, Vancouver.

Mirrlees, T 2019, 'The Military-Entertainment Complex', in Z Cope & I Ness (eds), *The Palgrave Encyclopedia of Imperialism and Anti-Imperialism*, 2nd edn online, Palgrave Macmillan, London.

Mirrlees, T 2021, '"Marveling" the World with Hollywood Militainment: The U.S. Air Force and Captain Marvel Go Higher! Further! Faster!', in D Y Jin (ed), *The Routledge Handbook of Digital Media and Globalization*, Routledge, New York, pp. 41–53.

Morris, C 2022, 'After 20 years, the U.S. Army Is shutting Down its Recruitment Video Game, "America's Army"', *Fast Company*, 11 February, <https://www.fastcompany.com/90720653/after-20-years-the-u-s-army-is-shutting-down-its-recruitment-video-game-americas-army> (accessed 22 November 2022).

Robinson, K S 2021, *The Ministry for the Future*, Orbit Books, London.

Ronson, J 2004, *The Men Who Stare At Goats*, Simon & Schuster, New York.

Singer, P W & Cole, A 2015, 'How to Write About World War II', *The Atlantic*, 30 June, <https://www.theatlantic.com/international/archive/2015/06/ghost-fleet-world-war-III/397301/> (accessed 22 November 2022).

Stahl, R 2009, *Militainment, Inc.: War, Media and Popular Culture*, Routledge, New York.

Stahl, R 2014, 'Life Is War: The Rhetoric of Biomimesis and the Future Military', *Democratic Communiqué*, vol. 26, no. 2, pp. 122–37.

Stahl, R, Kaempf, S, Alford, M & Secker, T 2022, 'Theaters of War: How the Pentagon and CIA Took Hollywood', *Media Education Foundation*, < https://go.mediaed.org/theaters-of-war> (accessed 22 November 2022).

Sullivan, J 2020, 'SWJ Book Review: Burn-In: A Novel of the Real Robotic Revolution', *Small Wars Journal*, 7 March, <https://smallwarsjournal.com/jrnl/art/swj-book-review-burn-novel-real-robotic-revolution> (accessed 22 November 2022).

US Army 2009, 'Future Soldier 2030 Initiative', *Wired*, <https://www.wired.com/images_blogs/dangerroom/2009/05/dplus2009_11641-1.pdf> (accessed 22 November 2022).

US Marine Corps 2016, *Science Fiction Futures: Marine Corps Security Environment Forecast - Futures 2030–2045*, Marine Corps Warfighting Laboratory, Quantico, VA, <https://www.mcwl.marines.mil/Portals/34/Documents/FuturesAssessment/Marine%20Corps%20Science%20Fiction%20Futures%202016_12_9.pdf?ver=2016-12-09-105855-733> (accessed 22 November 2022).

Van Creveld, M 2020, *Seeing into the Future: A Short History of Prediction*, The University of Chicago Press, Chicago.

Wager, W 1999, *A Short History of the Future*, The University of Chicago Press, Chicago.

Weinberger, S 2006, *Imaginary Weapons: A Journey Through the Pentagon's Scientific* Underworld, Nation Books, New York.

Weinberger, S 2017, *The Imagineers of War*, Knopf, New York.

Wright, E O 2010, *Envisioning Real Utopias*, Verso, New York.

PART II

The Systemic Variables of the Future of Warfare

8

HOW OUR ACCELERATING INTERACTIONS IN CYBERSPACE HAVE SHIFTED GLOBAL POWER AND MADE A KINETIC WORLD WAR MORE LIKELY

The Riddle of Steel

Ivan Arreguín-Toft

Introduction

In this chapter, I review old theories (themselves most often amalgams of yet *older* theories) to highlight the political implications of a dangerous trend in international politics: something I call 'right shift'. It is dangerous because right shift will make major interstate war – possibly even world war – increasingly likely over the next decade. War is of course only *one* of the lethal challenges we as a species must overcome sooner rather than later, but the core of my contribution here comes down to this: power is not a ladder, it is a wheel; and to the extent we continue to insist that of the three core *domains* of power – kinetic, economic and ideational – that kinetic resides at the top and that ideational resides at the bottom of an internalized ladder of consequence, our future prospects as a species are likely to dim.

This, then, is the 'riddle of steel'. As summarized by the fictional villain Thulsa Doom in John Millius's 1982 *Conan the Barbarian*: "Steel isn't strong boy, *flesh* is stronger". As Thulsa Doom then patiently explains to our temporarily disabled hero – punctuated by his commanding a young follower to leap to her death as a demonstration of his power – skill and ideas matter much more than the fact or qualities of any weapon. In other words, the power of ideas – 'the pen' – can often be mightier than 'the sword'.

Realist international relations theory: an abridged review

As most contemporary students of International Relations (IR) theory know, we tend to lump IR theories into three broad camps: (1) Realism (and its variants); (2) Liberalism (and its variants); and (3) Social Constructivism[1] (and its variants). The third is honestly both the most interesting and confusing, since at its core social constructivism tells us why there really *are not* any theories; there are only things we wish to be true that we then imbue with authority. If we wish to assert, for

DOI: 10.4324/9781003299011-11

example, that interstate war (or the state itself as a form of political association) is inevitable or necessary, then we will find a language to support that wish. That language will in turn help us to select from the empirical world in ways that appear, again, to support our wish. Once internalized, or 'essentialized', this invented reality becomes, well, effectively real.

But this is another way of underlining that power is a wheel and not a ladder. What we worry about, or should worry about, is *injury* or *harm*. The idea that imminent physical injury, or injury rising to the level of death is somehow more important than economic or ideational injury, or injury which is less than lethal, is on its face absurd. Yet it is one of the many meanings we in mostly white, mostly male, mostly middle-class, mostly North American International Relations theory have been socialized to internalize. When we wish to say, for example, that we should be more worried about global thermonuclear war, or major conventional war, than about civil or ethnic war, or terrorism, or sexual violence in war; deeply embedded in this rank ordering is a simple algorithm: The more corpses a given form of violence can be expected to produce per unit of time, the more important.[2]

That is Realism in a nutshell. The provenance of the ideas which animate contemporary Realism extend back as least as far as the ancient Greeks (or so we have been taught); and in particular the Greek historian Thucydides's account of a war between Athens and Sparta. The first popular translation of Thucydides's account into English was published by Thomas Hobbes in the mid-17th century. Keeping in mind that the choices we make in what we remember and how we translate any given language into another are profoundly shaped by the times in which both the originator of the history and translator live, we should not be surprised that Hobbes's later *magnum opus* – *Leviathan* – imagined a world in which imminent lethal physical violence was made to serve as the 'Archimedean point'[3] in a geometry of human social relations. By the time of its publication in 1651, for example, Hobbes had lived through not one, but two religious wars: on the Continent, the Thirty Years' War (1618–1648); and in England, the English Civil War (1642–1651).

If we accept a correlation between a characterization of 'the times in which we live' as 'nasty, brutish, and short'[4] and understandings of coercion and politics that reify imminent lethal violence, it should be unsurprising that following World War Two, Realism and its variants were to gain prominence as ways of decoding international politics and informing foreign policy. In effect, a ladder, with fear of imminent *physical* death at the top rung.

A puzzle realist IR theory could not answer

If Realism and Neorealism are right, we should expect 'rational' states to attempt to acquire as much killing power as possible (and we see a lot of this). This association of rationality with doing whatever is necessary to avoid physical conquest then becomes essentialized. It becomes a kind of script that states come into existence with and cannot abjure. But this leads to at least one serious problem: if relative killing power is the most important attribute of a rational state, then an ally's or adversary's regime type should not matter. It should not matter whether a people live in oppression verging on slavery, as in North Korea, or whether they have a real say in their own foreign and domestic policy, as in Norway.

Yet in two related challenges, critics of Realism pointed out that regime type *did* matter. The first was an empirical observation by political scientist Michael Doyle, who noticed that while authoritarian regimes were agnostic about with whom they went to war (they would attack both democratic and authoritarian states), democratic states never fought *each other* (Doyle 1983). Realists cannot really account for this *within the bounds* of Realism because any rational state, regardless of its regime type, should remain focused on the rise of any rival with the capability to attack, destroy, or conquer it.

A second and related challenge came in the 1990s after political scientist Alexander Wendt attempted to introduce North American IR students to social constructivism in his landmark essay *Anarchy is What States Make of It* (Wendt 1992). Wendt's most accessible example of the problem for Realists comes in the form of a simple understanding of the importance of 'friend' and 'foe' in evaluating a threat:

> States act differently toward enemies than they do toward friends because enemies are threatening and friends are not. Anarchy and the distribution of power are insufficient to tell us which is which. U.S. military power has a different significance for Canada than for Cuba, despite their similar 'structural' positions, just as British missiles have a different significance for the United States than do Soviet missiles.
>
> (Wendt 1992, p. 397)

These challenges to Realism and its variants remain serious concerns, but while it is true that, as Wendt argues, North American International Relations theorists have inherited and maintained a socially-constructed world that makes interstate armed conflicts appear to be inevitable, it is not equally true that through a simple act of will we can alter that construction or escape its implications. To paraphrase Marx, we may not make our own reality 'as we please', but it is also true that we may not unmake the realities we inherit as we please either.[5]

Major interstate war is coming back

Powerful democratic states, such as France and later the United States, have always sought to export their idea of democracy and the core values attached (e.g. popular sovereignty, advancement by merit over birth, the rule of law, due process, innocent until proven guilty and so on) beyond their own territorial frontiers.

But it was not until Doyle's 'democratic peace' observation that we were able to re-imagine 'democratization' as a kind of national security long game. The logic is simple: if democratic states never attack each other, the greater the number of authoritarian states in the system, the higher the likelihood of interstate war.

And what we have seen since the disintegration of the USSR in 1991 has been striking. What had appeared in that liminal historical moment to be the triumph of the liberal-democratic idea, may have turned out to be its high-water mark. Since 1991, and in particular since 2001, the number of liberal-democratic states in the international system shifting to the political right has continued to rise (Arreguín-Toft 2022). Italy's recent democratic election of a fascist, Georgia Meloni, is only one recent case in point (Ben-Ghiat 2022). France and Austria have only narrowly avoided a similar fate in recent elections. Each new authoritarian regime increases the likelihood that the universe of interstate conflict dyads will contain an authoritarian-authoritarian, or authoritarian-democratic pair and, by extension, each shift to the right that results in a Duterte, Orban, Lukashenko, Erdogan, Putin, Meloni, Le Pen, Xi, or Trump government, makes interstate war more likely. After Putin's Russian Federation invaded Ukraine in February of 2022, we witnessed the most serious interstate war since 1990, when Saddam Hussein led Iraq into unprovoked aggression against tiny Kuwait. This 'authoritarian-democratic' conflict dyad is likely to become increasingly common as European and American polities – to say nothing of Indian – continue to shift to the political far right.

Information war, social media, and 'right-shift'

Cyberspace is to ideas what the container ship was to material goods. Each communications technology had a profound impact on the global distribution of power. Once the manufacturing capital of the world, in the 1990s the United States began to export manufacturing to states with lower-cost labour. This was only profitable because the transaction costs of shipping goods from labour-rich states had plummeted due to the advent of the container ship *and*, critically, the use of computers to manage loading and unloading these ships.

The same thing has happened with the Internet and with social media business models, which trade attention (and highly intimate personal data) for profit.[6] The Internet has lowered the cost of communicating ideas in real time to near zero. If in many circumstances the 'pen' is mightier than the 'sword', it follows that the Internet set the pen on fire. Essentially, those whose 'business model' depended on persuasion and conversion were going to be positioned to exercise tremendous influence – power – as a result of the advent and rapid distribution of Internet access. And like television and film, the 'information' speeding across cyberspace could be *visual* information; meaning that the person to be influenced need not be literate to be affected, persuaded, or converted.

This marks a critical global power shift in two senses: first, we continue to witness a slide to the political right in many democratic countries, which manifests as an erosion of due process and popular sovereignty in favour of autocratic rule (Harari 2018); and second, we see a power inversion of 'Davids' and 'Goliaths' due mainly to the low transaction costs associated with the transmission of ideas and information across space.

Right-shift

But why a shift to the 'right'? In the Internet's infancy the tech entrepreneurs building social media were often transported by their shared vision of the egalitarian implications they imagined were embedded in the instant, zero-cost connectivity they advanced.[7] According to Mark Zuckerberg, for example, Facebook's original mission was to 'connect the world' – rich and poor; and all faiths and nations. Creativity and innovation would be 'set free' by the elimination of gate keepers. But nothing like that happened; at least, not for long. For Facebook, now Meta, profits came from two sources: first, the sale of users' intimate personal data to third parties; and second, advertising revenue from clicks. It turns out that what people clicked on, on a web page, could be manipulated not only in terms of graphic design, but in terms of content. And for a particular audience demographic connecting via Facebook (to cite but one example), the content most likely to elicit a profitable click was 'the outrageous stories', the lies.

Interestingly, for those monetizing lies and outrage, there was a problem: users with a decent high-school education (or higher) did not click on the lies (except for entertainment value); whereas people with a flawed or limited education, invariably did (Martin 2017; Subramanian 2017). And the lies were not neutral. They were meant to support a world view which featured centrist and left-of-centre ideas and policies as dangerous and/or immoral.

This power to use visual communications media labelled as 'news' (appropriating journalistic authority) to create an alternate universe in which the only policies that made sense – policies illuminating a pathway from 'socialist tyranny, disaster and catastrophe', to making [blank] great again – had already been pioneered by Fox News in the 1990s (DellaVigna & Kaplan 2006). But ad engine algorithms powered by social media (Haidt 2022), and data collection ushered in an entirely new universe of manipulation possibilities and, largely asleep because a core pillar of democracy is majority rule, majority centre- and left-of-centre political parties in the world's democracies tended to discount the impact of disinformation and fake news on political outcomes. That is, until Britain's Brexit referendum and the US presidential election of 2016.

A global power shift

The power to persuade, motivate and convert is real and matters just as much as the power to kill. But the lethal implications of this relatively new communications technology, and the idea entrepreneurs who have made brilliant strategic use of it, have been far from obvious or even sufficiently discussed in terms of the future of war (Figure 8.1).

The first thing to notice about post-WWII armed conflicts is that in material terms, 'Davids' began to win more often than 'Goliaths' (Arreguín-Toft 2005, p. 4): Understand, these 'Goliaths' – France in Indochina and Algeria, Britain in India and Malaya, the United States in Vietnam and the USSR in Afghanistan – in every case had at least a ten-to-one material advantage in arms and population. Yet they were defeated by so-called 'backward peasants', most of whom deployed the power of ideas precisely because as non-state actors, they did not enjoy material killing power sufficient to achieve their political aspirations in direct physical violence. Goliaths still occasionally won – the United States in Grenada, Panama and Iraq (1991), and Britain (after 12 years!) in Malaya, in the Falklands/Malvinas and in Sierra Leone – but the writing was definitely on the wall.

What we witnessed was the beginning of a global power shift in which the power of ideas – in this case those surrounding the illegitimacy of the brutal politics of colonialism, and national self-determination as legitimate response – increasingly placed 'Goliaths' (most of whom represented democratic states) into a choice set with two options: either give up, or escalate killing to pure genocide. At the same time, and during the same historical period, the advent and deployment of thermonuclear weapons caused the same effect once it became clear that these weapons were decisively useful for imminent physical killing, but effectively useless for coercion because one could never be sure the killing could be restricted to anything less than species-level extinction. In other words, the rise of both nationalist-fuelled indirect warfare strategies (Arreguin-Toft 2005)

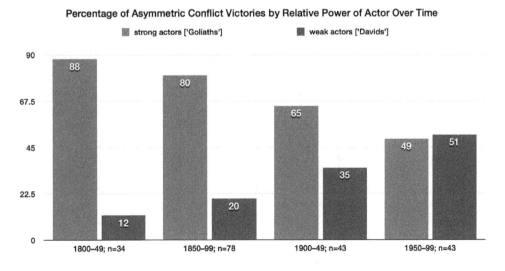

Figure 8.1   Percentage of conflict victories by relative power of actor over time, 1800–1999.

and the thermonuclear revolution turned the wheel and called the supposedly axiomatic connection between imminent physical killing power and coercive effectiveness into question.

This shift from kill-centric to idea-centric power is perhaps most accessibly recounted in the debates surrounding US strategy in Vietnam in the 1960s. In 1948, a year after its devastating loss of India, the British, having initially persisted in advancing a Malayan counterinsurgency strategy focused on identifying 'CTs' (communist terrorists) and killing them, shifted to a strategy of putting the idea of legitimacy ahead of killing. When they experienced success with this 'hearts and minds' strategy, they attempted to pass on what they had learned to the United States – then and still today the world's preeminent killing superpower. British strategy led with law enforcement supported by special operations forces; whereas the United States insisted on a kill-centric strategy (Shaw 2001). It did not work in Vietnam. It did not work in Iraq after 2003, and it did not work in Afghanistan after 2001.

Ideas continue to mobilize political violence: one can make an argument that the idea most likely to drive deliberate political violence globally today is the idea that women should have the same opportunities and choices as men (Inglehart & Norris 2003). And we are also beginning to see the emergence of ideas like 'climate justice' as potential levers of political change (O'Donnell 2022), including political violence.

The lethal power of the pen

Students of contemporary cyber conflict will be familiar with a debate over something called 'cyberwar'. In *Cyber War Will Not Take Place* (2013), Thomas Rid followed and expanded an earlier argument by Erik Gartzke (2013) to the effect that 'cyberwar' represented hyperbole and was unlikely to happen. Both arguments shared the same baseline: war is physically lethal, and that lethality is immediate. War is directed by a political agent and is intentional; whereas cyberattacks are 'never' lethal,[8] are directed by agents other than political and mostly intentional. In other words, both arguments internalized the ladder and were persuasive for audiences who likewise internalized the ladder.

This is a problem, because disinformation *is* manifestly lethal (consider the tens of thousands of US citizens who died unnecessarily from COVID-19 after being told that wearing a mask was pointless, or they could treat it by injecting bleach or by dosing with Ivermectin and so on). But disinformation tends to be lethal in ways that are indirect, unintentional and slow. In the case of disinformation campaigns directed against democratic states by Russia for example, it took the Soviet Union's KGB (now Russia's FSB) six *years* before its false claim that the HIV-AIDS virus had been secretly developed in a US military laboratory as a way to kill African Americans and gay men reached the mainstream (Ellick, Westbrook & Kissel 2018). That was in the 1980s. In 2016, it took the FSB only six *weeks* to succeed at convincing a number of Americans that Hillary Clinton and other elite Democrats were running a paedophile ring out of the basement of a Washington, DC area pizza restaurant (Comet Pizza does not have a basement, see Garrahan 2016; Ellick, Westbrook & Kissel 2018; Miller 2021). The explanation for this variation in disinformation effectiveness is twofold: first, by 2016, the ground for conspiracy theory acceptance in the United States and other democracies had been made much more fertile following two decades of accelerating income inequality (Leonhardt 2017). It is a problem hardly unique to the United States.

But second, smart phone penetration (The Economist 2005) and social media algorithms dramatically intensified the capability of political actors to manipulate reality and divide and confuse us. This is because the transaction costs of communicating by visual media have plummeted to almost zero, even as the number of those who can afford connected screens continue to rise. It is also because *visual* media, especially video, enjoy greater cognitive impact on our attention – and our sense of credibility – than text or voice.[9]

The ladder's toll: why the global distribution of power shifted

What I have attempted to do here is draw the reader's attention to the very real constructive and destructive power of ideas and identities. Recall that historically, whenever polities moved beyond their borders, they were usually led by merchants and clerics first, and only later followed by 'conquistadores'. The path dependency from which our current ladder conceptions of security suffers tend to make us – and by 'us' I mean the Global North – relatively more vulnerable to political actors skilled at persuasion and conversion, such as social media 'influencers' and religiously-inspired actors.

The implications are staggering: essentially, once weaponized, national self-determination led directly to an expansion in the number of causes for which rational people are willing to trade their physical existence. This new reality is a result of the *adversaries* of states possessing irresistible killing power (e.g. the United States, the Soviet Union) innovating around their relative material weaknesses and harnessing a different sort of power to exploit the so-called 'great powers' vulnerabilities.

It is a new reality brilliantly captured in a scene from Sir Richard Attenborough's *Gandhi* (1982), in which a young Gandhi is addressing a room of angry young men who are ready to escalate their claim to self-determination – independence from British colonial rule – to violence. The meeting was prompted by a new British law requiring the fingerprinting of all Indian men and women and establishing that only Christian marriages in a predominately Hindu and Muslim India would be acknowledged as legitimate. It also granted British police the right to enter an Indian home without permission or warrant. When the young men shout that they would be willing to kill to prevent such an insult, Gandhi famously replies that in that fight, he would be willing to die, but not to kill. The young men are puzzled, and Gandhi explains:

> I am asking you to fight. To fight against their anger, not to provoke it. We will not strike a blow, but, we will receive them. And through our pain we will make them see their injustice. And it will hurt, as all fighting hurts. But, we cannot lose. We cannot! They may torture my body, break my bones, even kill me. Then, they will have my dead body, *not* my obedience!

If the entire edifice of Western international politics rests on the Hobbesian notion that what we as humans all share in common is a fear of death first and foremost, then the spread of this idea – national self-determination being the follow-on to aristocratic honour and the secular analogue of religious faith – that your credible threat to kill me will not coerce my compliance, is the very death knell of that system of politics. What Cecil Rhodes once disparagingly referred to as that 'unctuous British rectitude' in the run-up to the Second South African War (1899–1902) was a vulnerability Gandhi was able to exploit, by placing Britain in a dilemma: a choice between being gored by the horn of Indian independence and a loss of British control, or the horn of mass murder. US Secretary of Defence Robert McNamara faced the same dilemma when the US Air Force suggested it be permitted to target the dikes guarding the Red River Valley in North Vietnam as a way to coerce the Democratic Republic of Vietnam to cease its support of insurgency in South Vietnam.

McNamara resigned rather than preside over what he felt would have been the deaths of as many as a million Vietnamese civilians.

But of course, not every state is led by people who are shy about mass murder or even genocide. In its day, the United States was happy to support the mass murder of indigenous Americans in the Plains Wars. The Soviet Union, now the Russian Federation, the People's Republic of China, Cambodia's Khmer Rouge, and contemporary Myanmar show no hesitation to commit mass murder in pursuit of political ends.

But crucially, the mass killing of noncombatants is *only* murder if the killers are targeting human beings. You cannot, for example, murder a goat or a tree. Outsiders instantly recognize the Rohingya as humans, but it is hardly clear that Myanmar's armed forces do. In Russian and Chinese states, there is also a long history of dehumanizing peoples who oppose – even only with ideas, art, faith – the ruling party's policies. Once dehumanized, as China's Uyghurs have been, the state acknowledges no limits on torture, slavery, sterilization and murder. North Americans still have difficulty recognizing people of colour as fully human, or women for that matter. My point is that 'human' is an idea, an identity and the *idea* that some people are people and others are not is subject to lethal and barbarous manipulation and redefinition (Rorty 1998).

Conclusions

In sum, global power has shifted from kill-centric to idea-centric as a result of our accelerating interactions in cyberspace; in large part because contemporary bandwidth enables image-based transmission of ideas and the distribution of access to that bandwitch has also increased. Ideas like 'a just cause' (legitimacy) have been understood since ancient times to be a force multiplier or divider (it is why coaches, kings, and generals are given to making speeches before critical contests). For states that have invested generations of wealth and human capital into the refinement of killing technologies in the service of conquest, deterrence or national defence, the power of ideas became a blind spot and now stands as a special challenge. In a climactic scene from James McTeague's 2006 film adaptation of Alan Moore's and David Lloyd's *V for Vendetta* graphic novel (Moore & Lloyd 2005), for example, the main villain fires a large-calibre revolver at V six times, apparently striking V with each shot, but not disabling V:

Creedy: Die! Die! Why won't you die? Why won't you die?
V: Beneath this mask there is more than flesh. Beneath this mask is an *idea* Mr. Creedy. And ideas, are, bulletproof!

In other words, you do not fight an idea with a gun, you fight it with a better idea, unless you are both willing and *able* to kill every person motivated by the idea or identity to which you object. To date, no one willing to commit genocide has succeeded and even a single survivor invariably makes an unwanted idea or identity much, *much* more powerful.[10]

Democracies the world over *have* great ideas – all were in fact founded on great ideas; on the power of the right over might. But the most kill-powerful democracies have, especially in this new century, steadily devalued idea power[11] in exchange for killing power.[12] Their authoritarian adversaries have not made this mistake. And in combination with private social media companies and unscrupulous domestic political minorities, their skilful attacks on democracies via dis- and misinformation have resulted in a palpable shift to the political right; first to anocracy and increasingly towards autocracy.

This cyber-accelerated right-shift means that there will soon be more authoritarian states, and should one of these be Britain, the United States, India or France (for cite but a few of the more kill-powerful democracies), expect a return to major interstate war and possibly a third *physical* world war.

There are only three ways to stop this democratic-state sleepwalking to Armageddon and none will be easy. First, democratic states will need to discipline (regulate) social media companies to criminalize and punish democracy-destructive algorithms that trade rage, intimate personal data and misinformation for profit. European tech regulators are already attempting this, but the going is too slow. Second, democratic states will need to seriously address the problem of income inequality, which invisibly scaffolds the despair and rage that manifest in such destructive ways both online and, increasingly, in the real world.[13] Third, democracies the world over need to pay more attention to the one-person-one-vote problem. Most of the actors using cyberspace to attack the 'majority rule' pillar of any functioning democracy are tiny minorities whose domestic and foreign policy preferences would never be enacted without serious compromise, if at all. The use of social media accelerated mis- and disinformation has changed this. As a result, in many democratic states, far-right minorities have innovated ever more harmful voter suppression policies.

Again, any one of these three policy trajectories will help, but in order to avoid a species-ending calamity we should insist on implementing all three. Global power has shifted from kill-advantaged states to idea-advantaged actors; some of whom are states such as Russia and China, and some of whom are wealthy conservative actors aiming to use the same techniques of social media accelerated disinformation to capture absolute power though what appears to be, but is not remotely, a democratic process.

Democracy has always been slow, tortured and frustrating in its insistence on deliberation and compromise as compared to autocracy, but history has made clear that over the long term, autocracies invariably end in ruin; their own and, in the near future possibly, the world's.

Notes

1 To which I would add, on an equal footing, feminist IR theory. Whereas social constructivists take gender, class, national origin, language, and a host of other biases into consideration when unpacking why it is we ask some questions or make some choices and not others, feminist IR theorists focus more narrowly on how *masculine* ('masculinist') understandings affect questions, choices, and outcomes.

2 There is a case to be made that humans are 'hard-wired' to give priority to some kinds of threats over others; and by hard-wired, I mean that concern for these threats has been 'naturally selected' in the Darwinian sense. For a brilliant analogous argument regarding territory, see Johnson and Toft (2014).

3 I am indebted on this point to the brilliant Professor Bernard Manin (now Emeritus Professor of Politics at New York University), who called to our attention in seminar not only Hobbes's love of (and faith in) mathematics as a hedge against uncertainty and madness at a time of Europe's and England's most lethal (per capita) wars, but Hobbes's effort to appropriate the universality and objectivity of mathematics as authority in *Leviathan*. For a contemporary example of the instrumental use of the universality-objectivity of mathematics as a persuasive tool, see O'Neil (2016).

4 Interestingly, former US president Donald J Trump repeatedly relied on similar language in support of the same objective: justifying absolute rule.

5 The full quotation is: "Men make their own history, but they do not make it as they please; they do not make it under self-selected circumstances, but under circumstances existing already, given and transmitted from the past" (Marx 1994).

6 On the farming of highly intimate personal data for corporate profit, see especially Zuboff (2019) and Johnson (2022).

7 No better single work of technology philosophy more presciently captures this dynamic than Langdon Winner's (Winner 1989).

8 This turns out not to be true, though most readers would agree the exception tends to prove the rule (at least so far). See Goodin (2000). For a description of a hypothetically much greater lethality from a cyberattack, see Clarke and Knake (2010, pp. 62–8). The authors are well aware that non-physical cyber-harm represents a serious threat to national security, but you do not get government policy reform (and resources) with the threat of 'pizzagates' as compared to the threat of lethal, immediate, intentional and mass physical injury.

9 Pioneering work on this theme, attendant as it was on the advent of television broadcasting, is McLuhan and Fiore (1967).

10 When Rome's genocide against Christianity sought to highlight the helplessness of Christians and destroy Christian popularity by systematically torturing and murdering them in the Coliseum as entertainment, it had the opposite effect: Christians began volunteering to be eaten alive by lions or impaled or burned alive, and the religion's popularity soared (Kelly 2006, Chapter 5).

11 By far the most brilliant entry in this category remains Paul Fussell's masterpiece *The Great War in Modern Memory* (Fussell 1975). Fussell's history brilliantly recalls the visceral shock that followed the outcome of the clash, in World War One, between 'the machine' (heavy artillery, automatic weapons) and human virtues such as honor, loyalty and bravery.

12 For the United States, this trend – not only over-use of armed force abroad, but harrowing under-investment in diplomacy since 2001 – has been empirically verified in the *Military Intervention Project*, a detailed database of every U.S. military intervention since 1776. See especially Kushi and Toft (2022).

13 In the United States, the disinformation-fueled January 6th assault on the Capitol resulted in at least five deaths and hundreds of physical injuries, *as well as* enduring trauma to survivors who escaped physical injury. More recently Paul Pelosi, the 82-year-old husband of U.S. Speaker of the House Nancy Pelosi, was assaulted in his San Francisco home by a man who had posted a number of conspiracy theories on social media and had come to the Pelosi home in search of Speaker Pelosi. See Holpuch (2022) and Browning, Holpuch and Broadwater (2022).

References

Arreguín-Toft, I 2005, *How the Weak Win Wars: A Theory of Asymmetric Conflict*, Cambridge University Press, Cambridge – New York.

Arreguín-Toft, I 2022, 'Big Data and AI Can Either Defend Democracy – or Destroy It," *The National Interest*, 29 July.

Ben-Ghiat, R 2022, 'The Return of Fascism in Italy', *The Atlantic*, 23 September.

Browning, K, Holpuch, A & Broadwater, L 2022, 'Live Updates: Here's Intruder Seeking Speaker Pelosi Attacked Her Husband With a Hammer', *The New York Times*, 28 October.

Clarke, R & Knake, R 2010, *Cyberwar: The Next Threat to National Security and What to Do About It*, Ecco, New York.

DellaVigna, S & Kaplan, E 2006, 'The Fox News Effect: Media Bias and Voting', *NBER Working Paper*, no. 12169, National Bureau of Economic Research (April).

Doyle, M 1983, 'Kant, Liberal Legacies, and Foreign Affairs', *Philosophy and Public Affairs*, vol. 12, no. 3, pp. 205–35.

Ellick. A B, Westbrook, A & Kessel, J M 2018, 'Operation Infektion', *The New York Times*, 12 November.

Fussell, P 1975, *The Great War in Modern Memory*, Oxford University Press, Oxford – New York.

Garrahan, M 2016, '"Pizzagate" Exposes Real Consequences of Posting Fake News', *Financial Times*, 9 December.

Gartzke, E 2013, 'The Myth of Cyberwar: Bringing War in Cyberspace Back Down to Earth', *International Security*, vol. 38, no. 2, pp. 41–73, https://doi.org/10.1162/ISEC_a_00136.

Goodin, D 2000, 'A Patient Dies After a Ransomware Attack Hits a Hospital', *Wired*, 19 September.

Haidt, J 2022, 'Yes, Social Media Really is Undermining Democracy: Despite what Meta Has to Say', *The Atlantic*, 28 July.

Harari, Y N 2018, 'Why Technology Favors Tyranny', *The Atlantic*, October, <https://www.theatlantic.com/magazine/archive/2018/10/yuval-noah-harari-technology-tyranny/568330/> (accessed 30 December 2022).

Holpuch, A 2022, 'What We Know About the Attack on Nancy Pelosi's Husband', *The New York Times*, 28 October.

Inglehart, R & Norris, P 2003, 'The True Clash of Civilizations', *Foreign Policy*, no. 135 (March–April), pp. 63–70. JSTOR, https://doi.org/10.2307/3183594 (accessed 14 May 2023).

Johnson, D D P & Toft, M D 2014, 'Grounds for War: The Evolution of Territorial Armed Conflict', *International Security*, vol. 38, no. 3, pp. 7–38, http://dx.doi.org/10.1162/ISEC_a_00149.

Johnson, K 2022, 'Meta's VR Headset Harvests Personal Data Right Off Your Face', *Wired,* 13 October.

Kelly, C 2006, *The Roman Empire: A Very Short Introduction*, Oxford University Press, Oxford – New York.

Kushi, S & Toft, M D 2022, 'Introducing the Military Intervention Project: A New Dataset on U.S. Military Interventions, 1776–2019', *Journal of Conflict Resolution*, online first, pp. 1–28, https://doi.org/10.1177/00220027221117546.

Leonhardt, D. 'Our Broken Economy, In One Simple Chart', *The New York Times* (7 August 2017). https://www.nytimes.com/interactive/2017/08/07/opinion/leonhardt-income-inequality.html, accessed on 15 May 2023

Martin, G 2017, 'Inside the Fake News Factory of Macedonia', *Wired*, 15 February.

Marx, K 1994 [1852], *The Eighteenth Brumaire of Louis Bonaparte*, International Publishers Co., New York.

McLuhan, M & Fiore, Q 1967, *The Medium Is the Massage: An Inventory of Effects*, Gingko Press, Berkeley, CA.

Miller, M E 2021, 'Pizzagate's Violent Legacy', *The Washington Post,* 16 February.

Moore, A & Lloyd, D 2005, *V for Vendetta*, DC Comics, New York.

O'Donnell, L 2022, 'Pakistan Leads Charge for Climate Justice at COP27', *Foreign Policy*, 9 November, <https://foreignpolicy.com/2022/11/09/cop27-pakistan-climate-loss-damage-floods-aid/> (accessed 30 December 2022).

O'Neil, C 2016, *Weapons of Math Destruction: How Big Data Increases Inequality and Threatens Democracy*, Broadway Books, New York.

Rid, T 2013, *Cyberwar Will Not Take Place*, Oxford University Press, New York.

Rorty, R 1998, 'Human Rights, Rationality, and Sentimentality', in R Rorty (ed), *Truth and Progress. Philosophical Papers,* Cambridge University Press, Cambridge – New York, vol. 3, pp. 167–85.

Shaw, G D T 2001, 'Policemen vs. Soldiers, the Debate Leading to MAAG Objections and Washington Rejections of the Core of the British Counter-Insurgency Advice', *Small Wars and Insurgencies,* vol. 12, no. 2, pp. 51–78, https://doi.org/10.1080/714005393.

Streich, P & Levy, J 2007, 'Time Horizons, Discounting, and Intertemporal Choice', *Journal of Conflict Resolution,* vol. 51, no. 2, pp. 199–226, https://doi.org/10.1177/0022002706298133.

Subramanian, S 2017, 'Inside the Macedonian Fake-News Complex', *Wired*, 15 February.

The Economist 2015, 'Planet of the Phones', *The Economist*, 26 February.

Tickner, J A 1992, 'Man, the State, and War: Gendered Perspectives on National Security', in J A Tickner (ed), *Gender in International Relations: Feminist Perspectives on Achieving Global Security*, Columbia University Press, New York, pp. 115–122.

Toft, M D 2006, 'Issue Indivisibility and Time Horizons as Rationalist Explanations for War', *Security Studies,* vol. 15, no. 1, pp. 34–69, https://doi.org/10.1080/09636410600666246.

Wendt, A 1992, 'Anarchy is What States Make of It: The Social Construction of Power Politics', *International Organization,* vol. 46, no. 2, pp. 391–425, https://doi.org/10.1017/S0020818300027764.

Winner, L 1989, *The Whale and the Reactor: A Search for Limits in an Age of High Technology*, University of Chicago Press, Chicago.

Zuboff, S 2019, *Surveillance Capitalism: The Fight for a Human Future at the New Frontier of Power*, Public Affairs, New York.

9

STATE FRAGILITY AS A MAJOR CHALLENGE TO THE EXISTING WORLD ORDER

"Too Fragile to Hold the World"

Iveta Hlouchova

Introduction

In 2004, Francis Fukuyama (2004, p. 92) stated that: "Since the end of the Cold War, weak and failing states have arguably become the single-most important problem for international order". This assertion is partially true, given the amount of attention and resources committed to addressing this issue in the post-9/11 security environment, even though state fragility has been affecting the global security environment and international security in one way, shape or form, despite not being labeled as state fragility at the time. Given the fact that state fragility is a spectrum rather than a static condition of a political entity, many different security-related threats, challenges, and risks originate in the unstable environment of fragile states.

The common understanding in academic circles, as well as among practitioners, has been that, for well over the past decade, countries characterized by weak state capacity or weak state legitimacy represent major sources of security threats at the local, regional, and often also global level. Amongst these threats are poverty (which tends to be concentrated in fragile states), activities of transnational organized crime, corruption, weapons proliferation, violent extremism and terrorism, mass migration, humanitarian catastrophes, pandemic disease, and environmental degradation. All these security challenges (and many more) are viewed as emerging from and exacerbated by the conditions present in fragile states. During the COVID-19 pandemic and in its immediate aftermath, state fragility has become even more serious in terms of how it affects both state and human security. In many countries around the world, personal freedoms were restricted for the public good in the context of the health emergency. The pandemic also created conditions ripe for an economic crisis, as businesses shut down, consequently destabilizing the social fabric of many countries. Combined with severe natural disasters caused by the accelerating effects of human-made climate change, state resilience has been severely reduced. That gave a recruitment boost to extremist movements and groups participating in transnational organized crime activities which found a safe haven in fragile states.

This chapter explores the phenomenon of state fragility from the perspective of what major security threats and challenges it poses to the future global security environment and what it means for the future of warfare. In the first section, the definition of state fragility developed by the Fund for Peace (FFP) is discussed, providing the conceptual framework of this chapter. The issue of state fragility as a

DOI: 10.4324/9781003299011-12

major source of many various security threats and challenges is analysed in the next section, focusing on both traditional security threats and challenges emanating in the context of fragile states (transnational terrorism, transnational organized crime, WMDs proliferation, privatized forms of violence) and security issues that hold great potential to destabilize global security and the entire world order (corruption, mass migration, conflicts over resources, food insecurity, etc.). Special attention is placed on the trend of rising autocracy around the world in the context of state fragility and how that can pose an existential threat on the local, regional, as well as global levels, due to its intensity and destabilizing effects. All the above-mentioned security challenges are intertwined, often originating in fragile states, and leading to a weakening of state apparatus, even in countries long considered strong in terms of state capacity. Consequently, this threatens the entire world order built on the importance of human rights and freedoms and of democratic values for maintaining international peace and stability. The Westphalian sovereign state, the bedrock of the modern international system, is crumbling under the weight of the unprecedented scale and complexity of state fragility in today's world. In the following part of the chapter, the issue of state fragility as a major sources of security risks, along with what that means for the future of war and for new demands on the capabilities of armed forces, is analysed. In the concluding section, policy recommendations and recommendations on further research are formulated.

The concept of state fragility

State fragility is generally understood as "the absence or breakdown of social contract between people and their government" (USIP 2018a). The state's prime function is to provide security to the people living within its borders. For that purpose, the state monopoly on the legitimate use of force and violence within a given territory represents the key characteristic of the principle of state sovereignty. In his essay *Politics as a Vocation* (1918) Max Weber emphasized a monopoly on the *legitimate* use of force as the essential quality of a state. Such a monopoly on the use of force includes not only the authority to kill and imprison but also to create and enforce the laws and rules to which citizens must adhere to (Gerth & Wright Mills 1946, p. 79). Weber identified three types of authority, or sources of legitimacy of political leaders (traditional, charismatic and rational-legal), that enable them to exercise a legitimate monopoly on the use of force. All three types imply a consent of the people, however, are also directly challenged in an environment of a fragile state, especially when the source of the legitimacy on the use of force is questioned or directly contested. In the context of a fragile state, a system of supplied security is created in which actors other than the government provide security and safety to citizens (warlords and their private militias, self-defense forces, gangs, etc.). Robert Rotberg considers the loss of control over the monopoly on the legitimate use of force to be the most fatal form of a state failure/fragility, as, with that, the state loses control over parts of its territory (Rotberg 2003). The loss of the state monopoly on the legitimate use of force and violence then inevitably raises a question which is critically important to address properly the dilemma of mitigating threats that originate in fragile states, i.e., did state fragility lead to an increase in violence in the environment of a fragile state, or was it the high levels of violence that ultimately led to exacerbated state fragility?

Stewart Patrick then argues that a state's propensity to weakness or even failure is determined by dynamic feedback among four sets of variables: (1) a state's baseline level of institutional resilience; (2) the presence of long-term drivers ("risk factors") of instability; (3) the nature of the state's external environment (whether positive or negative); and (4) the occurrence of short-term shocks/"triggering" events (Patrick 2011, p. 8). How each of the four variables interact and relate to each other determines not only the level of state fragility, but also what the major challenges to (and opportunities for) its management are.

A lot of criticism has also pointed to different aspects of the concept of state fragility, where scholars have questioned the values and assumptions underpinning it. Oftentimes scholars criticize the normative character of the concept in terms of how powerful state actors manipulate and instrumentalize it to meet their foreign policy goals (see, for instance, Bøas & Jennings 2007, pp. 475–85). Other scholars then question the analytical validity and utility of the concept of state fragility itself, given how it is built upon the Western notion of a state (see, for instance, Ziaja & Fabra Mata 2010). Somewhere between these two are scholars asserting that the concept of state fragility is a political invention meant to serve as a label to legitimize Western policy interventions in countries facing violence and profound poverty (Grimm, Lemay-Heber & Nay 2016).

The FFP think tank has been publishing their annual Fragile State Index[1] for well over the past decade. As an instrument to measure state fragility, it was designed some 25 years ago and since then periodically refined to incorporate lessons learned and best practices in order to adequately reflect the changes taking place in the global security environment. Individual causes and expressions of state fragility change from case to case, but what remains constant is the essence of state fragility, i.e., a state's resilience is weakened and a state itself struggles to fulfil its core, principal political, security, economic and social functions associated with the idea of a sovereign state. FFP's Fragile State Index (FSI) is based on a conflict assessment framework known as "CAST", using both qualitative and quantitative research methods on data from public sources (Fund for Peace 2022a). There are several major weaknesses the FSI suffers from. First, in states where there is no public data available, some critically important issues about the state of vulnerability/fragility cannot be assessed properly. Another major weakness of the FSI methodology is the numerical score given to a state by analysts. Some aspects can be overlooked, under/over-estimated, subject to confirmation bias.

The FSI is developed based on 12 indicators measured on a one to ten score scale. This allows analysts to measure the condition of a state at any given moment to determine the propensity of a state to collapse or fail. Each indicator also helps identify what major security threats and challenges originate in an environment of state fragility. The FFP evaluates the state of five core state institutions (government, military, police, judicial system, state structures) and factors in the possibility of a surprise or chance (Table 9.1).

The FFP also identifies longer-term trends in their annual reports on state fragility. These trends enable scholars to determine what security threats will be the most challenging ones to address. With that, the FSI helps prioritize where to commit capabilities and resources of state as well as non-state actors in the near future as part of prevention or mitigation strategies.

Table 9.1 The categories and individual indicators underpinning the FFP's Fragile State Index

Cohesion Indicators	Economic Indicators	Political Indicators	Social Indicators	Cross-cutting Indicators
Security apparatus	Economic decline	State legitimacy	Demographic pressures	External intervention
Factionalized elites	Uneven economic development	Public services	Refugees and IDPs	
Group grievance	Human flight and brain drain	Human rights and rule of law		

Source: Fund for Peace 2022a.

(In)security in fragile states

There are security threats and challenges commonly associated as originating in and/or thriving in fragile states, such as transnational terrorism, activities of transnational organized crime, weapons proliferation, large-scale migration, mass violations of human rights, including genocides, pandemic diseases, environmental degradation, energy insecurity, the so-called youth balk and lack of socioeconomic opportunities, corruption, and many others. There has also long been the assumption that weak governance and its spillover consequences emanate only in the "developing" world. The last three years of the COVID-19 pandemic, however, rolled back the progress made in many fragile states in terms of building their institutional resilience and state capacity. They also clearly showed that states in the developed world are not as resilient as previously thought. The increasing scale and complexity of state fragility today is "unprecedented" (USIP 2018b).

Each of the FSI indicators helps identify how closely and intricately is state fragility linked with stability, security and warfare. When a state is unable to provide public services, it generally also does not have the capacity to deal effectively with major risks, such as armed conflicts, and as such a state is not able to defend itself against threats. For this very reason, fragile states are often affected by conflicts which tend to reoccur in the territory of a fragile state, as the government does not have the capacity (or will) to address the root causes and grievances that led to it and/or to prevent an outbreak of violence. Political instability tends to be one of the defining features of state fragility. That is commonly manifested in various forms of politically motivated violence, stemming from ethnic, religious, or other intercommunal enmity. The environment of fragile states provides a fertile breeding ground for extremism, particularly in societies where polarization is high and in which past group grievances have not been resolved. Such polarization is often further exacerbated by widespread government and private sector corruption, nepotism, clientelism and patronage networks based on kin. Low levels of socioeconomic development, uneven distribution of economic benefits and lack of trust in the government that is unable (or unwilling) to provide basic services contribute to perceived attractiveness of extremist messages, as well as citizens' involvement in different forms of illegal economy ordinary people resort to in order to gain sources of income. Other contributing factors involve the inability of the government to solve disputes and enforce the rule of law. Frustrated population provides a solid recruitment pool for insurgent, terrorists, vigilantes, and criminal organizations alike.

Within a fragile state, terrorist organizations thrive in the parts of a state territory where the government is not able to project its power and control over. Conditions of state fragility drive terrorist recruitment efforts, as frustrated people look for alternative sources of actual self-realization. The ideology of terrorist organizations is often attractive to inhabitants of fragile states, as it provides them with an alternative explanation for the injustice and mistrust they feel towards the government. To terrorist organizations, fragile states often provide a form of ideological validation. For instance, the Democratic Republic of the Congo (DRC) was not viewed as a typical recruitment target, yet the Islamic State's Central African Province (ISCAP) managed to establish a solid presence in the country, with its branch called the Allied Democratic Forces (ADF) (Weiss & O'Farrell 2021). Be it for opportunistic (primarily monetary) reasons, or the ideas and beliefs the Islamic State preaches, it managed to get relatively high following in the impoverished country. Terrorist organizations also enjoy safe havens and freedom of movement in fragile states. Lack of interests and enforcement from the government allow them to regroup, rearm, establish themselves, test their governing skills and/or money-making activities. Such a safe haven yields ripe opportunities for establishing training camps, control and command structures, and for plotting terrorist attack around the globe, just as al-Qaeda did when it enjoyed its protection by the Taliban regime in

Afghanistan in the 1990s. The Taliban retook control of Afghanistan after the 20-year insurgent struggle in August 2021, capitalizing precisely on the inability, lack of interest and/or lack of serious commitment by the then Afghan national government and its international backers to increase Afghanistan's resilience in a long run. With Taliban back in power in Kabul, al-Qaeda has been yet again establishing and rebuilding itself (see, for instance, UNSC 2022).

Criminal networks, human traffickers and gangs benefit from fragile states for similar reasons, namely lack of enforcement, freedom of movement, and freedom to prey on citizens. High levels of violence, high crime rates and absence of the rule of law create the demand for the services of human traffickers as people start looking for a way out to protect and support themselves and their families.

There are several security threats and challenges inextricably connected to state fragility, that deserve to be addressed specifically, given their urgency and the scale and intensity of their first-, second-, and third-tier consequences: food and water insecurity (and natural disasters), energy insecurity, a full-scale conventional military invasion, the presence of nuclear weapons in fragile states, corruption (and activities of organized crime), rising autocracy and democratic backsliding around the world and instability in urban centers. All these security threats and challenges often represent, and will continue to represent, one of the root causes of other security challenges emanating from the environment of fragile states, such as violent extremism (Islamic, far-right, etc.) or mass migration, and therefore governments and the international community must be ready to tackle them. They also overlap and further strengthen each other's negative impacts and consequences. The list is not exhaustive and requires further research.

Food and water insecurity, along with conflicts over (strategic) natural resources, have been recognized as a major security issue already some time ago. However, against the backdrop of the latest developments (Russian re-invasion of Ukraine in 2022, the sanctions that followed and the Russian blockade of the exports of Ukrainian grain to countries around the world, also massive natural disasters caused primarily by man-made climate change, such as severe droughts in Madagascar or the Horn of Africa or the unprecedented floods in Pakistan, Nigeria or St. Louis, Missouri) food and water security, along with energy security, has gained renewed spotlight urgency. Coupled with ineffective government management in many countries around the world, including states long considered strong or (more or less) stable and resilient, and due to severe droughts or floods, food prices were rising steadily, leading to widespread hunger. This can lead to mass migration of frustrated people, provoking conflicts over resources and a collapse of social cohesion. Humanitarian action increasingly had to engage with enduring and recurrent food insecurity rather than episodic events and this had a number of consequences (Pain 2015, p. 123). This leads to the questioning of the purpose and instruments of intervention aiming to enable a shift from a simple response to the symptoms of food insecurity through emergency food supplies to more ambitious attempts to address some of the proximate causes of food insecurity through interventions to provide broader livelihood support and even to try to reduce vulnerability to food insecurity (Pain 2015). Food insecurity has increasingly been understood as a multifaceted issue. Importantly, hungry and frustrated individuals tend to support radical/extremist/populist politicians, thereby deepening state fragility. Food insecurity, natural disasters, and the resulting public frustration already led to massive government protests and, in some places, like Syria, to civil wars with dangerous spillover effects.

In fragile states, governments lack legitimacy in the eyes of citizens and institutions fail to provide basic public goods. As the latest FFP's FSI analytical report indicates, this has become an increasing issue for the states long considered as stable (Western countries). There has been "an erosion in public confidence in democratic institutions and an increase in social and political polarization in both rich and poor countries across the globe, which has contributed to the rise of authoritarianism" (Fund for Peace 2022b, p. 10). FFP also holds that:

previously, state fragility was seen as something to be contained and mitigated in the developing world so that it does not spread to the rich countries. Now, however, we are discovering that fragility can flow both ways. War in Europe can lead to food crises in Africa. A pandemic can just as easily spread from North to South. Same with xenophobic nationalism and violent extremism. Fragility is something that must be addressed everywhere all at once, and core to that strategy must be a focus on social and political cohesion and inclusiveness.

(Fund for Peace 2022b, p. 11)

Clearly, if developing and even some developed countries themselves continue to become more and more fragile, as they fall for aspiring autocrats and continue to roll back citizen's rights and freedoms, the conditions of state fragility around the world will continue to deteriorate, especially if the food and energy prices remain high and volatile and if severe natural disasters occur. The developed countries have long been major donors of humanitarian assistance, development aid and other state resilience-building support. If they themselves become less resilient and more fragile, their priorities will shift to internal stability issues. Global security instability will only increase in such a scenario, all the way to a point where the existence of humanity as such will be threatened with more nuclear-armed states becoming even more fragile. For instance, in Pakistan, according to the FSI, the level of state fragility has been gradually reduced over the past decade, yet the country remains severely weak in several important aspects to state fragility and resilience. However, factionalization of elites, group grievance, demographic pressures and external intervention all remain steadily dangerously high (Fund for Peace 2022c). Even though Pakistan has a long tradition of tolerating, if not supporting, in its territory activities of numerous terrorist organizations targeting other countries (the Afghan Taliban, Lashkar-e-Taiba, al-Qaida, Tehreek-e-Labaik to name just a few), it is also battling domestic terrorism of its own (Tehrik-i-Taliban Pakistan, ISIS). Ever since the civilian government acquired enough power to govern (at least nominally), the country has been governed by shaky coalitions of ineffective politicians, even as the country's military and the intelligence agency ISI (Inter-Services Intelligence) remain the real power brokers. After the massive floods that hit the country in the summer of 2022, millions of people were in an urgent need of humanitarian assistance which the government was not able to provide (UNICEF 2022). This can lead to an increase in the number of citizens looking for an outlet for their frustration and finding it in the ideologies of violent extremist/terrorist organizations. The risk of a terrorist organization acquiring a nuclear weapon in the territory of Pakistan is still high (Kalb 2021).

Corruption will most likely continue to be a major security issue going forward, including in Western countries, hampering any effective responses to state fragility at home and abroad. It is mainly the "golden handcuffs" type of corruption employed by Russia, itself a fragile state, that poses an enormous risk to established, yet vulnerable democracies. The power of the Russian mafia at home[2] and abroad and its ability to corrupt states all over the global is both a driver of state fragility and its expression and it represents one of the most serious security risks the international community faces today. Corruption then becomes an instrument purposefully weakening adversaries. Moreover, corruption contributes to other international security threats, such as symbiotic relationships between states and transnational organized crime networks, facilitation for terrorist organizations, permeable international security regimes and acute economic disruptions. As pervasive corruption is a key feature of fragile states, exploiting this vulnerability and increasing corruption in already fragile states will continue to represent a form of geopolitical competition (Marc & Jones 2021) in a form of proxy warfare.

The future of warfare and armed forces preparedness

From a military perspective, state fragility has been recognized as the Achilles' heel of collective security, as well as a threat to national security of Western countries mainly in the post-9/11 security environment, and it will continue to be so. Not only due to the traditional security threats originating in fragile states (violent extremism, terrorism, organized crime), but also because increasing state fragility domestically can thwart or severely undermine prevention and mitigation strategies employed externally, due to the lack of political will to intervene abroad. State fragility has long been, and will continue to be, a driver of conflict. It is important to continue to prioritize indirect approaches whenever possible – primarily through building the capacity of partner governments and their security forces (to prevent costly and controversial direct military intervention) and over-the-horizon military capabilities – surveillance, reconnaissance and solid intelligence-gathering networks in remote areas. The unchanging nature of security threats and challenges emanating in fragile states demand that armed forces develop and maintain readiness to deploy mobile special operation forces (SOF) units combined with air support (mainly surveillance and weaponized unmanned aerial vehicles (UAVs), covert operations (sabotage, etc.), cyber capabilities, as well as services outsourced to the private military and security companies, should they be deployed in the environment of a fragile state.

Information space is yet another critically important domain to maintain military readiness in. Effective information operations and psychological operations are critically important to be carried out to counter the disinformation and propaganda spread around by malicious actors, be it directly in the areas of operation, or back at home. De-polarization of societies diminishes their fragmentation and strengthens resilience of a state.

Moreover, David Kilcullen (2013) identified four megatrends that, in his view, will determine the future of warfare. Kilcullen emphasizes that, as all four interact with each other, they create a whole new security environment with a very specific type of warfare that will become prevalent and will become new hotspots of armed conflicts in the near future. He calls it "the coming age of urban guerilla" (Kilcullen 2013). The four megatrends are: (1) rapid population growth; (2) accelerating urbanization; (3) littoralization[3]; and (4) increasing interconnectedness. These interconnected coastal megacities full of young people lacking means of socioeconomic realization and being on the front line of rising sea levels, food and water insecurity and energy insecurity will also represent centers of state fragility to which military forces may be deployed, if necessary, due to the fact that, as weapons proliferate, nonstate actors may possess some of the conventional military capabilities that ought to be solely in the hand of a state (see Felbab-Brown 2014; House 2014). This fact requires that the armed forces continue to develop capabilities and skills suitable to engage in urban warfare. It also demands incorporating elements of law enforcement into their ranks for the purposes of community policing and, consequently, social development. As Vanda Felbab-Brown (2014, pp. 95–6) stated, "increasingly perceptions of public safety and the state's effectiveness and accountability will be determined by how effectively the state devises responses to crime and insecurity in urban spaces". This is not to say that urban centers will be the only hotspots in the future, but it is important to focus on urban unrest both abroad and domestically to be able to build/maintain state resilience. Crime groups and gangs exploit fragile states to pursue their own profit-driven agendas. Instances like the 2010 Tivoli Incursion in Kingston, Jamaica, during which the military alongside police forces attempted to arrest Christopher "Dudus" Coke, a powerful leader of the Shower Posse drug cartel, will be a common occurrence in the near future. The arrest mission turned into a three-day urban battle and a siege of Coke's housing complex and resulted in dozens of civilian casualties.

At the same time, it is important to maintain conventional military dominance, because, as the world witnessed Russia launching an unprovoked military invasion of Ukraine in February 2022, or Azerbaijan directly targeting the territory of neighboring Armenia in September 2022, fragile states can also be conquering states. Conventional military readiness and territorial defense must, thereby, remain the most critical capability of state armed forces. However, as even a conventional military of fragile states (crumpled under the weight of corruption or fractionalization of elites) can, ultimately, fail to succeed in major military maneuvers, due to problematic logistics, supply shipments, as well as incapable/unskilled personnel at all levels of operation. That will make them an attractive target for guerrilla-style attacks. Conventional military tactics will, most likely, be replaced by more paramilitary or insurgency-style operations, carried out simultaneously with attacks in the cyber domain, to counter the asymmetrical threats originating in fragile states. Hybrid forms of warfare will remain the dominant form of waging an armed conflict into the future. That requires the use of military (both conventional and unconventional) and non-military tools in an integrated campaign. Hybrid warfare is designed to achieve surprise, seize the initiative, and gain psychological as well as physical advantages utilizing diplomatic means; sophisticated and rapid information, electronic and cyber operations; covert and occasionally overt military and intelligence action; and economic pressure (IISS 2015).

Domestically, it is also necessary for state security forces to maintain their political neutrality and to create a clear sanctions system with a strong deterrence potential to prevent members of security forces from taking part in any seditious or treasonous activity or from providing their expertise and know-how to anti-government groups with political agenda domestically, that would only contribute to make the state they serve even weaker. Military forces will also be required to assist with mass migration flows.

Security forces also play a critically important role in the fight against corruption, both in the area of operations and domestically. Cleaning up one's own house is necessary to be able to effectively implement anti-corruption measures abroad. Corruption within the upper command echelons can gradually diminish combat readiness and preparedness of the military force everywhere. Corruption also poses a major security risk in the context of energy insecurity where governments must commit significant resources to protecting strategic resources and strategic infrastructure (including food stockpiles and reservoirs of potable water), as conflicts over resources are expected to arise more often soon. Other countries may seek to take control of the precious sources of strategic resources (water, food, etc.) as they become scarcer globally. Energy insecurity resulting from state fragility (be it domestic or foreign) can result in limited logistical capabilities of the armed forces as well. Therefore, appropriate measures, such as transitioning to more environmentally friendly alternatives of military transportation fuel and means, must be implemented without delay.

Given the nature of the security threats and challenges originating in fragile states, maintaining effective civil-military cooperation capabilities will be even more important into the future. In this regard, however, it is important to find an appropriate balance between clearly separating civilian personnel and civilian projects from the military ones and providing them appropriate levels of protection, so that civilians do not become targeted by violence or by accusations of espionage. Humanitarian assistance and natural disaster response capabilities readiness levels must be maintained as well because the likelihood of the need to be deployed in environments of fragile states is steadily increasing. Ultimately, a comprehensive whole-of-government and whole-of-society approach is required to help build resilience domestically and abroad.

Conclusion

As the past couple of years have shown, state fragility is becoming an even more serious security issue than it ever was. There, indeed, is a long history of security threats and challenges coming from the environments of fragile states. Those were mostly approached as a matter of the developing world. Increasingly, it is becoming clear though, that countries in the developed world are not immune from the perils of state fragility either. The modern world order, built on Western ideas and norms, will only hold as long as the states underpinning it do. The world order where humanitarian assistance and development aid, however imperfect, is being delivered may cease to exist as the attention of the major donors turns inwards to protect themselves and build their own state resilience or if those donors disappear as states completely.

Deciding upon whether state fragility is a national security issue or an international issue greatly depends on the nature of threat emanating from a fragile state environment. In a fragile state, traditionally, the strongest effects were felt locally (lack of socio-economic and educational opportunities, poverty, lack of competent workforce, lack of incentive for investment, non-existent basic commodities, widespread frustration and a sense of hopelessness among the population) with their spillover effects being felt primarily transnationally (activities of organized crime, terrorism, and migration flows). Different actors seek to instrumentalize or even weaponize state fragility in other countries in terms of weakening their resilience to external interference and good governance domestically to further their foreign policy objectives, often at the backdrop of grand imperialist projects.

In order to be able to conduct mission efficiently in the future, armed forces must maintain high levels of readiness and operability of their expeditionary force, mainly SOF and ISR units. Seeking to maintain conventional military dominance for deterrence purposes is critically important as well, specifically because future warfare will combine both conventional and nonconventional tactics and skills. In particular, attention should be focused toward developing and sustaining quality urban warfare capabilities (including how to tackle crime) and effective civil-military relationships. Ensuring interoperability with allies and partners is a must as well. Armed force must basically maintain the capabilities they already have, but also develop new ones for the domestic front, within a clear legal framework. Informational, psychological, and CBRN capabilities and readiness to assist with migration flows and natural disasters response are necessary now more than ever. From the perspective of energy insecurity emanating from fragile states, protection of strategic resources stockpiles, along with food and water supplies, is critical for the state survival. Ultimately, the military must be ready to assist in civilian awareness and preparedness initiatives to ensure that people know how to act in case of an armed conflict, a blackout, a nuclear disaster or food/water insecurity situations without panicking.

The wide range of security threats and challenges originating in fragile states may spread armed forces too thin. Therefore, it is also necessary to judge and decide upon the strategic significance of fragile states on a case-by-case basis and prioritize the needs and capabilities from there. Essentially, survival and resilience of one's own state should always be the number one priority.

Notes

1 Originally titled Failed States Index.
2 After the Cold War, corruption has become the center of Russian politics and even more so following Putin's rise to power in 2000. Putin formulated an interesting relationship with criminal groups in which,

in essence, criminals and legitimate businesses may be able to operate in Russia free of interference by law enforcement services, if they pay protection money to the government and do not oppose or criticize the Russian government (Kassab & Rosen 2018). Putin instrumentalized the transnational activities of Russian organized crime to achieve his foreign policy goals and used them rather skillfully.

3 The tendency for civilizational development to cluster along coastlines.

References

Bøas, M & Jennings, K M 2007, '"Failed States" and "State Failure": Threats or Opportunities?', *Globalizations*, vol. 4, no. 7, pp. 475–85, https://doi.org/10.1080/14747730701695729.

Felbab-Brown, V 2014, 'Crime, Low-Intensity Conflict, and the Future of War in the Twenty-First Century', in I Trauschweizer & S M Miner (eds), *Failed States and Fragile Societies: New World Order?*, Ohio University Press, Athens, OH, pp. 89–116.

Fukuyama, F 2004, *State-building: Governance and World Order in the 21st Century*, Cornell University Press, Ithaca, NY.

Fund for Peace 2022a, 'Indicators', *The Fund for Peace*, <https://fragilestatesindex.org/indicators/> (accessed 9 September 2022).

Fund for Peace 2022b, 'Fragile State Index Annual Report 2022', *The Fund for Peace*, <https://fragilestates-index.org/wp-content/uploads/2022/07/22-FSI-Report-Final.pdf> (accessed 10 September 2022).

Fund for Peace 2022c, 'Country Dashboard: Pakistan', *The Fund for Peace*, <https://fragilestatesindex.org/country-data/> (accessed 8 November 2022).

Gerth, H H & Wright Mills, C (eds) 1946, *From Max Weber: Essays in Sociology*, Oxford University Press, New York.

Grimm, S, Lemay-Hebert, N & Nay, O (eds) 2016, *The Political Invention of Fragile States: The Power of Ideas*, Routledge, Abingdon & New York.

House, J M 2014, 'The Past and Future of Insurgency: Protracted Warfare and Protracted Counterinsurgency', in I Trauschweizer & S M Miner (eds), *Failed States and Fragile Societies: New World Order?*, Ohio University Press, Athens, OH, pp. 49–61.

IISS 2015, *Military Balance*, <https://www.iiss.org/publications/the-military-balance/the-military-balance-2015> (accessed 17 November 2022).

Kalb, M 2021, *The Agonizing Problem of Pakistan's Nukes*, The Brookings Institution, 28 September, <https://www.brookings.edu/blog/order-from-chaos/2021/09/28/the-agonizing-problem-of-pakistans-nukes/> (accessed 10 November 2022).

Kassab, S & Rosen, J D 2018, *Corruption, Institutions, and Fragile States*, Palgrave Macmillan, London.

Kilcullen, D 2013, *Out of the Mountains: The Coming Age of the Urban Guerrilla*, Oxford University Press, Oxford & New York.

Marc, A & Jones, B 2021, *The New Geopolitics of State Fragility*, The Brookings Institution, 29 September 29, <https://www.brookings.edu/blog/order-from-chaos/2021/02/03/the-new-geopolitics-of-state-fragility/> (accessed 10 November 2022).

Pain, A 2015, 'Food Insecurity in Fragile States and Protracted Crises', in I Christoplos & A Pain (eds), *New Challenges to Food Security: From Climate Change to Fragile States*, Routledge, Abingdon & New York, pp. 123–39.

Patrick, S 2011, *Weak Links: Fragile States, Global Threats, and International Security*, Oxford University Press, Oxford & New York.

Rotberg, R 2003, *When States Fail: Causes and Consequences*, Princeton University Press, Princeton, NJ.

UNICEF 2022, *Devastating Floods in Pakistan*, <https://www.unicef.org/emergencies/devastating-floods-pakistan-2022> (accessed 18 November 2022).

UNSC 2022, *Thirtieth Report of the Analytical Support and Sanctions Monitoring Team Submitted Pursuant to Resolution 2610 (2021) Concerning ISIL (Da'esh), Al-Qaida and Associated Individuals and Entities*, United Nations Security Council, S/2022/547, <https://www.securitycouncilreport.org/atf/cf/%7B65BFCF9B-6D27-4E9C-8CD3-CF6E4FF96FF9%7D/S%202022%20547.pdf> (accessed 18 November 2022).

USIP 2018a, *Fragile States Fail Their Citizens and Threaten Global Security*, United States Institute of Peace, Task Force on Extremism in Fragile States, 5 September, <https://www.usip.org/blog/2018/09/fragile-states-fail-their-citizens-and-threaten-global-security> (accessed 12 September 2022).

USIP 2018b, *How Extremists Exploit Fragile States*, United States Institute of Peace, Task Force on Extremism in Fragile States, 6 September, <https://www.usip.org/blog/2018/09/how-extremists-exploit-fragile-states> (accessed 12 November 2022).

Weiss, C & O'Farrell, B 2021, 'Analysis: The Islamic State's Expansion in the Congo's Ituri Province', *Long War Journal*, 9 September, <https://www.longwarjournal.org/archives/2021/09/analysis-the-islamic-states-expansion-into-congos-ituri-province.php> (accessed 18 November 2022).

Ziaja, S & Fabra Mata, J 2010, 'State Fragility Indices: Potentials, Messages and Limitations', *IDOS Briefing Paper*, no. 10/2010, German Institute of Development and Sustainability, <https://www.idos-research.de/en/briefing-paper/article/state-fragility-indices-potentials-messages-and-limitations/> (accessed 9 September 2022).

10

LAWFARE IN THE 21ST CENTURY

Lauren Sanders

Introduction

The discourse on the use of the law to wage war – and its labelling as lawfare – has risen exponentially during the 21st century. Linked to the increasing codification of rights during armed conflict, and increasing codification of international legal mechanisms more generally, there are many more avenues to leverage legal mechanisms to achieve political and strategic aims as part of a military strategy.

This chapter will explore how the law has been used to achieve military outcomes and effects, referring to contemporary examples, whether relying upon formal legal mechanisms or relying upon expectations of an opponent's compliance with the law. Lawfare has been observed across the spectrum of operations: in hybrid or 'grey-zone' operations and during situations of armed conflict, and in both highly coordinated and ad hoc ways. As a strategic tool, lawfare seeks to influence the outcome of military operations at the political level, but it is also a tool that can be leveraged to cause tactical and operational effects (Dunlap 2017). This usage has been described in both positive and negative terms (Dill 2017); reflecting that the law can be leveraged in compliance with principles underpinning the international rules-based order and intent of the prevailing corpus of law, or with malfeasance and malintent as a methodology to undermine an opponent's adherence to that same rules-based order – all with the intent of influencing the outcome of military actions (Trachtman 2017).

The term 'lawfare' is applied to formal legal proceedings launched either domestically or internationally to seek to achieve this outcome, but also includes the conduct of actions that rely upon specific legal authorities: such as the conduct of Freedom Of Navigation Operations (FONOPS) relying upon the obligations expressly contained within *United Nations Law of the Sea Convention* (UNCLOS); or exploitation of an opponent's tactical rules of engagement, which incorporate laws of armed conflict obligations upon that party. It is also used to force particular actions, or inaction, by utilising legal obligations (and an actor's expected compliance with that obligation). In this way, the action is not merely related to the juridification of war, but in the use of law and specific legal permissions or prohibitions to buttress military actions and cause military effects. Increasingly, the effect sought is to legitimise action, or delegitimise an opponent's action, in pursuit of popular support for military outcomes.

 DOI: 10.4324/9781003299011-13

Contemporary use of the term 'lawfare'

It is relevant to note that there is no distinct understanding of lawfare, its purposes and whether or not it is a desirable feature of contemporary warfare (Brunera & Faix 2018). Given this absence of an accepted definition, it is useful to briefly identify how the term has developed and been used, to understand how the use of the law to influence military operations is variously understood. The history of the term has changed since its first appearance in the 1970s (Werner 2010). It has entered into common usage, having variously been used to refer to social justice issues, human rights concerns and to ground activist's causes by tying their cause to legal proceedings, thus lending them legitimacy. It has even been used to describe acts as broad as climate activism, and to the fight for women's rights on abortion. First used in a new age journal in Australia in 1975, to call for the use of the law to replace instances of war (Sadat & Geng 2010, citing Carlson and Yeomans), it is defined as "the strategic use of legal proceedings to intimidate or hinder an opponent".

Setting aside the non-warfare related interpretations of this term, lawfare has risen to prominence to describe the use and misuse of legal mechanisms to undermine the actions undertaken by parties opposing state or non-state actors, whether in competition phases or during the conduct of hostilities. The term has been variously used to describe the use of the law as a tactic; and in the semiotic combination of the terms of war and law, incorporate concepts of power, influence and legitimacy (Scharf & Pangon 2010). However, for these purposes, this chapter will refer to its contemporary and pure form: the concept of 'lawfare' as a military one. It describes the use of the law to gain an advantage over an enemy during, or in the lead-up to, the conduct of conflict. Perhaps the most widely accepted (and cited) definition of lawfare in this context is the evolved version of lawful espoused by former US Air Force Judge Advocate General Charles Dunlap, who has described it as "[t]he strategy of using—or misusing—law as a substitute for traditional military means to achieve an operational objective" (Dunlap 2009, p. 35). It is this formulation of lawfare that will be explored.

While first appearing in doctrinal discussion in the 1970s in Chinese literature (Werner 2010); there has been a schism in the approach of commentary on the use of lawfare in the 2000s (Williams 2010; Kittrie 2016). Specifically, the value-neutral description of lawfare as a military effect, as described by Dunlap (2017); is compared to the malfeasant exploitation of the law to achieve a military outcome (Werner 2010). These two types of lawfare have been characterised as instrumental lawfare (normatively neutral) versus compliance-leverage disparity lawfare (those cases where the law is misused) (Kittrie 2016; Chang 2022). In the case of the latter, the term focuses upon the exclusively pejorative use of the law, as compared to the effects-based description of the law as another tool or tactic available to all actors in the former.

The use of 'illegitimate' lawfare in the early 2000s was generally levelled against non-state actors (Horton 2010); while in more recent times, the focus of commentators on lawfare shifted to that of states – the most prevalent example being how the Russian Federation systematically utilises international legal mechanisms to achieve strategic goals and outcomes (Shiffman 2022). This is arguably reflective of the shift in commentary upon the differing character of contemporary conflicts, being those of an international, or internationalised non-international armed conflict, rather than those of a pure non-international character (Mia 2022).

Current commentary has, however, shifted to observe lawfare in more-value neutral terms; and contemplating that the use of lawfare might be a legitimate tactic. Reference to the norms-based concepts of the rule of international law, which is premised on cooperation, create lawfare as "an ideology embedded within the international political system" (Scott cited in Guilfoyle 2019), and thus one that can be used for 'good' or 'bad', depending on the effect desired. Regardless of scholarly debate about its desirability, or its limits, the use of the law to achieve military effects is a readily observable and regular occurrence in the international legal order (Williams 2010).

Lawfare as a tactic

In the same way that scholars are re-considering the use of the term 'grey-zone' as a contemporary description of hybrid conflict (Hobbs 2021), the well-utilised phenomenon of leveraging legal mechanisms to achieve military ones is nothing new (Berman cited in Ansah 2010). Rather, there have been documented rises in the capacity for states and non-state actors to utilise legal mechanisms to achieve military outcomes, simply because the international legal regulation of armed conflict has become increasingly codified in the post-modern period to date (Voetelink 2017). In spite of the challenges faced by such codification becoming quickly outdated when reflecting technological development (Crootof 2018), this trend appears to be continuing with attempts to influence future international legal regulation.

Across the three levels of war, recent examples of the use of the law to achieve military effects demonstrate the expansive use of lawfare during situations of armed conflict, as an opportunity to achieve physical effects and intangible effects (such as influence operations).

Tactical lawfare

Utilising well-accepted doctrinal terminology, tactical operations are those that translate combat power into engagements, battles or skirmishes, nested within operational and strategic effects (Krause 1990). Tactical use of lawfare is typically perfidious, specifically that the reliance upon a protected status will prevent an enemy from undertaking military action in response. Understanding the rules of engagement and purposefully obfuscating one's status to enable an advantage is a regular tactical level lawfare ploy.

For example, the Taliban misused the law of armed conflict to achieve tactical advantage over International Security Assistance Forces (ISAF) (Chang 2022). Placement of military objects within protected places by Taliban, a tactic subsequently copied by ISIS, is one method by which this exploitation occurred. Knowing that their enemy would be obliged to follow, and would comply with, their laws of armed conflict obligations not to attack civilian objects, or not attack if collateral damage would be disproportionate to the potential damage of targeting those military objects, the Taliban protected themselves by purposefully hiding within civilian populations. In this way, the tactic was a "substitute for conventional air defense" (Chang 2022).

While less influential in terms of the value of influencing strategic operations, the use of litigation is also 'exponentially effective', because of the relative disparity in funding capacity for lawsuits. As Samson contends, "one lawsuit can silence thousands who have neither the time nor the financial resources to challenge well-funded terror financiers or the vast machine of the international judicial system" (Samson 2009).

Complaints of war crimes and torture against ISAF soldiers in Afghanistan were also a stated tactic of Al Qaeda; whose intent was largely to undermine through distraction of resources in inquiry and investigation and undermining the credibility and local support for coalition soldiers of the ISAF mission (Lebowitz 2010). The counter-lawfare action in response to this tactic was deliberate planning to avoid such situations, which linked the 'hearts and minds' ISAF objectives to the legal ones. The adoption of robust precautionary measures, arguably in excess of strict legal obligations, such as the adoption of COMISAF Tactical Directives, demonstrated the ability to defeat this perfidious use of the law by the adversary (Lewis 2014). Complaints of breaching this protection, when not deserved, however, is a conflation of the extension of policy in the application laws of armed conflict. This is an example of counter-lawfare where a legal-adjacent remedy is applied to counter an exploitation of the law, rather than being a strict legal obligation.

Operational lawfare

The operational level of war is often claimed to have been 'discovered' by Moltke, because it represents a military campaign separated from the political, insofar as it is the preserve of military professionals to run a sequential, simultaneous or a series of military actions to achieve a particular campaign aim (Krause 1990). Typically defined by time, geography and phases, the impact of lawfare upon the operational level is more widespread than specific tactical actions. Consequently, the type of lawfare that is effective in an operational sense are those actions that have a significant impact on denuding an opponent's freedom of action, capabilities or manoeuvre.

An example of an operational use of lawfare was the impact upon the movement of resources to support the Assad regime during the Syrian conflict. Pressure from the US government upon a commercial shipping insurance company to withdraw insurance from *MV Alaed* prevented the ship from sailing. This vessel was delivering gunship helicopters from Russia to Assad's Syrian regime; but was prevented from doing so because of this regulatory requirement to be insured prior to sailing, or the commercial company would risk being boarded and thus prevented from further voyages. Worried about the impact of physical interception, this method leveraged available diplomatic pressure, focused upon a legal regulatory outcome, to achieve an operational-level effect. The effect was far more wide-reaching than a simple tactical action, given the supply lines of helicopter gunships produced a campaign-wide impact upon the regime's ability to conduct air operations. This was a demonstration of military outcome utilising legal-adjacent actions that have operational effects (Chang 2022).

Similar examples can be seen in leveraging of commercial contracts, such as the purchase of satellite imagery that was precluded from being sold to any party other than the US government (prior to the beginning of the Afghanistan conflict) (Randerson 2001). Denial of this valuable intelligence resource produced an ongoing operational advantage to ISAF forces throughout the conflict. Use of sanctions to prevent the Iraqi Air Force purchasing aircraft and spare parts delivery in 2003 is another example of operational level lawfare (Chang 2022).

Although a potentially useful operational lawfare tactic, in some situations, deference to the rules-based order makes lawfare options unavailable to states or actors seeking to reinforce the international order. An example is that of the constraint of FONOPS – in allowing intercepted vessels to continue unimpeded to support the common-good goal of free navigation of the high seas – such as the *MV So San* incident. Despite being capable of detaining the vessel and its cargo, the United States allowed it to continue to Yemen from North Korea, with the knowledge it contained a cargo of Scud missiles that would likely be utilised for furthering the conflict (Guilfoyle 2019). In this instance, the risk of destabilising the legal order was deemed to be greater than the specific operational advantage sought.

Strategic lawfare

Strategic actions are those that are concerned with the 'art and science' of employing national power (Krause 1990). Noting that these are sometimes synonymous with political objectives, the strategic use of the law to achieve military effects is perhaps the least controversial and most readily identifiable use of the law in contemporary warfare.

In an ongoing and blatant example of strategic lawfare in the 21st century, both Russia and Ukraine have adopted multi-faceted lawfare strategies in response to Russia's 2014 and 2022 unlawful occupations. Russia has sought to utilise legal terms to justify its unlawful invasion, whereas Ukraine has used legal mechanisms to seek to prevent the ongoing war.

Tropin suggested in 2021 that centralised state coordination of lawfare measures in Ukraine would assist in defeating unlawful actions of the Russian Federation. In 2022, the Ukrainian government announced its lawfare strategy:

> The legal front is inconspicuous, [...] Its key feature is that there is no noticeable disproportion in weight with the enemy. [...] Where there are no weapons, there is international law, sanctions and a tribunal. [...] And on this front, Ukraine (state bodies and state-owned enterprises) is fighting quite well.
> [...]
> We are moving from the sometimes chaotic hit-skip tactics to a well-thought-out, comprehensive and coordinated legal defense of our rights and interests, and for this purpose we have involved leading foreign legal advisers who help to develop a strategy for legal confrontation.

(Ukraine Ministry for Justice 2021)

In a very public and purposeful way, Ukraine has done just that, to pressure the Russian Federation to cease their war (Woods et al. 2022). At least nine complaints before the European Court of Human Rights, complaints before the International Tribunal for the Law of the Sea, the International Court of Justice (ICJ), and the Permanent Court of Arbitration; in addition to arbitral disputes relating to Bilateral Investment Treaties (Chang 2022).

By December 2022, the use of lawfare by Ukraine has been successful in many of these cases insofar as it has defeated Russian information operations and delegitimised any claims of legal justification for their occupation of Crimea and further acts of aggression in the Donetsk and Luhansk regions. Based upon claims of alleged genocide being committed against Russian residents of these regions, the Ukrainian Government brought a case against Russia before the International Court of Justice to clarify that these claims were false, relying upon the terms of the *Genocide Convention* that enables the ICJ to adjudicate disputes relating it; in this case being to adjudicate on the non-existence of genocide, and to nullify the claims of 'fulfilment' of the Convention by the Russian occupation of Ukraine (*Dispute Relating to Allegations of Genocide (Ukraine v Russian Federation)*) (ICJ 2022). Despite the case still not having been heard in December 2022, the overwhelming and unprecedented support of over 40 states making interventions in support of Ukraine demonstrates that contemporary lawfare also provides states opportunities to aid in the conflict without themselves becoming belligerent parties.

Use in situations other than armed conflict: lawfare and the 'grey zone'

In the same way that the term lawfare is a contemporary restatement of actions that have been undertaken for centuries; the term 'grey zone' has been applied to operations for far longer than the term has been used to describe hybrid operations, or the competition phase prior to the commencement of a situation of armed conflict (Hicks et al. 2019). However, the use of lawfare in the grey zone, is arguably more relevant in contemporary international relations, given the prominence of the current rules-based order's reliance on the United Nations Charter as the mechanism to ensure that any lawful use of force remains the preserve of the State.

The use of Russia's attempts to hide its initial occupation of Crimea in 2014 by falsely making claims of legitimate self-defence of its Russian-Crimean occupants demonstrate a case in point. While Russia's 'little green men' were consolidating their military position prior to any lawful response being mounted by the international community, Russia was denying the actions were conducted by its military personnel, and thus seeking to avoid legal responsibility for their actions under the principles of *jus ad bellum* as also reflected in accepted customary international law contained in the 2001 *Articles of State Responsibility for International Wrongful Acts*. This represents a contemporary example of grey zone lawfare by a state actor (Hobbs 2021). It enabled Russia to exploit international law by obfuscating attribution for their actions and thus buy time before the international legal regime was able to respond to its acts of aggression.

While much commentary on grey zone operations focuses on the use of information or influence operations and the law, grey zone lawfare operations are not merely limited to such operations. Physical acts, based upon expansionist interpretations of the law, are further examples of grey zone lawfare. The use of lawfare by China in the South China Sea is such an example. In this context, Guilfoyle (2019, p. 1000) notes that the "[l]aw may be a useful tool in consolidating gains or defeating a rival's claims". That is, China is using the law as an alternative for warfare to achieve its aims of territorial expansion. Challenges to sovereignty are thus being defeated with legal mechanisms rather than a physical use of force. China's legitimisation of its expansion to the 'nine-dash-line', was attempted through manufacture of islands (which have subsequently been determined to be rocks 'incapable of sustaining human habitation or an economic life of its own', following UNCLOS arbitration processes) (Davenport 2022). China's subsequent disregard of this outcome demonstrates that, like some military techniques, when desired outcomes are not achieved, the tactic may be abandoned by its proponent (Guilfoyle 2019). Regardless, this is one of the starkest, and oft-cited examples of lawfare in the competition phase and outside of armed conflict in recent years.

The response to these actions by other states, has been to leverage legal mechanisms to seek recourse for their actions: Freedom of Navigation Operations, known as 'FONOPS', which are regularly undertaken by US, Australian, Philippine and Japanese naval vessels seek to counter Chinese actions in the South China Sea. This counter-lawfare action seeks to reinforce the innocent transit and navigation rights under UNCLOS to free navigation in archipelagic sea lanes and on the high seas – the 'global [oceanic] commons' – and to undermine Chinese lawfare efforts to expand territorially (Mitall 2022). In this way, counter-lawfare operations are capable of counteracting malfeasant lawfare campaigns.

Lawfare can also be used to preserve future military actions. Positioning of legal arguments to protect against future threats can be seen in the use of law developing in relation to property rights in outer space. For example, the use of litigation by state-sponsored companies to challenge decisions made in the interests of national security represents a more insidious example of lawfare, simply because the claimed threat – a future, unrealised and hypothesised threat to national security, are difficult to substantivate. For example, in the 2019 case of *Huawei v the US*, the Chinese-owned communication company challenged American domestic national security legislation to seek to retain its ability to operate domestically in the United States (Goldenzeil 2021). This case was run to enable continued operations of a company that is ostensibly conducting military intelligence operations by one state against another, in the competition phase of conflict. This type of warfare is more systematised, planning to preserve future military actions, albeit less direct in terms of operational effect.

State versus non-state actor and non-government actor use of lawfare

Reflecting a change in the basic premise that all laws must be backed by potential enforcement action by states; the rise of the influence of public perception on the conduct of conflict has given rise to the impact of lawfare (Dill 2017). In this way, the ability of non-state actors to utilise the law as a tool is also enhanced.

The use of universal jurisdiction is a case in point. There are many examples of states shielding their personnel from prosecution when those individuals have been accused of committing atrocity crimes during armed conflicts that state has been party too. Universal jurisdiction is a method to prosecute such cases when the state is unwilling or unable to act as prosecutions can be launched by third party states with not traditional jurisdictional nexus to the offender, victims or geographic location of the crime. While objectively a good thing, when used to initiate vexatious complaints against individuals, and political leaders in particular, this use of the jurisdiction when aligned to third party state (or civilian) political intent is met with considerable, and understandable, resistance. In such cases, the jurisdiction is being utilised to undermine or circumvent the purpose of the law. However, if used, as a tool of lawfare, to bring to account individuals who might otherwise escape accountability for their actions then universal jurisdiction can promote compliance with the laws of armed conflict by states that would otherwise allow their citizens to perpetrate atrocity crimes on their behalf with impunity.

The most strident complaint against the use of universal jurisdiction is the capacity of this legal doctrine to be used against a state by its enemies to impact the capacity or will of its political leaders or armed forces to conduct certain activities. For example, in 2009, Belgium passed expansive universal jurisdiction laws that would allow the presentation of criminal charges by citizens, without requiring government involvement; applying broad jurisdictional bases for such prosecutions. The United States was concerned that this would enable politically motivated prosecutions of their leaders and military personnel (Ralph 2009). This concern resulted in pressure by the United States government to withhold funding that would effectively render NATO Headquarters in Brussels inoperable (Ralph 2009). This response is, in a sense, a further example of lawfare in response to a domestic state's peacetime laws. The pressure was exerted to ensure that US personnel and leaders could not be the subject of potential future criminal proceedings for alleged breaches of universal jurisdiction offences, which was contended as a potential limitation on future operational freedom of action.

Use of the law by supra-national organisations in pursuit of political aims has also been labelled lawfare in some settings. Israeli commentators suggest that the application of the Office of the Prosecutor to the International Criminal Court (ICC) to institute proceedings in the matter of Palestine is a partisan demonstration of lawfare and *mala fides* application of the law. This claim is on the basis of the Submission of former ICC Prosecutor, Fatou Bensouda, progressing a referral made by the Palestinian National Authority to rule on the lawfulness of the territorial claims within the occupied territories (Derri 2021). In this way, the law was used as part of a calculated strategy seeking to favour one side of the conflict over the other, based upon an external, partisan interpretation of the situation.

The Palestinian Authority have acknowledged their lawfare strategy, published in a New York Times op-ed (President of the Palestinian Authority Mahmoud Abbas, cited by Chang 2022), which, among other points, identified the purpose of attempts to join the UN was to internationalise their conflict and open access to claims utilising international legal mechanisms such as UN mechanisms and the ICJ, as well as bodies adjudicating human rights treaties obligations. Here, the use of the law to influence political and warfare objectives is concurrent.

Lawfare is also a tool available to states that wish to support a particular armed conflict, but not enter it as belligerent parties. Australia and the Netherlands, for example, have pursued prosecutions in the International Civil Aviation Organization relating to the downing of flight MH17 by Russian-backed actors (Payne 2022). This was followed by a domestic universal jurisdiction trial against three of the alleged perpetrators involved in procuring the missiles for the attack. While there is a jurisdictional link and basis for seeking justice for the Dutch and Australia people who were killed in that crash, both countries have stated that their additional intention in the proceedings is to influence ongoing Russian aggression in Ukraine. The categorisation of this type of lawfare as positive, or a misuse of the law, is purely dependent upon your perspective. It is a positive use of available legal mechanisms calculated to influence military operations that are inherently unlawful and a challenge to the current rules-based global order; but a misuse of the law in impeding upon Russia's sovereign integrity over its citizens, seeking extradition in contravention to its Constitution. In this instance, the weight of the international community is supportive of the former position.

Law as a tool in military and security doctrines

The term 'lawfare' is not widely used as a specific military tactic reduced to military doctrine, although reports of China adopting a specific lawfare doctrine demonstrates that this contemporary trend is becoming more codified and systematic in its use in the 21st century. A survey of the publicly available military doctrines of NATO, the United States, the United Kingdom, Australia and Canada reveals that the term itself does not appear. NATO refers to lawfare only tangentially during conference debates (Brunera & Faix 2018), while US military scholars have called for a codification or indoctrination of the principle to give certainty to how the United States might utilise the tactic (Logan 2017). US presidential statements have impliedly referred to lawfare in the negative sense, in referring to the use of international legal mechanisms and terrorism as equal threats to the state (Horton 2010). Noting the scepticism and, in some cases, demonisation of the use of legal mechanisms to enforce international human rights in official US government texts, particularly where those actions relate to the conduct of the US military (Waters 2010), it seems unlikely that a formal adoption of lawfare as a tactic, even in a value-neutral sense, will be forthcoming.

On the other hand, Chinese and Russian doctrine refer to the concept, with the Chinese describing it as part of its 'three warfares' doctrine (*san shong zhanfa*) (Goldenzeil 2021); and Russia referring to legal means to defend its national interests, notably before resorting to violent means (Military Doctrine of the Russian Federation cited in Voyger 2018). Chinese use of lawfare has openly focused upon manipulating the international community through aggressive application and exploitation of the prohibitions and permissions of the laws of war to their advantage.

Contrary to the Ukrainian example, discussed above, other states, such as Pakistan, have noted the increasing pressure to counter acts of lawfare by their opponents (Dawn 2021), but have not gone as far as calling for a systemisation or indoctrination of lawfare in response. Given the negative connotations associated with the term, despite attempts of making the term value-agnostic, it seems unlikely that formal doctrines of lawfare will be forthcoming by other states. Rather, lawfare will continue as part of either ad hoc or deliberate strategies to utilise the law linked to operational effects, without being positively declared as such by states.

Concluding observations

The above examples demonstrate that the use of the law to influence the conduct of military operations is neither a novel, nor an irregular occurrence. It is one that is accessed by both states, and non-state actors. It is used with equal prevalence by states attempting to undermine the rule of law and international legal order, as those espousing its importance; and is as regularly used during shaping operations prior to the commencement of armed conflict, as it is during the conduct of hostilities.

However, despite being a long-standing practice, it is increasingly becoming more entrenched as a deliberate and coordinated strategy. The leveraging of legal mechanisms to influence supply lines; the use of litigation to block future intelligence sources; and demarcation of future territorial claims feature in current and future uses of the law. However, the dualist nature of lawfare's definition, supports apprehension that codifying a policy of lawfare could flag an intent to misuse or misapply the law (or accept other states' actions in doing so). Consequently, most states are unlikely to entrench this concept as one written into their military doctrines, rather they will continue to enact it as the need arises, albeit in a considered, planned and coordinated way.

Thus, the use of lawfare as a tactic to legitimise military action will inevitably continue; and the manner of its use will align with its current trajectory:

1 It will be increasing coordinated with other operations; specifically, influence and information operations – given the concomitant increase in impact of these lines of effort on military campaigns.
2 It will increasingly become a concerted, planned effort in and of itself, to encourage both popular and international political support for a conflict. Its coordination with other political means of communication and technological platforms (specifically, social media) will be central to the operations' success.
3 Its use will not only continue as a defensive, or responsive tactic, but increasingly to preserve future options and freedom of military manoeuvre; with such considerations extending to rights in the cyber and space domains in particular. As such, future international legal regulation related to armed conflict will continue to be closely tied to the military plans of the near future for influential states.

Finally, the use of the law in positing patently fallacious legal positions, will continue. The invocation of judicial mechanisms (or threat thereof) is cause-agnostic. It is the outcome of the legal mechanism that represents the decision on merits of a case. While in some circumstances this could be considered vexatious use of the law, lawfare will increasingly be utilised as a litmus test to identify the acceptable limits on conduct in grey zone and during armed conflict. Such cases are not necessarily representative of an unwelcome manipulation of these legal mechanisms. On the contrary, they allow for the testing and strengthening of the values and norms that society writ large benefits from, when other actors – both state and non-state – seek to derail the stability offered by the extant rules-based order.

References

Ansah, T 2010, 'Lawfare: A Rhetorical Analysis', *Case Western Reserve Journal of International Law*, vol. 43, no. 1, pp. 87–119.

Brunera, T & Faix, M 2018, 'The Attribution Problem as a Tool of Lawfare', *Obrana A Strategie*, no. 1, pp. 79–96 <https://www.obranaastrategie.cz/en/archive/volume-2018/1-2018/articles/the-attribution-problem-as-a-tool-of-lawfare.html#:~:text=International%20law%20prescribes%20conditions%20for, responsible%20for%20actions%20of%20individuals> (accessed 12 October 2022).

Chang, E 2022, 'Lawfare in Ukraine: Weaponizing International Investment Law and the Law of Armed Conflict Against Russia's Invasion', *INSS Strategic Perspectives*, no. 39, <https://www.ndu.edu/News/Article-View/Article/3121206/lawfare-in-ukraine-weaponizing-international-investment-law-and-the-law-of-arme/> (accessed 5 October 2022).

Crootof, R 2018, 'Jurisprudential Space Junk: Treaties and New Technologies', in C Giorgetti & N Klein (eds), *Resolving Conflicts in the Law: Essays in Honour of Lea Brilmayer,* Brill/Nijhoff, Boston, MA & Leiden, pp. 106–29.

Davenport, T 2022, '"Lawfare" in the South China Sea Disputes', *The Interpreter*, 1 April, <https://www.lowyinstitute.org/the-interpreter/lawfare-south-china-sea-disputes> (accessed 12 October 2022).

Dawn 2021, 'Speakers for Developing Lawfare', *Dawn*, 16 July, <https://www.dawn.com/news/1635323%20July%2016> (accessed 21 October 2022).

Derri, A 2021, 'The ICC's Prosecutor in the Service of Palestinian Lawfare', *Israel Affairs,* vol. 27, no. 1, pp. 105–20, https://doi.org/10.1080/13537121.2021.1864852.

Dill, J 2017, 'Abuse of Law on the Twenty-First-Century Battlefield: A Typology of Lawfare', in M Gross & T Meisels (eds), *Soft War: The Ethics of Unarmed Conflict*, Cambridge University Press, Cambridge & New York, pp. 127–42.

Dunlap, C J 2009, 'Lawfare: A Decisive Element of 21st Century Conflicts?', *Joint Force Quarterly*, no. 54, pp. 34–9.

Dunlap, C J 2017, 'Lawfare 101: A Primer', *Military Review,* May–June, pp. 8–17.

Goldenzeil, J 2021, 'Law as a Battlefield: The U.S., China, and the Global Escalation of Lawfare', *Cornell Law Review*, vol. 106, no. 9, pp. 1085–171, <https://live-cornell-law-review.pantheonsite.io/wp-content/uploads/2021/09/Goldenziel-final11234.pdf> (accessed 21 October 2022).

Guilfoyle, D 2019, 'The Rule of Law and Maritime Security: Understanding Lawfare in the South China Sea', *International Affairs*, vol. 95, no. 5, pp. 999–1017, https://doi.org/10.1093/ia/iiz141.

Hicks, K, Friend, A, Frederici, J, Shah, H, Donahoe, M, Conklin, M, Acka, A, Matlaga, M & Sheppard, L 2019, *By Other Means. Part One: Campaigning In The Grey Zone,* Centre for Strategic and International Studies, London, <https://csis-website-prod.s3.amazonaws.com/s3fs-public/publication/Hicks_GrayZone_interior_v4_FULL_WEB_0.pdf> (accessed 31 December 2022).

Hobbs, D 2021, *Conflict in the Grey Zone – Nothing New Under the Sun (Tzu)*, Atlantic Treaty Association of the United Kingdom, London, <https://atauk.org/index.php/2021/01/19/conflict-in-the-grey-zone-nothing-new-under-the-sun-tzu/> (accessed 12 October 2022).

Horton, S 2010, 'The Dangers of Lawfare', *Case Western Reserve Journal of International Law*, vol. 43, no. 1, pp. 163–80.

ICJ 2022, 'Dispute Relating to Allegations of Genocide (Ukraine v Russian Federation*)'*, *International Court of Justice*, <https://www.icj-cij.org/public/files/annual-reports/2021-2022-en.pdf> (accessed 31 December 2022).

Kittrie, O F 2016, 'The Chinese Government Adopts and Implements a Lawfare Strategy', in O F Kittrie (ed), *Lawfare: Law as a Weapon of War*, Oxford University Press, Oxford, pp. 161–196, https://doi.org/10.1093/acprof:oso/9780190263577.003.0004.

Krause, M D 1990, 'Moltke and the Origins of the Operational Art', *Military Review*, vol. LXX, no. 9, pp. 28–44.

Lebowitz, M 2010, 'The Value of Claiming Torture: An Analysis of Al-Qaeda's Tactical Lawfare Strategy and Efforts to Fight Back', *Case Western Reserve Journal of International Law*, vol. 43, no. 1, pp. 357–92.

Lewis, L 2014, *Improving Lethal Action: Learning and Adapting in U.S. Counterterrorism Operations*, CNA Centre for Naval Analyses, Arlington, VA, <https://www.cna.org/archive/CNA_Files/pdf/cop-2014-u-008746-final.pdf> (accessed 22 October 2022).

Logan, T 2017, *International Law and the Use of Lawfare: An Argument for the U.S. To Adopt a Lawfare Doctrine*, Master of Science in Defence and Strategic Studies Thesis, Missouri State University, Springfield, MO.

Mia, I 2022, 'The Armed Conflict Survey 2022: Editor's Introduction', *Armed Conflict Survey*, viewed 20 November 2022, <https://www.iiss.org/publications/armed-conflict-survey/2022/armed-conflict-survey-2022> (accessed 20 November 2022).

Mitall, T 2022, 'Troubled Waters: FONOPS, UNCLOS, and Global Commons', *Observer Research Foundation*, 30 June, <https://www.orfonline.org/expert-speak/troubled-waters-fonops-unclos-and-global-commons/> (accessed 29 December 2022).

Payne, M 2022, *Australia and the Netherlands Institute MH17 Proceedings*, Parliament House, Canberra, 14 March.

Ralph, J 2009, *Defending the Society of States: Why America Opposes the International Criminal Court and its Vision of World Society*, Oxford University Press, Oxford.

Randerson, J 2001, 'US government Buys Up Rights to Satellite Pictures of Afghanistan', *New Scientist*, 17 October, <https://www.newscientist.com/article/dn1444-us-government-buys-up-rights-to-satellite-pictures-of-afghanistan/> (accessed 12 October 2022).

Sadat, L N & Geng, J 2010, 'On Legal Subterfuge and the So-Called "Lawfare"', *Case Western Reserve Journal of International Law,* vol. 43, no. 1, pp. 153–63.

Samson, E 2009, 'Warfare Through Misuse of International Law', *BESA Center Perspectives Paper*, no. 73, The Begin-Sadat Center for Strategic Studies, <https://besacenter.org/warfare-through-misuse-of-international-law/> (accessed 12 October 2022).

Scharf, M & Pangon, S 2010, 'Introduction: Lawfare!', *Case Western Reserve Journal of International Law,* vol. 43, no. 1, pp. 1–10.

Shiffman, S 2022, 'Great Power Use of Lawfare' Is the Joint Force Prepared?', *Joint Force Quarterly*, no. 107, pp. 15–20.

Trachtman, J P 2017, 'Integrating Lawfare and Warfare', *Boston College International & Comparative Law Review*, vol. 39, pp. 267–82.

Tropin, Z 2021, 'Lawfare as Apart of Hybrid Wars: The Experience of Ukraine in Conflict with Russian Federation', *Security and Defence Quarterly*, vol. 33, no. 1, pp. 15–29, https://doi.org/10.35467/sdq/132025.

Ukraine Ministry for Justice 2021, 'About Lawfare Project History,' *Law Confrontation with Russian Federation,* 26 January, <https://lawfare.gov.ua/t> (accessed 20 October 2022).

Voetelink, J 2017, 'Reframing Lawfare', in P Ducheine & F Osinga (eds), *Netherlands Annual Review of Military Studies,* T.M.C. Asser Press, The Hague, pp. 237–54.

Voyger, M 2018, 'Russian Lawfare – Russia's Weaponisation Of International And Domestic Law: Implications For The Region And Policy Recommendations', *Journal on Baltic Security*, vol. 4, no. 2, pp. 1–8, https://doi.org/10.2478/jobs-2018-0011.

Waters, M 2010, '"Lawfare" in the War on Terror: A Reclamation Project', *Case Western Reserve Journal of International Law,* vol. 43, no. 1, pp. 237–334.

Werner, W G 2010, 'The Curious Career of Lawfare', *Case Western Reserve Journal of International Law,* vol. 43, no. 1, pp. 61–72.

Williams, P 2010, 'Lawfare: A War Worth Fighting', *Case Western Reserve Journal of International Law,* vol. 43, no. 1, pp. 145–52.

Woods, N, Simpson, T, Akande, D & Koh, H 2022, *Ukraine: What's At Stake*, Blavatnik School of Government, Oxford University, London, 1 March, <https://www.bsg.ox.ac.uk/events/ukraine-whats-stake> (accessed 12 October 2022).

11

PRIVATIZATION OF WARFARE

Elke Krahmann

Introduction

Since the emergence of the first modern private military and security companies (PMSCs) in the 1990s, the privatization of warfare has gained momentum with important consequences for contemporary and future wars. On the one hand, the contracting of military and security services has become increasingly routine and regulated in Western democracies and international interventions led by the United Nations (UN), NATO, and the European Union (EU). On the other hand, the industry is continually seeking to expand its client base to countries in Africa, Asia, and Latin America, and to novel technologies and services, such as drones and cybersecurity. However, PMSCs and new mercenaries like the Russian 'Wagner Group' are not the only private and commercial actors who are changing the nature of warfare. Globalization and digitalization offer privateers, volunteers, and hackers additional opportunities for involvement in international conflicts.

When the Angolan government hired the South African company Executive Outcomes for military combat services in 1995, few politicians and even fewer scholars knew how to categorize the firm. Executive Outcomes fought for profit like mercenaries, but it was a legally registered company and subject to business regulations. To understand the newly emerging firms, the early literature differentiated them based on corporate structure, legal status, customers, services, and frontline distance (Mandel 2002; Singer 2003). Today, it is accepted that most PMSCs work for a diverse set of clients, serve in a multitude of functions, and adapt their services in response to changing customer demands and business opportunities. The most widely cited definition stems from the *Montreux Document on pertinent international legal obligations and good practices for States related to operations of private military and security companies during armed conflict* (ICRC 2009a), a nonbinding commitment that has been signed by 58 countries, the UN, NATO, and the EU. It states that

> 'PMSCs' are private business entities that provide military and/or security services, irrespective of how they describe themselves. Military and security services include, in particular, armed guarding and protection of persons and objects, such as convoys, buildings and other places; maintenance and operation of weapons systems; prisoner detention; and advice to or training of local forces and security personnel.
>
> (ICRC 2009a, p. 9)

DOI: 10.4324/9781003299011-14

Two features separate most PMSCs from mercenaries as defined by Article 47 of Protocol I additional to the 1949 Geneva Conventions: (1) they are incorporated and (2) they do not engage in combat. Additionally, it is useful to distinguish PMSCs from privateers and volunteers. Privateers are also motivated by profit, but they have a governmental license to engage in warfare independently from national armed forces at their own costs and benefits. By contrast, volunteers are motivated by political reasons rather than money. International volunteers are typically incorporated into military structures, for instance, in the form of volunteer corps.

In sum, private military and security actors come in many guises, and their number and ability to influence international and civil wars has expanded significantly over the past three decades. Companies offering military and security support have become indispensable for many governments and international organizations engaged in military operations abroad. Executive Outcomes disbanded at the turn of the millennium amidst criticism that the company undermined the state monopoly on violence, but mercenaries and combat PMSCs have been making a comeback in national and international conflicts such as in Ukraine, Mali, and the Central African Republic. New fields of operation are bringing about new problems and concerns for the future.

The following four sections examine the privatization of warfare and its consequences in further detail. The first section outlines how PMSCs serve as force multipliers in international military operations. The second section explores why failed, failing, and autocratic states are increasingly turning to mercenaries and combat PMSCs for assistance. The third looks at newly emerging markets and actors, including the operation of drones and cybersecurity. Finally, the chapter discusses the implications of these developments for the practice and theory of war.

Military support for international interventions

The military interventions in Iraq and Afghanistan have fundamentally changed not only the PMSC industry, but also the nature of warfare. Central to this transformation has been a massive expansion of military and security contracting for international operations. While in the Vietnam war, there were six times as many United States (US) soldiers as contractors in the field, the ratio decreased to 1.4:1 in Afghanistan and 1:1 in Iraq (Schwartz 2010, p. 5). Simultaneously, the industry has increased its range of services and functions. In the 1990s, PMSC contracts were confined to logistics and base support at home and during the pre-invasion phases. In the 2000s, security for convoys and bases abroad, military maintenance, intelligence collection, and drone operation brought contractors into the theater of war. Armed protection was the fastest-growing service sector in Iraq and Afghanistan, often breaking down the formal divisions between civilian and military personnel, and between defensive and offensive action (ICRC 2009b, p. 38).

Since the end of the multilateral interventions in Iraq and Afghanistan, PMSCs have attracted less public attention. The withdrawal of international forces from these countries has not heralded the decline of the industry, but has contributed to its diversification and consolidation. New lines of business in maritime security, cybersecurity, and drones have appeared (Maurer 2018; Liss 2020). Some firms have merged with corporations from the defense industry and IT sectors to increase their competitiveness. Others have partnered with local security providers, especially where national laws prohibit the employment of international PMSCs (Krahmann & Prem 2017).

The United States is the largest employer of PMSCs, closely followed by the United Kingdom (UK) (Avant 2005; Kinsey 2009; Stanger 2011). Primary reasons have been neoliberal reforms and reductions in the armed forces and military budgets after the end of the Cold War. Both countries hire PMSCs for the full breadth of military support services, including transport, logistics, maintenance, training, risk analysis, and intelligence. The US government also employs armed security contractors to protect civilian personnel, military bases, and logistic convoys. Other Western industrialized countries, such as Canada, Germany, the Czech Republic, Denmark, and Sweden, have followed their examples (Krahmann 2010; Berndtsson 2014; Spearin 2014; Bureš 2015). Due to public opposition to a weakening of the state monopoly on violence, the scale and scope of outsourcing was initially more restrictive in Europe than in the United States. Even the British armed forces continue to draw a line at hiring armed guards for international missions. However, the joint missions in Iraq and Afghanistan, financial and capability gaps, and changes in doctrine and military culture have facilitated more permissive attitudes toward contracting in Europe (Leander 2013).

In Asia, China is by far the largest potential market for military and security services. The Chinese government has already incorporated private companies into its international security strategy, assigning them an active role in intelligence gathering and unarmed protection for Chinese investments and personnel abroad (Ghiselli 2020; Lu 2020). It is estimated that up to 40 Chinese security firms operate globally (Lu 2020, p. 177). Many of the largest companies have close connections with the Chinese government, the Communist Party or the People's Liberation Army (PLA). The Zhongjun Junhong Group, for example, emerged from the security branch of the People's Armed Police. Chinese law requires armed security firms to be at least 51% state-owned and it prohibits the international sale and possession of arms (Lu 2020, p. 178). Since the law limits the kinds of services that Chinese security firms can supply abroad, some companies collaborate with local firms to provide armed protection. So far, the Chinese government rejects the idea of hiring armed PMSCs or mercenaries because of concerns about its international image and its ability to control of such actors. An exception has been made in the case of armed guards onboard Chinese ships (Masuhr & Friedrich 2020, p. 3). Moreover, the 11th Chinese People's Political Consultative Conference (CPPCC) National Committee suggested in 2012 that it would be desirable to create Chinese companies 'similar to Blackwater' to provide security in high-risk environments (Lu 2020, pp. 176–7).

International organizations, such as the UN, NATO, and the EU, are often forced to rely on private companies for the protection of embassies and civilian staff. In recent years, they have also begun to hire PMSCs for logistics, infrastructure support, demining services, the operation of drones, and intelligence analysis during multilateral military interventions and peacekeeping missions (Pingeot 2012, 2014; Østensen 2013; Giumelli & Cusumano 2014; Krahmann 2016). All three organizations are not yet prepared to hire contractors as peacekeepers or in combat roles, but the choice between private peacekeeping or no peacekeeping at all may lead to a change of mind in the not too far future, according to some analysts (Brooks 2000).

The negative and positive consequences of employing PMSCs to support military interventions are widely debated. PMSCs engaged in armed security provoke unsurprisingly the strongest controversies. When Blackwater employees killed 17 civilians and wounded 20 in a shootout at Nisour Square in Bagdad in 2007, the international community was shocked. Blackwater was only the most notorious company. Other PMSCs like Aegis, DynCorp, Triple Canopy, and EOD Technology were equally criticized for aggressive posturing, recklessness, and the indiscriminate use of weapons (Commission on Wartime Contracting 2011). The practice of hiring local security companies in countries that lack adequate regulation and oversight is a serious problem. Local firms in conflict regions frequently have links with militias and rebel groups, or they exploit and harass the civilian population (Krahmann 2016). On the other hand, PMSCs help to address manpower and capability shortfalls in military interventions. They act as force multipliers, allowing soldiers to focus on combat operations and they provide technical expertise and local knowledge that national armed forces may not have.

Mercenaries and combat PMSCs

In contrast to the wide variety of companies and functions known today, the early image of the industry was shaped by two combat corporations: Executive Outcomes and Sandline International. Showcases for the ability of these private military companies (PMCs) to conduct battalion- or even brigade-sized military operations were the civil wars in Angola and Sierra Leone during the 1990s. Executive Outcomes gained its reputation by successfully recapturing oil facilities from National Union for the Total Independence of Angola (UNITA) rebels at the behest of the Angolan government (Howe 1998). In Sierra Leone, the two companies helped to reinstall the ousted civilian government by training loyal militia forces and providing tactical support (Shearer 1998).

Despite international opposition to mercenary firms and the dissolution of Executive Outcomes and Sandline International around the turn of the millennium, PMCs and mercenaries have not disappeared. Two sets of clients shape the renewed demand for combat services. The first group are fragile or failed governments, such as in Mali, Nigeria, Libya, Sudan, Mozambique, and the Central African Republic. The motivations and conditions for the employment of private combat forces have not changed significantly since the civil wars in Angola and Sierra Leone. Drivers are weak national police and military structures, ethnic and religious divisions, and violent conflicts among local groups competing for political power (Branović 2011). In these contexts, PMCs can help to assert the authority of democratically elected governments and they can guard national resources and international businesses (Kinsey & Krieg 2021). Between 1990 and 2007, at least 28 failing or failed states have contracted PMCs for front-line functions, such as combat and military operations (2.7%), military assistance (17.4%), and operational support (16.6%) (Branović 2011, p. 26).

The other group of customers are autocratic or authoritarian regimes, notably Russia and the United Arab Emirates (UAE). These regimes hire mercenaries and PMCs not only to increase their military capabilities, but also because they offer plausible deniability, independence from national police and armed forces, fewer official military losses, combat experience, and international reach. Lack of manpower and confidentiality are major reasons for the oil-rich UAE with a population of only ten million, but the ambition to act as a regional power and a counterbalance to Iran and the Muslim Brotherhood. Already in the1990s, the UAE co-financed the training of the Bosnian armed forces by the American company MPRI. It also deployed PMCs in Yemen, Somalia, and Libya (Krieg 2022, p. 153). In 2015, the UAE thus reportedly dispatched a 1,800-member battalion to Yemen that had been assembled and trained by Blackwater-founder Eric Prince and his new company Reflex Responses (R2) (Hager & Mazzetti 2015).

For Russia, the main attraction appears to be the plausible deniability afforded by mercenaries and PMCs. While the 1,350,000-strong Russian military has significant weaknesses in structure, equipment, and motivation, the government has used mercenaries primarily to assist allied authoritarian regimes and pro-Russian forces in neighboring countries. The Russian Wagner Group was thus established in 2014 by Yevgeny Prigozhin, a businessman closely linked to President Putin, to fight with allies in Syria and to support pro-Russian militias in Ukraine. Following the Russian invasion in eastern Ukraine in 2022, at least 5,000 Wagner Group employees engaged in offensive military operations, progressing as far as Kyiv with alleged orders to assassinate the Ukrainian president Zelenskiy (BBC 2022). In addition, the group appears to have fought on the government's behalf in Sudan, Libya, and Mali. Since PMCs are illegal in Russia, most companies serving in military functions and operations are registered as defense or security firms, including the Wagner Group, RSB Group, Orel-Antiterror, MAR, Moran Security Group, Center-Redoubt, Feraks, Slavonic Corps Limited, and ENOT Corp. (Kokoshin 2018, p. 317). However, according to Østensen & Bukkvoll (2018, p. 3), the preceding companies "seem more ready for direct combat, more ideologically motivated (some of them) and less inclined to providing logistics and other support services than most Western PMSCs".

The track record of PMCs and mercenaries is problematic in both contexts. To pay for commercial combat forces, failed and failing states often sell rights to the exploitation of natural resources to governments or international corporations associated with these firms. Due to insufficient national regulations or the breakdown of the rule of law, they are also unable to curtail human rights violations by PMCs. Autocratic states not only exploit existing weaknesses in national and international laws, but also have a strong interest in maintaining a market where combat forces can operate secretly and with impunity. By sending PMSCs and mercenaries as support, they hope to create new alliances with non-democratic governments. These alliances can be strengthened by industry networks, such as the involvement of Erik Prince in the Chinese PMSC Frontier Services Group (Lu 2020, pp. 178–9). PMCs and mercenaries are rarely decisive for victory, but they can have negative effects on onset, duration, levels of violence, and compliance with international law (Akcinaroglu & Radziszewski 2013; Petersohn 2014, 2021).

Drones, cyber warfare, and hackers

It is the nature of business to seek new customers and functions to maximize turnovers and profits. Three developments have acted as motors of market expansion in the military and security service industry. First, competition among PMSCs has grown significantly since 1990s. Whereas a small number of American and British PMSCs dominated the market initially, it has since transformed into a global industry. Post-Cold War instability and multilateral military interventions have contributed to the creation of local and regional PMSCs in Europe, Asia, the Middle East, Africa, and Latin America. Second, the lack of success in Afghanistan, Iraq, and Libya has led to declining demand for commercial support for large-scale multilateral military interventions. National security strategies are instead shifting toward remote or hybrid forms of warfare. Third, technological innovations, such as automated weapons and drones, as well as the rise of cyberwarfare are creating new business opportunities. PMSCs not only adapt to these forces of supply and demand, but also play an active role in shaping them. They venture into new service sectors, offer new kinds of technologies and advertise at international military conventions. Two sectors specifically hold the promise of further growth and profits: automated weapons systems (AWS) and cybersecurity. Accordingly, there have been a growing number of mergers and collaborations between defense corporations, PMSCs, and cybersecurity firms.

Several factors make the provision and operation of AWS and cybersecurity particularly attractive for private businesses. Combining supply and services in package deals helps to guard a company's confidential knowhow and creates a dependence among clients that guarantees repeated contracts. AWS and cybersecurity also minimize the risk of physical harm and protect the civilian status of the operators. The ability to sell these technologies and services on both civilian and military markets reduces their price and makes them affordable to a wide range of state and non-state clients. Their utility for remote warfare is an added value for many military customers. AWS and cyberwarfare simultaneously disguise and protect the aggressor. Like PMSCs in general, both features also help to reduce public opposition to participation in military conflicts.

Due to the preceding factors, the extent of government contracting for automated weapons and cybersecurity is difficult to appraise. The US military has outsourced the piloting of drones and the analysis surveillance material since 2010 (Mahoney 2020, p. 9). It is estimated that contractors make up at least 10% of the staff employed to assess video material for US military and intelligence agencies (Mahoney 2020, p. 9). Due to manpower shortages, manufacturer employees regularly step in to fly weapon-capable drones for the US Navy and Air Force. However, US law prohibits civilians to make or execute decisions about the deployment of lethal weapons. PMSCs have operated surveillance drones for border controls by the EU's Frontex agency, and they have monitored rebel movements for the UN peacekeeping operation MONUSCO in the Democratic Republic of Congo.

Public information about the commercial provision of cybersecurity is equally limited. The available data is skewed toward the United States, creating the possibly misleading impression that American firms dominate the global market (Weiss 2022, p. 278). It is estimated that about 100 firms have the capabilities to shape international cyberwarfare, including defense contractors (e.g. Airbus, Northrop, Lockheed Martin, Raytheon, and Thales), cybersecurity firms (e.g. CrowdStrike, Endgame, FireEye, and Kaspersky), and PMSCs (e.g. G4S, the Constellis Group, CACI, CSC, Booz Allen Hamilton, and L3-Harris) (Swed & Burland 2021; Weiss 2022, p. 279). Private firms are only permitted to work in defensive cybersecurity functions according to US law. However, several US think tanks and commissions have proposed legalizing 'active' cyber defense involving access to external computer systems or networks to exploit vulnerabilities and diminish function (Broeders 2021, p. 1). In fact, it is believed that firms like Zerodium, Hacking Team, NSO Group, and Azimuth already carry out offensive operations (Weiss 2022, p. 276).

Hacker groups have emerged as another private actor in the field of cyberwarfare (Jopling 2018). Some of these groups are considered privateers or state proxies due to their close relationships with national intelligence and military agencies. It can be assumed that many hackers are at least partially motivated by profit, although nationalism or blackmail by government agencies may be supporting factors in their recruitment. An example is 'Cozy Bear', a Russian hacker group believed to be affiliated with the Russian Foreign Intelligence Service. The group has carried out cyberattacks against Western businesses and government agencies, including the US State Department, the White House, the Pentagon, the Dutch Ministry of General Affairs, and the Norwegian government. Additional targets are elections, media, public services, and critical infrastructure, such as energy supplies and air transport. The preceding groups can be distinguished from hacker communities with political motives, such as Anonymous, which has declared a 'cyber war' on Russia after its invasion of Eastern Ukraine in 2022.

Implications for the practice and theory of warfare

Despite their differences, the private actors outlined above share many implications for contemporary and future wars. This section outlines major political, military, and legal consequences before reflecting on several broader transformations in warfare.

The political decision to go to war is always difficult. Foremost, there is the cost of war to consider in terms of finance, military resources, reputation, and the lives of soldiers and civilians. In addition, politicians must assess the potential gains and the likelihood of success. Private military and security actors can influence these factors in ways that make decisions in favor of war easier. They can reduce the cost of war, especially if there is sufficient market competition and if clients avoid becoming dependent on selected providers. In particular, cyber capabilities are 'cheap and easy to acquire' commercially (Maurer & Hoffman 2019, p. 8). Private suppliers can also increase military capabilities and supply specialist expertise or combat experience. They can help to reduce losses among regular military personnel and, thus, public opposition to war. Private actors can deflect international sanctions by offering plausible deniability. Finally, they can enhance the likelihood of victory by acting as force multipliers.

The outsourcing of military functions can also come at political cost, including diminished democratic control, accountability, and legitimacy. Three decades of neoliberal privatization policies and enhanced regulation, however, have significantly curtailed public opposition to military and security contracting in Western democracies. Most democratic governments still rule out the employment of combat forces, but the dividing line between armed security and combat is increasingly blurred. Since autocratic regimes have discovered the many advantages of using PMSCs and mercenaries in combat operations, international demand is likely to increase in the future.

The military consequences of hiring PMSCs and other force multipliers are equally divers. The wars in Afghanistan, Iraq, Sierra Leone, and Angola have shown that PMSCs and mercenaries can quickly fill critical gaps in military capabilities, ranging from air transport, communication, and logistics to armed security and combat. Private military and security service providers also facilitate the implementation of new military strategies, such as hybrid and remote warfare. Private actors are particularly suited for hybrid conflicts because they grant plausible deniability. They additionally serve as a link between military and civilian technologies and sectors. By operating drones and providing cybersecurity far away from the battlefield, private actors also contribute to remote warfare. Both hybrid and remote warfare have the potential to alter the balance between offence and defense because they lower the cost of pre-emptive strikes.

In the long run, however, commercially motivated military and security providers have demonstrated a tendency to exploit excessive dependence on their services by inflating prices or lowering standards (Commission on Wartime Contracting 2011, pp. 75–80). PMSCs and mercenaries also have an incentive to extend war duration if they are not remunerated based on success (Akcinaroglu & Radziszewski 2013). Finally, their position outside the operational and legal structures of national armed forces often makes them difficult to control, increasing the potential for friendly fire or violence against civilians. PMSCs and mercenaries can thus impact negatively on the success and public acceptance of military operations.

The legal context fundamentally shapes the consequences of outsourcing warfare. However, contemporary national and international laws are fairly permissive. They are often limited to licensing requirements for domestic security firms and the general prohibition of mercenaries, whereas military and security service exports remain unregulated. Attempts to establish international legal standards, such as the *UN Draft of a possible Convention on Private Military and Security Companies (PMSCs)*, have failed due to opposition from major client states like the United States and the United Kingdom (UN 2010). Even the *First Additional Protocol to the Geneva Conventions* (ICRC 1977), which prohibits the hire of mercenaries since 1977, has had little effect on the industry because private military and security personnel usually fall outside its six cumulative criteria. The *Montreux Document* (2009) highlights that there are international laws applicable to PMSCs, but the document is not legally binding and has only been recognized by 61 signatories. Even weaker is the status of the *Tallinn Manual*. It is merely a "resource for legal advisers and policy experts dealing with cyber issues" (CCDCOE n.d.). Industry efforts to establish an international standard for PMSCs in the form of the *International Code of Conduct* (ICoC), controlled by the International Code of Conduct Association, are also voluntary. Even if it is accepted that existing international laws also pertain to commercial military and security service providers, they are difficult to apply because the privatization and hybridization of warfare undermines legal categories, such as the distinctions between combatants and non-combatants, and between offence and defense, as well as thresholds for the use of force and armed attacks.

In the current legal context, it is very difficult to hold international PMSCs and mercenaries accountable. The burden of prosecution normally falls to the state where a crime was committed, but war or weak institutions often curtail the ability to carry out due legal process in these countries. Even if a client state accepts the judicial responsibility for military and security contractors, effective prosecution regularly fails because of the difficulty of collecting evidence abroad or because the accused simply 'disappear' before they can be brought to justice. The conviction of Blackwater personnel for killing Iraqi civilians by an American court was a notable, but rare exception. In addition, covert military operations and new technologies that cause low levels of damage raise fundamental questions concerning the legal definition of war and national self-defense under international law (Maurer & Hoffman 2019, p. 10).

Beyond the practical consequences of hiring private actors in contemporary and future wars, the preceding developments necessitate new thinking about warfare. Two trends stand out that challenge analytical categories and theories of war. The first are the increasingly tenuous divisions between war and peace, and between war and crime. If classical military actors, weapons, and strategies of war are not only complemented, but also replaced by civilian and commercial ones, the question arises what we mean by war. The leading databases in the discipline, the Correlates of War project and the Uppsala Conflict Data Program, still define war as armed conflicts with a total of at least 1,000 battle-deaths during each year. Although militarized interstate disputes have been added as a category to capture conflicts "composed of incidents that range in intensity from threats to use force to actual combat short of war", the definition omits covert actions and non-official forces (Jones et al. 1996, pp. 163, 169). Private military and security service providers are excluded from these databases in several ways: (1) they are not part of national armed forces and are therefore not counted among official fatalities; (2) most of them do not engage in combat, but only enable and support combat missions; (3) they may operate (semi)independently from military command structures; and (4) they sometimes engage in clandestine or criminal missions. The preceding differences are reinforced by automated weapons and cyberwarfare because they often aim at civilian instead of military targets. It is thus increasingly common that private actors like PMSCs or hackers attack other private actors like energy firms, hospitals, or airports. In short, our understanding of war as a military enterprise and of national or subnational armed forces as its main actors reflects only a fraction of contemporary and future warfare.

The latter highlights another fundamental transformation: the (re)privatization of warfare. On the one hand, this development has been facilitated by states due to the perceived advantages of externalizing the cost of war. Private actors are not only hired to support or replace uniformed soldiers in warfare, but also responsibilized for their own security and protection from international attacks. Already in the Iraq War, the international intervention forces led by the US military no longer considered themselves responsible for protecting the civilian population after the Iraqi police and military had been dissolved. Similarly, ships attacked by pirates in the Gulf of Aden and businesses blackmailed by international hackers are told to protect themselves (Broeders 2021, p. 8). On the other hand, PMSCs, mercenaries, hackers, and ideologically motivated groups are using globalization and digitalization for their own purposes. The future of war is thus likely to be characterized by an ever-growing range of non-state actors with their own motives, interests, and weapons. Some speak of the 'democratization' of war in the sense that private and civilian actors are taking international security and conflicts into their own hands. However, democracy has little to do with it because their actions are not based on political decisions. The rise of private military and security actors rather leads to an expansion of warfare from the military and political spheres to economic and social domains.

Elke Krahmann

References

Akcinaroglu, S & Radziszewski, E 2013, 'Private Military Companies, Opportunities, and Termination of Civil Wars in Africa', *Journal of Conflict Resolution,* vol. 57, no. 5, pp. 795–821, https://doi.org/10.1177/0022002712449325.

Avant, D 2005, *The Market for Force: The Consequences of Privatizing Security,* Cambridge University Press, Cambridge, https://doi.org/10.1177/0022002712449325.

Berndtsson, J 2014, 'Realizing the 'Market-State'? Military Transformation and Security Outsourcing in Sweden', *International Journal,* vol. 69, no. 4, pp. 542–58, https://doi.org/10.1177/0020702014542813.

Branović, Ž 2011, 'The Privatisation of Security in Failing States: A Quantitative Assessment', *Geneva Centre for the Democratic Control of Armed Forces (DCAF) Occasional Paper,* no. 24, DCAF, Geneva.

Broeders, D 2021, 'Private Active Cyber Defense and (international) Cyber Security - Pushing the Line?', *Journal of Cybersecurity,* vol. 7, no. 1, pp. 1–14, https://doi.org/doi:10.1093/cybsec/tyab010.

Brooks, D 2000, 'Messiahs or Mercenaries? The Future of International Military Services', *International Peacekeeping,* vol. 7, no. 4, pp. 129–44, https://doi.org/doi:10.1080/13533310008413867.

Bureš, O 2015, *Private Security Companies: Transforming Politics and Security in the Czech Republic,* Palgrave Macmillan, Basingstoke.

CCDCOE n.d., 'The Tallinn Manual', *NATO Cooperative Cyber Defence Centre of Excellence,* <https://ccdcoe.org/research/tallinn-manual/> (accessed 20 November 2022).

Commission on Wartime Contracting 2011, *Transforming Wartime Contracting: Controlling Cost and Reducing Risks,* Commission on Wartime Contracting in Iraq and Afghanistan, Final Report to Congress, Arlington, <https://www.hsdl.org/?abstract&did=685405> (accessed 20 November 2022).

Ghiselli, A 2020, 'Market Opportunities and Political Responsibilities: The Difficult Development of Chinese Private Security Companies Abroad', *Armed Forces & Society,* vol. 46, no. 1, pp. 25–45, https://doi.org/10.1177/0095327X18806517.

Giumelli, F & Cusumano, E 2014, 'Normative Power Under Contract? Commercial Support to European Crisis Management Operations', *International Peacekeeping,* vol. 21, no. 1, pp. 37–55, https://doi.org/10.1080/13533312.2014.885709.

Hager, E B & Mazzetti, M 2015, 'Emirates Secretly Sends Colombian Mercenaries to Yemen Fight', *New York Times,* 26 November, <https://www.nytimes.com/2015/11/26/world/middleeast/emirates-secretly-sends-colombian-mercenaries-to-fight-in-yemen.html> (accessed 20 November 2022).

Howe, H M 1998, 'Private Security Forces and African Stability: The Case of Executive Outcomes', *Journal of Modern African Studies,* vol. 36, no. 2, pp. 307–31, https://doi.org/10.1017/S0022278X98002778.

ICRC 1977, *Protocol Additional to the Geneva Conventions of 12 August 1949, and Relating to the Protection of Victims of International Armed Conflicts (Protocol I),* International Committee of the Red Cross, Geneva, <https://ihl-databases.icrc.org/applic/ihl/ihl.nsf/INTRO/470?OpenDocument> (accessed 20 November 2022).

ICRC 2009a, *The Montreux Document on Pertinent International Legal Obligations and Good Practices for States Related to Operations of Private Military and Security Companies During Armed Conflict,* ICRC, Geneva, <https://www.icrc.org/eng/assets/files/other/icrc_002_0996.pdf> (accessed 20 November 2022).

ICRC 2009b, *Interpretive Guidance on the Notion of Direct Participation in Hostilities Under International Humanitarian Law,* ICRC, Geneva, <http://www.icrc.org/eng/assets/files/other/icrc_002_0990.pdf> (accessed 20 November 2022).

Jones, D M, Bremer, S & Singer, J D 1996, 'Militarized Disputes, 1816–1992: Rationale, Coding Rules and Empirical Patterns', *Conflict Management and Peace Science,* vol. 15, no. 2, pp. 163–212, https://doi.org/10.1177/073889429601500203.

Jopling, L 2018, *Countering Russia's Hybrid Threats: An Update,* NATO Parliamentary Assembly Special Report 166 CDS 18, Brussels, <https://www.nato-pa.int/document/2018-countering-russias-hybrid-threats-jopling-report-166-cds-18-e> (accessed 20 November 2022).

Kinsey, C 2009, *Private Contractors and the Reconstruction of Iraq,* Routledge, London.

Kinsey, C & Krieg, A 2021, 'Assembling a Force to Defeat Boko Haram: How Nigeria Integrated the Market into its Counterinsurgency Strategy', *Defense & Security Analysis,* vol. 37, no. 2, pp. 232–49, https://doi.org/10.1080/14751798.2021.1919356.

Kokoshin, A A 2018, 'The 'Hybrid War' Phenomenon in the Coercive Component of Current World Politics', *Science and Society,* vol. 88, no. 5, pp. 313–19, https://doi.org/10.1134/S101933161805009X.

Krahmann, E 2010, *States, Citizens, and the Privatization of Security*, Cambridge University Press, Cambridge.

Krahmann, E 2016, 'NATO Contracting in Afghanistan: The Problem of Principal-Agent Networks', *International Affairs,* vol. 92, no. 6, pp. 1401–26, https://doi.org/10.1111/1468-2346.12753.

Krahmann, E & Prem, B 2017, 'Private Security and Military Actors', in RA Denemark & R Marlin-Bennett (eds), *International Studies Encyclopedia,* Blackwell, Oxford, https://doi.org/10.1093/acrefore/9780190846626.013.279

Krieg, A 2022, 'The UAE's 'Dogs of War': Boosting a Small State's Regional Power Projection', *Small Wars & Insurgencies*, vol. 33, no. 1–2, pp. 152–72, https://doi.org/10.1080/09592318.2021.1951432.

Leander, A (ed) 2013, *Commercialising Security in Europe: Political Consequences for Peace Operations,* Routledge, London.

Liss, C 2020, 'Non-State Actors in the Maritime Domain: Non-State Responses to Maritime Security Challenges', in L Otto (ed), *Global Challenges in Maritime Security. An Introduction,* Springer, Cham, pp. 211–28.

Lu, Z 2020, 'A Bridge Too Far: China's Overseas Security and Private Military and Security Companies', *China: An International Journal*, vol. 18, no. 3, pp. 169–81, https://doi.org/10.1353/chn.2020.0035.

Mahoney, C W 2020, 'United States Defense Contractors and the Future of Military Operations', *Defense & Security Analysis*, vol. 36, no. 2, pp. 180–200, https://doi.org/10.1080/14751798.2020.1750182.

Mandel, R 2002, *Armies Without States: The Privatization of Security*, Lynne Rienner, Boulder, CO.

Masuhr, N & Friedrich, J 2020, 'Mercenaries in the Service of Authoritarian States', *CSS Analyses in Security Policy,* no. 274, November, ETH/CSS, Zurich, https://doi.org/10.3929/ethz-b-000448842.

Maurer, T 2018, *Cyber Mercenaries: The State, Hackers, and Power*, Cambridge University Press, Cambridge.

Maurer, T & Hoffman, W 2019, *The Privatization of Security and the Market for Cyber Tools and Services*, Business and Security Series no. 3, DCAF Geneva Centre for Security Governance, Geneva.

Østensen, Å G 2013, 'In the Business of Peace: The Political Influence of Private Military and Security Companies on UN Peacekeeping', *International Peacekeeping*, vol. 20, no. 1, pp. 33–47, https://doi.org/10.1080/13533312.2012.761872.

Østensen, Å G & Bukkvoll, T 2018, *Russian Use of Private Military and Security Companies – the Implications for European and Norwegian Security,* FFI-RAPPORT 18/01300, Norwegian Defence Research Establishment (FFI), Kjeller.

Petersohn, U 2014, 'The Impact of Mercenaries and Private Military and Security Companies on Civil War Severity Between 1946 and 2002', *International Interactions,* vol. 40, no. 2, pp. 191–215, https://doi.org/10.1080/03050629.2014.880699.

Petersohn, U 2021, 'Onset of New Business? Private Military and Security Companies and Conflict Onset in Latin America, Africa, and Southeast Asia from 1990 to 2011', *Small Wars and Insurgencies*, vol. 32, no. 8, pp. 1362–93, https://doi.org/10.1080/09592318.2020.1866404.

Pingeot, L 2012, *Dangerous Partnership. Private Military & Security Companies and the UN*, Global Policy Forum and Rosa Luxembourg Foundation, New York, <https://reliefweb.int/report/world/dangerous-partnership-private-military-and-security-companies-and-un> (accessed 25 November 2022).

Pingeot, L 2014, *Contracting Insecurity: Private Military and Security Companies and the Future of the United Nations,* Global Policy Forum and Rosa Luxemburg Foundation, New York, <https://www.business-humanrights.org/sites/default/files/media/gpf-dangerous-partnership-full-report-jun-2012.pdf> (accessed 20 November 2022).

Schwartz, M 2010, *Department of Defense Contractors in Iraq and Afghanistan: Background and Analysis,* Congressional Research Service (CRS) Report for Congress, Washington DC, <https://apps.dtic.mil/dtic/tr/fulltext/u2/a524085.pdf> (accessed 20 November 2022).

Shearer, D 1998, *Private Armies and Military Intervention*, Oxford University Press, Oxford.

Singer, P W 2003, *Corporate Warriors: The Rise of the Privatized Military Industry*, Cornell University Press, Ithaca, NY.

Spearin, C 2014, 'Canada and Contracted War: Afghanistan and Beyond', *International Journal: Canada's Journal of Global Policy Analysis*, vol. 69, no. 4, pp. 525–41, https://doi.org/10.1177/0020702014546703.

Stanger, A 2011, *One Nation Under Contract: The Outsourcing of American Power and the Future Foreign Policy,* Yale University Press, New Haven, CT.

Swed, O & Burland, D 2021, *Cyber Mercenaries: Review of the Cyber and Intelligence PMSC Market*, Report of the working group on the use of mercenaries as a means of violating human rights and impeding the exercise of the rights of peoples to self-determination, <https://www.researchgate.net/

publication/355469898_Cyber_Mercenaries_Review_of_the_Cyber_and_Intelligence_PMSC_Market> (accessed 20 November 2022).

UN 2010, *Draft of a Possible Convention on Private Military and Security Companies (PMSCs) for Consideration and Action by the Human Rights Council*, Annex to the report of the working group on the use of mercenaries as a means of violating human rights and impeding the exercise of the right of peoples to self-determination, A/HRC/15/25, United Nations, <https://www2.ohchr.org/english/issues/mercenaries/docs/A.HRC.15.25.pdf> (accessed 20 November 2022).

Weiss, M 2022, 'The Rise of Cybersecurity Warriors?', *Small Wars & Insurgencies*, vol. 33, no. 1–2, pp. 272–93, https://doi.org/10.1080/09592318.2021.1976574.

12

TERRORISM

The Never-Changing Chameleon

Anastasia Filippidou

Introduction

The presence of terrorism has remained constant over the years, but in the modern era, its methods have shifted from promulgating ignored grievances onto the international arena to direct large-scale attacks on the national security of powerful states. Depending on access to resources, capability, as well as quantity and quality of membership, terrorism can oscillate between an exceptional irritant to a national and international trauma. Owing to the plethora of means and narratives, what in the past could have been minimised as an unlikely incredibility, now it can demand to be taken seriously and demands to be prepared for it accordingly. Numerous challenges render the prediction of future terrorism difficult, including identifying and selecting real indicators of change amid the clamour of conflicting signals and indicators, deciding how to interpret public pronouncements, addressing the logic of the situation and appreciating the choices to be made and accepting their consequences. This matters because states often become, especially at the beginning of terrorist campaigns, the helpless witnesses to the consequences of their own policies, and it is often late in the day when states see with any clarity the nature of their choices.

With reference to the fundamentals of terrorism, inequality, injustice and interests fuel and will continue to nourish perceived and real grievances that terrorists may hijack to garner support to achieve their goals. Regarding the means of terrorism, depending on accessibility and reliability, terrorists and violent extremists will continue to use anything they can get their hands on. This may vary from something as basic as a knife to access to the latest technological advances, like biotechnology and augmented reality, which in turn provides them with new opportunities to continue their work. Additionally, the risk is not of defeating a major power but the realisation of a new type of vulnerability. The 9/11 attacks, for instance, created a reality of a future war that was different from anything that had happened before.

A plethora of competing realities precludes the adoption of a commonly agreed definition of terrorism, and as a generally accepted fact, it is not a preoccupation of this chapter. Schmid et al. (2011) in the *Routledge Handbook of Terrorism Research* provide an account on the definitional challenges of terrorism. This chapter explores the future of terrorism and it does so by focusing on the paradoxical duality of the phenomenon of terrorism, which is its consistency and at the same time its chameleonic nature. The constant element refers to the causes and fundamentals

DOI: 10.4324/9781003299011-15

of terrorism, and the changing character concentrates on the means and tactics of terrorism. The chapter then focuses on the consequences and implications of this duality on future terrorism and concludes with the provision of a model of future trends.

The constancy of terrorism: causes and fundamentals

Future terrorism has a revealing past but if everything flows and the world is but a series of constant transformations, making it impossible, as Heraclitus argued, to step into the same river twice, then looking at the past to predict the future can only give a partial picture that may lead to a false certainty when dealing with a complex phenomenon like terrorism. Arendt (1970, p. 6) posits that predictions are never anything but projections of present automatic processes and procedures, that is of occurrences that are likely to come to pass if people do not act and if nothing unexpected happens. Thus, any action, purposeful or accidental, would disrupt these processes and procedures within whose frame the prediction moves and where it finds its evidence.

Terrorism as a phenomenon has been linked to vagueness, opacity and discord, as it has been associated either with the ultimate sacrifice or with a heinous crime, all depending on the eyes of the beholder. Terrorism is motivated by causes that are considered as just by the perpetrators and it is expressed through violence and destructive means. Inasmuch as terrorists consider their causes just then any means to achieve these are considered justifiable. The just cause gives them their constancy, while the means to achieve that just cause will be anything they can get their hands on, which gives them their adaptability and chameleonic nature. For terrorists, one thing worse than taking their chance and failing is failing to take the chance. The above makes impossible an exhaustive list of causes of terrorism, which in turns makes it a Herculean task to accurately predict terrorism.

Previous models and types of future terrorism have been replaced by blurred concepts and a range of speculative possibilities. Demographic pressures, environmental degradation, resource accessibility, along with conflicting ideologies, ethnonational aspirations and interpretations of religion are not new, but the scale and impact are idiosyncratic of current situations and future trends. The intensity and effects of these phenomena are going to be experienced unevenly across different regions and countries, further accelerating causes for conflict and straining counterterrorism efforts.

Unlike conventional armies and insurgents, terrorists do not need to hold territory. Their priority is to make others pay attention and to try and gain time and notional space, allowing them to secure support and means while their opponent is drained of patience and credibility. Paraphrasing Fanon (1961, Chapter 1), terrorism is not a rational confrontation of points of view, but the untidy affirmation of an original ideal propounded as an absolute. Another constancy is that the conflicting parties, obedient to the rules of Aristotelian logic, they both follow the principle of reciprocal exclusivity. The contradictions continue, as despite terrorism's destructive nature, it is a source of solidarity and act of socialisation for the members of terrorist organisations. In their perception and thence reality, it is their altruism and commitment to a cause that leads them down the pathway of radicalisation and engagement. These characteristics help make terrorism a lasting mode of asymmetric warfare. Thus, regarding the phenomenon of terrorism, there is no transformational discontinuity; it is its modus operandi that changes.

The chameleonic nature of terrorism: the means and tactics

Interlinked and interdependent reasons that are internal and external to terrorist groups constantly force organisations to adapt the way in which they operate. Internal motives include low retention of membership and loss of access to resources, while external reasons refer to the broader context within which a specific organisation is operating. Hezbollah's leaders, for instance, described their movement as a cross between an army, a guerrilla and a socio-political force, and believed they developed a new organisational model (Hoffman 2009, p. 1; Filippidou 2020). Ethnonationalist separatist terrorism, for instance, had to adjust its *modus operandi* over the recent years. Different internal and external reasons explain this shift, including successful countermeasures, failure to achieve the endgame leading to loss of members and support, but also the decision of independentist organisations to distance themselves from existentialist terrorist groups that were on the rise since 9/11. The realisation of the support base of separatist organisations in the 21st century around the world is that these organisations cannot bomb their way to independence, and thus use of violence would backfire. Otherwise, any short-term benefits would be contradicted by a bitter legacy and popular desire for revenge, which in turn would make political gains non-viable (Kalyvas 2006, p. 388). Hence, unsurprisingly in the wake of 9/11 separatist organisations, such as ETA (Basque country and Fatherland) in Spain and FLNC (National Liberation Front of Corsica) in France, declared permanent ceasefires confirming their transition to peaceful politics. Although separatist violence is in decline, the presence and participation of nationalists and separatists in their regional parliaments are on the increase, which is the case for the Basque Parliament, as well as the Corsican and Northern Ireland Assemblies.

The intent, endgame and access to resources often dictate the weapon of choice of terrorists, which in turn defines the type of the organisation. Weapons of mass destruction and mass casualties have not yet been adopted as weapons of choice for most of the organisations. Jenkins's (1975) aphorism that terrorists want "a lot of people watching, not a lot of people dead" holds true to this day in most cases of terrorism, apart from the existential ones. The choice of weapons will also depend on the threshold of tolerance of violence, the accessibility to necessary materials and the organisation's know-how. If the chosen weapons and their effects exceed the organisation's and its supporters' threshold of tolerance, then this will backfire. Moreover, the choice of weapon will attract commensurate countermeasures, which is, however, something a terrorist organisation wants to avoid.

Practical constraints prohibit terrorists getting hold of certain weapons. In the early 1990s, emphasis was laid on the threat of a nuclear terrorist attack. Even if sufficient fissionable material and knowledgeable engineers could be acquired, the risks for anyone trying to construct nuclear weapons would be very high. Terrorist organisations, apart from existential ones, will mainly try and operate in a grey zone, where the act is kept deliberately below the threshold of tolerance of violence that otherwise would cause the full wrath of a state, with all the possible security consequences.

Trends of terrorism: the 5Ds of future terrorism

Trends in terrorism mirror the broader contemporary national and international threats and crises, which is reflected in the plethora of terrorist typologies. Hobbes's *bellum omnium contra omnes* appears more current than ever. From energy and resources to religious inspired terrorism, and everything in between, is considered a critical vulnerability and threat. The motivation and causes of terrorism are generated by any agenda and narrative that happens to be adopted by the first social agent to represent a viable need. Terrorism as a phenomenon resembles what Scroggins (2004, p. 427) characterises as "a violent ecosystem capable of generating endless new things to fight about without ever shedding any of the old ones". Thus, Rapoport's framework revisited in *Waves of Global Terrorism* (Rapoport 2022), with all its unavoidable challenges decades after its inception, remains valid.

Global Terrorism Database (GTD 2022) shows a 1% decrease in the number of attacks and a 12% increase in terrorism deaths globally. The GTD, however, cannot provide a definitive answer to the question if terrorism has increased or decreased. Even if the number of deaths is decreasing, the overall geographic footprint is increasing. Terrorism is concentrated in specific locations, such as Sub-Saharan Africa, Middle East and Asia (GTD 2022). However, these locations are diverse, ambiguously defined and have contextual factors associated with them regarding terrorism. In Europe, terrorism is characterised mostly by non-lethal attacks with the number of attacks exceeding the people killed. The Islamic State (IS) is in decline since 2019 after the fall of the so-called IS Caliphate territorial control and the deaths of its leaders: al-Baghdadi and al-Qurashi in 2019 and 2022 respectively. Al Qaeda (AQ) attacks are in the hundreds, but the organisation has been declining. AQ-related groups are not insignificant, but they are concentrated in specific locations, like Somalia (GTD 2022). The global financial crisis and the refugee emergency has led, among others, to the increase of a fragmented extreme right-wing terrorism (ERWT), with a membership of technologically savvy young men, often in their teens, self-indoctrinated and self-initiated terrorists (Intelligence and Security Committee of Parliament 2022, pp. 2–3).

Terrorist organisations aim to control natural resources in weak states to either influence politics or to enrich themselves, or both. Based on current trends, conditions such as state fragility marred by chronic poverty, population bulge, lack of development and instability are more accurate predictors of countries at higher risk for terrorist campaigns than are religious or ideological indicators. A range of factors is behind current and future terrorism, which can be summarised into 5Ds, that is development, deprivation, decision-making, depletion and demographics. These 5Ds are not sufficient individually to trigger a terrorist campaign, as these factors may overlap and coexist in different degrees. Moreover, these factors exist within the broader regional and international context.

Grievances, perceived or real, can develop as people find themselves with no access or control over natural resources. As Collier (2000) argues, opportunities for primary commodity predation cause conflict. The location of natural resources, such as oil fields, is a key factor in setting priorities for territorial control. In his sombre but accurate article, Kaplan (1994) argued that future wars will be those of communal survival, aggravated or caused by environmental scarcity and depletion. These conflicts would be subnational, making it hard for states and local governments to protect their own citizens. Terrorism in the West has declined by 68%, whilst Sub-Sahara Africa suffered 48% of global terrorist killings (GTI 2022). The Sahel, for instance, is identified as a "serious concern" (GTI 2022, p. 886) with deaths from terrorism in the region increasing by 1,000% since 2007. Simultaneously, the region is experiencing the high effects of climate change with scarce water and food insecurity, weak governance and high population movement, thus attracting the attention of the IS.

Silke and Morrison (2022) advocate the clear impact of climate change on terrorism trends. Lake Chad, for instance, has been reduced to a fraction of its original size since the 1960s. The decrease of the lake's size by 90% has led to the loss of local livelihood (UN 2018), which in turn led to a sharp increase in population movement to urban areas. Nigeria, Niger, Cameroon and Chad have been strongly affected by the shrinking of Lake Chad, with a direct link to the emergence of the terrorist group Boko Haram (Silke & Morrison 2022, p. 884). The prognosis of this type of organisations is that they are likely to last because these are low-intensity conflicts, and the organisations are impervious to a negotiated settlement and they also carry the risk of contagion into neighbouring countries (Walter 2017). The longevity of these organisations is not owed to their successes but to the failures of the affected states and the lack of interest and will of the international community to deal with these organisations effectively and efficiently.

Violence in countries experiencing severe inequalities and low, if any, development, facing disputes over access and control of natural resources, with youth with no hope and with not much else to do, is not new. What is different is the direct correlation of the above conditions with the presence of terrorist organisations. According to the UN Panel of Experts' report (UN 2021, p. 22), al-Shabaab, formed in 2005 out of the old Union of Islamic Courts, and which has evolved in its operations and sourcing finances, is in a healthy financial position and remains entrepreneurial in nature benefiting from illegal taxation and other forms of extortion. The organisation has been damaging the environment through illegal charcoal exports, engages in illegal gold exports, as well as extorts Somalis for money. The vulnerability of Somalia to climate change is projected to increase, owing to its heavy dependency on its natural resources. This, along with the human-made depletion of natural resources linked to charcoal production, has increased its vulnerability to drought and desertification, leading to a big reduction in food security (UN 2021, p. 21). Emphasising complexity, according to the Panel's report, al-Shabaab provides communities with protection from flooding, thus becoming a service provider to communities that otherwise receive little attention from the government.

ERWT environmentalism has surfaced as an "ideological agent for de-humanising those perceived to threaten racial purity" (Macklin 2022, p. 991). Even though these ideas are not new, the coincidence of crises such as energy, finance, refugee and migration and urbanisation warns that ERWT will continue to rise at different degrees. This was evidenced in 2019 in the attacks on mosques in Christchurch in New Zealand with 51 dead, and in the El Paso attack with 22 people killed. The attacker at Christchurch called his attack an act of environmental defence against overpopulation (Tarrant 2019, p. 29), while the attacker at El Paso blamed the impact of overpopulation and overconsumption, resource depletion and pollution for his acts (Crusius 2019, p. 3). Therefore, when a terrorist attack catches a state by surprise, this is not because these attacks are inconceivable, but rather because the relevant data of threat is not reaching the right ears, at the right time, in the right way.

Adding to the complexity of the phenomenon of terrorism is that it can be opportunistic and a response to a situation rather than a pre-organised and well-thought political endeavour. Where there is instability and conducive political and economic opportunities, a terrorist group may form. Collier (2016) argues that greed and loot are more important than grievance and justice in explaining the incidence of violent conflicts. In turn, this brings the control of and access to natural resources to the epicentre (Kalyvas 2008, p. 351). Although opportunities for gain and loot can facilitate recruitment, this does not translate into deep ideological commitment to the cause and loyalty to the organisation, evidenced in the existence of a plethora of organisations with limited impact.

The longer a terrorist organisation survives, the more difficult it becomes to separate its fight for ideology from its fight for profit. This became obvious with the now demobilised FARC (Revolutionary Armed Forces of Colombia) who had long financed their struggle against the Colombian establishment through kidnapping, extortion and participation in the drug trade (InSight Crime 2022). The FARC had to abandon kidnappings in 2012 as a precondition to inclusive negotiations with the Colombian government (Filippidou & O'Brien 2020). Nevertheless, this loss of income was recovered by getting more involved in illegal gold mining. For 2015–2016, which is the last period the FARC were active, if all the criminal economies are added, the organisation is estimated to have earned \$580 million (InSight Crime 2022).

Nonetheless, there are strings attached even to loot. In poorer environments, members of organisations must accept a lengthy struggle before they can expect any profit, and this only after their turn comes (Weinstein 2005). Most of the FARC's profits were used to cover operating expenses, but a big portion of the profits was pocketed by FARC commanders (InSight Crime 2022). In the end, this profiteering within the organisation led to the formation of splinter groups and the decline of the organisation as such. However, in this case, adding to the complexity of counterterrorism, winning is neither the endgame nor is it desirable. The *raison d'etre* of an organisation can be to just have the means to acquire legitimacy that it then can confer on actions, which otherwise would be punishable as mere crimes.

Even though there is a widespread assumption about global terrorism, geography still has a role to play. It is not always possible for technology to "trump terrain" (Porter 2015). Along with human-made barriers such as economic development, there are still natural barriers like mountain ranges and oceans that have an impact on accessibility and can limit or act as a shield of protection to terrorist organisations. Latin America is one of the most urbanised regions in the world with over 81% of its population living in cities (Statista 2022). Overall, urbanisation was considered a positive development, providing opportunities to people, bringing them out of poverty and promoting economic growth. However, there have been places where the rapid urbanisation put the environment under duress and put the citizens in a state of permanent competition over scarce resources without effective governance and with inadequate policing. This also created a fertile ground for political violence and terrorism, as a city is target rich, impact high, but limits the options of states' responses. Networked cities, where an attack can shut down transportation networks and city centres, give easy and quick access to media outlets and provide opportunities for financial gains, will always attract terrorists.

Additionally, with population movement forced by war or dire economic conditions, the displaced people tend to gather into cities, augmenting tensions as witnessed in Lebanon which as of 2020 became home to 1.5 million Syrian refugees of a total population of 4.4 million. All this in a country that according to the World Bank (2021) is experiencing one of the most severe economic crises worldwide since the 19th century. With its history of prolonged civil war and numerous conflicts, Lebanon is named by the World Bank a fragility, conflict and violence state with a growing wariness of potential triggers to violent extremism and social unrest (World Bank 2021). According to a US Army study, megacities are "the epicentres of human activity on the planet and, as such, they will generate most of the friction which compels future military intervention" (Harris et al. 2014). This and similar studies are nothing new, which raises the question of why megacities are still ineffective when facing a terrorist attack. The immediate response to the Manchester Arena attack in 2017, for instance, is criticised as a catalogue of multi-level failings, including security and medical provision at the Arena and shortcomings in emergency services' readiness and response (Manchester Arena Inquiry 2021, p. 15).

National and international responses to terrorism also dictate the shape of future terrorism. Successful counterterror measures and a transformation in security affairs may force terrorist groups to turn to more basic weapons and operations. Alternatively, inadequate counterterrorism can make terrorist organisations focus on high technology and cybersecurity, wherever possible. The attacks by lone actors and violent Islamist groups have been characterised by simplicity such as the use of knives and driving trucks into crowds. These basic weapons are difficult to detect, and without the need for a specialised know-how from the terrorists to make them work. Nonetheless, the above does not mean that terrorists' endgame comes closer to materialisation. The digital age has proven to be a great facilitator for recruitment, fundraising and planning attacks. Emerging technologies such as facial recognition, artificial intelligence and social media can make it harder for terrorist organisations to hide and sustain their campaigns. However, these technological advances also provide opportunities to terrorists, provided they can get hold of these (Parker & Sitter 2015).

Information warfare affects tangible and intangible aspects, as it is designed to disable systems dependent upon flows of information, and it also aims to influence ideas by interfering with the content of information. A strength of netwars is that it creates strong social ties and facilitates the promotion of a shared story, a narrative about terrorists' purpose and *modus operandi*, merging identity and ideology. Following that, the narrative unifies and gives meaning to events and thus shapes responses (Freedman 2017, p. 228). Thus, terrorists can cause as much damage and disruption with a laptop as they can with a physical attack. Digital technology is just a means, thus the point for them is to be able to link the damage caused to a political purpose and to persuade supporters and opponents. This is a challenge they are less successful with. However, throughout history, terrorist organisations have tried to use the latest technology available at the time to achieve their goals. Thus, the use of the latest technology by terrorists is a constancy, but the mode of technology changes constantly.

Hobbes's dictum on "the war of all against all" is reflected on both the ways and the character of terrorism, as there are numerous and varied terrorist organisations that claim to fight for the same cause. This in turn renders loyalty and commitment to an organisation nonbinding. Hence, states face a more fractious and impulsive type of terrorism making it more challenging to be constantly prepared for and to handle effectively. Freedman (2017, p. 196) argues, what led to increased Sunni support for the fight against AQ was not because of a shift in attitudes by the people, but a decision by some Sunni leaders to collaborate with the US military despite any distaste for the occupation.

Complexity and terrorism: taking advantage of the limits of complex systems

Future terrorism is difficult to predict as it depends on choices that have not been made yet and in uncertain circumstances and within a complex internal and external environment. Terrorists are becoming more skilful and flexible operationally looking even more at softer civilian targets with less protection, such as Boko Haram and the Chibok schoolgirls kidnapping in Nigeria. This is especially the case as harder targets like politicians and security services become better protected. Still, a terrorist organisation even if it dedicates great and systematic effort to control physically and psychologically the narrative, the situation and its members, it cannot maintain this control over all these different elements indefinitely and survive long term. Adding to the complexity is that terrorism in addition to the plethora of existent causes it may just occur because of aggressive and opportunistic actors. Thus, a terrorist attack may be a surprise because of a deceptive military operation, but also owing to a lack of a triggering crisis.

Even for terrorists, organisational performance relies on their ability to manage complex networks of interdependencies that are constantly evolving over time. These complex challenges refer to tangibles, for instance access to materiel, and intangibles, including members' commitment and loyalty. Managing this complex network determines the capacity of the organisation to sustain large-scale systemic failures, like the arrest of its leadership and the general decline of the organisation. Depending on the context, if a single tangible or intangible element, internal or external to the organisation, fails, it may cause a ripple effect and it may affect subsequent elements and therefore lead to a systemic failure. If, for instance, a cell of a terrorist organisation is compromised, this may lead to the decline or even collapse of the entire organisation. Additionally, if a specific element of an organisation is constantly targeted and is removed, everything attached to this element will also be affected and be removed, creating in this way a structural gap. Repeating this process in a strategic manner may lead to further disconnect, ultimately bringing the organisation to its knees. In the case for instance where the communications of a terrorist organisation are targeted, this will also affect among others its recruitment ability. In this regard, the effort could be to identify the specific affected element to avoid future repetition of the same pattern.

However, the said pattern is one out of many provided within a complex network, in which case the broader organisation is not affected but only the risk of experiencing the same pattern is. Furthermore, systemic failures in terrorist organisations are often due to mundane reasons and minor disturbances. The reason, for instance, for a terrorist organisation's low membership retention may just be generational. It is different to enter an organisation young and carefree and different for somebody with family obligations to remain in an organisation. Thus, when deciding on counterterrorism measures, it is necessary to identify and take into consideration network effects by controlling the way in which the different components and elements of a terrorist organisation interact.

On an individual level, a useful factor that can help identify future terrorism trends is the internal locus of control (Rotter 1954), which affects risk-taking behaviour. It is a personality attribute reflecting the degree to which terrorists perceive events to be under their control. This is in opposition to the external locus of control where people believe events to be under powerful others or under outside forces (Rotter 1954). Internal locus of control is a useful example of a generalised expectancy which applies to a wide variety of situations. Those with a high internal locus of control believe they have a significant personal control over their behaviour and are therefore more likely to assume responsibility for their decisions and their actions, and they tend to be less conforming and less obedient and more independent. Lopez-Garrido (2020) argues that people with an internal locus of control are better at resisting social pressure to conform or obey, because they take responsibility for their actions. This is reflected in terrorists' behaviour irrespective of organisational typology, and when it is combined with a belief in a perceived or real just cause, it is easy to understand why terrorism will remain an attractive approach for a percentage of the population.

Future Trends: 5Ds as a predictive model

Following from the above analysis, the chapter proposes a predictive model of future terrorism. The suggestion is that the combination of data on the 5D of development, deprivation, decision-making, depletion and demographics along with the proposed model below could help identify future terrorism trends. The model aims to identify countries and areas at a higher terrorism risk, depending on the degree and the extent of the existence of the 5Ds. It establishes how different components interact and can lead to terrorism. As mentioned earlier, these 5Ds are not sufficient by themselves to lead to terrorism, as these factors may overlap and coexist in different degrees and ways. Within this context, the 5Ds become a threat multiplier enabling and facilitating terrorism (Figure 12.1).

As highlighted by the GTD (2022), the different locations facing terrorism have contextual factors associated and these occur over time. Owing to the complexity of current threats and of terrorism, the relationship between the different factors is dynamic and the relationship between each component is particular to each situation. At times, the 5Ds may form a causal relationship, while in others, they act as a trigger. The complex interaction between terrorism and the 5Ds creates a vicious circle, as demonstrated in the model above. The presence of 5Ds will increase insecurity in the affected area, which in turn can aggravate natural disasters, creating a fertile ground for terrorist organisations. These can be dealt with through strategic and tactical measures at different levels and at different entry points, depicted in the model. Simultaneously, the different factors and

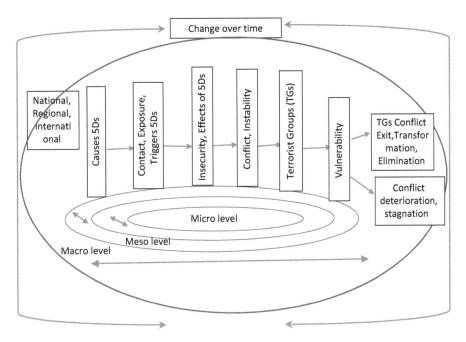

Figure 12.1 Predictive model of future terrorism.

relationships between all three levels of macro, meso and micro are all relevant when assessing terrorist threat. The causes, triggers, effects of the 5Ds and insecurity act as predisposition factors for terrorism. For this predisposition to lead to terrorism, an individual must be motivated for the cause to the point of joining an organisation. This in turn can lead to vulnerability. However, as Brown (2015) argues, vulnerability and insecurity are on the opposite ends, as insecurity is a debilitating awareness of one's limitations, while vulnerability is the ability to see one's potential for growth. Vulnerability happens when a person outgrows insecurity. This type of vulnerability can lead an individual to join a terrorist organisation. Additionally, the model provides entry opportunities, and the strategic and tactical counterterrorism entry points will vary depending on the specific situation and conditions.

Conclusion: terrorism's conditional future

The influences and factors examined in this chapter intersect in a complex manner making difficult solid and detailed predictions on the specifics of future terrorism. Predicting future terrorism may run the risk of giving voice to alarmism, in turn leading to unnecessary expenditure and ineffective countermeasures. The reality is that decision makers are defined and limited by their experiences and often miss what becomes obvious in hindsight. Then again, the types of future terrorism may also be dictated by the demands for political survival of governments. A terrorist organisation, for instance, operating in a distant region of a country might be ignored or get less attention, compared to a campaign in the country's major cities. Examining future trends of terrorism can validate Thucydides's (1980) idea that decision makers seem to be quite unique in the ability to consider the future as something more certain than what is before their eyes, and to see uncertainties as realities, simply because they would like them to be so.

It is unrealistic to expect an exhaustive list of causes in a complex phenomenon like terrorism. Thus, the 5Ds identified and discussed above should really be 5Ds plus one. The latter is necessary to accommodate Taleb's (2007) "black swan" of an unexpected event of magnitude and consequence with its dominant role in history. The chapter highlights that even though terrorist tactics constantly change, as a phenomenon, it remains constant. Terrorism, be it religiously inspired or extreme right wing, is a globally networked, merciless and willing threat, and as a multi-strand and multi-faceted phenomenon, there is a need for a fusion of means and measures to deal with it effectively.

Assuming there is opportunity and will, as discussed under the 5Ds, terrorism will remain a weapon of choice. If there is a perceived or real just cause, which gives terrorism constancy, and available forms of violence, which provide the chameleonic nature of terrorism, then there will always be place at different degrees for terrorist organisations. The exact mode of future terrorism would be speculative, but the hope is that still it will be sufficiently familiar to be manageable with the adoption of appropriate measures. Within this context, even though terrorism has ancient roots, it remains an emergent problem with complex systems and patterns arising out of a multiplicity of interactions. Future terrorist trends and means will include creative repetition, while states will need to avoid responses of non-creative repetition but focus on intentional adaptation, which is at the heart of emergent strategy and approaches.

References

Arendt, H 1970, *On Violence* Harcourt, New York.

Brown, B 2015, *Daring Greatly: How the Courage to Be Vulnerable Transforms the Way We Live, Love, Parent and Lead*, Penguin Life, London.

Collier, P 2000, 'Economic Causes of Civil Conflict and Their Implications for Policy', in C Crocker, F Hampson & P Aall (eds), *Managing Global Chaos*, United States Institute of Peace, Washington, DC, pp. 143–82.

Collier, P 2016, 'The Cultural Foundations of Economic Failure: A Conceptual Toolkit', *Journal of Economic Behavior & Organisation*, vol. 126, part B, pp. 5–24, https://doi.org/10.1016/j.jebo.2015.10.017.

Crusius, P 2019, *The Inconvenient Truth*, <https://randallpacker.com/wp-content/uploads/2019/08/The-Inconvenient-Truth.pdf> (accessed 10 August 2022).

Fanon, F 1961, *Les Damnés de la Terre* [Wretched of the Earth], Éditions François Maspéro, Paris.

Filippidou, A 2020, 'The Oxymoron of a Benevolent Authoritarian Leadership: The Case of Lebanon's Hezbollah and Hassan Nasrallah', *Terrorism and Political Violence*, vol. 34, no. 3, pp. 585–604, https://doi.org/10.1080/09546553.2020.1724967.

Filippidou, A & O'Brien, T 2020, 'Trust and Distrust in the Resolution of Protracted Social Conflicts: The Case of Colombia', *Behavioural Sciences of Terrorism and Political Aggression*, vol. 14, no. 1, pp. 1–21, https://doi.org/10.1080/19434472.2020.1785524.

Freedman, L 2017, *The Future of War: A History*, Allen Lane, London.

GTD 2022, 'A Look Back at 2020: Trends from the Global Terrorism Database', *Global Terrorism Database*, July, <https://www.start.umd.edu/look-back-2020-trends-global-terrorism-database-gtd> (accessed 5 November 2022).

GTI 2022, *Global Terrorism Index. Key Findings in 6 Charts*, <https://www.visionofhumanity.org/global-terrorism-index-2022-key-findings-in-6-charts/#:~:text=The%202022%20Global%20Terrorism%20Index, terrorism%20is%20becoming%20less%20lethal> (accessed 12 September 2022).

Harris, M, Dixon, R & Bailey, M 2014, 'Megacities and the United States Army', *Preparing for a Complex and Uncertain Future*, June, <https://www.semanticscholar.org/paper/Megacities-and-the-United-States-Army%3A-Preparing-a-Harris-Dixon/184ab2df1396c05105a4c9cb7f058173b2c6d4d> (accessed 13 August 2022).

Hoffman, F G 2009, 'Hybrid vs Compound War: The Janus Choice of Modern War: Defining Today's Multifaceted Conflict', *Armed Forces Journal*, 1 October, <http://armedforcesjournal.com/hybrid-vs-compound-war/> (accessed 1 November 2022).

Insight Crime 2022, *Colombia FARC*, <https://insightcrime.org/colombia-organized-crime-news/farc-profile accessed July 2022> (accessed 1 November 2022).

Intelligence and Security Committee of Parliament 2022, *Extreme Right-Wing Terrorism*, <https://isc. independent.gov.uk/wp-content/uploads/2022/07/E02710035-HCP-Extreme-Right-Wing-Terrorism_ Accessible.pdf> (accessed 1 November 2022).

Jenkins, B M 1975, *Will Terrorists Go Nuclear?*, RAND, Santa Monica, CA.

Kalyvas, S N 2006, *The Logic of Violence in Civil War*, Cambridge University Press, Cambridge.

Kalyvas, S N 2008, 'The New US Army/Marine Corps Counterinsurgency Field Manual as Political Science and Political Praxis', *Perspectives on Politics*, vol.6, no. 2, pp. 351–3, https://doi.org/10.1017/S1 537592708080675.

Lopez-Garrido, G 2020, 'Locus of Control: Definitions and Examples', *Simply Psychology*, 13 September, <www.simplypsychology.org/locus-of-control.html> (accessed 3 November 2022).

Macklin, G, 2022, 'The Extreme Right, Climate Change and Terrorism', *Terrorism and Political Violence*, vol. 34, no. 5, pp. 979–96, https://doi.org/10.1080/09546553.2022.2069928.

Manchester Arena Inquiry 2021, *Manchester Arena Inquiry, Volume 1: Security of the Arena*, <https://files. manchesterarenainquiry.org.uk/live/uploads/2021/06/17164904/CCS0321126370-002_MAI-Report-Volume-ONE_WebAccessible.pdf> (accessed 2 October 2022).

Parker, T & Sitter, N 2015, 'The Four Horsemen of Terrorism: It's Not Waves, It's Strains', *Terrorism and Political Violence*, vol. 28, no. 2, pp. 197–216, http://dx.doi.org/10.1080/09546553.2015.1112277.

Porter, P 2015, *The Global Village Myth: Distance, War, and the Limits of Power*, Hurst, London.

Rapoport, D C 2022, *Waves of Global Terrorism: From 1879 to the Present*, Columbia University Press, New York.

Rotter, J B 1954, *Social Learning and Clinical Psychology*, Prentice-Hall, New York.

Schmid, A P (ed) 2011, *The Routledge Handbook of Terrorism Research*, Routledge, London & New York.

Scroggins, D 2004, *Emma's War: Love, Betrayal and Death in the Sudan*, Vintage Books, New York.

Silke, A & Morrison, J 2022, 'Gathering Storm: An Introduction to the Special Issue on Climate Change and Terrorism', *Terrorism and Political Violence*, vol. 34, no. 5, pp. 883–93, https://doi.org/10.1080/095465 53.2022.2069444.

Statista 2022, *Latin America & Caribbean: Urbanisation from 2010 to 2020*, <https://www.statista.com/ statistics/699089/urbanization-in-latin-america-and-caribbean> (accessed 15 August 2022).

Taleb, N N 2007, *The Black Swan: The Impact of the Highly Improbable*, Allen Lane, London.

Tarrant, B 2019, *The Great Replacement*, <https://img-prod.ilfoglio.it/userUpload/The_Great_Replacement-convertito.pdf> (accessed 14 August 2022).

Thucydides 1980, *Ιστορία του Πελοποννησιακού Πολέμου* [History of the Peloponnesian War], ΕΣΤΙΑ, Athens.

UN 2018, 'The Tale of a Disappearing Lake', *UN Environment Programme*, <www.unep.org/news-and-stories/story/tale-disappearing-lake> (accessed 14 August 2022).

UN 2021, *The Final Report of the Panel of Experts (the Panel) on Somalia (S/2021/849)*, <https://frc.gov.so/ wp-content/uploads/2021/12/S_2021_849_E.pdf> (accessed 14 August 2022).

Walter, B 2017, 'The New New Civil Wars', *Annual Review of Political Science*, vol. 20, no. 1, pp. 469–86, https://doi.org/10.1146/annurev-polisci-060415-093921.

Weinstein, J M 2005, 'Resources and the Information Problem in Rebel Recruitment', *The Journal of Conflict Resolution*, vol. 49, no. 4, pp. 598–624, https://doi.org/10.1177/0022002705277802.

World Bank 2021, *Lebanon Sinking into One of the Most Severe Global Crises Episodes, Amidst Deliberate Inaction*, <https://www.worldbank.org/en/news/press-release/2021/05/01/lebanon-sinking-into-one-of-the-most-severe-global-crises-episode> (accessed 22 July 2022).

13

DETERRITORIALIZATION AND VIOLENT NETWORKS

Sebastian Kaempf

Introduction

Warfare – due to the political structure of the international system over the past centuries – has tended to be conducted by hierarchically organised military actors, ranging from empires and states to classical guerrillas and insurgents (van Creveld 1991; Kaldor 1999). Over the past two decades, however, a new breed of amorphous non-state military actors has started to emerge, which – at different points of their existence – have sought to compensate for their strategic inferiorities vis-à-vis conventional militaries by adapting a more horizontally organised, deterritorialised and networked nature and forms of operations.

While the need for militarily inferior actors to adapt is nothing new in the history of warfare, I argue that the contemporary manifestations of these dynamics afford us an early glimpse of what the future of warfare might hold regarding deterritorialisation and violent networks. First, the institutional organisation (from questions of membership to financing and decision-making) of non-state violent actors, such as al-Qaeda, the so-called Islamic State and Boko Haram, is increasingly mimicking the decentralised, networked logic of both the global economy and contemporary information technology. Second, their military operations (including kinetic and non-kinetic elements) are increasingly displaying a network logic, from communication strategies to recruitment and violent attacks taking place outside traditional chains of command.

In short, merely pointing to how this new breed of non-state military actors is exploiting novel and decentralised technologies such as blockchains, the darknet or encryption codes obfuscates the wider and more profound transformations that are taking place. Instead, I argue that we are witnessing the amorphous rise of military actors whose networked and horizontal structural advantage lies in their ability to more fundamentally disrupt the conventional military power of our times.

By making this argument, the chapter proceeds in the following way. Part one focuses specifically on the interactive dynamics of asymmetric warfare. Asymmetric constellations in warfare are inherently unstable as they require innovation on part of militarily inferior actors. In the course of the 19th and 20th centuries, these innovations manifested themselves in guerrillas, partisans and insurgents coming to successfully exploit factors such as space and time and combining defensive strategies alongside offensive tactics. This asymmetric form of warfare proved to be successful in disrupting the power of conventional armies of both empires and states, especially during anti-colonial struggles. Whereas counter-insurgents tended to hold the upper hand against insurgents in early 20th-century conflicts, by the end of the century, this balance has become reversed. Importantly for my argument in this chapter, though, is that the success brought about by these innovations occurred *in spite of* non-state armed groups displaying hierarchically organised structures.

Over the past 20 years, as I will show in parts two and three, it is with regard to the organisational structure of non-state armed groups where some of the most significant innovations have occurred. A number of non-state armed groups show early traces of a more horizontal, rather than hierarchical, structure which follows the decentralised, networked logic not dissimilar to other net-worked characteristics and elements of today's global system. In part four, this will be illustrated by looking at new networked forms of institutional organisation, recruitment and membership, financing, military operations and communication practices. Taken together, these innovations point to the emergence of a new breed of amorphous non-state military actors who seek to disrupt existing hierarchical power structures – and battlefield asymmetry – through their deterritorialised and networked nature.

The interactive dynamics of asymmetric warfare and innovation pressures

War, as Carl von Clausewitz famously defined it in his magnum opus *On War*, is the continuation of politics by other means (Clausewitz 1984, p. 75). It consists of two opponents who both have decided to use military means to seek to impose their will on their opponent. Clausewitz developed this understanding out of a realisation that, at the most basic level, war consists of interaction. It is never waged upon a passive object, but on another subject who reacts and responds, seeking to outdo the opponent in return:

> War is not an exercise of the will directed at inanimate matter, as is the case with the mechanical arts, or at matter which is animate but passive and yielding, as is the case with the human mind and emotions in the fine arts. In war, the will is directed at an animate object that reacts.
>
> (Clausewitz 1984, p. 149)

For Clausewitz, this interactive dynamic lies at the heart of war itself, leading him to compare war to a wrestling match: "War is nothing but a duel on a larger scale. Countless duels go to make up war, but a picture of it as a whole can be formed by imagining a pair of wrestlers" (Clausewitz 1984, p. 75). Key to his observation was that within a wrestling match, both wrestlers, by engaging with one another, take on positions, forms and shapes that each would not have been able to hold just by themselves.

Written at the time of major inter-state conflicts (in particular in the context of the 19th-century Napoleonic wars), considerable debate has emerged over the validity of his work in an age in which inter-state conflict has increasingly been displaced by war between state and non-state ac-tors. War today is less and less waged between two wrestlers who are alike in terms of their organisation, military capacity, strategy and tactics. Rather, the symmetry of conventional war has given way to asymmetric conflicts which are not waged between two similar wrestlers (i.e. states), but between – to continue drawing on his metaphors – a wrestler (state) and a dwarf (non-state actor). Post-Clausewitzeans have therefore charged that Clausewitz's relevance for today's age has diminished (van Creveld 1991; Enzensberger 1993), whereas neo-Clausewitzeans posit that his insights still ring true even in the age of asymmetric conflicts (Gray 1999; Strahan 2007).

Unfortunately, both sides in this debate have ignored the fact that Clausewitz's writings prior to *On War* not only have focused exclusively on asymmetric conflicts, but also that these early writings had laid many of the foundations for his own thinking about the interactive dynamic of war which then came to lie at the heart of *On War* (Kaempf 2011). In other words, had Clausewitz's widow not published *On War* posthumously and against his will, he only would have been known to us (if at all) as the first systematic theorist of modern asymmetric conflict.

Clausewitz's *Bekenntnisdenkschrift* ['Confession Memorandum'] (1812) and *Meine Vorlesungen ueber den Kleinen Krieg* ['My Lectures on Small Wars'] (1810/1811) resulted from his analyses of the non-state armed resistance against Napoleon (Vendee and the Iberian Peninsula). It is here that he observed how the interactive dynamics of asymmetric conflicts are inherently unstable as they impose pressure for considerable innovation on part of the militarily inferior actors. Their successes, he realised, lay in their ability to turn the inherent logic of state warfare on its head: instead of pursuing an offensive strategy paired with defensive tactics (as state militaries tend to do), guerrillas could prevail if they adopted a defensive strategy alongside offensive tactics (Clausewitz 1966a, 1966b).

The foundations laid in his earlier works formed the groundwork of his philosophical thinking we tend to associate with *On War* – even though only a short chapter in *On War* actually engages with asymmetric conflict (probably because he could not see guerrilla warfare as a self-standing from warfare). And yet, it is these insights that influenced the strategic development of the first self-standing theories of guerrilla warfare written and practiced by T E Lawrence and Mao Zedong (Heuser 2002; Kaempf 2011).

Both Lawrence and Mao inherently understood that in order to prevail in an asymmetric wrestling match, innovation required guerrillas to turn the logic of symmetric state warfare on its head. With state militaries pursuing offensive strategies and defensive tactics (i.e. seeking confrontation and decisive victories), guerrillas had to operate in an overall defensive mode while pursuing offensive tactics (i.e. avoiding full-on confrontations and applying hit-and-run strategies on the margins). With state armies needing to win a war through the elimination or – at the minimum – through the military defeat of their opponent's armed forces, guerrillas could win by not being defeated. In other words, exploiting the factors of space and time became seen as the core recipe for success for guerrilla warfare (Lawrence 1962; Mao 1992).

It is this constellation between Clausewitz's analysis of asymmetric conflict and Lawrence's and Mao's ability to put them into practice and to develop them further in their writings that formed the basis of the successes of non-state armed forces against state actors during the 20th century. It demonstrated the ability of non-state armed groups to disrupt the power of conventional armies of both empires and states, from the age of decolonisation all the way to more recent forms of insurgencies. The success brought about by these innovations has been tremendous: whereas counterinsurgents tended to hold the upper hand against insurgents in early 20th-century conflict, by the end of the 20th century, this balance has become reversed (Atran, Sheikh & Gomez 2014). Importantly though, the success brought about by these innovations occurred *in spite of* non-state armed groups displaying hierarchically organised structures. What we are witnessing more recently, however, is further innovation on part of non-state violent actors who increasingly started adapting the logics of networks and deterritorialisation.

The rise of networks

To understand the rise and strength of violent networks, we need to understand them in the broader context of how the rise of networks per se has been disrupting traditional state power in international politics in recent years. State power is hierarchically structured and institutionalised – the result of sovereign states emerging and consolidating over time to become the main power brokers in the international system (Tilly 1975).

Networks, of course, display the exact opposite characteristics from states: decentralised and horizontal. And even though networked actors are nothing new in international politics (see the Order of the Knight Templars, the Hanseatic League or the Rothschild banks), they were not able to substantially rival, let alone disrupt state power (Owen 2015). It is this power balance that is undergoing significant changes today as advances in digital information technology have radically lowered the barrier of entry to collective action, have vastly increased the importance of networks and have enabled different forms of organisation and behaviour compared to what was possible for non-digital networks (Castells 2000; Shirky 2008; Blenker 2011). What this means, according to Anne-Marie Slaughter, is that states, with their traditional forms of hi-erarchy and control, are beginning to lose out to self-organising networks (Slaughter 2009, pp. 94–113).

The point I am making here is threefold. First, the core features that make networked actors powerful are that their power runs counter to traditional features of power. As Taylor Owen demonstrates in his seminal study on *Disruptive Power*, the characteristics that "once made states weak – a lack of structure, instability, decentralized governance, loose and evolving ties – are precisely what makes [networked] groups [...] powerful" (Owen 2015, p. 38). Networked actors are disrupting traditional state power because they are formless, unstable and collaborative.

Second, early prominent examples of the disruptive power of networks can be found in actors ranging from Anonymous, Bitcoin, Wikileaks all the way to the Arab Spring. These digitally ena-bled actors all gain their power because of, rather than in spite of, their non-hierarchical nature. They tend to be formless, i.e. they are operating under different ideas of conventional leadership and what it means to be a member; they defy the very boundaries that encumber traditional in-stitutions; their communication tends to be highly decentralised; and they are oftentimes loosely connected. They thrive on instability, uncertainty and confusion. And their networked structure enables them to interact and collaborate according to what Yochai Benkler calls 'ad hoc volunteer-ism' (Blenker 2011).

Third, the rise of networks and their disruptive potential is not confined to only a few areas or forms of politics. Rather, it impacts on most, if not all aspects of international politics, including warfare. What we can see – and what will follow in the final section – is the beginning of the rise of non-state violent networks, a development that is testament to significant innovation on part of terrorist organisation, resistance fighters and insurgents.

The networked dimension of non-state armed groups

Before outlining the innovation regarding the networked nature, networked nature that we can already witness amongst some non-state violent groups today, an important qualification is needed first. Whereas some non-violent civil society actors like Bitcoin or Anonymous are already quin-tessentially networked actors, we are yet to see the emergence of an equivalent type of (non)state military actor who operates purely and exclusively in form of a network. Neither al-Qaeda 2.0 nor the so-called 'Islamic State' are purely networked actors. Having said this, what we can detect over the course of the past 20 years or so is a growing incorporation and adaption of networked elements and characteristics by non-state violent groups – as they see the disruptive potential vis-à-vis their (state) military opponents. It is this beginning of an innovative adaption on part of these actors which allows us to get a glimpse of what the future of warfare might hold. A future where guerrillas, terrorist organisations and insurgents – in response to the military asymmetries they are facing – will steadily strip themselves further of their traditionally hierarchical forms of organisation and increasingly operate according to networked logics.

This innovation has been closely connected to the ways in which digital communications technology has empowered non-state armed groups vis-à-vis states. Until the emergence of digital media technology in the early 2000s, most state-of-the-art media technology had tended – at first – to predominantly favour empires and states, not non-state military actors. For example, the invention of the telegraph in 1794, radio airwaves in the 1890s, television in 1927 or the first version of the Internet constituted media platforms that – because of their infrastructural nature, costs, maintenance and need for large numbers of highly-specialised professionals – could, at the time of their inception, only be afforded by a small number of rich and politically powerful actors, such as empires, states, the church and media conglomerates (Rid & Hecker 2009; Kaempf 2013). Non-state actors simply lacked the capacities to build, let alone maintain and operate, such vast and costly media platforms. On occasion and only with a significant delay, trickle-down effects would make some of these media technologies affordable to non-state actors (such as the printing press or radio technology), but only with delays.

This pattern meant that with each new media platform innovation between the 19th and 20th centuries, state actors have tended to sustain an asymmetric structural advantage over non-state actors regarding their capability to mass-mediatise their wars. The innovations in media technology have thereby tended to retain if not even widen the corridor of action for states more than they did for irregular forces or rebels (Rid & Hecker 2009, pp. 125–41).

This discrepancy furthermore meant, as Thomas Rid and Marc Hecker have shown, that non-state actors for most of the 19th and early 20th centuries perceived the empire's and state's communication facilities as a military target that could be physically attacked to weaken the armies of states and empires (for instance, by cutting down telegraph masts as could be seen by Arab rebels during World War I). Thus, being unable to afford and use such cutting-edge technology themselves, non-state armed groups tended to target and destroy such communications technology (Rid & Hecker 2009, pp. 1–13).

Alternatively, following the World War II, irregulars slowly but successfully began using and manipulating state-owned or state-controlled mass media outlets as a weapon to attack the moral support and cohesion of opposing political entities (see, for instance, the way in which the North Vietnamese used US television channels to relay images of the 1968 Tet Offensive; the events around Black Hawk Down in Somalia in 1994; or al-Qaeda on 9/11). So here we see an evolution in strategic thinking amongst non-state armed groups: rather than necessarily destroying the enemy's communications technologies, they started using and manipulating them for their own purposes.

Therefore, prior to the digital media revolution in 2002 irregulars tended to use traditional mass communication platforms as either military targets or weapons – a sign of the extent to which the structural form and trajectory of the various information revolutions spanning the last few centuries had benefitted the armies of states and empires rather than irregular forces (Kaempf 2013).

The emergence of the latest information revolution, digital media, however, has reversed this historical trend. The different structural nature of digital new media platforms, combined with its low (entry) costs and commoditised applications, constitutes the first media revolution which has benefitted non-state and irregular groups far more than it has governments and counter-insurgents (Gillmor 2010, pp. 1–13). For irregulars, this new information technology constitutes neither a target nor a weapon, but has come to serve as an extended strategic operating platform built around the logic of networks (Rid & Hecker 2009).

Trends towards networked forms of operation by non-state armed groups

Before illustrating some of the pivotal areas where networked dimensions have started to appear, it is important to re-emphasise that no non-state armed group has yet emerged, which fully and exclusively operates as a network. What can be observed (and what will be illustrated below), however, is a trend towards an increasing incorporation and adaption of network elements by these groups in recent years. And the areas where innovative moves towards more networked elements have been most prominent are with regard to communication practices, institutional organisation, recruitment and membership, financing, and military operations. I will engage with three of them below.

Institutional organisation

Two important and interrelated phenomena regarding changes in institutional organisation can be witnessed: the move towards increasing decentralisation of command and control and increasing deterritorialisation.

An early and perhaps the most prominent example here has been al-Qaeda post-9/11. Following its devastating losses in the early phase of 'Operation Enduring Freedom' (where the coalition's superior technology and firepower had eliminated, according to al-Qaeda's own estimates, about 80% of its mujahideen fighters), chief al-Qaeda strategist al-Suri became instrumental in pushing al-Qaeda's strategic shift towards increasing decentralisation. Fixed bases, even taxing mountainous terrain, and safe sanctuaries in friendly states became seen as untenable, and the organisation's own hierarchical structure became seen as making them easy targets for intelligence gathering and leadership decapitation attempts (Rid & Hecker 2009, pp. 190–1). In response, al-Qaeda shifted from what al-Suri called an 'organisation for operations' to an 'operative system' which offered templates for self-recruited activists and entrepreneurs who could operate – anywhere – on their own or with trusted accomplices. This was the emergence of what analysts have identified as al-Qaeda 2.0 or al-Qaeda as a network (Bergen 2002; see also chapters by Bousquet and Kilcullen in this book). Connections and organisational links between individual units and the al-Qaeda leadership were thus avoided and general guidance replaced direct orders (Rid & Hecker 2009, p. 192). Individualised cells were set up that were completely separated from one another and based on decentralisation, connected merely through a common aim, name and programme of beliefs. As Rid and Hecker show, the US-led coalition's asymmetric military superiority forced al-Qaeda to abandon classical insurgent strategies and hierarchical forms of organisation and to instead focus on two main components that they hoped would offer better resilience because of their more horizontal, networked nature: First, a 'guidance centre', i.e. al-Qaeda central, which "supervises and distributes ideological material, a doctrinal programme, educational items, and communiqués" and second, the use of so-called "resistance cell units" which established themselves "spontaneously and without central command and control" (Rid & Hecker 2009, p. 192).

In many ways, the so-called 'Islamic State' has both mimicked many of al-Qaeda 2.0's features of decentralisation and deterritorialisation and taken them further. This has, depending on its circumstances, taken different shapes. In particular, ISIS has shown innovative flexibility in its institutional organisation across time. Because it had started off as a network (comprising extremist jihadists and former members of Iraq's Baath regime), by the time ISIS began its insurgency on the ground in its successful campaign to temporarily carve out territory and establish the Caliphate, it never fully 'lost' its networked nature: it operated militarily along the two axes of a clear command and control centre and a looser, networked form of waging war (Muenkler 2015; Reuter 2015;

Singer & Brooking 2018). However, by the time it had lost most of its territorial gains, it then flexibly switched back to operating through a deterritorialised, networked form of organisation which encourages spontaneous, independent and self-organising cells to stage attacks on its behalf without central command and control (Muenkler 2015).

Membership and recruitment

Traditional actors with their hierarchical forms of organisation tend to hold a tight control over who can become a member or not; be this over questions of citizenship, of joining the armed forces, or with regards to the rules and expectations of a member's behaviour. As indicated, this has been the case in IR in general, but also with regards military actors, both state and non-state armed groups alike. Networks, on the other hand, turn this traditional logic on its head because networked actors hold a comparative advantage vis-à-vis hierarchically organised actors. Anyone can, through their actions, link themselves into the network. There is no formal application process, let alone a central committee which decides about membership applications. Anonymous is a case in point: anyone can join them, for a shorter or longer durations, by acting out and participating in their activities (Owen 2015). The network itself does not even need to know the geolocation or real identity of those participating. One becomes part of the network simply by taking actions on behalf of the network itself.

And while neither al-Qaeda nor Boko Haram, nor the Islamic State have taken on full and genuine network structures, they have encouraged supporters to increasingly operate through spontaneous, independent, self-organising forms of 'membership' without traditional central command and control elements. Al-Qaeda started doing this following its territorial losses in Afghanistan in 2001 (see above). And the Islamic State has actively encouraged individuals across the world to act on its behalf without, for example, the need to first having to undergo military training in ISIS camps inside the Caliphate (a significant departure from older al-Qaeda practices). As long as individuals act in accordance with the overarching ideology and doctrine, they can advance the objectives of the networked organisation. This became even more pronounced following IS's loss of geographical territory in Syria and Iraq in 2015 and 2016 as the result of the international alliance's military action against it. It was at this point that the IS leadership formally declared that sympathisers should not seek to join the fight inside the diminishing Caliphate, but instead should seek to carry the fight to enemies within their respective home countries. For instance, Abu Muhammad al-Adnani, official ISIS spokesman, stated in 2015:

> The smallest action you do in their heartland is better and more enduring to us than what you would if you were with us. If one of you hoped to reach the Islamic State, we wish we were in your place to punish the Crusaders day and night.
>
> (Reuters 2016)

As a partial consequence of these efforts, between 2014 and 2016, there was a 67% increase in attacks and a nearly 600% increase in deaths from terrorism inside OECD countries (Schippa 2017).

A similar phenomenon has played itself out with regard to recruitment. On the one hand, ISIS has relied on very traditional forms of recruitment not dissimilar to previous practices by non-state armed groups, such as radicalisation in prisons or the recruitment of young followers in Iraq and Syria. On the other hand, the exploitation of social networks has enabled ISIS to adapt and modernise older, traditional forms of recruitment. Its success in attracting an estimated 40,000 foreigners (men, women and children) from over 82 countries to join its ranks has largely been attributed to its ability to radicalise and mobilise recruits via social networks. These innovative networked forms of gaining followers, however, need to be seen as part of the wider communicative apparatus (often called a 'virtual Caliphate' or 'cybercaliphate') that ISIS has used to spread its ideas and influence (Lesaca 2017). This latter point will be illustrated in the next subsection. What is important to note here, though, are the increasing networked dimensions that have come to underpin crucial areas such as recruitment and membership by non-state armed groups.

Communication and propaganda

In the past, non-state armed groups and terrorist organisations were able to plan, execute and capture/document their attacks, but they had to rely on other gatekeepers (e.g. media organisations) to disseminate their attacks to the wider public. With the rise of social media, however, these actors have gained the ability to also disseminate their attacks. Social media, in this sense, has empowered non-state armed groups. And while the shift from the first (bin Laden) to the second al-Qaeda generation (al-Baghdadi) already demonstrated a change in the ways in which non-state armed groups were strategically employing social media for the purposes of communication and propaganda, the clearest, most advanced and most sophisticated example of these innovations can be found in the case of the Islamic State.

Despite the 'hype' around the Islamic State's revolutionary way of using media and despite some claims about ISIS being a flat and 'leaderless' network, what we can see instead is the hybrid nature of how ISIS organises its communication and propaganda. On the one hand, it operates in classical, hierarchical terms: it has a central media committee (al-Hayat, al-Furqan, al-Itisam and Ajnad) which oversees various media sub-committees and holds tight controls over the central narrative of ISIS media productions. This enables a consistent branding, produced in professional ways, which is disseminated through different platforms (Internet, darkweb, social media, bots), formats (film, magazines, newsletters, modified interactive video games) and languages to specified target audiences (inside the Caliphate, to the wider Muslim world, to foreign sympathisers and enemy populations). It also directly integrates its media production into its on-the-ground warfighting in ways not seen before (Ingram 2015; Friis 2018). For instance, when, early on in its military campaign, ISIS took the city of Mosul, social and conventional media were overflowing with news of ISIS sweeping across Northern Iraq. It helped fuel the sense of the Islamic State's momentum, generating a sense that Northern Iraq had simply collapsed in the face of the onslaught. This ability, through an incredibly sophisticated communications strategy, to dominate social and conventional media meant, according to Jared Cohen, the then Director of Google's internal think tank), that ISIS had become the "first terrorist group to hold both physical and digital territory" (cited in Singer 2016).

On the other hand, IS's approach to communication and propaganda also has an important decentralised, horizontal dimension to it. The group actively encourages its sympathisers to not just promote, share, and 'like' its centrally produced media contents, but to also directly produce and create media items themselves, without this content having to be vetted by an ISIS committee prior to its release. Most famously, this can be seen in the examples of suicide bombers in France or Belgium live-broadcasting their attacks on streaming platforms and linking these attacks to ISIS itself. Other examples are the co-opting of hashtags, members sharing memes they have produced, or ISIS fighters posting regular updates on their own social media channels. This networked logic is owed to the nature of digital media itself, but it also is a deliberate strategic move that enables

ISIS to grow its community and to reach much wider audiences. It is the group's members and supporters whose social media activities and presence exponentially increase the reach of ISIS communications (Ingram 2015, pp. 734–5). What this means is that ISIS, in contrast to al-Qaeda (with its closed Internet forums and its need to vet members), operates its communication and propaganda elements in both, hierarchically-controlled and horizontally-generated, open, networked ways. Organisationally speaking, it is a hybrid approach to propaganda and communication. This constitutes a significant departure from past practices by other groups, but also one that cannot be described as entirely being driven by network logics yet.

The elements of institutional organisation, membership and recruitment, as well as communication and propaganda are by no means the only areas where innovative moves towards more networked characteristics can be observed. Others include financing through cryptocurrencies, the discussion of ideology, the refinement of tactics and strategies. What they all indicate, however, is a trend towards an adaptation of networked structures by non-state armed groups in recent years.

Conclusion and outlook

When a giant fights a dwarf, the asymmetry of the contest is inherently unstable as it requires the weaker military actor to be innovative in order to prevail. In the not-so-distant past, the answer to this asymmetric constellation has been the systematic development (in theory and in practice) of guerrilla warfare, which proved to be successful because of its exploitation of the factors of space and time, as well as its focus on offensive tactics and defensive strategy. This enabled non-state armed groups to turn the strengths of state warfare into liabilities. It also proved Clausewitz right: warfare is never waged upon a lifeless mass, but on an actor who responds and innovates. Crucially, the innovation brought about by Lawrence, Mao and others (via Clausewitz) occurred *in spite of* non-state actors retaining a hierarchical form of organisation.

What we are seeing today is the beginning of different and novel form of innovation in the organisational nature of non-state armed groups. The rise of networked, horizontal forms of organisation, enabled by and mirrored on the logic of social media, are offering a new gravitational pull for non-state armed groups precisely because of their disruptive potential. What used to make states strong in the past (hierarchical forms of organisation) is turned into weaknesses by networked forms of organisation. This disruptive potential can be seen across all facets of social and institutional life, including warfare. This is not to say that non-state armed groups have emerged that are genuinely and consistently operating as networks yet (in contrast to other actors like Anonymous or cryptocurrencies like Bitcoin). But, as I have tried to show, we can see the beginning of a move on part of some actors (beginning with al-Qaeda and then subsequently, and to a larger extent, with ISIS), who have started incorporating elements of a network logic into their operations, from their organisational forms to questions over membership, financing, recruiting, communications and operations. What we are seeing, therefore, is a further push towards decentralisation, horizontal organisation and deterritorialisation on part of non-state armed groups in ways we have not seen in the past. Whether this trend continues, it is difficult to say. As the saying goes, predictions are difficult to make, especially when they concern the future.

And yet, there are strong indications that what we are seeing today might just be the beginning of something new. The power of networks lies in their potential to disrupt the power of states and their forms of warfare. And finding ways to disrupt the centre of gravity of their adversaries has always appealed to disadvantaged non-state military actors. It is also not surprising, therefore, that both al-Qaeda and ISIS started pushing in this direction precisely at those moments when they had suffered heavy respective military losses and at a time when networked forms of organisation had started to rise elsewhere. Violent networks are prone to further proliferate and escalate their activities in the future, especially given that emerging technologies, from blockchains, to the Internet of Things, swarming, nano-technologies etc. favour the push towards increasing deterritorialisation and the expansion of networked forms of organisation. It is therefore more than likely that in the future, states will have to get used to facing non-state adversaries who are not just guerrillas, but networked actors who employ guerrilla and terrorist strategies.

References

Atran, S, Sheikh, H & Gomez, A 2014, 'Devoted Actors Sacrifice for Close Comrades and Sacred Cause', *PNAS*, vol. 111, no. 50, pp. 17702–3, https://doi.org/10.1073/pnas.1420474111.

Bergen, P L 2002, *Holy War, Inc.*, Touchstone, New York.

Blenker, Y 2011, 'Networks of Power, Degrees of Freedom', *International Journal of Communication*, vol. 5, pp. 721–55.

Castells, M 2000, 'Information Technology and Global Capitalism', in W Hutton & A Giddens (eds), *On the Edge: Living with Global Capitalism*, Jonathan Cape, London, pp. 52–75.

Clausewitz, Carl von 1966a, 'Bekenntnisdenkschrift', in W Hahlweg (ed), *Carl von Clausewitz: Schriften – Aufsaetze – Studien – Briefe*, Vandenhoeck & Ruprecht, Göttingen, pp. 644–90.

Clausewitz, Carl von 1966b, 'Meine Vorlesungen Über den Kleinen Krieg, Gehalten auf der Kriegs-Schule 1810 und 1811', in W Hahlweg (ed), *Carl von Clausewitz: Schriften – Aufsaetze – Studien – Briefe*, Vandenhoeck & Ruprecht, Göttingen, pp. 205–588.

Clausewitz, Carl von 1984, *On War*, trans. M Howard & P Paret, Princeton University Press, Princeton.

Enzensberger, H-M 1993, *Aussichten auf den Buergerkrieg*, Suhrkamp, Frankfurt a. M.

Friis, S M 2018, '"Behead, Burn, Crucify, Crush": Theorizing the Islamic State's Public Displays of Violence', *European Journal of International Relations*, vol. 24, no. 2, pp. 243–67, https://doi.org/10.1177/1354066117714416.

Gillmor, D 2010, Mediaactive, available at http://mediaactive.com/wp-content/uploads/2010/12/mediactive_gillmor.pdf, accessed on 14 May 2023.

Gray, C S 1999, *Modern Strategy*, Oxford University Press, Oxford.

Heuser, B 2002, *Reading Clausewitz*, Pimlico, London.

Ingram, H J 2015, 'The Strategic Logic of Islamic State Information Operations', *Australian Journal of International Affairs*, vol. 69, no. 6, pp. 729–52, https://doi.org/10.1080/10357718.2015.1059799.

Kaempf, S 2011, 'Lost Through Non-Translation: Bringing Clausewitz's Writings on "New Wars" Back in', *Small Wars & Insurgencies*, vol. 22, no. 4, pp. 548–73, https://doi.org/10.1080/09592318.2011.599164.

Kaempf, S 2013, 'The Mediatisation of War in a Transforming Global Media Landscape', *Australian Journal of International Affairs*, vol. 67, no. 5, pp. 586–604, https://doi.org/10.1080/10357718.2013.817527

Kaldor, M 1999, *New and Old Wars: Organized Violence in a Global Era*, Polity Press, Cambridge, MA.

Lawrence, T E 1962, *Seven Pillars of Wisdom: A Triumph*, Penguin, Harmondsworth.

Lawrence, T E 1994, 'Guerrilla Warfare', in G Chaliand (ed), *The Art of War in World History From Antiquity to the Nuclear Age*, University of California Press, Berkeley – Los Angeles – London, pp. 880–90.

Lesaca, J 2017, *Armas de Seducción Masiva*, Ediciones Península, Barcelona.

Mao, Z 1992, 'On Guerrilla Warfare', in S B Griffith (ed), *Mao Tse-Tung on Guerrilla Warfare*, The Nautical & Aviation Publishing Company of America, Baltimore, MD, pp. 41–115.

Muenkler, H 2015, *Kriegssplitter: Die Evolution der Gewalt im 20. und 21. Jahrhundert*, Rohwolt, Berlin.

Owen, T 2015, *Disruptive Power: The Crisis of the State in the Digital Age*, Oxford University Press, Oxford.

Reuter, C 2015, *Die Schwarze Macht. Der "Islamische Staat" und die Strategen des Terrors*, Deutsche Verlags-Anstalt, München.

Reuter 2016, 'Islamic State Calls for Attacks on the West During Ramadan in Audio Message', *Reuters*, 21 May, <https://www.reuters.com/article/us-mideast-crisis-islamicstate/islamic-state-calls-for-attacks-on-the-west-during-ramadan-in-audio-message-idUSKCN0YC0OG> (accessed 12 March 2020).

Rid, T & Hecker, M 2009, *War 2.0: Irregular Warfare in the Information Age*, Praeger Security International, Westport, CT.

Schippa, C 2017, *The State of Terrorism in Wealthy Countries, Explained with Numbers*, <https://www.weforum.org/agenda/2017/11/state-of-terrorism-in-oecd-countries/> (accessed 11 January 2019).

Shirky, C 2008, *Here Comes Everybody: The Power of Organizing without Organizations*, Penguin Press, New York.

Singer, P W 2016, 'War Goes Viral', *The Atlantic*, November, <https://www.theatlantic.com/magazine/archive/2016/11/war-goes-viral/501125/> (accessed 2 November 2022).

Singer, P W & Brooking, E T 2018, *LikeWar: The Weaponization of Social Media*, Houghton Mifflin Harcourt, New York.

Slaughter, A-M 2009, 'America's Edge: Power in the Networked Century', *Foreign Affairs*, vol. 88, no. 1, pp. 94–113.

Strahan, H 2007, *Clausewitz's On War: A Biography*, Grove Press, New York.

Tilly, C (ed) 1975, *The Formation of National States in Western Europe*, Princeton University Press, Princeton.

Van Creveld, M 1991, *The Transformation of War*, The Free Press, New York.

PART III

Concepts and Theories of Future Warfare

14

UNDERSTANDING WESTERN PERCEPTIONS OF WAR AND INSECURITY

Unravelling Hybridity

David Snetselaar and Sebastiaan Rietjens

Introduction

The concepts of hybrid threats and hybrid warfare have become *en vogue* in the international security arena. They are frequently used as a policy tool in declarations and framework documents (e.g. the EU's *Joint Framework on Countering Hybrid Threats*), to establish new organizations (e.g. European Centre of Excellence for Countering Hybrid Threats) and to analyse contemporary cases (e.g. the 2014 Annexation of Crimea). Generally, hybridity refers to multidimensional activities that are coordinated, part of an integrated campaign with a strategic goal, often deceptive, and that exploit the border between war and peace (Weissmann 2021). Meanwhile, however, these concepts are considered highly problematic since they lack a common definition and use contested terminology. Some commentators even argue that hybrid concepts are "poorly constructed new theories that more often than not cloud rather than clarify" (Stoker & Whiteside 2020, p. 3). This led Johnson (2018) to argue that, despite the growing body of literature on hybrid concepts, there is still a need to better understand them, in order to detect them, build resilience against them, and ultimately combat them. This chapter contributes to this call and aims to introduce the reader to the concept of hybridity, its origin, critiques, as well as its current use.

In the chapter we use 'hybridity' as an overarching term, as opposed to making a distinction between hybrid war(fare), hybrid threats, hybrid conflict, etc. We start the chapter by tracing the origin and development of hybridity, including the multitude of definitions of the concept. Subsequently, in the Section 'Critiques and Debate' we outline the ongoing debate and critiques on hybridity. We then continue by showing how hybridity found its way into the current institutional and policy landscape in Section 'Hybrid Realities'. In the concluding Section, we introduce the concept of resilience as a way to counter hybrid threats and provide some suggestions for further research.

Tracing and defining hybridity

To unravel hybridity and understand how it emerged and changed over the past decades, it is important to understand the context that it originated in, namely, US military thought in the 1990s and 2000s. At that time, the US military realized its operational concepts were inadequate to respond

DOI: 10.4324/9781003299011-18

to the harsh reality on the battlefield, which became painfully clear during the Iraq and Afghan wars. According to Freedman (2017, p. 222), the "US military had clung to an ideal type derived from the classical model and then faced a more unruly form of warfare for which it was poorly prepared and from which it struggled to extricate itself". Military theorists developed different concepts to capture the variety of threats the United States faced, and specifically the blurring between different types of threats. In 2005, Lieutenant General James Mattis and military theorist Frank Hoffman argued that future conflict would not likely present neat distinctions between the traditional, irregular, catastrophic, and disruptive threats identified by the newly published National Defence Strategy. Rather, future opponents would pick and choose a combination that best suited them. "This unprecedented synthesis" is what they referred to as hybrid warfare (Mattis & Hoffman 2005, p. 2).

Hoffman was not the first to coin the term 'hybrid war', but his work played an important role in conceptualizing notions of hybridity and starting an intellectual debate.[1] Of particular relevance is Hoffman's often cited *Conflict in the 21st Century: The Rise of Hybrid Wars*. In this publication Hoffman defined hybrid wars as wars that "can be conducted by both state and a variety of non-state actors" and that "incorporate a range of different modes of warfare, including conventional capabilities, irregular tactics and formations, terrorists acts including indiscriminate violence and coercion, and criminal disorder" (Hoffman 2007, p. 14). Hybrid threats or challengers, in turn, are those adversaries who resort to hybrid warfare. Used in this way, Hoffman explains that the "term 'Hybrid' captures both their organization and their means. Organizationally, they may have a hierarchical political structure, coupled with decentralized cells or networked tactical units. Their means will also be hybrid in form and application" (2007, p. 28).

According to Fridman (2018, p. 31), Hoffman's ideas are themselves "based on a hybrid of different strategic ideas and theories". Hoffman, for example, draws upon concepts of *unrestricted warfare* (Liang & Xiangsui 2002), *fourth-generation warfare* (Lind et al. 1989), *compound warfare* (Huber 2005), and the aforementioned 2005 *National Defence Strategy*. Besides engaging existing theories and strategic ideas to conceptualize hybrid war, Hoffman also offered an empirical basis by analysing, amongst others, Hezbollah's war against Israel in 2006. He considered Hezbollah to be a prototypical hybrid actor. As a non-state actor, Hezbollah was able to use advanced and heavy weaponry, deploy a well-trained and organized fighting force, construct a strong defensive, and deploy guerrilla tactics all in an urban environment (Caliskan 2021, p. 24). Hoffman's objective was seemingly to come up with a concept that addressed the combination of different modes of warfare at an operational-tactical level that would help the US military adapt and prepare for future opponents without relying, as it had done, on technological superiority. The result, according to Fridman (2018, pp. 31–7), was a concept that was evidence-based, engaged with previous strategic thinking, was operationally applicable, and addressed timely and relevant policy questions.

Following the publication of his seminal paper, Hoffman's concepts quickly gained traction within the US military. Given its operational appeal and its intent to improve the US military's performance on the future battlefield, Hoffman's concept of hybrid war became "extremely popular within US military circles, generating an enormous amount of literature on the subject" (Fridman 2018, p. 37). But while Hoffman's work was recognized within the military and political establishment, the US military remained reluctant to formally adopt notions of hybridity in their doctrinal publications. Around 2010, Hoffman's work also became popular within NATO (Caliskan 2021, pp. 45–7). At that time a Capstone Concept was developed to analyse the challenges posed by hybrid threats and explore adequate counter policies and strategies (Lasconjarias & Larsen 2015, p. 5). This presented the first "comprehensive and methodological attempt to reconceptualize hybrid warfare and hybrid threats and elevate these concepts to the level of strategy" (Fridman 2018, p. 104).

Following the Capstone Concept until 2013, NATO member states committed relatively few resources to countering hybrid threats. This changed drastically, however, when Russia annexed Crimea in 2014. Russia's action came as a "wake-up call for European security" (Lasconjarias & Larsen 2015, p. 7) and "had a huge impact on both the popularity and the content of the concept" (Caliskan 2021, p. 28). Not only did Russia's hybrid actions receive a lot of attention in the media and academic literature, NATO members revitalized the concepts of hybrid warfare and, in particular, hybrid threats. NATO and the EU members made countering hybrid threats a priority and their interpretation and use of hybridity greatly expanded its meaning. While NATO had previous applied the concept at a strategic level, it now included the combination of military and non-military means and shifted its focus from non-state actors such as Hezbollah, al-Qaeda, and Chechen rebels as prototypical hybrid actors to state actors like Russia, China, Iran, and North Korea (Caliskan 2021, pp. 43–4).

After the annexation of Crimea in 2014, notions of hybridity became associated with Russia in particular (Caliskan 2021, p. 28). Not only did the Crimean crisis quickly become a schoolbook example of hybrid warfare, Russia was thought to have developed a new hybrid approach to war. Illustrative of this understanding is the so-called Gerasimov Doctrine. In 2013, the Chief of the General Staff Valery Gerasimov published a paper analysing the nature of contemporary conflict and in particular the significance of non-military means. While in fact more diagnostic than prognostic and drawing upon observations from recent Western interventions in the Middle East, Gerasimov's article has often been interpreted as the basis for the Kremlin's hybrid strategy to annex Crimea – a view that has been debated by scholars.[2] Fridman (2018) demonstrated that *gibridnaya voyna* (the Russian translation of hybrid war) only appeared after 2014 and mostly in reference to the use of the term 'hybrid warfare' in the West. Furthermore, Fridman argued that *gibridnaya voyna* represented something different than Hoffman's and NATO's interpretations of hybrid war. *Gibridnaya voyna* is "solely based on non-military means and is intended to undermine and subvert the adversary without the recourse to military force" (Fridman 2018, p. 155). These differences speak to the way concepts of hybridity have become entangled with international events and shaped by different traditions in military thinking.

Recently, commentators and practitioners seem to agree that hybrid war and hybrid threats take place below the threshold of warfare and aim to undermine a target's political system. This resonates well with the definition that Nilsson et al. (2021, p. 2) provide. They describe hybrid war *and* hybrid threats together as denoting:

> Adversaries or antagonists who aim to achieve outcomes without a war, to disrupt, undermine or damage the target's political system and cohesion through a combination of violence, control, subversion, manipulation and dissemination of (mis)information.

Indeed, the lack of clear definitions and the interchangeable use of the terms 'hybrid war', 'hybrid warfare' and 'hybrid threats', has made it very difficult to make a useful distinction. According to Caliskan (2021, p. 52), these concepts can be distinguished as follows:

> In theory hybrid threats denote the actor who employs hybrid means. The use of 'hybrid warfare' or 'hybrid war' largely depends on the connotations attached to 'warfare' and 'war'. While hybrid warfare represents an operational concept that is conducted via hybrid threats, hybrid war denotes the strategic manifestation of the operational ideas underpinning hybrid warfare.

Table 14.1 Summary of hybrid activities

Activity	Examples
Propaganda	Enabled and made cheaper by social media, also targeted at home
Fake news	'Lisa' was portrayed as a Russian-German raped by migrants
Strategic leaks	Macron emails leaked 48 hours before the French election
Funding organizations	China opened Chinese think tank in Washington
Political parties	Russia supports sympathetic European parties on right and left
Organized protest movements	Russian trolls organized both pro- and anti-protests in Houston mosque case
Cyber tools	Espionage is an old tactic with new, cyber means. Attack has
Espionage	targeted critical infrastructure, notably in Estonia in 2007.
Attack	Manipulation is next frontier, changing information without the
Manipulation	holders knowing it.
Economic leverage	China sought to punish South Korea for accepting U.S. anti-missile system
Proxies and unacknowledged war	Russian 'little green men' in Ukraine slid into actual combat
Paramilitary organizations	Russian 'Night Wolves' bikers intimidate civilians

Source: Adapted from Treverton (2018, p. 10)

Notwithstanding, Caliskan acknowledges that "in practice, it is extremely difficult to draw a clear line" between hybrid threats, war, and warfare. This is also the reason why we use 'hybridity' as an overarching concept. Taking together, notions of hybridity have become more than a concept (strategic, tactical, or otherwise), but also represent a discourse and practice of countering perceived threats. In this context, hybridity is often understood as the activities of (primarily) state actors and their proxies that operate in a grey zone between war and peace and intentionally exploit the vulnerabilities of Western democratic societies to exert influence, disrupt, and generally undermine the interest and values of target societies. These activities range from disinformation campaigns, industrial espionage, leveraging energy dependencies, and weaponizing migration, to sabotaging critical infrastructure and disrupting supply chains. To illustrate the wide range of hybrid activities, Treverton (2018) provides a summary of different types of hybrid activities and includes several examples. This summary is depicted in Table 14.1.

Critiques and debate

Since the 2000s, concepts of hybridity have been the subject of substantial critique and debate. Much of the critique centres around the novelty of 'hybrid warfare'. Proponents of hybridity argue that it has a long history citing examples such as the Peloponnesian War or the French involvement in Vietnam and Algeria. Because of this, Murray and Mansoor (Mansoor 2012, p. 1) see hybridity as useful in "thinking about war past, present and future". And, while these concepts themselves may not be new, Lasconjarias and Larsen (2015, p. 1) stress that the "changing dynamics within the international security environment [...] make this type of warfare look different". Opponents, on the other hand, argue that hybridity is historically indistinct. Stoker and Whiteside, for example, dispute the representation of historical cases by hybridist and point out that "[t]he strongest argument that hybridist can make is that all wars are hybrid, but to varying degrees. [...] But if all wars are *hybrid wars*, the term is redundant, similar to saying *violent wars*" (Stoker & Whiteside 2020, p. 23, emphasis in original).

The disputed historical basis for hybridity relates to broader critiques regarding its analytical vagueness and inconsequent use. Johnson, for example, argues that the term 'hybrid warfare' has lost "the sharpness that would have made it valuable" (Johnson 2018, p. 143). In his view, the term has become so broad that adding 'hybrid' to 'warfare' seems largely irrelevant: "[W]hat observers are trying to describe is a character of warfare as it currently exists, which represents a change from the immediate post-Cold War era". A complicating factor according to Caliskan (2021, pp. 40–2) is the inconsequent use of the term that blurs key distinctions and exacerbates the conceptual vagueness. He points out that while Hoffman initially focussed on the convergence of different modes of warfare at an operational-tactical level, subsequent applications of hybridity conflated strategic, operational, and tactical levels. According to Stoker and Whiteside (2020, p. 19) this is problematic because the discussion on hybrid war can be boiled down to 'the usage of tactical means' and is thus a faulty basis for strategy. They also express their concern over the blurring between war and peace by concepts of hybridity. In their view, concepts of hybridity

> Cause more harm than good and contribute to an increasingly dangerous distortion of the concepts of war, peace, and geopolitical competition, with a resultant negative impact on the crafting of security strategy for the United States and its Allies and partners around the world.
>
> (Stoker & Whiteside 2020, p. 2)

In addition to the abovementioned critiques, concepts of hybridity have specifically been criticized as a means to study Russian foreign policy and military strategy. Moreover, many scholars have questioned the existence of a Russian hybrid strategy and the annexation of Crimea as a prototype case hereof. Renz (2016), for example, argues that Russia's strategy in Crimea was neither new nor did it represent a war-winning formula that could be replicated elsewhere. Though Russia's apparent successful use of non-military instruments like disinformation was unexpected in Western perceptions, it would be incorrect to assume that this is new. In fact, scholars like Fridman (2018) show that the use of such instruments has played an important role in Russian military thinking for decades. "The idea that Russia is waging a 'hybrid war' against the West", according to Renz "oversimplifies Russian foreign policy thinking and tells us little about the goals and intentions behind such a presumed approach" (Renz 2016, p. 294). Renowned Russia expert Mark Galeotti is similarly sceptical of hybrid concepts as an appropriate framework to understand Russia's actions since 2014. Instead of hybrid warfare, Galeotti (2019a, pp. 49–57) makes the argument to use existing concepts like political warfare to understand Russia's policies and strategies.

The critiques outlined above are by no means exhaustive, but they raise the question of why hybridity remains so popular. According to Johnson (2018, p. 143), this is "because reality dawned: there was a shock realisation that the West's optimistic and unrealistic expectations were being shattered by the challenges of the West's rivals". In a similar vein, Caliskan (2021, p. VII) argues that hybridity has become a strategic communication tool, "a term to make sense of what happened in Crimea and to disguise the strategic shock experienced by NATO". He adds that NATO continues to use hybridity to raise awareness, secure defence budgets and foster closer NATO-EU collaboration. And finally, Fridman (2018, p. 1) concludes that the concept of hybrid war "had initially been intended to offer a better understanding of contemporary conflict [but] has been weaponized, becoming a tool in internal manoeuvring for finance, public opinion and political power". The critical analysis of these scholars shows how hybridity has travelled from a niche debate in US military strategy to become a key term in European security discourses, reflecting vested interests.

As such, hybridity itself becomes a relevant and interesting research subject to better understand Western perceptions of contemporary and future war, conflict and international security.

Hybrid realities

To better understand these perceptions, this section addresses what we refer to as hybrid realities. By this we not only mean the perceived threats identified as 'hybrid', but also the responses these threats have triggered. To do so, we first address the development of new counter-hybrid policies and strategies primarily at EU and NATO level. We then turn to the institutional changes and show what organizations have emerged in the wake of the hybrid discourse. Thirdly, we discuss three concrete challenges that have been labelled as 'hybrid' across various domains.

Policy and strategy

Following the annexation of Crimea in 2014, notions of hybridity were step-by-step integrated into EU and NATO security policies and strategies. The declaration issued at the Wales Summit held that same year recognizes the need to ensure that NATO is "able to effectively address the specific challenges posed by hybrid warfare threats" (NATO 2014). To address these challenges, the declaration states that the Alliance needs to possess the necessary tools and capabilities. Since then, NATO developed a three-pronged strategy to address hybrid threats, namely, (1) to be prepared, (2) to deter, and (3) to defend against hybrid threats (NATO 2022). Though the responsibility to respond to hybrid threats primarily lies with the targeted nation, crucially, the Warsaw Summit Declaration (NATO 2016) states that "[t]he Council could decide to invoke Article 5 of the Washington Treaty" in response to a hybrid attack. Another key aspect of NATO's strategy in this area is cooperation beyond the Alliance, particularly with the EU. In 2016, the leaders of both organizations issued a joint statement on strengthening the strategic partnership between the two organizations in a number of areas, including countering hybrid threats (Bajarūnas 2020, p. 64).

The EU similarly developed a policy to address the challenges of hybrid threats. One of the key documents is the *Joint Framework on Countering Hybrid Threats* published in 2016 (Bajarūnas 2020). The Joint Framework recognizes that the "European Union's security environment has changed dramatically" and that the Union needs to "adapt and increase its capacities as a security provider" (European Commission 2016, p. 2). Similar to NATO, the EU places the primary responsibility with member states and envisions a facilitating and coordinating role for the Union. The framework aims to "facilitate a holistic approach that will enable the EU, in coordination with Member States, to specifically counter threats of a hybrid nature by creating synergies between all relevant instruments and fostering close cooperation between all actors" (European Commission 2016, p. 3). Like NATO's strategy, the EU framework takes a three-pronged approach focussing on: (1) improving awareness, (2) building resilience, and (3) preventing, responding to, and recovering from crisis. Another key document is the Joint Communication *Increasing Resilience and Bolstering Capabilities to Address Hybrid Threats* (European Commission 2018). The document addresses improving resilience by, amongst others, threat detection, strategic communication, cybersecurity, and addressing hostile intelligence activities.

At a national level, EU and NATO Member States have implemented so-called comprehensive security concepts. According to Bajarūnas, these concepts build on the experience of countries like Finland and Norway with their respective approaches to comprehensive security and total defence. These concepts reflect a so-called whole-of-government approach that entails "the well-functioning coordination of various institutions at the government level; strong links between government, civil society and the private sector; a well-tuned legal base; civilian–military coop-eration; and constant preparation, training, exercises and education" (Bajarūnas 2020, p. 63).

Institutional changes

Besides developing policies and strategies to counter hybrid threats, the EU and NATO have es-tablished various dedicated organizations to counter hybrid threats. One of the most well-known and often cited actions is the establishment of the European Centre of Excellence for Countering Hybrid Threats (hereafter Hybrid CoE) in 2017. The Centre was established at the initiative of the Finish government with the support of nine participating states, which have since then expanded to a total of 31 countries (NATO 2022). Operating under auspices of the EU and NATO, the Hybrid CoE has positioned itself as an authoritative centre of knowledge and expertise. Besides conduct-ing and collecting relevant research, the centre coordinates between participating states and offers a range of trainings and exercises designed to educated representatives of the participating states, improve and test specific tools or mechanisms, and to strengthen the relationships between partici-pating states and key partners (Hybrid CoE 2022).

In addition to jointly establishing the Hybrid CoE, the EU and NATO have also individually taken steps. In 2018, for example, NATO created so-called Hybrid Support Teams to "provide tailored targeted assistance to Allies upon request, in preparing against and responding to hybrid activities" (NATO 2022). Another example is NATO's Joint Intelligence and Security Division, set up to raise awareness among Allies and improve the detection and attribution of hybrid threats. Besides these new initiatives, NATO's efforts to counter hybrid threats also include contributions from existing organizations like its Centres of Excellence on Strategic Communications, Coopera-tive Cyber Defence, and Energy Security (NATO 2022).

The EU has similarly taken concrete actions. For example, a key outcome of the Joint Frame-work was the establishment of the EU Hybrid Fusion Cell. The cell was created as part of the EU Intelligence and Situation Centre to help improve situational awareness and facilitate intelligence sharing within the EU and with key partners such as the Hybrid CoE (European Commission 2016, p. 4). The Joint Framework (European Commission 2016, pp. 4–5) and the Joint Communication (2018, pp. 6–7) both mention the East StratCom Task Force, established in 2015 to address Russian disinformation campaigns. The EUvsDisinfo project showcases the Task Force's communication products, including a weekly Disinformation Review and a database of disinformation messages. The project's objective is to "better forecast, address, and respond to the Russian Federation's ongoing disinformation campaigns" and to "increase public awareness and understanding of the Kremlin's disinformation operations, and to help citizens in Europe and beyond develop resistance to digital information and media manipulation" (EUvsDisinfo 2022).

Finally, at a national level, EU and NATO member states have also taken concrete steps to-wards countering hybrid threats. In addition to the implementation of the abovementioned com-prehensive security concepts, counter hybrid efforts have led to new initiatives. One such initiative is the Counter Hybrid Unit established in 2018 by the Dutch Ministry of Defence (Snel 2022). Collaborating with partners from different governmental departments, the Unit seeks to contribute to a whole-of-government approach to counter hybrid threats.

Domains

To illustrate the variety of hybrid realities that have come to characterize Western security policies and practices, this section discusses three concrete 'hybrid' cases.

Knowledge security

In May 2020, two Dutch universities signed an agreement with the Chinese telecommunication company Huawei for a research project called DREAMS Lab (Snetselaar 2023). Huawei agreed to fund the Free University of Amsterdam (VU) and the University of Amsterdam (UvA) to conduct a four-year study on the use of Artificial Intelligence to optimize search engine technology. The project drew a lot of public attention when a journalist working for the Financial Daily (a Dutch newspaper) began publishing about the project. The journalist questioned the VU and UvA's decision in the light of the debate on Huawei's role in the rollout of 5G (van Wijnen 2020). Objections to the research project included the risk of the Chinese state being able to access sensitive data on advanced AI-technology via Huawei. In addition, collaborating with Huawei was considered undesired on ethical grounds. The company was accused of developing surveillance technology for the Chinese authorities in Xinijang province, making it complicit in the oppression of the Uyghurs – an ethnic and Muslim minority in China.

The news reports triggered a heated debate in the media, politics and in academia (Snetselaar 2023, pp. 8–9). Politicians called on government to end the project and academics urged the universities to reassess their decision, but the project was not aborted. Nonetheless, the project helped raise awareness and catalysed the development and implementation of knowledge security policies by universities and government ministries. These policies aim to mitigate the risk of espionage, undesired knowledge transfers, censorship and the misuse of dual-use technologies (Snetselaar 2023, p. 12).

In the context of the rivalry between the United States and China, research projects like DREAMS Lab are considered part of China's strategy to obtain the technology it needs to become a global power (Snetselaar 2023). Issues like intellectual property theft and corporate espionage have been sources of tension in Sino-Western relations for years. Paramount cases include corporate espionage at the Dutch micro-chip company ASML (van Dijk 2021) and the theft of classified data on the design of the US F-35 fighter jet (The Economist 2010).

Energy security

The offshore pipeline Nord Stream 2 has been controversial since approval was given for its construction in 2015. The pipeline would allow Germany to increase the amount of natural gas it could import directly from Russia and was 'purely economic' according to former Chancellor Angela Merkel (Hofman 2022). However, redirecting the flow of natural gas would cut transfer fees for countries like Poland and Ukraine and meant that Russia could cut off its supply of gas to these countries without jeopardizing its supply to the rest of Europe (The Economist 2021a). The United States has also strongly opposed the project. Not only does it have an interest in selling more American gas to the continent, it has also repeatedly warned against becoming too dependent on Russia for gas. Furthermore, the Nord Stream 2 project contradicted the EU's policy to diversify its energy supplies (The Economist 2019).

Though the pipeline was completed in 2021, it never came into use (Hofman 2022). Following the Russian invasion of Ukraine in early 2022, the supply of natural gas became a focal point of the crisis between Russia and the West. Later that year, both Nord Stream 1 and 2 were hit by what was suspected to be Russian sabotage. The sabotage of the pipelines raised concerns over hybrid threats and the need to improving the resilience of European critical infrastructure. In a press release, for example, the European Commission stated that "Russia's war of aggression against Ukraine has brough new risks, physical and cyber-attacks, often combined as a hybrid threat" and that the "sabotage of the Nord Stream gas pipelines and other recent incidents made it clear that the resilience of the EU critical infrastructure is under threat" (European Commission 2022, p. 1).

Instrumentalization of migration

In the fall of 2021, an influx of migrants seeking to cross the Polish-Belarusian border sparked fears in the EU of a new migrant crisis. The crisis was orchestrated by the Belarusian regime in retaliation to EU's refusal to recognize Alexander Lukashenko's re-election and the imposition of sanctions (The Economist 2021b). Lukashenko's regime was offering visas and flight tickets to migrants from the Middle East and Africa. Upon arrival in the Belarusian capital, Minsk, the migrants were brought to the Polish-Belarusian border near Lithuania, where they were told to cross over into the EU. In response, both Poland and Lithuania declared a state of emergency and Poland reportedly deployed as many as 12,000 troops to the border (Kerres 2021). At the border, the migrants faced violence on both sides, caught in a no-man's land and out of reach of humanitarian aid organizations (van Verschuer 2021).

With thousands of refugees trapped in dire conditions and growing fatalities, the crisis caused discord and division in the EU over a proper response. This, commentators argued, was precisely what Lukashenko wanted (Kerres 2021). The instrumentalization of the irregular migrant flows by the Belarusian regime was a form of hybrid warfare, as explained by High Representative Josep Borrell (2021): "The world is full of hybrid situations where we face intermediate dynamics of competition, intimidation, and coercion. What we are seeing today in the Polish and Lithuanian border with Belarus is a typical example of that". Five months later, the EU published its new Strategic Compass that identified the instrumentalization of irregular flows of migration as one of the hybrid means used by state and non-state actors against the EU (EEAS 2022, pp. 22, 34).

Looking forward, building resilience

Taken together, where does the above leave hybridity and what insight does it give into Western perceptions of contemporary and future war? To begin with, the above demonstrates how hybridity became a key term in European security discourses and has become institutionalized in the security architecture of Europe. This architecture is being adapted to better deal with the great variety of present threats ranging from espionage and unwanted knowledge transfers, to leveraging energy dependencies and the sabotaging critical infrastructure, and to the instrumentalization of irregular migration flows that cause division and discord. And while the Russian invasion of Ukraine underlines the fact that conventional military threats remain, NATO's *2022 Strategic Concept* and the EU's *Strategic Compass for Defence and Security* identify building resilience to hybrid threats as a priority for Western security. This implies that in the near future at least, hybridity will remain an important aspect of how future war and security are understood and acted on in the West.

To better understand these threats and how they are responded to, more empirical research is needed to allow for sound evidence-based thinking in policy and decision making (Rietjens 2022). To this end, future research could focus on resilience as the ability of a society or a system to resist and respond to hybrid threats (Freedman et al. 2021, p. 41). Such research should not only seek to give insight into the practical challenges of building resilience, but should also seek to critically reflect on the politics of resilience, the various interests that are at stake, and what alternative understandings there are.

Notes

1 According to Caliskan (2021, p. 23) the term was first used by Lieutenant Robert G. Walker in 1998 in his master thesis. The term later also featured in the master thesis of Major William J. Nemeth in 2002. The first time Hoffman appears to mention the term is in the article he co-authored with Lieutenant General James N. Mattis in 2005.
2 For the discussion on the Gerasimov Doctrine see amongst others Galeotti (2019b) and Renz (2016, p. 286).

References

Bajarūnas, E 2020, 'Addressing Hybrid Threats: Priorities for the EU in 2020 and Beyond', *European View*, vol. 19, no. 1, pp. 62–70.

Borrell, J 2021, *Foreign Affairs Council (Defence): Remarks by the High Representative Joseph Borrell at the Press Conference*, European External Action Service, <https://www.eeas.europa.eu/eeas/foreign-affairs-council-defence-remarks-high-representative-josep-borrell-press-conference_en> (accessed 14 September 2021).

Caliskan, M 2021, *Hybrid Warfare Through the Lens of Strategic Theory: Based on Interviews with NATO Officials*, Université Catholique de Louvain, Louvain.

EEAS 2022, *A Strategic Compass for Security and Defence*, European External Action Service, Brussels.

European Commission and the High Representative of the Union for Foreign Affairs and Security Policy, 2016. Joint framework on countering hybrid threats: a European Union response. *Joint Communication to the European Parliament and the Council.* Brussels, April 6, JOIN(2016) 18 final.

European Commission 2018, *Increasing Resilience and Bolstering Capabilities to Address Hybrid Threats*, European Commission, Brussels.

European Commission 2022, *Critical Infrastructure: Commission Accelerates Work to Build Up European Resilience*, European Commission, Strasbourg.

EUvsDisinfo 2022, *About*, <https://euvsdisinfo.eu/about/> (accessed 12 September 2022).

Freedman, J, Hoogensen Gjørv, G & Razakamaharav, V 2021, 'Identity, Stability, Hybrid Threats and Disinformation', *Icono14*, vol. 19, no. 1, pp. 38–69.

Freedman, L 2017, *The Future of War: A History*, Public Affairs, New York.

Fridman, O 2018, *Russian 'Hybrid Warfare', Resurgence and Politicization*, Oxford University Press, Oxford.

Galeotti, M 2019a, *Russian Political War, Moving Beyond the Hybrid*. Routledge, London & New York.

Galeotti, M 2019b, 'The Mythical 'Gerasimov Doctrine' and the Language of Threat', *Critical Studies on Security*, vol. 7, no. 2, pp. 157–61, https://doi.org/10.1080/21624887.2018.1441623.

Hoffman, F G 2007, *Conflict in the 21 st Century: The Rise of Hybrid Wars*, Potomac Institute for Policy Studies, Arlington, VA.

Hoffman, F G 2022, 'Scholz: Geen Goedkeuring Voor Ingebruikname Nord Stream 2', *NRC*, 22 February.

Huber, T M (ed) 2005, *Compound Wars: That Fatal Knot*, US Army Command and General Staff College Press, Fort Leavenworth, KS.

Hybrid CoE 2022, *Training and Exercises*, <https://www.hybridcoe.fi/training-and-exercise/> (accessed 12 September 2022).

Johnson, R 2018, 'Hybrid War and Its Countermeasures: A Critique of the Literature', *Small Wars and Insurgencies*, vol. 29, no. 1, pp. 141–63, https://doi.org/10.1080/09592318.2018.1404770.

Kerres, M 2021, 'Hoe Moet De Europese Unie Omgaan Met de Hybride Oorlogsvoering Van de Wit-Russiche President Loekasjenko?', *NRC*, 9 November.

Lasconjarias, G & Larsen, J 2015, *NATO's Response to Hybrid Threats*, NATO Defence College, Rome.

Liang, Q & Xiangsui, W 2002, *Unrestricted Warfare: China's Master Plan to Destroy America*, Pan American Publishing Company, Panama City.

Lind, W S, Keith, N, Schmitt, J F, Sutton, J W & Wilson, G I 1989, 'The Changing Face of War : Into the Fourth Generation', *Marine Corps Gazette*, vol. 73, no. 10, pp. 22–6.

Mansoor, P R 2012, ' Introduction: Hybrid Warfare in History', in W Murray & P R Mansoor (eds), *Hybrid Warfare: Fighting Complex Opponents from the Ancient World to the Present*, Cambridge University Press, Cambridge, pp. 1–18.

Mattis, J N & Hoffman, F G 2005, 'Future Warfare: The Rise of Hybrid Wars', *U.S. Naval Institute Proceedings*, vol. 131, no. 11, pp. 18–19.

NATO 2014, *Wales Summit Declaration*, <https://www.nato.int/cps/en/natohq/official_texts_112964.htm> (accessed 12 September 2022).

NATO 2016, *Warsaw Summit Communiqué*, <https://www.nato.int/cps/en/natohq/official_texts_133169.htm> (accessed 12 September 2022).

NATO 2022, *NATO's Response to Hybrid Threats*, <https://www.nato.int/cps/en/natohq/topics_156338.htm> (accessed 12 September 2022).

Nilsson, N, Weissmann, M, Palmertz, B, Thunholm, P & Häggström, H 2021, 'Security Challenges in the Grey Zone: Hybrid Threats and Hybrid Warfare', in M Weissmann, N Nilsson, B Palmertz & P Thunholm (eds), *Hybrid Warfare, Security and Asymmetric Conflict in International Relations*. Bloomsbury Academic, London, pp. 1–18.

Renz, B 2016, 'Russia and "Hybrid Warfare"', *Contemporary Politics*, vol. 22, no. 3, pp. 283–300, https://doi.org/10.1080/13569775.2016.1201316.

Rietjens, S 2022, 'Coming to Grips with Hybrid Warfare', *International Journal of Intelligence and Counter-Intelligence*, online first, pp. 1–6, https://doi.org/10.1080/08850607.2021.1993435.

Snel, C 2022, 'Hybride Dreiging Aan de Orde Van de Dag', *Alle Hens*, no. 8. https://magazines.defensie.nl/allehens/2022/08/03_hybride-dreiging

Snetselaar, D 2023, 'DREAMS Lab: Assembling Knowledge Security in Sino-Dutch Research Collaborations', *European Security*, vol. 23, no. 2, pp. 233–51, https://doi.org/10.1080/09662839.2022.2127317. https://www.tandfonline.com/doi/full/10.1080/09662839.2022.2127317.

Stoker, D & Whiteside, C 2020, 'Blurred Lines: Gray-Zone Conflict and Hybrid War—Two Failures of American Strategic Thinking', *Naval War College Review*, vol. 73, no. 1, pp. 12–48.

The Economist 2010, 'War in the Fifth Domain, Are the Mouse and Keyboard the New Weapons of Conflict', *The Economist*, 1 July.

The Economist 2019, 'The Nord Stream 2 Gas Pipeline Is a Russian Trap', *The Economist*, 16 February.

The Economist 2021a, 'Why Nord Stream 2 Is the World's Most Controversial Energy Project', *The Economist*, 15 July.

The Economist 2021b, 'What Is Happening on the Poland-Belarus Border?', *The Economist*, 9 November.

Treverton, G F 2018, *The Intelligence Challenges of Hybrid Threats*, Centre for Asymmetric Threat Studies, Swedish Defence University, Stockholm.

van Dijk, B 2021, 'ASML Vreest Dat Dieven Gestolen Bedrijfsgeheimen Gaan Exploiteren in China', *Het Financieel Dagblad*, 3 June.

Verschuer, N van 2021, 'Migranten "Werden als een Bal Heen en Weer Gekaatst"', *NRC*, 10 October.

Weissmann, M 2021, 'Conceptualizing and Countering Hybrid Threats and Hybrid Warfare: The Role of the Military in the Grey Zone', in M Weissmann, N Nilsson, B Palmertz & P Thunholm (eds), *Hybrid Warfare, Security and Asymmetric Conflict in International Relations*. Bloomsbury Academic, London, pp. 61–82.

Wijnen, J F van 2020, 'Amsterdamse Universiteiten Werken Samen Met Omstreden Techgigant Huawei', *Het Financieel Dagblad*, 25 August.

15

IRREGULAR AND UNCONVENTIONAL WARFARE

David Kilcullen

This chapter examines the future of irregular and unconventional warfare (UW). It first defines key concepts, then offers an overview of trends in unconventional conflict and how these intersect with the wider context for future warfare. It examines irregular and UW in great-power competition (GPC) and explores Russian and Chinese approaches to irregular warfare. Finally, it identifies implications for practitioners and policy-makers.

Key concepts

United States doctrine defines UW as "operations and activities [to] enable a resistance movement or insurgency to coerce, disrupt, or overthrow a government or occupying power by operating through or with an underground, auxiliary, and guerrilla force in a denied area" (US DoD 2014, p. xi). UW covers

> A broad spectrum of military and paramilitary operations, normally of long duration, predominantly conducted through, with, or by indigenous or surrogate forces who are organized, trained, equipped, supported, and directed in varying degrees by an external source. It includes, but is not limited to, guerrilla warfare, subversion, sabotage, intelligence activities, and unconventional assisted recovery.
>
> (US DoD 2010, p. 259)

UW – called Special Warfare (SW) in Australian, British and sometimes American usage – dates to the Second World War. Intelligence services use the terms Special Activities or Covert Action to describe similar operations by intelligence personnel, conducted independently or in concert with military forces (Stoltz 2022, p. 7).

Irregular warfare (IW) is a more recent concept, dating to 2005 in US military usage. The IW annex to the 2020 *National Defence Strategy* describes it as

> A struggle among state and non-state actors to influence populations and affect legitimacy. IW favours indirect and asymmetric approaches, though it may employ the full range of military and other capabilities, in order to erode an adversary's power, influence, and will. It

includes the specific missions of unconventional warfare (UW), stabilization, foreign internal defence (FID), counterterrorism (CT) and counterinsurgency (COIN).

(US DoD 2020)

IW involves both state and non-state armed groups and seeks to influence populations and perceptions.

Finally, hybrid threat in US doctrine is "the diverse and dynamic combination of regular forces, irregular forces and/or criminal elements, all unified to achieve mutually benefitting effects. Synchronized and synergistic hybrid threat actions can take place in the information, social, political, infrastructure, economic and military domains" (TRADOC 2015). Hybrid threats are described as innovative, adaptive, globally connected, networked and embedded in complex human and physical terrain. They involve a mix of traditional, re-purposed and advanced technologies (including, potentially, weapons of mass destruction) and seek to saturate an entire operating environment, forcing opponents to react to multiple simultaneous threats. The aim is simultaneously to create economic instability, foster lack of trust in existing governance, attack information networks, cause humanitarian crises and physically endanger opponents.

Strategic and technological context

Since the end of the Cold War – more precisely, since the one-sided US victory over Iraq in 1991 showed opponents how *not* to fight the United States – IW has been driven by adversaries' need to avoid US dominance in traditional warfare (Kilcullen 2020, pp. 19–20). Selection pressure – the need to survive in a battlespace ecosystem dominated by US forces – has driven adversaries towards asymmetric adaptation, seeking to sidestep US mastery of one particular warfighting approach that has come to be seen as 'conventional'. Strategically, conventional warfare emphasizes direct force-on-force combat on the battlefield, de-emphasizing political and economic warfare, war termination or post-conflict stabilization; operationally, it prefers rapid decisive high-tech campaigns to protracted wars of attrition; tactically, it favours precision-guided munitions, intensive intelligence, surveillance and reconnaissance (ISR) and information dominance using space-based communications and global connectivity to achieve a 'system-of-systems' effect. Hybrid threats and IW actors offset this through signature manipulation (using ambiguous, covert or clandestine action to prevent detection) and avoidance behaviour (stepping outside western conceptual boundaries of 'warfare') to reduce risk. The goal is to render US conventional dominance irrelevant.

This adaptation is occurring within a complex, cluttered, connected, increasingly urban and littoral battlespace shaped, since the turn of the 21st century, by extraordinarily rapid proliferation of wearable/handheld communications and computing technologies (such as smartphones), which give hybrid and non-state actors levels of lethality and precision once available only to nation-states. A side effect of this connectivity explosion is ubiquitous technical surveillance (UTS) – proliferation of surveillance cameras, smartphones, internet-enabled infrastructure, citizen journalists, open-source intelligence, location-tracking and closed-circuit television – which increasingly renders clandestine activity impossible for all but short periods (Katz 2020). As a result, delayed attribution rather than long-term concealment is the most many IW actors can hope to achieve.

Another effect is that distributed operations, employing collaborative engagement – where sensors, shooters and controllers are dispersed across multiple locations, coordinating via decentralized electronic means – are increasingly common (Wade & Reames 2004; Mullins et al. 2006).

Autonomous systems are proliferating, while cyber and electromagnetic activities (CEMA) are becoming more lethal as a greater proportion of critical civil and military infrastructure is online (Scarborough 2018; Firedome 2021).

Emerging IW operational style

These conditions shape an operational style common to most modern, and likely future IW actors. It includes ubiquitous combat action, distributed across the full breadth and depth of an operational area, using 'leaderless resistance' to avoid centralized headquarters or command-and-control facilities targetable by a conventional adversary. It involves IW actors deploying acephalous swarms of combat groups, remote or stand-off control nodes – where sensors, controllers and shooters are separated in space or located outside a combat theatre altogether – or coordinating via one-way broadcast to self-synchronized actors. Given the urbanizing character of conflict, this involves 'infestation' of urban terrain, as combatants seek cover by embedding in physical structures, hollow and interior spaces and friendly or oblivious populations.

A typical combat group, operating in this manner, might comprise 20–50 personnel, with a mix of heavy and light weapons including direct- and indirect-fire systems, drones and loitering munitions, soft-skinned and armoured vehicles, and – in some cases – CEMA capabilities. Military hardware may be blended with civilian vehicles or off-the-shelf electronics. Some groups may be entirely land-based, while others employ crewed or autonomous watercraft or aircraft. Groups can operate as independent combat teams, aggregate effects by swarming a target, or cooperate with other groups in a self-synchronized manner. The mix of capabilities, mobility mechanisms, signatures and protection levels within the team creates flexibility, enabling it to move rapidly between fights, maintain a light logistics tail, fight mounted or dismounted and concentrate or disperse, as the battle develops.

Future IW actors are likely to build on these observed trends. They will field large numbers of small, cheap, stealthy, multi-role platforms rather than a few expensive, sophisticated, single-role platforms. They are likely to employ modular organizations, in which individuals and groups mirror each other's capabilities and can aggregate to attack targets or rapidly disaggregate into smaller, stealthier teams to fit the terrain and the tactical situation. They will favour collaborative and remote engagement to increase survivability against conventional adversaries. They will optimize for speed and stealth, and as a result will tend to lack the combat weight to stand and fight against conventional forces.

Enduring tactical characteristics of IW – raiding, improvised explosive or incendiary devices, ambushing, baited attacks, sabotage and subversion – will not necessarily change as new technologies emerge. Rather the means, speed and geographical reach of these tactics will change. IW actors will still emerge organically from local populations and operate on their home turf, well-adapted (and highly effective) within specific terrain and environmental conditions, but ineffectual outside that niche. This, with their lack of combat weight, will distinguish irregular fighters from regular militaries who must cover a wider range of contingencies. At the force level, IW actors may employ armoured vehicles, but will continue to optimize for indirect rather than direct protection: using speed, stealth and mobility to avoid being seen or hit (Lind 2008, pp. 10–13).

As more sophisticated technologies proliferate, IW actors may employ 'cyber-kinetic' operations – where CEMA has direct lethal effects, while kinetic engagements target information objectives – turning cyberspace into an adjunct manoeuvre space alongside air, space, land, maritime, information and electromagnetic domains (Goud 2015; Ivezic 2015). A form of integrated cyber-kinetic combined arms manoeuvre is emerging, in which CEMA enables physical manoeuvre, which facilitates follow-on cyber action and so on (Greengard 2010, pp. 20–2). Improvisable capabilities such as 3-D printed weapons, ammunition, incendiaries, explosives, communications devices and spare parts are increasingly available to IW actors (DEFCAD n.d.). Technological 'hugging' – in which IW actors exploit widely-used technologies such as GPS or cell phone systems, knowing that conventional adversaries rely on the same technologies and are thus unlikely to disrupt them – will be increasingly prevalent. Some IW actors are developing rudimentary counter-space capabilities – GPS jamming, high-altitude radio reflectors or balloon-based systems for communications and ISR, or employing space-based systems such as Starlink for targeting (Dukowitz 2022).

Autonomous vehicles and loitering munitions will allow future IW actors to operate across air, maritime and littoral environments previously dominated by state-based militaries, though remaining largely land-centric. On land, IW actors will rarely seek to hold terrain: rather than stand in the open against state-based militaries who would crush them in direct engagements, they will exploit a flexible, stealthy, mobile operational style for survivability. Instead of direct force-on-force combat, IW actors will seek to influence terrain and population indirectly, creating 'no-go' and 'no-see' areas, controlling cities through interdiction of routes and disruption of critical commodities (such as food, water, fuel and data), creating 'commuter insurgencies' based in peri-urban terrain that raid into an urban core, and making tactical use of terrorism to shape a conventional adversary's deployment.

Remote UW will be increasingly practiced by IW actors and state sponsors. In remote UW, rather than physically deploy a mentoring team into a denied area, sponsors use internet, mobile phone or radio and satellite communication to support partners from a distance. At present, remote techniques supplement rather than replacing face-to-face contact. However, IW actors will increasingly engage with sponsors remotely, instead of physical presence. Likewise, sponsors will maintain 'virtual persistent presence' between deployments, building remotely-enabled communications with local partners (Lopez 2019; Kimmons 2020).

Irregular warfare in great-power competition

The United States formally recognized GPC as a driver for global conflict in 2015, although competition with Russia and China had been increasing for almost a decade by then (Congressional Research Service 2022). Rather than self-motivated guerrilla and terrorist groups – as during the Global War on Terrorism (GWOT) – western militaries increasingly face proxy threats. Russia and Iran are the principal sponsors of irregular proxies, with Russian state-controlled military companies, paramilitaries and militias active from Syria and Georgia to Ukraine, Libya and Mozambique. Iran sponsors irregular forces in Iraq, Afghanistan, Yemen and Syria, directly and through its Lebanese proxy Hezbollah. China engages less in sponsorship of proxy forces, preferring to build its own IW capabilities and developing influence via Unrestricted Warfare (URW) and 'Three Warfares' (discussed below).

Factors shaping IW under GPC

Since key players in GPC are nuclear-armed, the dynamics of deterrence discourage direct conflict, displacing competition into surrogate and hybrid activity, hence promoting irregular and UW. This does not mean that conventional combat or, indeed, battlefield nuclear weapons are off the table: through miscalculation, or conflict over core national interests, large-scale combat operations among great powers remain a real possibility. At the same time, however, the risk of escalation across the nuclear threshold is severe enough that rivals will continue to avoid vertical escalation (in which a belligerent increases the intensity of conflict in one location), preferring to seek advantage through horizontal escalation, in which an adversary widens a conflict to new geographies, targets, domains or categories of competition, without necessarily raising intensity in any one area (Fitzsimmons 2019, pp. 95–134).

As an example, in a hypothetical war over Taiwan, Washington might be wary of escalating conflict in and around the Taiwan Strait, lest Chinese anti-ship missiles destroy American vessels or force them out of the region. Likewise, Beijing might be reluctant directly to engage US naval forces or garrisons on Guam or Okinawa for fear of triggering a massive response. This might prompt US SOF – or IW actors sponsored by them – to target Chinese military assets or state-controlled economic interests in, say, Africa or Latin America, to impose costs on China and compel a change in Beijing's strategy. Conversely, China might employ IW actors including maritime militias, operating under cover of a fishing fleet, to blockade Taiwan's offshore islands, triggering a crisis without an invasion and thereby making it harder for any US president to generate support for intervention in response. Each power, in this hypothetical scenario, would be using IW methods via horizontal escalation to enact a cost imposition strategy – across the categories of time, space, materiel and reputation – to change its adversary's strategic calculus without risking direct conflict (Lee 2021).

A second factor shaping IW under GPC is the emergence of space as a warfighting domain, especially suborbital and orbital navigation, ISR and communications satellites (Broad 2021; Dolman 2022, pp. 82–90). The United States, China and Russia all possess advanced space and counterspace capabilities (Weeden & Samson 2022). China has fielded a navigational constellation equivalent and, in some ways, superior to GPS (Tsunashima 2020). China's space station includes a military module; in 2021 Beijing demonstrated a fractional orbital bombardment system using a hypersonic glide vehicle to deliver a warhead from space anywhere on the earth's surface, a capability more advanced than any acknowledged by Russia or the United States (Lee & Singer 2021; Rogoway 2021). Over-reliance, to the point of abject dependence, on space-based systems for targeting, communications and navigation is thus now an enormous vulnerability for conventional militaries.

The risk that a great-power adversary might disable space systems, dislocating defences at the outset of a future conflict, drives militaries and IW actors to new operating methods. For militaries, the need to 'fight unplugged' by reducing dependence on space-based systems will push SOF and UW teams to operate over longer distances and durations, with less contact and support from home base, greater autonomy and more reliance on traditional communications and navigation systems, such as high-frequency radio or enhanced LORAN for navigation and targeting (Sutton 2021; Offermans 2022). Long-range reconnaissance, generation of intelligence mission data (IMD) for precision strike or support networks for battle damage assessment, aircrew recovery and communications will become more prominent SOF tasks. For self-sponsored or proxy IW actors, hugging adversary systems will be harder, while slower and stealthier methods of command, control and communication will increase in importance. All sides will conduct pre-conflict operational preparation of the environment (OPE) to create local support networks that can remain viable if space systems are knocked out (Kuyers 2013). Against this background each major power will employ IW differently.

Russian irregular warfare

Moscow's principal IW actor is the GU (Main Directorate) of Russia's General Staff, commonly known by its pre-2020 acronym, GRU. GRU has operated since 1918 and is the premier covert action arm of the Russian state (Leonard 1999). In western terms, it sits between a SOF organization and an intelligence service; Russians use the term 'special services' to describe organizations like GRU, whose main function is political warfare – covert influence and manipulation – rather than intelligence (Watling 2022). Key features of Russian IW include:

- ***Decisive shaping***. Russian planners treat the pre-conflict phase of a campaign as decisive, seeking to secure objectives before, or ideally instead of, kinetic action.
- ***Cross-domain coercion***. Russian IW weaponizes multiple categories of coercion including military or paramilitary forces, CEMA, economic and political warfare, and information operations, confronting adversaries with multiple simultaneous challenges (Adamsky 2015).
- ***Disruptive ambiguity***. Conscious of UTS, Russian IW does not seek to be covert or clandestine, but rather exploits cluttered and complex environments and ambiguous status to disrupt adversary decision-makers, delaying or preventing a response.
- ***Escalate to de-escalate***. Once commanders commit to combat, they no longer prioritize stealth, instead emphasizing speed, surprise and violence of action. Borrowing a concept from Russian nuclear strategy, in this type of campaign SOF, supported by irregular actors, may seize critical nodes at the outset via *coup de main*, with conventional forces rapidly reinforcing to consolidate, allowing political leaders to negotiate from a position of strength, while obfuscating or downplaying actions to de-escalate.
- ***Weaponization of western norms***. Having presented a *fait accompli,* Russian leaders use military action to set conditions for political success, playing back western norms – responsibility to protect, territorial integrity, self-determination, protection of civilians – to weaken responses.

Some or all of these features were evident during Russian operations in Georgia (2008), Crimea (2013–2014) and Syria (from 2015). Russia's 'special military operation' in Ukraine seems at first glance a departure from this pattern. But as information emerges about initial Russian actions, it seems increasingly clear that the operation was intended to repeat the earlier pattern – which we might call the 'Crimea model' – on a massive scale.

During ten months from April 2021, Russia used troop exercises, CEMA and political and economic warfare to intimidate and divide Ukraine from US and NATO backers, even as western leaders offered Russia a series of diplomatic concessions (Daalder & Lindsay 2022). Russian intelligence seems to have concluded there would be limited Ukrainian military opposition, NATO would not offer serious resistance, and many Ukrainians would welcome, or at least not oppose, an invasion (Reynolds & Watling 2022). Russian analysts saw the shaping phase as successful, rendering the risk of intervention acceptable (Watling & Reynolds 2022).

Accordingly, Russian troops launched a heliborne assault on Hostomel airfield, west of Kyiv, at dawn on 24 February 2022 (Marson 2022a). Speed and surprise were key to this operation, rather than stealth. The aim appears to have been to seize the runway intact, allowing aircraft carrying armoured vehicles, artillery and reinforcements to land, then launch a ground assault into Kyiv (Airlive 2022). Simultaneously, a large armoured column crossed the Belarusian border, driving for Hostomel with the goal of relieving the *coup de main* force on the airfield. Had this succeeded, Russian armour could have been in downtown Kyiv early on the first morning of the war, delivering a deadly shock to a government which Russian analysts had assessed as extremely fragile. A shadow administration, possibly under a pro-Russian oligarch, had allegedly been prepared to step in after the collapse and negotiate peace (Borger 2022; Moscow Times 2022). This would have given Moscow immense negotiating leverage, possibly prevented a NATO response and ended the war before sanctions had time to take effect. If this was Russia's intent, then the campaign plan followed the 'Crimea model' closely – suggesting the invasion in 2022 was not a departure from that model, but an attempt to execute it at scale.

In the event, the assault failed – in part because Ukrainian SOF managed to hold one end of the runway, shoot down several helicopters, and rally local militia to defend one side of the airfield (Trofimov 2022). This delayed the Russian landing force long enough for anti-armour from Ukraine's territorial forces to blunt the assault into Kyiv, while Ukrainian artillery cratered the runway, forcing Russian transport aircraft to orbit without landing (Marson 2022b). One, possibly two, aircraft were shot down with heavy loss of life, while the relief column from Belarus stalled short of its objective (Demerly 2022). Of note, ISR provided remotely via secure communications links, with remote UW technologies (discussed earlier) enabled western services to maintain an advisory relationship with Ukrainian partner forces throughout the effort, and later to feed IMD enabling long-range precision strike (Harris et al. 2022).

Russia's approach to Ukraine in 2022, combined with its history of IW and hybrid warfare, represents one future pathway for IW/UW; China offers another.

Chinese irregular warfare

China, as noted, does not currently sponsor armed IW actors to the same degree, or in the same way, as Russia, having largely ceased such sponsorship at the end of the 1980s. Beijing instead emphasizes development of PLA capabilities and domains (such as space warfare, hypersonic and anti-shipping missiles) alongside conventional modernization (Stephens 2022). China engages in infrastructure exploitation (militarizing islands in the South China Sea, constructing dual-use port facilities across the Indo-Pacific, exploiting financial leverage for economic and diplomatic advantage) rather than directly sponsoring armed IW actors – with exceptions, notably in northeast India (Morris 2011; Bhattacharya 2020). China's ally in South Asia, Pakistan, has filled the role of IW sponsor on China's behalf, mentoring regional actors such as the Taliban and Kashmiri separatists, enabling leaders in Beijing to keep their hands clean. Chinese maritime militia undertake what some analysts call 'people's war at sea', applying a form of state-sponsored IW suited to Chinese goals in the Indo-Pacific, intimidating rivals and blocking adversaries from contested locations (Erickson & Kennedy 2015; Erickson 2017).

Chinese SOF do not treat UW as a core mission as western forces do, and in a future greatpower conflict they would perform tasks such as long-range/low-profile reconnaissance, *coup de main* operations, or raids on strategic targets (Blasko 2015). These would look similar to Russian actions around Hostomel described earlier. The UW function, in Chinese IW, is performed by paramilitary forces such as maritime militia, People's Armed Police, intelligence services working through local Chinese populations or front businesses and private military companies. Chinese companies, since 2018, have been required to cooperate with intelligence services inside China and abroad, under national intelligence legislation (Hoffman & Kania 2018). Many commercial firms maintain Communist Party cells and people's militia units, making them assets for Chinese IW, while the military controls numerous companies (US DoD 2021). Chinese commercial entities thus form a conduit for IW, creating a permissive operating environment for SOF and conventional forces in the event of conflict. Private military companies – presenting as commercial security firms protecting Chinese companies' assets and personnel – provide an even more direct pathway for IW, while their relationships with local communities and governments help develop support and influence networks (Avdialani 2021; Markusen 2022). This is evident in the Pacific, Southeast Asia, Africa and Latin America (Arduino 2022). Commercial penetration of strategic areas can thus be seen as part of OPE, positioning China for influence ahead or instead of a future conflict.

China's 'three warfares' – psychological, legal and public opinion warfare – can be considered a form of non-kinetic IW, operating through a distributed influence network (Kania 2016). Organizations like the Chinese Communist Party's United Front Work Department conduct influence campaigns exploiting overseas Chinese and local elites to advance key messages or cover for covert or clandestine operations (Bowe 2018). China's 'Thousand Talents' programme – forced underground and renamed after US scrutiny in 2018 – recruited international scientists to work on military projects, creating an enduring influence network abroad while accelerating technology transfer, as does a successor program (Fedasiuk 2020; Strider Technologies 2022). Influencers on social media within China and via Chinese-speaking communities overseas engage in 'astroturfing', generating the appearance of grass-roots support for Beijing, while taking direction from the Communist Party and being paid for each post (King, Pan & Roberts 2017). Civilian–military integration in cyberspace is a key priority for Beijing, with up to ten million individuals in cyber-militias operating under the direction of the military's Strategic Support Force (Inkster 2016; Lyall 2018). In GPC, the three warfares set conditions for military operations: "legal warfare to provide the basis for launching an attack, public opinion warfare to delegitimize the adversary, and psychological warfare to demoralize the adversary" (Knoll, Pollpeter & Plapinger 2021).

The 2020 *National Defence Strategy* identifies China and Russia, with Iran, as

> Willing practitioners of campaigns of disinformation, deception, sabotage, and economic coercion, as well as proxy, guerrilla, and covert operations. This increasingly complex security environment suggests the need for a revised understanding of IW to account for its role as a component of great power competition.
>
> (US DoD 2020)

As this brief overview suggests, IW will be extremely important in GPC, particularly in the cost-imposition and shaping/counter-shaping efforts preceding combat engagement. Adapting to this reality implies the need for western innovation.

Implications and conclusions

As the foregoing analysis suggests, while long-standing sources of IW – jihadist terrorism, state weakness, intrastate conflict and ethno-sectarian unrest – are likely to persist, the resurgence of GPC adds important new drivers of conflict. As Ukraine increasingly becomes a proxy conflict between NATO and Russia, as Russia is driven into China's orbit, and tension over Taiwan grows, the dynamics of nuclear deterrence will encourage great powers to pursue competition through irregular and unconventional means. These may involve lethal combat, in the mode of traditional proxy wars, among sponsored surrogate forces. They may involve cyberwarfare, information warfare and cyber-kinetic operations, conducted online by state actors or cyber-irregulars sponsored by states. Cross-domain coercion will see IW techniques applied to economic warfare (using energy as a weapon, sabotaging critical infrastructure, dislocating supply chains to disrupt agriculture and industry, manipulating currencies and shaping commercial engagements to further IW objectives) and to political warfare, including election interference, sponsorship of dissident and separatist groups, and promotion of unrest within an adversary's society.

Warfare, as noted, increasingly takes place in a crowded, cluttered, highly connected, predominantly urban and coastal environment, against a mix of state and non-state adversaries applying irregular methods to overwhelm us with a massive number of simultaneous challenges. This implies that western militaries need to get out of the defensive crouch of the GWOT, during which they saw themselves as countering and defending against irregular adversaries who held the initiative. Instead, western forces will need to proactively exploit adversary weaknesses, operating in a more offensive manner, to impose hybrid and irregular challenges on great-power adversaries. To do this in a contested space-warfare environment, future SOF and related IW/UW organizations will need to master the art of the light footprint forward, operating in small independent teams, widely dispersed across a littoral, multi-domain environment characterized by cross-domain coercion from great-power adversaries, along with enduring non-state threats such as terrorist networks. In dealing with this set of challenges, national resilience, societal cohesion and civic strength at home will become critical defence missions – but since military forces do not normally hold the lead in domestic security, these will need to be located within a whole-of-nation resilience strategy.

IW/UW organizations, under these conditions, will need to invest in enduring relationships with partners across strategically important regions, as part of a broad OPE strategy. This will likely involve a mix of remote-UW and on-scene engagement with partners, involving digital overwatch teams in a home base, paired (or alternating through multiple rotations) with field teams. The increasing prevalence of UTS will require substantial effort on communications security (COMSEC) and operational security (OPSEC), including training for partner forces. Cyber-kinetic integration – combining manoeuvre with firepower and CEMA – will become standard, as IW actors engage in protracted shaping and counter-shaping efforts to impose costs in time, space, materiel and reputation to change an adversary's calculus. Operating in contested or denied environments, where space warfare capabilities are used to blind and dislocate adversaries, will demand the ability to 'fight unplugged', rapidly improvise capabilities on the spot and operate in stealthy, dispersed, autonomous small teams with much less reach-back support than today's militaries became accustomed to during the GWOT. Innovation, and the ability to rapidly repurpose assets to generate field-expedient capabilities will become a core SOF skill.

This in turn will require updates to doctrine, organization, training and education, materiel and equipment, leadership, personnel, facilities and interoperability – in effect, a complete overhaul of capability. Traditional UW/SW and IW approaches will need updating for the range of techniques available to state-sponsored adversaries, with a focus on support to resistance movements and exiled governments whose territory is occupied by a great-power adversary, and deterrence through denial – convincing an adversary not to attack through conspicuous whole-of-nation resilience, total national defence and preparation for resistance warfare. Supporting such a 'porcupine strategy' will demand security force assistance to approved partners (domestic and overseas), support to resistance groups whether on-scene or remote and collaboration with other national agencies (Timbie & Ellis 2022). In the event of conflict, multi-domain special operations (covert, clandestine, ambiguous or overt) will rely on a foundation of relationships and capabilities developed earlier, during pre-conflict shaping and OPE. IW and UW techniques will be central to this effort, along with collection and dissemination of IMD and support to strategic strike. All this suggests that, while irregular warfare and UW will undergo changes due to the factors identified in this chapter, both forms of conflict will remain central and enduring features of warfare.

References

Adamsky, D 2015, *Cross-Domain Coercion: The Current Art of Russian Strategy*, Institut Français des Relations Internationales, Paris.
Airlive 2022, *Russian Air Assault on Gostomel Airport*, <https://youtu.be/dD7tVaB2-2M> (accessed 4 December 2022).
Arduino, A 2022, 'Chinese Private Security Firms Are Growing Their Presence in Africa: Why it Matters', *The Conversation*, 8 August.

Avdialani, E 2021, 'For China, Private Military Companies are the Future', *The National Interest,* 8 November.

Bhattacharya, R 2020, 'How China's "Aid" To Rebel Groups Sustained Northeast Insurgency', *The Quint,* 1 July, <https://www.thequint.com /voices/opinion/northeast-india-sustained-insurgency-covert-chinese-support-weapons-supply#read-more> (accessed 4 December 2022).

Blasko, D J 2015, 'Chinese Special Operations Forces: Not Like "Back at Bragg"', *War on The Rocks,* 1 January.

Borger, J 2022, 'Kremlin Dismisses Ukraine's Offer to Free Putin Ally in Prisoner Exchange', *The Guardian,* 13 April.

Bowe, A 2018, *China's Overseas United Front Work: Background and Implications for the United States,* US-China Economic and Security Review Commission, Washington, DC.

Broad W J 2021, 'How Space Became the Next "Great Power" Contest Between the U.S. and China', *The New York Times,* 24 January.

Congressional Research Service 2022, *Renewed Great Power Competition: Implications for Defense—Issues for Congress,* Congressional Research Service, Washington, DC.

Daalder, I H & Lindsay, J M 2022, 'Why Putin Underestimated the West', *Foreign Affairs,* 7 April, <https://www.foreignaffairs.com/articles/russian-federation/2022-04-07/why-putin-underestimated-west> (accessed 4 December 2022).

DEFCAD n.d., *The World's Largest 3-D Gun Repository,* <https://defcad.com> (accessed 4 December 2022).

Demerly, T 2022, 'Reports: "Two Russian Il-76s Shot Down" in Ukraine, Combat Erupts in Kyiv', *The Aviationist,* 26 February.

Dolman, E C 2022, 'Space Is a Warfighting Domain', *Æther: A Journal of Strategic Airpower & Spacepower,* vol. 1, no. 1, pp. 82–90.

Dukowitz, Z 2022, 'How Elon Musk's Starlink Satellites Make Drone Operations Possible for Special Ukrainian Drone Unit', *UAV Coach,* 30 March, <https://uavcoach.com/ukraine-starlink/> (accessed 4 December 2022).

Erickson, A S 2017, *Understanding China's Third Sea Force: The Maritime Militia,* Harvard Fairbanks Center for Chinese Studies, Cambridge, MA, 8 September.

Erickson, A S & Kennedy, C M 2015, 'Meet the Chinese Maritime Militia Waging a "People's War at Sea"', *The Wall Street Journal,* 30 March.

Fedasiuk, R 2020, 'If You Want to Keep Talent Out of China, Invest at Home', *Foreign Policy,* 17 September.

Firedome 2021, 'Top Cyber Attacks on IoT Devices in 2021', *Firedome,* 30 November.

Fitzsimmons, M 2019, 'Horizontal Escalation: An Asymmetric Approach to Russian Aggression?', *Strategic Studies* Quarterly, vol. 13, no. 1, pp. 95–134.

Goud, N 2015, 'What Is a Cyber-Kinetic Attack?', *Cybersecurity Insiders,* <https://www.cybersecurity-insiders.com/what-is-a-cyber-kinetic-attack/> (accessed 4 December 2022).

Greengard, S 2010, 'The New Face of War', *Communications of the ACM,* vol. 53, no. 12, pp. 20–2, https://doi.org/10.1145/1859204.1859212.

Harris, S, Sonne, P, Lamothe, D & Birnbaum, M 2022, 'U.S. Provided Intelligence That Helped Ukraine Sink Russian Warship', *The Washington Post,* 5 May.

Hoffman, S & Kania, E 2018, 'Huawei and the Ambiguity of China's Intelligence and Counter-Espionage Laws', *ASPI Strategist,* 13 September.

Inkster, N 2016, *China's Cyber Power,* Routledge, London.

Ivezic, M 2015, 'The World of Cyber-Physical Systems & Rising Cyber-Kinetic Risks', *Cyber-Kinetic Security,* 31 March.

Kania, E 2016, 'The PLA's Latest Strategic Thinking on the Three Warfares', *China Brief,* vol. 16, no. 13, <https://jamestown.org/program/the-plas-latest-strategic-thinking-on-the-three-warfares/> (accessed 4 December 2022).

Katz, B 2020, *The Intelligence Edge: Opportunities and Challenges from Emerging Technologies for U.S. Intelligence,* Center for Strategic and International Studies, Washington, DC.

Kilcullen, D 2020, *The Dragons and the Snakes: How the Rest Learned to Fight the Rest,* Oxford University Press, New York.

Kimmons, S 2020, 'New Normal for Indo-Pacific Partners May Include Larger Virtual Presence', *Army News Service,* 22 May, <https://www.army.mil/article/235865/new_normal_for_indo_pacific_partners_may_include_larger_virtual_presence> (accessed 4 December 2022).

King, G, Pan, J & Roberts, M 2017, 'How the Chinese Government Fabricates Social Media Posts for Strategic Distraction, Not Engaged Argument', *American Political Science Review,* vol. 111, no. 3, pp. 484–501, https://doi.org/10.1017/S0003055417000144.

Knoll, D, Pollpeter, K & Plapinger, S 2021, *China's Irregular Approach to War: The Myth of a Purely Conventional Future Fight*, Modern Warfare Institute, West Point, NY, 27 April, <https://mwi.usma.edu/chinas-irregular-approach-to-war-the-myth-of-a-purely-conventional-future-fight/> (accessed 4 December 2022).

Kuyers, J 2013, '"Operational Preparation of the Environment": "Intelligence Activity" or "Covert Action" by Any Other Name?', *American University National Security Law Brief*, vol. 4, no. 1, pp. 21–40, <https://ssrn.com/abstract=2398500> (accessed 4 December 2022).

Lee, D 2021, *Cost Imposition: The Key to Making Great Power Competition an Actionable Strategy*, Modern Warfare Institute, West Point, NY, 8 April, <https://mwi.usma.edu/cost-imposition-the-key-to-making-great-power-competition-an-actionable-strategy/> (accessed 4 December 2022).

Lee, T A & Singer, P W 2021, 'China's Space Program Is More Military Than You Might Think', *Defense One*, 16 July, <https://www.defenseone.com/ideas/2021/07/chinas-space-program-more-military-you-might-think/183790/> (accessed 4 December 2022).

Leonard, R W 1999, *Secret Soldiers of the Revolution: Soviet Military Intelligence, 1918–33,* Greenwood Press, Westport, CT.

Lind, A 2008, *Semi-Active Suspension Systems Using Magneto-Rheological Fluids*, Forsvarets Forskningsinstitutt, Oslo, <https://www.researchgate.net/publication/240625298_Semiactive_suspension_systems_using_magneto-rheological_fluids/link/0a85e52fccc55181b6000000/download> (accessed 4 December 2022).

Lopez, C T 2019, *Persistent Engagement, Partnerships, Top Cybercom's Priorities*, US Department of State, 14 May, <https://www.defense.gov/News/News-Stories/Article/Article/1847823/persistent-engagement-partnerships-top-cybercoms-priorities/> (accessed 4 December 2022).

Lyall, N 2018, 'China's Cyber Militias', *The Diplomat*, 1 March, <https://thediplomat.com/2018/03/chinas-cyber-militias/> (accessed 4 December 2022).

Markusen, M 2022, *A Stealth Industry: The Quiet Expansion of Chinese Private Security Companies*, Center for Strategic and International Studies, Washington, DC.

Marson, J 2022a, 'The Ragtag Army That Won the Battle of Kyiv and Saved Ukraine', *The Wall Street Journal*, 20 September.

Marson, J 2022b, 'Putin Thought Ukraine Would Fall Quickly. An Airport Battle Proved Him Wrong', *The Wall Street Journal*, 3 March.

Morris, L 2011, 'Is China Backing Indian Insurgents?', *The Diplomat*, 22 March.

Moscow Times 2022, 'США назвали нового возможного главу марионеточного правительства в Киеве' [United States Named New Possible Head of Puppet Government in Kiev], *Moscow Times*, 15 February.

Mullins, K, Troyerb, B, Wadeb, R, Skibbac, B & Dunn, M 2006, 'Collaborative Engagement Experiment', in *Proceedings of the SPIE 6230–37: Unmanned Systems Technology VIII*, 62300V (12 May 2006); https://doi.org/10.1117/12.664613 <https://apps.dtic.mil/sti/pdfs/ADA449482.pdf> (accessed 4 December 2022). Event: Defense and Security Symposium, 2006, Orlando (Kissimmee), Florida, United States.

Offermans, G 2022, *eLoran - Alternative PNT for Submerged and GNSS Denied Environments*, Conference Presentation, DISTEC-UDT, Rotterdam, 8 June.

Reynolds, N & Watling, J 2022, 'Ukraine through Russia's Eyes', *RUSI Commentary*, 25 February, <https://rusi.org/explore-our-research/publications/commentary/ukraine-through-russias-eyes> (accessed 4 December 2022).

Rogoway, T 2021, 'China Tested A Fractional Orbital Bombardment System That Uses A Hypersonic Glide Vehicle: Report', *The War Zone,* 18 October.

Scarborough, S 2018, *CEMA and the Internet of Things*, conference presentation, 30 August, <https://youtu.be/QZpBakOTTb4> (accessed 4 December 2022).

Stephens, W 2022, *China's Space Program Through the Lens of Irregular Warfare Theory*, China Aerospace Studies Institute, Montgomery, AL.

Stoltz, W A 2022, *A Regrettable Necessity: The Future of Australian Covert Action*, Australian National University, National Security College, Canberra.

Strider Technologies 2022, *The Los Alamos Club: How the People's Republic of China Recruited Leading Scientists from Los Alamos National Laboratory to Advance Its Military Programs*, <https://www.strider-intel.com/wp-content/uploads/Strider-Los-Alamos-Report.pdf> (accessed 4 December 2022).

Sutton, M 2021, *Special Operations Forces (SOF): Dual Redundancy for Denied Environments—from System to Soldier*, <https://www.orolia.com/wp-content/uploads/2021/07/Special-Operations-Forces-Dual-Redundancy-for-GPS-GNSS-Denied-Environments-Final_0-1.pdf> (accessed 4 December 2022).

Timbie, J & Ellis, J O Jr 2022, 'A Large Number of Small Things: A Porcupine Strategy for Taiwan', *Texas National Security Review*, vol. 5, no. 1, pp. 83–93, https://doi.org/10.15781/gkaw-3709.

TRADOC 2015, *Training Circular TC 7–100.4, Hybrid Threat Force Structure Organization Guide*, US Army Training and Doctrine Command, <https://odin.tradoc.army.mil/TC/TC_7-100.2_Opposing_Force_Tactics/TC_7-100.4_Hybrid_Threat_Force_Structure_Organization_Guide> (accessed 4 December 2022).

Trofimov, Y 2022, 'Ukraine's Special Forces Hold Off Russian Offensive on Kyiv's Front Lines', *The Wall Street Journal*, 4 March.

Tsunashima, T 2020, 'In 165 Countries, China's Beidou Eclipses American GPS', *Nikkei Asia*, 25 November, <https://asia.nikkei.com/Spotlight/Century-of-Data/In-165-countries-China-s-Beidou-eclipses-American-GPS> (accessed 4 December 2022).

US DoD 2010, *Department of Defense Dictionary of Military and Associated Terms,* Joint Publication 1–02, US Department of Defence, Washington, DC.

US DoD 2014, *Special Operations*, Joint Publication 3-05, US Department of Defence, Washington, DC.

US DoD 2020, 'Summary of the Irregular Warfare Annex to the National Defense Strategy', *US Department of Defence*, <https://media.defense.gov/2020/Oct/02/2002510472/-1/-1/0/Irregular-Warfare-Annex-to-the-National-Defense-Strategy-Summary.PDF> (accessed 4 December 2022).

US DoD 2021, 'DOD Releases List of Chinese Military Companies in Accordance with Section 1260H of the National Defense Authorization Act for Fiscal Year 2021', *US Department of Defence*, 3 June.

Wade, R L & Reames, J M 2004, 'Collaborative Engagement', *Proceedings of the SPIE*, vol. 5422, pp. 398–404, https://doi.org/10.1117/12.553048.

Watling, J 2022, 'The Kaleidoscopic Campaigning of Russia's Special Services', *RUSI Commentary*, 20 September, <https://rusi.org/explore-our-research/publications/commentary/kaleidoscopic-campaigning-russias-special-services> (accessed 4 December 2022).

Watling, J & Reynolds, N 2022, *The Plot to Destroy Ukraine*, RUSI, London.

Weeden, B & Samson, V (eds) 2022, *Global Counterspace Capabilities: An Open Source Assessment,* Secure World Foundation, Washington, DC.

16

THE FUTURE OF PROXY WARS

Vladimir Rauta and Giuseppe Spatafora

Introduction

The future of proxy wars is already here, and the present of proxy wars feels at home in the past. Proxy wars are a regular feature of modern conflict (Mumford 2013), and, perhaps, "the most successful kind of political war" being waged today (Barrons in Roberts 2019, p. 11). As some have observed, "war by proxy is a strategy depended on now as never before" (Stevenson 2020). Others have even argued that the strategic objectives of states "are likely to be played out in proxy wars" (de Soysa 2017) to such an extent that "proxy warfare will shape twenty-first century conflict for the foreseeable future" (Rondeaux & Sterman 2019, p. 3).

The topic has gained "a degree of public attention which it has perhaps not enjoyed since the end of the Cold War" (Marshall 2016, p. 184), with proxy wars shaping contemporary conflict debates for academics and practitioners alike (Rauta 2021a, p. 113). Political violence of many guises has become synonymous with proxy wars, be it in the context of the Syrian civil war (2011–ongoing) or the Russian invasion of Ukraine (2022–ongoing). If the Syrian civil war "typifies the age of proxy war like no other conflict" (Stevenson 2020), the Russo-Ukrainian inter-state war shows the escalatory potential of simmering proxy wars (Spatafora & Rauta 2022). Moreover, the entire histories of some recent wars, like Libya (2011–2014; 2014–2020) or Yemen (2014–ongoing), sit in the shadow of proxy wars. Scholarship on proxy wars has grown considerably into a sub-field of study (Karlén et al. 2021; Moghadam, Rauta & Wyss 2023; Rauta 2021a), just as this type of war entered the lexicon of transatlantic national security and defence policy.

Given that "proxy wars are not going away" (Byman 2018), how do we assess their future? Is it correct to expect fighting "to shift from explicit conflicts between states to proxy wars, conducted at arm's length with a buffer of deniability" (Warrell 2020)? Or do proxy wars contribute to the contested idea "that humanity is past the era of war", at least in the traditional sense of state-on-state conventional fighting (Fazal & Poast 2019)? In this chapter, we propose a middle-ground between arguments that see delegation of war to proxies as the future of war and those who see it as a thing of the past. While arguments proclaiming an era of "new proxy wars", "semi-proxy wars", or "quasi-proxy wars" are far-fetched, the empirical phenomenon "has exhibited important patterns of change in recent years" (Moghadam & Wyss 2018). These are key to making sense of where proxy wars are today and where they might be headed in the future.

DOI: 10.4324/9781003299011-20

In this chapter, we advance an argument that balances continuity and change in a discussion about the future of proxy wars. Specifically, we use the recently updated *External Supporter Dataset* (ESD) to assess current trends in proxy wars and to consider their future implications (Meier et al. 2022). ESD is the most complete and updated global dataset focusing on forms of external participation in conflict by actors other than the primary warring parties. It includes both state and non-state actors, and spans across interstate and intrastate conflicts between 1975 and 2017. ESD lists a significant number of forms of external support, including weapons supplies, training and expertise, intelligence sharing, as well as troop support and the sharing of territory and infrastructure for joint operations. ESD allows us to study current trends in proxy warfare and to anticipate future ones. Although some forms of external support such as troop provision do not fall under the mainstream understanding of proxy wars as indirect intervention (Mumford 2013; Rauta 2018, 2021b), ESD allows us to compare the two strategies, and understand when actions via proxy happen in isolation and when they are combined with direct intervention.

We offer two tentative empirical and theoretical links: actor diversity and process complexity. With an argument that is in equal parts actor-centric and process-centric, we aim to provide a corrective to accounts of proxy war dynamics misinformed by the past, and then present set of conjectures on possible future trajectories of proxy wars. The chapter is structured as follows. First, we briefly situate our focus on actor diversity and process complexity within the debate. Second, we show how current trends on who wages proxy wars and who fights proxy wars highlight key empirical features which are likely to be relevant in the future. Third, we evaluate the place proxy wars hold on the wider spectrum of conflict by offering some observations about the interaction between proxy wars, counterterrorism (CT) and counterinsurgency (COIN) campaigns, and great power competition.

Proxy wars, actor diversity, and process complexity

Proxy wars are conflicts between two (or more) actors in which at least one of them entrusts another party to fight on their behalf. The external party (usually referred to as the *sponsor* or *principal*) delegates combat action to an agent (known as the *proxy*) and provides some form of military, economic, or diplomatic assistance to help the latter fight. As such, we can think of proxy warfare as an indirect military strategy that substitutes direct military confrontation with the opponent. The study of this phenomenon has grown tremendously and has coalesced into what is now proxy war studies: a research sub-field with a distinctive intellectual disciplinary orientation, galvanised around a notion of relative conceptual autonomy and, more importantly, one that embraces intellectual and theoretical diversity, interdisciplinarity and methodological pluralism (Moghadam, Rauta & Wyss 2023).

The progress and cumulation of the debate have been recently evaluated in comprehensive ways and they need not be relitigated in this chapter (Karlén et al. 2021; Rauta 2021a, 2021b). To briefly summarise the state of the field, we know that proxy wars are by no means a new phenomenon, with important historical antecedents: the Thirty Years' War (1618–1648), the American War of Independence (1775–1783), the Russian Civil War (1917–1922) and the Spanish Civil War (1936–1939). We know that proxy wars are very common: research has estimated that almost two-thirds of all rebel groups active since World War II have received external support (San-Akca 2016); and data on external support to insurgencies over the last two centuries demonstrate that the odds of groups receiving aid have increased from about one in five to about four in five (Grauer & Tierney 2018).

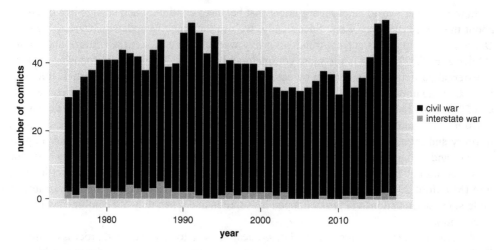

Figure 16.1   Conflict trends, 1975–2017.

Source: Authors' calculations on ACD data.

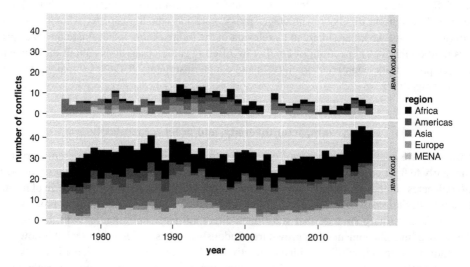

Figure 16.2   Proxy war trends by region, 1975–2017.

Source: Authors' calculations on ESD data.

Data from ESD show that, over the past four decades, most conflicts have had a proxy element. Figure 16.1, derived from the Armed Conflict Dataset (ACD) (Pettersson et al. 2021), displays the trend in conflicts from 1975 to 2017, showing a peak in the number of conflicts per year around 1990, followed by a decline over the post-Cold War period and a new uptick in violence after 2010. Figure 16.2, using ESD data, which distinguishes between proxy wars (i.e., conflicts with an element of indirect external support) and wars without proxy features, shows that most conflicts listed in Figure 16.1 had a proxy element. More than 80% of civil wars and 72% of interstate wars recorded between 1975 and 2017 have experienced external meddling in the form of support to conflict actors (Meier et al. 2022). Proxy wars too tend to decline after the end of the Cold War, only to surge again over the past decade. This suggests a correlation between periods of heightened strategic competition and the use of proxy strategies, as we discuss in the "Process Complexity" section. Finally, Figure 16.2 indicates where proxy wars tend to take place: while a sizeable proportion of them takes place in Asia (including Afghanistan) and is constant throughout the period, it is a surge in proxy conflicts in Africa and the Middle East what is driving the recent global growth of conflicts.

We know that proxy wars are waged because they are cost-effective, risk-averse and deniable. They are, as US President Dwight Eisenhower infamously put it, "the cheapest insurance in the world" (Mumford 2013, p. 40), whilst being "a superficially seductive policy option" (Hughes 2014, p. 523). We know that proxy wars tend to be covert (Carson 2018), although it is "usually easy to find out who is backing whom" (Stevenson 2020). We know that the notion sometimes implies symmetry whereby two sides fight each other indirectly through proxies. Finally, we also know that proxy wars make conflicts longer (de Soysa 2017; Roberts 2019), deadlier and more severe (Lacina 2006; Salehyan, Siroky & Wood 2014), as well as more likely to recur (Karlén 2017).

These findings, we argue, could benefit from two further empirical and theoretical links: actor diversity and process complexity. Why the two are a missing piece of the proxy war puzzle is explained in the extant literature by the relative infancy of this debate (Karlén et al. 2021), by the continuous politicisation of the label of "proxy war" (Rauta & Stark 2022), and the prevalence of some theoretical perspectives such as the principal-agent theory (Salehyan 2010; Salehyan, Gleditsch & Cunningham 2011). Our emphasis on these two links is informed by the need to tap into the variation proxy wars show today – a key aspect likely to hold for the future. Proxy wars are not just an interaction between a powerful state and a weaker proxy, nor do they simply follow the logic of "my enemy's enemy is my friend". Proxy wars involve a range of actors in vastly different roles which, much like in civil wars, "foster an apparently massive, though variable, mix of identities and actions – to such a degree as to be defined by that mix" (Kalyvas 2003, p. 475). Proxy wars come about in radically different ways across geostrategic contexts and evolve and terminate following *sui generis* modes. Proxy wars do not "hijack" only civil wars but overlap with inter-state wars and they hold key implications for a future spectrum of war including COIN, as well as great power competition and war. As we show next, actor diversity and process complexity are already evidenced by current trends and their careful consideration allows for a more stable discussion on the future of wars by proxy. Taken together, they permit a correction of some flawed assumptions behind proxy wars today and the drawing of a more stable foundation for understanding what lies ahead.

Proxy wars and actor diversity

As discussed previously, proxy wars follow an indirect military strategy through the employment of a proxy as a third party (Rauta 2018, p. 475; Karlén et al. 2021, p. 2051; Rauta 2021b). Whilst these definitions offer a core set of features of the phenomenon, much of the debate has been operating on some assumptions that could benefit from nuance for a correct assessment of both the present and the future of wars by proxy. Specifically, we have come to presuppose that the delegating actor tends to be a state, and the proxy a non-state actor. In doing so, we have ignored the empirical diversity behind answers to two questions relevant to the future: Who wages proxy wars? Who fights proxy wars?

Who wages proxy wars? Features of sponsors

When it comes to who wages proxy wars, most proxy conflicts recorded since 1975 (94%) involve state supporters. As Figure 16.3 shows, the ten most frequent state sponsors include great, middle

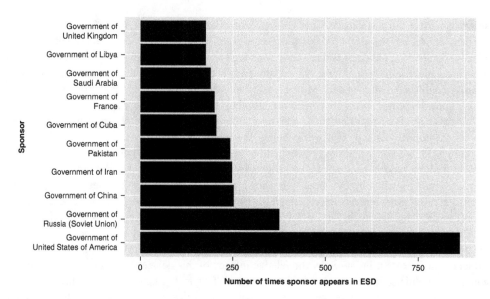

Figure 16.3 Most frequent state sponsors, 1975–2017.

Source: Authors' calculations on ESD data.

and weak powers. This is unsurprising for the logic of proxy wars is rather straightforward, appealing to strong and weak states alike.

For states, the advantages of delegation to proxies emerge from its lower costs. While states can directly intervene with their military forces against any perceived adversaries, intervention carries significant costs, including military losses and the risks of escalation (San-Akca 2016). Instead, by supporting a warring faction via a proxy strategy, states can avoid direct combat and only accept the costs of subsidising or training of one side. Proxy war is, therefore, "the least bad option" when the direct deployment of armed forces is deemed too expensive (Groh 2019). Moreover, foreign states can exploit the proxy's competences: local actors know the territory and the battlefield better than the state's own forces, may have specialised knowledge or skills and possess higher legitimacy vis-à-vis the population and foreign audiences (Salehyan 2010). In short, proxy wars allow state sponsors to reap the benefits of the proxy's competencies while depressing the costs of fighting.

Despite the presence of both major and non-major powers, ESD data show some interesting shifts, likely to hold for the future. Specifically, the permanent members of the United Nations Security Council (UNSC) have been the most frequent external supporters over the last decade, replacing regional powers such as India, Iran, and Pakistan that took centre stage after the beginning of the 21st century (Meier et al. 2022).

In fact, the top panel of Figure 16.4 reflects the trends in Figure 16.2, whereas the bottom panel runs contrary to it, showing an increase in non-P5 sponsorship when the number of proxy wars declines. The implications for the future are significant, especially given the shift towards multipolarity and great power competition. Yet, the data comes with an important blind spot: it assumes a direct relationship between state sponsors and proxies when proxy wars include many hierarchical and heterarchical relationships between sponsors themselves. Recently discussed as "complex conflict delegation" (Karlén & Rauta 2023; Karlén et al. 2021, pp. 2058–60), the issue of chains of delegation is key to the future of proxy wars not least given the

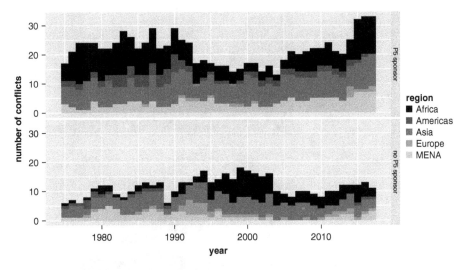

Figure 16.4 Disaggregating state sponsors: P5 vs other states.

Source: Authors' calculations on ESD data.

multi-actor conflict settings of contemporary proxy wars. For example, the United States' program of backing the opposition to Syrian President Bashar al-Assad involved training bases in neighbouring Jordan and Turkey, acting also as trans-shipment points for lethal support (Cloud & Abdulrahim 2013). It is, therefore, plausible to infer the future transformation of single conflict delegation into complex proxy wars involving *composite principals* (several states jointly supporting a proxy), *multiple principals* (several states individually supporting a proxy), and *chains of subordinate or specialised principals* (a state delegating to another state which further delegates to a proxy).

Next, discussions of the future of proxy wars need to recognise that non-state actors may also be principals and wage proxy wars themselves. Non-state sponsors make up 21% of all observations of proxy war. The most active non-state sponsors over the past decade include transnational movements such as al-Qaeda, Burma's Kachin Independence Army (KIO), Hezbollah and the Eritrean People's Liberation Front (EPLF). Al-Qaeda famously supported the Taleban against other Afghan groups during the 1990s and against the US-led coalition and new Afghan government in the 2000s. Hezbollah (itself part of Iran's proxy delegation chain) has been Hamas's strongest backer in Gaza. Both Hezbollah in Lebanon and the Kurdish YPG in Syria have employed proxies to reach out to local communities. In the Democratic Republic of Congo, the state's armed forces have a history of backing local militias to fight against rebels such as the Democratic Forces for the Liberation of Rwanda (FDLR), a practice which drove FDLR itself to "cultivate local allies and proxies of their own", thereby complicating the prospects of resolving the conflict (Arieff 2019, p. 9). These actors possess significant economic and military power, surpassing that of some state actors, and are therefore capable of having their own proxies. However, there are some significant differences between them and state actors. Specifically, non-state sponsors use proxies as "political ancillaries" to "address their organisational shortcomings" such as governance and legitimacy deficits (Moghadam & Wyss 2020, pp. 122–3). These trends are likely to persist in the near future as the battle for political legitimacy in certain territories ensues, especially is the Middle East and Sub-Saharan Africa where state authority is strongly contested, and non-state actors seek to present themselves as legitimate governments (Huang 2016). Moreover, given the growing power of

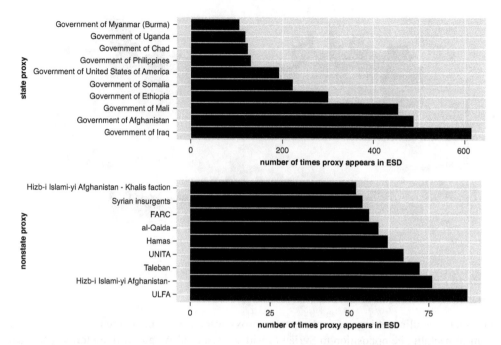

Figure 16.5   Most frequent state and non-state proxies.

Source: Authors' calculations on ESD data.

some non-state actors, including Private Military Contractors (PMCs), vis-à-vis states, we may see a further increase in the proportion of proxy wars waged by non-state sponsors, even if state actors are likely to remain the most common type of sponsor for the foreseeable future.

Who fights proxy wars? Proxy characteristics

As most definitions of proxy wars suggest, proxies are often equated with non-state actors (San-Akca 2016). During the Cold War, the typical proxies were rebel groups engaging in guerrilla warfare or terrorism, such as the Viet Cong, the Irish Republican Army (IRA), the Mujahedeen in Afghanistan or the Contras in Nicaragua. Prominent proxies over the past decade include the Syrian Democratic Forces (SDF) and the People's Republics in Donetsk and Luhansk. However, the most common recipients of support since 1975 (59% of all observations in ESD) are states actors, the most frequent since 1975 being Iraq, Afghanistan, and Mali (see Figure 16.5).

Importantly, this calculation excludes not only direct troop support, but also all forms of humanitarian assistance, support in peacetime and state-to-state arms transfers, which are part of the regular workings of the global economy (Meier et al. 2022). Hence, these states do fit the definition of proxy actors: they fight on behalf of a third party in exchange for support. The reasons why states and non-state actors become proxies are comparable: the material resources and expertise they receive as part of the transaction allow them to gain an advantage over adversaries, finance their war effort and organisational structure and increase the chances of victory (Salehyan 2010, p. 501). These benefits incentivise state and non-state actors alike to become proxies even though conflict delegation may entail some loss of autonomy. The critique that those actors are not proxies because they would likely fight even without external support – such as states seeking to suppress an internal insurgency – stems from a misrepresentation of proxy wars during the Cold War, which regarded proxies as mere pawns in the chessboard of great powers, deprived of agency. Instead, all proxies have their own reason to engage in combat; fighting on behalf of a third party may compound or add to their own interest, but not annul it.

From the perspective of the proxy, the future of this form of war looks bright. Several conjectures are plausible if we reconsider the degree to which proxy actors themselves shape the strategic environment of delegated war. Be they states or non-state actors, proxies have historically been key to determining the trajectory of the wars they fight. It is worth re-emphasising that even at the height of superpower competition in Africa during the Cold War, proxy wars were hardly the result of external puppeteering. This is relevant to the future of proxy wars not because we necessarily anticipate a new Cold War, but because for proxies, fighting delegated war is a complex endeavour. Proxies seek support either through rebel diplomacy (Huang 2016) or by making the most of the opportunities of social media (Zeitzoff 2017). They shift and modify behaviour to attract new or more support from external backers. As discussed above, the general appeal of the strategy of war by proxy and its cost-effectiveness makes it attractive for several states which opens the window for potentially more proxy wars. Proxies compete with one another for external support, as when the Free Syrian Army and the Syrian Democratic Forces vied for the attention of the United States in the early phase of the Syrian civil war. This makes proxy wars more likely as the barriers for seeking and receiving support are lowered. Proxies also end their relationships with supporters – external or internal – as was the case with the Janjaweed militias who often turned against the government of Sudan. What this implies for the future is perhaps an age of more transactional proxy relationships, individually shorter in length, yet cumulatively more dangerous. This might lend itself to an embrace of proxy strategies in an ad hoc fashion and in the absence of some grand strategic objective, patterns the likes of which are already emerging in some countries in the Middle East, as evidenced by the Iranian network of proxies already performing specialised and different functions across Iraq, Syria, and Yemen (Carmi 2017, p. 6).

Proxy wars and process complexity

Just like the type of actors engaged in proxy wars blur traditional categories, whereby sponsors are states and proxies are non-state actors, so the processes and contexts in which proxy wars unfold are complex, multifaceted, and intersecting. Proxy wars do not take place in isolation, but rather are closely connected to other phenomena, such as CT, strategic competition, and interstate war, which have been on the rise in recent decades.

First, both the growth in the number of conflicts and the parallel rise in proxy wars are linked to the growth of CT and COIN efforts after 9/11. The "by-with-through" approach to CT developed by Western states relies on the support for allies on the ground, both state and non-state actors (Elias 2018). This approach entails the use of proxy forces, and carries with it the benefits (lower costs, local ownership, higher legitimacy), but also the costs (principal-agent dilemmas) associated with this strategy. The United States, for instance, supported the governments of Afghanistan and Iraq, as well as Syrian insurgents, to deter and downgrade the terrorist threat posed by al-Qaeda and Daesh. At times, the need to empower local actors significantly reduced Washington's leverage: proxies, despite their weakness vis-à-vis patrons, could resist unwanted requests as they were indispensable to the implementation of the "by-with-through" approach (Elias 2018). The Afghani government's resistance to far-reaching reforms as part of the effort contributed to the US decision to seek a deal with the Taliban in 2020. However, the approach of dealing with CT and COIN by proxy will likely continue. As the 2022 US National Security Strategy puts it, "we will increase cooperation and support to trusted partners, shifting from a strategy that is 'U.S.-led, partner-enabled' to one that is 'partner-led, U.S.-enabled'" (The White House 2022). Likewise, the UK's most recent *Integrated Operating Concept* proposes fighting against adversaries "utilising proxies and deniable para-military forces" (Ministry of Defence 2021, p. 6). Hence, efforts to reduce direct military presence, relying instead on action by proxy, are bound to be more and more frequent.

Second, proxy wars tend to be embedded in regional and great-power competition. As we already pointed out, the number of proxy wars was high during the 1980s, at the height of US-Soviet competition, and peaked again after 2010, as strategic competition between regional and global power struggle gradually brought the post-Cold War unipolar moment to an end. Often, competing states support rival factions in civil war: the United States and the USSR squared off in Nicaragua (1981–1989), El Salvador (1979–1991), and Angola (1975–1991) (Karlén et al. 2021, p. 2068). In both Vietnam and Thailand, the United States and China assisted opposing sides of the conflict (Carson 2016). More recently, the United States and Russia supported, respectively, the Syrian opposition and the Assad government, even as they both fought the Islamic State (IS). The trend is not limited to the global superpowers. The civil war in Yemen is the theatre of a regional context between Saudi Arabia, who leads a coalition supporting the Sana'a government, and Iran, who instead supplies the Houthi rebel faction (Stark 2020). And civil wars in sub-Saharan Africa tend to experience "competitive interventions" between rival governments interested in weakening each other (Anderson 2019; Duursma & Tamm 2021). As this trend is on the rise, proxy wars have the potential to turn into the modal form of great-power confrontation, given the high costs and the risks of escalation of direct conflict, as the situation in Ukraine is making painfully clear. States might be likely to use a wider array of proxies, including cyber actors and PMCs, the latter of which has already been extensively deployed by Russia: the Wagner Group, closely tied to but not part of Russia's armed forces, has played a significant role in Libya, the Central African Republic and Ukraine, sometimes engaging directly against US-backed actors (Marten 2019).

Finally, the lines between action by proxy and its alternative strategy, direct military confrontation, are often blurred and are likely to remain so. Regional actors often intervene in civil wars in ways that blend forms of indirect and direct support, "providing funding, weapons, and/or intelligence support to local actors, for example, while at the same time deploying Special Forces on the ground to train and sometimes fight alongside local actors or conducting drone strikes or other types of airstrikes" (Karlén et al. 2021, p. 2061). Moreover, proxy war can give way to direct intervention and vice versa. A foreign state supporting a rebel group with weapons and training can escalate its level of involvement by sending its troops to fight the incumbent government, effectively turning the intrastate conflict into an interstate war (Gleditsch, Salehyan & Schultz 2008). For instance, in the spring of 2014, Russia supplied the Donbas separatists indirectly, only to escalate its involvement and send a full-fledged force to forestall the collapse of the separatists against the Ukrainian government forces in the summer. The same conflict witnessed a subsequent case of "de-escalation" from direct intervention to proxy warfare: In 2015, after Russia signed the Minsk agreement and withdrew its troops from Ukraine, it "de-escalated" to indirect support to the self-proclaimed People's Republics in Luhansk and Donetsk (Käihkö 2021). Similarly, in Vietnam (1972), Iraq (2011), and Afghanistan (2020), the United States shifted from military to training missions, ending its phase of direct engagement in combat and moving to an advisory role.

The interaction between proxy war and direct intervention may become a central element in future warfare. As the bottom-right panel in Figure 16.6 shows, we are witnessing a marked increase in the number of conflicts that experience both proxy war (i.e., indirect support) and troop support

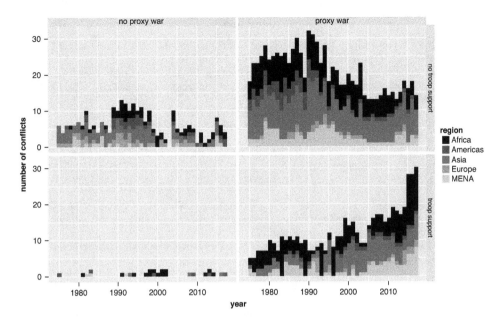

Figure 16.6   Proxy wars and direct interventions, 1975–2017

Source: Authors' calculations on ESD data.

(i.e., direct intervention). The trend is on the rise in all regions of the world. The trend suggests that, on the one hand, more and more states may be incorporating proxy warfare as part of their military strategy, in close coordination with their own armed forces; and on the other hand, both state and non-state actors see additional opportunities to bridge between proxy war and military intervention, as Russia did in Ukraine in 2022. If this trend sustains itself, we are heading for a world in which proxy warfare is more and more prominent.

Conclusion

Over the past decade, conflicts in Afghanistan, Libya, Yemen, Syria, among others, have been characterised by the interference of external state and non-state actors. The prominence of external meddling and conflict delegation has drawn the attention of scholars and policymakers to the phenomenon of proxy warfare. In this chapter, we offered some observations on the future of proxy wars starting from the past and current trends, because, as argued above, to get the future of proxy wars right, we first must get their present right. By focusing on the actors involved and the broader strategic processes shaping proxy war calculations, we show that the strategic logic of indirect war is likely to appeal to a range of state and non-state actors and to be employed on a spectrum of future war. However, we should not infer that all wars will be delegated, nor that ahead lies an era of new proxy wars that make war redundant. The intellectual trap behind such thinking is as dangerous as that negating agency to proxies during the Cold War. Will proxy warfare become the modal form of conflict? Who will be the main sponsors and proxies and how will the relationship between them pan out? The tentative answer is that while proxy warfare offers significant strategic advantages, it will not render direct confrontation obsolete: there are certain strategic objectives for which the use of proxies cannot supersede national armies. At the same time, the power will increasingly shift towards non-state actors, both as proxies and as sponsors.

References

Anderson, N 2019, 'Competitive Intervention, Protracted Conflict, and the Global Prevalence of Civil War', *International Studies Quarterly*, vol. 63, no 3, pp. 692–706, doi:10.1093/isq/sqz037.

Arieff, A 2019, *Democratic Republic of Congo: Background and US Relations*, Congressional Research Service Report R43166. Washington, DC, <https://crsreports.congress.gov/product/pdf/R/R43166/43> (accessed 29 October 2022).

Carmi, O 2017, 'Deconstructing and Countering the Iran Threat Network', The Washington Institute, *Policy Notes*, no. 42, <https://www.washingtoninstitute.org/policy-analysis/deconstructing-and-countering-iran-threat-network> (accessed 29 October 2022).

Carson, A 2016, 'Facing Off and Saving Face: Covert Intervention and Escalation Management in the Korean War', *International Organization*, vol. 70, no. 1, pp. 103–31, doi:10.1017/S0020818315000284.

Carson, A 2018, *Secret Wars: Covert Conflict in International Politics*, Princeton University Press, Princeton & Oxford.

Cloud, D S & Abdulrahim, R 2013, 'U.S. Training Syrian Rebels; White House "Stepped up Assistance"', *Los Angeles Times*, 21 June, <https://www.latimes.com/world/la-xpm-2013-jun-21-la-fg-wn-cia-syria-20130621-story.html> (accessed 29 October 2022).

Duursma, A & Tamm, H 2021, 'Mutual Interventions in Africa', *International Studies Quarterly*, vol. 65, no. 4, pp. 1077–86, doi:10.1093/isq/sqab023.

Elias, B 2018, 'The Big Problem of Small Allies: New Data and Theory on Defiant Local Counterinsurgency Partners in Afghanistan and Iraq', *Security Studies*, vol. 27, no. 2, pp. 233–62, doi:10.1080/09636412.2017.1386935.

Fazal, T M & Poast, P 2019, 'War Is Not Over: What the Optimists Get Wrong About Conflict', *Foreign Affairs*, <https://www.foreignaffairs.com/world/war-not-over> (accessed 29 October 2022).

Gleditsch, K S, Salehyan, I & Schultz, K 2008, 'Fighting at Home, Fighting Abroad: How Civil Wars Lead to International Disputes', *Journal of Conflict Resolution*, vol. 52, no. 4, pp. 479–506, doi:10.1177/0022002707313305.

Grauer, R & Tierney, D 2018, 'The Arsenal of Insurrection: Explaining Rising Support for Rebels', *Security Studies*, vol. 27, no. 2, pp. 263–95, doi:10.1080/09636412.2017.1386936.

Groh, T L 2019, *Proxy War: The Least Bad Option*, Stanford University Press, Stanford, CA.

Huang, R 2016, 'Rebel Diplomacy in Civil War', *International Security*, vol. 40, no. 4, pp. 89–126, doi:10.1162/ISEC_a_00237.

Hughes, G 2014, *My Enemy's Enemy: Proxy Warfare in International Politics*, Academic Press, Portland, OR & Sussex.

Käihkö, I 2021, 'A Conventional War: Escalation in the War in Donbas, Ukraine', *The Journal of Slavic Military Studies*, vol. 34, no. 1, pp. 24–49, doi:10.1080/13518046.2021.1923984.

Kalyvas, S N 2003, 'The Ontology of 'Political Violence': Action and Identity in Civil Wars', *Perspectives on Politics*, vol. 1, no. 3, pp. 475–94, doi:10.1017/S1537592703000355.

Karlén, N 2017, 'The Legacy of Foreign Patrons: External State Support and Conflict Recurrence', *Journal of Peace Research*, vol. 54, no. 4, pp. 499–512, doi:10.1177/0022343317700465.

Karlén, N & Rauta, V 2023, 'Dealers and Brokers in Civil Wars: Why States Delegate Rebel Support to Conduit Countries', *International Security*, vol. 47, no. 4, pp. 107–146, doi:10.1162/ISEC_a_00461.

Karlén, N et al 2021, 'Forum: Conflict Delegation in Civil Wars', *International Studies Review*, vol. 23, no. 4, pp. 2048–78, doi:10.1093/isr/viab053.

Lacina, B 2006, 'Explaining the Severity of Civil Wars', *Journal of Conflict Resolution*, vol. 50, no. 2, pp. 276–89, doi:10.1177/0022002705284828.

Marshall, A 2016, 'From Civil War to Proxy War: Past History and Current Dilemmas', *Small Wars & Insurgencies*, vol. 27, no. 2, pp. 183–95, doi:10.1080/09592318.2015.1129172.

Marten, K 2019, 'Russia's Use of Semi-State Security Forces: The Case of the Wagner Group', *Post-Soviet Affairs*, vol. 35, no. 3, pp. 181–204, doi:10.1080/1060586X.2019.1591142.

Meier, V, Karlén, N, Pettersson, T & Croicu, M 2022, 'External Support in Armed Conflicts. Introducing the UCDP External Support Dataset (ESD), 1975–2017', *Journal of Peace Research*, online first, doi:10.1177/00223433221079864

Ministry of Defence 2021, *Integrated Operating Concept*, <https://www.gov.uk/government/publications/the-integrated-operating-concept-2025> (accessed 29 October 2022).

Moghadam, A, Rauta, V & Wyss, M (eds) 2023, *The Routledge Handbook of Proxy War*, Routledge, London & New York.

Moghadam, A & Wyss, M 2018, 'Five Myths about Sponsor-Proxy Relationships', *Lawfare* (blog), 16 December, <https://www.lawfareblog.com/five-myths-about-sponsor-proxy-relationships> (accessed 29 October 2022).

Moghadam, A & Wyss, M 2020, 'The Political Power of Proxies: Why Nonstate Actors Use Local Surrogates', *International Security*, vol. 44, no. 4, pp. 119–57, doi:10.1162/isec_a_00377.

Mumford, A 2013, 'Proxy Warfare and the Future of Conflict', *The RUSI Journal*, vol. 158, no. 2, pp. 40–6, doi:10.1080/03071847.2013.787733.

Pettersson, T, Davies, S, Deniz, A, Engström, G, Hawach, N, Högbladh, S, Sollenberg, M & Öberg, M 2021, 'Organized Violence 1989–2020, with a Special Emphasis on Syria', *Journal of Peace Research*, vol. 58, no. 4, pp. 809–25, doi:10.1177/00223433211026126.

Rauta, V 2018, 'A Structural-Relational Analysis of Party Dynamics in Proxy Wars', *International Relations*, vol. 32, no. 4, 449–67, doi:10.1177/0047117818802436.

Rauta, V 2021a, 'Framers, Founders, and Reformers: Three Generations of Proxy War Research', *Contemporary Security Policy*, vol. 42, no. 1, pp. 113–34, doi:10.1080/13523260.2020.1800240.

Rauta, V 2021b, '"Proxy War" - A Reconceptualisation', *Civil Wars*, vol. 23, no. 1, pp. 1–24, doi:10.1080/13698249.2021.1860578.

Rauta, V & Stark, A 2022, 'What Does Arming an Insurgency in Ukraine Mean?', *Lawfare* (blog), 3 April, <https://www.lawfareblog.com/what-does-arming-insurgency-ukraine-mean> (accessed 29 October 2022).

Roberts, J 2019, 'Targeting and Resistance: Reassessing the Effect of External Support on the Duration and Outcome of Armed Conflict', *Civil Wars*, vol. 21, no. 3, pp. 362–84, doi:10.1080/13698249.2019.1648631.

Roberts, P 2019, 'The Future Conflict Operating Environment Out to 2030', *RUSI Occasional Paper*, RUSI, London, <https://static.rusi.org/201906_op_future_operating_enviroment_web.pdf> (accessed 29 October 2022).

Rondeaux, C & Sterman, D 2019, 'Twenty-First Century Proxy Warfare: Confronting Strategic Innovation in a Multipolar World Since the 2011 NATO Intervention', *New America*, <https://www.newamerica.org/international-security/reports/twenty-first-century-proxy-warfare-confronting-strategic-innovation-multipolar-world/> (accessed 29 October 2022).

Salehyan, I 2010, 'The Delegation of War to Rebel Organizations', *Journal of Conflict Resolution*, vol. 54, no. 3, pp. 493–515, doi:10.1177/0022002709357890.

Salehyan, I, Gleditsch, K S & Cunningham, D E 2011, 'Explaining External Support for Insurgent Groups', *International Organization*, vol. 65, no. 4, pp. 709–44, doi:10.1017/S0020818311000233.

Salehyan, I, Siroky, D & Wood, R M 2014, 'External Rebel Sponsorship and Civilian Abuse: A Principal-Agent Analysis of Wartime Atrocities', *International Organization*, vol. 68, no. 3, pp. 633–61, doi:10.1017/S002081831400006X.

San-Akca, B 2016, *States in Disguise: Causes of State Support for Rebel Groups*, Oxford University Press, New York.

Soysa, I de 2017, 'Proxy Wars: Implications of Great-Power Rivalry for the Onset and Duration of Civil War', in W R Thompson (ed), *Oxford Research Encyclopedia of Politics*, Oxford University Press, Oxford & New York, doi:10.1093/acrefore/9780190228637.013.526.

Spatafora, G & Rauta, V 2022, 'Ukraine: How Putin Used a Long Proxy Conflict to Justify Invasion', *The Conversation* (blog), 25 February, <https://theconversation.com/ukraine-how-putin-used-a-long-proxy-conflict-to-justify-invasion-177652> (accessed 29 October 2022).

Stark, A 2020, 'The Monarchs' Pawns? Gulf State Proxy Warfare 2011-Today', *New America*, <https://www.newamerica.org/international-security/reports/the-monarchs-pawns/> (accessed 29 October 2022).

Stevenson, T 2020, 'In the Grey Zone: Proxy Wars', *London Review of Books*, <https://www.lrb.co.uk/the-paper/v42/n20/tom-stevenson/in-the-grey-zone> (accessed 29 October 2022).

The White House 2022, *The Biden-Harris Administration's National Security Strategy*, <https://www.whitehouse.gov/wp-content/uploads/2022/10/Biden-Harris-Administrations-National-Security-Strategy-10.2022.pdf> (accessed 29 October 2020).

Warrell, H 2020, 'Future of Warfare: High-Tech Militias Fight Smouldering Proxy Wars', *Financial Times*, 20 January, <https://www.ft.com/content/ab49c39c-1c0c-11ea-81f0-0c253907d3e0> (accessed 29 October 2022).

Zeitzoff, T 2017, 'How Social Media Is Changing Conflict', *Journal of Conflict Resolution*, vol. 61, no. 9, pp. 1970–91, doi:10.1177/0022002717721392.

17

REMOTE WARFARE

Drivers, Limits, Challenges

Neil C Renic

Introduction

Remoteness is an important feature of contemporary armed conflict.[1] States, particularly Western actors, have grown averse to large-scale deployments of their own forces to the battlefield. Instead, lesser forms of military commitment are favoured: support of local and regional partners through a supply of training, equipment and intelligence; the use of private military contractors; discreet Special Forces operations; and air power (both crewed and uncrewed aircraft). Contemporary examples of 'remote warfare' include the 2011 intervention into Libya by NATO forces, US-led coalition action against the Islamic State in Iraq and Syria, as well as the ongoing reliance on armed drone strikes in Pakistan, Somalia, Yemen and Niger.

While the modern practice of remote warfare is now well established, important debates regarding its novelty, morality and utility remain unsettled. *Is it new*: is this mode of warfare merely the latest expression of a longstanding drive toward increasingly distanced violence, or does it represent a more fundamental disjuncture from what has come before? *Is it moral*: should remote warfare be favoured over alternatives as a more virtuous application of violence, or do its military and political benefits come, too often, at the expense of civilian safety? Finally, *is it effective*: does this distanced and dislocated way of fighting increase or undermine the likelihood of victory?

Answering these questions is necessary to understanding not only past and current trends in remote warfare, but also future ones. Remoteness is likely to remain an important feature of armed conflict, for both Western and non-Western actors. In order to properly evaluate what that role will and should be, clarity on its novelty, morality and effectiveness is needed.

In this chapter, I limit my analysis to the air power component of 'remote warfare' – the considerations driving adoption, particularly in the West; its value and limits as a mode of armed conflict; and the moral challenges it generates in relation to civilian harm. Remote warfare is more than air power, but air power has played a critical role in its development and practice. Air power has also been important in shaping, and sometimes distorting, the debate over the value and virtue of this mode of violence.

Remote warfare is best understood in evolutionary, rather than revolutionary terms; as the culmination of longstanding political and technological trends in Western warfare towards increasingly distanced, data-centric and lower-risk violence. These trends have intensified in contemporary remote warfare and will likely intensify further as remote technologies advance. In terms of its morality, remote warfare is not inherently problematic. It does, however, entail moral trade-offs. Too often, the force protection goals that drive remote warfare are pursued and met at the expense of increased – and unacceptable – harm for civilians on the ground. The moral status of future remote military operations will be determined by how well or poorly such harms are mitigated. The effectiveness of remote warfare is also mixed. While there are real tactical and political benefits to this way of war, there are also limits – remote warfare mitigates many of the challenges that afflict more intensive combat operations, but it is no military cure-all. This reality is unlikely to dissuade interested actors, both Western and non-Western, who will continue to invest in remote warfare in the years ahead.

Is it new?

Is contemporary remote warfare a continuation of, or break from, the practices and doctrines that precede it? Establishing this is complicated by the sheer abundance of concepts now used to characterise some or all of its features. Grey zone warfare (Hoffman 2016; Rauta & Monaghan 2021), post-heroic warfare (Luttwak 1995; Enemark 2013), surrogate warfare (Krieg & Rickli 2018; Karagiannis 2021), vicarious warfare (Waldman 2018), risk-transfer war (Shaw 2005), riskless war (Kahn 2002; Kaempf 2014), radically asymmetric war (Renic 2021) – these terms and others are similar enough to make difficult a clear account of the character and distinctiveness of remote warfare.[2]

Exacerbating this classification challenge is the historical ubiquity of remoteness in war. For as long as armed conflict has been waged, participants have availed themselves of technologies – early projectile weapons, firearms, artillery, missiles, aircraft – that exploit and intensify the physical distance between adversaries. The historical antecedents of remote warfare also go beyond the technological. Parallels have been drawn, for example, between the imperial and colonial policing of the past and the remote warfare of the present. These linkages can be observed in relation to both means (use of proxies and a preference for air power over significant ground forces) and ends (violence directed against indigenous adversaries to uphold national or international hierarchies) (Satia 2014; Moran 2015, pp. 2–3; Akhter 2019, p. 64).

Remote warfare is best understood as a distillation of trends that extend back into history and continue to inform, to different degrees, all modern war. Take the ongoing Russo-Ukrainian war: an inter-state armed conflict with hundreds of thousands of fighters on both sides, featuring direct, attritional, sometimes face-to-face fighting, with substantial casualties. Not fundamentally dissimilar from the industrialised warfare of the first half of the 20th century. Yet remoteness also plays an important role in the conflict. Both Russian and Ukrainian militaries are heavily dependent on rocket and artillery systems that fire from dozens of kilometres away; armed drones have been utilised, and Western proxy support in the form of military equipment, financing and sanctions has played a critical role.

As this should reinforce, remote warfare is less a specific mode of war, than a continuum. Virtually all contemporary conflicts feature some degree of remoteness and no conflict is entirely remote. The remote warfare of today is not a new phenomenon, but it is an evolved one, distinct in the intensity of its realisation. Few things highlight this as clearly as the air power utilised by Western forces in remote operations.

Air power serves a number of functions in remote warfare, including surveillance. Prior to the US invasions of Iraq and Afghanistan, airborne surveillance consisted primarily of still photographs (Michel 2019, p. 16). The war on terror necessitated a new approach, however. To better confront the stateless, dispersed group of fighters it now faced, the US implemented a rotation system, harnessing advancements in satellite technology and drones to monitor suspected terrorists continuously and in real time, for weeks if needed (Michel 2019, p. 20). Aiding this were improvements in communication. The kill-chain – a concept that identifies the complete structure of an attack (find, fix, track, target, engage and asses targets) – is now a kill web, "a flexible and persistent network of capabilities spanning global distances and woven together by arrays of streaming data" (Schultz 2022, p. 28).

This links to another distinctive feature of contemporary remote warfare – the data-driven nature of targeting. Targeted killing, like remote warfare, is not a new phenomenon. What is new are the big data and mass surveillance programs that now sustain it. 'Big data' refers to the range of technological advances that have enabled the collection, storage and analysis of massive amounts of diverse data at unprecedented speed. This data plays an important role in many aspects of remote warfare, including signature strikes. These strikes are launched against individuals whose identities are not known; but who are alleged to display, through their conduct, "characteristics associated with terrorist activity" (Bowcott 2012, p. 19). In addition to visual indicators, these signatures are data-based – with calls, emails and other forms of electronic communications collected and analysed to determine whether individuals are liable to lethal targeting (Gibson 2021, p. 190).

When evaluating the distinctiveness of contemporary remote warfare, we should finally consider its increasingly riskless dimensions. The Western reliance on air power in general, and armed drone strikes in particular, has enabled the imposition of violence at radically reduced levels of physical risk. It is estimated that between November 2002 and June 2014 98% of the targeted killings conducted remotely by US forces in Pakistan, Yemen and Somalia were executed via armed drones (Zenko & Kreps 2014, pp. 9–10).[3] This method of killing, carried out by human operators sometimes based 7,000 miles away,[4] enables conditions of unprecedented risk asymmetry:

> By prolonging and radicalising pre-existing tendencies, the armed drone goes to the very limit: for whoever uses such a weapon, it becomes *a priori* impossible to die as one kills. Warfare, from being possibly asymmetrical, becomes absolutely unilateral [...].
>
> (Chamayou 2015, pp. 12–13)

Contemporary remote warfare is not a fundamentally new phenomenon, but rather a refinement of longstanding trends. The same will be true of future remote warfare. Going forward, the air power component of this mode of violence will be shaped, to a significant degree, by the mutually reinforcing quality of the technologies that enable it. Big data will play an increasingly central role in such operations, necessitating the integration of AI and self-learning algorithms that can outpace humans in their capacity to structure, process and analyse gathered information. The ongoing pursuit of speed in combat operations will generate further pressure to develop and integrate military AI.

None of these changes, however, will meaningfully alter the basic structure of war. Regardless of future developments in AI and autonomy, war will remain something prosecuted by and against humans. Technological inertia is a driving and shaping force, but it does not void agency – human actors will decide whether and how to impose remote warfare in the future, and human actors will be accountable for such choices. War will also continue to be riven by uncertainties, no matter the sophistication of the surveillance and big data technologies at hand. Fog and friction is a feature of war, not a bug. And most importantly, no advance in distanced killing, data-centric targeting, or risk mitigation will alter the fact that war is fought for, and ultimately resolved by, politics.

Is it moral?

One enduring criticism of remote warfare is that it is immoral. These criticisms take a number of forms, two of which I will examine in this section: first, that the physically distanced and increasingly riskless character of remote warfare is ethically problematic; and second, that those who practice it fail to sufficiently uphold their duty of civilian protection.

One very basic objection to this mode of warfare is that it is cowardly. To bomb targets from afar, to kill without accepting a minimal degree of reciprocal vulnerability, is viewed by some as an ignoble way of war. This perceived degradation of martial virtue is typified by the drone:

> [...] the attempt to eradicate all direct reciprocity in any exposure to hostile violence transforms not only the material conduct of armed violence technically, tactically, and psychically, but also the traditional principles of a military ethos officially based on bravery and a sense of sacrifice. Judged by the yardstick of such classical categories, a drone looks like the weapon of cowards.
>
> (Chamayou 2015, p. 17)

This is not a new objection in war. For as long as ranged technologies have been employed in battle, they have been opposed by some as a threat to the ethical standards of the time. These objections are grounded in a particular conception of martial virtue and the warrior ethos, which holds physical risk, and a willingness to endure injury and death in combat, as the primary determinant of ethical status (Renic 2020, pp. 59, 168). What is to be made of such a charge? Is remote warfare virtueless, and if so, should it matter?

We should firstly be careful not to overstate the historical and contemporary influence of this critique. War has never been organised or waged around a principle of true fairness; quite the opposite. War "is about winning, which means killing the enemy on the most unequal terms possible" (Junger 2010, p. 140). This has always been true, regardless of the temporary discomfort generated by battlefield innovations in ranged killing.

The valorisation of face-to-face violence has also been challenged by the changing character of war, including a strengthening regard for the life of the fighter. Most rightly look back with disgust at the cannon fodder treatment of ordinary soldiers in the First World War. Today, for both moral and political reasons, casualty avoidance is a priority for most warring parties, particularly liberal democratic states. Leaders have a duty to reduce the combat risks to their own side as much as feasible. Military values have evolved to reflect these shifting priorities, holding compliance with the rules and standards of the battlefield, in addition to a willingness to face injury and death, as key markers of an ethical fighter.[5]

Some might also question, with some justification, the relevance of a warrior ethos-based objection to remote warfare. For most, the moral status of any mode of war should be judged not on the basis of its courage or cowardice, but rather on its adherence to, or contravention of, the explicit rules of war, particularly the principle of non-combatant immunity.

How does remote warfare stack up when we replace physical courageousness with civilian protection as the applicable moral standard? We should firstly consider military alternatives. The use of significant ground forces for military occupation is a morally fraught endeavour. It is likely to entail active combat and generate unavoidable harm for nearby civilians. Physical proximity to the adversary also creates pressures – fear, agitation, anxiety, confusion, etc. – that incentivise rule-breaking. Given the less than optimal moral record of human agents in war, should we not welcome modes of conflict that lessen the physical commitment of one party?

The air power dimension of remote warfare has long been framed as a morally, as well as militarily, superior way of fighting. Commander Stephen J Townsend, when referring to US-led coalition action against ISIS, challenged anyone to find a more "precise air campaign in the history of warfare" (Townsend 2017). Remote warfare has been further improved, some argue, by the introduction of the armed drone. This includes the counter-terrorist, targeted killings carried out by the United States throughout the now decades-long war on terror. According to Strawser, "drones do better at both identifying the terrorist and avoiding collateral damage than anything else we have" (cited in Shane 2012). Some have gone as far as to suggest that drones are "the most humane form of warfare ever" (Lewis 2013). If true, then drone-centric remote warfare is not only morally permissible, but morally obligatory.

Much of this praise is overblown, exaggerating the benefits and understating the limits and drawbacks of remote warfare. Firstly, remoteness in war, as noted above, is a continuum. Contemporary remote warfare is often conducted in conjunction with, not instead of, on-the-ground fighting. It is coalitional, with security actors, supported by Western powers, doing the bulk of the fighting. These partners have at times lacked the capacity, training, or inclination, to comply with the rules of war, and civilians have suffered as a consequence (Walpole & Karlshøj-Pedersen 2019; Keck 2022).

Claims regarding the moral superiority of air power should also be met with some scepticism. The Bureau of Investigative Journalism has worked to detail the civilian cost of remote drone warfare. According to their data, up to 2,200 civilians have been killed by US strikes since 2002 in Afghanistan, Somalia, Yemen and Pakistan (TBIJ 2022), a figure that exceeds those provided by official sources.

The 2014 campaign against ISIS further highlights the tension between remote warfare and civilian protection. Motivated partly by concern over combat casualties, the United States and its Coalition partners ruled out deploying their own ground troops, beyond a small contingent of special forces. On-the-ground combat was instead left to the Iraqi Army and Kurdish Forces, supported by a Coalition air campaign (Gouré 2017). This preservation of Western troops, however, came at a high price. According to One eighteen-month study, one in five Coalition air strikes resulted in a civilian death, a rate 31 times higher than official reports at the time (Khan & Gopal 2017).

Remote warfare, at present, is closer to risk-transfer than risk-free. The physical risk it mitigates for the belligerents in question is too often shifted onto those civilians unfortunate enough to be within or near the battlefield (Amnesty International 2019; Shiban & Molyneux 2021). The reality of US remote warfare was recently detailed in a New York Times report, based on confidential military assessments of over 1,300 civilian casualties since 2014. In sharp contrast to the humane framing offered by defenders of air war, the documents revealed a campaign of "deeply flawed intelligence, [and] rushed and often imprecise targeting" (Khan 2021).

Can future remote warfare better align with the moral vision of discriminate and proportionate violence advanced by its proponents, and if so, what must change? Firstly, operating standards must improve. In 2013, Obama introduced more restrictive rules for US drone strikes, including a 'near certainty' standard that targets were lawful and non-combatants would not be harmed during the attack (Obama 2013). The evidence suggests that this standard can be incorporated into remote warfare more broadly without degrading operational performance (Lushenko, Raman & Kreps 2022).

These changes should also come with greater transparency. The secrecy that has long characterised the remote warfare of the United States and others has helped sustain targeting practices that fall short of the moral standards we should demand. Going forward, practitioners and policymakers should commit more fully to comprehensive and transparent post-strike investigations, incorporating the good work already done in this context by local activists, NGOs and journalists. NGOs and IGOs play an important role in conflict zones, assisting local populations in protection efforts, providing lines of communication between belligerents and civilians and calling out violations when necessary (Allen, Bell & Machain 2021). These voices should be amplified, as should the voices of those communities within which such strikes take place. The remote warfare of the future will benefit, morally, from greater interaction with these external sources of accountability.

A deeper scepticism of the technological features of remote warfare is also needed. This includes military AI and autonomous weapons systems, innovations routinely praised for their potential to ethically improve the battlefield. According to Larry Lewis, head of the Centre for Autonomy and Artificial Intelligence:

> AI could review imagery and other intelligence to reduce the number of civilians mistakenly identified as combatants. They could monitor areas and provide a double check of existing collateral damage estimates, particularly as things can change over time. AI-driven unmanned systems would allow those systems to take on risk and use tactical patience, which can reduce risk to civilians.
>
> (cited in Watts & Biegon 2019)

There are reasons for caution, however. From its genesis, the promise of military AI and autonomous violence has exceeded the reality, and if this technology is deployed on the battlefield in the absence of necessary safeguards, civilians are likely to suffer. Questions have also been raised regarding the alleged 'inhumanity' of autonomous killing and its potential to degrade the moral status of both the recipients and dispensers of violence. Many further doubt the capacity of these weapons systems to accurately interpret legal standards such as 'direct participation in hostilities' and *hors de combat*. If this technology is integrated into future remote warfare uncritically then the moral challenges of the present will persist or intensify.

Lastly, future remote warfare must take better account of the unintended but foreseeable moral harms associated with such operations. As already noted, a principal driver of remote warfare is force protection – the surest way to safeguard one's own forces is to remove them entirely from the conflict theatre. One potential outcome of this prioritisation of combatant safety, however, is 'casualty displacement'. This refers to circumstances in which adversaries, unable to effectively strike back against military targets, redirect more of their violence onto civilians (Renic & Kaempf 2022). To be clear, no degree of force protection justifies the enemy to target and murder non-combatants. It is worth considering, however, whether those who embrace remote warfare bear any responsibility for the conflict conditions they incentivise. If so, are they morally obligated to reduce these incentivises, even if that necessitates a deprioritisation of force protection and shift away from remote operations? At a minimum, the existence of casualty displacement, as well as other forms of 'blowback', should be recognised when evaluating the moral desirability of remote warfare in the years ahead.

Remote warfare is not *inherently* problematic. Neither Just War nor the laws of war prohibit fighting from a militarily and politically safe(r) distance. But there are serious moral challenges to contend with, challenges that if ignored may exacerbate the vulnerability of the already vulnerable. Overwhelming reliance on air power and partner-forces in war creates inescapable risks for civilian populations, risks that should be carefully weighed when considering the appropriateness of violence. In some cases, the likely risks of remote warfare will be acceptable, particularly when compared to more conventional operations. In other cases, however, the foreseeable harm to civilians will be high enough to morally invalidate any resort to force, remote or conventional. Future remote warfare, and warfare more broadly, will be morally improved if it is anchored to a stronger presumption against violence within international politics.

Is it effective?

In order to judge the effectiveness of remote warfare, we should consider its political drivers, and specifically, the enduring assumption that liberal democratic publics have a limited tolerance for combat casualties. The conventional wisdom has long held that Western support for military operations, particularly those conceived as 'wars of choice', rather than necessity, is contingent on a relatively low level of combat death (Freedman 2006, p. 7).[6]

Obama's advocacy for 'multilateral retrenchment' was motivated by a perception of American overcommitment, typified by lengthy and frustrating military engagements in Iraq and Afghanistan. In 2012, Obama declared "the end of long-term nation-building with large military footprints" in favour of "innovative, low-cost, small-footprint approaches" (Obama 2012). More recently, Biden vowed to "maintain the fight against terrorism in Afghanistan from over the horizon" (Sherwood-Randall 2021). Remote warfare, it is assumed, will allow policymakers to avoid the criticism that more publicised and risk-intensive operations invariably draw. Armed drones, in particular, are favoured for their perceived discretion. Liberal democratic war requires some degree of public buy-in; this may be harder to secure and sustain for large-scale, complex and viscerally costly operations. A major appeal of drones is the assumption that they can be used with "domestic impunity, minimal international response and low political risk and cost" (Dunn 2013, p. 1238).[7]

Once could consider remote warfare effective to the degree that it allows policymakers to wage wars that *should* be waged, but *could not* otherwise be waged due to public discomfort with combat casualties. What this fails to answer, however, is whether remote warfare should be waged at all, and when waged, can it be successful? In cases where the answer to one or both is no, then the perception of low political risk is a dangerous one. It incentivises policymakers to embark on and continue imprudent or immoral military operations, and erodes the democratic guardrails that are essential to holding those who wage war accountable.

There are very real benefits to remote warfare. Significant ground forces generate significant challenges for the West, both military and political. The risks assumed are a mission pressure – too much death can undermine public support. Ground forces may also intensify resentment from local populations, and perpetuate the impression that such interventions are imperial and predatory. The assumption, however, that remote warfare can necessarily transcend these challenges is mistaken. Too often, these operations yield short-term tactical success, while failing to secure deeper strategic objectives. Examples include Libya (Watson & McKay 2021, p. 16) and Syria (Hatahet 2021), where remote warfare has been criticised for its inability to affect positive political outcomes. In both cases, Western support for local actors had a destabilising effect on the region, intensifying animosity between rival factions and undermining rather than facilitating the attainment of peace.

Criticism can also be levelled against the aerial strikes that constitute the primary direct involvement of Western powers. In the FATA region of Pakistan, drone strikes damaged "the social fabric of society" and contributed to "an atmosphere of lawlessness and chaos in which terrorism and militancy thrive[d]" (Aslam 2011, p. 324). Such violence, uncoupled as it is from cost – or at least the perception of cost – can also be difficult to bring to a close. Too often, remote warfare facilitates a drift from limited, temporally bounded war, to open-ended risk management. The latter reframes violence as *anticipatory*; future risks, not current threats, are the focus. Those targeted are similarly reconceptualised:

> [...] the adversary is no longer seen as an enemy with opposed political objectives who needs to be fought [...] but rather as a potential offender whose nefarious activities need to be managed, policed and reduced to a level of acceptable risk.
>
> (Schmitt 2020, p. 6)

One problem with such an approach, and the remote modes of warfare that best facilitate it, is that it sets the stage for permanent action, or what has come to be termed 'forever war'. It is important to be clear here, as the term 'forever war' is frequently critiqued on the basis of its alleged imprecision. Forever war is more accurately termed 'endless war', i.e. war without ends. Wars assume an endless character when two conditions are met: First, when belligerents lack the capability to achieve their set strategic objectives; and second, when the belligerent, despite an inability to secure victory, is not at risk of defeat (Sterman 2021). While Biden has been praised for improving US drone policy in the wake of the Trump years (Hartig 2022), questions remain over the willingness of the United States to make the moral and legal adjustments necessary to bring the 'forever wars' properly to a close (Rosen 2022).

There are many critiques of remote warfare, not all of them good. One complaint sometimes voiced is that this mode of violence is 'too easy'. It has become unmoored from the traditional expectations of risk and cost, and in doing so, transformed into something morally objectionable, even sordid. This is not, by itself, an adequate basis for objection, particularly when the 'ease' referred to includes a reduction in the number of injured and dead combatants on that side of the conflict. But the 'too easy' question does provide an entry point into discussing important aspects of remoteness, including its utility in future armed conflict. Cost – especially visceral, bloody cost – clarifies the thinking in war. It encourages, and sometimes forces, reflection, on whether the anticipated gains of military action are truly worth the anticipated price. Ideally, when the cost is deemed too high, poorly conceived missions will be reconsidered. Remote warfare can distort this process by deluding those who fight into falsely assuming that both risk and cost can be transcended, fundamentally and enduringly. Such thinking too often leads to sub-optimal approaches that prioritise poor strategy, or no strategy. It may lead policymakers to wrongly gamble on wars that should not be started and are unlikely to be won.

Unfortunately, there is little evidence to suggest that this calculus will meaningfully alter going forward. Those with the capacity to do so will continue to utilise remoteness under the assumption that it can secure goals at a reduced military and political cost. This assumption is, and will likely remain, an inflated one.

Conclusion

At the time of writing this chapter, Russia's illegal invasion of Ukraine continues, the largest inter-state conflict in Europe since the Second World War. As the conflict reveals, states retain an appetite for physically and financially costly military action, at least when the objectives are sufficiently ambitious. As it further highlights, however, large-scale, conventional warfare is a serious, and potentially ruinous, gamble for states. Remote operations are and will remain attractive to actors sensitive to the risks and costs of more intensive military engagement. This chapter has sought to better clarify the historical, contemporary, and future trends of this mode of war.

The remote warfare practiced today by a growing number of states is an evolution in distanced and lower-risk violence. While not new, this mode of war is distinct from its historical antecedents, in terms of both the technologies harnessed and the combat risks averted. These features of remote warfare are not inherently immoral but do necessitate moral trade-offs – too often, physical and political risk is reduced by warring parties at the expense of civilian safety.

Remote warfare bypasses some of the problems that beset more intensive ground operations, but we must not forget that war remains a political contest, one that cannot be won by distance or technology alone. States that ignore this reality invite military defeat or the frustrating stagnation of perpetual war. These limits should be better recognised as remote warfare further evolves, extending to new actors and incorporating new technologies.

Notes

1 'Remoteness' can refer to the inter-personal – the growing physical and emotional detachment between military forces and the civilians upon whose behalf they fight, or between those same forces and those they seek to kill. It can also characterise on-the-ground conditions – military strategies of risk management and minimisation that prioritise 'bunkerisation' and troop protection at the expense of more direct engagement with enemy forces (Waldman 2018, pp. 3–4).
2 For a more complete list of terminology used in reference to this type of political violence, see Watson & McKay 2021, p. 10 and Biegon, Rauta & Watts 2021, p. 427.
3 The remaining 2% of strikes were comprised of crewed aircraft attacks and ground raids (Zenko & Kreps 2014, pp. 9–10).
4 For more detail on the 'remote-split operations' development that made this distancing of force possible, see Schultz 2022, pp. 35–7.
5 As I argue elsewhere, updates in the warrior ethos still leave a more fundamental moral question unresolved: whether the violence of the stronger party may be so one-directional in remote warfare as to undermine the moral basis for its *permissiveness* (Renic 2020).
6 Some dispute this claim, arguing that the casualty aversion of the American public has long been overstated (Lacquement 2004).
7 According to Mumford (2013, p. 43), drones "nullify the twentieth-century belief in 'boots on the ground' as a proxy-war necessity".

References

Akhter, M 2019, 'The Proliferation of Peripheries: Militarised Drones and the Reconfiguration of Global Space', *Progress in Human Georgraphy*, vol. 43, no. 1, pp. 64–80.
Allen, S, Bell, S R & Machain, C M 2021, 'Air Power, NGOs, and Collateral Killings', *Foreign Policy Analysis*, vol. 17, no. 2, pp. 1–17, https://doi.org/10.1093/fpa/oraa025.
Amnesty International 2019, 'US Military Shows Appalling Disregard for Civilians Killed in Somalia Air Strike', *Press Release*, Amnesty International, 1 October, <https://www.amnesty.org/en/latest/press-release/2019/09/us-military-shows-appalling-disregard-for-civilians-killed-in-somalia-air-strike/> (accessed 12 July 2022).
Aslam, W 2011, 'A Critical Evaluation of American Drone Strikes in Pakistan: Legality, Legitimacy and Prudence', *Critical Studies on Terrorism*, vol. 4, no. 3, pp. 313–29, https://doi.org/10.1080/17539153.2011.623397.
Biegon, R, Rauta, V & Watts, T F A 2021, 'Remote Warfare: Buzzword or Buzzkill?', *Defence Studies*, vol. 21, no. 4, pp. 427–46, https://doi.org/10.1080/14702436.2021.1994396.
Bowcott, O 2012, 'Drone Attacks in Pakistan are Counterproductive, Says Report', *The Guardian*, 25 September.
Chamayou, G 2015, *A Theory of the Drone*, trans. J Lloyd, The New Press, New York – London.
Dunn, D H 2013, 'Drones: Disembodied Aerial Warfare and the Unarticulated Threat', *International Affairs*, vol. 89, no. 5, pp. 1237–46, https://doi.org/10.1111/1468-2346.12069.

Enemark, C 2013, *Armed Drones and the Ethics of War: Military Virtue in a Post-Heroic Age,* Routledge, London.

Freedman, L 2006, 'Iraq, Liberal Wars and Illiberal Containment', *Survival,* vol 28, no. 4, pp. 51–65, https://doi.org/10.1080/00396330601062709.

Gibson, J 2021, 'Death By Data: Drones, Kill Lists and Algorithms', in A McKay, A Watson & M Karlshoj-Pedersen (eds), *Remote Warfare: Interdisciplinary Perspectives*, E-International Publishing, Bristol, pp. 187–97.

Gouré, D 2017, 'The Air War That is Defeating ISIS', *Real Clear Defense*, 8 August, <https://www.realclear-defense.com/articles/2017/08/08/the_air_war_that_is_defeating_isis_111992.html> (accessed 13 February 2019).

Hartig, L 2022, 'The Biden Drone Playbook: The Elusive Promise of Restrained Counterterrorism', *Just Security*, 17 October, <https://www.justsecurity.org/83586/assessing-bidens-counterterrorism-rules/> (accessed 13 November 2022).

Hatahet, S 2021, 'The Limitations and Consequences of Remote Warfare in Syria' in A McKay, A Watson & M Karlshoj-Pedersen (eds), *Remote Warfare: Interdisciplinary Perspectives*, E-International Publishing, Bristol, pp. 173–86.

Michel, A H 2019, *Eyes in the Sky: The Secret Rise of Gorgon Stare and How It Will Watch Us All*, Houghton Mifflin Harcourt, New York.

Junger, S 2010, *War*, Fourth Estate, London.

Kaempf, S 2014, 'Post-Heroic US Warfare and the Moral Justification for Killing in War', in C E Gentry & A E Eckert (eds), *The Future of Just War. New Critical Essays*, The University of Georgia Press, Athens, GA – London, pp. 79–97.

Kahn, P 2002, 'The Paradox of Riskless Warfare', *Philosophy & Public Policy Quarterly*, vol. 22, no. 3, pp. 2–7.

Karagiannis, E 2021, 'Russian Surrogate Warfare in Ukraine and Syria: Understanding the Utility of Militias and Private Military Companies', *Journal of Balkan and Near Eastern Studies*, vol. 23, no.4, pp. 549–65, https://doi.org/10.1080/19448953.2021.1888603.

Keck, T 2022, 'Don't Forget Your Friends: Risks and Opportunities in Security Partnerships', *Just Security*, 9 June, <https://www.justsecurity.org/81822/dont-forget-your-friends-risks-and-opportunities-in-security-partnerships/> (accessed 12 July 2022).

Khan, A 2021, 'Hidden Pentagon Records Reveal Patterns of Failure in Deadly Airstrikes', *New York Times,* <https://www.nytimes.com/interactive/2021/12/18/us/airstrikes-pentagon-records-civilian-deaths.html> (accessed 14 May 2023).

Khan, A & Gopal, A 2017, 'The Uncounted', *The New York Times Magazine*, 16 November, <https://www.nytimes.com/interactive/2017/11/16/magazine/uncounted-civilian-casualties-iraq-airstrikes.html?_r=0> (accessed 11 February 2019).

Krieg, A & Rickli, J 2018, 'Surrogate Warfare: The Art of War in the 21st Century?', *Defence Studies,* vol. 18, no. 2, pp. 113–30, https://doi.org/10.1080/14702436.2018.1429218.

Lacquement, R A 2004, 'The Casualty-Aversion Myth', *Naval War College Review*, vol. 57, no. 1, pp. 38–57.

Lewis, M 2013, 'Drones: Actually the Most Humane Form of Warfare Ever', *The Atlantic*, 21 August, <https://www.theatlantic.com/international/archive/2013/08/drones-actually-the-most-humane-form-of-warfare-ever/278746/> (accessed 11 June 2022).

Lushenko, P, Raman, S & Kreps, S 2022, *How to Avoid Civilian Casualties During Drone Strikes – At No Cost to National Security*, Modern War Institute, 10 February <https://mwi.usma.edu/how-to-avoid-civilian-casualties-during-drone-strikes-at-no-cost-to-national-security> (accessed 12 February 2022).

Luttwak, E N 1995, 'Toward Post-Heroic Warfare', *Foreign Affairs*, vol. 74, no. 3, pp. 109–22.

Moran, J 2015, *Remote Warfare: Developing a Framework for Evaluating Its Use*, Remote Control Project, London.

Mumford, A 2013, 'Proxy Warfare and the Future of Conflict', *RUSI Journal*, vol. 158, no. 2, pp. 40–6, https://doi.org/10.1080/03071847.2013.787733.

Obama, B 2012, 'Remarks by the President on the Defense Strategic Review', *The White House*, 5 January <http://www.whitehouse.gov/the-pressoffice/2012/01/05/   remarks-president-defense-strategic-review> (accessed 12 July 2022).

Obama, B 2013, 'Remarks by the President at the National Defense University', *The White House*, <https://www.whitehouse.gov/the-press-office/2013/05/23/remarks-president-national-defense-university> (accessed 11 July 2022).

Rauta, V & Monaghan, S 2021, 'Global Britain in the Grey Zone: Between Stagecraft and Statecraft', *Contemporary Security* Policy, vol. 42, no. 4, pp. 475–97, https://doi.org/10.1080/13523260.2021.1980984.

Renic, N 2020, *Asymmetric Killing: Risk Avoidance, Just War, and the Warrior Ethos*, Oxford University Press, Oxford.

Renic, N & Kaempf, S 2022, 'Violence Re-Directed: Due Care and the Moral Challenge of Casualty Displacement Warfare', *International Relations* [online first], https://doi.org/10.1177/00471178221105598.

Rosen, B 2022, 'Ending Perpetual War', *Just Security*, 25 October, <https://www.justsecurity.org/83749/ending-perpetual-war/> (accessed 14 November 2022).

Satia, P 2014, 'Drones: A History from the British Middle East', *Humanity*, vol. 5, no. 1, pp. 1–31, https://doi.org/10.1353/hum.2014.0002.

Schmitt, O 2020, 'Wartime Paradigms and the Future of Western Military Power', *International Affairs*, vol. 96, no. 2, pp. 401–18, https://doi.org/10.1093/ia/iiaa005.

Schultz, T P 2022, 'Remote Warfare: A New Architecture of Air Power', in P M Haun, C F Jackson & T P Schultz (eds), *Air Power in the Age of Primacy: Air Warfare Since the Cold War*, Cambridge University Press, Cambridge, pp. 26–53.

Shane, S 2012, 'The Moral Case for Drones', *The New York Times*, 15 July, <https://www.nytimes.com/2012/07/15/sunday-review/the-moral-case-for-drones.html> (accessed 12 July 2022).

Shaw, M 2005, *The New Western Way of War*, Polity Press, Cambridge, MA.

Sherwood-Randall, L 2021, 'Remarks as Prepared for Delivery by Assistant to the President for Homeland Security, Dr. Liz Sherwood-Randall on the Future of the U.S. Counterterrorism Mission: Aligning Strategy, Policy, and Resources', *The White House*, <https://www.whitehouse.gov/briefing-room/speeches-remarks/2021/09/09/remarks-by-assistant-to-the-president-for-homeland-security-dr-liz-sherwood-randall-on-the-future-of-the-u-s-counterterrorism-mission-aligning-strategy-policy-and-resources/> (accessed 12 July 2022).

Shiban, B & Molyneux, C 2021, 'The Human Cost of Remote Warfare in Yemen', in A McKay, A Watson & M Karlshoj-Pedersen (eds), *Remote Warfare: Interdisciplinary Perspectives*, E-International Publishing, Bristol, pp. 110–31.

Sterman, D 2021, 'Defining Endless Wars', *New America*, January, <https://www.newamerica.org/international-security/reports/defining-endless-wars/> (accessed 11 July 2022).

TBIJ 2022, 'Drone Warfare', *The Bureau of Investigative Journalism*, <https://www.thebureauinvestigates.com/projects/drone-war> (accessed 11 July 2022).

Townsend, S J 2017, 'Reports of Civilian Casualties in the War Against ISIS Are Vastly Inflated', *Foreign Policy*, 15 September, <https://foreignpolicy.com/2017/09/15/reports-of-civilian-casualties-fromcoalition-strikes-on-isis-are-vastly-inflated> (accessed 12 July 2022).

Waldman, T 2018, 'Vicarious warfare: The Counterproductive Consequences of Modern American Military Practice', *Contemporary Security Policy*, vol. 39, no. 2, pp. 181–205, https://doi.org/10.1080/13523260.2017.1393201.

Walpole, L & Karlshøj-Pedersen, M 2019, *Remote Warfare and the Practical Challenges for the Protection of Civilians Strategy*, Oxford Research Group, London.

Watson, A & McKay, A 2021, 'Remote Warfare: A Critical Introduction', in A McKay, A Watson & M Karlshoj-Pedersen (eds), *Remote Warfare: Interdisciplinary Perspectives*, E-International Publishing, Bristol, pp. 7–33.

Watts, T & Biegon, R 2019, *Conceptualising Remote Warfare: The Past, Present, and Future*, Oxford Research Group, London, <https://www.oxfordresearchgroup.org.uk/conceptualising-remote-warfare-the-past-present-and-future> (accessed 12 November 2022).

Zenko, M & Kreps, S 2014, 'Limiting Armed Drone Proliferation', *Council on Foreign Relations, Centre for Preventive Action*, <https://cfrd8-files.cfr.org/sites/default/files/pdf/2014/06/Limiting_Armed_Drone_Proliferation_CSR69.pdf> (accessed 4 April 2019).

18

VICARIOUS WAR AND THE UNITED STATES

Imperial Antecedents and Anticipations

Thomas Waldman

Introduction

The concept of vicarious war describes an approach to the use of force characterized by efforts to achieve objectives on the cheap. Belligerents using force vicariously seek to purchase strategic success without the usual high price tag in terms of blood, treasure, military resourcing and political capital, or, at a wider societal level, to use war to achieve national ends but in a manner that does not place significant demands on the people. The term is employed as an overarching metaphor that seeks to capture the notion of war fought by a society at arm's length, at a remove (Waldman 2021).

This can manifest itself in behaviour at all levels and in all spheres of war, from the tactical to the strategic, from individual soldier to wider populace. It is variably enabled and willed by all major societal actors, whether political and military elites or ordinary citizens. As more a strategic predisposition than a predetermined set of military modalities, it can take on many different guises in different contexts. For this reason, it is difficult to predict the precise form vicarious war may take in the future, which will depend on the character of belligerents, the circumstances of its application and the wider strategic, socio-political and material conditions shaping its manifestation.

Operationally, some vicarious approaches have always been and will likely remain available in theory, such as less societally invasive forms of military mobilization or methods of conflict delegation. Otherwise, new opportunities and instruments might appear that promise to limit the sacrifices involved: this might be in the form of new technologies or ways of employing existing capabilities, and occasionally bold strategic thinkers will claim to have discovered less costly routes to objectives, perhaps through clever coercive threats or dynamic schemes of manoeuvre. Whether societies chose to avail themselves of these things has always depended on circumstances. But as often there is no choice to be had – many actors simply lack the capacity to even consider vicarious approaches as a serious option, while others may be fighting for core interests that demand serious commitment, direct engagement and societal sacrifice. Rather, war fought in a truly vicarious manner has historically tended to be predominantly associated with strong states pursuing forms of imperial or hegemonic projects abroad – this relationship is likely to endure.

Where states accrue significant power, wealth and territory, and control relatively large areas in an imperial fashion, this produces a distinct mix of strategic requirements, motivating incentives,

DOI: 10.4324/9781003299011-22

emerging opportunities and changing socio-cultural patterns that work to sustain these patterns. For the United States, since the middle of the 20th century, albeit building on earlier precedents, the pursuit of primacy – sustaining and expanding US-led liberal hegemony – has functioned as the underlying condition driving its prosecution of vicarious war. In coping with the contemporary dilemmas of policing the *Pax Americana,* its leaders have sought militarized measures that are economically affordable, socially acceptable, legally permissible, politically viable and also, it is hoped, strategically effective. Such behaviour is likely to persist so long as America harbours hegemonic ambitions, even as other regional powers emerge to stake claims and expand influence into zones far beyond their borders. As rivalry between great powers re-emerges across the geopolitical landscape, the prospect of major war has become a serious pre-occupation among strategists, but the future could equally be marked by the proliferating vicarious interventionism of existing and aspiring empires.

This chapter will use the imperial lens to unlock clues regarding the fundamental underlying conditions and drivers that predispose and permit societies to wage this form of war. This should serve as a reliable basis to make tentative observations regarding whether vicarious war has a future and if so, what that might look like; it will also assess the likely consequences for states employing vicarious approaches and international affairs more broadly. In this light, the concept of vicarious war can be employed to capture how certain approaches allow powerful states to prosecute aggrandizing military campaigns, whether regionally or globally, but without the level of direct societal involvement, visceral military engagement, public contestation, rigorous accountability and meaningful investment of resources or political capital that traditionally applies when states go to war. As the chapter unfolds, broad observations based on evidence from historical empires will be brought together with more substantive insights from the imperialistic practices of the United States, the preeminent contemporary exponent of vicarious war and as such our best guide to possible futures.

Caveat lector: conceptual qualifications

In its modern guise, vicarious war has much in common with forms of war discussed in earlier chapters of this handbook, such as remote, proxy and surrogate warfare. Accounts bearing similarities to the argument here present recent developments around evolving forms of western warfare as bound up with the imperatives of contemporary globalized, privatized and mediatized risk society (Krieg 2016; Heng 2018); others see them as strongly associated with political pressures generated by the fallout from gruelling Western campaigns in the wider Middle East, the peculiar demands of waging the long war on terror, or the possibilities inherent in new weapons systems such as armed drones (Biegon et al. 2021, pp. 431–3). So, in this telling, states such as America

> Have acted instinctively to diminish the domestic social footprint of often contentious foreign operations by exploiting stand-off systems, minimising ground-force operations, and using special operations forces and professional soldiers, as well as subcontractors and proxies, instead of conscripts or reservists wherever possible.
>
> (Levite & Shimshoni 2018, p. 104)

In the aftermath of costly wars, there has been a shift towards tech-enabled economization, specialization, privatization and remoteness. While in no way dismissing the merit of these studies, I want to argue that deeper factors are at work and explore the bigger picture associated with the modalities of force in service of imperial projects – this should help us identify key underlying structural factors less tethered to immediate operational experiences or specific scenarios. As such, contrary to many existing accounts, I am concerned as much with continuity as change, the logic of imperial force as opposed to its grammar. But before proceeding, it is important to make explicit some underlying assumptions and highlight caveats lest the conclusions be judged overly determinist.

Debates over empire and imperialism, in general and specifically in the American context, cover countless volumes: there is not space to wade into these debates in detail. Attempts to establish definitions quickly lead down conceptual rabbit holes; therefore I follow leading studies which adopt a fairly broad understanding of empire capable of accommodating a range of historical cases and centred around how 'core' or 'metropolitan' states maintain hierarchical control over the sovereignty of other 'peripheral' states (Doyle 1986); or as Porter usefully puts it: empire concerns the "exercise of dominance over another state's domestic policies, whether in the foreground or implicitly in the background" (Porter 2020). This makes comparison with other empires in history relevant and is capable of embracing contemporary forms of American empire, however 'neo-imperial', 'informal' or 'lite' (Ignatieff 2003). There are meaningful transhistorical comparisons to be made and the United States can be usefully studied through an imperial lens. The motivation behind this imperial framing is not ideological but analytical; to explore how the dynamics of US hierarchical global domination shapes the nature of its war-making practices – this offers insights that can be applied to other cases and into the future.

While vicarious war historically tends to be strongly associated, if not exclusively or deterministically, with powerful imperial states, this does not mean it is the only form of war employed by them or that some empires, due to the happy confluence of protective geography and benign external environments, have not experienced long periods of largely peaceful existence. Moreover, land-based empires expanding into contiguous regions have, especially in the initial stages of conquest, employed brutally large-scale campaigns fought with conscripts (yet typically reverting to vicarious forms to maintain dominance). Similarly, imperial ambition alone is insufficient to explain the emergence of vicarious modes of war. Evolving socio-political conditions and prevailing norms or the status of military-strategic thought, and the influence of prominent events, can play a role in either promoting or precluding it. The imperial factor is conditioning rather than determinative.

Linked to this, while vicarious approaches dominate imperial practice, strategic planners may nevertheless continue to prepare for, or even wage, major wars – the two can coexist. American vicarious war has evolved over decades as its power and imperial ambition expanded. The path to contemporary forms was neither straightforward nor linear, and it was partially interrupted by the demands of large-scale war, most notably in the Second World War, Korea, Vietnam and twice in Iraq; the post-9/11 war on terror also seemed to augur a new appetite for service and sacrifice. Such episodes are best understood not only as exceptions confirming the rule, but also as drivers towards ever more vicarious forms: they often emerged in circumstances shaped by vicarious interventions; they were typically fought, at least initially, according to the hope that shortcut strategies might resolve matters bloodlessly; they served as incubators for technological advances and innovative approaches that would later be applied in more independent ways; and, in their aftermath, they spurred strategists to devise approaches to further reduce risks and costs.

Caveat imperator: empire and models of American mobilization

Whatever caveats we might raise, the converging requirements, incentives and opportunities that imperial power brings, somewhat counterintuitively perhaps, lead such states to increasingly rely on vicarious approaches. Other drivers result from the less obvious political and social dynamics of empire and a continuing, often misguided, faith in the presumed effectiveness of these approaches relative to the magnitude of the hegemonic ambition.

Imperial dominion can, of course, bring great rewards, in plunder, prestige, trade and security. Regarding the latter, dangers are essentially pushed further away. However, empire creates new interests to be protected and new threats, both real and perceived, to be countered. Imperial projects by default entail forms of external force projection and inevitably get caught up in the 'self-propelling dynamic of empire': expanding frontiers entail growing commitments and new vulnerabilities (Porter 2015, p. 61). As Kumar (2020, p. 51) notes, conflict and antagonism appear to be built into the very structure of empire and Howe similarly observes that colonial conquest meets resistance almost everywhere (Howe 2002, p. 94). Domination over far-flung territories thus requires the occasional or sometimes frequent exercise of force to discipline rule-breakers, quash rebellions and pacify the frontiers.

This can place great demands on military establishments, not least in terms of the logistical feats required to protect imperial possessions – this entails vast efforts, drains resources and generates all manner of political questions at home. Especially for sea-borne empires presiding over faraway territories, it is difficult to sustain large infantry forces over vast oceans. Moreover, fighting at long distances from home places untenable burdens on citizen-soldiers: sending large numbers of a nation's young men overseas for extended periods to fight obscure frontier wars has long been an unpopular and politically unsustainable proposition.

Yet where empire creates problems for strategists, so it seemingly provides some of the solutions – typically through forms of vicarious military interventionism. However external domination is achieved the effect is usually to encourage parsimonious warfighting approaches. Certainly, the capacity of vicarious methods to put out fires while maintaining internal stability and growth over extended periods is impressive. Further possibilities arise from the influxes of wealth gained from monopolized trade, control of natural resources, the booty of empire and new populations to tax. Plentiful resources can allow imperial states to amass powerful armaments with which to conduct "campaigns small in scope but spectacular in results" (Keegan 2004, p. 357). US neo-imperial domination is perhaps less crude or directly exploitative, but it has not been shy in reaping economic gains by adopting mercantilist, protectionist policies or exploiting its domination of global financial institutions and the dollar's status as the world's reserve currency (Porter 2020, pp. 87–93).

But more important is the ability of empires to sponsor politically low-risk types of military organization or mobilization that distance the prosecution of imperial war from the home population. This results in a general reliance on a mix of specialized professional forces, mercenaries, privateers, proxies and clients to protect and advance the empire's interests (Porch 2005). Conscripts or large professional forces have been employed by (especially land-based) empires throughout history, but generally only on a small scale and rarely over the long-term. Rather, 'light-footprint' approaches allow imperialists to effectively maintain tolerable security over extensive territories and even achieve impressive victories by relying on local lackeys, often equipped with their patron's superior armaments. The ancient maritime trading empire of Carthage eschewed citizen militias and used its wealth to hire foreign mercenaries which "indulged the inclinations of a citizenry indifferent to martial values" (Bernstein 2007, p. 69). Rome resisted as far as possible, but in its dying days desperately implemented a process of self-defeating delegation. Britain's mid-Victorian imperial policy relied on minimalist force commitments, widespread delegation and rule by proxy.

As we move along a stylized spectrum from less to more vicarious models of mobilization – to simplify, from conscript forces to professional volunteer forces, elites professionals, mercenaries, proxy delegation, and reliance on allied or client state forces – the historical record suggests these require a significant measure of power and wealth to employ *on a sustained and systematic basis*. This does not mean all imperial states will utilize them; likewise, weak states on occasion might look to hire mercenaries to defend against immediate threats (as the United States did as a young nation). Nevertheless, alongside the expanding burdens of imperial control, there would be a tendency towards vicariousness. It is possible to observe how these models, often layered on top of one another, have been progressively adopted by the United States as we move towards the contemporary era (albeit, as noted, with periodical retreats), characterized by shifts from a reliance on citizen-soldiers, to volunteers, to elite professionals and secretive paramilitary operators, to proxies and private security companies, and even potentially to autonomous warfighting machines and robots.

The nation has come to rely on minimalist, coercive force in disparate military interventions as part of its wider liberal hegemonic project. New interventions or stand-alone strikes can be launched almost effortlessly, while existing commitments can be prolonged through an enduring small-scale presence. Vicarious measures enable the unceasing management of disparate threats, both small and large, across expansive geographies. Even the 2003 Iraq War was fought according to vicarious rationales: as Porter (2021) notes, the Bush administration thought "war would work, quickly, cheaply and overwhelmingly. The assumption of a lightning strike at minimal cost". And of course the Iraq War unfolded in a region still heavily shaped by the legacies of imperial campaigns almost a hundred years earlier (Waldman 2007, pp. 64–5). Indeed, Poast (2021) and Satia (2022) have compared the practices of modern liberal empire with the imperial policing model implemented by the British in the early 20th century. As Satia argues, growing democratization and enfranchisement, combined with anti-war attitudes following the carnage of the First World War, meant the British had to devise new budget-conscious techniques "to escape the check of Britons concerned about taxes, demobilization, and imperial expansion and violence", resulting in a form of 'covert empire'. The combination of superior technology, secrecy and propaganda used to evade scrutiny would be taken forward by its successor American empire after 1945. Moreover, in an age of strong anti-colonial sentiment, the United States has had to go to even greater lengths than empires before it to cloak the coercive apparatus exercised to sustain hegemony. Covert agencies, drones and locally recruited armies are central to this, while a largely complicit media perpetuates elite myths around the 'surgical' and 'humane' forms of violence employed to police the periphery.

Caveat emptor: the empire strikes back

In the European wars of empire, the fighting often involved a clash pitting vicarious against non-vicarious ways of war; between aristocratic officers sent to lead foreign forces armed with repeating rifles against warriors adopting tribal or 'heroic' methods armed with spears; between imperialists fighting limited wars of avaricious ambition against natives fighting for their homelands, and in some cases, their survival. This foreshadows the kinds of adversaries America has found itself fighting across the frontiers of its informal empire. Indeed, the parallels between the interminable campaigns of European imperialism and modern American 'forever wars' are stark, and not least concerning the domestic consequences of external expansionism.

Due to the reliance on professionals, privateers and proxies, citizens who are spared the burdens of fighting become increasingly sedentary and unwarlike. Metropolitan populations welcome the prestige that comes with domination but are unwilling to accept serious sacrifice to sustain distant campaigns. Officials and merchants who have grown rich on the spoils of empire are "reluctant to leave their business and good life behind" (Gat 2006, p. 306). But this does not necessarily entail opposition to further domination or aggrandizement. In fact, many stand to profit from territorial expansion and control of new markets, especially if the burden can be shifted onto others. Furthermore, vicarious interventionism itself can sustain the societal militarism that provides the cultural context in which these practices thrive. If most citizens do not experience war's costs directly and are only cognisant of its short-term benefits, it becomes something they begin to romanticize and even actively desire through ignorance of its real consequences. During the European colonial period, people at home would consume whitewashed tales of its heroes and generals, its proconsuls and proxies, largely unconcerned by the carnage wrought in foreign societies by perpetual wars fought in their name. Especially when wedded to comforting rationalizations of benevolent intent, the idea can emerge that the nation is only capable of wielding a righteous sword.

Imperial domination can thus fuel nationalistic jingoism and a civic militarism urging new conquests. In the late Roman Republic, the growing popularity of gladiatorial contests was symptomatic of a population less and less exposed to the reality of fighting due to growing military professionalization but that nevertheless wanted to experience battles and triumphs vicariously. Elites exploited this public appetite for militaristic spectacle to advance their own agendas. Ominously, these developments accompanied creeping authoritarianism and the growing power of military-political leaders, prefiguring the ultimate collapse of the republican system itself.

Despite the extent of empire, the mass of the metropolitan public can be surprisingly 'imperially ignorant' and display scant interest in their nation's behaviour abroad beyond a voyeuristic fascination with demonstrations of martial prowess or tales of daring-do. This kind of apathetic uncritical attitude results in little serious examination of aggrandizing campaigns far from home, which much of the population might not even realize are taking place. The generally low-cost manner of their prosecution further serves to limit domestic awareness or opposition (Porter 1996, p. 105). Meanwhile, the growth of increasingly unaccountable centralized control is a product of the accumulation of extraordinary powers and a more general accretion of elite prerogatives and moral authority flowing from the necessity of confronting persistent military emergencies. In this way, bolstered by narratives glorifying triumphs, papering over failures or inflating threats, the political leadership is able to distance itself from responsibility for the costs of empire.

Yet while the intent of vicarious war is to 'distance' the costs and consequences of war from the imperial centre, rarely have states been able to so insulate themselves from the indirect (and sometimes direct) repercussions of remote aggression. The presumed distance can soon collapse in unexpected ways. Sometimes, the methods employed abroad eventually ended up being turned against domestic populations as militarized foreign policy morphs into forceful suppression of internal dissent. As Benton describes in relation to the British empire, "harsh practices used to control imperial hot spots also surfaced back home. Wartime emergency powers applied in the empire were adapted in the United Kingdom to repress dissent" (Benton 2022). So there is an irony in the process whereby imperialists seeking to spread purportedly enlightened values – then the white man's burden and the *mission civilisatrice*, today forceful democracy promotion and the Freedom Agenda – often ended up curtailing liberties at home due to the exigencies of empire abroad. In mid-2020, the harsh response to widespread protests in American cities worryingly reflected these patterns (Morefield & Porter 2020).

The importation of repressive militarized measures from periphery to core and the steady deterioration of accountability structures around the use of force is reflected in the American experience, concomitant with growing imperial ambition. While the American people have long maintained an ambiguous relationship with the wars of the nation, the vicarious distancing between society and war truly starts to become apparent during the Cold War as the United States enormously expanded its foreign commitments, overseas bases and imperial reach. This was largely a function of the arrogation of executive power and elitist secrecy demanded by the global confrontation with communism. Congress often dragged its feet in terms of responding to or restraining executive military adventurism, and in some cases actively connived in allowing this situation to persist. Continuing apathy (even following a burst of democratic assertion in the 1970s) meant there was little pressure on representatives to claw back a meaningful voice for ordinary people. Such patterns would continue to be apparent to the contemporary era.

American wars today are increasingly fought in the shadows and ordinary citizens are not expected to shoulder the major burdens of US belligerency. They barely register as blips on the radar of public attention. Moreover, a dearth of in-depth reporting on foreign affairs in mainstream media entrenches apathy and ignorance: drone strikes and night raids are just incredibly difficult to report on and a short dispatch will struggle to meaningfully interrogate second-order effects or convey how they form part of broader campaigns (Demmers & Gould 2018, pp. 364–81). The 'ending endless wars' agenda resonates with some voters when prompted: there are always critics of empire, even if only among marginal dissident minorities mostly preoccupied with harmful domestic repercussions (Howe 2002, p. 87). Beyond this, most military operations today are largely out of sight, out of mind (Baron 2019). As a result, intervention has become untethered from the constitutional and democratic restraints that traditionally served to check the use of force. Alongside an expansion of legal authorities and the dilution of oversight processes, policymakers have chosen strategic approaches that enable them to circumvent potential political obstacles as well as accountability for their decisions (Goldsmith & Waxman 2016, pp. 7–21).

Vicarious war is thus perfectly suited for a modern demagogue like former President Trump. He was able to seemingly fulfil his campaign promise of ending costly wars while simultaneously overseeing numerous operations around the globe. When it suited, he exploited the popular appetite among his nationalist base for triumphal displays of American military muscle, publicly glorifying in actions such as the targeted assassination of an Iranian general or air strikes against Syrian chemical weapons facilities. Vicarious war affords leaders the option of militaristic activism without accountability. This bodes ill if Trump, or someone of his ilk, returns to the White House. But the issue applies to any administration by virtue of its inherited role as preserver of US primacy – a consistent feature of US foreign policy since 1945 (Porter 2018).

What does this all mean for the future? A decent measure of the wisdom of any use of force is the extent to which it can command broad public support. According to Mead, the jostling tumult of democratic decision-making can have a beneficial effect on foreign policy as it ensures actions broadly reflect the wishes of wider society (Mead 2001, pp. 84–6). Likewise, a central theme of Freedman's (2022) recent study on command is that autocracies tend to make catastrophic decisions due to a lack of reliable feedback mechanisms between military and political leaders. Furthermore, if there is truth to the political science contention that democracies are more likely to be successful in war (Reiter & Stam 2002), then the extent to which vicarious methods dilute the efficacy of oversight structures or allows policymakers to evade or subvert democratic processes could be hugely damaging for American security. These same dynamics may also contribute to growing international instability when applied to developments in other states.

Caveat mundus: a new age of empire?

Vicarious warfare is a shape-shifter, adapting to fit the concerns and opportunities of imperial actors seeking to apply force in this evasive manner. Ultimately, whether and how it continues to define the strategic pursuits of powerful states in the international system will be determined by the confluence of unfolding realities in several critical spheres and the broader evolution of the geopolitical environment. Somewhat worryingly, especially in light of the foregoing discussion, it appears that the world is moving towards what Mankoff has dubbed a 'new age of empire'. While states such as Iran and Turkey have been seeking to extend their regional influence – making extensive use of proxies and drones, as we might expect – the major aspirants for imperial domination of a more extensive kind are Russia and China. The early evidence suggests trajectories that mirror patterns we have outlined above, albeit in the distinctive geographic, socio-political and historical contexts of the states concerned.

Since at least the mid-2000s, Russia under Vladimir Putin has been engaged in an increasingly aggressive policy of reasserting its influence across the territories of its former empire, lost with the collapse of the Soviet Union in 1991. It has expanded its footprint not only in its internal empire (Chechnya) and near-abroad (Georgia) but also further afield in the Middle East and Africa, mainly through the activities of Kremlin-aligned mercenaries such as the infamous Wagner group, dependent clients and loosely controlled separatist forces. Building on the landgrabs of 2014, the large-scale invasion of Ukraine in 2022 represents the latest and most important phase of Russia's imperialist revisionism. While likely motivated by some mix of genuine security concerns and atavistic territorial greed, the imperialistic nature of the move is inescapable. Putin's aim of dominating through force sovereign territories deemed part of a so-called *Russky Mir* ('Russian world') has been described as the "death throes of an imperial delusion" (Watling 2022). Putin's willingness to commit large troop numbers and sustain massive casualties might on the surface contradict the overarching argument here, but on closer inspection familiar imperial logics of violence are at work.

First, employing vicarious methods offers no guarantee of success and in fact can prove enormously strategically counterproductive. As the United States itself experienced repeatedly, states are often inadvertently dragged into commitments far more costly than planned. Putin calculated that a daring assault spearheaded by elite VDV paratroopers – supplemented by cruise missile and drone strikes, cyber attacks and coercive envelopment – would rapidly break Ukrainian resistance. When this failed and the 'special military operation' settled into a slogging match in the east and south, vicarious rationales persisted – Russia mostly relied on stand-off force through long-range artillery barrages and Putin long persisted in his refusal to issue a general mobilization, instead coercively inducing conscripts into signing up for extended deployments. He also instituted forms of 'stealth mobilization' employing Ukrainian separatists, Chechen militants, Wagner mercenaries, impoverished ethnic minorities and even criminals (MacFarquhar 2022). Even the large-scale, if still 'partial', September mobilization was implemented in ways intended to minimize the impact on politically consequential segments of society. In short, Putin hoped to keep his expansionist campaign distanced from Russian society. Amid widespread opposition to the chaotic drafts, mounting casualties, strikes against Russian targets and the growing impact of sweeping western economic sanctions, that will prove increasingly difficult, but Putin's tight control of the media has meant he has been able to downplay setbacks and feed the public a steady diet of nationalistic displays of (illusory) Russian military might. Russian democracy had long been something of a mirage, but with this war the last vestiges of accountability are fading – and with that, strategic sense. But just as other empires crumbled following failed imperial campaigns, so defeat may in the long run offer the best chance for Russia's democratic renewal.

China has not launched territorial conquests on the scale of Putin's recent gambit, but its behaviour is no less worrying, especially given the much greater reserves of power it has at its disposal. Interestingly, China's imperial moves mirror those of the United States, characterized by the synergistic merging of commercial and state interests driving expansion and the establishment of outposts to serve as lily-pads to project power into the periphery, all accompanied by soothing narratives of benevolent intent designed to limit resistance – hence a Sinocentric 'community of common destiny' that has been 'chosen by heaven' is destined through 'unprecedented changes' to replace the US-led international rules-based order (Rolland 2020). China's purported commitment to non-intervention is giving way to growing political meddling, economic coercion, involvement in civil wars, arms transfers and aggressive actions in its near-seas (Tierney 2021): state-aligned private security companies protect Chinese interests along its belt and road (Yuan 2021); maritime militias form the vanguard of its militarized island-building in the South China Sea; and cyberwarriors launch attacks and spread misinformation across global networks. As in Britain and America before it, the demands of empire will justify extraordinary domestic measures and the further curtailing of freedoms. Tidsall (2021) describes Chinese premiere Xi Jinping as a "totalitarian control freak with imperial fantasies" overseeing "a techno-fascist surveillance state".

Of course, it is precisely these developments associated with China's rise that have prompted the United States to reorient its foreign policy in an effort to protect its hegemonic global status and this is likely to be conducted through indirect means (Mumford 2013). Biegon and Watts (2022, p. 954) argue that "the turn towards more 'remote' modalities of policing the periphery cannot be detached from perceptions of strategic competition with China" and that will be "integral to the retooling of American primacy" going forward. Some neo-conservative commentators have even explicitly appealed to earlier colonial models as useful ways to control "the frontiers of the pax Americana" (Boot 2019).

The more that states pursue quixotic imperial adventures, the more likely it is that they will spark unnecessary crises or stumble into military misadventures, especially if there are multiple contending empires vying for domination across overlapping territories. Many of the most dangerous crises during the Cold War emerged in contexts shaped by vicarious interventionism as the Soviet and American empires sought to assert control over their spheres, satellites and subalterns. Some expect the most likely confrontations between China and the United States to occur in the context of proxy wars in far-flung states rather than direct clashes over hot spots such as Taiwan (Hoffman & Orner 2021; Tierney 2021).

But just as vicarious war evolved to fit the requirements of empires past, so it will manifest itself in new forms in the decades ahead shaped by the opportunities afforded by new technologies such as artificial intelligence, leveraged through new strategies of cyber coercion and remote unconventional warfare and supported by new techniques of propaganda and media manipulation. The proliferation of imperially motivated interventionism will make for a perpetually unstable and conflictual world, and given past experience, this will all have hugely costly consequences for local populations around the globe. Meanwhile, democratic structures in some of the world's largest states will be further eroded, thus potentially exacerbating the 'democratic recession' of recent times. In itself, this is perhaps less consequential for (and may suit the leaders) of authoritarian states that never really welcomed popular participation in the decisions of government, but it will strike at the very heart of republican and liberal democratic systems. The fundamental paradox at the heart of liberal empire is that at the same as it seeks to coercively promote its principles around the world so it weakens them from within.

References

Baron, K 2019, 'Do Americans Really Want to End the 'Forever Wars?' Survey Says…', *Defense One*, 10 September, <https://www.defenseone.com/policy/2019/09/do-americans-really-want-end-forever-wars-survey-says/159760/> (accessed 25 September 2020).

Benton, L 2022, 'Evil Empires: The Long Shadow of British Colonialism', *Foreign Affairs*, July/August, <https://www.foreignaffairs.com/reviews/evil-empires> (accessed 22 June 2022).

Bernstein, A H 2007, 'The Strategy of a Warrior-State: Rome and the Wars Against Carthage', in W Murray, M Knox & A Bernstein (eds), *The Making of Strategy: Rulers, States, and War*, Cambridge University Press, Cambridge, pp. 56–84.

Biegon, R, Rauta V & Watts T 2021, 'Remote Warfare – Buzzword or Buzzkill?', *Defence Studies*, vol. 21, no. 4, pp. 427–46, https://doi.org/10.1080/14702436.2021.1994396.

Biegon, R & Watts T 2022, 'Remote Warfare and the Retooling of American Primacy', *Geopolitics*, vol. 27, no. 3, pp. 948–71, https://doi.org/10.1080/14650045.2020.1850442.

Boot, M 2019, 'Why Winning and Losing Are Irrelevant in Syria and Afghanistan', *The Washington Post*, 30 January, <https://www.washingtonpost.com/opinions/global-opinions/the-us-cant-win-the-wars-in-afghanistan-and-syria--but-we-can-lose-them/2019/01/30/e440c54e-23ea-11e9-90cd-dedb0c92dc17_story.html> (accessed 13 July 2022).

Demmers, J & Gould L 2018, 'An Assemblage Approach to Liquid Warfare: AFRICOM and the 'Hunt' for Joseph Kony', *Security Dialogue*, vol. 49, no. 5, pp. 364–81, https://doi.org/10.1177/0967010618777890.

Doyle, M 1986, *Empires*, Cornell University Press, Ithaca, NY.

Freedman, L 2022, *Command: The Politics of Military Operations from Korea to Ukraine*, Penguin, London.

Gat, A 2006, *War in Human Civilisation*, Oxford University Press, New York.

Goldsmith, J & Waxman, M 2016, 'Legal Legacy of Light-Footprint Warfare', *Washington Quarterly*, vol. 39, no. 2, pp. 7–21, http://dx.doi.org/10.1080/0163660X.2016.1204305.

Heng, Y 2018, 'The Continuing Resonance of the War as Risk Management Perspective for Understanding Military Interventions', *Contemporary Security Policy*, vol. 39, no. 4, pp. 544–58, https://doi.org/10.1080/13523260.2018.1494670.

Hoffman, F & Orner, A 2021 'Return of Great Power Proxy Wars', *War on the Rocks*, 2 September, <https://warontherocks.com/2021/09/the-return-of-great-power-proxy-wars/> (accessed on 3 September 2021).

Ignatieff, M 2003, *Empire Lite: Nation-Building in Bosnia, Kosovo and Afghanistan*, Vintage, London.

Keegan, J 2004, *A History of Warfare*, Pimlico, London.

Krieg, A 2016, 'Externalising the Burden of War: The Obama Doctrine and US Foreign Policy in the Middle East', *International Affairs*, vol. 92, no. 1, pp. 97–113, https://doi.org/10.1111/1468-2346.12506.

Kumar, K 2020, *Empires*, Polity, Cambridge, MA.

Levite, A E & Shimshoni J 2018, 'The Strategic Challenge of Society-Centric Warfare', *Survival*, vol. 60, no. 6, pp. 91–118, https://doi.org/10.1080/00396338.2018.1542806.

MacFarquhar, N 2022, 'Desperate for Recruits, Russia Launches a "Stealth Mobilization"', *The New York Times*, 10 July, <https://www.nytimes.com/2022/07/10/world/europe/russia-recruits-ukraine-war.html> (accessed 11 July 2022).

Mead, W R 2001, *Special Providence: American Foreign Policy and How It Changed the World*, Alfred A. Knopf, New York.

Morefield, J & Porter P 2020, 'Revenge of the Forever Wars', *New Statesman*, 10 June, pp. 13–14.

Mumford, A 2013, 'Proxy Warfare and the Future of Conflict', *The RUSI Journal*, vol. 158, no. 2, pp. 40–6, https://doi.org/10.1080/03071847.2013.787733.

Poast, P 2021, 'Imperial Policing Reduz: The Folly of Staying the Course in Afghanistan', *Modern War Institute*, 8 April, viewed on 15 April 2021, <https://mwi.usma.edu/imperial-policing-redux-the-folly-of-staying-the-course-in-afghanistan/>.

Porch, D 2005, 'Imperial Wars: From the Seven Years War to the First World War,' in C Townshend (ed), *The Oxford History of Modern War*, Oxford University Press, New York, pp. 94–116.

Porter, B 1996, *The Lion's Share: A Short History of British Imperialism 1850–1995*, Pearson, Harlow.

Porter, P 2015, *The Global Village Myth: Distance, War, and the Limits of Power*, Hurst & Company, London.

Porter, P 2018, 'Why America's Grand Strategy Has Not Changed: Power, Habit, and the U.S. Foreign Policy Establishment', *International Security*, vol. 42, no. 4, pp. 9–46, https://doi.org/10.1162/isec_a_00311.

Porter, P 2020, *The False Promise of Liberal Order*, Polity, Cambridge, MA.

Porter, P 2021, 'Unipolar America: another imperial delusion ends', *Engelsberg Ideas*, 3 September, viewed 12 June 2022, <https://engelsbergideas.com/essays/unipolar-america-another-imperial-delusion-ends/>.

Reiter, D & Stam A C 2002, *Democracies at War*, Princeton University Press, Princeton.

Rolland, N 2020, 'China's Vision for a New World Order', NBR Special Report No. 83, *The National Bureau of Asian Research*, 27 January, <https://www.nbr.org/publication/chinas-vision-for-a-new-world-order/> (accessed 14 June 2022).

Satia, P 2021, 'Not Humane, Just Invisible: A Counternarrative to Samuel Moyn's "Humane"', *Los Angeles Review of Books*, 3 December, <https://lareviewofbooks.org/article/not-humane-just-invisible-a-counter-narrative-to-samuel-moyns-humane/> (accessed 17 December 2021).

Tidsall, S 2021, 'In China's new age of imperialism, Xi Jinping gives thumbs down to democracy', *The Guardian*, 12 December, viewed on 7 January 2022, <https://www.theguardian.com/commentisfree/2021/dec/12/xi-jinping-china-beijing-new-age-of-imperialism>.

Tierney, D 2021, 'The Future of Sino-US Proxy War', *Texas National Security Review*, vol. 4, no. 2, pp. 49–73, http://dx.doi.org/10.26153/tsw/13198.

Waldman, T 2007, 'British Post-Conflict Operations in Iraq: Into the Heart of Strategic Darkness', *Civil Wars*, vol. 9, no. 1, pp. 61–86, https://doi.org/10.1080/13698240601159066.

Waldman, T 2021, *Vicarious Warfare: American Strategy and the Illusion of War on the Cheap*, Bristol University Press, Bristol.

Watling, J 2022, 'Operation Z: The Death Throes of an Imperial Delusion', *RUSI Special Report*, 22 April, <https://www.rusi.org/explore-our-research/publications/special-resources/operation-z-death-throes-imperial-delusion> (accessed 28 April 2022).

Yuan, J 2021, 'China's Private Security Companies and the Protection of Chinese Economic Interests Abroad', *Small Wars & Insurgencies*, vol. 33, no. 1–2, pp. 173–95, https://doi.org/10.1080/09592318.2021.1940646.

19

POST-MODERN WARFARE

Artur Gruszczak

Introduction

The concept of post-modern warfare emerged as a form of contestation of the conventional thoughts accompanying the transformation and reorganisation of military and non-state armed groups in the late 20th century. It was a reaction to post-modernist interpretations of the security environment after the end of the Cold War, inspired by the speed of globalisation, unstoppable networking and the increasing impact of technology. In the security field, it reflected the advantages and limitations of the technology-driven Revolution in Military Affairs (RMA). Post-modernist scepticism, relativist discourse and a polemical approach have been reinforced by the post-RMA theorising of warfare.

The assumption that post-modernity refers to the period which follows modernity and exhibits novel shapes and forms of reality in its social, cultural, political and technological dimensions is the starting point for the conceptualisation of post-modern warfare. It argues that wars of the past, waged principally by the modern nation-states, entered the inevitable path of transformation, requiring a profound reconsideration of the use of violence and military force and reinterpretation of armed conflicts according to different categories and arguments. Hence, the Clausewitzian understanding of war – like Smithian economic theory, the Fordist production model and the Weberian concept of the state – was challenged by metaphors, representations and discourses of subjectivity, indeterminacy, relativism and heterogeneity.

Post-modern warfare reflects the changing character of military confrontation and warfighting determined by technology, complexity and cognition. It features technology-driven defence innovation and modernisation as the sources of military overmatch, placing the emphasis on information management and the accumulation of knowledge. It highlights the power of networks in bringing together various categories of actors and engaging them in the rapidly changing security environment. Post-modern warfare epitomises the accelerated transformation of the complex space of military confrontation towards cognitive frameworks, which aim to reduce unpredictability and gain more leverage from asymmetrical engagements.

This chapter discusses post-modern warfare as a dimension of post-Cold War antagonisms and conflicts. Triggered by technological advancements and nurtured by the complexity and vagueness of the security environment, it has evolved through a three-stage process. These stages,

DOI: 10.4324/9781003299011-23

corresponding to subsequent generations of post-modern warfare, will be examined according to drivers, dynamics, and potentialities of the use of coercion, manipulation and force to remake the ontological structuring of the global security arena.

Post-modernity and warfare

Post-modernity encouraged a view of the world as consisting of a plurality of heterogeneous spaces and temporalities, of cultures and discourses (Heller & Fehér 1988, pp. 1–5). It fostered language trade-offs with the real world encapsulated in overarching 'metanarratives'. Post-modernism embraces "indeterminacy rather than determinism, diversity rather than unity, difference rather than synthesis, complexity rather than simplification" (Rosenau 1992, p. 8). It entails an emotional, affective approach to reality and a sensitivity towards the human condition. It reflects on existential issues, such as dehumanisation (in terms of degradation and savagery, as well as the replacement of soldiers by AI-driven military systems); non-discrimination (based on race, gender, worldview); protection (of population, nature, climate, etc.); and perception of war (awareness-building by media, main narratives, value-laden interpretations, etc.).

The end of the Cold War and the transformation of the global security system favoured new approaches and conceptions exploring and explaining emerging or evolving patterns of coercion, aggression and armed conflict. Christopher Coker argued, with a sense of irony, that 'endism' – as a post-Cold War 'season fad' driven by Fukuyama's acclaimed essay – was substituted with the prefix 'post' to designate discontinuity between the past and the future (Coker 1998, p. 7). Indeed, post-modernism – as Best and Kellner (2001, p. 2) put it – "calls attention to discontinuities and ruptures, and signals that an extensive range of novelties are appearing that require fresh analyses, theories and practices". However, a strategic perspective on global security in the early 1990s displayed many characteristics unambiguously associated with the modern war system. Large-scale mechanised combat systems, nuclear weapons, counterinsurgency forces and national security strategies were still of paramount importance for global security and international order.

Accordingly, mainstream theoretical deliberations on security voiced considerable reservations concerning the utility of post-modern ideas for the analysis of the nascent post-Cold War security system. Leading security scholars, like Stephen Walt, argued that

> Post-modern approaches have yet to demonstrate much value for comprehending world politics [...] In particular, issues of peace and war are too important for the field to be diverted into a prolix and self-indulgent discourse that is divorced from the real world.
>
> (Walt 1991, p. 223)

The eccentric concepts and interpretations offered by outstanding post-modernist thinkers such as Baudrillard ("the first Gulf War did not take place") or Lyotard ("war as a structure of thought"), did not help War Studies, which is conservative by default, accept the post-modern outlook.

However, the debate on the transformation of war (as well as of politics, society and economy), stirred by the chequered career of the concept of RMA, encompassed more and more post-modern arguments and propositions. What facilitated greatly the inclusion of post-modern discourse in that debate was the emphasis placed on the technological factor and the belief that modernisation signifies a gradual yet inevitable exit from the modern world. Justifying the use of the label 'post-modern war', Chris Hables Gray argued:

> Modern war as a category is used by most military historians, who usually see it as starting in the 1500s and continuing into the middle or late twentieth century. [...] The new kind of war, while related to modern war, is different enough to deserve the appellation 'postmodern'.
>
> (Gray 1997, p. 22)

The concept of post-modern war (PMW) has aspired, then, to critically interact with the leading theories, as well as to keep the post-modern interpretation and explanation active in the debate on current and future conditions of warfare. The post-modern perspective is future-oriented by default, as it galvanises unorthodox reflections on the essence of warfare and its evolution. It puts the emphasis on the creation of the space of confrontation and stimulation of hostilities by the application of advanced technologies of information and disinformation, knowledge management and awareness building. The perception of warfighting through the prism of trail-blazing tech-nologies and high-tech military weapons (having both advantages and flaws) shifts the focus to the cognitive dimension: making sense of military confrontation and interpreting its varieties and idiosyncrasies. Motivations for violence and manifestations of destructiveness, regardless of their origins, are born in an individual's consciousness, which is shaped by natural and artificial sensors supplying information and knowledge. Accordingly, post-modernity seems to embrace a struggle between "warriors of knowledge, not warriors of war" (Coker 1992, p. 193).

Post-modernist explanations of transitions from the conventional wars of the modern age stemmed from the affirmation of technology and its impact on ways and means of warfighting. Gradually, the high-tech 'hype' gave way to a more insightful reflection on the changing character of warfare and the relevance of the domain. Agents – to employ post-modernist vocabulary – expe-rienced growing difficulties in mastering the increasing complexity of the military confrontation. The expansion of cyberspace (mirroring post-modernist 'hyper-reality' and 'hyper-space') and the weaponisation of information and mass communication, mostly via social media, have shown that technologies matter insofar as they shape the mindsets and performances of belligerents. Hence, post-modern warfare has been engaged in relentless efforts to exploit technologies – being fruits of modernisation – to manage ambiguity, indeterminacy and fragmentation, as typical features of the post-modernist approach.

First-generation PMW

The early PMW concepts were entrenched in the modern world system of sovereign nation-states pursuing their vital interests in a volatile security environment delimited by international legal norms, bounded rationality and the peripheralisation of violence. Even though those concepts challenge various aspects of the modern world, they seem to be intimately connected to the evolu-tionary logic of the Westphalian system.

The first-generation concepts of PMW underlined continuity in the evolution and transforma-tion of warfare in the 20th century. They conceived the post-modern elements, such as military high-tech, cyberspace, networking, identity politics and post-heroism, as additional layers built into the traditional system of modern warfare. There was a unanimity of modernist and post-modernist thinkers as to technology as a game changer, a force behind the deep transformation of the military domain and the ensuing shift to post-modern warfare. This point was shared by the proponents of the RMA, it being the consequence of the transformation of war. Van Creveld (2000, p. 341) indicated in this regard "unlimited trust in, and dependence on, modern technology". Robins and Webster (1999, p. 151) underlined "a recurrent faith in a 'technical fix' to the problem of war". C H Gray depicted PMW as a conventional, technoscientific and technophilic war. It could be seen as a systemic activity developed in both the conventional ('real') and electronic battlefields (which converge into a battlespace), scientifically determined by computer models, game theories and tailored management techniques.

Illustrative of the first-generation PMW concept, Steven Metz's description of the changing nature of armed conflicts focused on technological advancement, mostly in the military domain, that triggers organisational change through interconnectedness, the expansion of networks, dispersion of power and proliferation of information and knowledge. Key resources are unevenly distributed, causing disproportions and leading to asymmetric conflicts. Those conflicts, called 'informal wars', emerge as a result of the declining effectiveness of states. These wars "grow from the culture of violence [...] flowing from endemic conflict, crime, the drug trade, the proliferation of weapons and the trivialization of violence through popular culture" (Metz 2000, p. 48).

The attempt to provide empirical examples of post-modern warfare is a contentious issue. For C H Gray, following Fredric Jameson (1984, pp. 84–5), the Vietnam War was the first PMW (Gray 1997, pp. 158–67). Likewise, Michael Bibby (1999, p. 167) saw that war as "foundational to the emergence of postmodernity". For Van Creveld (2000, pp. 351–2), the Israeli-Arab "War of Attrition" (1969–1970) was the "first electronic war", in which electronic circuits, sensors, guided missiles and, ultimately, the broad range of weapons deployed were connected to computers and operated remotely. Other scholars mention the conflicts of the late 20th century: the obvious case of the (first) War in the Gulf (1990–1991), and not so obvious wars in Chechnya and Kosovo (Moore 2010).

The Gulf War was the most spectacular representation of first-generation PMW. The 'hyperreal' media coverage offered by CNN, virtualisation of the battlefield, massive use of 'smart' weapons and the strong tendency towards the replacement of humans by automated systems were put into effect, mostly due to cybernetics, information management and the introduction of a new military architecture based on C4I2: command, control, communication, computerisation, intelligence and interoperability. The first War in the Gulf demonstrated that PMWs were formed by technoscience underpinning digital realism in the military realm and a rhetorical and cultural discourse clarifying the contradictions of warfare. In Keller's words, "the Gulf War deployed both a new mode of high-tech warfare and a new experience of war as a hyperreal media event, as a postmodern political spectacle [...]" (Keller 1999, p. 218).

The reliance on high-tech systems reflected an unwillingness to accept fatalities in combat operations, especially in Western societies. Edward Luttwak coined the term 'post-heroic warfare' for the depiction of armed activities aimed at avoiding casualties, as a result of demographic tendencies and value shifts in post-modern societies and the revision of the meaning of heroism and sacrifice (Luttwak 1995). His observations coincided with the discussion on the post-modern military and the post-modern soldier. The former was focused on army culture, military bureaucracy, civil-military relations and the legitimisation of the national discourse of war (Bondy 2004, pp. 39–41). The latter takes a great deal of care of his or her body, health, well-being and the prolongation of life (Coker 2007, p. 70). The soldier is even subject to intense pharmacological stimulation and medical treatment in order to augment physical or cognitive abilities in order to mitigate the effects of staying in a warzone, as well as to heal emotional scars when discharged as a veteran (Kamieński 2013, 2016).

The post-heroic warrior is haunted by the need for 'responsible survival', the ability to avoid a 'heroic death', in order to "satisfy a desire for adventure and to have a meaningful personal experience" (Battistelli 1997, p. 471). Hence, safeguarding the military so as to minimise the risk of deaths and injuries was one of the key purposes of PMW.

Post-heroic accents were found in the Clinton administration's sensitivity over the protection of civilians as well as the military personnel deployed in missions overseas (Kaempf 2018, Chapter 4). Force protection was one of the priorities during peace-enforcement operations in Haiti, Somalia and the Balkans, as well as during the disarmament crisis in Iraq (Operation Desert Fox of 1998). NATO's intervention in Kosovo, the last large-scale international military operation prior to 9/11, was highly determined by a policy of 'riskless warfare', a 'no-boots-on-the-ground' strategy based on the maximisation of air dominance and information superiority. The acceleration of the allied military operation was enabled by the widespread use of satellite surveillance, unmanned aerial reconnaissance, precision guided missiles and Internet-based strategic communication.

First-generation PMW accompanied the turbulent post-Cold War global security environment by propagating confidence in military high-tech as the game changer in the transformation of war in the late 20th century.

Second-generation PMW

Just before the beginning of the Kosovo intervention, Mary Kaldor published her book *Old and New Wars*, which resonated immediately in the War and Security Studies communities. Using the simple dichotomy of 'old' and 'new' wars, Kaldor introduced a novel and inspiring perspective that saw wars as a type of organised violence that was a side-effect of globalisation, security privatisation and the expansion of cyberspace. She preferred the term 'new wars' to 'post-modern wars' because the latter was mostly associated with virtual wars and wars in cyberspace (Kaldor 1999, p. 2).

The emergence of new wars was facilitated by the transformation of the modern nation-state, the erosion of its autonomy and the questioning of its traditional monopoly of legitimate organised violence. New wars were more about identity politics than about military technologies, doctrines and network-centric enablers; they epitomised the clash of ideas about social, cultural, political and economic change. They involve a plethora of belligerents: dispersed units of the armed forces, police squads, insurgents, paramilitary groups, local armed mobs commanded by warlords, criminal gangs and mercenaries (or private military contractors).

Kaldor did not underrate technology as a driver of new wars. She underlined the enormous impact of information and communication systems on states and societies. However, she considered this factor as auxiliary, and sometimes secondary, to societal efforts aiming to overcome barriers on the path to cosmopolitan politics and human security. New wars did not "represent a progressive displacement of humans by technology" (Keller 1999, p. 227); they epitomised uncontrolled violence unleashed by ferocious gangs, ruthless thugs, self-proclaimed militias and terrorists which could not be stopped or restrained by high-tech solutions.

Second-generation PMW, substantially shaped by the critique of the RMA, accentuated profound alterations in the military, social, political and economic domains galvanised by cultural shifts, technoscientific progress, and the heavy investment in communication infrastructure, fostering the expansion of the mass (electronic) media. The widespread use of the Internet by the population and of the advanced C4ISR (command, control, communication, computers, intelligence, surveillance, reconnaissance) systems by the army transformed warfare into a complex battlespace saturated with multiple networks facilitating the coordination of hostilities yet also elevating risk of collateral damage.

Complex networks emerged as a result of the triple revolution produced by social networks, the personalised Internet and always-available mobile connectivity (Rainie & Wellman 2012, p. ix). These three components mostly contributed to the emergence and maintenance of the so-called conflict ecosystem, in which multiple competing entities are seeking to maximise their survivability and influence (Kilcullen 2006, p. 122). The technoscientific hype associated with first-generation PMW also spread to non-state violent actors, especially terrorist networks and organised criminal syndicates. These eagerly employed new technologies to better coordinate their structures and ramp up their capabilities when it came to engaging in a violent confrontation with the state. The jihadist network created by al-Qaeda became a paradigmatic case of the new-generation terrorist groups.

The war on terrorism, launched in response to 9/11, was another incentive for reconsidering the theorems of first-generation PMW (see Bondy 2004, pp. 35–6). The conventional reaction of the Bush administration, lagging behind the dynamics of jihadi networks, reduced the terrorist threat to a military campaign in remote Afghanistan. Conservative voices heralded the exhaustion of the post-modernist argument on the basis of its relativism and anti-patriotism. They pointed out the objectiveness and tangibility of the war on terror and highlighted just cause and moral clarity as commonly shared beliefs. Counterinsurgency doctrines, emphasising the need to gain and maintain control over an area of conflict and over the population residing there, hailed the 'kinetic' actions taken by force providers.

This counter-post-modernist movement did not disavow post-modernist arguments. The wars in Afghanistan and Iraq shifted the centre of gravity to social structures, religious beliefs, the shaping of identity, language and narratives and cultural awareness. The 'hardware' of modern warfare gave way to the 'software' of PMW. Seen from the Foucauldian angle, knowledge of local communities, their customs, beliefs and lifestyles, was the factor of power and control over the population. It also reflected the heterogeneity of behavioural patterns and relativity of tactical goals and strategic objectives pursued by actors in the conflicts. The Human Terrain System, introduced into the Afghan conflict by the US command in the mid-2000s, was based on an ethnographic and anthropological insight into – in David Petraeus's words – fighting in "the kind of wars we must master" (McFate & Laurence 2015, p. 3). Technology was employed to strengthen the Human Terrain Teams, mostly by the massive use of biometrics and computerised registries of personal and other data relevant for situational awareness. 'Casualty-phobia' was noticeable in the Bush administration as well. Several hundred thousand US troops, sent to Afghanistan and then to Iraq to engage against the Taliban regime and the brutal dictatorship of Saddam Hussein, were deployed, commanded and engaged in operations with due respect to the principle of casualty aversion (Kaempf 2018, Chapters 5 and 6).

The striving for a 'riskless warfare' was strongly linked to the Western states, but omitted non-state entities. Risk was outsourced to private military companies (PMCs), which confirmed the arguments voiced by Coker and Kaldor in the 1990s that the privatisation of war completes the marketisation of politics. Tasks associated with the risk of casualties and weapons damage were outsourced to PMCs, such as Blackwater, KBR or Dyncorp (see the chapter by Krahmann in this book).

Second-generation PMW was marked by the widening of the discrepancy between the 'late-modern' belief in the utility of high-tech military applications and the growing awareness of their flaws and shortcomings. It endorsed the suggestive argument that 'new wars' can be fought in an expanded and crowded space in which advanced technologies do not guarantee victory but are still useful as enablers of influence operations and cognitive warfare.

Third-generation PMW

Third-generation PMW concepts highlighted the dialectical relation between the progressive and modernising function of technology and conventional (pre-modern and modern) patterns of power and organised violence. They pointed to "hybrid identities, flexible hierarchies, and plural exchanges through modulating networks of command" which stimulate the emergence and consolidation of "complex regimes of differentiation and homogenization, deterritorialization and reterritorialization" (Hardt & Negri 2000, pp. xii–xiii). They took from the concept of hybrid wars the deep conviction that in war paradoxes and contradictions are clearly visible and that the spectrum of combat activities tends to overstretch. They borrowed from the effect-based operations (see Vego 2006) the understanding of post-asymmetry as a dialectic intertwining of warfare and anti-warfare, which "shifts our focus from targets and damage to behavior and the stimuli that alter behavior" (Smith 2002, p. xi). Most importantly, they aspired to redefine war with reference to a wide spectrum of antagonisms and hostilities unfolding in a battlespace determined by 'hybrid' connections between technology, communication and culture (see Dickson 2004; Kay 2017; Gruszczak 2018).

Although philosophical and sociological reflection on post-modernism evolved towards a next stage dubbed 'post-post-modernism' (Nealon), 'pseudo-modernism' or 'digimodernism' (Kirby), or 'metamodernism' (van den Akker, Vermeulen, Freinacht), marking mutations of the varieties of post-modernity, third-generation PMW followed the topical subjects discussed from the beginning of the 21st century. On the one side, they hailed artificial intelligence (AI) and its innovative applications in defence. On the other, they accentuated the impact of conventional cultural patterns, religious zeal and mass communication on mobilisation for and the conduct of war. The discourse on third-generation PMW implied a problematic dialectic of a limiting and debounding of warfare (Ehrhart 2017, p. 270). This discourse is needed to explain some striking continuities with the modern era and for avoiding a paradox trap caused by the ambivalence of modernisation and technological expansion.

Ambiguity, liquidity and flexibility, which are characteristic of post-modern thinking, continuously permeate warfare, bringing about blurred distinctions between peace and war, fact and fake, information and disinformation, kinetic and non-kinetic operations. Accordingly, US Army Major Larry A Kay defined post-modern warfare as:

> Multi-domain, borderless competition dominated by the ability of state and non-state actors to manipulate information through metanarratives to decisively overwhelm or undermine adversaries, focusing on non-combatants for sources of internal and adversarial political dissidence.
>
> (Kay 2017)

It was taken for granted that AI-centric third-generation PMW has clear advantages over human-centric second-generation PMW. Likewise, human-to-human communication became virtualised, constituting a substantial part of cyberspace and depending increasingly on technical interfaces. It began evolving towards the human-to-AI hybrid cognitive symbiosis emerging in the complex ecosystem powered by algorithms. Hence, algorithmic warfare was introduced to the discourse on PMW. Surveillance, profiling, mapping, image analysis and pattern recognition were examples of the wide range of algorithm-driven methods employed in warfare. Algorithms were considered as constitutive of a distinct security logic reshaping the existing practices of awareness building, decision-making, targeting and securitisation (Amoore & Raley 2017, p. 8). Algorithms define and determine actionable security choices (military orders) in armed conflicts, as well as in operations below the threshold of war. Moreover, they are used for steering and calibrating communication systems and (dis)information campaigns so as to enhance disruptive and destabilising tendencies. Strategic communication, intelligence and planning structures do not avoid targeting political parties, governments or ethnic, racial and religious communities. For example, algorithms and social media were used as a means of manipulation of the 2016 US presidential race, the Brexit referendum in the United Kingdom and the aborted process of Catalan independence.

Third-generation PMW emerged in the era of post-truth and fake news. The first-generation motif of mediatisation of warfare by 'hyper-real' depictions and military imaginaries gave way to the weaponisation of social media. The modern take on information as a tool of political warfare was substituted by disinformation and meta-disinformation. 'War by other means', as it accompanied first-generation PMW, was overshadowed by 'war by other memes' (Singer & Brooking 2018). The Internet became a global platform for expansive and predatory social media, which revolutionised information warfare. The flood of lies, hoaxes, fake news and conspiracy theories, amplified by deception, disinformation and misperceptions, had a huge impact on states' security, strategic communications and situational awareness. Some willingly adapted themselves to the new information ecosystem, reinforcing the old ways and means (as in the case of Russia's active measures) or setting up specialised units for covert operations (such as China's PLA Unit 61398, Iran's APT39 or Russia's 'Cozy Bear'). Others, like the United States or the United Kingdom, enhanced their cyber-defence capabilities by deploying a coordinated set of protective measures and tools and investing in new solutions. Crowdsourcing, a popular practice in cyberspace, was utilised in order to maximise the potential of social media users to raise security awareness and obtain intelligence. Activist projects, like Fifth Estate, CyberGuerrilla, Cryptome or WikiLeaks, became important providers of sensitive data. Investigative journalism groups, like Bellingcat, The Intercept or The Insider, became influential OSINT (open-source intelligence) producers.

The return of the 'technological hype' typical of first-generation PMW was accompanied by an outburst of 'hyper-real' representations of warfare, augmented by social media. Third-generation PMW has questioned the ability of the military to command and control the multi-domain architecture of the evolving battlespace. Therefore, the relevance of the mental processes of interpretation and comprehension of the perceived reality set the direction of the evolution of post-modern warfare.

PMW of the future: towards the next generation

The future of PMW is predestined by the advancing counter-evolution of warfare in terms of a scientific way of perceiving, analysing, understanding and conducting it. Post-modern scepticism, subjectivism and relativism aptly exploit the shortcomings and occasional failures of the application of the predominant concepts of the 21st century, such as hybrid warfare, counterinsurgency, mosaic warfare or effect-based operations. PMW is not a genuinely novel type of armed conflict; it blends and reshuffles certain ingredients and features of dominant concepts of 21st century warfare in an unconventional way. PMW reflects the complexity and diversity of a human civilisation doomed to the escalating clash between the drivers of globalisation and technology-led modernisation, and the forces fiercely defending structural and organisational patterns of traditional political, cultural, economic and social relations.

A next-generation (next-gen) PMW would seem to incite unconstrained violence affecting civilians, as well as various categories of belligerents: the military, insurgents, armed gangs and paramilitary groups. An extensive catalogue of methods of warfare and the variety of methods for the conduct of hostilities will blend 'online' and 'offline' warfare regulated by streams of immense data flows. The allocation of key resources, such as information, knowledge, power and capital, will be determined by technological drivers enabling the ever-increasing violent confrontation between units enmeshed in a complex theatre of operations wired with information and communication networks. Technologies are secondary when it comes to the way in which warfare is conducted (strategic culture), but they are absolutely crucial as drivers of organised violence and protracted conflicts. A microchip, a CPU, the remote access to ICT networks and geospatial positioning are the essential components of the ecosystem of next-gen PMW.

Characterised by a multi-layered structure, next-gen PMW will take place in territorial, spatial, cognitive, virtual (cyber-spatial) and hyper-real (reproductive) spheres. I will explain each of those in the following. Territory is a remnant of first-generation PMW and represents the physical, geographical and corporeal dimensions of warfare. Humans are still the living embodiments of hostilities, destined to occupy a fragment of territory and have the basic resources at their constant disposal. Critical infrastructure is also established within a given territory. Hardware is installed in given locations and needs to be safeguarded by physical means. Next-gen PMW will focus on taking hold of and maintaining this across key locations of infrastructural nodes.

The spatial domain, containing air space and outer space, is critical for communication, surveillance and reconnaissance, as well as for the ability to conduct stand-in and stand-off strikes. The use of drones for remote targeting and lethal strikes will consolidate the post-modern trend of riskless warfare waged by post-heroic operators. Massive surveillance, eavesdropping and intelligence-led acquisition of data, mostly by satellites orbiting the Earth, will be crucial for creating maximally effective real-time battlespace awareness. The spatial 'suprastructure' will be equally imperative to informational precision (global positioning systems, smart grids), and communication (extensive wireless networks). The latter can be illustrated by Elon Musk's Starlink project and its engagement in the war in Ukraine in 2022. In response to the destruction of cables and cell towers by the Russian forces in the first days of the invasion, Musk delivered Starlink satellite kits to Ukraine, ensuring broadband communication and access to the Internet.

The virtual domain is going to be dominated by an ever-expanding cyberspace. The Internet will spill over into new territories in the global peripheries, enabling the diffusion of ideas and beliefs which may trigger new forms of political radicalism and cultural backlash against post-modern values. The relativity and ambiguity of messages generated on the Internet, which is typical for 'liquid security' and 'chaoplexic' reality (see Bousquet in this volume), will be looming large in the next stages of (dis)information operations. The vertical dimension of the Internet will be increasingly exploited by a host of state and non-state actors seeking to capitalise on malicious activities. The acquisition of classified information and intelligence, transactions of illegal goods, including weapons, and capital raising via blockchain technologies are opportunities offered by the encrypted layers of the Darknet as part of a virtual battlespace. The cyber-spatial sphere opens up further opportunities for better preparedness and more effective training and simulation of operational processes. Virtual reality and augmented reality (see Liaropoulos in this volume) have been increasingly utilised during the military activities of the Western coalition in Iraq and NATO/ISAF forces in Afghanistan. In the future battlespace saturated with AI-driven semi-autonomous combat systems, a high-fidelity simulation of weapons performance, combat environments, command chains and the behaviour of an adversary in multiple scenarios, will aim to reduce risk and optimise military organisation in network configurations with sensors and shooters.

Social media will be massively exploited by belligerent actors. The hyperproduction of information based on texts, images and videos provided by witnesses, often accidental observers, has been of the utmost significance for situational assessment and awareness building in the battlespace. Crowdsourced intelligence utilising the potential of individual and collective actors (public, private, commercial, state-affiliated) will enable the processing of scattered data and bringing about of an accurate, reliable and time-sensitive product available to everyone. The evidently unstoppable expansion of social media tends to create a mosaic depiction of warfare which for some (like intelligence services) will facilitate greatly the understanding of the logic of a confrontation, while for others it will blur the overall perception of warfare, thus provoking uncertainty and anxiety. In this regard, next-gen PMW is going to exist as a layer added to the mosaic warfare concept, which assumes the building of an overwhelming advantage through the employment of a large volume and variety of weapons from different classes, sizes and types – each fighting in a specific way which is hardly legible for the enemy.

A next-generation PMW should be conceived as an architecture of complex networks permeating warfare activities unfolding in the future. The practically unbreakable linkages between actors, hostilities and crucial assets will shape future warfare as a sequential combination of dispersed acts of hostility performed between interconnected units which engage in information-powered operations in uncertain and volatile environments. Next-gen PMW will be waged by state and non-state actors primarily involved in network building, capital raising, information management and intelligence acquisition. Territorial control over selected areas is relevant, yet not indispensable, for the belligerents who will exploit protracted political and social instability, the delegitimisation of legal authority, information anarchy on social media, indoctrination and deception.

Conclusion

Since the beginning of the 21st century, the understanding of post-modern warfare has engaged with the very foundations of post-modernity by emphasising diversity, heterogeneity, 'liquidity' (Bauman) and risk (Beck) as principal features of conflicts. It points out the relevance of information and communication for shaping the domains of warfare yet at the same time draws attention to the deformation and mystification of reality caused intentionally by anonymised belligerents, or unconsciously by billions of users of social media.

The post-modern outlook for the future of warfare accentuates the fragility of the global commons and the desperate need to rescue them from degradation and depreciation caused mostly by the states. Accordingly, warfare as an organised way of employing military violence is losing its traditional meaning as the major threat to stability, well-being and human development. It becomes secondary to the global market, competition for economic resources, supply chains, critical information and communication avenues. The global 'tug of war' does not necessarily involve military force; it rather seeks to disengage belligerent actors from costly, damaging and disturbing warfighting activities, or to channel hostilities into non-military encounters. This resembles future wars as portrayed by Mark Galeotti (2022, p. 4): "Wars without warfare, non-military conflicts fought with all kinds of other means, from subversion to sanctions, memes to murder, may be becoming the new normal".

References

Amoore, L & Raley, R 2017, 'Securing with Algorithms: Knowledge, Decision, Sovereignty', *Security Dialogue*, vol. 48, no. 1, pp. 3–10, https://doi.org/10.1177/0967010616680753.

Battistelli, F 1997, 'Peacekeeping and the Postmodern Soldier', *Armed Forces & Society*, vol. 23, no. 3, pp. 467–84, https://doi.org/10.1177/0095327X9702300308.

Best, S & Kellner, D 2001, *The Postmodern Adventure. Science Technology and Cultural Studies at the Third Millennium*, Routledge, London & New York.

Bibby, M 1999, 'The Post-Vietnam Condition', in M Bibby (ed), *The Vietnam War and Postmodernity*, University of Massachusetts Press, Amherst, MA, pp. 143–71.

Bondy, H 2004, 'Postmodernism and the Source of Military Strength in the Anglo West', *Armed Forces & Society*, vol. 31, no. 1, pp. 31–61, https://doi.org/10.1177/0095327X0403100103.

Coker, C 1992, 'Post-modernity and the End of the Cold War: Has War Been Disinvented?', *Review of International Studies*, vol. 18, no. 3, pp. 189–98, https://doi.org/10.1017/S026021050011722X.

Coker, C 1998, 'Post-Modern War', *RUSI Journal*, vol. 143, no. 3, pp. 7–14.

Coker, C 2007, *The Warrior Ethos: Military Culture and the War on Terror*, Routledge, London – New York.

Dickson, K D 2004, 'War in (Another) New Context: Postmodernism', *Journal of Conflict Studies*, vol. 24, no. 2, pp. 78–91.

Ehrhart, H-G 2017, 'Postmodern warfare and the blurred boundaries between war and peace', *Defense & Security Analysis*, vol. 33, no. 3, pp. 263–275, https://doi.org/10.1080/14751798.2017.1351156.

Galeotti, M 2022, *The Weaponisation Of Everything. A Field Guide To The New Way Of War*, Yale University Press, New Haven, CT & London.

Gray, C H 1997, *Postmodern War. The New Politics of Conflict*, The Guilford Press, New York & London.

Gruszczak, A 2018, 'Violence Reconsidered. Towards Postmodern Warfare', in A Gruszczak & P Frankowski (eds), *Technology, Ethics and the Protocols of Modern War*, Routledge, London & New York, pp. 26–40.

Hardt, M & Negri, A 2000, *Empire*, Harvard University Press, Cambridge, MA.

Heller, A. & Fehér, F 1988, *The Postmodern Political Condition*, Columbia University Press, New York.

Jameson, F 1984, 'Postmodernism or the Cultural Logic of Late Capitalism', *New Left Review*, no. 146, pp. 53–92.

Kaempf, S 2018, *Saving Soldiers or Civilians? Casualty-Aversion versus Civilian Protection in Asymmetric Conflicts*, Cambridge University Press, Cambridge.

Kaldor, M 1999, *New and Old Wars. Organized Violence in a Global Era*, Stanford University Press, Stanford, CA.

Kamieński, Ł 2013, 'Helping the Postmodern Ajax: Is Managing Combat Trauma through Pharmacology a Faustian Bargain?', *Armed Forces & Society*, vol. 39, no. 3, pp. 395–414, https://doi:10.1177/0095327X12451558.

Kamieński, Ł 2016, *Shooting Up: A Short History of Drugs and War*, Oxford University Press, New York.

Kay, L 2017, 'Innovation of Military Thought in the Postmodern Warfare Era', *Small Wars Journal*, 2 February, <https://smallwarsjournal.com/index.php/jrnl/art/innovation-military-thought-postmodern-warfare-era> (accessed 20 June 2022).

Keller, D 1999, 'From Vietnam to the Gulf: Postmodern Wars?', in M Bibby (ed) *The Vietnam War and Postmodernity*, University of Massachusetts Press, Amherst, MA, pp. 199–236.

Kilcullen, D 2006–2007, 'Counter-Insurgency Redux', *Survival*, vol. 48, no. 4, pp. 111–30, https://doi 10.1080/00396330601062790.

Luttwak, E N 1995, 'Toward Post-Heroic Warfare', *Foreign Affairs*, vol. 74, no. 3, pp. 109–22.

McFate, M & Laurence, J H 2015, 'Introduction: Unveiling the Human Terrain System', in M McFate & J H Laurence (eds), *Social Science Goes to War. The Human Terrain System in Iraq and Afghanistan*, Oxford University Press, Oxford – New York, pp. 1–44.

Metz, S 2000, *Armed Conflict in the 21st Century: The Information Revolution and Post-Modern Warfare*, Strategic Studies Institute, U.S. Army War College, Carlisle, PA.

Moore, C 2010, *Contemporary Violence. Postmodern War in Kosovo and Chechnya*, Manchester University Press, Manchester.

Rainie, L & Wellman, B 2012, *Networked. The New Social Operating System*, The MIT Press, London & Cambridge, MA.

Robins, K & Webster, F 1999, *Times of the Technoculture. From the Information Society to the Virtual Life*, Routledge, London & New York.

Rosenau, P M 1992, *Post-Modernism and the Social Sciences. Insights, Inroads, and Intrusions*, Princeton University Press, Princeton, NJ.

Singer, P W & Brooking E T 2018, *LikeWar: The Weaponization of Social Media*, Houghton Mifflin Harcourt, New York.

Smith, E A 2002, *Effects Based Operations: Applying Network Centric Warfare in Peace, Crisis, and War*, Command and Control Research Program, Washington, DC.

Van Creveld, M 2000, 'Technology and War II: Postmodern War?', in C Townshend (ed), *The Oxford History of Modern War*, Oxford University Press, Oxford – New York, pp. 341–59.

Vego, M N 2006, 'Effects-Based Operations: A Critique', *Joint Force Quarterly*, no. 41, pp. 51–7.

Walt, S 1991, 'The Renaissance of Security Studies', *International Studies Quarterly*, vol. 35, no. 2, pp. 211–39.

PART IV

Structural Complexity

20

THE PERSISTENT APPEAL OF CHAOPLEXIC WARFARE

Towards an Autonomous S(War)M Machine?

Antoine Bousquet

Introduction

Throughout the modern era, Western militaries have drawn upon the corpus of contemporaneous scientific understandings of reality and their paradigmatic technological models to inform the organisation of their forces and outline the horizon of their future development. The armed forces successively absorbed the influence of mechanistic, thermodynamic and cybernetic conceptions and the associated figures of the clock, engine and computer in their pursuit of mastery on the battlefield. In the closing two decades of the last century, the military mind increasingly came under the sway of a new scientific regime catalysed by the discoveries of chaos theory and complexity science. Organised around the figure of the network, chaoplexic warfare affirms distributed information processing, emergent self-organisation, and decentralised operations as the means to navigate creatively the turmoil of war.

Initially carried to the commanding heights of the US military by the doctrine of network-centric warfare (NCW), chaoplexic warfare survived NCW's fall from grace in Iraq and Afghanistan. It continued to irrigate the subsequent theories and practices of counterinsurgency and counter-terrorism devised during the War on Terror, albeit without yielding any more decisive outcomes against non-state adversaries characterised by their own network forms. With the global security agenda having resolutely shifted to an era of rekindled great power competition in the midst of a new technological wave of artificial intelligence and robotics, chaoplexic conceptions remain the conceptual fount upon which the latest doctrinal proposals of mosaic warfare, decision-centric warfare, and hyperwar draw. This chapter will review the enduring influence of chaoplexity upon military thought, examining the persistence of its appeal as a future vision of war despite its inconclusive results to date, and analyse the tensions and perils attendant to the incipient realisation of an autonomous s(war)m machine.

The four regimes of the scientific way of warfare

As proposed in *The Scientific Way of Warfare* (Bousquet 2022), we can distinguish four moments in the development of military organisation. Each of these corresponds to a broad historical period during which a coherent array of scientific conceptions inform a particular approach to the

	Key technology	Scientific concepts	Form of warfare
Mechanism	Clock	Force, matter in motion, linearity, geometry	closer order drill, rigid tactical deployments
Thermodynamics	Engine	Energy, entropy, probability	mass mobilisation, motorisation, industrialisation
Cybernetics	Computer	Information, negentropy, negative feedback, homeostasis	command and control, automation
Chaoplexity	Network	Information, non-linearity positive feedback, self-organisation, emergence	decentralisation, swarming, autonomy

Figure 20.1   The four regimes of the scientific way of warfare.

Source: Author's creation.

problems of control and order on the battlefield. Associated with a corresponding technology that doubles as both tool and metaphor, each regime denotes a distinct form of warfare with its specific features and privileged operational principles (see Figure 20.1).

Situated within the seventeenth and eighteenth centuries, the mechanistic era revolved around the clockwork metaphor, promulgating an understanding of the world as perfectly ordered by a divine mechanism set in motion by its creator. Mechanistic warfare reached its apogee with Frederick the Great's army as the pristine embodiment of a ticking leviathan on the field of battle. Via a process of intense drilling that shaped troops into obedient cogs, an intricate choreography of metronomic firearm volleys and complex tactical deployments was performed on the instruction of the enlightened monarch. With individual soldiers stripped of any capacity for initiative and absent the means for the commander to exert meaningful control after the onset of battle, the mechanistic approach to warfare was devoid of any flexibility and responsiveness to the contingencies of combat. Success rested above all upon meticulous advance planning and the endurance of its moving parts in the face of battlefield attrition.

The industrialisation and motorisation of society correspond to the advent of the thermodynamic age in which science turned to the study of energy, advancing a dynamic, unstable understanding of the universe and the irreversibility of fundamental processes within it. The notion of entropy, in particular, inscribed an immutable tendency towards decay and disorder. Alongside it came a probabilistic approach to scientific problems, undermining the tidy linearity and precise predictability of mechanistic models. Thermodynamic warfare unleashed volcanic forces into war, with rival nation-states mobilising, concentrating and discharging all available energies in their feverish collisions. From the onset of the French revolutionary wars to the development of nuclear weaponry, a vertiginous escalation in the intensity of destruction took place. While the development of command economies and total war brought unprecedented levels of central planning to the conduct of war, several armies experimented in this era with tactical decentralisation to navigate the turmoil of the industrial battlefield.

Although World War II marked the apotheosis of thermodynamic escalation, it simultaneously constituted the threshold of a new regime. Cybernetics established a science of control and communications organised around the concept of information and embodied in the advances in electromagnetic telecommunication and computational technology. Information became conceptualised as the negation of entropy and thus as an island of order in a dissipating world. Vast command and control architectures were established to secure a Cold War threatening to spiral at any moment into an apocalyptic nuclear conflict, promising centralised authority and stabilising self-regulation through negative information feedback. In the elusive quest for predictability, scientific methodology was applied more systematically than ever to warfare with the comprehensive treatment of tactical and strategic questions by operations research and systems analysis. Yet cybernetic warfare eventually experienced a chastening reversal with the Vietnam War, its sophisticated analytical techniques and military systems floundering when faced with a resourceful asymmetric adversary.

In the midst of the Cold War, scientists were busy extending the informational paradigm and pushing beyond the strictures of early cybernetics. From an exclusive focus on systems characterised by stability and self-regulation, they turned to processes of dynamic change and creative disruption. Through the exploration of non-linear mathematics, chaos theory discovered new inherent limits to scientific prediction, simultaneously revealing a secret order to seemingly random phenomena. At the edge of this intricately patterned effervescence, scientists found life itself in the guise of complex adaptive systems and their collective intelligences. A new understanding of order as the emergent property of distributed interactions between autonomous agents was illuminated and repeatedly identified in nature and society. Buoyed by the proliferation of decentralised telecommunication links and social organisations, the network established itself as a ubiquitous figure of thought by the final decade of the 20th century. Yet if the network arrived to change the world, "[it] came not in peace but with swords" (Arquilla 2007, p. 203). By the early 21st century, violent non-state actors had established the power of reticular organisation in humbling hierarchical states and confounding their best efforts at eradicating them. For its part, the US military had been pursuing throughout the 1990s the realisation of a "revolution in military affairs" (RMA) which, by the end of the decade, had become thoroughly infused with chaoplexic thinking. Under the banner of network-centric warfare, armed conflict was reimagined as "a complex, adaptive system where non-linear variables continuously interact" (Gray 2002, p. 105) and military force is best organised from the bottom-up.

Chaoplexic warfare meets the war on terror

Originally conceived with peer state competitors in mind, NCW was suddenly reoriented towards meeting the challenge of a Global War on Terror launched in the wake of the September 11 attacks. The speed and decisiveness of the successive invasions of Afghanistan and Iraq initially appeared to validate entirely this self-proclaimed new theory of war. The moment of triumph was short-lived. Iraq soon descended into a vortex of civil war that the Coalition appeared powerless to arrest. In response, military leaders undertook a major shift away from the 'light footprints' of nimble ground forces supported by air power to visible 'boots on the ground' tasked with 'winning the hearts and minds' of the local population.

The counterinsurgency moment was, in one sense, a spectacular reversal of NCW. Yet it was simultaneously a reaffirmation of chaoplexic principles that were called upon once again to make sense of the new challenge and devise an appropriate response to it. A refrain would return throughout: "it takes a network to beat a network, and our network must be better" (Transformation Warfare 2007). This mantra would be shared in equal measure by the special forces-led counterterrorist apparatus that grew in increasing scale and sophistication throughout the same period. Indeed, rather than mutually exclusive, the strategies of counterinsurgency and counterterrorism ran concurrently in both Iraq and Afghanistan, united by a common allegiance to chaoplexity.

The doctrinal expression of the new counterinsurgency (COIN) approach coalesced under the US Army Field Manual 23–4 (United States Army 2006). The manual advocates a "systems thinking" approach to insurgency, drawing upon "the perspective of the systems sciences that seeks to understand the interconnectedness, complexity, and wholeness of the elements of the systems in relation to one another" (p. 4–3). Contemporary insurgencies are conceived as networked organisations powered by "interconnectedness and information technology" (p. 1–4). They are correspondingly "difficult to destroy" and "tend to heal, adapt, and learn rapidly" (p. 1–17). COIN is therefore an "extremely complex form of warfare" (p. 1–27) that must blend kinetic force with "weapons that do not shoot" that can win over with the local population (p. 1–28). The "human terrain" of the occupied countries is itself essentially composed of "adaptive social networks," such as tribes, that have to be courted and nudged so as to sever their functional relations to the insurgency (p. 3–5). In this operational environment, decentralised command and control that fosters the "initiative of subordinates" is required to realise "a COIN force that can adapt and react at least as quickly as the insurgents" (p. 1–26). Overall, the final text counts no less than 218 references to "network(s)," 72 mentions of "complex(ity)," and 89 instance of variations on "adaptive" or "adaptation." Within a couple of months of publication, the Bush administration would announce a surge of 20,000 troops tasked with implementing the new doctrine in Iraq.

While the extent of the contribution made by the troop surge and pivot to COIN remains an object of contention, the security situation in Iraq did improve manifestly over the course of 2007, allowing for a drawdown to be initiated by the end of the following year. All the while, the situation in Afghanistan was rapidly deteriorating, eventually leading to the announcement of its own surge in December 2009. Following its toppling in 2001, the Taliban had evolved into an increasingly decentralised movement and successfully shifted tactics towards the use of improvised explosive devices. General Stanley McChrystal, the commander entrusted with rescuing the Afghan war, observed that the new Taliban "keeps dispersed insurgent cells motivated, strategically wired, and continually informed, all without a rigid – or targetable – chain of command". In sum, "just like their allies in al-Qaeda, this new Taliban is more network than army". This could of course only mean one thing: "to defeat a networked enemy we had to become a network ourselves" (McChrystal 2011, p. 67). Reviewing the military's response in Iraq and Afghanistan, McChrystal proudly touted the constitution of an "effective" counter-network: "decisions were decentralised and cut laterally across the organisation," "traditional institutional boundaries fell away," the network "constantly self-analysed, revisiting its structure, aims, and processes," and "continually grew the capacity to inform itself" (McChrystal 2011, p. 70).

Although appointed to oversee the deployment of an additional 30,000 troops, the choice of McChrystal belies the popular notion of a wholesale shift to a less kinetic campaign intent on building relations with the local population. In his earlier role, McChrystal had led for five years Joint Special Operations Command (JSOC), the organisation responsible for coordinating the actions of special operations forces from across the US military. During that time, he directed a relentless campaign of kill-or-capture raids against terrorist and insurgent networks in Iraq that only intensified with the surge, a pattern subsequently reproduced in Afghanistan. It is therefore erroneous to construe the Iraqi and Afghan surges as unalloyed strategic reorientations from counterterrorist manhunt to population-centric counterinsurgency when, in reality, the former was only ratcheted up alongside the new emphasis on public diplomacy and influence operations. Here again, in the most shadowy corner of the War on Terror, we observe chaoplexic principles in action.

As Steve Niva (2013) recounts, JSOC established itself as a truly joint command under McChrystal, systematically breaking down bureaucratic barriers to forge connections between the military's elite units, ranging from the Navy SEALs to the Army's Delta Force and the Air Force's Special Tactics Group. With the support of Secretary of Defence Donald Rumsfeld intent on outflanking the CIA in the conduct of covert anti-terror operations, McChrystal was able to circumvent the institution's hierarchical strictures and set up a common information-sharing infrastructure. The result was "a networked form of organisation composed of interconnected sets of decentralised and largely autonomous components that combine and work together on the basis of shared information and strategy" (Niva 2013, p. 191). Building up its capacity in Iraq between 2003 and 2006, JSOC accelerated its operations under the surge, moving beyond its previous, more limited, decapitation strategy. As McChrystal explained (Filkins 2009): "the aim was to go after the middle of their network – in a regular army, their senior non-commissioned officers. We tried to cause the network to collapse." "Cued to a powerful and decentralised all-source intelligence apparatus," a high-speed tempo of operations could be sustained by exploiting any information obtained through a raid on a given target to rapidly set in motion another targeting cycle (Flynn et al. 2008, p. 57). As Niva (2013, p. 192) concludes, through "organisational decentralisation and tactical autonomy," JSOC emerged as "a self-synchronised force experimenting with new forms of network-oriented hunt-and-kill operations."

While these manhunt operations were pursued assiduously, notching high-profile targets as such Abu Musab al-Zarqawi or Osama bin Laden, these did not translate into strategic success. Insurgent and terrorist organisations proved highly resilient and even the intensified efforts to extirpate their networks during the troop surges were only temporarily able to hold back the tide. Nor did COIN sufficiently alter the ambient conditions that provided a steady flow of recruits and resources to the insurgents. In Iraq, Sunni factions bid their time until the American withdrawal in late 2011 before resuming their attacks on the Shia-led government. By 2014, the spill-over from the neighbouring civil war in Syria had set the stage for the dramatic capture of major cities by the self-proclaimed Islamic State, an outgrowth of the al-Qaeda in Iraq network led by al-Zarqawi. Coalition efforts to decisively defeat the Taliban were no more fruitful. A signalled commitment to withdrawal led to a similar lull in attacks on international forces that merely served as a prelude to the Afghan government collapsing before even the completion of the final drawdown in summer 2021.

On the two main fronts on which the Global War on Terror was waged after September 11, the best efforts of the network-enabled US military amounted to strategic failures, whatever the tactical successes attained over opponents with vastly inferior resources. Yet, by the early 2010s, the American state was already shifting its attention away from the fight against international terrorism and its regional theatres towards a resurgence of great power competition. The renewed prospect of inter-state war called for a reorienting of the military machine supported by a new raft of advanced technologies and corresponding doctrinal overhauls. Sure enough, chaoplexity would once again serve as a central touchstone for imagining the future of war.

Plus ça change… the unsurpassed horizon of chaoplexic warfare

Concerned with both the rise of China and Russia's resurgence, the United States has pointedly rearticulated its grand strategic narrative over the past decade, as ratified by the 2018 National Defence Strategy: "inter-state strategic competition, not terrorism, is now the primary concern in US national security" (Mattis 2018, p. 1). This strategic alignment has been accompanied by a concerted push to winning the race for the next raft of advanced technologies to shape the future of war. At the end of 2014, the Pentagon announced a Third Offset Strategy to restore a competitive military advantage perceived to be eroding dangerously (Hagel 2014). The policy gestured at two previous offset strategies enacted during the Cold War through the development and implementation of key technological innovations. The First Offset involved the acquisition of strategic and tactical nuclear weapons to balance the Soviet Union's superiority in conventional forces in the European theatre during the 1950s. The Second Offset, pursued from the late 1970s after the Soviets attained nuclear parity, sought to exploit breakthroughs in precision weaponry, sensors and stealth – the very advances that would galvanise the RMA movement. The Third Offset, compelled by the diffusion of Second Offset innovations to rival states, has cast its net widely at a raft of technologies including robotics, machine learning, big data, directed energy, hypersonics, miniaturisation and additive manufacturing. One primary focus emerges, however, in the words of Deputy Defence Secretary Robert Work: "artificial intelligence and autonomy will lead to a new era of human-machine collaboration" (Pavluk & Cole 2016). Yet, as Work insisted, "technology is never, never the final answer" and defence institutions must therefore "incorporate those technologies into new operational and organisational constructs" (Gentile et al. 2021, p. 35).

Responding to this exhortation, DARPA (2017) introduced a new concept called "mosaic warfare" with the stated objective of acquiring "a new asymmetric advantage – one that imposes complexity on adversaries by harnessing the power of dynamic, coordinated, and highly autonomous composable systems". Highlighting the vulnerability and inflexibility of modern forces whose components have to fit each other precisely in the manner of a puzzle, the Pentagon's lead R&D agency outlined the vision of a modular, interoperable and resilient military whose interchangeable pieces could combine as a constantly shifting mosaic. "The goal is to fight as a network to create a chain of effects – or, more accurately because these effects are not linear, 'effects webs' – to deter and defeat adversaries across multiple scales of conflict intensity". By combining all the elements (be they manned, remotely controlled or fully autonomous) in a "system of systems", new capabilities and behaviours are expected to emerge, surprising the adversary on the battlefield and confounding any modernisation efforts through their unpredictability. Mosaic warfare promises to deliver operations at "continuous speed" for constant adaptation to the circumstances of battle and support "multi-domain battle" waged simultaneously across the arenas of land, see, air, space and cyberspace (Grayson 2018).

A related stream of writings invokes a new "decision-centric" approach to warfare that seeks to gain a decision-making advantage on the adversary via a "distributed force design" and a command and control structure "combining human command with AI-enabled machine control" (Clark et al. 2020, p. vi). Decision-centric warfare is favourably contrasted with network-centric warfare which "focused on improving US military decision-making by centralising it." NCW thus presupposed an "unfettered situational awareness" delivered to theatre commanders by a secure infostructure, a benefit thought to be foreclosed in future contested environments. Consequently, "network-centric warfare is not well-suited to an adversarial context" with degraded communications correspondingly depleting combat power (Clark et al. 2021, p. 19). Finally, "whereas network-centric warfare assumes a high degree of clarity and control, decision-centric warfare embraces the fog and friction inherent in military conflict" (Clark et al. 2020, p. iv). The proposed new approach thus asserts itself by appealing to the unquestioned virtues of chaoplexity and disparaging NCW despite the latter's own historical, if inconsistent, advocacy of decentralisation.

A central assumption within decision-centric warfare is that state competitors have identified network access as a key vulnerability and can be expected, in any future conflict, to target it with the full gamut of available kinetic, electromagnetic and cyber weapons. As such, the new thinking promotes a "context-centric" infrastructure supported by decentralised wireless networks rather than a single overarching network that might serve as a single point of failure. Depending on the available communication links, the command and control architecture will reshape itself, enabling discrete operations to be carried without the requirement for system-wide information-sharing. A related construct refers to an "Internet of Battle Things" (Kott et al. 2016) that conceives of future conflictual spaces as saturated by pervasive computing, communication and sensing through the ubiquitous connectivity of AI-equipped entities, with data networks managing and reconfiguring themselves autonomously as a function of needs and availability.

This concern with minimising critical reliance on unhindered data links is one of the drivers in the concerted push towards autonomous weapons, along with the promise of greater speed and agility in the battlespace. In particular, the development of swarm robotics involving large numbers of small, low-cost, autonomous robots has revived concepts of "fire-ant warfare" warfare first proposed in the 1990s (Libicki 1994). One widely cited report (Scharre 2014, p. 20) envisions the fielding of "billions of tiny, insect-like drones" and rehearses the familiar chaoplexic litany of emergent behaviour, collective intelligence, adaptation and self-healing networks. Yet another publication (Ryan 2018, p. 12) highlights how "the new [sic] and interdisciplinary research areas of AI, complex adaptive systems, and swarm optimisation indicates the potential for self-organised robot swarms to be used in future conflict."

In addition to a reliance on autonomous platforms, the vision of decision-centric warfare rests upon the future articulation of AI with human cognition. Machine learning algorithms are expected to assist local commanders with a range of force element combinations and tactics to achieve their goals, allowing for courses of action that would not have been otherwise conceived and will not be anticipated by the enemy. Over time, past performance will allow commanders to accept machine recommendations without scrutiny, accelerating even further the decision-making process and imposing insoluble dilemmas to the adversary (Clark et al. 2020). In the longer term, an informational fusion of human and machine through brain-computer interfaces is anticipated. The development of "direct neural enhancements of the human brain for two-way data transfer" supporting a "read/write capability between humans and machines" thus holds the potential to "revolutionise tactical warfighter communications, speed the transfer of knowledge throughout the chain of command, and ultimately dispel the 'fog' of war" (Emanuel et al. 2019, p. v).

The allure of AI has brought forth familiar dreams of martial omnipotence through techno-logical supremacy. A four-star Marine Corps general and an AI entrepreneur have outlined their shared vision (Allen & Husain 2017) of a future "hyperwar" defined by "the unparalleled speed enabled by automating decision-making and the concurrency of action that will become possible by leveraging artificial intelligence and machine cognition". Postulating a revolution in artificial intelligence that will "fundamentally change the human condition" and thereby the "profoundly human undertaking" that is war, they foresee AI being "deployed at scales sufficient to essentially enable an infinite supply of tactical, operational, and strategic decision-making." By "collapsing the decision action cycle to fractions of a second," hyperwar will be "a type of conflict where human decision-making is almost entirely absent." Directing "swarms of complex, autonomous systems" operating in both the kinetic and cyber realms, the AI-augmented strategic commander will attain "a qualitatively unsurpassed level of situational awareness and understanding." The upshot will be nothing less that the capacity to "consistently dominate [and] overmatch the enemy's capacity to respond."

In all this, the main operative concept remains, as ever, that of information, binding ever more tightly the constituents of the war machine. As with previous incarnations of chaoplexic warfare, it remains uncertain whether the present proposals for the adoption of AI and robotic systems can achieve the desired decentralisation and emergent adaptation. Simonetti and Tripodi (2020, p. 127) express the concern that the new technologies and the corresponding acceleration in the tempo of the battlespace "may overcentralise command and control functions at the political or strategic level" and effectively prohibit the meaningful conduct of mission-oriented operations. With reaction times that preclude meaningful human tactical input, the levels of war could become dramatically compressed with the upper echelons drawn to exert their authority as low down the chain of command as the tempo of battle and prerogatives of AI permit. Yet, from another perspective (Payne 2021, p. 192), the AI swarm might just as conceivably institute a 'supercharged' form of mission command in which the speed and opacity of its distributed deliberations systematically exclude any hierarchical intercession.

War at the edge of control... and beyond

As of today, the ideal of chaoplexic warfare remains the unsurpassed horizon of military thought, its incantatory power seemingly undimmed by the repeated setbacks incurred in its previous applications. Since they began permeating military thinking in the 1980s, chaoplexic conceptions have become an exhortation tirelessly repeated through the overlapping waves of manoeuvre warfare, network-centric operations, counterterrorism, COIN and mosaic warfare, each iteration promising anew to realise their promise. Yet chaoplexic warfare must at this point appear to the jaded eye as a revolution perpetually deferred. The perennial calls for the decentralisation of military operations only serve to underline the fact that it is never achieved. As for the supposed dominance that the turn to chaoplexity was to deliver, it has proven stubbornly elusive.

A first explanation for this eternal return can be sought in the innate tension between a state military's inherently hierarchical character and chaoplexic warfare's project of radical decentralisation. Quite simply, so long as armed forces act as an instrument at the behest of a state authority, they must necessarily adhere in some fundamental measure to the hierarchical principles that are the very essence of the state form. Civilian control, strategic planning and bureaucratic accountability are all merely different expressions of the war machine's capture by the state apparatus (Deleuze & Guattari 2003). As such, any decentralising moves must eventually conflict with chains of command and legal responsibilities. This obviously explains why non-state actors, while almost never purely horizontal organisations, have been the truest practitioners of chaoplexic warfare. Unhampered by the constraints of legality, popular accountability or even strategic coherence, transnational jihadism has constituted a fissiparous yet enduring war machine that has proven both atrociously creative and endlessly resilient in the face of concerted state efforts at eradicating it. In this sense, chaoplexic warfare constitutes a horizon forever out of reach for state militaries. Indeed, we should certainly dread the prospect of any military so fully emancipated from state control as to no longer have any purpose apart from itself.

Military thinkers are not unaware of this tension, at the very least intuitively, and the most sophisticated analysts among them have endeavoured to find in it a virtue. Arquilla and Ronfeldt (2000, pp. 49, 86) thus assert that, while decentralisation should be vigorously encouraged, it is necessary to maintain "central strategic control" and pursue "hybrids of hierarchies and networks." Whether or not a middle passage can ever be successfully negotiated, the opposition between hierarchies and networks is set to remain a constitutive tension in military thought and practice for the foreseeable future, with the exhortations to be more chaoplexic unlikely to be silenced.

A second, more straightforward, reason may also account for the disappointing outcomes generated by two decades of war under the sign of chaoplexity. There is no doubt that the US military has developed information-enabled capabilities at the tactical and operational levels that can execute combined arms operations with a speed, precision and power that has no match today. Over the course of the War on Terror, it adapted repeatedly, overhauling its doctrine in response to the challenges it faced. And yet, neither tactical virtuosity nor institutional learning could salvage a flawed strategy. The lightning invasions of Afghanistan and Iraq were followed by a dawning realisation that, as many had warned at the outset, the subsequent occupations would be a much taller order. Naïve assumptions, held by at least some within the political and military leadership, about the pacified democratic societies that would spontaneously emerge after the toppling of the incumbent regimes were mercilessly dispelled by the intractable realities of insurgency, international terrorism and civil war. Despite the turn to counterinsurgency and the supposed priority placed on 'winning hearts and minds,' the presence of occupying forces and recurrent civilian casualties continued to generate armed opposition faster than it could be decimated. Even the narrow goal of securing some geopolitical advantage upon departure from Afghanistan and Iraq could not be attained by the exertions of the most powerful army in history. While the inquest into the failings of the two major American wars conducted in the early 21st century is now a matter for historians, many will have already drawn the conclusion that they were either so injudicious in their conception or so compromised in their initial execution as to have been beyond rescue.

This in turn raises a more fundamental consideration about the nature of power and control in the chaoplexic age. The vibrant transmutability of reticular organisation is observable everywhere in our ever more interconnected world, pulling in remote locations and disparate entities into tangled causal complexes via the continuous flows of information criss-crossing the planet. While opportunities to profit from the rippling perturbations of these dynamic complexes abound, these are necessarily contingent and transient – and the perils are no less plentiful. It therefore speaks of a particular hubris to believe that the embrace of the network form will deliver the certainty and mastery necessary to shape the world in one's image. Nothing in the non-linear sciences offers such guarantees.

In seeking to appropriate the network form and its attendant powers, militaries have repeatedly come up against the limits that their institutional frameworks and mindsets impose on any attempts to radically decentralise their operations. Piecemeal implementations of mission command have resulted, here and there, in highly effective tactical deployments in which substantial autonomy has been granted to their individual agents. The generalisation of these various experiments in surfing at the edge of control within armed forces shaped in the hierarchical image of their state masters remains stubbornly elusive, however.

And yet, we plausibly stand at the cusp of a radical transformation in war. The former Deputy Secretary of Defence Robert Work even dares to imagine that it will change the 'nature of war,' a taboo thought among faithful devotees of Clausewitz (Freedberg 2017). Perhaps it will not even be apposite to speak any longer of what is to come as 'war,' insofar as our historical experience of it has always been one in which humans are the main protagonists. For in our pursuit of the scientific way of warfare, we have arrived at a juncture at which our machines seem poised to take centre stage.

To be sure, today's military theorists (Scharre 2016, p. 151) place their hope in "human-machine teaming" and the figure of the "centaur," those "hybrid human-machine cognitive architectures [that] will be able to leverage the precision and reliability of automation without sacrificing the robustness and flexibility of human intelligence." Work (2015) thus expresses the belief that "artificial intelligence and autonomy will allow entirely new levels of what we refer to as man-machine symbiosis on the battlefield." Under this alluring vision, humans will set overarching strategic goals, determine relevant mission objectives with the assistance of machine learning algorithms modelling and simulating all the possible courses of action, and instruct autonomous platforms to complete the mission, maintaining oversight as they swarm the battlespace and devise contingent tactical responses at the speed of light. In the domain of cyberspace, a throng of bots, worms and viruses will battle to protect and defend the flows of information necessary for situational awareness and the exertion of command and control while disrupting, corrupting and misleading the adversary's own infostructure – all of which will again be conducted at speeds and scale far exceeding human comprehension. As these new orders of battle encounter each other, setting in motion spiralling interactions whose non-linear effects are inherently unknowable, disquieting questions about the nature of control within human-machine symbiotes will inevitably arise. Indeed, those with a view from the edge already worry (Ilachinski 2017, p. 233) that "as autonomous systems increase in complexity, we can expect a commensurate decrease in our ability to both predict and control such systems."

Pointing on the horizon is a fully autonomous (s)war(m) machine whose control would be totally immanent to itself – in other words, for which there would be no outside from which to exert control over it. This would surely be the realm of "a purely tactical mode of operability" (Guha 2010, p. 173), unhampered by strategic or political considerations and constrained ethically only in so far as its emergent behaviour could be said to have its own ethos. Crucially, the emergence of such an unbounded martial condition is not premised on the speculative advent of a general artificial super-intelligence that would outstrip our own and develop its own deliberate anthropomorphic designs in opposition to our will. The stumbling, groping evolutionary intelligence of the animal swarm will suffice so long as its algorithmic decision loops become untethered from any rationale external to it, relentlessly pursuing their tactical becoming in a blind pursuit of survival. Nor is this potentiality even first and foremost the function of any specific technological development. For it ultimately rests upon the insistent impulse to surrender ourselves wholesale to chaoplexic warfare in the plenitude of its concept. And so the disquieting question must be asked: what if war at the edge of control served no other master than itself?

References

Allen, J R & Husain, A 2017, 'On Hyperwar', *Proceedings*, vol. 143, no. 7, pp. 30–7.

Arquilla, J 2007, 'Of Networks and Nations', *The Brown Journal of World Affairs*, vol. 14, no. 1, pp. 199–209.

Arquilla, J & Ronfeldt, D 2000, *Swarming and the Future of Conflict*, RAND, Santa Monica, CA.

Bousquet, A 2022, *The Scientific Way of Warfare: Order and Chaos on the Battlefields of Modernity*, 2nd edn, Hurst Publishers, London.

Clark, B, Patt, D & Schramm, H 2020, *Mosaic Warfare: Exploiting Artificial Intelligence and Autonomous Systems to Implement Decision-Centric Operations*, Center for Strategic and Budgetary Assessments, Washington, DC.

Clark, B, Patt, D & Walton, T A 2021, *Implementing Decision-Centric Warfare: Elevating Command and Control to Gain an Optionality Advantage*, Hudson Institute, Washington, DC.

DARPA 2017, *Strategic Technology Office Outlines Vision for 'Mosaic Warfare'*, <https://www.darpa.mil/news-events/2017-08-04> (accessed 12 September 2022).

Deleuze, G & Guattari, F 2003, *A Thousand Plateaus*, Continuum, London.

Emanuel P et al. 2019, *Cyborg Soldier 2050: Human/Machine Fusion and the Implications for the Future of the DoD*, DoD Biotechnologies for Health and Human Performance Council, Alexandria, VA.

Filkins, D 2009, 'Stanley McChrystal's Long War', *The New York Times Magazine*, 18 October.

Flynn, M T, Juergens, R & Cantrell, T L 2008, 'Employing ISR SOF Best Practices', *Joint Force Quarterly*, no. 50, pp. 56–61.

Freedberg, S J 2017, 'War Without Fear: DepSecDef Work on How AI Changes Conflict' *Breaking Defense*, 31 May, <https://breakingdefense.com/2017/05/killer-robots-arent-the-problem-it-unpredictable-ai/> (accessed 12 September 2022).

Gentile, G et al. 2021, *A History of the Third Offset, 2014–2018*, RAND, Santa Monica, CA.

Gray, C S 2002, *Strategy for Chaos: Revolutions in Military Affairs and the Evidence of History*, Frank Cass, London.

Grayson, T 2018, 'Mosaic Warfare and Multi-Domain Battle', *DARPA D60 Symposium*, <https://youtu.be/33VAnIEjDgk> (accessed 12 September 2022).

Guha, M 2010, *Reimagining War in the 21st Century: From Clausewitz to Network-Centric Warfare*, Routledge, London.

Hagel, C 2014, *Reagan National Defense Forum Keynote*, 15 November, <https://www.defense.gov/Newsroom/Speeches/Speech/Article/606635/> (accessed 12 September 2022).

Ilachinski, A 2017, *AI, Robots, and Swarms: Issues, Questions, and Recommended Studies*, CAN, Arlington, VA.

Kott, A, Swami, A & West, B J 2016, 'The Internet of Battle Things', *Computer*, vol. 49, no. 12, pp. 70–5, https://doi.org/10.48550/arXiv.1712.08980.

Libicki, M 1994, *The Mesh and the Net: Speculation on Armed Conflict in a Time of Free Silicon*, National Defense University Press, Washington, DC.

Mattis, J 2018, *Summary of the 2018 National Defense Strategy of the United States of America: Sharpening the American Military's Competitive Edge*, <https://dod.defense.gov/Portals/1/Documents/pubs/2018-National-Defense-Strategy-Summary.pdf> (accessed 12 September 2022).

McChrystal, S A 2011, 'Becoming the Enemy', *Foreign Policy*, no. 185, pp. 66–70.

Niva, S 2013, 'Disappearing Violence: JSOC and the Pentagon's New Cartography of Networked Warfare', *Security Dialogue*, vol. 44, no. 3, pp. 185–202, https://doi: 10.1177/0967010613485869.

Pavluk, J & Cole, A 2016, 'From Strategy to Execution: Accelerating the Third Offset', *War on the Rocks*, 9 June, <https://warontherocks.com/2016/06/from-strategy-to-execution-accelerating-the-third-offset/> (accessed 12 September 2022).

Payne, K 2021, *I, Warbot: The Dawn of Artificially Intelligent Conflict*, Hurst Publishers, London.

Ryan, M 2018, *Human-Machine Teaming for Future Ground Forces*, Center for Strategic and Budgetary Assessment, Washington, DC.

Scharre, P 2014, *Robotics on the Battlefield Part II: The Coming Swarm*, Center for a New American Security, Washington, DC.

Scharre, P 2016, 'Centaur Warfighting: The False Choice of Humans vs. Automation', *Temple International and Comparative Law Journal*, vol. 30, no. 1, pp. 151–65.

Simonetti, R M & Tripodi, P 2020, 'Automation and the Future of Command and Control: The End of Auftragstaktik?', *Journal of Advanced Military Studies*, vol. 11, no. 1, pp. 127–46, https://doi.org/10.21140/mcuj.2020110106.

Transformation Warfare 2007, *Transformation Warfare '07*, Virginia Beach Convention Center, Virginia Beach, VA.

United States Army 2006, *Field Manual 3–24: Counterinsurgency*, The United States Army, Washington, DC.

Work, R 2015, *Remarks at the CNAS Inaugural National Security Forum*, 14 December, <https://www.cnas.org/publications/transcript/remarks-by-defense-deputy-secretary-robert-work-at-the-cnas-inaugural-national-security-forum> (accessed 12 September 2022).

21

ETHNIC CONFLICT AND MODERN WARFARE

Dani Belo and David Carment

Introduction

In this chapter, we examine the broader tendencies and consequences that ethnic conflict has for future warfare as states engage in hybrid tactics and grey zone strategies to support ethnic kin (Carment & Belo 2019, 2022).[1] We argue that the instrumentalization of ethnic-based movements as a platform for cross-border intervention is becoming a norm in contemporary international conflicts. We demonstrate this through an analysis of Russia's grey zone interventions in Georgia, Ukraine, and the Baltic States. Our presentation of the evidence builds on Walt's idea of strategic empathy (Walt 2021). Strategic empathy is necessary to overcome some basic errors in the strategic analysis of adversarial behaviour. These errors include fundamental misattribution, premature closure, selection bias, and faulty analogistic thinking (Carment 2014; Walt 2022). As Carment argues, understanding an adversary's motivation is an essential ingredient in decision-making and far superior than reasoning through analogy or one-sided blaming (Carment 2014; Carment & Belo 2022b).

Alongside the ethnic-based component of grey zone interventions, we identify two other common elements of modern grey zone engagements. First, there is a clear desire to revise or preserve the traditional regional balance of power. Second, even though kinetic operations have become an inseparable component of grey zone conflict, political and economic campaigns, as well as cyber operations, play a greater role in achieving foreign policy outcomes. We conclude by identifying some of the reasons why grey zone conflict has become a more central part of modern warfare and the implications therein for conflict management and the future of war.

Intervention in ethnic-based movements

Ethnic conflicts that involve large-scale warfare are typically either secessionist, in which external states and other international actors are drawn into a conflict, or irredentist, in which two or more states enter into war over an irredentist claim (Carment et al. 2006).[2] Ethnic conflict can be generated internally and then externalized. In other instances, ethnic conflict weakens state structures, inviting external intervention. Sometimes the conflict process involves a more subtle and complex series of interactions such as diffusion and horizontal escalation (Carment et al. 2006).

DOI: 10.4324/9781003299011-26

Ethnic conflict shapes warfare in several important ways. First, states are more likely to fight ethnic wars with neighbours. Generally, but not always, the states involved will be territorially adjacent. Since so few states can project their military across the globe, borders are integral to warfare strategies. Many, but not all, are dyadic (Carment & James 1995). Further, disputes over territory are more likely than non-territorial disputes to involve the use of force, and more likely to reach higher levels of severity. Ethnic conflicts in neighbouring countries can draw states in to defend ethnic kin (Carment & James 1995).

Second, ethnic mobilization serves as a background cause and clarifies and hardens the fundamental lines of political, social, economic, and national cleavage. Warfare involving non-state actors is reflected in exclusion of some ethnic groups from power, and by the systematic favouring of others.

Third, repeated failures in inclusionary nation-building within multiethnic states facilitate unmet grievances. Both the objectives and key political actors of those strategies become targets of armed groups. A weak state will have difficulty controlling competing group interests through formal institutional structures. The end result is a downward spiral in which the injection of ethnic differences into political loyalties and the politicization of ethnic identities become the basis for exclusion and suppression.

Fourth, increasingly international legal regimes do not inhibit ethnic warfare. In a seminal study, Jackson and Rosberg developed the idea of the inhibited state as a way of explaining the maintenance of African boundaries during the Cold War (1982). Weak states supported norms on the inviolability of state boundaries because there was a common interest in international rules and institutions based on mutual vulnerability. A similar view provided by Donald Horowitz (1985, 2010, p. 275) argues that "[T]rans-border ethnic affinities more often promote restraint in supporting separatists or intervention on? behalf of a central government fighting to suppress separatism. Fear of contagion and domino effects is widespread". Today, for reasons we outline below, international legal regimes and norms no longer regulate state behaviour to the same extent.

Finally, it has become more common for powerful nations to outsource their operations across international borders on the physical battlefield. Such support has a deleterious impact on conflict reduction and deterrence. Indeed, a key reason why these conflicts are immune to resolution is due to the level and kinds of support warring parties receive from third parties (Carment, Nikolko & Belo 2019).

The rise of grey zone conflict, and interventions in ethnic conflicts therein, is a natural outcome of a weakened international legal order in conjunction with the emergence of a multipolar system in which deterrence is more difficult to apply and enforce (Mearsheimer 1990). From this perspective, ethnic conflicts constitute a security dilemma for states that are not easily resolved through 'conventional' deterrent techniques (Harvey 1998). Not only is there the challenge of how states should engage in 'self-defence' in response to grey zone techniques and strategies, there is also the increasing problem that rival states in a multipolar system will take opposing sides in a local conflict (Carment & Belo 2022c).

The instrumentalization of ethnic-based grievances and movements for strategic purposes has become common in grey zone conflicts. In other words, the permeability of international borders and technological advancements have enabled states to use ethnic-based movements as platforms for achieving political goals, without relying on kinetic operations. The use of cyber and information operations enables interveners to forego the domestic and international political, as well as economic, costs of large-scale military interventions. Chazan and Horowitz (1991) note that these common costs include domestic political backlash, international sanctions, as well as international reputation costs.

Moreover, the benefit of such conduct, as we show below, is the creation of plausible deniability by state sponsors when confronted by the targets of the attack, their allies, and international institutions. A crucial factor is ambiguity in international law regarding such support which in turn has created a situation in which external states can act with impunity.[3] Concurrently, a key drawback of the grey zone conflict format is its protracted nature, often transforming into a 'frozen conflict'. As a consequence, such conflicts become resistant to decisive resolution as they often entail the harmonization of numerous highly-polarized interests. (Carment, Nikolko & Belo 2019; Carment & Belo 2022b, 2022c).

Protractedness is related to the fact that intervention in ethnic-based movements is motivated by both affective and instrumental reasons (Carment et al. 2006). The latter category focuses on a desire to gain balance of power advantages in relation to adversaries or a revision in local alliance structures. By contrast, intervention based on affective reasons relies on ideological dimensions including cross-border ethnic affinity or re-connection with 'historic lands.'

Heraclides (1990) finds that one of the indicators of affective reasons for third-party interventions in ethnic-based movements is the disproportionate economic, material, and geopolitical losses compared to any affective gains. In other words, because ideological outcomes or gains may be difficult to measure, and are clear only to the intervener, high monetary and material investment in their pursuit may appear disproportionately large and thus, irrational to other actors.

There are several intensities of commitment through which an intervener may become involved in ethnic based-movements: (1) low involvement, starting with simple transactional participation, including humanitarian involvement; (2) medium involvement, characterized by extended nonmilitary contributions, such as providing sanctuary, a base of operations, financial assistance or vital access to communications; and (3) high level of physical involvement, such as the deployment of troops.

As noted by Chazan and Horowitz (1991), support for secessionism, relative to irredentism, is a more effective and flexible tool of influence as it is considerably easier for a state to use its support selectively and reverse it when concessions are given. The comparison between secessionism and irredentism is based on overt material and political support across international borders. Irredentism is relatively costly to support in terms of international reputation and the potential consequences as the endeavour requires the undermining of the territorial integrity of another state (Carment & James 1995).

In contrast, the relative flexibility, and therefore effectiveness, of support for a secessionist movement, is based on the relative absence of deep ties and long-term commitments, which are required for the support of an irredentist movement. Plausible deniability is easier to establish by the intervener as the local movement may only desire more autonomy from their national government.

Into the grey zone

As conventional wars have become increasingly costly in terms of human lives, infrastructure, and economic impact, powerful states have adapted their arsenals to decrease the cost of intervention across international borders (Hoffman 2007; Carment & Belo 2022c). As we show below, under modern conditions, states are more likely to use the permeability of international borders, advanced cyber technology and information tools, and international legal blind spots to support ethnic kin as opposed to physically intervening into a conflict (Mazarr 2015; Carment & Belo 2022a). This strategy is considered 'grey zone' in the sense that it fits between the highest and lowest levels of involvement in the Heraclides typology we outlined in the previous section. Indeed, the exact relationship between states that support ethnic kin and the strategies they deploy have significantly changed over the last few decades with military operations involving many substate actors to avoid the threshold of a direct state-to-state attack which could generate a legitimate conventional military response.

In grey zone conflict, states rely on low-intensity tools and tactics, such as propaganda, the use of ethnic-based non-governmental organizations as well as cyber space to achieve strategic and tactical outcomes (Carment & Belo 2018). A key limitation of low-intensity grey-zone tools and tactics is the incremental pace at which they can achieve outcomes (Mazarr 2015; Bhatia 2018, p. 25). Thus, in circumstances where strategic or tactical goals must be achieved within a window of opportunity, the use of limited kinetic operations is possible. In the following sections, we show how this form of modern warfare plays out in the context of ethnic conflict. We identify three components of grey zone conflict. They are: (1) ethnic-based movements as intervention platforms; (2) power balancing; and (3) economic, political, and cyber tactics. We illustrate how each of these components has been applied through an examination and comparison of Russia's interventions in Georgia, Ukraine, and the Baltic States.

Ethnic-based movements as intervention platforms in grey zone conflict

The idea of ethnic-based movements as intervention platforms illustrates how the social and political exclusion of national minorities can become organized into secessionist or irredentist movements. These movements provide the necessary permissive conditions for subsequent grey zone strategies. These findings are summarized in Row 1 in Table 21.1.

Table 21.1 Summary table of grey zone conflict engagements

	Grey Zone Case Studies		
	Ukraine	*Baltic States*	*Georgia*
• Ethnic conflict as an intervention platform	• Cultural affinity toward Moscow, the Soviet era, and the Russian language are the focal points for the mobilization of diaspora communities toward secessionism in the Donbas region, as well as irredentism in Crimea and Southern Ukraine. • Ukraine's increasingly restrictive minority-language laws created a permissive environment for Moscow's intervention. • Protection of ethnic diaspora entrenched in Russia's foreign policy doctrine.	• Ethnic diaspora communities, predominantly Russian, experience social, political and economic exclusion across the Baltic region without a crystalized secessionist or irredentism movement. • Nationalizing Latvian and Estonian states prevent diaspora groups from citizenship. • Russia sees ethnic diaspora in the Baltic region as marginalized.	• Abkhazia and South Ossetia demand to separate from Georgia. • A secessionist movement mobilized in the region in the 1950s.

(Continued)

Table 21.1 (Continued)

	Grey Zone Case Studies		
	Ukraine	*Baltic States*	*Georgia*
• Power balancing	• The Ukraine-Russia conflict escalated the Russia-NATO standoff. • OSCE and Normandy format had limited success.	• The Ukraine-Russia conflict escalated Russia-NATO standoff. Moscow became increasingly vigilant and sensitive regarding balance of power relative to NATO in the Baltic region.	• Russian peacekeepers authorized by UNSC Resolution 934 allowing Russia to station 'peacekeepers' in Abkhazia through the mandate of the Commonwealth of Independent States. • Russian peacekeepers became 'protectors' of Abkhazia from Georgia.
• Political, economic and cyber dimensions	• Grey zone political and economic pressure campaigns in Ukraine undertaken by Russia starting in 2004. • Russia-Western political and economic pressure campaigns since 2007. • Non-military means of intervention dominate; kinetic operations are secondary. • Political and war materiel support for non-state actors by Russia. • February 2022 kinetic intervention by Russia in northern, eastern and southern Ukraine.	• Grey zone political intervention predominantly in the form of monetary support for local organizations such as the Moscow House and Orthodox Church undertaken by Russia since early 2000s. • Local authorities in the Baltic region target Russia-affiliated organizations and media. • Only non-military means used for intervention. • Battle of narratives between local anti-Soviet national history and pro-Moscow narratives.	• Grey zone tools and tactics, including in cyber space and economic pressure used against Georgia from April to July 2008. • Unconventional tools and tactics deployed as 'shaping operations' for short kinetic intervention in August 2008.

In the case of Georgia, the nation-building project in the sub-region of Abkhazia emerged as resistance to perceived Georgian imperialism Many in Abkhazia, and not just ethnic Abkhaz, saw their security as potentially undermined by ethnic diversity. As a consequence, the return of ethnic Georgians following the 1992–1993 war was restricted to the Galli region through legislation (Clogg 2008, pp. 308–11). The sub-regions of Abkhazia and South Ossetia had become mobilized toward secession as early as the 1950s but it was not until the late 1990s that the likelihood of warfare in pursuit of that goal began to emerge.

In a second example, Ukraine's unitary structure following the collapse of the Soviet Union, provided the legal and legislative foundation for Kyiv to influence local cultural-linguistic policy in the regions. However, it also contributed to the mobilization of the local population toward secessionism and irredentism. In this case, the permissive conditions for the rise of irredentism in Crimea were present before the collapse of the Soviet Union. The first Crimean parliament backed a new constitution on May 6, 1992. The document defines the peninsula as a 'sovereign state' which would be able to control its international relations and law enforcement (Sasse 2007). However, in 1995, Ukraine's President Kuchma attempted to take personal control of the situation in Crimea, over which he claimed the Kyiv government was losing power. He abolished the post of the President of Crimea, thereby Removing THE pro-Moscow Crimean leader Meshkov from his post (Solchanyk 2000).

In the post-Soviet era, the southern and eastern regions of Ukraine built robust transnational mechanisms of political cooperation with Russia. For example, in 2013 alone, the Kremlin-funded Russkiy Mir (Russian World) Foundation opened three offices with the largest one in the Gorlovka State Pedagogical Institute of Foreign Languages in Horlivka, Donetsk Oblast. From Russia's perspective, its protection of 'stranded' compatriots in Ukraine was a mission bestowed upon its leadership after Russians became one of the most divided ethnic groups in the world (Birka 2022, p. 55).

As in Crimea, the Donbas region had significant cross-border socio-economic linkages to Russia that were often threatened by an increasingly nationalizing Ukrainian state. Moscow-backed organizations such as Russkiy Mir were present in the region. Once the Euro Maidan protests culminated in the removal of President Yanukovych, the new pro-European leaders were determined to block the activities of such organizations. In other words, such organizations became a security concern for Kyiv as it perceived them to be elements of Moscow's soft power (Feklyunina 2016, pp. 775–8). The threatened cross-border linkages, and pre-existing ethnic-based movements in Eastern and Southern Ukraine, created permissive conditions for Moscow's interventions.

The challenges of socio-economic exclusion of the Russian diaspora have not been confined to Ukraine, however. In the Baltics, as our third example, approximately 300,000 people, most of them ethnic Russians, found themselves in the category of 'non-citizens' after the breakup of the Soviet Union. Following the independence of Latvia and Estonia from the Soviet Union, their respective governments began a rapid process of cultural nationalization. In tandem, this turned into a weakening of the Russian language and cultural symbolism that were considered inseparable from the Soviet identity. Even though ethnic-based movements did not crystalize in the Baltic region toward formal secessionism, the socio-economic exclusion of Russian minorities, including access to segments of the labour market and positions of political power (see Aasland & Fløtten 2001), created permissive conditions for Moscow to intervene as a 'protector.' Moreover, with the onset of the 2022 conflict in Ukraine, the challenge of the stranded diaspora was exacerbated when Latvia and Estonia closed their borders to Russia.[4]

Latvia's situation has perhaps been the most acute. Even though ethnic minorities constitute approximately 35% of the Latvian population, Riga began a rapid process of socio-cultural nationalization following its independence declaration in November 1990. For example, some Latvians have celebrated the Day of the Legionnaires which honours Latvian soldiers who fought on the side of Germany against the Soviet Union during the Second World War.[5]

The presence of Moscow-affiliated entities in Latvia, such as cultural and religious organizations, enabled the local conflict over diaspora issues to transform into an international dispute involving Russia. For example, Moscow House is considered the largest Russian culture centre in Latvia. It is financially supported by the Moscow City Council. According to the Latvian government, its activities were "harming the Latvian state and its citizens" (The Lithuanian Tribune 2012). Moreover, according to the Latvian government, the Russian Orthodox Church has become one of the promoters of Russia's foreign policy priorities and interests.

In sum, socio-economic conditions in varying degrees, and the exclusion of ethnic diaspora groups in Georgia, Ukraine, and the Baltic nations have created conditions that were seen in Moscow as permissive to engage in grey zone conflict. Even though ethnic-based movements provide a platform for external intervention, the goals of state interveners may also be instrumental, or strategic in nature, including a desire to shift the balance of power against adversaries.

Power balancing

In grey zone conflict, the foreign policy goals of intervention are both strategic and tactical in nature. In other words, grey zone conflict focuses on engagement against other great powers below the threshold of war, but often manifests in localized proxy conflicts (Carment & Belo 2022b). In turn, grey zone conflicts carry consequences for the broader security architecture involving shifts in the local balance of power among non-state ethnic-based groups as well as the external state interveners that support them. These findings are summarized in Row 2 in Table 21.1.

For example, Russia's military and unconventional operations in Georgia were an early indicator of a hardening in Moscow's foreign policy posture regarding former Soviet republics. Moscow showed readiness to operationalize its June 2000 Foreign Policy Concept (FPC), in which Russia indicated the priority to preserve its traditional sphere of influence following waves of NATO enlargement (Global Security 2012).

In relation to Ukraine, and to a lesser extent the Baltic region, Moscow has indicated a desire to preserve its traditional sphere of influence. In pursuit of this goal, Russia has supported several local ethnic-based movements in Ukraine. In the Baltic region, ethnic-based movements have not yet crystallized, but Moscow's actions have indicated that socially and politically excluded diaspora groups provide an effective platform to discredit local governments. In other words, Moscow has generally relied on tools and tactics below the threshold of open and overt warfare to achieve its foreign policy outcomes while avoiding the cost of direct fighting.

Political, economic, and cyber tactics

The political, economic, and cyber components of grey zone conflict are summarized in Row 3 of Table 21.1. Moscow's intervention in Georgia, on behalf of the secessionist territory of Abkhazia, was one of the earliest examples of 21st century grey zone conflict. Russia's five-day operation in August 2008 relied primarily on an extensive shaping operation using unconventional tools and tactics, most notably in cyber space, followed by targeted and limited military involvement. Although Russia used a limited military incursion into Georgia in support of Abkhazia, much of its efforts focused on 'shaping operations' meant to create disorganization within the government in Tbilisi and the security apparatus.

A goal of Russia's cyber operations in Georgia before the military intervention was to disrupt the coordination of Georgia's military and disable effective communication between central organs of government in Tbilisi and the population. These operations could be characterized as denial of service (DoS) (US Military 2009). The hacking operations, which began on 19 July 2008, disabled most websites operated by Georgia's government by 10 August 2008. The completion of these cyber operations corresponded with the beginning of Russia's kinetic operations in Abkhazia. By

11 August 2008, Georgia's government was largely unable to communicate with either military or civilian organs of government as well as the local population using the internet (Institute for War and Peace Reporting 2014).

Russia's intervention in support of 'stranded' diaspora across eastern and southern Ukraine began as early as the 2004–2005 Orange Revolution. Moscow's interventions have taken the form of propaganda to mobilize ethnic kin, as well as unconventional kinetic operations. With Russia's material support, separatist forces had several successes on the battlefield against the Ukrainian Armed Forces. The battle of Illovaysk in August 2014 forced the Ukrainian Army into total retreat, giving control over the entire surrounding territory to the separatists.

To increase the battlefield effectiveness of rebel forces and its own fighters, Russia employed malware in the Donbas to collect battlefield intelligence, retrieved locational data from mobile network devices used by Ukrainian artillery troops, and hacked CCTV cameras behind the adversaries' lines (Kostyuk & Zhukov 2019). Moreover, the pro-Moscow group CyberBerkut disseminated disruptive hacks and disinformation to create disorganization among pro-Ukraine supporters, their leaders, and the local Ukrainian Armed Forces groups (Croft & Apps 2014).

The covert Crimean operation used swiftness and the element of surprise to establish a fait accompli in the operational environment in Crimea, thus making any counter-actions by Ukraine nearly impossible. Using the 16,000 troops stationed in Crimea and special unmarked military units to capture and disarm Ukrainian soldiers located at strategic locations, Russia deployed a covert military operation (Carment & Belo 2019).

Even though the February 2022 intervention by Russia has escalated substantially between March and April, the original intent of this military incursion was to be a limited 'operation', being far short of a total military-to-military confrontation. The February 2022 intervention in Ukraine exacerbated the already difficult situation for the Russian-speaking diaspora throughout Ukraine. For example, Kyiv began censorship of predominantly Russian-language media sources (Patil 2022). Even though many Russian-speaking civilians from eastern and southern Ukraine fled west, and some to Russia, many civilians chose to remain in the territories that were annexed by Moscow in September 2022 (Sullivan 2022). Such loyalty by the Russian diaspora is not confined to these regions. This begs the question of what happens to the Russian diaspora that remains in Ukraine and must live in a rapidly nationalizing Ukrainian state. In many cases, the Russian intervention compelled local politicians in predominantly Russian-speaking areas like Odesa to reject anything Russian (Skorkin 2022). This challenge is also applicable to the stranded diaspora in the Baltic states.

Russian-language media has become an increasingly important source of leverage of Moscow's grey zone operations in Latvia. Major Russian media channels are under the direct or indirect control of Moscow. The ethnic-based marginalization of minorities enabled such media to focus on themes such as 'rampant Russophobia', a 'resurgence of fascism', and the 'ethnic cleansing of local Russian populations'. In the long run, it aims to capture the hearts and minds of the Baltic peoples, especially those of minority backgrounds. However, following the February 2022 intervention in Ukraine, the activities of the above channels were substantially curtailed by the Latvian government.

In 2022, Russia pursued the occupation of the 'Novorossiya' territory in southeastern Ukraine, thereby establishing a land-based bridge to Crimea (Carment & Belo 2022a). Even though Russia's strategy has shifted toward kinetic operations, the intervention in Ukraine should be examined in the context of Russia's push to shift the regional balance of power in its favour. In other words, the 2022 intervention in Ukraine is one component in Russia's foreign policy pursuits, which in the majority take place in the grey zone. However, the rationale for this change in strategy in February 2022 was twofold.

First, the value of NATO remaining outside of Ukraine was much greater for Russia than the value of Kyiv's alliance membership for the West. This is the case in terms of strategic value and ideological dimension for Russia. In general, Russia's perception of its near abroad has been increasingly influenced by the Endowment Effect (Belo 2020). Under this effect, states place a greater value on assets they perceive to currently or previously own relative to those they have never claimed. In other words, with its military and political retreat following the collapse of the Soviet Union, Moscow has placed significant value on the loss of its traditional sphere of influence compared to the West, which has been increasing its relative influence. As a consequence, Russia is willing to invest more in the fight relative to NATO and its allies.

Second, there was a shift in American resolve to confront, rather than tolerate, a frozen conflict (Carment & Belo 2022b). From Moscow's perspective, the war materiel and training supplied by the West only made Russian operations more imminent while Ukraine was relatively weak. In other words, Russia had the incentive to strike before Ukraine became stronger as the result of material and weapons supplies and training from the West. Indeed, Angela Merkel admitted as much when she stated in December 2022 that "the 2014 Minsk Agreement was an attempt to buy time for Ukraine. Ukraine used this time to become stronger. Ukraine in 2014–2015 and Ukraine today are not the same" (Thumann 2022). The decision to arm Ukraine thus far created more insecurity than a lasting peace, as the move only emboldened Kyiv to try and take back the Donbas by force, rather than pursue dialogue with the separatists to grant more political autonomy to the territories while remaining within Ukraine. For example, following the removal of Yanukovych, Ukraine's acting president Oleksandr Turchinov announced the beginning of an anti-terrorist operation using the military and volunteer battalions in Donbas to reinstate Kyiv's control over the territory. (Carment, Nikolko & Belo 2019, p. 130) Another example includes the July–August 2014 offensive on Luhansk and Donetsk Oblast by Ukraine's Armed Forces which resulted in the retaking of the city of Lysychansk (BBC 2014).

Table 21.1 summarizes the individual ethnic-based components of each intervention case as well as elements of grey zone conflict focused on respectively, balance of power shifts and political, economic and cyber warfare.

Conclusion

In this chapter, we showed how ethnic conflict serves as a permissive condition for states to pursue grey zone conflict interventions. Strategies encompassing lower cost political, economic, and cyber warfare allow states to avoid direct confrontation while minimizing culpability.

The central problem revealed in this study is the absence of effective deterrence strategies to counter modern warfare where ethnic conflict combines with grey zone strategies. This is particularly true in circumstances where the actors involved are not only states but groups that often lack the commitment to finding peaceful solutions related to territorial control. While it is possible that frequent success in the use of reforms, concessions, and accommodation to manage internal challenges will lead to the curtailment of grey zone strategies, such outcomes are unlikely for three reasons.

First, few international institutions are designed to counter grey zone conflict (Carment & Belo 2019, 2018, 2022c). Even though Russia's 2022 intervention in Ukraine may signal increasing reliance on kinetic force, the majority of international disputes still take place in the grey zone. Therein, a central problem is international law's preoccupation with high-level military and security affairs while doing little to tackle the political and identity-driven dimensions of ethnic conflict such as minority rights protection or partition in more extreme cases.

International law relies heavily on post-Second World War international legal instruments, such as the Geneva Conventions, without supplementing them to fit the modern grey zone conflict environment. As a consequence, for example, when the integrity of the Ukrainian state was first challenged by secessionist surges in Crimea and Donbas, the hope of a harmonized non-violent settlement to resolve this conflict diminished rapidly. Individual nations, alliances and international organizations did not have the institutional instruments to address the violence on the ground or any of the political considerations around it (Carment, Nikolko & Belo 2019).

Second, great powers who rely on grey conflict are willing to bear a high risk of confrontation in the pursuit of their strategic goals. For example, in the lead-up to the Russian intervention in 2022, according to the Biden Administration, there were 3,000 close-contact incidents between American and Russian forces (Clem & Finch 2021). These flashpoints needed to be managed as they created room for military accidents, miscalculations, and errors (Deutsche Welle 2021). Some of these incidents were quite worrying and included sending US strategic bombers carrying nuclear weapons within 12 miles of the Russian border (Reuters 2021).

Third, to avoid confrontation between rival states, intervention across international borders occurs far below the threshold of open warfare (Carment & Belo 2022c). This transformation raises the question of how decades-old international legal frameworks such as Article Five of the North Atlantic Treaty and Articles 51 and 2(4) of the UN Charter can respond to the new challenges. In other words, what constitutes an 'attack', and what is an effective deterrent mechanism? NATO established the Comprehensive Approach in 2008, which recognizes the necessity to combine military and civilian resources to mitigate modern unconventional threats. However, the approach must be fully integrated into the security doctrine of individual nations, alliances, and international organizations to show any meaningful effect.

Moreover, as grey zone conflicts inherently involve military and civilian elements working in tandem to achieve foreign policy outcomes, this environment poses a direct challenge to the 1949 Article 51 (3) Additional Protocol I. In a whole-of-society approach to fighting, many of the groups and individuals involved do not engage directly in any fighting as participants of militaries or state-sponsored militias with insignias. Consequently, their actions are difficult to attribute to specific nations. The international legal regime does not have a robust formula through which actions of all non-state conflict participants can be reliably identified, attributed, and addressed.

Looking ahead, even though Russia's military intervention in Ukraine and elsewhere on its periphery indicates that contemporary grey zone conflicts may incorporate more violence, warfare on its own is unlikely to determine grand strategic outcomes among great powers and blocs. In other words, the complete military defeat of any major global power will continue to be unlikely because of nuclear weapons risks. This means grey zone conflicts, and the use of tools and tactics of warfare below the threshold of warfare will continue to be the dominant conflict format through which foreign policy goals are pursued. As a response, nations, alliances, and international organizations must create robust deterrence, conflict management mechanisms, and international behaviour regulations that fit this perpetual, incremental, and low-intensity conflict format.

Notes

1 Though not synonymous we use the terms 'ethnic kin' and diaspora interchangeably. See Carment et al. (2006) for a fuller interpretation of these terms.
2 A secessionist conflict is the formal and informal aspects of political alienation in which one or more ethnic groups seek a reduction of control or autonomy from a central authority through political means. The term separatist is also used. An irredentist conflict is the claim to the territory of an entity - usually an independent state - wherein an ethnic ingroup is in a numerical minority. The original term *terra irredenta* means territory to be redeemed.

3 Mearsheimer (1990) argues that the appeal to polarizing ethnic sentiment and the pursuit of interstate ethnic wars is generated by the need for leaders to mobilize the population in the face of a threatening international environment. Horowitz (2005) argues that the unwillingness to engage in political and economic reform in an ethnically divided society is reframed as an identity-based conflict creating opportunities for ethno-nationalists to stay in power through ethnic warfare conducted across borders.

4 For example, the Estonian government has aimed at key identity markers such as the victory in the 'Great Patriotic War', a term for the Second World war widely used in Russia.

5 The Soviet Union occupied the Baltic region in June 1940 following the August 1939 Molotov-Ribbentrop Pact with Nazi Germany.

References

Aasland, A & Fløtten, T 2001, 'Ethnicity and Social Exclusion in Estonia and Latvia.' *Europe-Asia Studies*, vol. 53, no. 7, pp. 1023–49, doi: 10.1080/09668130120085029.

BBC 2014, 'Ukraine Conflict: Part of Luhansk "Retaken" from Rebels', *BBC*, 8 July <https://www.bbc.com/news/world-europe-28363086> (accessed 1 February 2023).

Belo, D 2020, 'Conflict in the Absence of War: A Comparative Analysis of China and Russia Engagement in Gray Zone Conflicts', *Canadian Foreign Policy Journal*, vol. 26, no. 1, pp. 73–91, doi: 10.1080/11926422.2019.1644358.

Belo, D & Carment, D 2020, 'Unilateralism and Competitive Multilateralism in Gray-zone Conflict', *[Air University] Wild Blue Yonder* Journal, <https://www.airuniversity.af.edu/Wild-Blue-Yonder/Article-Display/Article/2292990/unilateralism-and-competitive-multilateralism-in-gray-zone-conflict-a-compariso/> (accessed 12 January 2023).

Bhatia, K 2018, 'Coercive Gradualism Through Gray Zone Statecraft in the South China Seas', *Joint Force Quarterly,* no. 91, no. 4, pp. 24–31.

Birka, I 2022, 'Thinking Diaspora Diplomacy After Russia's War in Ukraine', *Space & Polity*, vol. 26, no. 1, pp. 53–61, doi: 10.1080/13562576.2022.2104632.

Carment, D. 2014, *The False Promise of Policy Making Through Analogy*, <https://npsia.wordpress.com/2014/03/08/the-false-promise-of-policy-making-through-analogy-sudetenland-and-the-crimea-2/> (accessed 2 February 2023).

Carment, D & Belo, D 2018, *War's Future: The Risks and Rewards of Grey Zone Conflict and Hybrid Warfare*, Canadian Global Affairs Institute, Calgary.

Carment, D & Belo, D 2019, *Protecting Minority Rights to Undermine Russia's Compatriot Policy*, Canadian Global Affairs Institute, Calgary.

Carment, D & Belo, D 2022a, 'The Russia-West Standoff: "Locked into War"', Institute for Peace and Diplomacy, <https://peacediplomacy.org/2022/01/28/the-russia-west-standoff-locked-into-war/> (accessed 23 September 2022).

Carment, D & Belo, D 2022b, 'The Ukraine Crisis: More War or Shared Responsibility?', *iaffairscanada*, <https://iaffairscanada.com/2022/the-ukraine-crisis-more-war-or-shared-responsibility/> (accessed 1 February 2023).

Carment, D & Belo, D 2022c, 'Let's Stop Pretending Canada Isn't at War in Ukraine', *Policy Options*, 18 March, <https://policyoptions.irpp.org/magazines/lets-stop-pretending-canada-isnt-at-war-in-ukraine/> (accessed 3 February 2023).

Carment, D & James, P 1995, 'Internal Constraints and Interstate Ethnic Conflict: Toward a Crisis-Based Assessment of Irredentism', *Journal of Conflict Resolution*, vol. 39, no. 1, pp. 82–109, doi: 10.1177/0022002795039001004.

Carment, D, James, P & Taydas, Z 2006, *Who Intervenes? Ethnic Conflict and Interstate Crisis*, Ohio State University Press, Columbus, OH.

Carment, D, Nikolko, M & Belo, D 2019, 'Gray Zone Mediation in the Ukraine Crisis: Comparing Crimea and Donbas', in J Wilkenfeld, K Beardsley & D Quinn (eds), *Research Handbook on Mediating International Crises*, Edward Elgar Publishing, Cheltenham - Northampton, MA, pp. 124–40, doi: 10.4337/9781788110709.00016.

Chazan, N & Horowitz, D 1991, *Irredentism and International Politics,* Lynne Rienner, Boulder, CO.

Clem, R & Finch R 2021, 'Crowded Skies and Turbulent Seas: Assessing the Full Scope of the NATO-Russian Military Incidents', *War On The Rocks*, 19 August, <https://warontherocks.com/2021/08/crowded-skies-and-turbulent-seas-assessing-the-full-scope-of-nato-russian-military-incidents/ > (accessed 26 January 2023).

Clogg, R 2008, 'The Politics of Identity in Post-Soviet Abkhazia: Managing Diversity and Unresolved Conflict', *Nationalities Papers*, vol. 36, no. 2, pp. 305–29, doi: doi.org/10.1080/00905990801934371.

Croft, A & Apps P 2014, 'NATO Websites Hit in Cyber Attack Linked to Crimea Tension', *Reuters*, 16 March. <https://www.reuters.com/article/us-ukraine-nato-idUSBREA2E0T320140316> (accessed 26 January 2023).

Deutsche Welle 2021, 'Moscow Claims US Spy Plane Endangered Aeroflot Jet', *Deutsche Welle*, 12 May, <https://www.dw.com/en/moscow-claims-us-spy-plane-nearly-caused-mid-air-catastrophe/a-60027286> (accessed 20 January 2023)

Feklyunina, V 2016, 'Soft Power and Identity: Russia, Ukraine and the "Russian world(s)"', *European Journal of International Relations*, vol. 22, no. 4, pp. 773–96, doi: 10.1177/1354066115601200.

Global News 2016, 'Latvians Honour WWII Nazi Allies in Legionnaires Day Memorials', *GlobalNews.ca*, 16 March, <https://globalnews.ca/news/2581869/latvians-honour-wwii-nazi-allies-in-legionnaires-day-memorials/> (accessed 23 January 2023).

Global Security 2012, *Foreign Policy Concept of the Russian Federation June 28, 2000*, GlobalSecurity.Org, <https://www.globalsecurity.org/military/library/report/2000/russia-fp-2000.htm> (accessed 8 October 2022).

Harvey, F 1998, 'Deterrence Failure and Ethnic Conflict: The Case of Bosnia', in D Carment & P James (eds), *Peace in the Midst of* Wars, University of Pittsburgh Press, Pittsburgh, PA, pp. 23–264.

Heraclides, A 1990, 'Secessionist Minorities and External Involvement', *International Organization*, vol. 44, no. 3, pp. 341–78, doi: 10.1017/S0020818300035323.

Hoffman, F 2007, *Conflict in the 21st Century: The Rise of Hybrid Wars*, Potomac Institute for Policy Studies, Arlington, VA.

Horowitz, D. (1985) *Ethnic Groups in Conflict*, California University Press, Berkeley.

Horowitz, D 2010, 'Irredentas and Secessions: Adjacent Phenomena, Neglected Connections', in K Cordell & S Wolff (eds), *Routledge Handbook of Ethnic Conflict*, Routledge, London – New York, pp. 155–64.

Institute for War and Peace Reporting 2014, *Russia's War with Georgia: 2008 Timeline*, Institute for War and Peace Reporting, 4 August, <https://iwpr.net/global-voices/russias-war-georgia-2008-timeline> (accessed 23 January 2023).

Jackson, R & Rosberg, C 1982, 'Why Africa's Weak States Persist: The Empirical and the Juridical in Statehood', *World Politics*, vol. 35, no. 1, pp. 1–24, doi: 10.2307/2010277.

Kostyuk, N & Zhukov, Y M 2019, 'Invisible Digital Front: Can Cyber Attacks Shape Battlefield Events?', *The Journal of Conflict Resolution*, vol. 63, no. 2, pp. 317–47, doi: 10.1177/0022002717737138.

Mazarr, M J 2015, *Mastering the Gray Zone: Understanding a Changing Era of Conflict*, US Army War College, Carlisle, PA.

Mearsheimer, J 1990, 'Why We Will Soon Miss the Cold War', *Atlantic Monthly*, August.

Patil, A 2022, 'Critics Say a New Media Law Signed by Zelensky Could Restrict Press Freedom in Ukraine', *The New York Times*, 30 December, <https://www.nytimes.com/2022/12/30/world/europe/zelensky-journalism-law-free-speech.html> (accessed 23 January 2023).

Radio Liberty 2015, 'Pentagon: 12,000 Russian Soldiers In Ukraine', *Radio Liberty*, 3 March <https://www.rferl.org/a/ukraine-us-commander-hodges-12000-russian-troops/26880574.html> (accessed 23 January 2023).

Reuters 2008, 'Georgia Says Russian Jet Shot Down Its Drone (2008)', *Reuters*, 21 April, <https://www.reuters.com/article/us-georgia-russia-drone-idUSL2153087320080421> (accessed 1 February 2023).

Reuters 2021, 'Moscow Says U.S. Rehearsed Nuclear Strike Against Russia This Month', *Reuters*, 23 November, <https://www.reuters.com/world/russia-notes-significant-increase-us-bomber-activity-east-minister-2021-11-23/> (accessed 1 February 2023).

Sasse, G 2007, *The Crimea Question: Identity, Transition, and Conflict*, Harvard University Press for the Harvard Ukrainian Research Institute, Cambridge, MA.

Skorkin, K 2022, 'What Next for Ukraine's Formerly Pro-Russian Regions?', *Carnegie Endowment for International Peace*, 12 December, <https://carnegieendowment.org/politika/88542> (accessed 23 January 2023).

Solchanyk, R 2000, *Ukraine and Russia: The Post-Soviet Transition*, Rowman & Littlefield, Lanham, MD.

Sullivan B 2022, 'Ukrainians Navigate a Perilous Route to Safety Out of Besieged Mariupol', *NPR*, 31 March, <https://www.npr.org/2022/03/31/1089705434/ukraine-russia-war-mariupol-zaporizhzhia> (accessed 23 January 2023).

The Lithuania Tribune 2014, 'Russian Historian Alexander Dyukov - Persona Non-Grata in Lithuania for Whitewashing Soviet Crimes', *The Lithuania Tribune,* 14 August, <https://lithuaniatribune.com/russian-historian-alexander-dyukov-persona-non-grata-in-lithuania-for-whitewashing-soviet-crimes/> (accessed 23 January 2023).

Tapon, F 2018, 'The Bronze Soldier Explains Why Estonia Prepares for a Russian Cyberattack', *Forbes Magazine*, 7 July, <https://www.forbes.com/sites/francistapon/2018/0707/the-bronze-soldier-statue-in-tallinn-estonia-give-baltic-headaches/?sh=429fb22f98c7> (accessed 23 January 2023).

Thumann, M 2022, 'Hassnachricht aus Moskau', *Die Zeit*, 22 December, <https://www.zeit.de/2022/53/angela-merkel-russland-krieg-wladimir-putin> (accessed 23 January 2023).

US Military 2009, 'Georgia's Cyber Left Hook', www.army.mil., 7 April, <https://www.army.mil/article/19351/georgias_cyber_left_hook> (accessed 23 January 2023).

Walt, S W 2021, *Geopolitics and Empathy*, Belfer Center, <https://www.belfercenter.org/publication/geopolitics-empathy> (accessed 1 February 2023).

Walt, S 2022, 'Ukraine Is the World's Foreign Policy Rorschach Test', *Foreign Policy*, 18 October, https://foreignpolicy.com/2022/10/18/ukraine-is-the-worlds-foreign-policy-rorschach-test/ (accessed 31 January 2023).

22

JUST WAR THINKING AND WARS OF INFORMATION

War, Not-War, and the Places Between

Valerie Morkevičius

Introduction

Although information warfare has captured the public's attention, neither international relations realists nor just war thinkers have explored the subject in depth. This lack of attention to emerging strategies is not unprecedented. While classical realists like Morgenthau were concerned that nuclear weapons could fundamentally alter the nature of international politics, contemporary realists' emphasis on structure downplays the significance of technological change (Scheuerman 2009; Drezner 2019). Of course, the ability to develop new technology is a component of power: "most sophisticated technologies... invariably get incorporated into the most advanced weaponry", so states who fall behind face an unfavorable asymmetry of power (Mearsheimer 2001, p. 61). Yet realists see innovators' gains as ephemeral (Pape 2001). Consequently, realists find claims that technology drives strategic behavior or even battlefield outcomes "overstated" (Lieber 2000, p. 72). Tactics and strategies change, but the overall logic of the grand strategic landscape remains rather constant.

Similarly, ethicists occasionally identify an emerging technology as radically disruptive – claiming it has 'exploded' the existing just war framework (to borrow Michael Walzer's term). However, like realists, just war thinkers are more likely to imagine war's ethical problems as perennial. While debates abound as to whether AI and 'killer robots' are revolutionary technologies of this sort, most contemporary thinkers imagine that the ethical dilemmas information warfare poses can be addressed within the existing just war framework (Gross 2012; Lucas 2019).

In this, they follow their predecessors. Historical just war thinkers rarely (if ever) mentioned specific weapons. When they did so, it was to illustrate a general ethical dilemma, not to analyze the technology. The story of the crossbow appears to be an exception to the trend of silence. Yet although the Lateran in 1139 Council banned its use, at least against Christians, theologians central to the just war tradition never incorporated the ban (Russell 1977, p. 243; Johnson 1981, p. 129).

Viewing war's problems as perennial prevents overreaction and enables realists and just war thinkers alike to draw from history when faced with complex and dramatic changes. However, since both groups see themselves as participating in a tradition of statecraft aimed at managing the disorder of the international system, it behooves us to think through how such changes might be harnessed in ways that are both ethically and strategically wise.

DOI: 10.4324/9781003299011-27

This chapter attempts to frame an ethical realist approach to information warfare. First, it disambiguates information-technical warfare (cyberwar) from information-psychological warfare, in a way that suggests the actions of trolls and bots can rightly be understood as acts of war short of war. Hence, the rules of *jus in vi*, which largely parallel the traditional *jus in bello* rules, apply. Second, it distinguishes between two strategies of information-psychological warfare – denial and deception – arguing that while the former is generally permissible, the latter is not always so. Third, it advances a consequentialist argument against lying as a means of political coercion. It concludes with a caution: while kinetic warfare – by conventional or cyber means – may be devastating, information-psychological warfare's consequences may be much worse.

Information warfare: technical and psychological means

'Information warfare' in American strategic parlance includes two disparate sets of practices (Ford 2010). First, it describes information-technical warfare, where cyber tools disrupt or destroy an opponent's infrastructure. This involves blocking communications, wiping financial data, interfering with power generation and generally wreaking havoc with anything connected to the Internet. While the revolutionary nature of cyber warfare is hotly debated, norms have already emerged regarding its use, as expressed in the Tallinn Manual.

Second, the term can describe the information-psychological strategies China and Russia have advanced by adapting cyber means. While psychologically manipulating members of an opposing military is an ancient concept, the idea of employing such means to directly influence an opponent's public is relatively new. E H Carr observed that within 20 years of the first use of propaganda aimed at the opponent's civilians during World War I, its peacetime use had reached a level of "intensity unsurpassed in the war period" (Carr 1964, p. 124). Despite ever more proliferation of information-psychological warfare, it remains an "essentially lawless" realm where "chaos reigns" (Nye 2011, p. 156; Lin 2019, p. 189).

Information-psychological warfare endeavors to change how states and leaders are perceived by domestic and international publics, thus affecting an opposing state's internal cohesion and international reputation (Kalpokas 2017). It carefully studies the opponent's society to identify vulnerable social cleavages and decision-making frameworks that can then be manipulated (Ajir & Vailliant 2018, p. 73). Although this strategy predates the internet, contemporary information warfare exploits developments in the cyber-domain: social media's mass reach "amplifies" its scale, "not only in terms of space, but also in terms of the degree of resonance and the nature of impacts on social life" (Lopatina 2014, p. 156).

But are such informational tactics war? Is the language of just war the appropriate idiom to adopt? Thomas Rid terms cyber war an oxymoron, arguing "acts of war" must "rather immediately and directly result in casualties" (Rid 2012, p. 9). While Gartzke's definition is broader, encompassing non-lethal kinetic effects, his emphasis on the physicality of coercion also leads him to question whether information-psychological warfare should be classed as war at all (Gartzke 2013).

John Stone, by contrast, suggests that "war demands no necessary causal connection between what are really three distinct phenomena [...] all war involves force, but force does not necessarily imply violence – particularly if violence implies lethality" (Stone 2013, p. 103). Mid-20th-century Protestant theologian Paul Ramsey similarly separated power — namely the ability to control others' actions, by coercion if necessary – from force and violence (Ramsey 2002, p. 5). Even cyberattacks that do not *directly* cause massive casualties… could still serve as an effective means of political coercion or brute force" (Liff 2012, p. 403).

Fundamentally, debating whether information warfare fits into the bi-modal categories of war or not war is a distraction (Lupton & Morkevičius 2019). It is more useful to envision a continuum ranging from ideal peace to total war (Whetham 2016). The international relations literature on coercion already imagines the world this way, recognizing that formal definitions of war are arbitrary. Hence, this literature recognizes numerous coercive actions between peace and war, including covert action, assassination and even bombing campaigns.

Kinetic force is not necessary for coercion, nor is the threat of such force. The strategies of compellence and deterrence provide helpful analogies. A compellent threat "that leaves something to chance" invokes the specter of force – but (if successful) never actually resorts to it (Schelling 1980, p. 187). Instead, it relies on psychological manipulation. Ramsey likewise argued that devastating nuclear threats against cities only appeared immoral, as those making them were (secretly) aware that they would not carry them out (Ramsey 2002, p. 304). While deterrence may kinetically be preferable to war, psychologically it forces many – including civilians – to bear a heavy burden. If coercion means forcing someone to act in ways they might otherwise not, psychological manipulation fits the bill. Information-psychological efforts aimed at undermining states' domestic cohesion and international soft power capabilities are grave enough to warrant characterization as uses of coercive force.

Governing the gap: from *jus ad bellum* to *jus ad vim*

This space between war and peace is governed by the normative framework of *jus ad vim* (the justness of force short of war). While the concept is relatively new to the just war literature, the roots of *jus ad vim* extend into the historical tradition (Brunstetter 2021). Classical just war thinkers in the Western tradition justified all legitimate uses of force using similar logics. Thus, Augustine treated corporal punishment, the death penalty and war as alike in their moral character. So long as the individuals using force in each case act not "as avengers of their own injuries, but defenders of public well-being", he argued they should be seen as "ministers of the law", not murderers (Augustine 1994, p. 222). Implicitly, Augustine did not see war and peace as distinct moral spheres. Applying *jus ad vim* to information warfare allows us to use familiar principles to analyze the effects of new technologies and tactics, rather than getting lost in questions of whether their use constitutes war.

Just as traditional just war reasoning begins by asking *ad bellum* questions about the justifiability of going to war, *jus ad vim* asks us whether engaging in coercion is justifiable. We must consider whether we are responding to a serious wrong (just cause), whether we are truly motivated by that just cause, rather some other more profane aim (right intention), and whether the decision to use such tactics has been made via appropriate channels (legitimate authority). We must also consider two pragmatic principles which serve as additional restraints: proportionality and likelihood of success.

The *jus in vi* principles determine *how* coercive force may be used. The traditional *jus in bello* principles of distinction and proportionality are central to evaluating what the legitimate use of a particular tactic would look like.

The principle of distinction protects non-combatants from becoming direct targets of harm. The principle of double effect modifies this injunction. Thus, actions aimed at a military target, yet result in unintended (although not necessarily unexpected) harm to civilians, can be permissible. Some scholars argue that because uses of force short of war respond to lesser wrongs than those justifying war, the *jus in vi* should permit "less moral latitude for inflicting unintended harm on noncombatants, where 'harm' is not simply measured in deaths, but also in human rights concerns that deeply affect civilian lives" (Brunstetter 2017). I partly disagree. Assuming the bar for using coercion against another is met, given a choice between tactics indirectly causing civilian injury and death and tactics directly resulting in economic or property damage, the latter seems ethically preferable, if strictly limited by concerns about proportionality, necessity and order (Morkevičius 2017).

Proportionality in this context encourages the economy of force: the harms caused by a specific action must not outweigh the expected benefits. In the case of *jus in vi*, proportionality additionally requires avoiding tactics that could lead to unnecessary escalation, particularly when increasing amounts of coercion or violence are unlikely to effectively further a moral end (Lupton & Morkevičius 2019, p. 52).

Finally, the principles of *necessity* and *order* are important ethical restraints. When we consider actions that directly impact non-combatants, we must ask if they are necessary, or if other means could be equally effective. Furthermore, if war (and conflicts short of war) are justly aimed only at peace, then tactics that significantly undermine order are morally impermissible. This includes attacks that would frustrate hopes of achieving peace post-bellum (by violating trust, for example), as well as attacks that sow widespread disorder akin to humanitarian disaster.

Information warfare: denial and deception

Having argued that some kinds of non-kinetic attacks are rightly called war, while others fall into the continuum between war and peace governable by *jus in vi*, we can map the moral contours of information warfare. Information warfare can be pursued using two broad strategies: denial and deception. The former involves withholding information. In the cybersphere, denial could be as straightforward as maintaining robust network security, so that opponents cannot access one's systems. This tactic differs only in method from classical examples of denial. One has no ethical obligation to tell one's opponent anything (nor to provide them the means to find out).

Strategies of deception are ethically more complex. Deception manipulates the opponent's view of reality in several ways: concealing, spinning, and lying (Mearsheimer 2013, p. 10). Concealment and spin can sometimes be permissible, but lying is unjustifiable, for reasons drawn both from a pragmatic perspective and from virtue ethics.

Concealment

If denial is simply not sharing information, concealment is making it harder for one's opponent to find it. Many theologians and philosophers accept that concealment may be necessary, even laudable, if used to good ends. For example, casuists argued that while deception through concealment is not inherently good, it "might be justified in a case in which strict allegiance to such a principle would lead to disaster: one could attempt to forestall an impending calamity and yet avoid the direct lie" (Stone 2006, p. 115). Similarly, the 14th-century Islamic jurist al-Misri argued that "giving a misleading impression" is a form of deception that is not morally harmful "if required by an interest countenanced by sacred law", such as defending oneself or rescuing another from oppression (Al-Misri 1997, p. 748). Acceptable tactics could involve plays on words – for example, telling a murderer at the door that one's friend is not *here*, when they are in the next room. And while the Hindu tradition considers *kutayuddha* – tactics of concealed, or hidden war – less honorable, such means are permissible in cases where open means of fighting would be ineffective (Roy 2021, pp. 144, 146).

In conventional warfare, one might wear a uniform printed with pixelated designs to conceal oneself. A cyber-enabled ambush might use code to jam a state's air defense systems, effectively blinding it to an incoming strike, as Israel did when it attacked a nuclear reactor under construction in Syria in 2007. One has no ethical obligation to be visible to one's opponent, and hence, this sort of behavior is permissible. As Aquinas (1991, p. 246) put it, ambush is a permissible misdirection, as when "someone may be deceived by what we say or do because we do not reveal our thoughts or intentions to him". From this perspective, ambushes are not really deception at all, because complete transparency is not required.

Still, some kinds of concealment are impermissible. Consider Walzer's example of French partisans posing as farmers harvesting a field. When a patrol of German soldiers passes, the 'farmers' spring up and attack them with machine guns that had been hidden in their potato sacks. Walzer – although deeply sympathetic to the partisans' cause – decries this ambush as morally wrong. In his view, the problem is that the ambush was "prepared behind a political or moral, rather than natural, cover" (Walzer 2000, p. 287). The Islamic tradition makes a similar distinction. Although Islamic jurists found ambush to be generally permissible, Malik notes that night ambushes were expressly forbidden unless a people had already been invited to Islam (Morkevičius 2018, p. 79). As in Walzer's example, the justification hinges on people's expectations. A people who had never before been confronted could not possibly expect to be vulnerable to a night attack.

A cyber parallel could involve using malicious code to disrupt an opponent's air defense systems not simply to make one's own aircraft invisible, but to make them appear to be civilian planes. Similarly, an information operation that employs sock puppets (accounts using fictitious identities) or that creates fake webpages masquerading as reliable media or government sites can be thought of as engaging in this sort of illegitimate concealment.

Put simply, it is one thing to hide behind a rock wall or a piece of disruptive code, but it is quite another to pretend to be something you are not. It is this deception that transforms the ambush in Walzer's story from something laudable to something impermissible. In conventional warfare, this type of deception is abhorrent because it endangers non-combatants by making the opponent more likely to treat them as potential threats; the same could apply to information-technological warfare as well (Cohen 2016, p. 1312). In the case of information-psychological warfare, concealment is morally problematic when it undermines individuals' trust in each other – particularly when it leads to mistrust in trustworthy sources of information whose identities have been stolen and abused for malicious purposes. This sort of action dangerously undermines civil order.

Spin

While concealment involves hiding information, spinning involves selectively presenting it – highlighting some bits, downplaying others – to further one's interests. Spin tells the truth selectively to *imply* something else, affecting the way the other perceives the world. In warfare, spin can involve managing public relations to put one's own actions in the best possible light. The language of 'collateral damage' and 'surgical strikes' is a permissible sort of spin, attempting to sanitize our accounts of violence, rendering our actions more palatable.

Nonetheless, there are ethical boundaries here too. Acceptable spin must be somewhat transparent. The audience should be aware that they are in a context where they may be encountering spin. We know advertisers want to sell us products; we know opinion columnists want to persuade us to accept their view; we know spokespeople want to cast government policy positively. This consciousness means we can choose to "ask the spinner for additional information, do independent research on the spinner's story, or listen to counter-spinners, who are usually not in short supply when it comes to foreign policy" (Mearsheimer 2013, p. 18).

Furthermore, acceptable spin does not involve the intent to tell a false story. Because tactics like overselling and blame-shifting frequently move beyond selective truth telling, these variants of spin are ethically risky. Overselling involves exaggerating the opponent's "aggressiveness or offensive capabilities" (Schuessler 2015, p. 16). This sort of spin is similar to advertising, and audiences should often be able to recognize it, but it can slide into impermissible lying if threats or events are simply invented.

Blame-shifting uses two potential strategies to try to shift responsibility for hostilities to the adversary (Schuessler 2015, p. 15). First, one can simply wait for a pretext to use force, rather than trying to diffuse tensions. Second, one can engage in 'counterfeit diplomacy' while concealing one's active preparation for war. The first tactic is not itself deceptive, although it may produce a distorted narrative that misplaces the blame for the conflict. Ultimately, the ethical problem there is not deception, but rather a violation of last resort due to the failure to seek non-coercive means of resolving the conflict.

The second form of blame-shifting involves deliberate deception. Participating in a diplomatic conference with apparent good will, but no real intention of reaching an agreement, is the same type of deception as the ambush that troubled Walzer. Such a political ruse cheapens trust in diplomacy, making others less likely to engage in reciprocal efforts to reduce tensions in the future. Ultimately, this undermines order. Counterfeit diplomacy cannot be ethically permissible, firstly because it is deceptive and secondly because it does not aim at peace (or even de-escalation).

Concealment and spin can be used ethically within the limits imposed by *jus in bello* or *jus in vi* principles. While spin may directly target non-combatants, it can be permissible if it meets the requirements of proportionality, necessity, and a concern with order. As I have argued above, many forms of spin may be able, at least in theory, to meet these requirements. Spin relying on blame-shifting or counterfeit diplomacy may not.

Lying

Lying poses the gravest ethical problems. Philosopher Sissela Bok defines a lie as "any intentionally deceptive message", whether made verbally or in writing, or "conveyed via smoke signals, Morse code, sign language, and the like" (Bok 1999, p. 13). Augustine likewise described lying nearly two millennia earlier as having one thing in his mind while uttering "another in words, or by signs of whatever kind" (Augustine 1887, p. 458). One can say many untrue things without lying (how else could we tell jokes or write fiction?) – so long as one does not *intend* to deceive the other (Augustine 1887, p. 458; Bok 1999, p. 206). Because intending to deceive defines lying, one can lie by using "facts – even true facts – to imply that something is true, when [one] knows that it is not true" and thus to "purposely [lead] the listener to a false conclusion without explicitly stating that conclusion" (Mearsheimer 2013, p. 16).

Mearsheimer identifies two distinct categories of lies: selfish lies and "strategic lies" serving the "good of the collectivity" (Mearsheimer 2013, p. 11). Although he declares selfish lies deplorable, he asserts that strategic lies "can do good things for a country, although there is always the possibility that they will do more harm than good" (Mearsheimer 2013, p. 24). Machiavelli would have approved.

I argue, however, that strategic lies on the level of information operations generally (perhaps always) do more harm than good, drawing on consequentialist claims. Mearsheimer fails to adequately weigh the damage caused by pervasive lying, partly because he fails to imagine the scale of cyber-enabled information warfare. The lies spread as deliberate cyber-enabled information operations can not only reach farther, quicker, but can also generate an almost impenetrable web of lies, thanks to the ways algorithms structure individuals' information silos. Hannah Arendt also worried about the effects of public lying, but thought even the most capable totalitarian state could not generate a web of lies broad enough to prevent citizens from eventually bumping up against reality, even if it used computers (Arendt 1972, p. 7). Unfortunately, today's trolls and bots may do just what Arendt feared, creating a world in which "truth that can be relied upon disappears entirely from public life, and with it, the chief stabilizing factor in the ever-changing affairs of men" (Arendt 1972, p. 7).

What's wrong with lying?

Some theologians and philosophers claim lying is simply always wrong. For Augustine and Aquinas, lying cuts the liar off from God who personifies Truth. For Kant, the problem is that lying fails to respect the other. Similar bans on lying can be found in the Hindu *Dharmasutras* and the *Code of Manu*, as well as in the work of Islamic legal scholar Malik ibn Anas, who argued that a believer can be a miser or a coward, but never a liar (Rao 2013; ibn Anas 2014, p. 416). More recently, Sissela Bok uses virtue ethics to argue that

> Deceit and violence [...] are the two forms of deliberate assault on human beings. Both can coerce people into acting against their will. Most harm that can befall victims through violence can come to them also through deceit. But deceit controls more subtly, for it works on belief as well as action.
>
> (Bok 1999, p. 18)

However, many just war thinkers and all realists are consequentialists. And there are consequentialist arguments in favor of lying in certain circumstances. Rahab's story in the book of Joshua has long been used, including by Augustine's contemporary John Chrysostom at the end of the 4th century, to justify lies told for good aims. In the story, a woman named Rahab saves the lives of two Israelite spies hiding in her house by misdirecting the soldiers looking for them, then helping them escape through her window as the soldiers charge off in the wrong direction. More recently, American evangelicals referenced Rahab's story to justify the Bush administration's dishonest claims about weapons of mass destruction on the eve of the Iraq War (Kellner 2007, p. 641). Plato's parable of the Noble Lie and Machiavelli's advice in *The Prince* reflect the same logic (Newey 1997). Recent attempts have even been made to reconcile Augustine's deontological condemnation of lying with his consequentialist account of war to justify political lies told for good ends (Decosimo 2010).

Consequentialist arguments justifying lying can also be found in other traditions. The 8th-century Islamic scholar al-Shaybani claimed that lying could be permissible to "remove some injustice or oppression from yourself or from your brother" (al-Shaybani 2002, p. 392). Likewise, al-Ghazali thought lying might be permissible in some contexts, as "a precaution against some wrong; or in the struggle against enemies to prevent them from espying the secrets of the realm" (Al-Ghazli 2013, p. 86). As in Christian theology, intent matters: "whenever the purpose is sound, the intention is truthful, and the desire purely for the good, one is both truthful and perfectly truthful, regardless of what the utterance happens to be" (al-Ghazali 2013, p. 86).

From a consequentialist perspective, lying on the scale of a disinformation campaign likely violates the proportionality principle. The long-term costs are phenomenal. First, lying damages those who craft and propagate lies. An Augustinian might say this is because lying credibly requires suppressing part of one's self. Just as the evil in war, in Augustine's eyes, lies in the hate and lust killing arouses in the killer, the evil in lying is what it does to the liar. For Kant, a liar "annihilates his dignity as a man" (Bok 1999, p. 32). Even Mearsheimer recognizes that lying has "a corrupting effect on individuals as well as the broader society in which they live" (Mearsheimer 2013, p. 7).

Practically speaking, disinformation campaigns launched against others ultimately undermine one's own society. Decades of domestic misinformation generated a state of "informational learned helplessness" in the Russian public, which led Russians to be more susceptible to Covid-19 disinformation – some of which had actually circled back to Russia from its own overseas campaigns (Nisbet & Kamenchuk 2021).

Second, disinformation campaigns brutally harm the target's society. Democracies are especially susceptible. Widely proliferating lies undermine the public's ability to make informed choices, cripple the policy-making process, and ultimately corrode faith in democracy (Bok 1999, p. 27). A well-informed public (not to mention policy makers) is essential to democracy. But if the idea of truth comes to have no meaning, individuals become cynically agnostic as to whether any given proposition is true or false (Arendt 1972). Indeed, evidence suggests individuals consuming a significant amounts of disinformation come to distrust *all* sources of information, struggle to form stable opinions, and ultimately are drawn to whatever emotional or dramatic narratives capture their imagination (Lucas & Pomeranzev 2016).

Russian disinformation campaigns successfully exploit polarization in democratic societies, leading to increased social tensions and even, as seen in responses to Covid-19, policy paralysis (Jankowicz 2020). "Factual truth", after all, "provides the ground of the public space itself" (Birmingham 2010, p. 75). Without shared truths, democratic politics becomes impossible. Imagine two individuals who agree the planet is rapidly warming. One believes human activities are responsible; the other does not. Assuming both agree that a warming planet means rising sea levels, they can nonetheless rationally discuss practical responses to the problem, perhaps finding a middle ground in building sea walls. If, on the other hand, they disagree as to whether the planet is warming at all, the policy process will be paralyzed. For this reason, "trust is a social good to be protected just as much as the air we breathe or the water we drink" (Bok 1999, p. 26). Societies deeply rent by polarization may be at peace in a technical sense, but if political collapse or civil war looms, they cannot be said to be at peace in any meaningful sense. If, as Augustine and others have argued, the only just purpose of any war is to aim at peace, such tactics cannot be permissible.

But paralysis is not the worst of it. Contemporary disinformation campaigns are no longer "satisfied with lying, but deliberately [propose] to transform… lies into reality" (Birmingham 2010, p. 74). For example, Russian disinformation campaigns targeted disaffected eastern Ukrainians to generate support for Russian-installed separatist governments; simultaneous disinformation campaigns targeted Ukraine's allies to discredit Ukraine as a corrupt, unreliable, violent partner (Patrikarakos 2017). Such information warfare campaigns fail the proportionality test. If, as Walzer suggests, states' right to self-defense arises from the value of the common life we build together within their borders, any strategy that destroys that common life is a serious act of aggression, whether by physical or psychological means (Walzer 2000, p. 55).

Conclusion

Conventional warfare is horrific. Buildings are destroyed. Landscapes are devastated. Lives are lost and irrevocably altered. Material things can be rebuilt or replaced, but repairing broken social bonds or rebuilding social trust is more challenging. Yet human beings are strangely resilient and remarkably empathetic. And so – although it is admittedly difficult – reconciliation is possible. Broken lives are put (mostly) back together again. Life continues.

Everything we know about post-conflict reconciliation suggests that truth-telling is central to the process after conventional wars (Lu 2002; Hehir 2019). This is not only a matter of bringing perpetrators to justice for past crimes. Arriving at a shared truth of past horrors is the foundation on which more just social and political institutions can be reconstructed for the future, hopefully leading to a more stable peace.

Yet disinformation campaigns subvert the very *idea* of truth. How does one re-institute shared truth in a society shredded by pervasive lies? Why would those who believed falsehoods alter their beliefs, especially if those urging them to do so are their former opponents or even outsiders? After all, ordinary people spread disinformation peddled by trolls and bots not because they are collaborators, but because they *believe* it. Recognizing one has been duped is psychologically traumatic and potentially socially costly. Consequently, even individuals who start to see the "holes in the web", as Arendt would put it, are likely to try to look away for as long as possible.

So far, despite its bloodless appearance, information-psychological warfare has been remarkably successful at undercutting effective political action and undermining social trust. The Internet (and the devices which put it right in our pockets) have made these tactics cheaper and more far-reaching than ever before.

Yet a dystopian post-truth future is not inevitable. The effectiveness of disinformation campaigns against democracies can be limited by improving media literacy and critical thinking skills across society. If successful countermeasures emerge, malevolent actors may abandon this tactic. Furthermore, if it can be demonstrated that such campaigns backfire against those who launch them, it may be possible to develop a strong normative consensus against their use. States are, after all, self-interested. Ultimately, ethical concerns alone will be insufficient to prevent continued or even expanded use of such tactics, but ethical concerns coupled with strategic ones just might.

References

Ajir, M & Vailliant, B 2018, 'Russian Information Warfare: Implications for Deterrence Theory', *Strategic Studies Quarterly*, vol. 12, no. 3, pp. 70–89.

Al-Ghazli, A H 2003, *On Intention, Sincerity, and Truthfulness* (Book XXXVII of the Revival of the Religious Sciences), trans. A F Shaker, Islamic Texts Society, Cambridge.

Al-Misri, A N 1997, *Reliance of the Traveler*, trans. N H M Keller, Amana Publications, Beltsville, MD.

Al-Shaybani, I M 2002, *The Islamic Law of Nations: Shaybani's Siyar*, trans. & ed. M Khadduri, Johns Hopkins University Press, Baltimore, MD.

Arendt, H 1972, *Crises of the Republic,* Harcourt Brace and Company, New York.

Augustine 1887, 'On Lying,' in P Schaffer (ed), *Nicene and Post Nicene Fathers: First Series, Volume III — St. Augustine: On the Holy Trinity Doctrinal Treatises, Moral Treatises,* The Christian Literature Company, Buffalo, NY, pp. 457–80.

Augustine 1994, 'Against Faustus the Manichaean,' in M Tkacz & D Kries (eds), *Political Writings*, Hackett Publishing, Indianapolis, IN, pp. 221–2.

Birmingham, P 2010, 'A Lying World Order: Political Deception and the Threat of Totalitarianism', R Berkowitz, J Katz & T Keenan (eds), *Thinking in Dark Times: Hannah Arendt on Ethics and Politics*, Fordham University Press, New York, pp. 73–8.

Bok, S 1999, *Lying*, Vintage Books, New York.

Brunstetter, D 2017, 'Justice After the Use of Limited Force: Victory and the Moral Dilemmas of Jus Post Vim,' in A R Hom & C O'Driscoll (eds), *Moral Victories: The Ethics of Winning Wars*, Oxford University Press, Oxford, pp. 214–230.

Brunstetter, D 2021, *Just and Unjust Uses of Limited Force: A Moral Argument with Contemporary Illustrations,* Oxford University Press, Oxford.

Carr, E H 1964, *The Twenty Years Crisis,* Palgrave, London.

Cohen, S 2016, 'Are There Limits to Military Deception?' *Philosophia*, vol. 44, pp. 1305–18. https://doi.org/10.1007/s11406-017-9826-z.

Decosimo, D 2010, 'Finding Augustine's Ethics of Public Lying in His Treatments of Lying and Killing', *The Journal of Religious Ethics*, vol. 38, no. 4, pp. 661–97, https://doi.org/10.1111/j.1467-9795.2010.00458.x.

Drezner, D 2019, 'Technological Change and International Relations', *International Relations*, vol. 33, no. 2, pp. 286–303. https://doi.org/10.1177/0047117819834629.

Ford, C A 2010, 'The Trouble with Cyber Arms Control', *The New Atlantis*, no. 29, pp. 52–67.

Gartzke, E 2013, 'The Myth of Cyberwar: Bringing War in Cyberspace Back Down to Earth', *International Security*, vol. 38, no. 2, pp. 41–73, https://doi.org/10.1162/isec_a_00136.

Gross, M 2012, *Moral Dilemmas of Modern War,* Cambridge University Press, Cambridge.

Hehir, A 2019, 'Lessons Learned? The Kosovo Specialist Chambers' Lack of Local Legitimacy and Its Implications', *Human Rights Review*, vol. 20, pp. 267–87, https://doi.org/10.1007/s12142-019-00564-y.

Ibn Anas, M 2014, *Al-Muwatta of Imam Malik Ibn Anas: The First Formulation of Islamic Law*, Diwan Press, Bradford.

Jankowicz N 2020, *How to Lose the Information War: Russia, Fake News, and the Future of Conflict*, Bloomsbury Publishing, London.

Johnson, J T 1981, *Just War Tradition and The Restraint of War,* Princeton University Press, Princeton.

Kalpokas, I 2017, 'Information Warfare on Social Media: A Brand Management Perspective,' *Baltic Journal of Law and Politics*, vol. 10, no. 1, pp. 35–62, https://doi.org/10.1515/bjlp-2017-0002.

Kellner, D 2007, 'Bushspeak and the Politics of Lying: Presidential Rhetoric in the "War on Terror"', *Presidential Studies Quarterly*, vol. 37, no. 4, pp. 622–45, https://doi.org/10.1111/j.1741-5705.2007.02617.x.

Lieber, K A 2000, 'Grasping the Technological Peace: The Offense-Defense Balance and International Security', *International Security*, vol. 25, no. 1, pp. 71–104, https://doi.org/10.1162/016228800560390.

Liff, A P 2012, 'Cyberwar: A 'New Absolute Weapon'? The Proliferation of Cyberwarfare Capabilities and Interstate War', *Journal of Strategic Studies*, vol. 35, no. 3, pp. 401–28, https://doi.org/10.1080/0140239 0.2012.663252.

Lin, H 2019, 'The Existential Threat from Cyber-Enabled Information Warfare', *Bulletin of Atomic Scientists*, vol. 75, no. 4, pp. 187–96, https://doi.org/10.1080/00963402.2019.1629574.

Lopatina, N V 2014, 'The Modern Information Culture and Information Warfare', *Scientific and Technical Information Processing*, vol. 41, no. 3, pp. 155–8, https://doi.org/10.3103/s0147688214030034.

Lu, C 2002, 'Justice and Moral Regeneration: Lessons from the Treaty of Versailles', *International Studies Review*, vol. 4, no. 3, pp. 3–25, https://doi.org/10.1111/1521-9488.t01-1-00261.

Lucas, G 2019, *Ethics and Cyber Warfare,* Oxford University Press, Oxford.

Lucas, E & Pomeranzev, P 2016, *Winning the Information War. Techniques and Counter-strategies to Russian Propaganda in Central and Eastern Europe,* The Center for European Policy Analysis, Washington, DC.

Lupton, D & Morkevičius, V 2019, 'The Fog of War: Violence, Coercion, and the Jus Ad Vim', in J Galliott (ed), *Force Short of War in Modern Conflict: Jus Ad Vim,* Edinburgh University Press, Edinburgh, pp. 36–56.

Mearsheimer, J J 2001, *The Tragedy of Great Power Politics*, W.W. Norton, New York.

Mearsheimer, J J 2013, *Why Leaders Lie: The Truth about Lying in International Politics*, Oxford University Press, Oxford.

Morkevičius, V 2017, 'Coercion, Manipulation, and Harm: Civilian Immunity and War,' in M L Gross & T Meisels (eds), *Soft War: The Ethics of Unarmed Conflict*, Cambridge University Press, Cambridge, pp. 33–48.

Morkevičius, V 2018, *Realist Ethics: Just War Traditions as Power Politics,* Cambridge University Press, Cambridge.

Newey, G 1997, 'Political Lying: A Defense,' *Public Affairs Quarterly*, vol. 11, no. 2, pp. 93–116.

Nisbet, E C & Kamenchuk, O 2021, 'Russian News Media, Digital Media, Informational Learned Helplessness, and Belief in COVID-19 Misinformation', *International Journal of Public Opinion Research*, vol. 33, no. 3, pp. 571–90, https://doi.org/10.1093/ijpor/edab011.

Nye, J S 2011, *The Future of Power,* Public Affairs, New York.

Pape, R A 2001, *Technological Sources of War and Peace: Why Structural Change Ended the Cold War Peacefully,* unpublished manuscript, University of Chicago, Chicago.

Patrikarakos, D 2017, *War in 140 Characters: How Social Media Is Reshaping Conflict in the Twenty-First Century,* Hachette, London.

Ramsey, P 2002, *The Just War: Force and Political Responsibility*, Rowman and Littlefield, Lanham, MD.

Rao, R N 2013, 'Navigating 'Truthfulness' as a Standard for Ethical Speech: Revisiting Speech in Ancient India', *China Media Research*, vol. 9, no. 1, pp. 26–33.

Rid, T 2012, 'Cyber War Will Not Take Place', *The Journal of Strategic Studies*, vol. 35, no. 1, pp. 5–32, https://doi.org/10.1080/01402390.2011.608939.

Roy, K 2021, *Hinduism and the Ethics of Warfare in South Asia: From Antiquity to the Present*, Cambridge University Press, Cambridge.

Russell, F 1977, *The Just War in the Middle Ages*, Cambridge University Press, Cambridge.

Schelling, T 1980, *The Strategy of Conflict*, Harvard University Press, Cambridge, MA.

Scheuerman, W E 2009, 'Realism and the Critique of Technology', *Cambridge Review of International Affairs*, vol. 22, no. 4, pp. 563–84, https://doi.org/10.1080/09557570903325504

Schuessler, J M 2015, *Deceit on the Road to War: Presidents, Politics, and American Democracy*, Cornell University Press, Ithaca, NY.

Stone, J 2013, 'Cyber War Will Take Place!', *The Journal of Strategic Studies*, vol. 36, no. 1, pp. 101–8, https://doi.org/10.1080/01402390.2012.730485.

Stone, M W F 2006, 'Truth, Deception, and Lies: Lessons from the Casuistical Tradition', *Tijdschrift voor Filosofie*, vol. 68, no. 1, pp. 101–31.

Walzer, M 2000, *Just and Unjust Wars,* Basic Books, New York.

Whetham, D 2016, 'Cyber Chevauchées', in F Allhoff, A Henschke & B J Strawser (eds), *Binary Bullets: The Ethics of Cyberwarfare*, Oxford University Press, Oxford, pp. 75–88.

23

GENDER IN FUTURE WARFARE

Lindsay Clark

Introduction

On the day I am writing this, thousands of men are attempting to flee Russia to avoid being drafted into service in the war against Ukraine. They are fleeing specifically because they are men. Their maleness makes them, according to the draft in Russia, appropriate individuals for soldiering. This is just one way in which warfare is gendered. It has been gendered for as long as it has been conducted, and for as long as international politics has been patriarchal (and sometimes misogynistic (Smith 1993)). If warfare has been gendered for millennia, are we likely to see a change in this in the future of warfare? What does it mean for the traditional connection between maleness (and masculinity) and soldiering that there are increasing numbers of women in armed forces and in unofficial violent groups? What about the introduction of increasingly automated and even autonomous robotic systems on the battlefield? Where does that leave men and women soldiers? What does it mean for the types of policies which result in or limit warfare in the future? These are some of the questions which this chapter aims to introduce and discuss.

It is necessary to pause here to outline what I mean by the term 'gender'. We tend to think about the category of 'man' or 'woman' as mapping onto specific biological difference: sex organs, chromosomes, hormones etc. This is generally understood (although contested) as an individual's 'sex'. Gender is related to sex but tends to be viewed as a social construction, a performance, of what society says makes a 'man' or 'woman.' This social construction often relies on individuals labelled 'men' behaving in ways that are viewed as 'masculine' and 'women' behaving in ways that are viewed as 'feminine'. Importantly these categories of male and female, man and woman, masculine and feminine are viewed as mutually exclusive (one cannot be male and female at the same time) and hierarchical (masculinity is hierarchically superior to femininity). This is not to argue that this perspective is right – feminist and queer scholarship which has successfully questioned the basis of these claims. However, the narratives about what makes a man, what makes a woman, what is feminine, what is masculine, continue to have important political, social, and cultural salience. As I have noted elsewhere, 'being a 'man' or a 'woman' is less about the body that you have and more about the 'stories' that are told' (Clark 2019). These stories enable us to make sense of the categories of gender categories, a move which is "profoundly political because it polices the ways that individuals are allowed to behave in a manner that invites violence in the case of transgression [...]" (Clark 2019, p. 38; see also Zalewski 2000; Sylvester 2002). How we articulate and understand gender also has implications for where, how and by whom warfare can be conducted.

Making men

The story of war and gender can begin with today's news of the men fleeing Russia: for example, why is it only the men? This feels self-evident, only the men are being called up to fight. But *why* are only the men being called up? War has historically and traditionally been fought by men.[1] This shows in the way we do not speak of 'male soldiers' but we do differentiate 'women soldiers' or 'female soldiers' and until recently, in states like the US and UK women were not permitted to take part the violent elements of warfare (in the USA 2015, and in the UK 2017). Whilst they might have been permitted to serve in 'gender appropriate' roles such as nursing or support work, roles which include 'closing' with the enemy (killing) have been closed in these states to women until surprisingly recently. (The situation in armed rebel groups is slightly different – and will be addressed in more detail in the section 'Where are the women?')

State-based war, then, is something which has historically been conducted by men – and this is in part because the traits associated with being a good soldier are traits which are associated with masculinity and therefore associated with individuals biologically determined as men. Demonstrating masculinity means demonstrating traits such as bravery, aggression, strength, rationality, which are also traits associated with being a good soldier or warrior – hence the connection between masculinity and the military. These traits are situated in opposition to traits associated with femininity (and therefore femaleness) – weakness, emotionality, passiveness and pacifism etc. Here, it is important to note that it is not that women cannot demonstrate masculine traits or men demonstrate feminine traits, but the connection between these traits and masculinity and femininity has a powerful disciplinary effect on individual and collective actions. For example, in military training soldiers may still be critiqued for failing by being called a 'woman' or a 'wimp'. Or if someone is tough and powerful, we say they have 'balls', connecting those traits with male genitalia. The connection between masculinity, maleness and military service has spawned its own literature into 'military masculinities' which has explored the changing but durable nature of masculinity as a core concept in the conduct of warfare (e.g. Cohn 1999; Higate 2003; Hockey 2003; Duncanson 2009; Taber 2011; Chisholm & Tidy 2017). These masculinities impact on the way soldiers (male or female) are expected to behave and feel about warfare – they play out through personal interactions (the narratives of the 'band of brothers'), through training (using gendered and sexual slurs against failing recruits) and through the use of weaponry: "carrying a gun was like having a permanent hard-on" (Grossman 2009, loc. 2333).

This masculinization of war also plays out at a macro-level beyond the individual soldier – aggressive foreign policies are deemed more masculine than peaceful ones, and because of the cultural valorisation of masculinity, masculine policies are understood as 'better' policies (Zalewski & Parpart 1998; Hooper 2001). Gendered logics and narratives therefore underpin when we go to war, why we go to war, how that war is conducted, who or what is targeted and how categories such as 'combatant,' 'enemy' and 'civilian' are constructed. Of particular interest for this chapter is the way gendered logics intersect with technologies of war – how these technologies are used, who they are used by, how their use is articulated and understood. Technological developments can affect how gender functions in war and will continue to do so as warfare develops in the future. One of the recent technological phenomena used by militaries in warfare is the drone, described by Peter Singer as "the most important weapons development since the atomic bomb" (Singer 2011, p. 10; see also Coker 2013) and this will be the technological focus for this chapter. One of the most pertinent things for thinking about the relationship between drones and gender in warfare is that conducting drone warfare does not require crew members to demonstrate a high level of physical fitness or strength. In comparison to other roles, where killing requires physical strength and interaction, these traditional masculine warrior traits are less important to successfully crewing drones than, for example, taking part in close-combat special forces operations. This means that arguments about women's comparative lack of physical strength vis-à-vis their male counterparts cannot be considered a barrier to women's inclusion in drone crews.

Where are the women?

The above subtitle reflects the ground-breaking work done by feminist IR scholar Cynthia Enloe (2010, 2000) to illuminate women's involvement in, and integral part in international politics including warfare. Women's stories are an important starting point for understanding violent conflict (Afshar & Eade 2004; D'Costa et al. 2006). Whilst women experience much of the suffering which results from warfare (Hynes 2004; Kirby 2013), this highlighting of women's perspectives is not just about women's victimhood. It is also an important way of 'talking about women's agency: "Women are capturing hostages, engaging in suicide bombings, hijacking aeroplanes, and abusing prisoners" and it is necessary to find ways of speaking about and making sense of these phenomena' (Sjoberg 2007, p. 1; see also Clark 2021; Åhäll 2012).

The involvement of women in violence, including state-sanctioned violence, such as participating in the military, remains complicated (Howard III & Prividera 2004). Even where their physical stature or strength cannot be used to argue against women's inclusion – arguments are made which focus on their sexual difference (and therefore disruptive desirability) and capacity to 'get themselves' pregnant to 'avoid deployment' (Taber 2011; Drury 2014). Whilst drone warfare can do nothing about the former, pregnancy is no longer a barrier to active drone service – and women can be and are members of armed drone crews. However, in my own interviews, the women made up such a small number that they requested gender anonymity and in journalistic accounts of female drone crews, their involvement is often sensationalized (e.g. Maurer 2015). Similarly, popular culture representations of the same demonstrate that where women's physical weakness cannot be used to suggest an unfitness for warfare then femininity's connection with emotions is mobilized (e.g. Brant 2017; for analysis see Clark 2021).

Women's participation in warfare *outside* of state militaries has a long and more nuanced history. Feminist scholarship has illuminated the range of conflicts, roles and rationales women have for joining violent non-state groups (i.e. Trisko Darden 2015; Henshaw 2016; Trisko Darden et al. 2019; Loken & Matfess, 2022). One of the key challenges this scholarship has faced is addressing the narratives that women are always reluctant warriors, coerced/forced into killing, usually for personal reasons. This research has carefully debunked these common myths and opened the door to new gender-attentive ways of understanding women's participation in violence. However, it remains important to be attentive to the work of gender, even in circumstances where men and women are apparently engaged in combat on equal footing. Cynthia Enloe notes her bafflement on reading the statement: "Now that the war is over, Esmeralda has had her IUD removed", where Esmeralda is "a Salvadoran woman who spent many of her young adult years as a guerrilla in the Farabundo Marti National Liberation Front, the FMLN" (Enloe 1993, p. 1). The end of the Cold War-induced civil war in El Salvador signalled to the men there the need to "urge" their women to "imagine her post-war life as one devoted to being a good mother" despite the fact that the post-war environment included particularly high levels of domestic violence (Enloe 1993, p. 1). Enloe's careful attention to a short statement in an article demonstrates the way women's involvement in violence, even non-state violence, is often framed as exceptional rather than a new gender-equal norm.

I am sensitive to Henshaw's claim that "scholarly research tends to perpetuate [...] the stereotype that conflict is the domain of men" (Henshaw 2016, pp. 39–40) and Trisko Darden et al.'s statement: "women's participation in armed conflict is in fact profoundly routine" (Trisko Darden et al. 2019, p. 1). I agree that empirically women are, and in some contexts always have been, part of armed conflict. However, this empirical reality is not yet reflected in the stories we tell about warfare or to make sense of warfare. Nor is it reflected in the way we interact with technology – think about the female voice of the assistant 'Alexa' in comparison to the way Arnold Schwarzenegger played the terminator. Whilst these examples might seem to exist in a different space from the war-focused debates of this chapter what they enable us to do is to consider the way in which war, even saturated with modern distancing technologies, is a profoundly social event. As social beings, the way we *make sense* of war, and the novel technologies being developed for war, remain anchored in these tenacious myths about war as a masculine/male space.

Part of the continued resistance to women in combat roles is related to an often-unacknowledged gendered logic that men are the protectors and women are the protected (analysis of the rescue of Jessica Lynch by Howard III & Prividera 2004 is useful here). In her seminal work, *Women and War*, Jean Elshtain (1995) articulates the two roles as the 'just warrior' and the 'beautiful soul' – the former, the masculine role, risking life and limb to protect the latter, who is beautiful and dutiful and therefore worthy of saving. Similarly, part of the resistance to the use of drones because they will 'feminize' the using military and result in moral deskilling, is a result of the potential for drones to disrupt this hallowed gendered logic through the absence of risk (Vallor 2013; for analysis see Clark 2019). With this is a concurrent disruption of the role of the protector, the just warrior, challenging what it means to take part in war, as the following sections explain.

Masculinity and risk

One of the benefits (from a forces protection perspective) of using armed drones is that it is possible to conduct lethal strikes whilst placing one's own forces at very little risk of physical harm. Whilst asymmetry between opposing sides in a conflict is nothing new, many scholars have argued that the 'extreme' asymmetry between the militaries currently using armed drones and their enemies is concerning (Enemark 2015; Renic 2020; Jeangène Vilmer 2021). There are ethical, legal and strategic reasons why this might be considered concerning, but of particular interest for this chapter is the gendered implications. As noted above, traditional narratives of warfare offer a clear gendered delineation between the just warrior and beautiful soul, and as part of that the just warrior is expected to risk injury or death in the performance of his role. In so doing, the just warrior demonstrates the bravery which is part of his identity, and which is part of the reason for the celebration of his role. In negating the physical risk to drone crews to such an extreme extent, these individuals do not have access to the same traditional narratives through which to make sense of their experiences of combat, including killing. Indeed, interview data collected from former drone crews indicates a complicated relationship with identities such as 'hero' and 'warrior':

There is no concept of heroism or warrior-ship in the military. All members will act to save themselves and others- that is not heroic-that is our job
Absolutely, he is an unrecognised warrior
I've never seen myself as a warrior… it's the wrong word, I don't think you can be a warrior if you're not there[2]

These quotes demonstrate the emotional and political tension around gendered terms such as 'hero' and 'warrior' at the intersection of war and new technologies.[3] Some of this tension potentially arises from the way in which the lack of risk to the drone crews repositions them within the protector/protected gendered logic, and it is this logic which stands to be further challenged because of technological developments in future war.

Gendering future drones

It is generally expected that future warfare will see increasing levels of automation, and perhaps autonomy in drones resulting in what are often referred to as lethal autonomous weapons systems (LAWS) and sometimes as 'killer robots' (Human Rights Watch 2012). For the future of warfare, the difference between automation and autonomy is important and nuanced. In an 'automated' weapons system 'predetermined parameters' will be used to 'fire automatically at a target' (Jakob Kellenberger cited in Backstrom & Henderson 2012, p. 488). In an 'autonomous system' it is possible that the system would have 'the capability of a weapon to independently identify targets and to trigger itself' (Krishnan 2009, p. 5). There is an ongoing debate regarding whether LAWS will ever be 'fully' autonomous, what it means to say a system is 'fully autonomous' and whether those systems could ever be used ethically and legally (i.e. Pagallo 2011; Sharkey 2011, 2012; Beard 2014; Sparrow 2016). However, the general consensus is that war technologies are going to gradually include more automatic and then more autonomous elements.

As part of this move towards autonomous weapons systems there have been concurrent developments in artificial intelligence (AI). AI is not the same as autonomy but AI in some measure is required for the development of autonomous systems. And it is from the perspective of AI that major policy debates are being held in the US about the development of LAWS – the current, but contested leader, in military robotics (closely challenged by China). This debate is at least partly outlined in a report delivered by the National Security Commission on Artificial Intelligence (NSCAI) published in March 2021. In this report (NSCAI 2021), the Commission outlines its hopes and fears for the future development of AI and its potential uses in military contexts. I refer to this report in this chapter as a means of illuminating some of the work that gender is doing in the development of US policy towards the development of more automated robotic systems and possible lethal autonomous weapons systems. There are three possible outcomes to this increased automation or autonomy in weapons systems as it relates to gender: (1) gender norms are disrupted, (2) gender norms are further sedimented or (3) gender norms remain the same.

If we begin with gender norms being disrupted, Donna Haraway, whilst not writing specifically about lethal autonomous robots, argued that the shift towards the use of robots had the potential to disrupt existing gender binaries and hierarchies. In her famous *Cyborg Manifesto* Haraway argues that the cyborg is a "hybrid of machine and organism, a creature of social reality as well as a creature of fiction" and importantly "The cyborg is a creature in a post-gender world […]" (Haraway 1991, pp. 149–50). Indeed, it is possible to argue that in displacing the masculinity of the frontline soldier with that of a frontline robot, LAWS have the potential to disrupt our narratives about how warfare is conducted, by whom and under what understanding.

Alternatively, Lena Moore critiques Christopher Coker (2002) for presenting the "assumption that while human beings have been interfacing with technology for centuries, if not longer, there is something exceptional about the kinds of new technologies and developments" that make them likely to disrupt gendered binaries in war in a way that preceding technological advances have not (Moore 2021, p. 8). To think about how Coker might make this assertion and why this might be problematic, it is useful to deploy Mary Manjikian's particular understanding of future war as not 'post-heroic' but rather one in which

> Future technological developments are incompatible with the hegemonic masculinist [...] because new technologies will not 'steal' the masculine role, but rather they will 'steal' the qualities of autonomy and agency away from soldiers through giving these qualities to the machinery itself.
>
> (Manjikian 2016, p.107)

My own research suggests that gender norms are very deeply sedimented and not easily disrupted by new technologies – rather, there is a tendency for potentially disruptive technologies to be co-opted by existing gendered structures. Drones have certainly made some sectors of the military uncomfortable – the lack of risk presents the possibility of being accused of cowardice (Monbiot 2012; Johnson 2014; Clark 2019), but masculinity and femininity are surprisingly resilient and adaptable concepts (Enloe 2017) – supporting the argument that gender norms will either be further sedimented or stay the same. Whilst AI and robotics might enable more women to take part in warfare without questions regarding their physical fitness (a questionable boon for womankind), the very construction of war is likely to remain highly gendered, and therefore heavily masculinized.

It therefore seems more likely LAWS, as a new actor in warfare will merely serve to replace the (masculine) human as the protector – so the binary itself remains, all that changes is who plays what role. In this situation the using troops become a feminized participant in war – their contribution to the success or otherwise of warfare may be viewed (perhaps inaccurately) as supplementary rather than essential. In this case, Manjikian argues "new technologies [...] have created a situation in which traditional 'heroic' qualities can no longer be identified in or practiced by those individual soldiers who carry out warfare" (Manjikian 2016, p. 107; see also Heyns & Borden 2017). Manjikian argues that this is because soldiers are losing some or much of their agency in warfare. Their ability to act as they choose (weighing up the possibilities, probable consequences etc.) is circumscribed by their position of relative powerlessness in comparison to technologies like drones: "it is difficult to see how a soldier might be said to be engaged in leadership or acting heroically if in many ways s/he is now "out of the loop" in a situation of conflict [...]" (Manjikian 2016, p. 117).

Similarly, when we look at the language of NSCAI report, the commission demonstrates considerable concern at the potential loss of the masculine superpower status of the US if it does not keep up with technological developments: the "US needs to reassert its masculinity through the development of LAWS and through the discussion of their use in profoundly masculine and rationalistic ways" (unpublished manuscript). Similarly, focus is turned to 'hard decisions', and 'far-sighted' 'executive' top-down leadership, in order to 'win' the AI (and autonomous weapons) race in international politics. This race, the report argues, is integral to the future of the US because LAWS equipped with AI are "the kind of discoveries for which the label 'game changing' is not a cliché" and represent "the most powerful tool for generations" and therefore: "The race to research, develop, and deploy AI and associated technologies is already intensifying strategic competition" (NSCAI 2021, pp. 1, 159). US efforts to develop AI equipped

LAWS then provide the means through which potentially displaced nationalistic masculinity can be demonstrated: the heroes will not be the side-lined soldiers but rather the "visionary technologists" (NSCAI 2021, p. 61).

I therefore agree with Heather Roff (2016) when she counters the use of Haraway's argument about the potential of the robot to change our thinking about warfare in the future. We must remember that robots are programmed by humans with all our intersectional biases – gendered, raced, classed, ableist – and this means that these robots will be programmed to be biased in their actions. Similarly, Roff argues that: "Masculine humanoid robots will be deemed ideal warfighters, while feminine humanoid robots will be tasked with research or humanitarian efforts" and therefore "Instead of using technology to free us from gendered practices and hierarchies, à la [Haraway] […] this machine will perpetuate domination and subordination" (Roff 2016, p. 1–2).

Conclusion

Warfare is, and always has been, a gendered social cultural phenomenon. Historically war has been the crucible in which men are made. Contemporary scholarship and technological advances have forced us to question whether this remains true. In response, I argue that whilst it is possible to de-centre the *man* from war (although he remains in a starring role), *masculinity* remains central to both how we understand men and how we understand war.

Despite technological progress which makes arguments about physical strength largely irrelevant, masculinity remains an integral part of the stories we tell to make sense of war. The introduction of remotely piloted drones has challenged our understandings of what it means to be a warrior – raising questions about distance, risk and bravery. However, masculinity is a persistent and malleable concept and its centrality to warfare means that these questions are being answered by gendered appeals to alternative forms of military masculinity.

I have therefore argued that future warfare is likely to follow the pattern of the preceding millennia. Even with the introduction of more automated, or even more autonomous robots within warfare challenging our understanding of hegemonic military masculinities, and even if women might be able to officially engage in a wider range of military roles, gender narratives and logics are remarkably tenacious and adaptable. The process of developing and using technology does not occur somehow outside of the social/cultural milieu in which war is also conducted, and therefore these new technologies are highly likely to be laced with either evident or subtle gendered logics to which it we must continue to attend.

LAWS have the potential to displace the male soldier as the actor in the protector/protected dynamic, but masculinity and femininity and their connection with logics such as protector/protected will likely maintain their gendered salience. Because of this, it remains essential that scholarship continues to pay close attention to the way gender and warfare intersect – because both have an important role in making the other concept meaningful. And these concepts, far from just being of scholarly use, have life and death implications for those involved in warfare.

Notes

1 This is not to say that women have not historically been involved in war, far from it, but rather that the stories we tell about war and the way we make sense of war, involve male soldiers.
2 Quotes from interview data collected by the author.
3 See, for example the debate around the awarding of medals to drone crews (Joyner 2013; Kesling 2013; Stewart 2013).

References

Afshar, H & Eade, D (eds) 2004, *Development, Women, and War: Feminist Perspectives. Development in Practice Reader*, Oxfam, Oxford.

Åhäll, L 2012, 'Motherhood, Myth and Gendered Agency in Political Violence', *International Feminist Journal of Politics*, vol. 14, no. 1, pp. 103–20, doi:10.1080/14616742.2011.619781.

Backstrom, A & Henderson, I 2012, 'New Capabilities in Warfare: An Overview of Contemporary Technological Developments and the Associated Legal and Engineering Issues in Article 36 Weapons Reviews', *International Review of the Red Cross*, vol. 94, no. 886, pp. 483–514, doi:10.1017/S1816383112000707.

Beard, J 2014, 'Autonomous Weapons and Human Responsibilities', *College of Law, Faculty Publications*, no. 196, <http://digitalcommons.unl.edu/lawfacpub/196> (accessed 22 October 2022).

Brant, G 2017, *Grounded*, Oberon Books, London.

Chisholm, A & Tidy, J 2017, 'Beyond the Hegemonic in the Study of Militaries, Masculinities, and War', *Critical Military Studies*, vol. 3, no. 2, pp. 99–102, doi:10.1080/23337486.2017.1328182.

Clark, L 2019, *Gender and Drone Warfare: A Hauntological Perspective*, Routledge, Abingdon – New York.

Clark, L C 2021, 'Delivering Life, Delivering Death: Reaper Drones, Hysteria and Maternity', *Security Dialogue*, vol. 53, no. 1, pp. 75–92, doi:10.1177/0967010621997628.

Cohn, C 1999, 'Missions, Men and Masculinities', *International Feminist Journal of Politics*, vol 1, no. 3, pp. 460–75, doi:10.1080/146167499359835.

Coker, C 2002, *Waging War Without Warriors?: The Changing Culture of Military Conflict*, Lynne Rienner, Boulder, CO.

Coker, C 2013, *Warrior Geeks: How 21st Century Technology Is Changing the Way We Fight and Think About War*, Hurst, London.

D'Costa, B D, Ackerly, B A & Stern, M et al. 2006, 'Marginalized Identity: New Frontiers of Research for IR?', in B A Ackerly, M Stern & J True (eds), *Feminist Methodologies for International Relations*, Cambridge University Press, Cambridge, pp. 129–52.

Drury, I 2014, '200 Women Troops Sent Home for Being Pregnant: MoD Won't Impose War Zone Pregnancy Tests due to "Privacy" Fears', *Daily Mail*, 16 February, <http://www.dailymail.co.uk/news/article-2560898/200-women-troops-sent-home-pregnant-MoD-wont-impose-war-zone-pregnancy-tests-privacy-fears.html> (accessed 28 August 2018).

Duncanson, C 2009, 'Forces for Good? Narratives of Military Masculinity in Peacekeeping Operations', *International Feminist Journal of Politics*, vol. 11, no. 1, pp. 63–80, doi:10.1080/14616740802567808.

Elshtain, J B 1995, *Women and war*, The University of Chicago Press, Chicago.

Enemark, C 2015, *Armed Drones and the Ethics of War: Military Virtue in a Post-Heroic Age*, Routledge, London – New York.

Enloe, C H 1993, *The Morning After: Sexual Politics at the End of the Cold War*, University of California Press, Berkeley, CA.

Enloe, C H 2000, *Bananas, Beaches and Bases: Making Feminist Sense of International Politics*, University of California Press, Berkeley, CA.

Enloe, C H 2010, *Nimo's War, Emma's War: Making Feminist Sense of the Iraq War*, University of California Press, Berkeley, CA.

Enloe, C 2017, *The Big Push: Exposing and Challenging the Persistence of Patriarchy*, Myriad Editions, Oxford.

Grossman, D 2009, *On killing: The Psychological Cost of Learning to Kill In War and Society*. rev. edn., Little, Brown and Co., New York.

Haraway, D 1991, 'A Cyborg Manifesto: Science, Technology and Socialist Feminism in the Late Twentieth Century', in D Haraway (ed), *Simians, Cyborgs and Women: The Reinvention of Nature*, Routledge, London – New York, pp. 149–81.

Henshaw, A L 2016, 'Where Women Rebel: Patterns of Women's Participation in Armed Rebel Groups 1990–2008', *International Feminist Journal of Politics*, vol. 18, no. 1, pp. 39–60, doi:10.1080/14616742.2015.1007729.

Heyns, C & Borden T 2017, 'Unmanned Weapons: Looking for the Gender Dimensions', in F Ní Aoláin, N Cahn, D F Haynes & N Valji (eds), *The Oxford Handbook of Gender and Conflict*, Oxford University Press, Oxford, pp. 376–85.

Higate, P (ed) 2003, *Military Masculinities: Identity and the State*, Praeger, Westport, CT.

Hockey, J 2003, 'No More Heroes: Masculinity in the Military', in P Higate (ed), *Military Masculinities: Identity and the State*, Praeger, Westport, CT, pp. 15–25.

Hooper, C 2001, *Manly States: Masculinities, International Relations, and Gender Politics*, Columbia University Press, New York.

Howard III, J W & Prividera, L C 2004, 'Rescuing Patriarchy or Saving "Jessica Lynch": The Rhetorical Construction of the American Woman Soldier', *Women and Language*, vol. 27, no. 2, pp. 89–97.

Human Rights Watch, 2012, *Losing Humanity: The Case Against Killer Robots*, Human Rights Watch, Amsterdam – Berlin.

Hynes, H P 2004, 'On the Battlefield of Women's Bodies: An Overview of the Harm of War to Women', *Women's Studies International Forum*, vol. 27, no. 5–6, pp. 431–45, doi:10.1016/j.wsif.2004.09.001.

Jeangène Vilmer, J-B 2021, 'Not so Remote Drone Warfare', *International Politics* (online first), doi:10.1057/s41311-021-00338-9.

Johnson, A 2014, 'ISIS to U.S.: 'Don't Be Cowards and Attack Us With Drones. . . Send Your Soldiers', *The National Review*, 8 September, <http://www.nationalreview.com/corner/384981/isis-us-dont-be-cowards-and-attack-us-drones-send-your-soldiers-andrew-johnson> (accessed 3 December 2017).

Joyner, J 2013, 'Distinguished Warfare Medal for Armchair Warriors', *Outside the Beltway*, 13 February, <http://www.outsidethebeltway.com/distinguished-warfare-medal-for-armchair-warriors/> (accessed 9 March 2015).

Kesling, B 2013, 'Combat Veterans, Senators Fight New Drone Pilot Medal', *The Wall Street Journal*, 11 March, <http://blogs.wsj.com/washwire/2013/03/11/combat-veterans-senators-fight-new-drone-pilot-medal/> (accessed 18 September 2014).

Kirby, P 2013, 'How Is Rape a Weapon of War? Feminist International Relations, Modes of Critical Explanation and the Study of Wartime Sexual Violence', *European Journal of International Relations*, vol. 19, no. 4, pp. 797–821, doi:10.1177/1354066111427614.

Krishnan, A 2009, *Killer Robots: Legality and Ethicality of Autonomous Weapons*, Ashgate, Farnham – Burlington, VT.

Loken, M & Matfess, H 2022, 'Women's Participation in Violent Non-State Organizations', in M Loken & H Matfess (eds), *Oxford Research Encyclopedia of International Studies*, Oxford University Press, Oxford, doi:10.1093/acrefore/9780190846626.013.712.

Manjikian, M 2016, 'Not All Soldiers: Hegemonic Masculinity and the Problem of Soldiers' Agency in an Age of Technological Intervention', in S Sharoni, J Welland, L Steiner & J Pedersen (eds), *Handbook on Gender and War*, Edward Elgar, Cheltenham – Northampton, MA, pp. 105–26.

Maurer, K 2015, 'She Kills People From 7,850 Miles Away', *The Daily Beast*, 18 October, <http://www.the-dailybeast.com/articles/2015/10/18/she-kills-people-from-7-850-miles-away.html> (accessed 2 February 2016).

Monbiot, G 2012, 'With its Deadly Drones, the US Is Fighting a Coward's War', *The Guardian*, 30 January, <https://www.theguardian.com/commentisfree/2012/jan/30/deadly-drones-us-cowards-war> (accessed 3 December 2017).

Moore, L 2021, *Posthuman War: Race, Gender, Technology, and the Making of U.S. Military Futures*, Cambridge University Press, Cambridge.

NSCAI 2021, 'Final Report,' *National Security Commission on Artificial Intelligence*, <https://www.nscai.gov/wp-content/uploads/2021/03/Full-Report-Digital-1.pdf> (accessed 20 December 2022).

Pagallo, U 2011, 'Robots of Just War: A Legal Perspective', *Philosophy & Technology*, vol. 24, no. 3, pp. 307–23, doi:10.1007/s13347-011-0024-9.

Renic, N C 2020, *Asymmetric Killing: Risk Avoidance, Just War, and the Warrior Ethos*, Oxford University Press, New York.

Roff, H M 2016, 'Gendering a Warbot: Gender, Sex and the Implications for the Future of War', *International Feminist Journal of Politics*, vol. 18, no. 1, pp. 1–18, doi:10.1080/14616742.2015.1094246.

Sharkey, N 2011, 'Automating Warfare: Lessons Learned from the Drones', *Journal of Law, Information & Science*, vol. 21, no. 2, pp. 140–54.

Sharkey, N E 2012, 'The Evitability of Autonomous Robot Warfare', *International Review of the Red Cross*, vol. 94, no. 886, pp. 787–99, doi:10.1017/S1816383112000732.

Singer, P W 2011, *Wired for War: The Robotics Revolution and Conflict in the 21st Century*, Penguin, New York.

Sjoberg, L 2007, 'Agency, Militarized Femininity and Enemy Others: Observations From the War in Iraq', *International Feminist Journal of Politics*, vol. 9, no. 1, pp. 82–101, doi:10.1080/14616740601066408.

Smith, J 1993, *Misogynies: Reflections on Myths and Malice*, new & rev. edn, Faber and Faber, London.

Sparrow, R 2016, 'Robots and Respect: Assessing the Case Against Autonomous Weapon Systems', *Ethics & International Affairs*, vol. 30, no. 1, pp. 93–116, doi:10.1017/S0892679415000647.

Stewart, P 2013, 'Pentagon Scraps Medal for Drone Pilots after Uproar', *Reuters*, 15 April, <http://www.reuters.com/article/2013/04/15/us-usa-pentagon-medal-idUSBRE93E12V20130415> (accessed 12 December 2022).

Sylvester, C 2002, *Feminist International Relations: An Unfinished Journey*, Cambridge University Press, Cambridge – New York.

Taber, N 2011,'"You Better Not Get Pregnant While You're Here": Tensions Between Masculinities and Femininities in Military Communities of Practice', *International Journal of Lifelong Education*, vol. 30, no. 3, pp. 331–48, doi:10.1080/02601370.2011.570871.

Trisko Darden, J 2015, 'Assessing the Significance of Women in Combat Roles', *International Journal: Canada's Journal of Global Policy Analysis*, vol. 70, no. 3, pp. 454–62, doi:10.1177/0020702015585306.

Trisko Darden, J, Henshaw, A L & Szekely, O 2019, *Insurgent Women: Female Combatants in Civil Wars*, Georgetown University Press, Washington, DC.

Vallor, S 2013, 'The Future of Military Virtue: Autonomous Systems and the Moral Deskilling of the Military', in *5th International Conference on Cyber Conflict, CYCON*, pp. 1–15.

Zalewski, M 2000, *Feminism After Postmodernism: Theorising Through Practice*, Routledge, London – New York.

Zalewski, M & Parpart, J L (eds) 1998, *The "Man Question" in International Relations*, Westview Press, Boulder, Co.

24

INTELLIGENCE AND AWARENESS

Rubén Arcos

Introduction

Even if discussing the future, including the future of conflict or warfare, may always be speculative, the following contention seems to be a safe prediction: "the competitive use of information will play a starring role in conflicts of all kinds" (Sims 2022, p. 441). This assumption about the role of intelligence in the 21st century leads to the question of how different future intelligence will be from intelligence as we know it today?

This chapter explores and discusses this question by considering intelligence mainly from a 'knowledge producer' perspective (Eriksson 2016), but also considering its counterintelligence/counterespionage and potential covert influence operations missions (see Treverton 1988; Daugherty 2006; Lowenthal 2006; Cormac 2018). Accepting that in the future, this triad of intelligence disciplines will continue to be undertaken by intelligence organizations in peace and war is an underlying assumption of the chapter.

Exploring the future of the intelligence function requires us to reduce several uncertainties connected to drivers of change (or continuity), not only in intelligence, but also associated with the future of societies which intelligence serves and the social context within which intelligence is produced. This includes, among other factors, the relative degree of competitiveness and decision advantages that intelligence will be able to provide in a digitally transformed world of big data processing and analysis of massive data and open-source information, cyber-enabled information operations, artificial intelligences, autonomous machines and decision algorithms.

The chapter holds the view that research and innovation projects for intelligence and decision-support systems will lead to new competitive edges in technological capabilities against adversaries, but that it is the combination of technological, conceptual/processual and organizational innovations that has the greater potential to produce disruptive changes in future warfare and intelligence (see Scharre 2016). These dynamic interactions of technological and doctrinal innovations, as well as organizational change in intelligence systems in response to future conflict and the strategic environment, can provide decision advantages against adversaries. Information technology and AI developments are now providing and will continue to provide support to intelligence analysts and customers for anticipating security challenges, violent conflicts and strategic early warning of crises.

DOI: 10.4324/9781003299011-29

Strategic anticipation to future conflicts and in warfare by intelligence and foresight however will very likely continue to have limits – even if assisted by supercomputing and artificial intelligence – but it is extremely unlikely that security decision-making will cease to require the support of national intelligence machineries, also in cooperation through transnational organizations and multinational frameworks.

At the same time, controlling and disrupting the adversaries' knowledge and intelligence activities is equally important. Intelligence is also about opposing and neutralizing hostile intelligence activities; and deception or stratagem (see Whaley 2007) has played and will continue to play a role in warfare, and thus needs always to be considered as a hypothesis by intelligence analysts and commanders. While intelligence deception targets intelligence analysts "through controlled human or technical collection channels", perception management activities using open channels can also have an influence on "the opinions and policies of foreign countries" and even on intelligence products (Dailey & Parker 1987, pp. xv–xx). These hostile activities can also be part of what more recently has been designated as cognitive warfare and potentially influence the thinking, decisions and actions of people (Government of Canada 2021).

Following this logic, the chapter first discusses the role of the intelligence function in peace and war and the missions of intelligence from a knowledge production perspective. It also addresses the role of armed forces or military intelligence and key reforms and developments in intelligence in recent years within NATO. Second, the chapter examines technology as a major driver of change in intelligence and shows how technological developments in the fields of artificial intelligence, machine learning and automation are called to play a key role in the future of the intelligence function. It then turns to discuss transformation processes in intelligence and tensions that can shape the future of intelligence and counterintelligence in warfare. Thirdly, the chapter elaborates on the need for adaptive intelligence functions and systems able to provide shared intelligence pictures to policymakers and commanders, while enabling the development of comprehensive approaches and responses, involving a set of stakeholders, to address future threats, conflicts and complex security phenomena. It argues that conflict will be increasingly waged in the information environment and the cognitive domain, and future warfare will permanently demand a role for intelligence and make intelligence services involved in these domains.

Intelligence as a decision support function

As a function, the purpose of intelligence is to provide situational awareness, explanations, predictions and strategic anticipation to support decision-making in peace and war. This conceptualization of intelligence under a functionalist approach can be identified in early theorizations such as the works of Harold D Lasswell (1942).

According to Francis Dvornik the origins of intelligence services can be traced back to "ancient cultural states of the Nile and the Middle East" and were triggered by the need of supporting political expansion (Dvornik 1974, p. 4). This need for intelligence drove the emergence of primitive services and nowadays is the need to know about the adversary's capabilities and intentions for offence and defense, the operating environment, the understanding of complex-decision problems, and/or advances in research, innovation and development applied to military technology. This triggers the need for intelligence and may unfold transformations in the way intelligence is produced and is organized. This need for intelligence in the future geopolitical and spatial competition, the planning and waging of operations in the different battlefields, the interpretation of signals 'exuded' (Goffman 1969) and information transmitted by hostile states on the likelihood of their future hostile actions is extremely unlikely to decline.

The 2019 National Intelligence Strategy (NIS) of the United States makes a distinction between 'foundational mission objectives' – strategic intelligence, anticipatory intelligence, and current operations intelligence – and 'topical mission objectives' – cyber threat intelligence, counterterrorism, counterproliferation and counterintelligence, including security – for the Intelligence Community (ODNI 2019, p. 7). Anticipatory intelligence was introduced as a mission objective in the 2014 iteration of the NIS. According to the 2019 NIS, "strategic intelligence is the process and product of developing the context, knowledge, and understanding of the strategic environment" for supporting national security policy-making and planning, and includes classical activities like assessing capabilities and intentions of state and non-state actors with an impact on national security, and also provides a "deep understanding of issues of enduring importance to the United States" and "in-depth assessments of trends and developments to recognize and warn of changes related to these issues that will affect the future strategic environment" (ODNI 2019, p. 8). On the other hand, anticipatory intelligence aims to "identify and assess new, emerging trends, changing conditions, and underappreciated developments to challenge long-standing assumptions, encourage new perspectives, identify new opportunities, and provide warning of threats to U.S. interests" (ODNI 2019, p. 9). It does so through foresight, forecasting and warning. Josh Kerbel, however, has emphasized on the difference between these future oriented approaches – forecasting (the future of security issues once they have already emerged), predicting, or (linearly) projecting – and proposed instead the following definition for anticipatory intelligence: "the intelligence process or practice whereby potentially emergent developments stemming from the increasingly complex security environment are foreseen via the cultivation of holistic perspectives" (Kerbel 2019). This approach understands anticipatory intelligence from a complex systems or complex adaptive systems theory (Kerbel 2020a, 2020b) and calls for applied creative thinking methods in intelligence, in addition to analytic thinking, for developing an understanding of the increasingly interconnected security environment (Kerbel 2017). A different approach to anticipatory intelligence can be found in some forecasting methods like superforecasting and crowdsourced forecasting (see Cortes, Thompson & Mandel 2021).

Military intelligence

As a product, armed forces intelligence can be seen as one of the differentiated, although not mutually exclusive, components of strategic intelligence, together with political intelligence, economic intelligence, scientific and technical intelligence among others, that is concerned mainly with providing processed and analyzed information on foreign nations' military forces as one of the key instruments of its national power to realize its strategic goals (Garst 1989). The uses of military intelligence include estimating the probable use of doctrine, strategy and tactics by foreign nations and the provision of relevant and timely products to decision-makers, planners and commanders to choose between alternative courses of action for countering military threats and conducting operations (Goldman & Maret 2016, p. 356).

As explained by Jensen, Whyte and Cuomo (2022, p. 144) "armed forces transmit, interpret, and use information to plan, organize, and apply violence in pursuit of political objectives". Military intelligence is produced in relation to armed violence, threats of military nature and operations in traditional armed conflicts, unconventional, hybrid and asymmetric warfare (Gruszczak 2016). According to the UK's intelligence machinery booklet, Defence Intelligence (DI) is part of the Ministry of Defence and conducts all-source intelligence analysis from both overt and covert sources. It provides intelligence assessments in support of policy-making, crisis management and the generation of military capability. These are used by the MOD, military commands and deployed forces, as well as other Government departments and to support the work of the Joint Intelligence Committee.

In addition to such assessments, DI collects intelligence in direct support of military operations, as well as in support of the operations of the Agencies.

(UK Government 2010)

In the United States, the Defence Intelligence Agency (DIA) explains its role within the intelligence community as the "Department of Defense combat support agency" that produces, analyzes and disseminates "military intelligence information to combat and noncombat military missions", serving "as the Nation's primary manager and producer of foreign military intelligence" and "being a central intelligence producer and manager for the secretary of defense, the Joint Chiefs of Staff and combatant commands" (DIA n.d.).

In 2017, NATO established its Joint Intelligence and Security Division (JISD) at NATO headquarters, in what was described as "the most significant reform in the history of Allied intelligence" (Freytag von Loringhoven 2017). The JISD of the International Military Staff (IMS) – the executive body that supports NATO's Military Committee (MC) role in providing military advise to the North Atlantic Council – delivers:

Intelligence support to all NATO Headquarters (HQ) elements, NATO member states and NATO Commands. It also provides strategic warning and situational awareness to all NATO HQ elements. The Division's core activities are: developing a NATO Intelligence framework, architecture and intelligence capabilities; providing customer-oriented policies and NATO Agreed Intelligence Assessments; advising on intelligence-sharing matters and conducting intelligence liaison activities.

(NATO 2022)

Other joint bodies with an analysis and advice mandate include the NATO Situation Centre and the C3 – consultation, command and control – Staff (NHQC3S) (NATO 2022).

Technology and other drivers of change for intelligence

According to Michael Herman, until the mid-19th-century intelligence was not associated with permanent government institutions and this change of status came from the new military technology of this period and its impact on command (Herman 2005, p. 2).

Technology has been, and will continue to be, a major driver of intelligence transformation for at least three main reasons: the applications of technological innovations in the field of intelligence have led to the emergence of different technical collection disciplines, or INTs (see Clark 2011) and competitive edges against adversaries; technologies have the potential to produce political, social and environmental transformations, sometimes leading to enduring changes in the security environment; they may create security vulnerabilities and opportunities for different hostile actors (the double-edged sword character).

Technologies affecting the capability of intelligence systems for fulfilling faster and better their mission objectives in peace and war constitute a strand of technology usually connected with advances in AI. They will impact intelligence by enabling the production and dissemination of analyses and assessment in a more accurate, timely and unbiased way, and by ultimately leading to informational dominance over adversaries through faster processing and exploitation of signals and overwhelming amounts of information.

A different technological strand is that affecting information security and the protection of information and secrets by breaking encryption systems (see NCSC 2020).

The 15th-anniversary logo of the Intelligence Advanced Research Projects Activity (IARPA) includes the tagline: "creating advantage through research and technology". IARPA sponsors innovative research on different areas in support of the United States Intelligence Community, including research in the areas of "artificial intelligence, quantum computing, machine learning and synthetic biology" (IARPA n.d. a). IARPA's mission statement highlights that it "does not have an operational mission and does not deploy technologies directly to the field" but facilitates "the transition of research results to our IC customers for operational application" (IARPA n.d. b).

New research and technologies applied to intelligence collection and analysis usually come associated as well with ethical concerns of different kind. With this regard, the "Artificial Intelligence Ethics Framework for the Intelligence Community" was released to provide an ethical compass to stakeholders in the intelligence community when adopting AI systems. The document is structured and provides a guide on ten issues with their associated key questions. For example, for the topical issue "Human Judgment and Accountability" an associated critical question is: "Given the purpose of the AI and potential consequences of its use, at what points, if any, are a human required as part of the decision process?"; for the topical issue "Mitigating Undesired Bias and Ensuring Objectivity," a key question is: "Do you know or can you learn what types of bias exist in the training data (statistical, contextual, historical, or other)?" (ODNI 2020, pp. 3–4).

Other than ethical aspects, applications of AI and machine learning bring a different set of questions associated with their effectiveness in providing information and decision-making advantages, which is particularly relevant in early stage innovations. A report of the Rand Corporation entitled "Evaluating the Effectiveness of Artificial Intelligence Systems in Intelligence Analysis" addressed the question: "How are AI system measures of performance connected with effectiveness in intelligence analysis?" and introduced a taxonomy of functional categories of these AI systems associated with the intelligence process for analyzing "how errors in AI system output for each of these functions might propagate to produce consequences" (Ish, Ettinger & Ferris 2001). The functional categories considered are: support to intelligence analysis through "automated analysis" of data (without human supervision), support to information collection, "information prioritization" and "evaluation support" (Ish, Ettinger & Ferris 2001, pp. 31–2).

Similarly, a different set of concerns are those associated with the vulnerabilities of AI systems to attacks and intentional disruptions by adversaries. For some experts, the next revolution (in Kuhnian sense of the term) in intelligence affairs will have machines not only in supporting roles for augmenting collection and analysis capabilities, but also as "intelligence consumers, decision-makers, and even targets of other machine intelligence operations" (Vinci 2020).

Transformation processes and tensions

Discussing over a decade ago on the future of intelligence, Wilhelm Agrell identified six processes of change for intelligence in the 21st century: (1) decreasing relevance of the dominant foreign intelligence/domestic intelligence divide; (2) new fields of knowledge with a relevance for intelligence; (3) lessening of exclusive sources and methods as top-of-mind intelligence capability due to the open-source revolution; (4) rise of new players producing and consuming intelligence;

(5) loss of intelligence institutions monopoly; and (6) information verification and knowledge validation vs information collection as the primary intelligence task (Agrell 2012, pp. 131–2).

Global connectivity and interdependence, digital transformation and communicative overabundance enabled by new information technologies and the emergence of the cyberspace "as a domain of operations" (NATO 2016) are certainly behind these transformation processes. Moreover, as stated in NATO's Secretary General Annual Report,

> Hostile powers do not have to take to the battlefield to inflict damage on their adversaries. They can make political and strategic gains in other ways, such as spreading disinformation, launching cyber-attacks, and using deception and sabotage. These hybrid or grey zone activities blur the line between peace and war and are used to destabilize and undermine affected countries.
>
> (NATO 2020a, p. 29)

Western democracies and societies have demonstrated their intrinsic vulnerabilities to foreign information manipulations and interference, but have also progressively developed different counter measures and responses; public opinions have been targeted in different countries by hostile powers showing how information and the digital communication environment can be weaponized by exploiting societal, political or economic vulnerabilities through disinformation.

Acts of Russian aggression against Ukraine have also triggered the release of 'public intelligence' (Dylan 2022) and military 'intelligence updates' by the UK Ministry of Defence through its Twitter account (Adam 2022). Even if in the war in Ukraine adversaries have engaged in predominantly conventional warfare, it is worth highlighting the extraordinarily important role of US and allied intelligence assistance to the Ukrainian forces. This shows that even 'primitive' forms of warfare require the dissemination of reliable intelligence (see Milanovic 2022).

Russian actions against Ukraine have also indicated that civilians can be targeted by authoritarian states not only through hybrid tactics, but also through deliberate violence aimed at civilian populations in the event of a war with the Russian Federation (Anthony 2022, p. 1).

We agree with Paul Scharre on the different contest that will continue to shape the future of warfare, and on those of them more probably related to intelligence and counterintelligence activities: *Hiding vs Finding; Understanding vs Confusion; Speed of Action vs Speed of Decision-Making; Shaping the Perceptions of Key Populations* (Scharre 2016, p. 22). Regarding the hiding vs finding challenge, Scharre argues that by leveraging the computing processing power "to sift through noise to detect objects, including synthesizing information gained from multiple active or passive sensors" the efforts of "those seeking to hide" will be increasingly difficult "because they must conceal their signature or actively deceive the enemy in multiple directions at once and potentially against multiple methods of detection" (Scharre 2016, p. 23). In the case of understanding versus confusion, the contest will be affected by technologies like AI for processing information on the battlefield and providing understanding against the adversaries' attempts to deceive and produce confusion through denial and deception (Scharre 2016, p. 24). The Federal Bureau of Investigation (FBI) warned on the use of AI-generated forgeries (deepfakes) in influence operations by foreign actors (FBI 2021) and researchers have discussed on their potential for military deception in 'ambiguity-increasing' operations (Geist & Blumenthal 2019).

Regarding the tensions speed of decision-making/speed of action, Scharre discussed the impact of different automation technologies and autonomous systems and the role of human vs machine decision-making, under the following logic:

Understanding the battlefield and reacting faster than the enemy can help in achieving a decisive edge over one's adversary, forcing the enemy to confront a shifting, confusing chaotic landscape. In recent times, this has been instantiated in the American military concept of an 'observe, orient, decide, act' (OODA) loop, where adversaries compete to complete this cycle faster than the enemy, thus changing the battle's conditions before the enemy can understand the situation and effectively respond.

(Scharre 2016, pp. 26–8)

Developments in AI and automation will certainly have an impact on the pace in which understanding is facilitated and warnings are provided by intelligence systems, conducting to headed decisions and actions.

The future of the intelligence function in the holistic whole-of-government, whole-of-society security paradigm

Discussing the need-to-know principle, General Stanley McChrystal reminded its basic underlaying assumption that some entity, being it a senior manager, state bureaucracy or an algorithm, really knows who does or does not need to know which pieces of information, and that is precisely this logic what might prevent the intelligence function to fulfill its mission with effectiveness:

> The organizational structures we had developed in the name of secrecy and efficiency actively prevented us from talking to each other and assembling a full picture [...] Functioning safely in an interdependent environment requires that every team possess a holistic understanding of the interaction between all the moving parts. Everyone has to see the system in its entirety for the plan to work.

(McChrystal et al. 2019, p. 141)

As stated by Gregory Treverton, the intelligence target, the 'threat', can cover a range in a spectrum with "those threats that come with threateners attached, people who mean us harm", at one end, and "threats without threateners" at the other end, that result from a set of individual actions with aggregated effects or from the interdependencies of different phenomena (Treverton 2009, pp. 143–4). That is to say, threats can stretch from foreign state threats, criminal and terrorist organizations, to pandemics coupled with infodemics or anthropogenic climate change. The intelligence issue is completely different (a secret, a mystery or a complexity) and will require different intelligence approaches and products to reduce uncertainty and address the threat (see Treverton 2014).

NATO has acknowledged that military means and responses are not currently enough to address some of the threats and challenges of the complex security environment, including the promotion of stability, the fight against terrorism and countering hybrid threats, calling for a comprehensive approach that includes also political and civilian instruments (NATO 2022b). Regarding hybrid warfare/threats, the preparedness pillar of NATO's strategy for countering hybrid warfare includes intelligence capabilities within the Joint Intelligence and Security Division for understanding, detection, and attribution of hybrid activities (NATO 2018). The response to hybrid threats has also driven and strengthen EU-NATO cooperation since the July 2016 Joint Declaration which identified an urgent need to "boost our ability to counter hybrid threats, including by bolstering resilience, working together on analysis, prevention, and early detection, through timely information sharing and, to the extent possible, intelligence sharing between staffs; and cooperating on strategic communication and response" (Tusk, Juncker & Stoltenberg 2016).

Understanding and addressing complex security phenomena, conventional and hybrid warfare/threats require intelligence functions and intelligence systems able to provide strategic anticipation to decision-makers and enable the development of comprehensive responses increasingly involving a set of different key stakeholders. However, while holistic, whole-of-government and whole-of-society responses, are generally accepted and prescribed, their realization similarly requires, adaptative, strategic information and intelligence systems in place able to facilitate the emergence of a "shared picture of the target" (Clark 2004, p. 17) between stakeholders within the intelligence community and also engaging those external stakeholders that should be involved in the response (Smith, Arcos & Lebrun 2021).

Information warfare and intelligence support to strategic engagement and communications

It is a fact that digitalization and new technologies have created opportunities for adversaries to conduct hostile activities in the information domain through disinformation and information manipulations, presenting challenges to intelligence anticipation, and emergent technologies will come associated with new security challenges as well. Protecting societies against cognitive warfare, perception management and unacknowledged interference activities will permanently demand a role for intelligence and make intelligence services involved in a constant struggle with potential adversaries in order to prevail in the information domain.

Societies have been experiencing an information revolution and intelligence services, similar to other organizations in government, are undertaking a digital transformation. Conflict is waged not only in physical environments but increasingly in the infosphere – as illustrated by the exploitation of the COVID-19 pandemic by state and non-state actors through disinformation aimed at deepening divisions within Western societies and NATO Allied nations (NATO 2020b) – and political and military authorities need assessments and warning on threats in this domain of the strategic environment. We believe that the information domain will have an increasingly key role in future warfare requiring intelligence to provide understanding and anticipation against adversaries.

As we have argued before, since humans make decisions based on our representations about the world emanating either from experience or from the information available through interpersonal symbolic interactions and through the different media – we cannot acquire direct experience on each and one of every international events and political development, and necessarily rely in the symbolic content transmitted by others – information can be weaponized or disseminated with a manipulative purpose for influencing our beliefs, understanding, attitudes or orientation toward objects (with positive or negative valence) and behaviors (Arcos & Smith 2021).

Digitalization and the information revolution have produced an information environment that have transformed our societies and practices on the production, dissemination and consumption of symbolic content, with the effect of creating opportunities for adversaries to influence civilian populations of foreign countries through perception management, reflexive control and disinformation. As a concept, information warfare is problematic, since information can be instrumentalized against and adversary, or for the conduct of warfare, in distinct forms (psy-ops based on intelligence and counterintelligence operations, cyber activities and others), activities and against different targets (military commanders, computer systems, intelligence systems, civilians); it involves "the protection, manipulation, degradation, and denial of information" (Libicki 1995, p. x).

In recent years, the term information warfare has been used frequently in the sense of weaponization of symbolic content through statements, (fake) news stories, images, memes, audios, videos and synthetic content (deepfakes). The European Parliament in a resolution of 1 March 2022 on the Russian military aggression against Ukraine condemned "the use of information warfare by Russian authorities, state media and proxies to create division with denigrating content and false narratives about the EU, NATO and Ukraine, with the aim of creating plausible deniability for the Russian atrocities" (European Parliament 2022, point 31), and the Council of the EU prohibited operators to broadcast, facilitate or contribute to broadcast, any content by RT and Sputnik and suspended any broadcasting license previously granted. RT and Sputnik are considered propaganda machines targeting civil society and "essential and instrumental in bringing forward and supporting the aggression against Ukraine, and for the destabilization of its neighboring countries" (Council of the EU 2022).

The information environment requires citizens, as consumers, creators and disseminators of information, content and opinion, to have competence in evaluating the reliability and competence of sources, distinguish between evidence and judgment, to be better equipped against hostile influence and interference through information. Computer-mediated communications, digital media and foreign information manipulations require civilians as citizens to be equipped with knowledge and skills, "traditionally associated with practitioners in the fields of security and intelligence" (Ivan, Chiru & Arcos 2021, p. 501) to understand the threat environment and build more resilient societies against old and new forms of information manipulations. This can be done by intelligence communities through openness policies and strategies (Díaz-Fernández & Arcos 2021), education programs, and interventions through engagement with key stakeholders in academia, industry, media, and public administration, aimed at building awareness on forms of foreign interference and covert influence (Ivan, Chiru & Arcos 2021).

At the same time, strategic communications require a supporting intelligence function across the communication process assessing future vulnerabilities likely to be exploited by disinformation and hostile narratives, informing though analyses effective counter-narratives, and providing support to other deterrence by denial efforts for countering future forms of disinformation (NATO 2020) that will capitalize on advances in AI and automation. AI has the potential to support the tracking of content flows across the information environment, where information originates from and is spread across different channels, by which actors, and support forensics by practitioners on potential uses of synthetic contents as documentary evidence in information warfare.

Conclusion

Intelligence is experiencing different developments that affect the whole intelligence process. Technologies like artificial intelligence and automation have the potential to transform the intelligence enterprise in the future in revolutionary ways and keep political authorities, military commanders and tactical units permanently informed on ongoing developments, providing them with predictions and statistical information on chances of success and failure of potential courses of action.

Data processing speed and intelligence communication speed, higher accuracy of intelligence judgments by mitigating human bias and errors can provide competitive advantages and reduce uncertainties, but not the elimination of uncertainty.

Traditional collection disciplines like HUMINT will not cease to be relevant for acquiring access to secret pieces of information, providing understanding on intelligence targets and contrasting the output or adding context to those pieces obtained from technical disciplines.

Future warfare will probably require a revolution in counterintelligence and security and the adaptation of capabilities and doctrines to neutralize enhanced intelligence systems by AI, machine learning and automation.

The expression of conflict in the information domain is acquiring an enduring character, and there is no reason to believe that hostile powers will cease to exploit in the future opportunities and the intrinsic vulnerabilities of democratic societies through disinformation and propaganda to divide societies and erode relationships between military allies, including by conducting covert influence activities through intelligence organizations. Intelligence and awareness will continue to be critical against future cognitive warfare operations of adversaries.

References

Adam, K 2022, 'How U.K. Intelligence Came to Tweet the Lowdown on the War in Ukraine', *The Washington Post*, 22 April, <https://www.washingtonpost.com/world/2022/04/22/how-uk-intelligence-came-tweet-lowdown-war-ukraine/> (accessed 6 December 2022).

Agrell, W 2012, 'The Next 100 Years? Reflections on the Future of Intelligence', *Intelligence and National Security*, vol. 27, no. 1, pp. 118–32, https://doi.org/10.1080/02684527.2012.621601.

Anthony, I 2022, 'An Ethical Response to An Unethical Adversary', *NDC Policy Brief*, no. 16, <https://www.ndc.nato.int/news/news.php?icode=1744> (accessed 6 December 2022).

Arcos, R & Smith, H 2021, 'Digital Communication and Hybrid Threats', *ICONO 14*, vol. 19, no. 1, pp. 1–14, https://doi.org/10.7195/ri14.v19i1.1662.

Clark, R M 2004, *Intelligence Analysis: A Target-Centric Approach*, CQ Press, Washington, DC.

Clark, R M 2011, *The Technical Collection of Intelligence*, CQ Press, Washington, DC.

Cormac, R 2018, *Disrupt and Deny: Spies, Special Forces, and the Secret Pursuit of British Foreign Policy*, Kindle edn, Oxford University Press, Oxford.

Cortes, K, Thompson, M & Mandel, D 2021, 'Report on the 2021 Anticipatory Intelligence Workshop', *Defence Research and Development Canada*, Contract Report DRDC-RDDC-2021-C302, <https://cradpdf.drdc-rddc.gc.ca/PDFS/unc379/p814106_A1b.pdf> (accessed 1 November 2022).

Council of the EU 2022, *Council Decision (CFSP) 2022/351 of 1 March 2022 Amending Decision 2014/512/CFSP Concerning Restrictive Measures in View of Russia's Actions Destabilising the Situation in Ukraine*, <https://eur-lex.europa.eu/eli/dec/2022/351> (accessed 1 November 2022).

Dailey, B D & Parker, P J (eds) 1987, *Soviet Strategic Deception*, D.C. Heath & Company, Lexington, MA & Toronto.

Daugherty, W J 2006, *Executive Secrets: Covert Action and the Presidency*, The University Press of Kentucky, Lexington, KY.

DIA n.d. *What Does DIA Do?*, <https://www.dia.mil/About/FAQs/> (accessed 1 November 2022).

Díaz-Fernández, A M & Arcos, R 2021, 'A Framework for Understanding the Strategies of Openness of the Intelligence Services', *The International Journal of Intelligence, Security, and Public Affairs*, vol. 23, no. 3, pp. 259–80, https://doi.org/10.1080/23800992.2021.2010365.

Dvornik, F 1974, *Origins of Intelligence Services: The Ancient Near East, Persia, Greece, Rome, Byzantium, the Arab Muslim Empires, the Mongol Empire, China, Muscovy*, Rutgers University Press, New Brunswick, NJ.

Dylan, H 2022, *How Has Public Intelligence Transformed the Way This War Has Been Reported?*, 1 March, <https://www.kcl.ac.uk/how-has-public-intelligence-transformed-the-way-this-war-has-been-reported> (accessed 6 December 2022).

Eriksson, G 2016, *Swedish Military Intelligence. Producing Knowledge*, Edinburgh University Press, Edinburgh.

European Parliament 2022, *European Parliament Resolution of 1 March 2022 on the Russian Aggression Against Ukraine (2022/2564(RSP))*, <https://eur-lex.europa.eu/legal-content/EN/TXT/PDF/?uri=CELEX:52022IP0052&from=GA> (accessed 1 November 2022).

FBI 2021, *Private Industry Notification 210310-001*, 10 March, <https://www.ic3.gov/Media/News/2021/210310-2.pdf> (accessed 1 November 2022).

Freytag von Loringhoven, A 2017, 'Adapting NATO Intelligence in Support of "One NATO', *NATO Review*, 8 September, <https://www.nato.int/docu/review/articles/2017/09/08/adapting-nato-intelligence-in-support-of-one-nato/index.html> (accessed 6 December 2022).

Garst, R D 1989, 'Components of Intelligence', in R D Garst (ed), *A Handbook of Intelligence Analysis*, Defence Intelligence College, Washington, DC, pp. 1–31.

Geist, E & Blumenthal, M 2019, 'Commentary: Military Deception: AI's Killer App?', *War on the Rocks*, 23 October, <https://warontherocks.com/2019/10/military-deception-ais-killer-app/>, (accessed 6 December 2022).

Goffman, E 1969, *Strategic Interaction*, University of Pennsylvania Press, Philadelphia, PA.

Goldman, J & Maret, S 2016, *Intelligence and Information Policy for National Security: Key Terms and Concepts*, Rowman & Littlefield, Lanham, MD.

Government of Canada 2021, 'The Invisible Threat: Tools for Countering Cognitive Warfare', *Fall 2021 NATO Innovation Challenge*, <https://www.canada.ca/en/department-national-defence/campaigns/fall-2021-nato-innovation-challenge.html> (accessed 17 December 2022).

Gruszczak, A 2016, *Intelligence Security in the European Union: Building a Strategic Intelligence Community*, Palgrave Macmillan, London & New York.

Herman, M 2005, *Intelligence Power in Peace and War*, Cambridge University Press, Cambridge.

IARPA n.d. a, *Research Programs*, <https://www.iarpa.gov/research-programs> (accessed 1 November 2022).

IARPA n.d. b, *About IARPA*, <https://www.iarpa.gov/who-we-are/about-us> (accessed 1 November 2022).

Ish, D, Ettinger, J & Ferris, C 2021, *Evaluating the Effectiveness of Artificial Intelligence Systems in Intelligence Analysis*, RAND Corporation, Santa Monica, CA, <https://www.rand.org/pubs/research_reports/RRA464-1.html> (accessed 1 November 2022).

Ivan, C, Chiru, I & Arcos, R 2021, 'A Whole of Society Intelligence Approach: Critical Reassessment of the Tools and Means used to Counter Information Warfare in the Digital Age', *Intelligence and National Security*, vol. 36, no. 4, pp. 495–511, https://doi.org/10.1080/02684527.2021.1893072.

Jensen, B J, Whyte, C & Scott, C 2022, *Information in War: Military Innovation, Battle Networks, and the Future of Artificial Intelligence*, Kindle edn, Georgetown University Press, Washington, DC.

Kerbel, J 2017, 'Are the Analytic Tradecraft Standards Hurting as Much as Helping?', *Research Shorts*, 14 September, <https://ni-u.edu/wp/wp-content/uploads/2021/08/NIU-ShortKerbel1.pdf> (accessed 1 November 2022).

Kerbel, J 2019, 'Commentary: Coming to Terms with Anticipatory Intelligence', *War on the Rocks*, 13 August, <https://warontherocks.com/2019/08/coming-to-terms-with-anticipatory-intelligence/> (accessed 1 November 2022).

Kerbel, J 2020a, 'Anticipatory Intelligence and Adaptive Influence: A New Paradigm for Foreign Policy Development', *Research Shorts*, 10 July, https://ni-u.edu/wp/wp-content/uploads/2021/09/NIUShort_07102020_20C_167.pdf> (accessed 1 November 2022).

Kerbel, J 2020b, 'Complexity, COVID, and the Failure of Strategic Incrementalism', *Research Shorts*, 1 October, <https://ni-u.edu/wp/wp-content/uploads/2021/09/NIUShort_10012020_20C304.pdf> (accessed 1 November 2022).

Lasswell, H D 1942, 'The Relation of Ideological Intelligence to Public Policy', *Ethics*, vol. 53, no. 1, pp. 25–34.

Lowenthal, M M 2006, *Intelligence: From Secrets to Policy*, 3rd edn, CQ Press, Washington, DC.

Libicki, M C 1995, *What Is Information Warfare?*, Institute for National Strategic Studies, National Defense University, Washington DC, <https://apps.dtic.mil/sti/pdfs/ADA367662.pdf> (accessed 1 November 2022).

Milanovic, M 2022, 'The United States and Allies Sharing Intelligence with Ukraine', *EJIL: Talk! Blog of the European Journal of International Law*, 9 May, <https://www.ejiltalk.org/the-united-states-and-allies-sharing-intelligence-with-ukraine/> (accessed 17 December 2022).

McChrystal, S with Collins, T, Silverman, D & Fussell, C 2019, *Team of Teams. New Rules of Engagement for a Complex World*, Kindle edn, Penguin Books, New York.

NATO 2016, *Warsaw Summit Communiqué Issued by the Heads of State and Government participating in the meeting of the North Atlantic Council in Warsaw*, 8–9 July 2016, <https://www.nato.int/cps/en/natohq/official_texts_133169.htm> (accessed 1 November 2022).

NATO 2018, *NATO Encyclopedia 2018*, NATO Public Diplomacy Division, Brussels, <https://www.nato.int/nato_static_fl2014/assets/pdf/pdf_2019_02/20190211_2018-nato-encyclopedia-eng.pdf> (accessed 1 November 2022).

NATO 2020a, *The Secretary General Annual Report 2019*, <https://www.nato.int/nato_static_fl2014/assets/pdf/2020/3/pdf_publications/sgar19-en.pdf> (accessed 6 December 2022).

NATO 2020b, *NATO's Approach to Countering Disinformation: A Focus on COVID-19*, <https://www.nato.int/cps/en/natohq/177273.htm> (accessed 6 December 2022).

NATO 2022a, *International Military Staff*, <https://www.nato.int/cps/en/natohq/topics_64557.htm> (accessed 6 December 2022).

NATO 2022b, *A "Comprehensive Approach" to Crises*, <https://www.nato.int/cps/en/natohq/topics_51633.htm> (accessed 1 November 2022).

NCSC 2020, 'Preparing for Quantum-Safe Cryptography', *National Cyber Security Centre*, <https://www.ncsc.gov.uk/pdfs/whitepaper/preparing-for-quantum-safe-cryptography.pdf> (accessed 1 November 2022).

ODNI 2019, *The National Intelligence Strategy of the United States of America 2019*, <https://www.dni.gov/files/ODNI/documents/National_Intelligence_Strategy_2019.pdf?utm_source=Press%20Release&utm_medium=Email&utm_campaign=NIS_2019> (accessed 1 November 2022).

ODNI 2020, *Artificial Intelligence Ethics Framework for the Intelligence Community*, v. 1.0 as of June 2020, <https://www.intelligence.gov/images/AI/AI_Ethics_Framework_for_the_Intelligence_Community_1.0.pdf> (accessed 1 November 2022).

Scharre, P 2016, 'Disruptive Change in Warfare', in *The Future of Warfare. Hearing Before the Committee on Armed Services United States Senate, One Hundred Fourteenth Congress, First Session,* November 3, 2015, US Government Printing Office, Washington, DC, pp. 19–30, <https://www.govinfo.gov/content/pkg/CHRG-114shrg99570/pdf/CHRG-114shrg99570.pdf> (accessed 19 September 2022).

Sims, J E 2022, *Decision Advantage: Intelligence in International Politics from the Spanish Armada to Cyberwar*, Kindle edn, Oxford University Press, New York.

Smith, H, Arcos, R & Lebrun, M 2021. Intelligence and Information: The Challenge of Hybrid Threats. *International Journal of Intelligence and Counterintelligence* (not published yet).

Treverton, G F 1988, *Covert Action: The CIA and the Limits of American Intervention in the Postwar World*, I. B. Tauris, London.

Treverton, G F 2009, 'Approaching Threat Convergence from An Intelligence Perspective', in M Ranstorp & M Normark (eds), *Unconventional Weapons and International Terrorism Challenges and New Approaches*, Kindle edn, Routledge, London & New York, pp. 141–62.

Treverton, G F 2014, 'The Future of Intelligence: Changing Threats, Evolving Methods', in I Duyvesteyn, B de Jong & J van Reijn (eds), *The Future of Intelligence: Challenges in the 21st Century*, Routledge, London & New York, pp. 27–38.

Tusk, D, Juncker, J-C & Stoltenberg, J 2016, *Joint Declaration by the President of the European Council, the President of the European Commission, and the Secretary General of the North Atlantic Treaty Organization*, 8 July 2016, <https://www.nato.int/nato_static_fl2014/assets/pdf/pdf_2016_07/20160708_160708-joint-NATO-EU-declaration.pdf> (accessed 17 December 2022).

UK Government 2010, *National Intelligence Machinery*, <https://assets.publishing.service.gov.uk/government/uploads/system/uploads/attachment_data/file/61808/nim-november2010.pdf> (accessed 1 November 2022).

Vinci, A 2020, 'The Coming Revolution in Intelligence Affairs: How Artificial Intelligence and Autonomous Systems Will Transform Espionage', *Foreign Affairs*, 31 August, <https://www.foreignaffairs.com/articles/north-america/2020-08-31/coming-revolution-intelligence-affairs> (accessed 1 November 2022).

Whaley, B 2007, *Stratagem: Deception and Surprise in War*, Artech House, Boston, MA & London.

25

CRIMINALITY AND DELINQUENCY

The Impact on Regional and Global Security

Daniela Irrera

Introduction

The study of warfare has always attracted the interest of scholars of political science and was predominantly deepened within the International Relations (IR) community. Irregular warfare and the use of violence by actors that differ from traditional ones, such as organised crime groups, as well as the assessment of the impact of various forms of criminality represent a more innovative and fascinating research trend that deserves greater consideration.

Coherent with the aims of the Handbook, this chapter focuses on how crime and delinquency may shape the future of warfare and amplify those tendencies that indicate an increasing relevance of criminal violence for armed confrontation and warfighting. Such intersections can be considered part of the differentiation and complexity of the domain of warfare and contribute to explaining its changeable structure.

The scholarly debate about the nexus between terrorism and organised crime can provide an insightful starting point. This nexus can be perceived as a strategic alliance of two influential non-state actors, able to exploit illegal markets and profit from the instability produced by failed and weak states, or civil and proxy wars, for their respective purposes. The ability of criminal networks to progressively increase their performance and interact with other subversive non-state actors that violently oppose the state (such as insurgents and paramilitaries) needs to be evaluated within a broader and comprehensive theoretical framework. To do so, this chapter seeks to answer the following questions: Does the use of violence by organised crime represent a consolidated threat rather than a contingent and temporary practice? Are regional variations relevant? What impact does this have on global and regional countermeasures?

The chapter is divided into three parts. First, the state of the art on the crime-terror nexus is discussed. Second, this nexus is analysed against additional threats, represented by insurgency, armed conflicts and political instability. In the final part, the focus shifts to the use of violence by organised crime groups, analysing major developments and recent trends.

Relations between organised crime, terrorism and insurgency

The literature on irregular warfare has focused on definitions but also on the assessment of the actors involved (Gray 2007; Olson 2009; Rogers 2016; Sheehan, Marquardt & Collins 2022).

DOI: 10.4324/9781003299011-31

Most investigations have shed light on the link between military organisations, tactics and combat performances, focusing on non-state armed groups challenging states (Ucko & Marks 2020). The political identity of the combatants, their objectives and the implications produced on security still require further research. The extent to which violence – associated with any subversive activities – is employed under a specific agenda and tactic needs a deeper investigation.

Over time, studies of the crime-terror nexus have consolidated within the IR scholarly community, producing theoretical and empirical insights and resulting in fascinating, if at times ambiguous, understanding (Dishman 2005; Ljujic, van Prooijen & Weerman 2017; Felbab-Brown 2019; Makarenko 2021).

This nexus connects two very different actors, each with distinct identities, aims and methods, who may sometimes share common grounds and objectives. The most relevant investigations have analysed how their different nature – mainly entrepreneurial for criminals and political for terrorists – may converge and produce various forms of connection. After the Cold War, particularly during the 1990s, both terrorist and organised crime groups changed their agendas and strategies following technological advancements and the expanded transnational dimensions of illicit markets (Makarenko 2000, 2004, 2009; Wang 2010). Makarenko particularly focused on the process through which such factors exerted an impact on the nature of subversive actors. A criminal or terrorist group can start adopting the tactics of the other for achieving a mutual benefit; it can proceed with the appropriation of those methods or tactics producing the merging of a criminal and terror group in a functional alliance; and finally, it can lead to an evolution through which the tactics and motivations of one entity can be transformed by the other. All different phases may be placed along a *continuum* and describe a variety of graduations, which depend on different conditions and causes (Makarenko 2004).

As has been observed, terrorists and criminals may cooperate for opportunistic reasons, for mutual profit and convenience, without necessarily producing (or requiring) a change in attitudes and nature (Williams 2002). Separating the nature from the performance may make the overall analysis of the nexus clearer. As for the nature, although there are several official or semi-official definitions of terrorism and organised crime provided by policymakers, practitioners and academics, they do not always catch all aspects of their identity and transformations.

Terrorist groups have been defined with respect to their identities and their violent features. They primarily seek to induce fear among the public, targeting innocent civilians or agents of the state, the military or political life more generally. According to Martin and Weinberg (2016), however, this definition is too restrictive, as terrorism is rather a multi-layered actor, made of different components, in which violence complements those acts aimed at producing political change.

An organised criminal group is defined in the United Nations Convention Against Transnational Organised Crime as a structured actor in which several persons exist for a period of time and act in concert, with the aim of committing one or more serious crimes or offences to obtain, directly or indirectly, financial or other material benefits (UN Convention 2000, art. 2). It is commonly associated with illegal activities that have as their preponderant purpose the accumulation of money or valuable material resources, although distinctions employed by criminology –corporate crime, blue-collar and white-collar crime – are less relevant when it comes to the analysis of the nexus.

Organised crime groups have also been investigated with respect to security threats. They may have a clandestine component, but can also appear more legitimised and supported by local communities because of the tangible benefits they can provide. In so doing, they are deeply political in their activities and benefit from the state's weakness and vulnerability. Analysis of the performance requires shifting the focus towards the use of violence and criminal tactics. The above-mentioned definitions have been employed for distinguishing terrorists from other non-state armed groups, such as paramilitary groups or private military companies (PMCs) employed by states for providing security services (Sullivan & Bunker 2005; Jones & Johnston 2013).

Following the transnational expansion of markets and services offered by the cyber environment, terrorist groups have adopted new structural forms, which are often very similar to those of organised crime syndicates. During the Cold War, terrorist organisations were composed of several individuals belonging to an identifiable organisation with a clear command and control structure, such as the Irish Republican Army (IRA) or the Basque separatist group ETA. By contrast, modern terrorist groups, such as al-Qaeda and the Islamic State (IS), seem to be sophisticated networks that combine mostly autonomous cells and structures (Hutchinson & O'Malley 2007). These terrorist groups are also more likely to engage in crimes such as drug smuggling, money laundering, theft, extortion and prostitution, although they do not consider themselves common criminals (Hoffman 2006; Hamm 2007).

Drug trafficking is definitively the largest source of income for both organised crime groups and terrorists, alongside robberies, extortion, kidnapping, arms trading and smuggling. However, such activities require extensive organisational capabilities and are likely to be engaged in by more organised terrorist groups rather than by individuals or stand-alone cells. To expand, terrorist groups may acquire expertise in conventional criminality that sometimes transcends their original political goal. Violent political groups who cease their operations, moreover, may find at their disposal not only unlawful expertise and skills, but also arms and infrastructures, and after the dismissal of their organisation may use what they possess to start a career in criminal markets (Hamm 2007; Hutchinson & O'Malley 2007).

Changes in nature and performance are therefore relevant for understanding not only how terrorists and criminals interact, but also for identifying connections with other actors, such as insurgents, in particularly troubled and conflictual environments.

From the nexus to several nexuses

Scholars in the fields of criminology and IR have contributed to a deeper understanding of the nexus as a security threat, but further research is still necessary on the different forms that this nexus may assume (Carrapico, Irrera & Tupman 2014).

Paoli and Fijnaut offered a tripartite conceptualisation of the crime-terror nexus, which includes three types of (a) interaction; (b) transformation/imitation and (c) similarities. For each type, they singled out different potential categories, going from zero (no interaction, transformation or similarity) to one (fusion, full transformation or complete overlap). They argued that only the 'heavier' categories of the first type – regular collaboration, alliance formation and fusion – presuppose the simultaneous existence of organised crime and terrorist organisations in each place and only occur rarely. Other types may happen more frequently, but they vary depending on a variety of facilitating factors and the different performances of organised crime and terrorism, as previously described (Paoli & Fijnaut 2022).

Other analyses have employed different categories (cooperation, coexistence, convergence) for including more flexible and changing features, and embracing various gradations of activity (Irrera 2016). Cooperation refers to the established alliances between terrorist and criminal groups. Short-term or *ad hoc* relations may be frequent and outweigh the risks that are mechanically associated with this set of relationships, especially if focused upon specific operational requirements. The alliances between the Fuerzas Armadas Revolucionarias de Colombia (FARC) and drug cartels in Colombia are a case in point.

Coexistence may be located in an intermediate position, producing a condition in which criminal and terrorist groups operate in the same business but explicitly prefer to remain separate entities unless union is rationally and functionally required through an occasional or temporary connection. It can happen during a conflict or in a nondemocratic political regime (e.g., in the Balkans during the 1990s), but not necessarily. Some of the features that build a situation conducive to organised crime also make it attractive to terrorist groups. The lack of border control and law enforcement and the eventual presence of certain types of infrastructure and services for operations may also be found in democratic states as well (e.g., Italy and Greece). The combined presence can amplify the threat to state structures – both weak or strong, democratic or undemocratic states – even if they do not explicitly act together and they may produce cross-border effects.

Convergence is more difficult to observe and investigate and may refer to a very frequent condition in which the two actors make use of their respective techniques for practical purposes, without necessarily establishing an alliance. Organised criminal networks have long used terror tactics to safeguard business interests and protect their working environments, but even the use of criminal expertise by terrorist groups to meet operational requirements is increasing. As previously seen, the transformations that have occurred in the global system have produced a change in the behaviour of subversive actors, bringing about more ephemeral and hybrid entities, as well as an increase in crimes and greater use of violence (Ruggiero 2019). Such changes at the intersections between terrorism and organised crime may be more evident in different regions, depending on the level of political stability, the occurrence of conflict and the parallel action of other subversive actors. The combination of different regional factors may determine variations of the nexus but also cause, in a sort of vicious circle, an escalation of violence and instability in a specific area (Makarenko 2007; Makarenko & Mesquita 2014).

Successive analyses have tried to identify those contexts in which alliances among subversive actors may more easily flourish, including institutional failure or instability, wars and civil conflicts. On the one hand, it is argued that in those contexts in which terrorist groups and organised criminal groups are already active and consolidated, it is more likely to lead to closer forms of cooperation between them. On the other hand, some exceptional conditions may facilitate their presence and even produce new forms or entities. These conditions can be observed in states affected by political, economic or social weaknesses; in states or regions in which competitive illicit markets are controlled in a large part or on the whole by existing organised crime syndicates; and in states or regions in which various forms of non-state armed groups (different from terrorists and criminals) are already active (Shelley & Picarelli 2005; Alesina, Piccolo & Pinotti 2019).

Conditions of ungovernability and conduciveness to terrorist or insurgent presence are those in which the presence of criminal networks opens the possibility of strategic alliances through which terrorists or insurgents can share logistical corridors, safe environments and access to sources of funding (Hansen 2012). In some cases, such as Afghanistan or Central Asia, ephemeral crime groups have been known to use profits to fund insurgencies or terrorist groups, benefiting from this temporary volatility. However, in most cases, the proliferation of connections among subversive groups can be observed in certain contexts more than in others, particularly in areas experiencing armed conflicts.

Evidently, the interconnections among criminals, terrorists and other armed groups can adopt several different, flexible forms that cannot be simply categorised under one single label. At the same time, there are some areas of the global system in which the use of terror tactics by criminals can be more visibly observed. Developments of performance require an analysis of historical and political trends, particularly in some troubled areas of the global system.

Organised crime, criminality and violence

The changes in the activities of organised crime groups and the increasing commitment to the use of violence are due to several factors, including the impact of regional variations, the effects of existing conflicts (Cornell 2005; O'Neill 2005) and political instability (Piazza 2008).

In the 1970s in Colombia, drug trafficking was already an enormous business, involving 30,000 to 50,000 small farmers and over 50,000 transporters and guards. Part of the profits was reinvested in the purchase of new land, the development of industrial laboratories, the creation of banks for managing money laundering and private airlines used for transport. In the populated regions of Barranquilla, Cali and Medellin cartels were able to build a sophisticated structure that ensured social stability and economic prosperity. Such a structure was evidently grounded on corruption, infiltration into institutions at all levels and intangible community support. Political scientists have interpreted the Colombian case through the lens of state failure (Kenney 2007). This is not only due to the widespread penetration of institutions by cartels through corruption, but also due to the capacity of criminals to exploit the territorial fragmentation and institutional weakness that afflicted the country and conquer the empty spaces left by state bodies. Throughout the 1980s, political and financial actors, police, army, justice and criminals coalesced in pursuing shared interests. In the same period, Colombia was dominated by extreme violence, perpetrated by left-wing terrorist groups (mainly FARC and Ejército de Liberación Nacional – ELN), complemented by paramilitary groups – the Autodefensas – deliberately supported by the state in the name of self-defence. The cartels coexisted alongside them and tolerated their involvement in drug trafficking (Sullivan & Bunker 2002). The fight they engaged in against the US Drug Enforcement Administration and its attempts to eradicate coca plantations did not change the powerful criminalisation process (Peceny & Durnan 2006).

After the end of the Cold War, changes in political regimes in several Latin American countries and in the relations between them and the US, as well as globalisation processes, contributed to modifications in this balance (Lessing 2017). Big Colombian cartels turned into a dozen smaller organisations with refined techniques and modernised transactions. Their capacity to dominate the drug routes in the region declined, favouring other actors, including Mexican cartels that during the Cold War played secondary roles and slowly increased their power. The Sinaloa, Jaurez and Tijuana cartels became extremely powerful and increasingly militarised. If Colombian criminals used an entrepreneurial approach that employed violence in an essentially functional way, Mexican criminals are closer to paramilitaries and more likely to use violence as a way of exercising power and intimidating all segments of society (Brophy 2008; Medel & Thoumi 2014).

Militarisation, increasing violence even against civilians and ambiguous relations with state institutions are contemporary trends that have been observed since the end of the Cold War in various regions and by different organisations. The Balkans are a paradigmatic example. In the 1990s, the weakness and disintegration of state institutions affected all post-communist societies in the region, exacerbated by ethnic fragmentation and instability. Civil wars between Serbs, Croats and Bosnians (1992–1995), followed by the Kosovo war (1999) and the Macedonian crisis (2001), reconfirmed that this region urgently needed political, economic and social assistance, beginning at the local level and addressing the most critical problems. The difficult transition process, the economic crisis and the sanctions opened a huge market for illegal goods (the trafficking of drugs, weapons, human beings, nuclear materials and stolen cars). The entire Balkan region became a large transit area to be used by criminals to bring drugs and other kinds of illicit goods to Europe.

The post-war settlement, notably, created an environment in which the promises of democratic political elections and economic reconstruction were extremely high, but also created an environment in which informal actors may easily establish patterns of behaviour that profit from state weakness and affect public interest (Politi 2001; Anastasijevic 2010). The legacy of communist political regimes, the influence of ethnic fragmentation and the need to face and manage a subtle transition to democracy led the Balkans through a difficult and troubled period of adaptation and evolution. The same conditions did not inhibit a variety of groups from exploiting nationalistic ties and ethnic cleavages to build terrorist groups and illegal armies (KLA, Serbian 'Tigers'), as well as criminal organisations that profited from illicit activities. This cluster of illegal actors flourished in all countries, building a criminal network that involved local police officers, civil servants, businessmen and former intelligence officers.

Central Asia has lived a similar experience, although it has produced different outcomes when it comes to political regimes and relations with Russia. The five post-Soviet republics of Kazakhstan, Kyrgyzstan, Uzbekistan, Tajikistan and Turkmenistan are affected by the convergent presence of the increased activity of organised crime groups after the collapse of the USSR and the emergence of transnational militant Islamist groups in the 1990s (Lewis 2014). The situation of serious economic uncertainty that Central Asia experienced after the Cold War attracted criminals and paramilitary, political and religious extremists to the area, all vying for economic advantage. Drugs rapidly became the most reliable currency for the acquisition of arms, munitions and provisions. Within the context of uncertainty, the clans in many countries became strong competitors with the state, since they were able to provide goods to satisfy the needs of local populations and thus to control the territory. Hence, this legitimisation contributed to strengthening criminals' influence bottom (Ceccarelli 2007; Irrera 2020).

In Central Asia, state institutions suffer from a lack of efficiency and the inability to provide assets and goods or to control the territory. This is the basis of the increasing roles of criminals, who also employ violence to maintain their control over the territory against other armed groups. A similar performance can be observed in some parts of the African continent and particularly in the Sahel, a large part of sub-Saharan Africa, which comprises many countries and areas (Mali, Niger, Chad, southern Algeria, southern Libya and Darfur) affected by civil armed conflicts, ethnic fragmentations and weak economies. Here, criminals have benefited from neopatrimonialism, the vertical distribution of resources around patron-client networks mainly based on a ruling political party or individual, which has favoured the spread of private use of public resources and boosted institutional corruption (Thompson 2004; Cammack 2007; Bach & Gazibo 2012).

The increasingly active roles of criminal organisations started to become visible in the 2000s and developed in all countries where drug trafficking, arms, human smuggling, kidnapping for ransom and goldfield mining are common. The absence of state control over the territory and its authority, associated with armed groups and mercenaries, to various degrees involved in the local conflicts, are additional relevant push factors that have contributed to completely subverting the societal systems (Micallef, Farrah & Bish 2019).

Following the end of the Cold War and changes in the security environment in many regions, a general trend can be observed in the performances of criminal groups. Troubled relations with state institutions and the necessity to regulate coexistence with terrorists and other armed groups have produced increasing militarisation and the use of violence to assert their power and dominance. Most recently, criminals have also profited from the networking opportunities offered by radicalisation. Much of the literature has focused on violent extremism and how it spreads in hotbeds like prisons. Especially in the West, and across Europe, prisons have been at the core of the attention of scholars and policymakers as hubs for the recruitment and proselytisation of jihadists. As has been observed, prisons are environments characterised by personal grievances, fragility and marginalisation. Individuals may find more opportunities to continue the struggle in prison. A common nationality, ethnicity and language can facilitate this activity of proselytism, producing more radicalised subjects (Marone & Olimpo 2019). Measuring and empirically evaluating this phenomenon is, however, very difficult, although it is sustained by the Radicalisation Awareness Network funded by the European Commission. Despite some very good research projects in prisons, the knowledge and data on people being or becoming radicalised during detention are limited. As already argued, criminals are usually far from political or ideological motivations. However, because of the increasing militarisation of their performance, radicalisation has become an additional powerful source of recruitment and a way to oppose states and other competitors.

These considerations on past and contemporary trends in the use of violence can be complemented by empirical data provided by the criminality score, measured within the Global Organised Crime Index. The score epitomises the average of the criminal markets' and criminal actors' scores and provides a clear representation of the impact of the nexus and its gradations in different regions.[1] In the Index, organised crime is defined as the set of illegal activities, conducted by groups or networks acting in concert, by engaging in violence, corruption or related activities to obtain, directly or indirectly, a financial or material benefit. Such activities may be carried out both within a country and transnationally (Figure 25.1).

Regions affected by the high impact of non-state armed conflict also suffer high levels of criminality. Asia reveals the highest levels of criminality overall (scoring 5.30 out of 10 on the criminality scale), closely followed by Africa (5.17) and the Americas (5.06). In the report that complements the Index, this is explained by the fact that Asia is a populous continent, rich with natural resources, infrastructural complexes and a strategic hub for the world's largest economic centres. The Western part, which also incorporates the Middle East (for the purposes of the

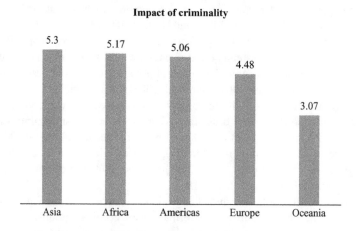

Figure 25.1 The impact of criminality in different regions.

Source: Author's creation, data from Global Organised Crime Index (2021).

Index) has a sub-score of 5.78 and is the most fragile region because of long-lasting conflicts and enduring violence. The combination of conflict, natural resources and weak democratic traditions is described in the Index and, for criminality data, as the most relevant transmitters of organised crime. In various regions, the interactions that criminals may develop with other armed actors may vary greatly, as well as the impact the nexus can have on the region in terms of stability and level of violence. Data reveals that criminality may impact all regions, even consolidated democracies, such as European countries, either as a traditional base for criminals or as a larger transit area. The challenges posed to states are marked by the global and regional spread and can be placed on a double level. It constitutes a threat to the state's capacity to provide security to its citizens and to the regional and international institutions' ability to manage cross-border flows.

Towards new and more sophisticated *nexuses*?

The main aim of this chapter has been to shed light on the use of violence by organised crime groups and on the impact that intersections between delinquency, terrorism and insurgency produced on the global and regional security agenda. Additionally, it has been intended to contribute to discussions about irregular warfare, particularly to an understanding of whether intersections between terrorism and organised crime may represent a novel kind of security threat.

The mainstream literature has identified the crime-terror nexus, referring to the strategic alliance between two non-state actors, both able to exploit illegal markets and influence policy-making on a global level, although they may have different agendas, approaches and methods. Interactions between criminals and terrorists can gradually and increasingly develop as the result of a variety of domestic, regional and global factors. Parallel to the increasing involvement of terrorists in criminal activities, the use of violence by organised crime groups is the most visible and impactful phenomenon. Scholars argue that a variety of internal structures (the level of organisation, networking capacities and continuity in the action) determine whether and to what degree terrorists and criminals will engage in various levels of criminal activity or violent attacks, respectively.

The nexus has been unpacked by focusing on the nature and performance of its main components and is largely based on the most recent literature. In particular, three large categories (coexistence, cooperation, convergence) have been employed to describe various gradations of intersections between the two actors. While cooperation expresses the traditional way to conceive the nexus, in terms of alliances, coexistence and convergence better represent the more practical use of terrorist techniques by criminals or the illicit activities by terrorists for funding in an occasional and functional perspective. Therefore, different variations of the nexus can be observed, depending on the regions and different environments.

They may find a privileged place to flourish in troubled contexts, affected by war, insurgency, as well as political, social and economic instability. The nexus first constitutes a threat to the state's capacity to provide security to its citizens and to the regional and international institutions' ability to manage cross-border flows. This is why it is listed among those issues of global concern that require a collective response. The changing nature of global security and the increasing effects of globalisation have contributed to a blurring of the distinction between politically and criminally motivated violence and to greater similarity in operations and organisation. The evanescence of traditional boundaries is currently marking the new manifestations of this nexus and requires policymakers to undertake a reconceptualisation of the phenomenon as a whole. In particular, the increasing militarisation in the performances of criminal groups can be observed in various regions, both as a consequence of the changes in the security environments and as a necessity to assert their power over adversary states, terrorists and other armed groups.

Countermeasures and counterstrategies have been developed by states and intergovernmental organisations following the changes in conflicts. Scholarly debates on conflict management, conflict transformation and post-conflict reconstruction have met with those about counterinsurgency (Barnett 2005; Bell 2011; Crossley 2018; Roth 2019). Since the end of the Cold War, in Western perception insurgents, violent terrorist networks and criminal organisations have been identified as among the most dangerous global threats. Considering that this is first a threat to the legitimacy and credibility of a state, part of the solution necessarily passes through the strengthening of the domestic political and social institutions in the distressed countries and the strengthening of capacities in the states to effectively respond to violence (Crenshaw 1983; Ciluffo 2000; Skuldt 2010). Another part deals with a paradigm change. Although the counterinsurgency doctrine is strictly linked to classical military doctrine, contemporary trends in countering irregular warfare may be differently oriented (Bell 2011). Tackling a new threat, such as the terror-criminality-warfare nexus and the variety of implications they produce, may require more than a military strategy. Rather, they may involve a more comprehensive strategy, in which the military dimension is complemented by humanitarian practices and peace interventionism.

Note

1 In the Global Organised Crime Index, criminal actors are mafia-style groups, criminal networks, state-embedded actors and foreign actors, whereas criminal markets are human trafficking, human smuggling, arms trafficking, flora and fauna crimes, nonrenewable resource crimes, as well as trade in heroin, cocaine, cannabis and synthetic drugs.

References

Alesina A, Piccolo S & Pinotti P 2019, 'Organized Crime, Violence, and Politics', *The Review of Economic Studies*, vol. 86, no. 2, pp. 457–99, https://doi.org/10.1093/restud/rdy036.

Anastasijevic, D 2010, 'Getting Better? A Map of Organized Crime in the Western Balkans', in W Benedek, C Daase, V Dimitrijevic & P van Duyne (eds), *Transnational Terrorism, Organized Crime and Peace-Building*, Palgrave Macmillan, London, pp. 149–68.

Bach D. & Gazibo M. (2012) (eds), *Neopatrimonialism in Africa and Beyond*, Abingdon: Routledge.

Barnett, M 2005, 'Humanitarianism Transformed', *Perspectives on Politics*, vol. 3, no. 4, pp. 723–40, https://doi.org/10.1017/S1537592705050401.

Bell, C 2011, 'Civilianising Warfare: Ways of War and Peace in Modern Counterinsurgency', *Journal of International Relations and Development*, vol. 14, no. 3, pp. 309–32, https://doi.org/10.1057/jird.2010.16.

Brophy, S 2008, 'Mexico: Cartels, Corruption and Cocaine: A Profile of the Gulf Cartel', *Global Crime*, vol. 9, no. 3, pp. 248–61, https://doi.org/10.1080/17440570802254353.

Cammack, D 2007, 'The Logic of African Neopatrimonialism – What Role for Donors?', *Development Policy Review*, vol. 25, no. 5, pp. 599–614.

Carrapico H, Irrera, D & Tupman, B 2014, 'Transnational Organised Crime and Terrorism: Different Peas, Same Pod?', *Global Crime*, vol. 15, no. 3–4, pp. 213–18, https://doi.org/10.1080/17440572.2014.939882.

Ceccarelli, A 2007, 'Clans, Politics and Organized Crime in Central Asia', *Trends in Organized Crime*, vol. 10, no. 3, pp. 19–36, http://dx.doi.org/10.1007/s12117-007-9011-z.

Cilluffo, F 2000, 'The threat posed from the convergence of organized crime, drug trafficking, and terrorism', *Testimony of the Deputy Director, Global Organized Crime Program, Director, Counterterrorism Task Force, Centre for Strategic and International Studies, Washington (DC) to the US House Committee on the Judiciary Subcommittee on Crime*.

Cornell, S E 2005, 'The Interaction of Narcotics and Conflict', *Journal of Peace Research*, vol. 42, no. 6, pp. 751–60, https://doi.org/10.1177/0022343305057895.

Crenshaw, M (ed), 1983, *Terrorism, Legitimacy, and Power: The Consequences of Political Violence*, Wesleyan University Press, Middletown, CT.

Crossley, N 2018, 'Is R2P Still Controversial? Continuity and Change in the Debate on "Humanitarian Intervention"', *Cambridge Review of International Affairs*, vol. 31, no. 5, pp. 415–36, https://doi.org/10.1080/09557571.2018.1516196.

Dishman, C 2005, 'The Leaderless Nexus: When Crime and Terror Converge', *Studies in Conflict & Terrorism*, vol. 28, no. 3, pp. 237–52, https://doi.org/10.1080/10576100590928124.

Felbab-Brown, V 2019, 'The Crime-Terror Nexus and its Fallacies', in E Chenoweth (ed), *The Oxford Handbook of Terrorism*, Oxford University Press, Oxford, pp. 366–83.

Gray, C S 2007, 'Irregular Warfare: One Nature, Many Characters', *Strategic Studies Quarterly*, vol. 1, no. 2, pp. 35–57.

Hamm, M S 2007, *Terrorism as Crime*, New York University Press, New York.

Hansen, W 2012, *The Crime-Terrorism Nexus*, ISN, Center for Security Studies, Zurich.

Hoffman, B 2006, *Inside Terrorism*, Columbia University Press, New York.

Hutchinson, S & O'malley, P 2007, 'A Crime–Terror Nexus? Thinking on Some of the Links Between Terrorism and Criminality', *Studies in Conflict & Terrorism*, vol. 30, no. 12, pp. 1095–107, https://doi.org/10.1080/10576100701670870.

Irrera, D 2016, 'The Crime-Terror-Insurgency "Nexus". Implications on Multilateral Cooperation', in S Romaniuk & S T Webb (eds), *Insurgency and Counterinsurgency in Modern War*, CRC Press, New York, pp. 39–52.

Irrera D 2020, 'Humanitarianism and the migration crisis', in Klaus Gerd-Giesen (ed), *Ideologies in World Politics*, Springer Nature, Springer VS Wiesbaden, pp. 33–50.

Jones, S G & Johnston, P B 2013, 'The Future of Insurgency', *Studies in Conflict & Terrorism*, vol. 36, no. 1, pp. 1–25, https://doi.org/10.1080/1057610X.2013.739077.

Kenney, M 2007, 'The Architecture of Drug Trafficking: Network Forms of Organisation in the Colombian Cocaine Trade', *Global Crime*, vol. 8, no. 3, pp. 233–59, https://doi.org/10.1080/17440570701507794.

Lessing, B 2017, *Making Peace in Drug Wars: Crackdowns and Cartels in Latin America*, Cambridge University Press, Cambridge.

Lewis, D 2014, 'Crime, Terror and the State in Central Asia', *Global Crime*, vol. 15, no. 3–4, pp. 337–56, https://doi.org/10.1080/17440572.2014.927764.

Ljujic, V, van Prooijen, J W & Weerman, F 2017, 'Beyond the Crime-Terror Nexus: Socio-Economic Status, Violent Crimes and Terrorism', *Journal of Criminological Research, Policy and Practice*, vol. 3, no. 3, pp. 158–72, https://doi.org/10.1108/JCRPP-02-2017-0010.

Makarenko, T 2000, 'Crime and Terrorism in Central Asia', *Jane's Intelligence Review*, vol. 12, no. 7, pp. 16–17.

Makarenko, T 2004, 'The Crime-Terror Continuum: Tracing the Interplay between Transnational Organised Crime and Terrorism', *Global Crime*, vol. 6, no. 1, pp. 129–45, https://doi.org/10.1080/1744057042000297025.

Makarenko, T 2007, 'Criminal and Terrorist Networks: Gauging Interaction and the Resultant Impact on Counter-Terrorism', in E Brimmer (ed), *Five Dimensions of Homeland and International Security*, Centre for Transatlantic Relations, The Johns Hopkins University, Washington, DC, pp. 57–72.

Makarenko, T 2009, 'Terrorist Use of Organised Crime: Operational Tool or Exacerbating the Threat?' in F Allum, F Longo, D Irrera & P Kostakos (eds), *Defining and Defying Organised Crime: Discourse, Perceptions, and Reality*, Routledge, London, pp. 180–93.

Makarenko, T 2021, 'Foundations and Evolution of the Crime–Terror Nexus', in F Allum & S Gilmour (eds), *The Routledge Handbook of Transnational Organized Crime*, Routledge, London, pp. 253–69.

Marone, F & Olimpio, M 2019, 'Jihadist Radicalization in Italian Prisons: A Primer', *Analysis*, ispionline, <https://www.ispionline.it/sites/default/files/pubblicazioni/analysis_ispi_2019_jihadist_radicalization_marone_olimpio.pdf> (accessed 23 December 2022).

Martin, S & Weinberg, L 2016, *The Role of Terrorism in Twenty-First-Century Warfare*, Manchester University Press, Manchester.

Medel, M & Thoumi, F 2014, 'Mexican Drug "Cartels"', in L Paoli (ed), *The Oxford Handbook of Organized Crime*, Oxford University Press, Oxford, pp. 196–218.

Micallef, M, Farrah, R & Bish, A 2019, *After the Storm, Organized Crime Across the Sahel-Sahara Following the Libyan Revolution and Malian Rebellion*, Global Initiative against Transnational Organized Crime, Geneva.

Olson, E T 2009, 'A Balanced Approach to Irregular Warfare', *The Journal of International Security Affairs*, vol. 16, pp. 3–6.

O'Neill, B 2005, *Insurgency and Terrorism: from Revolution to Apocalypse*, Potomac Books, Washington, DC.

Paoli, L & Fijnaut, C & Jan W (eds), 2022, '*The Nexus Between Organized Crime and Terrorism*, Edward Elgar Publishing, Cheltenham, pp. 48–84.

Peceny, M & Durnan, M 2006, 'The FARC's Best Friend: US Antidrug Policies and the Deepening of Colombia's Civil War in the 1990s', *Latin American Politics and Society*, vol. 48, no. 2, pp. 95–116, https://doi.org/10.1111/j.1548-2456.2006.tb00348.x.

Piazza, J A 2008, 'Do Democracy and Free Markets Protect Us from Terrorism?', *International Politics*, vol. 45, no. 1, pp. 72–91, https://doi.org/10.1057/palgrave.ip.8800220.

Politi, A 2001, 'The Threat of Organized Crime in the Balkans', *Southeast European and Black Sea Studies*, vol. 1, no. 2, pp. 39–63, https://doi.org/10.1080/14683850108454636.

Rogers, P 2016, *Irregular War: ISIS and the New Threat from the Margins*, I.B. Tauris, London – New York.

Roth, S 2019, 'Humanitarian NGOs', in T Davies (ed), *Routledge Handbook of NGOs and International Relations*, Routledge, London, pp. 267–82.

Ruggiero, V 2019, 'Hybrids: On the Crime-Terror Nexus', *International Journal of Comparative and Applied Criminal Justice*, vol. 43, no. 1, pp. 49–60, https://doi.org/10.1080/01924036.2017.1411283.

Sheehan, M A, Marquardt, E & Collins, L (eds) 2022, *Routledge Handbook of U.S. Counterterrorism and Irregular Warfare Operations*, Routledge, London.

Shelley, L I & Picarelli, J T 2005, 'Methods and Motives: Exploring Links Between Transnational Organized Crime and International Terrorism', *Trends in Organized Crime*, vol. 9, no. 2, pp. 52–67, https://doi.org/10.1007/s12117-005-1024-x.

Skuldt, A 2010, 'Terrorism and Foreign Policy', *Oxford Research Encyclopedia of International Studies*, https://doi.org/10.1093/acrefore/9780190846626.013.321

Sullivan, J P & Bunker, R J 2002, 'Drug Cartels, Street Gangs, and Warlords', *Small Wars and Insurgencies*, vol. 13, no. 2, pp. 40–53, https://doi.org/10.1080/09592310208559180.

Sullivan, J P & Bunker, R J 2005, 'Multilateral Counter-Insurgency Networks', in R J Bunker (ed), *Networks, Terrorism and Global Insurgency*, Routledge, London, pp. 183–98.

Thompson, A 2004, *An Introduction to African Politics*, London: Routledge.

Ucko, D H & Marks, T A 2022, *Organised Crime as Irregular Warfare*, National Defense University Press, Washington, DC, <https://ndupress.ndu.edu/Portals/68/Documents/strat-monograph/Crafting-Strategy-for-Irregular-Warfare_2ndEd.pdf?ver=mFY-dJC9aRGKfjz0E0KK5Q%3d%3d> (accessed 22 December 2022).

UN Convention 2000, *United Nations Convention Against Transnational Organised Crime*, A/RES/55/25, 15 November 2000, <https://www.unodc.org/documents/treaties/UNTOC/Publications/TOC%20Convention/TOCebook-e.pdf> (accessed 22 December 2022.

Wang, P 2010, 'The Crime-Terror Nexus: Transformation, Alliance, Convergence', *Asian Social Science*, vol. 6, no. 6, pp. 11–20.

Williams, P 2002, 'Cooperation Among Criminal Organizations', in M Berdal & M Serrano (eds), *Transnational Organized Crime and International Security: Business as Usual?*, Lynne Rienner, Boulder, CO, pp. 67–80.

PART V

Technoscience

26

CYBERNETICS AT WAR

Military Artificial Intelligence, Weapon Systems and the De-Skilled Moral Agent[1]

Elke Schwarz

Introduction

The drive towards greater automation and autonomy in weapons systems has a long history, whereby military aims and cutting-edge research in autonomy and artificial intelligence (AI) have traditionally co-evolved. Presently, most AI innovation is driven by the private sector, this was, however, not always the case. In the early years of AI development, AI and military technological advancement were intricately entwined. Turing's conception of computing machines evolved from his wartime work on decoding; John von Neuman's work on system design and programming derived from his high-level military work for the Manhattan Project; and some of Wiener's contribution to systems automation stemmed from wartime advances in automatic gun fire control (Noble 1999, pp. 152–3). But not all involved in this twinned development were at ease with the use of increasing automation, if not autonomy, in the context of warfare. Early philosophers of technology, including the father of cybernetics himself, Norbert Wiener, were uneasy in particular with the latent question of human control, especially as Wiener saw the temporal structures of cybernetic systems outpacing human cognitive abilities. What are the consequences, he asked, if we avail ourselves of a "mechanical agency with whose operation we cannot efficiently interfere once we have started it, because the action is so fast and irrevocable that we do have not the data to intervene before the action is complete" (Wiener 1960, p. 1356)? His answer was, unequivocally, that the consequences might be disastrous if we do not address the underlying moral questions.

As advances in machine learning and computational processing power continue to progress at an accelerated pace, this distance between machine and human capacities widens even further. In the decades between when Wiener first raised his concerns and today, military AI has become one of the fastest-growing areas of defence investment. At the time of writing, the global military AI market is estimated to be worth just under seven billion US dollars with a projected growth to $13.7bn by 2028 (Globe Newswire 2022b). The US National Security Commission on AI report published in 2021 suggests that the military AI R&D budget alone should be expanded to $8bn (NSCAI 2021, p. 730). This, in turn, drives autonomous weapons industry growth from an estimated $13.3bn in 2022 to a projected $19.6bn by 2026 (Globe Newswire 2022a). The promise of financial payoffs through investments in this area is substantial and runs in parallel with high hopes for fully networked military operations in future wars.

DOI: 10.4324/9781003299011-32

Although the US is by far the country with the largest investment in pioneering military AI initiatives, other countries are following suit. Another major player, China, is "pursuing AI-enabled systems and autonomous capabilities", which include AI-facilitated targeting technologies (Kania 2020). The UK has been making it a priority to transform "Defence into an AI ready organisation" to become "the world's most effective, efficient, trusted and influential Defence organisation for our size", in terms of AI (Ministry of Defence 2022, pp. 1–2). This includes adopting AI for every aspect, from logistics to targeting. In short, there is a global push to develop AI-enabled weapons systems which make it easier to identify potential targets at higher speeds and with more efficiency, as well as a belief, shared among policymakers and industry proponents alike, that such AI functions must be further developed in order to gain an upper hand in the ostensibly inevitable algorithmic context of future wars.

The vision is to expand the military AI ecology to facilitate "widespread integration of AI [in defence operations] by 2025" and divest "from military systems that are ill-equipped for AI enabled warfare" (NSCAI 2021, p. 9). Not all militaries have equally lofty ambitions, but the race for superior military AI is well underway, and with this, the realisation of greater autonomy in weapons systems where AI holds the key to faster, more efficient and ultimately more lethal action. In this constellation, the machine is cast as a superior decision-making agent, over the slow and deliberative processes implicit in human thought; a superior decision-making agent which inevitably comes to replace the human in a growing realm of tasks and decisions, including the targeting of enemies. This, in the story of AI, is a necessity as human cognitive capacities are no match for the speed and data-processing power of AI. The deference to AI authority is born out of a sense of both inferiority and expediency. Embedded within an AI environment, this deference becomes a necessity. This, in turn, bears consequences for conceptions of ethical decisions in war.

With this framing in mind, this chapter focuses less on the latest specifics of technological developments and AI capabilities in military contexts, instead foregrounding how digital military technology, including AI, mediates and shapes human thought and practices, specifically the capacity to act and decide as moral agents. My core claim is that as digital infrastructures and interfaces dominate the human (military) landscape, not only is human moral agency diminished, but ethical practices become cast in distinctly technological terms. This is a concerning development particularly when it comes to the future conduct of war and the use of force where the moral stakes are high.

I begin by tracing the role of AI in military operations as it is both in place today, and envisioned for the future, with a focus on the US context, before then moving on to exploring how the logic contained in these developments and visions for human decision making in collaboration with AI systems affect human agency. In the final section, I focus more specifically on the nexus of moral agency and AI, highlighting some of the key tensions between the logic of digital systems and ethical practices.

Military AI: between utopia and dystopia

The US and China are presently leading the way in shaping global ambitions for military AI use, with other military powers – Russia, France, the UK and Israel, among others – investing increasing sums in military AI and the global shift towards greater integration of AI into defence operations is well underway. As one of the key drivers of AI in military operations, the US is both vocal about its ambitions and representative of future global visions of AI for warfare. In 2018, the US established the Joint Artificial Intelligence Centre (JAIC) to serve as the Department of

Defence (DoD) hub for the digitisation of US warfare. The Centre's stated aim is to shift the DoD's "mindset and culture from a hardware-centric and industrial-age force to a software-driven and information-age one" (CDAO n.d.). The goal is to make the business of warfare lighter, more agile and, importantly, much faster. In general terms, AI for military purposes can be used to undertake tasks that involve *description* (pattern recognition, voice/object identification), *prediction* (the forecasting of future states) or *prescription* (analysis and subsequent decision).

Despite the emphatically ambitious agenda for military AI, the field is still young and clear pathways to understanding where the technology can serve most effectively are still ill-defined. Current applications of AI are typically sometimes classified by broad area of application; Taddeo et al. (2021, p. 1710), for example, suggest three broad categories for possible military AI uses: for support actions such as back office support, logistics and systems resilience; for 'non-kinetic' uses such as active offensive and defensive cyber operations, and for kinetic uses, including the use of AI for targeting operations and for autonomous weapons systems operations. The NATO Cooperative Cyber Defence Centre of Excellence categorises areas of AI application by system uses – logistics and personnel management, autonomous vehicles, data analytics and autonomous defence and weapons systems (Gray & Ertan 2021). A more fine-grained perspective with a focus on AI for weapons systems is offered by the US Defence Systems Information Analysis Centre (DSIAC), which categorises these in its 2022 State of the Art Report as "Autonomy, AI in perception, AI in guidance, navigation and control, mission and path planning, intelligent strategy, opponent modelling, cognitive electronic warfare" and distinguishes between AI use for air, sea and land systems (Chakour 2022, pp. 3–1). It is clear that defence operations might hope to use AI in various settings, but to date, few countries have a clear military AI strategy in place, and the technology itself is not widely rolled out, whether that is in non-kinetic or in kinetic systems. This means that the discussions about what AI can, and will, achieve in the military domain are to date largely based on speculative ambitions.

It is easy to see how AI can be effectively used to streamline infrastructural and logistical processes, such as supply chain management, optimised communications or the preventive maintenance of fighter jets to identify potential failure before they occur, such as France's F4 Rafale Predictive Maintenance project (Thales 2019). At this stage in the development of the technology, AI is particularly useful for applications that are narrow in scope and that take place within an environment of limited variables. For the faster and more efficient undertaking of non-combat activities and processes, AI promises to make unwieldy and logistically complex operations leaner and faster. This, with some caveats, is likely to be uncontroversial.

But when it comes to combat activities and the use of AI for tactical, operational and/or strategic gains, it is less clear whether AI gives an advantage, especially when it involves tasks that require complex knowledge and expertise-based reasoning in highly dynamic environments (Cummings 2017, pp. 5–6). However, the desire to implement AI within particularly these areas of military operations is becoming increasingly pronounced. This takes place along a gradient of human-machine interaction, from more to increasingly less human involvement in the decision and execution process. In terms of weapons capability, this ranges from weapon systems that are equipped with an AI module to find and track a manually configured target and suggest an action to the operator, for example an MQ-9 Reaper equipped with an Agile Condor Pod, to fully autonomous systems, capable of executing all critical functions – find, track and attack a target – without a human in the loop, such as the Turkish Kargu2 drone which made headlines in 2021 as the first publicly documented anti-personnel use of a fully autonomous lethal weapons system (UN Security Council 2021). In terms of broader strategic decision tasks, this again, can range from more narrow and specific tasks of AI-enabled data analysis of a specific terrain to confirm a decision made prior by a human, to a broad and sweeping vision of a full-spectrum, AI-driven ecology of interconnected domains in which the role of the human is less clear.

A number of programmes are in place that work towards these goals, such as the Pentagon's military AI pioneering Algorithmic Warfare Cross-Functional Team programme, better known as Project Maven, and other defence industry programmes that seek to pair advanced drone technology with intelligent capabilities. Since its inception in 2017, Project Maven's aim has been to connect the sensory input gathered by drones with the ability to identify and track potential targets in real-time to give the human intelligence for kinetic engagement at speed. Since then, various systems of this nature have been rolled out, trialled, tested and designed to meet the US military's objective of achieving 'decision dominance' with faster and more lethal action through AI (Freedberg Jr 2021). In August 2020, DARPA flew a trial mission in which "several dozen military drones and tank-like robots took to the skies and roads" (Knight 2021) with the aim of tracking down terrorist suspects in an urban environment. This was just one of many such exercises that indicate the Pentagon's determination to shift an increasing amount of decision-making, including lethal decision-making, to machines. Indeed, the suggestion put forward by General John Murray, among others, is that we may perhaps not need any direct human control over lethal AI systems after all, since that would impede the superior capacities of the technologies available (Knight 2021).

Expanding this logic of AI as an accelerator for a more pervasive battlefield, Project Convergence, another US programme, foregrounds data connectivity across domains for more comprehensive situational awareness, more efficient command and control and faster sensor-to-shooter action. Project Convergence is operated under the auspices of the Army Futures Command (AFC) and aims its efforts at "building the Army of 2030" in which the development of "innovative technologies to outpace near-peer adversaries in future battles" is emphasised (Lacdan 2022). To do this, the Programme "leverages a series of joint, multi-domain engagements to integrate artificial intelligence, robotics, and autonomy to improve battlefield situational awareness, connect sensors with shooters and accelerate the decision-making timeline" (AFC n.d.). In short, the programme seeks to leverage the capabilities of AI to connect domains, and allies, for faster lethal action. This, to date, is an experiment rather than a reality but the idea is gaining traction with other militaries as well.

The broader vision, of which Project Convergence is an important component, is to integrate all military functions into a highly networked, AI-enabled, machine-learning driven cross-domain operational context. Once again, the visions presented by the United States Department of Defence are illustrative of global aims and initiatives. In 2022, the US launched the Joint All Domain Control and Command (JADC2) strategy, which seeks to produce interlinked "warfighting capabilities to sense, make sense and act at all levels and phases of war, across all domains and with partners to deliver information advantage at the speed of relevance" (US Department of Defence 2022, p. 2), connecting Air Force, Navy, Marine Corps, Army and Space Force in one data universe. The premise for this is that traditional command and control activities, in which human judgement is typically instrumental, is no longer adequate "for the speed, complexity and lethality of future conflict" (Congressional Research Service 2022, p. 2). By leveraging AI, the vision is to "sense, make-sense and act" to "prompt high-speed operations" (BAE Systems n.d.).

Yet this vision of an effortless integration of AI into all military operations at all phases of war, especially where lethal decisions are at stake, is marred by both the complexities and uncertainties of the conflict environments and the myriad of ethical challenges that arise in any context of conflict. Particularly thorny here is the question of whether AI systems can, or indeed should, be taking on a significant role in critical selection and targeting functions, whether they should be making lethal decisions, be involved in "accelerated sensor-to-shooter timelines" (Shanahan 2019) or play a crucial role in predictive suspect selection and any other tasks in which the ethical stakes are patently high. The parameter 'speed' is paramount and plays a significant role as a focal point for military AI visions. If, as the NSCAI report suggests, it is detrimental that the US government "still operates at human speed, not machine speed" (NSCAI 2021, p. 24), and if the greatest perceived advantage of AI is that it compresses decision times from minutes to seconds, thereby exceeding any human decision capabilities, then what role can the human – whether operator or commander – play within such an infrastructure?

Hyperbolic narratives about the future potency – military and otherwise – of AI aside, the growing ubiquity of AI applications across military fields of use organises the present and future military habitus in ways that affect ethical practices. Not only through the implicit ethos of speed as a core value, but through a specific logic upon which AI output rests.

The artifice of military intelligence

At present, AI for complex military operations, such as enemy identification and targeting, lacks in robustness and reliability and is dependent on enormous levels of data and computational processing power, often neither of which are adequately available. In contrast to civilian areas of AI applications, appropriate data for contingent and highly dynamic environments in warfare is not available in sufficient quantities to be able to reliably train an AI system. While narrow AI might be used quite effectively in predictive maintenance or logistical operations, where the operational context is demarcated by a limited number of relatively stable variables, a more extensive use of AI in unpredictable, unruly and highly dynamic combat environments remains an aspiration rather than a viable reality. The reasons for this are many, but it bears keeping in mind that AI is essentially a statistical data processing programme premised on algorithms. It is an

> Entity (or collective set of cooperative entities), able to receive inputs from the environment, interpret and learn from such inputs, and exhibit related and flexible behaviours and actions that might help the entity achieve a particular goal or objective over a period of time.
>
> (Flaggella 2018)

This comprises both traditional, symbolic rule-based AI systems, as well as newer approaches to AI that draw on neural networks and advanced machine learning techniques. For these to work effectively, vast amounts of input data are needed on which algorithms are then trained. The availability of the input data is one arena which poses a challenge to military AI, accuracy and comprehensiveness of relevant data is another. Datasets can be biased from the outset, they can produce biased outcomes, data might be too discrepant, low-quality, incomplete or insufficient to produce an accurate world model upon which the AI is intended to work (Holland Michel 2021, p. 4). Moreover, computer vision, although improving at a rapid rate, remains still brittle as a tool for reliable recognition and examples where a system can be spoofed by making minute changes to an image abound, as was effectively shown by experiment in which hackers fooled an AI algorithm into consistently misidentifying a turtle as a rifle (Hutson 2018). This poses not only a security concern, but also raises questions of accuracy in the complex and dynamic world of warfare. Hardware and network provisions in military contexts can be slow and unwieldy in the best of times; yet in many cases, new systems are brought into operation before persistent and serious technical failures are fully addressed.

Taken together, these observations suggest that triumphant visions of a fast, fully intercon-nected and efficient military AI to lessen the fog of war are optimistic to say the least. Yet the chorus for a full-spectrum integration of AI technology into all modes of warfighting continues to swell amidst fears of losing the AI arms race. The faith in AI as a panacea overlooks the fact that AI has not yet proven to be particularly robust or consistently infallible. Increased computational processing speeds and the theoretical availability of vast amounts of data facilitate the illusion that the world can be rendered as data in all its facets, quickly, so that it can be acted upon. However, 'artificial' intelligence is only ever just that – an 'artificial' way of knowing and acting upon the world. Digital technologies render the world never quite fully as it is, as it appears to us humans, collectively or individually. The upshot of such a quantification of human life is that only those elements can be considered that do not resist transformation into utility-relevant data, for reasons of methodological smoothness and purity. In other words, the multiple, messy, unruly and aleatory dimension of humanity must be pressed into a data rationality for an ostensibly objective assess-ment. If this logic is applied to such complex and incalculable environments as battlefields and warzones, it is clear that the loss that is incurred is substantial.

An AI system calculates and approximates. The very AI paradigm, as Matteo Pasquinelli (2019, p. 2) highlights, is marked by "limits, approximations, biases, errors, fallacies and vul-nerabilities". What AI presents is a model of the world, an approximation of the perceived en-vironment, calculated based on input data. Machine learning, Pasquinelli notes, calculates "not an exact pattern, but the statistical distribution of a pattern" (Pasquinelli 2019, p. 4), truncating that which does not fit and pressing data into assorted categories through which an outcome can be achieved that is speedily actionable on the ground. AI is as such a "technique of informa-tion compression" (Pasquinelli 2019, p. 12). Phenomena that cannot be captured numerically remain invisible to the AI system, data that is too messy is rendered pliable, categorised and calculable – never without loss. In order to be able to function optimally, more data is neces-sarily always better. This logic requires an expanding sphere of input and output data to include ever-greater realms of the human world as data. In other words, more and more arenas need to be captured as data, categorised and classified, in order to be processed as relevant for an essentially expansive AI logic, to bring the world into line with ostensibly objective logics of machine optimisation and speed. In such an environment the human – as operator, commander or target – is pressed into a schema of optimised calculation and functionality in order to better align with machine logics.

It is against this logic that we might better understand the complexities of agency in the military AI-human-machine today. Rather than enhancing or amplifying human cognition through technol-ogy, military AI replaces it with a different and faster logical system of information processing and optimisation that serves the aim of producing knowledge about possible actionable targets at speed, "to the detriment of an informed engagement with relevant actors on the ground" (Suchman 2020, p. 6). In this, the machine co-produces a specific, more violent mode of military operations, one that prioritises lethal action. Putting AI technology at the edge of the weapons system is a logical next step in the technification of war, amplifying speed and embedding it ever deeper into war's social and political processes. The commander, hoping to gain strategic advantages with AI systems, too becomes increasingly reliant on the rationale of AI decision-making, at the expense of agency and control. If we take seriously the expansive character of AI as a logic, and the visions for a comprehensively networked military AI realm suggest we should, then neither fully explain-able nor highly narrow decision-assistance AI is likely to serve as safeguard that the human will be able to retain moral agency, in the AI wars of the future to come. This human-machine complexity bears a moral wager.

Ethics at the interface

There is by now an extensive and well-developed literature addressing the complex human-machine relationship in modernity, including the cognitive challenges humans face when working with computer technologies (Sharkey 2018). When AI and human reasoning form an ecosystem, the possibility for human control is limited. As humans, we have a strong bias in favour of computationally derived decisions, and we often lack the knowledge needed to reason well enough to assert proper control over an action, particularly when the utility of the action depends so heavily on speed. The work of Missy Cummings explores these limitations of human agency within the setting of intelligent decision support systems. She notes that although such systems can be useful in alleviating human fatigue, boredom and cognitive shortcomings, they can also impose a "measurable cost to human performance [...] such as loss of situational awareness, complacency, skill degradation and automation bias" (Cummings 2004, p. 1). In other words, a different cognitive loss for the human is amplified in this human–machine constellation. Cummings highlights the well-documented inclination of humans to afford the computer system a substantial role in determining a decision. Humans have "a tendency to disregard or not search for contradictory information in light of a computer-generated solution that is accepted as correct and can be exacerbated in time-critical domains" (Cummings 2004, p. 1). Here again, we might consider how the logic of computation decisions at speed functions to privilege quick action over more time-intensive deliberation. And although this could potentially be overcome for specific systems with targeted training, the complexity of AI systems makes this much harder to achieve, especially as they are designed with a non-human and time-critical logic at their foundation.

As the human operator then becomes a modular part in the digital system, the question of agency – including moral agency – becomes complicated. Granted, the role of the soldier has always been that of being an element in the wider war-machine, and this has steadily increased with the greater complexity of digital information systems. As digitalisation advances and, with AI, moves into the space for potentially lethal decisions in warfare, there is a risk that the role of human judgment as to where the limits of ethical acts are becomes equally modular and computational, whereby flattening out, streamlining and problem-solving become increasingly prevalent modes of decision-making. Shifting military AI ethics into the realm of engineering might seem an obvious move in a technological ecology but it turns ethics into a technical matter, and in doing so, into risk management, rather than ethics. The two cannot be equated.

The question of how to address the ethics of autonomous, AI-powered systems is indeed looming large and remains thorny – in the military realm as well as in the commercial sector. Initiatives to address the ethics of military AI, especially those that include targeting systems, remain, to date, in the early stages of development. The US has pioneered a set of five principles to guide the use of military AI in 2018. These principles were formally adopted by the Pentagon in 2020 (Lopez 2020). The UK has followed suite and developed its own set of five principles in a 2022 policy paper, which closely mirrors the five elements developed by the US (Ministry of Defence 2022). Far from solving ethical dilemmas or indeed ensuring exactly how the mandate of responsibility is to be met with complex technological systems, the principles are ultimately reverse-engineered to reflect that which critics and proponents alike are most worried about. So rather than address ethical issues, they provide a technical veneer by which the development process is to be guided. This approach to military AI ethics fits effortlessly with the shift of ethics into the technical realm.

Principle-based thinking is increasingly prevalent in discussions on the ethics of autonomous systems, including projects that aim to make 'moral' lethal weapons systems. Where the world is seen primarily in calculable terms, it is not a stretch to consider it a logical next step to make ethics programmable through codes to find solutions to complex, multiple and conflicting ethical issues within plural contexts. Such is the aspiration of the engineer – to solve problems through data and computation. Roboticist Ronald Arkin's work is perhaps the most emblematic of this move towards ethics as a programme in the contemporary context of weapons systems. For him, the possibility of building ethical modules into lethal autonomous weapons systems would serve as a safeguard against wrong-doing and as a way to address the ethics of a lethal situation. The 'ethical governor', a software and interface module, provides an analysis of a given potentially lethal situation and assesses, broadly speaking, whether the potential lethal action falls within the parameters of the Laws of War (LOW) and the Rules of Engagement (ROE) relevant to a mission. It then alerts an operator if there are any possible violations so that "operator responsibility can be maintained while a mission is actively underway" (Arkin & Ulam 2012, p. 4). The calculation is presented to the operator through a graphical user interface "that conveys the ethical governor's status to the operator, providing continuous information regarding an armed unmanned system's potential use of lethal force during the conduct of a mission", thereby providing "ongoing ethical situational awareness of potential LOW and ROE violations" (Arkin & Ulam 2012, p. 4). The proposed prototype interface is a relatively rudimentary set of online boxes which show the ethical governor's recommendation – permission to fire either denied or granted – for a given situation, and an option to click on a 'More Info' tab for an explanation as to why the governor suggests that permission might be denied ('Damaging cultural property prohibited'). The operator can then, together with a second operator, decide to override the recommendation, by entering a validation key and permitting the system to fire, thereby retaining responsibility over the lethal action. This process is meant to be completed in highly time-critical situations.

Here, then, ethics is understood in very limited parameters, as codable rules. The ethical principles included in the system are those of the laws of armed conflict (law) and the rules of engagement (rules). Both of these are informed by ethics, but ethics, especially in war, can hardly be reduced to these principles. The system's capacity would, for example, not be able to flag an instance in which the system misidentifies a disarming combatant for a legitimate target, mistakes a turtle for a rifle, or works according to parameters that set the acceptable collateral damage estimates too high. In all of this, the 'responsible' operator has very limited situational awareness, let alone sufficient cognitive abilities to appropriately assess the ethical implications of what is taking place on the ground in a highly dynamic, messy and every-changing context of conflict, particularly with a very crude interface as the only guide. Much of the decision-making already takes place through the machine. A prompt to lethal action, rather than an opportunity to survey the scene and assess the situation and conditions on the ground are the more likely outcome here. Arkin's discussion, beginning with the title of the paper, is cast in the language of engineering – "Overriding Ethical Constraints" – such that ethics itself ultimately appears as a constraint, to be solved as an engineering problem by the smooth functioning of the machine.

Conclusion: AI logics and ethical practice

The allure of AI as a panacea for the challenges of future war is powerful in the present moment, its fields of application envisioned as near limitless. At this stage, AI works best for narrowly set optimisation tasks and within a controllable environment with limited parameters. Whether and how the technology might work appropriately as a decision support system within a command-and-control setting, such as is envisioned in the JADC2 programme or indeed for targeting operations, is not yet clear. Research suggests that the risks that a commander or operator becomes overly dependent on the authority of an AI decision are high. Insufficient and inappropriate data about something as complex and dynamic as a warzone are, however, likely to make such systems unreliable and potentially harmful. Where the weight of this burden of harm is born is not clear in the complex digital sphere.

The temptation to see ethics as an engineering problem when warfare itself is cast predominantly as a matter of technological prowess, rather than a complex social challenge with uncertain dynamics is high. The allure of the ostensibly neutral, comprehensive and smooth functioning machine operation subsumes the difficult, indeterminable and often unsolvable terrain, necessary to traverse for ethical decision-making, into its systems logic. It suggests that with enough data and engineering ingenuity any problem can be solved, including the 'problem' of ethics. However, if war's end is to be the goal, ethical matters cannot be cast in those terms. Ethics is difficult and asks questions that have no clear answers, often no answers at all, only better or worse decisions for which human actors will be asked to take responsibility. Applying a set of codes or principles cannot be equated with ethical thinking or moral agency. No doubt, codes, rules or laws constitute a part of ethics in military practice, but ethics cannot be reduced to them alone.

To not lose sight of this aspect of ethics in military practice, an active honing of ethical skills is required. As military ethicist David Whetham notes,

One's surrounding environment has an enormous effect on ethical awareness and motivation to act [...] Therefore, normalising routine engagement with ethical issues is hugely important in shaping behaviour. This is sometimes referred to as 'ethical muscle memory', representing the idea that it is easier to do the right thing if you have engaged with a situation in advance and are already familiar with the ethical landscape of the problem.

(Whetham 2018, p. 75)

And precisely herein lies the crux. A military operator or commander, embedded in a network of digital decision infrastructures, some of which take on the function of making morally relevant decisions, has precisely those cognitive skills truncated which are required for ethical awareness. Both situational awareness and the ethical muscle memory atrophies when technologies shape the cognitive scope, knowledge base and capacity for moral action. The skill degradation Cummings alludes to in her study on human-machine teaming includes a degradation of the skill to think ethically about complex and changing environments.

It is clear that today AI engineering has different priorities and logics, which often are not well aligned at all with the cumbersome and unwieldy demands of social, political and ethical human life. One might, however, would do well to heed the words of Norbert Wiener who warned already in the 1960s that coupling together "two agencies essentially foreign to each other" – the human being and the technological system – may herald a future not of progress but disaster.

Note

1 This is an adaptation of the following article published in 2021: Elke Schwarz, 'Silicon Valley Goes to War: Artificial Intelligence, Weapons Systems, and Moral Agency', *Philosophy Today*, vol. 65, no. 3, Summer 2021, pp. 549–69, https://doi.org/10.5840/philtoday2021519407.

References

AFC n.d., *Project Convergence*, Army Future Command, <https://armyfuturescommand.com/convergence/> (accessed 16 December 2022).

Arkin, R & Ulam, P 2012, *Overriding Ethical Constraints in Lethal Autonomous Systems*, Georgia Institute of Technology Mobile Robot Laboratory Technical Report GIT-MRL-12-01,1–8.

BAE Systems n.d., *What Does JADC2 Stand for?*, <https://www.baesystems.com/en-us/definition/what-does-jadc2-stand-for> (accessed 1 December 2022).

Chakour, S 2022, *Artificial Intelligence (AI) for Weapons Systems*, Defense Systems Information Analysis Center (DSIAC) State of the Art Report (SOAR), September, DSIAC-BCO-2022–216.

CDAO n.d., *About the JAIC: The JAIC Story*, Chief Digital and Artificial Intelligence Office, <https://www.ai.mil/about.html> (accessed 1 December 2022).

Congressional Research Service 2022, *Joint All-Domain Command and Control (JDAC2)*, Congressional Research Service Report IF11493, 21 January, <https://crsreports.congress.gov/> (accessed 16 December 2022).

Cummings, M L 2004, 'Automation Bias in Intelligent Time Critical Decision Support Systems', in *Conference Proceedings of the American Institute of Aeronautics and Astronautics*, AIAA 2004–6313.

Cummings, M L 2017, *Artificial Intelligence and the Future of Warfare*, Chatham House, London.

Faggella, D 2018, 'What Is Artificial Intelligence? An Informed Definition', *Emerj: AI Research and Insight*, 21 December, <https://emerj.com/ai-glossary-terms/what-is-artificial-intelligence-an-informed-definition/> (accessed 16 December 2022).

Freedberg Jr, S 2021, 'Army's New Aim Is Decision Dominance', *Breaking Defense*, 17 March, <https://breakingdefense.com/2021/03/armys-new-aim-is-decision-dominance/> (accessed 16 December 2022).

Globe Newswire 2022a, 'Autonomous Military Weapons Global Market Report 2022: Featuring Key Players Lockheed Martin, Raytheon, Boeing & Others', *Globe Newswire*, 5 August, <https://www.globenewswire.com/news-release/2022/08/05/2493025/0/en/Autonomous-Military-Weapons-Global-Market-Report-2022-Featuring-Key-Players-Lockheed-Martin-Raytheon-Boeing-Others.html> (accessed 16 December 2022).

Globe Newswire 2022b, '13+Billion Artificial Intelligence (AI) in Military Market Is expected to grow at CAGR of over 12.9% during 2022–2028', *Globe Newswire*, 14 April, <https://www.globenewswire.com/news-release/2022/04/14/2422469/0/en/13-Billion-Artificial-Intelligence-AI-in-Military-Market-is-Expected-to-Grow-at-a-CAGR-of-over-12-9-During-2022-2028-Vantage-Market-Research.html> (accessed 16 December 2022).

Gray, M & Ertan, A 2021, *Artificial Intelligence and Autonomy in the Military: An Overview of NATO Member States' Strategies and Deployment*, NATO Cooperative Cyber Defence Centre of Excellence (CCDCOE), Tallinn.

Holland Michel, A, 2021. *Known Unknowns: Data Issues and Military Autonomous Systems*, United Nations Institute for Disarmament Research, Geneva.

Hutson, M 2018, 'A Turtle or a Rifle? Hackers Easily Fool AIs into Seeing the Wrong Thing', *Science*, 19 July, <https://www.sciencemag.org/news/2018/07/turtle-or-rifle-hackers-easily-fool-ais-seeing-wrong-thing> (accessed 16 December 2022).

Kania, E 2020, 'AI Weapons in China's Military Innovation', in *Global China: Assessing China's Growing Role in the World*, Brookings Institute Report, Washington, DC, <https://www.brookings.edu/research/ai-weapons-in-chinas-military-innovation/> (accessed 16 December 2022).

Knight, W 2021, 'The Pentagon Inches Toward Letting AI Control Weapons', *WIRED*, 10 May, <https://www.wired.com/story/pentagon-inches-toward-letting-ai-control-weapons/> (accessed 16 December 2022).

Lacdan, J 2022, 'Project Convergence 2022: Army to Work Closely with Allies in the Future Fight', *U.S. Army News Service*, 16 November, <https://www.army.mil/article/262055/project_convergence_2022_army_to_work_closely_with_allies_in_the_future_fight#:~:text=Project%20Convergence%20falls%20under%20the,peer%20adversaries%20in%20future%20battles> (accessed 16 December 2022).

Lopez, C T 2020, 'DOD Adopts 5 Principles of Artificial Intelligence Ethics', *U.S. Department of Defense News*, 25 February, <https://www.defense.gov/News/News-Stories/Article/Article/2094085/dod-adopts-5-principles-of-artificial-intelligence-ethics/> (accessed 16 December 2022).

Noble, D 1999, *The Religion of Technology: The Divinity of Man and the Spirit of Invention*, Penguin, London.

NSCAI 2021, *The Final Report*, National Security Commission on Artificial Intelligence, <https://www.nscai.gov/2021-final-report/> (accessed 16 December 2022).

Pasquinelli, M 2019, 'How a Machine Learns and Fails: A Grammar of Error for Artificial Intelligence', *Spheres: Journal for Digital Cultures*, no. 5, pp. 1–17.

Shanahan, J 2019, 'Lt. Gen. Jack Shanahan Media Briefing on A.I.-Related Initiatives within the Department of Defense', *U.S. Department of Defense News*, 30 August, <https://www.defense.gov/Newsroom/Transcripts/Transcript/Article/1949362/lt-gen-jack-shanahan-media-briefing-on-ai-related-initiatives-within-the-depart/> (accessed 16 December 2022).

Sharkey, N 2018, 'Guidelines for the Human Control of Weapons System', *International Committee for Robot Arms Control Briefing Paper*, April.

Suchman, L 2020, 'Algorithmic Warfare and the Reinvention of Accuracy', *Critical Studies on Security*, vol. 8, no. 2, pp. 175–87, https://doi.org/10.1080/21624887.2020.1760587.

Taddeo, M, Mceish D, Blanchard A, & Edgar, E 2021, 'Ethical Principles for Artificial Intelligence in National Defence', *Philosophy & Technology*, vol. 34, pp. 1707–29, https://doi.org/10.1007/s13347-021-00482-3.

Thales 2019, 'Thales to Develop New Connected Sensors for Rafale F4 Standard', *Thales Communication,* 28 January, <https://www.thalesgroup.com/en/worldwide-defence/radio-communications/news/thales-develop-new-connected-sensors-rafale-f4-standard> (accessed 16 December 2022).

UK Ministry of Defence 2022, 'Ambitious, Safe, Responsible: Our Approach to the Delivery of AI Enabled Capability in Defence', *MoD Policy Report*, 15 June, <https://www.gov.uk/government/publications/ambitious-safe-responsible-our-approach-to-the-delivery-of-ai-enabled-capability-in-defence/ambitious-safe-responsible-our-approach-to-the-delivery-of-ai-enabled-capability-in-defence> (accessed 16 December 2022).

UN Security Council 2021, *Letter Dated 8 March 2021 from the Panel of Experts on Libya Established Pursuant to Resolution 1973(2011) addressed to the President of the Security Council*, 8 March 2021, United Nations, Geneva.

US Department of Defence 2022, 'Summary of the JOINT All-Domain Command and Control (JDAC2) Strategy', *U.S. Department of Defence*, March, <https://media.defense.gov/2022/Mar/17/2002958406/-1/-1/1/SUMMARY-OF-THE-JOINT-ALL-DOMAIN-COMMAND-AND-CONTROL-STRATEGY.PDF> (accessed 16 December 2022).

Whetham, D 2018, 'An Introduction and Review: The King's College London Centre for Military Ethics', *Journal of Military Ethics,* vol. 17, no. 1, pp. 72–9, https://doi.org/10.1080/15027570.2018.1505440.

Wiener, N 1960, 'Some Moral and Technical Consequences of Automation', *Science,* vol. 131, no. 3, 1355–58, https://doi.org/10.1126/science.131.3410.1355.

27

DIGITIZING THE BATTLEFIELD

Augmented and Virtual Reality
Applications in Warfare

Andrew N. Liaropoulos

Introduction

Throughout history, warfare has been shaped by geopolitical, societal, economic, military and technological factors. These factors also appear in the current discussion about the future of warfare, a discussion triggered by the developments in relation to the Fourth Industrial Revolution. This revolution builds on the third one – the Digital Revolution, but is not simply an expansion of it. The Fourth Industrial Revolution blurs the distinction between physical, digital and biological domains. Emerging technology breakthroughs in areas as diverse as artificial intelligence, robotics, the Internet of Things (IoT), three-dimensional printing, nanotechnology and quantum computing, profoundly affect every aspect of our society (Schwab 2016). In common with the previous revolutions that reshaped society and transformed the character of war, the current one is also bringing significant changes in how modern armies train, organize and conduct operations (Hammes 2018; Raska, Zysk & Powers 2022).

Speculating on the future of warfare is truly a difficult task. Thinking about the next war is usually limited by projecting past experiences forward. It is a human tendency to think linearly about what might happen, based on what has happened. This chapter is not offering predictions but a critical analysis of what augmented reality (AR) and virtual reality (VR) offer in the modern battlefield. The chapter first approaches the reality spectrum in order to define key terms and differences. The emphasis is on AR, VR and the novel concept of metaverse. Having conceptualized a framework on what the above developments entail, the chapter then shifts its focus to the implications in the military domain. In the end, the broader question of whether AR and VR have an evolutionary or revolutionary impact on warfare is addressed. The purpose is to link the digital developments in the present battlefield with a holistic understanding of warfare in both technological and socio-political terms.

The reality spectrum

Over the past years, advances in information technology, artificial intelligence and high-resolution displays, offer us new ways to experience reality. Reality refers to the actual, physical world that exists and that we navigate every day. The reality spectrum extends from simple overlaying of data into the user's vision to full immersive three-dimensional virtual representations of reality. To begin with, reality includes both actual elements (e.g. physical objects like a device) and virtual (e.g. virtual assistants like Siri or Alexa, which do not actually exist, but are real since we interact with them). Thus, virtuality is not opposed to reality, but it is opposed to actuality (Farshid et al. 2018, p. 658).

In 1994, Paul Milgram and Fumio Kishino introduced the notion of the reality-virtuality (RV) continuum and the term mixed reality (MR) in their seminal work titled "A Taxonomy of Mixed Reality Visual Displays". Milgram and Kishino (1994) offered an overview of how technologies allow us to move from the real world – one side of the spectrum, to the virtual world – the other side of the spectrum and the types of augmented environments in between. In the past two decades, movies like *Minority Report* and the *Matrix* series of films have popularized the reality spectrum. *Minority Report* presented futuristic technologies like heads-up display that are being implemented nowadays and *Matrix* illustrated the idea of a computer-generated, three-dimensional space in which users are integrated. Likewise, the *Iron Man* films and *Pacific Rim*, demonstrated how soldiers operate in a digitally augmented battlefield, using encased suits (Stahl 2010; Tucker 2017).

Nowadays, devices like headsets and smart glasses that replace aspects of the real world with digital elements have become cheaper and accessible to millions of users. The rapid rise of these technologies also brought with them a number of new terms that are commonly used to describe how such technologies generate or modify reality. Thus, there is reference to augmented, enhanced, virtual, mixed, hybrid, assisted, extended and digital reality, not to forget the latest catchphrase – metaverse (Rauschnabel et al. 2022).

AR refers to the integration of the actual world with digital information about it. It involves an interactive experience of a real-world environment, where objects that exist in the real world are enhanced via computer-generated representations. It overlays digital content on a live view of the real world, thus it enhances reality. AR relies on data provided by satellite-based navigation systems and artificial intelligence to generate features. These digital features are delivered through smart glasses, headsets and portable devices such as smartphones (Graig 2013). Any smart device with a camera and the proper software can function as an AR training tool. The goal of AR is to highlight specific features of the physical world, increase understanding of those features and thus develop awareness that can be applied to real-world applications. AR allows its users to interact with the real world, while at the same time augmented digital content is added to the real world around them (Jacobsen 2021, p. 94).

VR refers to complete, three-dimensional virtual representations of the actual world or of objects within it. It is not a real world experience, but a computer-simulated environment, which can simulate places in the real world as well as imaginary ones, offering users the ability to immerse themselves into artificial environments that stimulate sensory experiences (Jacobsen 2021, p. 94). Thus, VR creates an artificial digital environment that completely replaces the real environment. In this digital and simulated environment, hearing and vision are created and delivered to the user by a digital device like a headset (Sherman & Graig 2003). AR overlays visual elements, sound and other sensory input into real-world settings to enhance the user's experience. In contrast, VR is entirely simulated and enhances fictional realities. AR uses the real world environment to project virtual information, whereas VR immerses users into an artificial environment generated by digital technologies.

In between, there is MR. The latter involves a combination of aspects from both real and virtual environments with the use of digital elements. MR enables the user to interact with both the virtual and physical world in real time. In contrast to AR, where the virtual objects are placed on a separate layer on top of the physical world, in MR the virtual objects can be mapped to the physical environment (Farshid et al. 2018; Quora 2018). Table 27.1 summarizes the typology of realities, the devices used and their applications.

Table 27.1 The reality spectrum

Reality Types	(a) Augmented Reality	(b) Mixed Reality	(c) Virtual Reality
Description	Combination of real-life and digital (offers only observation). Users interact and remain present in the real world.	Combination of real-life and virtual (enables real time interactions with the environment and the user).	Fully artificial /computer simulated environment. Users are fully immersed in a virtual environment, removed from the real world.
Devices	Mobile phones, tablets, smart watches, smart glasses	Headsets, translucent glasses	Headsets, data gloves
Application	Training, design and analysis, manufacturing, gaming, enhanced user experience, immersive learning		

The metaverse is a form of reality that combines aspects of social media, IoT, AR and VR in order to enable its users to interact virtually. The metaverse is a concept of a persistent, three-dimensional universe that combines virtual spaces, where users can meet, work and socialize. It is important to note that the term does not refer to a specific type of technology, but rather to a new and often notional way of interacting with existing digital technologies (Ravescraft 2022). Science fiction author Neal Stephenson first coined the term 'metaverse in' the 1992 novel titled *Snow Crash*. He defined metaverse as a computer-generated universe, where human avatars and software agents interact in a three-dimensional virtual space (Stephenson 1992, p. 23). The metaverse can be described as a synthesis of several technological entities that empower its users to 'live' within the digital realm (Rospigliosi 2022). The metaverse does not transmute into a single and unified digital entity, but rather to multiple virtual worlds that complement each other.

Over the past years, private companies and platforms have already developed applications and virtual worlds that emulate the logic of the metaverse. One can identify elements of the metaverse in existing virtual video game worlds like Second Life and Fortnite (Ravescraft 2022). Facebook's rebranding as Meta has made the metaverse the latest catchphrase in the digital industry. Meta's latest development is a VR platform called Horizon Worlds, where users can explore, build virtual communities and connect with audiences (Heath 2022; Meta 2022). The vision of a fully immersive Internet, where users, equipped with VR headsets and AR glasses, interact via avatars is still under development.

The evolution of the metaverse involves three phases: the digital twins, the digital residents and last surreality (The Wix 2022). The metaverse is a digital mirror of the physical world and digital twins are the building blocks of this new reality. Digital twins are digital replicas of physical entities, products, processes and systems. They provide a connection between a physical entity and its virtual counterpart. The connection is established by sensors which provide real-time data exchange. Digital twins mirror a lifelike digital reproduction of the actual world. The digital twin of an object enables us to completely recreate it with live data, but also evaluate it and reinsert it back into the system. Reality and virtuality coexist as two parallel spaces (Apte & Spanos 2021; Holopainen et al. 2022).

The second phase involves digital residents, the digital representatives in the virtual world, who develop content. Practically these are the digital avatars who produce insights in virtual spaces. Digital twins are responsible for reproducing a digital version of our world – the metaverse, which is then populated with avatars (Marr 2022). The last phase involves surreality, where a mature version of the metaverse will gradually absorb reality into itself. Even though the metaverse 'actualizes' the convergence of the physical and the virtual world, the latter might emerge as a place where people choose to exist in a more active way (The Wix 2022). In this phase, users will live and interact with the virtual objects integrated in the metaverse. Advanced holographic technology and high-quality head-mounted displays (HMDs) will blur the difference between real and virtual, thus materializing a state of surreality. In the same way that the Internet served as the backbone of cyberspace, the metaverse might function as the medium that will enable us to experience a new domain and a new reality, created by interconnected virtual worlds. Such a development will profoundly affect how societies, economies and governments function and how armies train and fight.

Applying the 'new realities' in the military

Technology has been integrated into military strategy and tactics since the beginning of time. The use of metallurgy, gunpowder, combustion engines and computers has all altered the way wars were conducted in the past (Van Creveld 1991). In many cases, the way technology is used in relation to warfare is unpredictable. When iPhones first entered the market, no one could imagine that in less than a decade they could serve as powerful encrypted communication tools that commanders use in order to communicate and interact with their soldiers in the battlefield. There is no doubt that AR and VR technologies enable the modern military to train (e.g., personnel training, flight training, weapons training), simulate battles and execute operations in a more sophisticated way. AR and VR devices and applications alter the way that soldiers access information and conduct operations. The examples are truly vast, since AR and VR have become routine aspects of military training. What follows below is a selective and critical analysis of what these technologies offer. The areas where AR and VR add value to the modern military include among others training, manufacturing, maintenance, repair, security system checks and operations.

To begin with, in the early 2000s, the Defence Advanced Research Projects Agency (DARPA) developed the Personalized Assistant that Learns (PAL) programme. This involved cognitive computing systems to make military decision-making more efficient and more effective at multiple levels of command. PAL aimed to reduce the need for large command staffs; and enable smaller, more mobile, and less vulnerable command centers. The use of the PAL programme was not restricted to the military domain, but also led to applications for civilian devices. In particular, it led to the 2007 launch of Siri Inc, later acquired by Apple and used in its mobile operating system. Furthermore, DARPA recently launched the Perceptually enabled Task Guidance (PTG) program to develop virtual task guidance assistants that can provide just-in-time visual and audio feedback to help human users expand their skillsets and minimize their errors. This program involves virtual task assistants that are able to automatically acquire task knowledge from instructions intended for humans, including checklists, illustrated manuals and training videos (DARPA 2021).

AR is applied in the high-tech helmet for the F-35 fighter jet, which includes a display that shows telemetry data and target information on top of video footage around the aircraft. In 2018, the US Army paid Microsoft $22 billion to develop a version of its HoloLens augmented reality system for warfighters, known as the Integrated Visual Augmentation System (IVAS). Likewise, in 2014, the Office of Naval Research and the Institute for Creative Technologies at the University of Southern California developed Project BlueShark, a system that allowed sailors to drive vessels and collaborate in a virtual environment (Hollister 2014). Another example is Project Avenger developed by the US Navy. It is a training program advanced in 2021 which aims to reduce the time of training by utilizing virtual reality headsets, artificial intelligence and advanced biometrics (Correll 2021). Finally, the US and the UK have developed synthetic environments for large-scale and sophisticated simulations. In particular, the US Army Synthetic Training Environment (STE) and the UK Ministry of Defence's Synthetic Environment (SE) offer multi-dimensional training and mission rehearsal capability, by combining live, virtual and constructive training environments into a single one (Datta 2022; Nash 2022).

In general, AR applications enhance operational and situational awareness, thus enabling commanders and soldiers to make better judgments of the issues at stake. In the form of smart glasses and other devices, AR presents data regarding spatial orientation, situational awareness, weapons targeting and digital terrain, in order to ensure safety, speed and coordination. AR devices allow soldiers to familiarize themselves with features such as night vision, thermal sensing and applications that measure vital signs during trainings (Virca 2021). Another field where AR is used, is for ground support, to treat medical casualties; in case a trained medic is absent. Often used for training purposes, AR is effective for warfare simulations, military sand tables, battlefield visualizations and other applications that project a realistic representation of military activities (Herrmann & Steed 2018).

The applications of VR in defense are also notable. VR enables the officers to create a simulation, to design a virtual battlefield, where they can exercise their tactics and attacks. This offers them a valuable experience of a life-threatening environment at less cost. A practical application of the above is the concept of the so-called enhanced soldier. Smart helmets allow the transmission of crucial information (e.g., maps and environmental factors) from commanders to ground forces and lead to significantly faster decisions and lower error rates. Since information is easily accessible and presented, this allows soldiers to continue to act according to the on-ground situation, without stopping to look at screens and coordinates. A VR headset enhances a soldier's capacity with extra information regarding the tactical situation. Likewise, night-and-day vision binoculars enable the infantry soldier to acquire nyctalopic vision, the ability to see in the dark and obviously have a tactical advantage (De Boisboissel & Le Masson 2021, p. 2).

One of the areas where AR and VR are vastly used in the military sector is that of immersive training. Such technologies provide officers flight and battlefield simulations, weapons simulations, vehicle simulations and virtual boot camps (Amorim 2013). We should bear in mind that VR simulations are a quite useful platform to train the younger generation of soldiers who have grown up spending hundreds of hours with Nintendo, Xbox and PlayStation computer games (Orvis et al. 2010). By utilizing VR soldiers can understand what to expect while firing a missile in combat circumstances. With immersive training soldiers can simulate and experience the stress of a parachute jump or the fear of confined spaces, like that in fighter jets, submarines and tanks (claustrophobia). Likewise, AR and VR applications simulate training for extreme conditions. These simulated scenarios enhance situational awareness, navigation, and they foster team-building activities, and development of survival and leadership skills in extreme environments like jungle, desert or arctic terrain. Such applications improve practical lessons for learning in rescue training, which is of central importance in real-life situations (Deloitte 2019, p. 20). AR systems provide complex three-dimensional environment for military operations, enabling soldier to adjust to various terrains. In the case of urban warfare, three-dimensional drawings of architectural designs and building facilities enhance combat capability by far (You et al. 2018, p. 3). Adding to the above, there is also the advantage of real time remote collaboration among different soldiers and units in a virtual environment. This does not only accelerate decision-making processes, but also reduces travel costs and the facilitation of logistics (Dodevska et al. 2018, p. 592).

VR technology offers significant benefit in the areas of weapon design and manufacturing. In relation to weapons development, VR applications are used to provide advance demonstration, so that developers and users can engage simultaneously in the virtual combat environment, test the design, operate a weapon system, and access its technical performance and tactical characteristics. This process speeds up the development cycle of the weapon system and provides a reasonable assessment of its operational effectiveness, in order to adjust it closer to the actual combat requirements (Liu 2018, p. 5).

Likewise, another example is the use of digital twins for the design and construction of navy ships and engines. VR is utilized in order to draw a digital ship model and a real time simulation platform enables the designer to monitor and analyze the way the various digital components and the engine integrate with the ship model (Deloitte 2019, p. 20). Another area where AR and VR instruments are applied is that of maintenance and repair. These technologies are useful for the maintenance of equipment without the need to study two-dimensional printed manuals, since instructions can be shown as layers over a real three-dimensional object. Thus, errors are limited and the usual time needed for maintenance is reduced to the minimum. Due to AR instruments, soldiers in the field can be remotely guided to repair equipment like a battle tank in real combat situation. Such instruments can detect, scan and recognize malfunctions, communicate with remote data centers to receive necessary data and guidance in order to proceed with the repair (Dodevska et al. 2018, p. 592). Such technologies can raise awareness to designers and technicians to take all necessary actions in the case of equipment malfunction and thereby reduce time and cost of repair.

Performing security system checks is of vital importance for modern armies. AR technologies facilitate a better understanding of complex weapon systems in many ways. They offer visualization of information, which facilitates a more comprehensive analysis of the system and they provide step-by-step instructions, which simplify procedures and finally real time security monitoring (Dodevska et al. 2018, p. 592). Another area where AR and VR technologies are applicable is that of medical training and on-the-ground emergency support. VR devices have been applied to train doctors and paramedics. The training provides a virtual environment where they can simulate on how to carry out life-saving operations in a real warzone. Such simulations improve response time and efficiency of response. The ability to remotely view a patient, permits on-field doctors to utilize a level of expertise that might otherwise be absent in the field (Deloitte 2019, pp. 21, 29).

VR has also major applicability in the field of clinical purposes, such as image-guided therapy, motor-skills rehabilitation, but also cognitive assessment and mental health therapy, like the post-traumatic stress disorder (PTSD). Regarding the latter, many veterans returning from their missions, had to cope with stress disorders that were caused during combat, because of injury or torture or even because of being imprisoned by the enemy. The virtual exposure therapy places veterans that are experiencing PTSD in a provocative, yet also controlled virtual environment, in order to confront their traumatic memories (Riverasaenz 2019, p. 2). Another area where VR technology is applied is that of cultural awareness. The evidence from conflicts that involved culturally diverse audiences, like those of Iraq and Afghanistan, revealed that a number of incidents were caused by miscommunication between the local population and the soldiers. Thus, more than 80 countries have developed web-based virtual cultural awareness training (VCAT) tools, which enable warfighters to practice interpersonal skills in a safe environment (TechLink 2017).

In terms of actual combat, a major advantage that AR offers is the so-called tactical augmented reality (TAR). This practically means improved situational awareness with TAR equipment (e.g., a helmet mounded AR display), permitting soldiers to replace the handheld global positioning system device and goggles. Such devices also include a thermal site on the weapon that is connected to the TAR eyepiece and a tablet on the soldier's waist. Such systems allow soldiers to see the target they are aiming at and the distance to it. The display can be split in two so that soldiers can see where their guns are pointing while also seeing the view from the frontal camera on the helmet. A soldier can see around a corner or over a wall without any risk of getting a headshot. TAR also includes a wireless network that allows soldiers to share information among their platoon members or input data whenever the situation changes (Kallberg et al. 2022).

The future of military training is the metaverse. It is only natural that the military has a strong interest in connecting and combining real and virtual worlds, mainly for training purposes, experimentation and mission rehearsal (Knight 2022; Vanorio 2022). After all, metaverse-related ideas are already part of some military systems, like the high-tech helmets that include AR displays. The military has developed simulations covering land, sea, air and space, flight simulators, tank simulators and successfully integrated these simulators for combined arms training. Nevertheless, moving from these simulations to a metaverse environment is not an easy task. For example, it is difficult to represent a dense urban environment in a simulation. Representing more than a few thousand people and vehicle entities is expensive and time-consuming. Additionally, each simulation uses its own format for terrain data, making it challenging to build perfectly correlated terrain (Datta 2022).

Adding to the above, the main difference between the military metaverse and the commercial ones is that the former has to deliver a high-fidelity digital twin of the real world. Virtual simulations of military missions require an accurate three-dimensional representation of a target area. In contrast to the commercial one, in a military metaverse, a digital twin is a necessity. Another difficulty in relation to materializing metaverse is security. In the military metaverse, a vast amount of sensitive data (e.g. biometrics) is collected and applied to create digital twins. Thus, data security is crucial in terms of preventing data breaches and the spread of malware. Finally, we should not underestimate the fact that the metaverse is mainly virtual, thus useful for training, whereas the military exists and produces results, mainly in the physical world. The hard reality of recent conflicts serves as a strong reminder that wars are (still) fought on land, sea and air and not solely in a virtual battlespace.

A revolution in the 'reality' of warfare?

As stated above, AR and VR offer numerous advantages that range from situational awareness and simulations, to training and maintenance of equipment. In common with previous cases of radical military innovation, the question that is inevitably raised is whether AR and VR applications have a revolutionary or evolutionary impact on the way military operations are conducted. A closer look at these technologies reveals the following challenges.

First, there are some technical and practical challenges regarding AR. These include connectivity issues, difficulty in the orientation and alignment of the real-world and simulated objects, low processing power and weak radio signals for deployed troops, weight issues for infantry and difficulties in seeing AR-generated objects in natural light. Adding to the above, the operational environment for AR and VR might include extreme heat, cold and humidity, thus environmental conditions that degrade the performance of electronic devices (Kallberg et al. 2022, p. 110).

Second, there is a challenge of information overload. Headsets, instant messaging and radio transmissions may produce a large amount of raw data that, if not properly structured, might add confusion instead of clarity in the decision-making process. Although not a new problem, if data are not properly filtered and constructed, AR instruments might be more of a hinder than an enhancement. Thus, the real challenge for AR technology is to reduce data load for both information systems and human operators in the battlefield (Dodevska et al. 2018, p. 592).

Third, dependence on AR and VR technologies might lead to overdependence and the latter is always a vulnerability when planning and executing operations. There are reasonable concerns that commanders might rely too much on AR to make decisions. Thus, any type of disruption or even worse destruction of AR systems will give the enemy a significant advantage (Kallberg et al. 2022, p. 108). Thus, although the advantages that technologies bring with them are always welcome, commanders and soldiers should always develop a variety of skill sets. For example, if transmissions are jammed, the infantryman should be able to reap a printed map.

Fourth, there are always security concerns regarding the communication and data storing by AR and VR systems. The soldiers trust the pixels that appear in a screen with their lives. Data manipulation and loss of integrity might lead to the failure of an operation and casualties (Kallberg et al. 2022, p. 107). As the metaverse is still very much in its infancy, the extent and scale of risks that are related to its integration with the military domain are still unknown. Nevertheless, existing challenges to cybersecurity are also expected to apply to the case of metaverse.

The above challenges only partly answer the question about the evolutionary or revolutionary impact of these technologies in the conduct of military operations in the near future. The reason is that the analysis so far is technology driven and does not link the technological developments with the socio-political ones. After all, technology is only one part of the equation and the transformational effects of AR and VR are only limited to the tactical and operational level, and not the strategic one.

The literature on RMA frames the revolutionary aspects in relation to emerging technologies, novel operational concepts and new force structures (Raska 2021, pp. 456–7) and undervalues the socio-political mode of warfare. Thus, over the past two decades, references on information warfare, network-centric warfare, cyber warfare and many more, abound. History teaches us that the course of the previous RMAs (Liaropoulos 2016) was not defined by the novel technologies that triggered changes in the way militaries fought, but was rather defined by the socio-political parameters of the actors involved. History is full of examples, where actors with similar technological capabilities chose different organizational concepts and formed different military doctrines (Sloan 2002). The reasons have to do more with strategic culture and less with technology. Thus, it is the socio-political parameters of the actors involved in a conflict that define whether hybrid war or cyber war is the most appropriate choice to enforce its will on the opponent, and not technology. Any effort to understand war, and even more to plan for a future one, has to take into account that war has several contexts – political, social, cultural – and not only the technological one.

Conclusions

Adapting to the changing character of war in the Fourth Industrial Revolution is a tremendous challenge for the military domain. There is no doubt that modern armies have long realized the huge potential of AR and VR in every aspect of warfare, from training and simulations, to manufacturing and gaining situational, but also cultural awareness in the real battlefield. Although some of these technologies are still under development, it is safe to argue that they provide an immersive way for training and optimizing operations. It is only a matter of time for modern armies to apply metaverse-related concepts in their everyday practice.

Nevertheless, placing the technological developments analyzed above in a broader strategic context forces us to rethink how AR and VR might shape the future of warfare. Since it is impossible to predict the future, all that is left to us, is to use the lessons of history and apply them critically in the present situation. Technology defines warfare, but does not determine wars. Technology has been the primary source of military innovation throughout history. It drives changes in warfare more than any other factor, but it does not win or lose wars on its own. History teaches us that we need to avoid technological determinism and embrace the fact that war is inherently complex and political in nature. Technology was, is and will always be one among the many factors that shape the conduct of warfare. Sophisticated technologies like AR and VR aim to optimize a soldier's situational awareness, shape perception, compress time and accelerate decision-making. In common with past technologies who promised to lift the fog of war, it is reasonable to question whether AR and VR will limit friction and uncertainty in future battlefield. It seems inevitable that tomorrow's soldiers will have their reality enhanced, but it is also certain that the reality of war is political and not technological. There is no doubt that technology has changed how the military fights wars and how it plans for wars, but the decision-makers cannot lose sight of the human and political domains of war regardless of any technological advances.

References

Amorim, J, Matos, C, Cuperschmid, A & Gustavsson, P 2013, 'Augmented Reality and Mixed Reality Technologies: Enhancing Training and Mission Preparation with Simulations', *NATO, STO-MP-MSG-111*, pp. 1–16 <https://doi: 10.14339/STO-MP-MSG-111–09-pdf>.

Apte, P & Spanos, C 2021, 'The Digital Twin Opportunity', *MIT Sloan Management Review,* 11 August, <https://sloanreview.mit.edu/article/the-digital-twin-opportunity/> (accessed 6 September 2022).

Correll, D 2021, 'Navy's New "Project Avenger" Flight Training Program Aims to Produce Stronger Aviators', *Navy Times,* 26 March, <https://www.navytimes.com/news/your-navy/2021/05/25/navys-new-project-avenger-flight-training-program-aims-to-produce-stronger-aviators/> (accessed 15 November 2022).

DARPA 2021, *Developing Virtual Partners to Assist Military Personnel*, 3 March, <https://www.darpa.mil/news-events/2021-03-03> (accessed 7 November 2022).

Datta, A 2022, 'What Is Military Metaverse and How Is it Different from Commercial Metaverse', *Geospatial World,* 29 June 2022, <https://www.geospatialworld.net/prime/interviews/what-is-military-metaverse-and-how-is-it-different-from-commercial-metaverse/> (accessed 28 September 2022).

De Boisboissel, G & Le Masson, J-M 2021, 'The Enhanced Soldier. Definitions', *Military Review Online Exclusive,* <https://www.armyupress.army.mil/Journals/Military-Review/Online-Exclusive/2021-French-OLE/Part-2-Definitions/> (accessed 1 September 2022).

Deloitte 2019, *Virtual, Augmented, and Mixed Reality for Defence and the Public Sector*, 11 July, <https://www2.deloitte.com/in/en/pages/about-deloitte/articles/vr-ar-mr.html> (accessed 2 September 2022).

Dodevska, Z, Mihić, M & Manasijević, S 2018, 'The Role of Augmented Reality in Defensive Activities', *8th International Scientific Conference on Defensive Technologies, OTEH 2018,* 11–12 October, Belgrade, <https://www.researchgate.net/profile/Srecko-Manasijevic/publication/328580806_The_Role_of_Augmented_Reality_in_Defensive_Activities/links/5c3b36ec92851c22a37167b0/The-Role-of-Augmented-Reality-in-Defensive-Activities.pdf> (accessed 1 September 2022).

Farshid, M, Paschen, J, Ekrisson, T & Kietzmann, J 2018, 'Go Boldly! Explore Augmented Reality (AR), Virtual Reality (VR), and Mixed Reality (MR) for Business', *Business Horizons*, vol. 61, no. 5, pp. 657–63, https://doi: 10.1016/j.bushor.2018.05.009.

Graig, A 2013, *Understanding Augmented Reality. Concepts and Applications,* Morgan Kaufman Publishers, San Francisco, CA.

Hammes, T X 2018, 'Technological Change and the Fourth Industrial Revolution' in G P Shultz, J Hoaglabd & J Timbie (eds), *Beyond Disruption: Technology's Challenge to Governance,* Hoover Institution Press, Washington, DC, pp. 37–73.

Heath, A 2022, 'Meta's Social VR Platform Horizon Hits 300,000 Users', *The Verge*, 18 February, <https://www.theverge.com/2022/2/17/22939297/meta-social-vr-platform-horizon-300000-users> (accessed 9 September 2022).

Herrmann, J & Steed, B 2018, 'Understanding Information as a Weapon. The Virtual Reality/Sand Table Model of Information Conflict', *Military Review Online Exclusive,* <https://www.armyupress.army.

mil/Journals/Military-Review/Online-Exclusive/2018-OLE/Understanding-Information/> (accessed 1 September 2022).

Hollister, S 2014, 'BlueShark: Where the US Navy Dreams up the Battleship Interfaces of Tomorrow', *The Verge*, 26 January, <https://www.theverge.com/2014/1/26/5346772/blueshark-us-navy-oculus-rift-virtual-interface> (accessed 15 November 2022).

Holopainen, M, Saunila, M, Rantala, T & Ukko, J 2022, '"Digital Twins" Implications for Innovation', *Technology Analysis & Strategic Management*, pp. 1–13, https://doi: 10.1080/09537325.2022.2115881.

Jacobsen, M (ed) 2021, *The Age of Spectacular Death*, Routledge, New York.

Kallberg, J, Beitelman, V, Mitsuoka, V, Pittman, J, Boyce, M & Arnold, T 2022, 'The Tactical Considerations of Augmented and Mixed Reality Implementation', *Military Review*, May-June, pp. 105–13, <https://www.armyupress.army.mil/Journals/Military-Review/English-Edition-Archives/May-June-2022/Kallberg/> (accessed 3 September 2022).

Knight, W 2022, 'The US Military is building its own metaverse', *Wired*, 17 May, <https://www.wired.com/story/military-metaverse/> (accessed 20 November 2022).

Liaropoulos, A 2016, 'Revolutions in Warfare: Theoretical Paradigms and Historical Evidence – The Napoleonic and First World War Revolutions in Military Affairs', *Journal of Military History*, vol. 70, no. 2, pp. 363–84.

Liu, X, Zhang, J. Hou, G & Wang, Z 2018, 'Virtual Reality and its Application in Military', *IOP Conf. Series: Earth and Environmental Science*, vol. 170, pp. 1–7, https://doi:10.1088/1755-1315/170/3/032155.

Marr, B 2022, 'How to Create Your Digital Avatar for the Metaverse', *Forbes*, 27 May, <https://www.forbes.com/sites/bernardmarr/2022/05/27/how-to-create-your-digital-avatar-for-the-metaverse/?sh=102c5c102f1d> (accessed 8 September 2022).

Meta 2022, *Launcing Horizon Worlds in More Countries in Europe*, 16 August, <https://about.fb.com/news/2022/08/launching-horizon-worlds-in-more-countries-in-europe/> (accessed 8 September 2022).

Milgram, P & Kishino, F 1994, 'A Taxonomy of Mixed Reality Visual Displays', *IEICE Transactions on Information and Systems*, vol. E77-D, no. 12, pp. 1321–29.

Nash, T 2022, 'The Force-on-Force Training Challenge', *Military Technology*, vol. XLVI, no. 2, pp. 8–11, <https://monch.com/ebooks/military-technology/2022/MilTech_02-2022/> (accessed 16 November 2022).

Orvis, K, Moore, J, Belanish, J, Murphy, S & Horn, D 2010, 'Are Soldiers Gamers? Videogame Usage among Soldiers and Implications for the Effective Use of Serious Videogames for Military Training', *Military Psychology*, vol. 22, pp. 143–57, https://doi: 10.1080/08995600903417225.

Quora 2018, 'The Difference between Virtual Reality, Augmented Reality, and Mixed Reality', *Forbes*, 2 February, <https://www.forbes.com/sites/quora/2018/02/02/ the-difference-between-virtual-reality-> (accessed 2 September 2022).

Raska, M 2021, 'The Sixth RMA Wave: Disruption in Military Affairs?', *Journal of Strategic Studies*, vol. 44, no. 4, pp. 456–79, https://doi: 10.1080/01402390.2020.1848818.

Raska, M, Zysk, K & Powers, I 2022, *Defence Innovation and the 4th Industrial Revolution*, Routledge, New York.

Rauschnabel, P A, Felix, R, Hinsch, C, Shahab, H & Alt, F 2022, 'What Is XR? Towards a Framework for Augmented and Virtual Reality', *Computers in Human Behaviour*, vol. 133, pp. 1–18, https://doi.org/10.1016/j.chb.2022.107289.

Ravescraft, E 2022, 'What Is Metaverse, Exactly?', *Wired*, 25 April, <https://www.wired.com/story/what-is-the-metaverse/> (accessed 7 September 2022).

Riverasaenz, J 2019, 'Technology and Warfare. Concepts and Integration', *NCO Journal*, 17 June, <https://www.armyupress.army.mil/journals/nco-journal/archives/2019/june/technology-and-warfare/> (accessed 3 September 2022).

Rospigliosi, P 2022, 'Metaverse or Simulacra? Roblox, Minecraft, Meta and the Turn to Virtual Reality for Education, Socialisation and Work', *Interactive Learning Environments*, vol. 30, no. 1, pp. 1–3, https://doi.org/10.1080/10494820.2022.2022899.

Schwab, K 2016, *The Fourth Industrial Revolution*, Penguin Random House, New York.

Sherman, W & Graig, A 2003, *Understanding Virtual Reality. Interface, Application and Design*, Morgan Kaufman Publishers, San Francisco, CA.

Sloan, E 2002, *The Revolution in Military Affairs*, McGill-Queen's University Press, Montreal.

Stahl, R 2010, *Militainment, Inc. War, Media and Popular Culture*, Routledge, New York.

Stephenson, N 1992, *Snow Crash*, Bantam Books, New York.

TechLink 2017, *The Military's Virtual Cultural Awareness Training Technology*, TechLink, 22 February, <https://techlinkcenter.org/news/military-virtual-cultural-awareness-training-technology/> (accessed 18 November 2022).

The Wix 2022, 'The Technologies That Power the Virtual World', *The Wix*, 15 September, <https://thewix.com.au/virtual-reality/the-technologies-that-power-the-virtual-world/> (accessed 16 September 2022).

Tucker, A 2017, *Virtual Weaponry. The Militarized Internet in Hollywood War Films,* Palgrave Macmillan, Cham.

Van Creveld, M 1991, *Technology and War. From 2000 B.C to the Present*, The Free Press, New York.

Vanorio, F 2022, 'Metaverse: Implications for Security and Intelligence', *NATO Defense College Foundation Paper*, <https://www.natofoundation.org/wp-content/uploads/2022/02/NDCF-Paper-Vanorio-110222.pdf > (accessed 8 September 2022).

Virca, I, Bârsan, G, Oancea, R & Vesa, C 2021, 'Applications of Augmented Reality Technology in the Military Education Field', *Land Forces Academy Review*, vol. XXVI, no. 104, pp. 337–47, https://doi:10.2478/raft-2021–0044.

You, X, Zhang, W, Ma, M, Deng, C & Yang, J 2018, 'Survey on Urban Warfare Augmented Reality, *ISPRS International Journal of Geo-Information,* vol. 7, no. 2, pp. 1–7, https://doi.org/10.3390/ijgi7020046.

28

QUANTUM WARFARE

James Der Derian and Stuart Rollo

Introduction

The transition from the machine-based industrial age to a new digital society and economy has already radically transformed the way we live and work, make war and seek security. It is predicted that the development and use of quantum technologies will not just quicken the winds of change, but completely revolutionise the way information is processed, with implications for society, economy and statecraft of a magnitude that we are perhaps not fully able to appreciate at this time. Still in its nascent stages, the development of quantum technology is today largely being fostered by states, with governments around the world providing the major source of funding for quantum research and influencing the direction of quantum developments. In this environment, the application of quantum technology to matters of international security competition warrants critical scholarly attention.

Quantum technology has the potential to influence international security on multiple levels. In the most visible and direct sense, it could produce breakthroughs in weapons, communications, sensing and computing technology that will recalibrate the strategic balance between military forces and reshape our broader conceptions of geopolitics in areas as diverse as critical resource supplies and nuclear deterrence. In a densely networked, information-saturated battlespace, in which visual media and messaging exerts unprecedented influence on geopolitics, quantum computers, communications, control and artificial intelligence (QC3AI) has the potential to further reduce the human element in future warfare, and accelerate trends of cyber and hybrid war.

The quantum revolution also holds profound implications for international security on the level of world order. The development of new, disruptive, expensive and research-intensive technologies will certainly affect global power distribution. In this sense, quantum technology is likely to exacerbate inequality of strategic capacity and power between the 'haves' and 'have-nots'. The realignment of world power propelled by developments in quantum technology that is most commonly envisaged by security experts would see the re-emergence of the kind of superpower rivalry that characterised the Cold War, although now between the United States and China, seeking advantage in their struggle for global economic and strategic supremacy through the development and deployment of power multiplying innovations in quantum technology. This logic, based on a classical worldview of Newtonian physics and Hobbesian politics, is embedded in the traditional

 DOI: 10.4324/9781003299011-34

realist world of International Relations. It invokes a world of unitary actors pursuing self-help strategies, bouncing off each other like billiard balls, with an underlying mechanistic equilibrium keeping the order intact if not necessarily just, peaceful or predictable.

There is also the strong possibility that the revolutionary character of this technology could have other unforeseen, or 'weird' in the parlance of quantum science, effects on world order. We have already witnessed how in an increasingly interconnected, networked and hypermediated environment, new actors are conjured into existence and entangled by acts of observation; security becomes an intersubjective affect; and what makes 'us' safe makes 'others' feel endangered. Quantum technology could amplify many of the networking trends that characterised the late stages of the digital revolution, and contribute to the reshaping of world order around a system of 'heteropolarity', wherein a wide range of new actors, operating simultaneously across diverse levels of power – individual, local, national and global – come to exert inordinate influence and reshape the international security environment.

The impact of past innovations based on quantum mechanics supports such speculations. If measured by the invention of the transistor, television, laser, computer, smart phones and the atomic bomb, quantum mechanics is not only the most scientifically successful, but also the most technologically transformative theory in modern physics (Orzel 2015). Like the harnessing of thermodynamics that produced the external (steam) and internal (gas) combustion engines, or of electrodynamics that led to electrification, the telegraph and radio, the quantisation of physics (and increasingly other fields of knowledge) has been characterised by a sequence of theoretical discoveries, experimental proofs, technological breakthroughs, economic disruptions and geostrategic applications. In the process, enormous wealth has also been produced: at the turn of the 20th century, it is estimated that already 30% of the Gross National Product of advanced economies came from innovations made possible by quantum mechanics (Folger & Le Gall 2001)

Now a new wave of quantum innovation is coming, faster than we thought, with the potential to transform war, peace and the international order. The third quantum revolution will be built upon quantum computers, communication, control and artificial intelligence that surpass their classical equivalents in speed, scale and capability.

We are today still in the early stages of this third quantum revolution, and the specifics of how it will impact international security remain uncertain. However, distinct quantum effects and trends are already beginning to present themselves. Here we offer a brief description of ongoing developments in the application of quantum scientific research to military hardware and discuss some of the ways in which interstate and multisector competition in this field could recalibrate the nature of power in world politics. We then go on to highlight a few of the most salient ways in which the dynamics of a third quantum revolution could force us to rethink of some of the core principles of international security.

From quantum ideas to quantum weapons

The origin story of quantum mechanics is, like many new revolutionary ideas, full of epiphanies and more than a few paradoxes (Der Derian & Wendt 2022). One noteworthy example is how quickly the international scientific collaboration of the greatest minds in physics during the interwar period degenerated into the national rivalries of the Second World War and then the superpower conflict of the Cold War. The pioneering work of theoretical quantum physicists like Niels Bohr, Werner Heisenberg, John Wheeler and J Robert Oppenheimer would become instrumental in the production of atomic weapons and the dawn of a nuclear age under the symbol of the mushroom cloud.

This pre-history weighs heavily on any consideration of the next quantum revolution. While the frontiers of research at global universities, major tech companies and quantum startups, the majority of funding by far comes from national governments, with a heavy weighting towards military and intelligence agencies. And while there has certainly been a high degree of international scientific cooperation, we are now seeing clear signs of an emergent 'quantum race' between the United States and China. As frictions between the world's two superpowers intensify, there is a mutual acknowledgement that technological prowess will be a key determinant of geostrategic, as well as economic, supremacy in the 21st century. Quantum is seen as a core critical technology by both countries in this struggle.

It is practically a truism to say that every powerful new technology is eventually weaponised. In fact, under modern conditions of extremely large, well-resourced, military-industrial-research networks, many of today's consumer technologies began their life as parts of military research and development projects (the Internet, the microwave, GPS and touch screens, just to name a few). There are, however, good reasons – not least the potential for an exponential leap in power – to consider what the weaponisation of quantum might mean before rather than after the fact. Just as founding international security experts W T R Fox and Bernard Brodie thought it necessary after World War II to coin new terms – 'superpower' and 'atomic power' – to denote the qualitative advantages of the nuclear-enabled (Brodie 1946), so too might we soon need to acknowledge the geostrategic superiority of the new 'quantum power'.

What might give rise to a quantum power? The first wave of innovation could be grouped across three categories: quantum computing, which will enhance logistics, decision-making and autonomous weapons systems; quantum communications, which can provide secure and unhackable information networks; and quantum sensing, which can produce more accurate and powerful radar, sonar and global positioning technologies.

Incorporating the probabilistic mechanisms of quantum physics into information processing quantum computing is the foundational innovation. Unlike a classical computer, which converts information into a binary structure of bits, made up of 1s and 0s, a quantum computer represents information in qubits, which, entangled in all possible states of superposition (both *0* and *1*), have already demonstrated exponential advantages over classical digital bits in binary states (either *0* or *1*). A quantum computer with 300 qubits could perform more calculations than there are atoms in the universe; a classically encrypted message that takes a digital computer thousands of years to crack could be deciphered by a quantum computer using Shor's algorithm in a few minutes. The ability of quantum computers to rapidly simulate and process complex systems, from weather patterns to chemical compounds, provides a host of new commercial, as well as strategic advantages.

However, it is also important to acknowledge at the outset that qubits are notoriously sensitive to environmental 'noise'; building a quantum computer as fault-tolerant as a classical computer is still years if not decades away; and, in general, new technologies, especially those thought to have disruptive or transformational potential, go through a hype cycle (Der Derian & Wendt 2022). But when such high stakes are involved, and with a long history of new thinking lagging behind technological change, this is the moment to identify the drivers of what might one day be referred to as the 'Quantum Revolution in Military Affairs'.

If one follows the money going into and out of governmental agencies, university departments and big tech labs, Quantum Artificial Intelligence (QAI) is the place to start. AI already plays a major role in military surveillance, targeting and decision-making (Maathuis 2022). The application of quantum computers to AI will greatly enhance the performance of lethal autonomous weapons systems like drones in their selection and engagement of targets, as well as vastly increased capacity for analysing large datasets that are now common in defence intelligence and cybersecurity operations. A lead in the development of quantum computing will confer a major advantage in the capacity to undertake or defend against cyberattacks. A quantum-based cyberattack could compromise the security of the entire network of a rival's digital commerce and communications if it remained operating on classical encryption standards. This threat has spurred research into Post-Quantum Cryptography (PQC) methods for protecting data that are less vulnerable to quantum computer hacking. The US National Institute of Standards and Technology is now several years into a public submissions process for evaluating quantum-resistant encryption algorithms upon which new public-key cryptographic methods will be based, and has developed guidelines for the migration of classical encryption systems to PQC protocols (Barker & Souppaya 2021).

Investment into the research and development of quantum computing has ballooned in recent years, and claims of approaching or achieving quantum supremacy, the point at which a quantum computer successfully solve problems that are unachievable by classical computers, have been made by research teams in both the United States and China (Gibney 2019; Zhong et al. 2020). While advances in this field are coming rapidly, a programmable quantum computer, capable of performing error correction and thus producing complete and reliable data outputs, is unlikely to be developed within the next five to ten years (Grumbling & Horowitz 2019).

The degree to which quantum computing comes to influence international security will be largely determined by the development of the capability to network quantum computers in the same way as conventional computers. The foundational research for the development of quantum networks is already underway, with the United States and China exploring both land and space-based quantum entanglement distribution. This would allow quantum computers to interlink with quantum sensing and communications systems, enhancing the ability to process data gained through sensors and in the decryption of intercepted sensitive material.

A functional network of quantum computers depends on quantum communications systems to transport and exchange quantum data (Grumbling 2019). The development of such quantum communications systems is today already well advanced. A subfield of quantum communications, quantum cryptography, also allows for communications that are impervious to interception by unwanted observers. This is an area of quantum research in which the Chinese government is a clear leader. It launched its first Quantum Experiments at Space Scale (QUESS) satellite in 2016, and completed its first quantum key distribution (QKD) optical network between Beijing and Shanghai in 2017. In January 2021, China announced the completion of a 4,600-km integrated quantum communications network capable of video, audio, text and file transmission across much of the country, using a combination of quantum satellites and optical cables (Xinhua News 2021).

The United States has enjoyed a clear advantage in intelligence gathering, communications and surveillance for the past 70 years. The breadth and effectiveness of American intelligence operations has been a considerable pillar of its global influence and power during this period. Breakthroughs in the field of quantum communications could immediately overturn, and if coupled with advances in quantum computing potentially invert, these advantages.

Although not as high-profile as quantum computing, quantum sensing is the most ready for military application today (Krelina 2021). By utilising the unique properties of quantum particles, primarily the entanglement of photons, new sensing systems are able to detect and measure the physical environment with much greater precision, including distortions in magnetic and electric fields, gravity and temperature. This has implications for the resilience and accuracy of GPS systems, radar and the detection of stealth weapons, including the latest generation of assault aircraft and nuclear submarines.

The implications for nuclear deterrence are significant. The maintenance of a reliable second strike capability is a major pillar of the underlying logic of mutually assured destruction. Should a nuclear-armed power suffer a nuclear attack, even to such an extent that their capacity to launch a retaliatory attack from their land-based nuclear arsenals is compromised, its nuclear submarine force ensures that any potential foe would suffer catastrophic retaliation. The impact that quantum sensing could have on submarine survivability has been identified as a serious issue for the US government and strategic planners (Sayler 2022). The furthest developed applied quantum sensor in this domain is the superconducting quantum interference device (or SQUID), which detects subtle electromagnetic disturbances. These have been in use since the early 1960s in biological sciences and medicine, but SQUIDs are now being developed as airborne devices to detect submarines. Conventional airborne detection devices are only effective in the range of a few hundred metres, while SQUID-based magnetometers could detect submarines at an estimated range of six kilometres or further (Kubiak 2020). This is a major improvement in sensitivity and range, but experts maintain that quantum sensing capabilities which could truly make the oceans transparent, and endanger the near-invulnerability of submarine based nuclear forces, will not be achieved in the near future (Kubiak 2020). Still, the potential for quantum sensing to confer such an advantage as to degrade the stealth capabilities of nuclear submarines, could cause a recalibration of strategic nuclear forces and their deterrent effect in years to come.

From superpower to quantum power rivalry

The quantum race between China and the United States, and how it will influence the global balance of power, has recently become the major focus of scholars as well as policy makers. And for good reason: China and the United States are the two clear leaders in several areas, including: investment into quantum research, production of quantum technology, quantum patents and number of quantum enterprises and start-ups. The quantum race is currently heralded as the technological tip of an ongoing strategic and economic competition between the two countries. Under these circumstances, and given the self-fulfilling nature of realist worldviews, a return to a bipolar Cold War-style system is dominant scenario for the future. However, the quantum race between the United States and China should not be so quickly subsumed by the so-called 'Thucydides trap', in which a rising power inevitably conflicts with a declining one. In several ways, the quantum race could prove bigger and beyond the intentions of any one power – super or not.

Multiple factors and multiple sectors are involved; many – but not all – support a bipolar outcome. The high barriers to entry ensure that only the wealthiest and most technologically advanced actors are capable of competing in the new quantum race. Supercooling facilities shielded from even miniscule levels of ambient environmental interference, critical raw materials, and large amounts of both financial and intellectual capital, in the form of mastery of quantum theory and engineering expertise, are all required at the frontiers of quantum technology. The development of more complex technologies with military applications, dependent on the mustering of resources and technical abilities possessed by fewer actors, concentrates the production of weaponry in the most advanced states. This can also increase their ability to exercise power over people, states and regions of the world who do not enjoy the same level of techno-industrial development. Quantum technology is likely to exacerbate this inequality of capacity and power between states. It is easy to see why the United States and China, as the world's most powerful states, have already established an imposing lead in the field.

The US government has greatly expanded its investment into quantum technology in recent years. Federal quantum R&D has grown from US$450 million in 2019, to US$710 million in 2021 (Subcommittee on Quantum Information Science 2021). Much of this funding flows to private and university research projects, but there has also been a proliferation of in-house federal agency research into quantum technology. Under the 'Three Pillars Model' established by the federal government, funding to create and sustain an American quantum ecosystem is split between civilian, defence and intelligence agencies. Quantum research is one of the Department of Defense's top modernisation priorities. Research coordination offices and funding streams have been established across the Army, Navy and Air Force, as well as through DARPA (Subcommittee on Quantum Information Science 2021). The American intelligence community has also been a major actor in quantum research and development. The National Security Agency has funded quantum research through its Laboratory for Physical Sciences since the 1990s. The CIA conducts its own quantum research and development in collaboration with academia and the private sector through the newly minted CIA Labs, and also directs strategic investment into quantum research through its In-Q-Tel fund. The Intelligence Advanced Research Projects Activity (IARPA), a cross-agency research collaboration that sits under the Director of National Intelligence, lists quantum as one of its four primary research areas, along with AI, machine-learning and synthetic biology, and both conducts and supports a wide range of quantum research, with a focus on quantum computing.

The United States is also integrating quantum R&D cooperation agreements into well-established alliances such as NATO, as well as into more recent strategic arrangements like the Australia–UK–US (AUKUS) security pact and the Quadrilateral Security Dialogue ('The Quad') between Australia, India, Japan and the United States. Cooperation with allied nations in quantum R&D could prove critical for the United States to keep up with China. Despite the major increase in federal investment into quantum, the United States is actually slipping in comparison to other nations. The United States remains the leading private market for quantum technology, with one billion dollars in total investment funding into quantum technology as of May 2021, which accounts for around two-thirds of the world's total private sector investments (Mahendran et al. 2021). But in quantum, the private sector is dwarfed by the state. Sovereign investment has truly exploded in recent years. In 2015, China had invested around $200 million into quantum technology, as of May 2021, that number had grown over 4,000% to almost $9 billion (Mahendran et al. 2021). Germany and France, the second and third largest state investors in quantum research and development, have each seen their total spending grow from $90 million and $55 million respectively to around $2 billion each during the same period. In these years, the United States has lost its lead. In 2015, it was the world's largest investor in quantum, totalling almost $350 million, by 2021 this investment had expanded to $1.8 billion, but the United States had slipped to fourth place in terms of state spending on quantum, as China established a massive investment lead (Mahendran et al. 2021).

Chinese leadership is keenly aware of the decisive role that technology will play in the 21st-century struggle for strategic and economic power. The need for military modernisation and technological development was prominently identified in China's most recent defence white paper, released in 2015 (State Council Information Office 2015). The following year, China released a National Innovation-Driven Development Strategy, which focused on the development of quantum, among other new technologies, as critical 'to achieve the Chinese dream of the great rejuvenation of the Chinese nation' (CSET 2016). President Xi Jinping has identified quantum science and technology as the frontier field in a new round of sci-tech and industrial revolutions, and stressed its role in accelerating the development of China's economy and national security (Xinhua News 2020). As a relative latecomer to the field, the Chinese government has invested heavily in its project to become the global leader in quantum science. As in the United States, quantum developments in China are deeply embedded in the national security establishment. While specific information on both funding amounts and research projects is difficult to ascertain, the People's Liberation Army is known to be supporting research into quantum technology through the National Defence Key Laboratories Fund, the Academy of Military Science and the National University of Defence Technology (Kania 2021).

There are, however, other, less binary scenarios to consider. While many observable trends of quantum competition in international relations indicate a new era of superpower rivalry, the possibility that this technology could be so revolutionary as to fundamentally reshape the underlying structure and interconnections of world order itself should not be discounted. The nature and potential of quantum technology make it qualitatively different from other major technological-military breakthroughs of recent history. The case of nuclear weapons is often presented in comparison, involving a race to develop a technology, already theoretically proven by physicists, which would give a major advantage in strategic affairs, and divide the world between nuclear 'haves' and 'have-nots'. Conceptualising the third quantum revolution as a simple repeat of the first is a mistake on multiple levels. Quantum actors have a clear asymmetrical potential in a way that the large state-actors of the nuclear weapons club do not. Private enterprise, with its complex, and sometimes conflictual, relationship with the state, is playing a much larger role in the early stages of the third quantum revolution. The race for quantum supremacy could, in fact, turn the logic of mutually assured destruction on its head. The advantages that quantum supremacy would confer are so great, that there is a clear strategic logic behind conducting pre-emptive strikes should it appear that a rival is developing an insurmountable quantum lead. Ian Bremmer has argued, along similar lines of concern first presented by Niels Bohr in his 'Open Letter to the UN' (Bohr 1950), that this poses a structural threat so great that governments must immediately prioritise sharing information on developments in quantum computing, because "even the threat of such a breakthrough could trigger World War III…" (Bremmer 2022, p. 172).

Quantum effects in international security

A technological revolution of this magnitude fosters new paradigms for the understanding, interpretation and conduct of warfare. But making the case for greater adoption of quantum perspectives within international relations and, indeed, throughout the social sciences, remains daunting. International relations theorists can readily visualise how opposing armies can fight each other and, irrespective of any deep knowledge of nuclear fission, the catastrophic consequences of a breakdown in nuclear deterrence have been vividly captured in popular culture. Even more esoteric threats to international peace and security from emergent technologies such as artificial intelligence and cyber – which are increasingly linked to new quantum developments – can at least be imagined in the form of thinking robots or villainous computer hackers. Quantum's potential disruptive impact is much harder to envision; it lacks a mushroom cloud equivalent.

A useful start for investigating quantum effects on the futures of war is through a brief genealogy of the so-called 'new wars', Mary Kaldor's umbrella concept along with a host of other terms seeking to give sense to the admixture of domestic, foreign and global conflicts that followed the end of the Cold War (Kaldor 1998). Some terms, like 'hybrid', 'irregular' and 'fourth-generation' signified a combination or a break while acknowledging continuities with past forms of warfare. In similar fashion, the 'post' prefix proliferated, to describe phenomena that built upon but went beyond past practices, like 'postindustrial', 'postmodern' and 'posthuman' wars. Other terms emphasised the spatial ('three-block', '3D' and '360-degree' war); the spectral ('TV', 'visual' or 'image' war); the temporal ('long', 'forever' and 'permanent' war); or the technical ('infowar', 'netwar' and 'cyberwar').

Just about every major war since the Gulf War has had a cyber element to it. To be sure, acts of primal if not always organised violence by and against tribes, nations and superpowers continue, all too often in the name of origin myths that would not be out of place in the bronze age. And the contemporary landscape of world politics is littered with casus belli that would not be unfamiliar to Clausewitz; or for that matter, to his eminent precursors like Machiavelli and Hobbes, who identified wars of gain (produced by imperial, economic and military struggles for dominance), wars of fear (prompted by perceptions of a rising power or threatening evil) and wars of doctrine (caused by the clash of monolithic faiths and universalist ideologies).

The threat of cyber-weapons and digital warfare, particularly in the realm of organised persuasive communications (the more subtle and modern art of propaganda) and foreign interference in domestic political mechanisms, has risen to prominence in the tensions between the United States, Russia and China in recent years. Both Russia and China see the United States as having been the example par excellence of this form of interventionist digital and communicative power for years, and the United States has, more recently, accused their own adversaries, most notably Russia, of having successfully pulled off their own major operations in this field in ways deleterious to American democracy. While today the threat of cyberwar is focused around powerful states, al-Qaeda, ISIS and other non-state actors repeatedly stress-tested the Westphalian system with new cyber-weapons in the first decades of the 21st century. Intent on challenging the state's monopoly on violence, insurgents, jihadists and private militias proved to be willing as well as able to use networked technology to wage asymmetric cyberwars – which in turn prompted over-reactions by states and further cycles of mimetic violence.

Recent examples of the interconnection between new digital technologies and conflict between state and non-state actors resulting in novel, complex and potent geopolitical externalities are myriad. Rather than resorting to the convention of bombs, it was revealed in 2010 that the United States and Israel inserted the Stuxnet virus to degrade the Iranian nuclear weapon programme; no matter that the virus proved to be less than a precise munition and rapidly spread to non-targeted industrial platforms. Wikileaks published the hacked information of thousands of embassy cables to make US diplomacy more transparent and democratic; no matter the collateral damage done to alliances and coalition efforts to overcome America's geopolitical rivals. Drones pursue a statistically 'cleaner' kill; no matter the inevitable errors, civilian casualties or the virtual terror induced upon whole populations.

It is safe to say that we have not seen the end – or the worst – of 'classical' forms of warfare, including cyberwar. With so many networked actors operating simultaneously across multiple levels of power, prediction, pre-emption or restriction of cyberwar is exceptionally difficult. Distinguishing intentional from accidental acts is hard. Knock-on effects will grow. The cyber-advantage might now go to the most technologically advanced powers, but the law of uneven development can give latecomers the edge. Which is why we should be asking now what cyberwar will look like when it goes quantum.

A preview can be found in the *quantum-like effects* produced in the highly mediated realm of information war and active measures. The quantum character of today's Ukraine-Russia conflict, in which multiple realities are being produced through networked global media, was demonstrated when Ukrainian President Volodymyr Zelensky, after appealing through live-feeds to almost every major Western parliament and the US Congress, appeared as a hologram at the largest big tech conference in Europe (France 24 2022). These appearances, and the many others like them, entail a broad appeal, but are tailored in subtle and dynamic ways exploiting the advantages of networked digital communications to target specific audiences (Keane 2022). Actors, events and narratives are being observed through digital parallaxes that shape perceptions around the world, now channelled more through social media platforms than through much tighter controlled and curated traditional media outlets. The primacy of the visual over the written transmission of information here is clear. When observational practices and visual imagery transmitted in near simultaneity through densely networked systems of multiple media produce powerful superpositional *e*ffects as well as entangled *a*ffects, it is time to assess the advantages of quantum over classical approaches to war and world politics.

The historical evolution of visual war tracks – but is not wholly determined – by new technologies of representation. From the first use of cameras in the Crimean, American Civil, and Franco-Prussian Wars, visual war has been part of official war-making. Tracking black budgets and gnomic bureaucratic acronyms in the United States after WWII and the beginning of the Cold War, one finds an early proliferation of national security organisations in which imagery plays a critical role. At the apex of surveillance and secrecy would be the National Reconnaissance Office, set up in 1960 but only officially (and accidentally acknowledged) in 1973, to collect image as well as signals intelligence for the US Department of Defense and other intelligence agencies, including the National Geospatial-Intelligence Agency, which was known as the National Imagery and Mapping Agency until 2003. Most recently, linking boots on the ground to eyes in the sky, Information, Surveillance, Target Acquisition and Reconnaissance (ISTAR) gives a technological edge and asymmetrical advantage to visual warriors. Operating across strategic levels and symbolic fields, visual war is tasked to oversee, foresee, and if necessary, pre-empt any potential threat; or in military parlance, to deter, disrupt and destroy the seen enemy.

The globalisation of the threat matrix through open and closed networks of information and imagery, many of them extra-terrestrial, augment regular, irregular, as well as hybrid warfare. No longer delimited by national borders, imminent threats and the ability to identify proximal foes from homogenous friends, visual war takes on an amorphous even spectral quality. As the modes of observation, representation and execution of war become complexly entangled on multiple screens and platforms, we must venture even further afield from the traditional social as well as physical sciences. This means recognising that while one particular kind of war might be in decline, global violence remains as a viable option in the face of intractable political differences, social injustices, cultural struggles for recognition. The emergence of the nation-state and the concomitant spread of reason, rights and prosperity might well have resulted in a global decrease in the level of state-on-state violence. But these metrics, based on linear Enlightenment demarcations of space and time, fail to account for the displacement, acceleration and perception of violent effects emanating from pre-, post- and non-state actors that shift identities and addresses with every attempt to deter, disrupt and destroy them.

Of these multiple permutations of 'new wars', visual war stands out as having the most quantum-like effects. Its reiterative and emergent violence does not lend itself to the assumptions of rational action, methods of linear regression or hopes for a progressivist future that drive much of contemporary international relations thinking today. States, democratic or not, might be inclined less to use violence to achieve political goals. However, now individuals with access to networked technologies for the preparation, execution and visualisation of violence, can do more damage to a system, be it state or corporate, organic or inorganic, physical or psychological, than any time in history. Following pathways worn by conditions of uneven development, visual war will continue to oscillate from classical to quantum and back again. Networked global media, as the trigger and transmitter, catalyst and conveyor of global events, has produced a multiverse of visual wars, a virtual realm but with all too real effects.

Conclusion

Physicists in 1939 had been fairly quick to recognise that the principles of quantum mechanics would lead to a revolution in energy; and, facing the possibility that Nazi Germany might get there first, most of them enlisted in the effort to produce nuclear weapons of mass destruction. Physicists and other scientists showed considerably less celerity in understanding how quantum principles applied to the invention of semiconductors and fibre-optics would lead to a second revolution, in information, with even more disruptive effects on society after the war. Potentially the most critical question for the future is how we respond to the paradoxes of a third quantum revolution: when quantum computing, communications, control and artificial intelligence (QC3AI) converge, will political and military decision-making – understood in quantum terms as 'the collapse of the wave function' – still necessitate human agency in the conduct of warfare and the pursuit of security? In the meantime, will international rivalry in the race to develop these and other powerful new technologies define a new bipolar Cold War. Or could they come to upend the current dynamics of world order entirely, ushering in a new heteropolarity?

It is vital that we pay close attention *now* to the deeper implications of quantum technological, political and social changes and develop new practical and ethical frameworks to guide us through a highly uncertain and potentially disruptive quantum future. Rather than wait for the new genie to leave the bottle, we must heed the words of Albert Einstein who, observing the gravity of the first quantum revolution, lamented that: "The unleashed power of the atom has changed everything save our modes of thinking, and thus we drift toward unparalleled catastrophe" (Einstein 1946, as cited in Crockatt 2016).

References

Barker, W & Souppaya, M 2021, *Draft White Paper on Migration to Post-Quantum Cryptography*, National Institute of Standards and Technology, <https://csrc.nist.gov/publications/detail/white-paper/2021/06/04/migration-to-post-quantum-cryptography/draft> (accessed 22 December 2022)

Bohr, N 1950, 'Open Letter to the United Nations', *Science*, vol. 112, no. 2897, 1–6. https://doi.org/10.1126/science.112.2897.1

Bremmer, I 2022, *The Power of Crisis: How Three Threats - and Our Response - Will Change the World,* Simon & Schuster, New York.

Brodie, B et al 1946, *The Absolute Weapon: Atomic Power and World Order,* Harcourt Brace, New York.

Crockatt, R 2016, *Einstein and Twentieth-Century Politics: 'A Salutary Moral Influence'*, Oxford University Press, Oxford.

CSET 2016, Translation of 'Outline of the National Innovation-Driven Development Strategy' [中共中央国务院印发《国家创新驱动发展战略纲要》, *Xinhua News Agency*, 19 May, <https://cset.georgetown.edu/research/outline-of-the-national-innovation-driven-development-strategy/> (accessed 22 December 2022).

Der Derian, J & Wendt, A 2022, *Quantum International Relations: A Human Science for World Politics,* Oxford University Press, New York.

Folger, T & Le Gall, M 2001, 'Physics' Best Kept Secret', *Discover Magazine*, 1 September, <https://www.discovermagazine.com/the-sciences/physics-best-kept-secret> (accessed 22 December 2022).

FRANCE 24 2022, 'Zelensky Hologram Appeals for Tech Firm Help', *France 24*, 17 June <https://www.france24.com/en/video/20220617-zelensky-hologram-appeals-for-tech-firm-help> (accessed 22 December 2022).

Gibney, E 2019, 'Hello Quantum World! Google Publishes Landmark Quantum Supremacy Claim', *Nature,* vol. 574, no. 7779, pp. 461–3, https://doi.org/10.1038/d41586-019-03213-z. PMID: 31645740.

Grumbling, E & Horowitz, M (eds) 2019, *Quantum Computing: Progress and Prospects*, National Academies Press, Washington, DC.

Kaldor, M 1998, *New and Old Wars: Organised Violence in a Global Era*, Polity Press, Oxford.

Kania, E B 2021, 'China's Quest for Quantum Advantage—Strategic and Defense Innovation at a New Frontier', *Journal of Strategic Studies*, vol. 44, no. 6, pp. 922–52, https://doi.org/10.1080/01402390.2021.1973658.

Mahendran et al 2021, 'Quantum Computing: Hype or Reality'*?*, *Deloitte*, <https://www2.deloitte.com/content/dam/Deloitte/au/Documents/deloitte-au-quantum-computing-hype-reality-290721.pdf> (accessed 22 December 2022).

Keane, J 2022, 'Metaverse Wars', *Eurozine*, 15 June, <https://www.eurozine.com/metaverse-wars/> (accessed 22 December 2022).

Krelina, M 2021, 'Quantum Technology for Military Applications', *EPJ Quantum Technology*, vol. 8, no. 24, pp. 1–53. https://doi.org/10.1140/epjqt/s40507-021-00113-y.

Kubiak, K 2020, 'Quantum Technology and Submarine Near-Invulnerability'. *European Leadership Network Policy Brief*, 11 December, <https://www.europeanleadershipnetwork.org/policy-brief/quantum-technology-and-submarine-near-invulnerability/> (accessed 22 December 2022).

Maathuis, C 2022, 'On Explainable AI Solutions for Targeting in Cyber Military Operations', *International Conference on Cyber Warfare and Security*, vol. 17, no. 1, pp. 166–75, https://doi.org/10.34190/iccws.17.1.38.

Orzel, C 2015, 'What Has Quantum Mechanics Ever Done For Us?', *Forbes* Magazine, 13 August, <https://www.forbes.com/sites/chadorzel/2015/08/13/what-has-quantum-mechanics-ever-done-for-us/?sh=212d483b4046> (accessed 22 December 2022).

Sayler, K M 2022, 'Defense Primer: Quantum Technology', *Congressional Research Service*, 15 November, <https://crsreports.congress.gov/product/pdf/IF/IF11836> (accessed 22 December 2022).

State Council Information Office 2015, *China's Military Strategy*, State Council Information Office of the People's Republic of China, <http://english.www.gov.cn/archive/white_paper/2015/05/27/content_281475115610833.htm> (accessed 22 December 2022).

Subcommittee on Quantum Information Science 2021, *National Quantum Initiative Supplement to the President's FY 2021 Budget. A Report by the Subcommittee on Quantum Information Science, Committee on Science of the National Science & Technology Council*, Executive Office of the President of the United States, < https://www.quantum.gov/wp-content/uploads/2021/01/NQI-Annual-Report-FY2021.pdf> (accessed 22 December 2022).

Xinhua News 2020, 'Xi Focus: Xi Stresses Advancing Development of Quantum Science and Technology', *Xinhua*, 17 October, <http://www.xinhuanet.com/english/2020-10/17/c_139447976.htm> (accessed 22 December 2022).

Xinhua News 2021, *China Realizes Secure, Stable Quantum Communication Network Spanning 4,600 km*, 7 January, <http://english.www.gov.cn/news/topnews/202101/07/content_WS5ff65c40c6d0f72576943611.html> (accessed 22 December 2022).

Zhong, H-S, Wang, H, Deng, Y-H, Chen, M-C, Peng, L-C, Luo, Y-H, Qin, J, Wu, D, Ding, X & Hu, Y 2020, 'Quantum Computational Advantage Using Photons', *Science*, vol. 370, no. 6523, pp. 1460–3. https://doi.org/10.1126/science.abe8770

29

LETHAL AUTONOMOUS WEAPON SYSTEMS AND THEIR POTENTIAL IMPACT ON THE FUTURE OF WARFARE

Austin Wyatt

Introduction

The development of increasingly autonomous weapon systems has been recognised by a number of states as the next likely Revolution in Military Affairs (RMA), an innovation that forces a shift in the paradigm of armed conflict. Such innovations are particularly disruptive in the context of hegemonic competition. While the prospect of removing humans from the horrors of warfare is tempting, it risks distracting from the significant ethical, legal and geopolitical challenges that stem from removing some humans from the decision to end the life of another human. This chapter will examine lethal autonomous weapon systems (LAWS) as a disruptive major military innovation. In doing so, it will evaluate global progress towards their deployment, present key legal and ethical arguments for and against their development and use, and consider their potential impact on the future of warfare.

Outlining the ongoing international debate surrounding LAWS

The first issue when one is asked to consider the future impacts of LAWS is that the question of what this term covers remains under contention both in the literature and at the United Nations. The most commonly cited definition, although it is in the process of being updated, is the definition contained in US Department of Defence's Directive 3000.09, which defines autonomous weapon systems as those that "can select and engage targets without further intervention by a human operator" (Wyatt & Galliott 2021a). The UK Ministry of Defence took a different stance referring to autonomous weapon systems as those with the capability to understand and interpret "higher level intent and direction" with the potential for unpredictable action (Development 2018). Despite the practical issues with a military pursuing a system that they could not necessarily predict, China took this approach even further arguing that they supported a ban but limiting their definition to only those systems that are intended to use force, have no human involvement in the "entire process of the task" and operate in an indiscriminate manner (Kania 2018). Definitions that limit LAWS to only include those systems with these kinds of distinctions do not account for the technological reality and were rightfully dismissed as a distraction by Jenks (2016). Moving away from government positions,

DOI: 10.4324/9781003299011-35

the three categories established by Human Rights Watch based on the level of human involvement in the Observe, Orient, Decide, Act (OODA) loop have also been widely utilised. The first category is semi-autonomous, or human-in-the-loop, systems, which are human-activated with a limited capacity to autonomously manoeuvre and/or engage designated target categories within geographic limitations. Supervised or human-on-the-loop systems can select and attack targets independent of human command yet include a mechanism that allows a human supervisor to interrupt or terminate the weapon's engagement process within a limited timeline. Finally, fully autonomous, human-out-of-the-loop systems are capable of true autonomous function once activated by a human operator (Wyatt & Galliott 2021a). Wyatt has undertaken a more detailed review of the ongoing debate surrounding how to define LAWS and defines autonomous weapons systems as a "weapon delivery platform, [informed by artificial intelligence], that is able to independently analyse its environment and make an active decision whether to fire without human supervision or guidance" (Wyatt 2020b).

This lack of definitional certainty is one of the main barriers to meaningful progress in the ongoing international discussions among the UN-sponsored Group of Government Experts on LAWS, which have been ongoing since 2014 (although only as formal GGE discussions since 2017) (Sayler 2021). Two main camps have formed in the academic and government literature around this issue. Those who oppose autonomous weapon systems argue that LAWS are incapable of operating in accordance with existing International Humanitarian Law (IHL, Laws of Armed Conflict or more colloquially the laws of war) and international human rights law. This is exacerbated by the creation of an 'accountability gap' in situations where the human is removed from the proximate, causal, real-time decision-making, with various potential responses being suggested including the expansion of commercial liability (Crootof 2015). Arguably the most compelling, and certainly the most problematic, of these is that it would be unethical and immoral to delegate the decision to end a human life to non-human entity, and that there is a fundamental disrespect for the dignity of human life in any use of a 'killer robot'.[1] According to this approach, the only ethically justifiable use of autonomy in the future battlespace is when such systems remain under Meaningful Human Control (MHC), which somewhat unhelpfully, also remains an epistemologically contested concept. While these are worthy and complex questions, it is notable that advocating for a pre-emptive ban on the development of LAWS as the only workable solution requires significant and unsupportable assumptions, principally that the enabling technologies can be effectively limited without interfering unduly in their use by the commercial sector, and that states will agree to sufficiently specific and measurable criteria that a such a ban could be feasibly enforceable. Acknowledging the extent of this ongoing debate, and expressing frustration with the absence of meaningful progress towards a resolution, should not divert one from a recognition that GGE participants are grappling with complex issues and that there are ethical and legal arguments on both sides of the debate.

Considering how close the world is to reliably deployable LAWS

Concurrent to the above debates, the underlying technologies have continued to be developed. Determining just how advanced progress is towards a LAWS demonstration point is complicated not only by the fact that 'autonomy' as a characteristic is neither binary nor easy to objectively assess, but also the political sensitivities associated with 'killer robots', which de-incentivises developing states from advertising their intentions (although this notably does not apply to private military firms). Setting aside a narrow focus on LAWS, however, it is possible to glean insights into the development of military applications of artificial intelligence (AI) and increasingly autonomous systems among leading militaries.

AI-enabled systems are certainly under active development. They have not, however, reached the point where 'killer robots' are a realistic possibility, at least without accepting a high risk of potentially lethal error. This is a problem that, as technology continues to develop, one can expect to see minimised in the near future, with multiple great power states actively developing related technologies (Wyatt 2021). Progress along the 'hardware' or technological part of this emerging major military innovation is difficult to objectively evaluate, particularly given the aforementioned lack of definitional or technical agreement. However, on the extent to which a system can independently control its 'critical functions' – how it moves through the battlespace, its target acquisition and identification processes, and how it engages the target – can give insight.

How a system moves through space, regardless of domain, is both the least controversial of these critical functions and the most the most reliant on dual-use technologies, such as GPS. Furthermore, these systems generally utilise similar propulsion and navigation sensors as their crewed counterparts, particularly in the aerial and maritime domains. For example, Uninhabited Underwater Vehicles designed for anti-submarine or anti-diver surveillance operations make extensive use of active and passive sonar arrays. In the ground domain, platforms draw on similar sensors to one would expect to find in civilian driverless vehicles including LIDAR (Mukhtar, Xia & Tang 2015), satellite positioning (Ryan 2018) and computer vision (Development 2018). For example, the 'follow-me' platforms (such as the Mutt) use the latter two technologies to follow a designated leader and avoid obstacles. Other platforms leverage GPS as part of a checkpoint navigation system, autonomously avoiding obstacles but remaining headed to a pre-set destination (Ivanova, Gallasch & Jordans 2016). What makes an autonomous system different is that it interprets the data from otherwise conventional sensors, compares it with its trained expectations and decides on how best to proceed. Unlike an automated system, which may be stymied by an unexpected obstacle or a closing of its intended pathway, an autonomous system is able to adapt within its 'experiences'. It is noteworthy that the more a system is required to adjust or interpret, the higher demands will be placed on its processing capacity and power supply, neither of which is unlimited. Furthermore, AI-enabled systems remain incapable of the sort of intuitive leap that an experienced human operator might have made in the same situation.

This inability, combined with the well-known 'black box' problem with complex AI (French & Lindsay 2022), has a significant effect on autonomous systems capacity to undertake reliable and explainable target identification and verification. Unfortunately, it is this package of critical functions that are the most ethically, legal and technically challenging as, when there is no human operator directly identifying and authorising a targeting decision, the international community's capacity to ensure accountability becomes questionable at best. For example, while modern computer vision technology can fairly reliably identify a human and even label basic behaviours (such as walking), that system cannot intuitively leap to a conclusion as to the intention of that human's actions (Sparrow 2015). This is less of a problem when the target is a military vessel, armoured vehicle or fighter aircraft, where the system can be explicitly trained to recognise legitimate military targets based on their visual, electromagnetic, radar or thermal characteristics. For complex urban fights or counter-insurgency operations, the inability of these systems to reliably identify humans or their intentions would place civilians and allied soldiers at increased risk (Wyatt & Galliott 2021b). Given the immense sensitivities involved in authorising the deployment of the first truly autonomous lethal system, it is highly unlikely that a state would do so in the immediate future given the known risks stemming from the current immaturity of underlying technologies. The prominence of Human–Machine Teaming (HMT) and Meaningful Human Control in relevant strategies, such as the Australian Army Robotic and Autonomous Systems Strategy, suggest that militaries have recognised the need to retain human oversight over target identification.

Finally, there is the actual persecution of a positively identified legitimate target. While the actual use of lethal force by a non-human entity presents serious ethical issues that deserve attention, there is a danger that a focus on this aspect of the 'kill chain' draws attention away from the target identification and verification critical functions. Despite the hype, a LAWS is essentially an advanced platform, granted one that further removes the human from the immediacy of the decision to use force than has been the case in prior innovations that increased this geographical and moral distance (such as precision-guided munitions and loitering munitions). Almost all uninhabited systems known to be in development utilise munitions that have been (or are designed to be) also deployed by crewed assets and thus should have undergone an Article 36[2] legal review (Wyatt 2021). The difference with autonomous weapon systems lies in their capacity to make the decision to fire a munition without direct human involvement, rather than simply guide an already launched munition or independently identify a target based on pre-determined criteria. It is important to note, however, that there are those who have argued that AI will never be accurate or reliable enough to meet the requirements of international humanitarian law.[3] On the other hand, some argue that there is a legitimate argument to be made that allowing LAWS to independently engage a target that has been identified as legitimate (in this case by a human supervisor) could be more accurate and present less risk of damage to civilians (Blanchard & Taddeo 2022). As the platform is incapable of feeling fear, stress or fatigue, and is guided by sensor data unavailable to the human soldier. Furthermore, autonomous systems are, by definition, more expendable than human soldiers and do not have a self-preservation instinct; therefore, they can expose themselves to enemy fire to engage more effectively, can engage their target directly with small arms (where the alternative may have been an artillery strike) and are better suited for dangerous or predictable patrolling tasks (Wyatt 2021).

But how do we use them? Emergent operational concepts for LAWS

It is also important to recognise that, particularly over the past four years, serious thought and experimentation has begun to occur focused on developing operational concepts for best leveraging the advantages of AI-enabled autonomous systems, including but not limited to weapon systems. Early attempts to generate operational concepts for the use of autonomous weapon systems included centaur or hybrid warfighting (Wyatt 2021), the use of supervised uninhabited surface or underwater vessels to protect crewed ships against surveillance or attack while in harbour and the use of adaptive swarming. However, at least for physical platforms, a consensus has formed around staying inside a HMT paradigm, although work continues on stand-alone autonomous system operational concepts, especially in the cyber domain. HMT is a paradigm based on the argument that a combat system is more effective in cases where the strengths of a human and an AI-enabled machine are enhanced through cooperation with one another. An admittedly human-centric approach that seems to preclude truly autonomous systems, proponents argue that in addition to being more effective than removing the human completely from a system's critical functions, HMT presents fewer ethical, legal and technological challenges (Wyatt 2020a). Unfortunately, but unsurprisingly, there also remains disagreement on where the boundaries of this paradigm are, and whether the human in such an arrangement really retains agency over the 'critical functions' or is simply there to bridge accountability and ethical gaps. This is the question that the concept of requiring such systems to retain Meaningful Human Control sought to resolve, based on the reasoning that to address some of the ethical and legal issues raised by such systems, humans had to retain a meaningful level of agency, understanding and control over the AWS they are teamed with. As noted above, however, there remains a lack of certainty about how the international community would objectively evaluate whether a given system met such a standard and a current failure to agree on where that standard should be set.

A clear example of this challenge are those operational concepts that envisage a mixed human AI combat team, with the autonomous weapon systems operated as 'loyal wingmen' that can fight in support of, and nominally under the direction (but not active supervision) of, their human team-mates (Wassmuth & Blair 2018). In theory, this would be more effective in high-tempo operations where direct supervision would be impractical and potentially dangerous, but the delay of a remote control link would fundamentally undermine the system's combat effectiveness even without accounting for electronic warfare. Instead, under this kind of operational concept, platforms such as the MQ-28 Ghost Bat would fly in support of conventionally crewed fighter aircraft. Immediately before an engagement, the human leader would enable the use of lethal force by the MQ-28s, likely bounded by a temporal or geographic limitation, which would then be capable of identifying and engaging targets without further human intervention.

Related approaches to incorporating armed autonomous platforms into human combat teams generally either limit the system's authorisation to engage targets (e.g., active protection systems on infantry fighting vehicles engage incoming ballistic projectiles not humans charging a vehicle),[4] or retain human supervision over the whole engagement period. An example of the latter is the use of the Super Aegis II (a supervised autonomous turret armed with a heavy machine gun and a loudhailer) at the Korean De-Militarised Zone, allowing a single soldier to remotely guard a wide section of the heavily mined zone, which would otherwise have to be patrolled. Importantly, these are not operational concepts for fully autonomous weapon systems, rather they limit the deployable systems to semi-autonomous and supervised systems, respectively. They are, however, still useful for understanding the development of relevant doctrine as the limitations are a response to legal and ethical challenges as well as technical limitations, rather than a reluctance to embrace fully autonomous weapon systems.

Disturbingly, we have already seen instances of criminal, terrorist and even state intelligence agencies make use of remote and AI-enabled weapon systems, unrestrained from the technical and moral requirements to limit unjust harm and protect against civilian injury, that are justly preventing their early use by ethical actors. As referenced earlier in this chapter, there are also states that have deliberately shaped their stated definitions of autonomous weapon systems to exclude their own efforts from any potential ban, whether that be by emphasising lethality as the defining characteristic or by adopting an unrealistic definition of full autonomy (Wyatt 2021).

One must also recognise that the future of warfare will not just be impacted by those systems that are capable of autonomously inflicting lethal damage on humans. HMT also includes the use of AI-enabled systems to enhance and augment soldiers or to remove them from dull, dirty or dangerous roles. One example is the proposed use of uninhabited (whether autonomous, semi-autonomous or remote operated) ground vehicles to haul an infantry unit's supplies and heavy weapons, reducing the load on the soldiers to increase their mobility and endurance. The same vehicle could then be utilised to extract wounded soldiers from dangerous locations under fire and return them autonomously to a casualty treatment point. This would otherwise require humans to expose themselves to fire to recover and treat the casualty, and risks a crewed helicopter or other extraction vehicle (which would also take longer as they are almost never deployed on-station in advance of a casualty). However, it is worth noting that there have already been several cases of remote operated systems that were clearly not designed to cause harm being jury-rigged as weapons in the field, for example by duct-taping explosives to the front of a bomb-disposal Uninhabited Ground Vehicle (UGV) (Wyatt & Galliott 2021b).

Some militaries have considered the potential applications of AI-enabled systems for improving their command-and-control mechanisms. Given the proliferation of precision strike capabilities, the comparatively static and vulnerable operational headquarters model is becoming an increasing liability. The use of a 'virtual assistant' AI-enabled system is intended to make such headquarters more agile and thus difficult to target by cutting down on the numbers of support personnel required for on-site processing and coordination of incoming and outgoing tactical information. These 'Lieutenant Siri' systems are anticipated to be able to analyse and prioritise incoming data in near real-time as an aid to the commander's decision making, speeding up the OODA process while simultaneously minimising the size of, for example, a battalion command post. Of course, the effectiveness of such systems would largely depend on a military's capacity to integrate them into the training processes of commanders, as they would need a significant level of familiarity and trust in the system.

A final exemplary emerging type of operational concept within an HMT paradigm are those intended to improve the efficiency, survivability and effectiveness of military logistics activities. The most obvious of these are the use of autonomous vehicles for the physical transport of materials and munitions, which although not as high profile as weapon systems, is arguably just as vital to the success of military operations. The Australian (Ryan 2018) and US armies (US Army 2017), for example, have invested in 'follow me' technologies for heavy supply vehicles, which are intended to largely remove the need for human drivers while retaining the capacity to intelligently respond to obstacles. In addition to resource and manpower efficiencies, this approach would remove soldiers from danger, supply convoy interdiction being a common strategy. Operational concepts for incorporating AI and autonomous systems into logistical activities also include non-physical systems. The potential for AI to revolutionise the way militaries conduct predictive maintenance and resupply has led to well-documented interest from a range of militaries including Singapore and the United States, while the Australian Navy ranks amongst those investigating 'digital twinning' to improve training, familiarisation, logistical supply and even damage control.

Overall, recognition of increasingly autonomous weapon systems as an emergent RMA has begun to translate into investment and experimentation in the operational concepts for their integration and use. While it is not yet clear which of these operational concepts will come to dominate the use of autonomous systems (or combination thereof), it is noteworthy that HMT has emerged to the extent that it has as a unifying mantra, even if its exact meaning varies between militaries.

Considering the impact of LAWS on the future of warfare

The culmination of the development of LAWS as a major military innovation will be illustrated by the first deployment of a completed innovation, combining the disruptive technology with an operational concept that enables it to undercut the dominant paradigm of conflict. It is worth noting that this is not simply a matter of a state becoming the first mover in deploying an autonomous system, states might take different approaches to developing related technologies or pair a matured autonomous system with distinct but non-disruptive operational concepts. Furthermore, a developer may be incentivised to limit exposure of their approach to autonomous systems to protect their operational advantage or, in the case of LAWS, avoid international scrutiny. Regardless, a point will come where a state deploys a fully autonomous weapon system in a manner that disrupts conventional balance balances, forcing other states to react to the resulting shift in relative power. This is called the demonstration point (Horowitz 2010) and it forces rival states to respond or cede comparative advantage to the first mover.

Granted, the first mover's advantage is likely to be fleeting (Silverstein 2013), particularly in case of a disruptive innovation with low proliferation barriers, as autonomous systems are hypothesised to be. Historically, major military innovations, including those described as RMAs, were typically resource or organisational capital intensive, restricting the capacity of states to respond to a demonstration point by attempting to catch up with the first mover. Faced with the emergence of aircraft carrier warfare, for example, a smaller state could theoretically attempt to overtake the first mover, but in practice would be restricted by their comparatively fewer resources to band wagoning together, allying with a great power early adopter, or investing in developing counter-innovations (Horowitz 2010). However, where these barriers to entry and early adoption are significantly lower (e.g., because the technical component of the innovation depends on dual use enabling technology or does not require a highly specialised skill set) one must consider the disruptive impact of rapid proliferation to multiple state and potentially non-state actors (as we have seen with remote operated armed drones).

Although it is impossible to definitively predict how this proliferation would impact the future of warfare, the history of both military and civilian disruptive innovation theory tempered by the unique characteristics of LAWS (and other forms of AI-enabled military technology) and initial state reactions to their early development in the context of prior known major military innovations, provide a clear basis for hypothesis. Among the defining features of RMA, and major military innovations more broadly, is that they herald a shift in the paradigm of how states project power and deter, including the conduct of warfare. Historically, this shift has resulting in a disruption in the international balance of power (Gilpin 1988), which has in turn enabled rising states to challenge the hegemony linked to that balance of power, noting that this has historically occurred in both a global and more limited regional context. This shift can allow a rising state to offset the traditional advantage of the existing hegemon, while smaller states attempt to imitate and emulate the more successful states to secure their own power base from their rivals, increasing the rate of diffusion (Goldman & Andres 1999). Challenged by this deterioration of its comparative advantage, the dominant state is prompted to adopt or improve upon that RMA to re-secure its position. The diffusion of major military innovation generates regional instability and precipitates, but is not necessarily sufficient to trigger, hegemonic war, as the dominant power reacts violently to the transition of power towards the rising power. Due to the comparatively low entry-level adoption barriers for this technology, as compared to prior major military innovations such as nuclear weapons, it is hypothesised that the emergence of autonomous weapon systems will have a profound and destabilising impact on the future of warfare.

From a grand strategy perspective, this potential for non-great power states to become effective early adopters represents a shift away from historical examples, again returning to the example of nuclear weapons, in that one cannot simply assume that middle and minor powers would be forced to align with a great power competitor to protect their own position. Instead, we could see Global South states exercise a greater level of independence as states attempt to balance competing great powers in their region while attempting to deter aggression from similarly sized neighbours. This of course runs the risk of creating a self-reinforcing cycle of arms acquisition and posturing as regional powers adopt and deploy systems for which there are no effective legal or normative controls to save a perceived security dilemma. The absence of mutually accepted norms around acceptable uses and responses to such systems, or effective treaty provisions banning their use, there is a significant risk of unintended or unexpected escalation, either due to a state reacting in an unexpected manner, or simply as the unanticipated result of a confrontation between two autonomous systems. Furthermore, the proliferation of remote, autonomous and AI-enabled uninhabited systems, especially given the dual-use nature of the enabling technologies, raises a significant risk of the use of such systems by violent non-state groups. The result of these factors would be a far less stable balance of power, particularly in the Asia-Pacific, and the creation of a multipolar competition space rather than a more traditional hegemonic transition of power.

Aside from the impact of such systems on regional stability and the likelihood of conflict, it is important to take a moment to undercut two inter-related and persistent myths in the discussion around autonomous weapon systems. First, there will be no Terminator or Dalek-style 'slaughter-bot' developed or deployed in the foreseeable future, despite the claims of some in the literature. One must remember that designers and potential end-users are rationale actors that are generally aware of the ethical concerns raised by LAWS (Galliott & Wyatt 2022) and extremely conscious of the fact that current technologies would not, and should not ever, allow for such systems. Second, and arguably more importantly, the rise of autonomous weapon systems will not lead to future wars becoming 'bloodless' or 'sterile', war remains a human endeavour even where humans do not make the final decision for a system to use lethal force. There will unfortunately always be human casualties of warfare, particularly amongst the civilian population in urban operations. In a way this approach is just as flawed as the first and ignores the significantly more likely, potential outcome of widespread deployment of such systems being that the balance of casualties simply shifts towards being further weighted on the technologically inferior combatant and civilians (Blanchard & Taddeo 2022). Importantly however, each of these arguments has some merit, there are significant ethical challenges raised by the prospect of releasing yet more human control over the decision to end a human life, and yet there is arguably a moral duty placed on leaders to utilise autonomous systems where they will protect the lives of soldiers, even if one limits their deployment to the dull, dirty and dangerous roles.

Proposing a normative stop-gap approach for reducing the risks of escalation

Minimising these potential destabilising effects of the emergence of increasingly autonomous weapon systems requires pre-emptive, but also meaningful action by the international community. It is easy to see the appeal of a pre-emptive ban on the development or use of LAWS under international humanitarian law, especially given the significant ethical and legal challenges that such systems pose. However, the failure of the international community to achieve significant progress towards such a ban suggests that it is unlikely to succeed, while the enabling technology continues to be developed.

In the absence of meaningful progress towards a legal instrument that is likely to be accepted and effective, the international community should pivot towards pursuing a normative approach, the first steps of which would include generating common, if not universal, definitions of LAWS and technical standards for their development and identification. These steps would create the basis for discussion and development of common practices and de-escalation protocols that would limit the potential for harm, even if only between a subset of states (such as the European Union or the Association of Southeast Asian Nations) (Wyatt & Galliott 2020). Somewhat unsurprisingly, the major benefit of adopting a normative approach is that it could enable technical experts from a smaller number of like-minded states to bypass the current deadlock at the United Nations and establish a harm-reducing technical baseline (Wyatt & Galliott 2021a). Such an approach could build on existing but unsettled concepts such as Meaningful Human Control or the 11 Guiding Principles affirmed by the Group of Governmental Experts on LAWS in 2019.[5] No approach is perfect, however, and a normative approach would lack the certainty, accountability and universal applicability of treaty-based international legal regulation. Instead of mandating behaviour norms merely guide actors and provide for mutual understanding and are therefore far more open to interpretation and selective application than international humanitarian law. Finally, there is a risk that adopting a normative approach to autonomous weapon systems may exacerbate the likelihood that states and manufacturers continue their practice of selectively describing systems in such a manner that they are easier to avoid being defined as an autonomous weapon system and can thus avoid any inconvenient restrictions (Bode & Watts 2021).

Overall, therefore, a normative approach to limiting the potential harm of uncontrolled proliferation of autonomous weapon systems is not an ideal solution. Ideally truly autonomous LAWS should be banned or at least heavily regulated under international humanitarian law. However, this is unlikely to occur and it is even more difficult to believe that any international legal instrument would be sufficiently effective or even accepted by the core developer-states of LAWS. The better part of a decade into efforts to generate such a ban, it is past time that the international community should push for technically based provisions for de-escalation and transparency before these systems begin to mature and proliferate.

Conclusion

The emergence of increasingly autonomous weapon systems presents both significant challenges and opportunities to military planners and threatens to disrupt the established paradigm of conflict. Aside from the well-covered ethical and legal challenges raised using a non-human entity to end human life, the emergence of a novel major military innovation for which there are no established behavioural norms or de-confliction procedures raises the risk of unexpected escalation and provocation, especially if the innovation rapidly proliferates following its demonstration point. At the core of arguments in favour of these systems is the belief that they will reduce risk to human soldiers, some have even argued that future warfare could be bloodless. While the former is a defendable, if optimistic position, the latter is just as unhelpful as those pushing a ban as the only solution to 'slaughterbots'. Paralysed by this debate, the international community risks missing its opportunity to limit the potential negative impacts of a future of warfare based around autonomous systems. Pushing for a pre-emptive legal ban is less important that implementing normative mechanisms that work before the demonstration point.

Notes

1 One example of this can be seen in Heyns (2017).
2 Article 36 of Additional Protocol I of the 1949 Geneva Conventions requires states to conduct legal reviews of all new weapons, means and methods of warfare in order to determine whether their use is prohibited by international law.
3 Sharkey (2012) quoted in Scholz & Galliott (2021).
4 This is, admittedly, a somewhat flawed example as Active Protection Systems are automated rather than autonomous, but it is still useful as an illustrative example.
5 These principles can be found at: Group of Governmental Experts (2019).

References

Blanchard, A & Taddeo, M 2022, 'Autonomous Weapon Systems and Jus ad Bellum', *AI & Society*, pp. 1–7, online first, https://doi.org/10.1007/s00146-022-01425-y.

Bode, I & Watts, T 2021, *Meaning-Less Human Control: Lessons from Air Defence Systems on Meaningful Human Control for the Debate on AWS*, Center for War Studies, University of Southern Denmark, Odense.

Crootof, R 2015, 'War Torts: Accountability for Autonomous Weapons', *University of Pennsylvania Law Review*, vol. 164, no. 6, pp. 1347–402.

Development 2018, *Joint Concept Note 1/18: Human-Machine Teaming*, Ministry of Defence, United Kingdom, London.

French, S E & Lindsay, L N 2022, 'Artificial Intelligence in Military Decision-Making: Avoiding Ethical and Strategic Perils with an Option-Generator Model', in B Koch & R Schoonhoven (eds), *Emerging Military Technologies*, Brill Nijhoff, Leiden, pp. 53–74.

Galliott, J & Wyatt, A 2022, 'A Consideration of How Emerging Military Leaders Perceive Themes in the Autonomous Weapon System Discourse', *Defence Studies*, vol. 22, no. 2, pp. 253–76, https://doi.org/10.1080/14702436.2021.2012653.

Gilpin, R 1988, 'The Theory of Hegemonic War', *The Journal of Interdisciplinary History*, vol. 18, no. 4, pp. 591–613, https://doi.org/10.2307/204816.

Goldman, E O & Andres, R B 1999, 'Systemic Effects of Military Innovation and Diffusion', *Security Studies*, vol. 8, no. 4, pp. 79–125.

Group of Governmental Experts 2019, *Guiding Principles Affirmed by the Group of Governmental Experts on Emerging Technologies in the Area of Lethal Autonomous Weapons System*, United Nations, Geneva.

Heyns, C 2017, 'Autonomous Weapons in Armed Conflict and the Right to a Dignified Life: An African Perspective', *South African Journal on Human Rights*, vol. 33, no. 1, pp. 46–71, https://doi.org/10.1080/02587203.2017.1303903.

Horowitz, M C 2010, *The Diffusion of Military Power: Causes and Consequences of for International Politics*, Princeton University Press, Princeton, NJ.

Ivanova, K, Gallasch, G E & Jordans, J 2016, *Automated and Autonomous Systems for Combat Service Support: Scoping Study and Technology Prioritisation*, Defence Science and Technology Group, Edinburgh, SA, Australia.

Jenks, C 2016, 'The Distraction of Full Autonomy & the Need to Refocus the CCW LAWS Discussion on Critical Functions', *SMU Dedman School of Law Legal Studies Research Paper*, no. 314.

Kania, E 2018, 'China's Strategic Ambiguity and Shifting Approach to Lethal Autonomous Weapons Systems', *Lawfare,* 17 April, <https://www.lawfareblog.com/chinas-strategic-ambiguity-and-shifting-approach-lethal-autonomous-weapons-systems> (accessed 20 October 2022).

Mukhtar, A, Xia, L & Tang, T B 2015, 'Vehicle Detection Techniques for Collision Avoidance Systems: A Review', *IEEE Transactions on Intelligent Transportation Systems*, vol. 16, no. 5, pp. 2318–38, https://doi.org/10.1109/TITS.2015.2409109.

Ryan, M 2018, *Man-Machine Teaming for Future Ground Forces*, Center for Strategic and Budgetary Assessments, Washington, DC.

Sayler, K M 2021, *International Discussions Concerning Lethal Autonomous Weapon Systems*, Congressional Research Service, Library of Congress, Washington, DC.

Scholz, J & Galliott, J 2021, 'The Humanitarian Imperative for Minimally-Just AI in Weapons', in J Galliott, D MacIntosh & J D Ohlin (eds), *Lethal Autonomous Weapons: Re-Examining the Law and Ethics of Robotic Warfare*, Oxford University Press, Oxford, pp. 57–72, https://doi.org/10.1093/oso/9780197546048.003.0005.

Sharkey, N E 2012, 'The Evitability of Autonomous Robot Warfare', *International Review of the Red Cross*, vol. 94, no. 886, pp. 787–99, https://doi.org/10.1017/S1816383112000732.

Silverstein, A B 2013, 'Revolutions in Military Affairs: A Theory on First-Mover Advantage', *CUREJ: College Undergraduate Research Electronic Journal*, vol. 4, no. 1, pp. 1–108.

Sparrow, R 2015, 'Twenty Seconds to Comply: Autonomous Weapon Systems and the Recognition of Surrender', *International Law Studies*, vol. 91, no. 1, pp. 700–28.

US Army 2017, *Robotic and Autonomous Systems Strategy*, The US Army, Fort Eustis, VA.

Wassmuth, D & Blair, D 2018, 'Loyal Wingman, Flocking, and Swarming: New Models of Distributed Airpower', *War on the Rocks*, <https://warontherocks.com/2018/02/loyal-wingman-flocking-swarming-new-models-distributed-airpower/> (accessed 20 October 2022).

Wyatt, A 2020a, 'Charting Great Power Progress Toward a Lethal Autonomous Weapon System Demonstration Point', *Defence Studies*, vol. 20, no. 1, pp. 1–20, https://doi.org/10.1080/14702436.2019.1698956.

Wyatt, A 2020b, 'So Just What Is a Killer Robot? Detailing the Ongoing Debate Around Defining Lethal Autonomous Weapon Systems', *Wild Blue Yonder*, 8 June.

Wyatt, A 2021, *The Disruptive Impact of Lethal Autonomous Weapons Systems Diffusion: Modern Melians and the Dawn of Robotic Warriors*, Routledge, London & New York.

Wyatt, A & Galliott, J 2020, 'Proposing a Regional Normative Framework for Limiting the Potential for Unintentional or Escalatory Engagements with Increasingly Autonomous Weapon Systems', in J

Galliott, D MacIntosh & J D Ohlin (eds.), *Lethal Autonomous Weapons: Re-Examining the Law and Ethics of Robotic Warfare*, Oxford University Press, Oxford, pp. 259–72, https://doi.org/10.1093/oso/9780197546048.003.0017.

Wyatt, A & Galliott, J 2021a, 'An Empirical Examination of the Impact of Cross-Cultural Perspectives on Value Sensitive Design for Autonomous Systems', *Information*, vol. 12, no. 12, pp. 1–21, https://doi.org/10.3390/info12120527.

Wyatt, A & Galliott, J 2021b, 'Toward a Trusted Autonomous systems Offset Strategy: Examining the Options for Australia as a Middle Power', *Australian Army Occasional Paper*, no. 2, Australian Army Research Centre, Canberra.

30

MILITARY NEUROENHANCEMENT[1]

Łukasz Kamieński

The mind of man is capable of anything – because everything is in it, all the past as well as all the future.
Joseph Conrad, Heart of Darkness and Other Stories, Ware: Wordsworth Editions 1999

The British historian Arnold Toynbee captured the deep-seated aspiration of *Homo sapiens* to surpass the boundaries of his biology: "It is characteristic of our human nature that we rebel against our human limitations and try to transcend them" (Toynbee 1964). The early ramifications of this revolt were Greek mythological heroes, such as Daedalus and Prometheus, who sought to exceed the human condition, and the archetypal superwarrior, Achilles. In the 20th century, reinvented superheroes made their way to popular culture: techno-modified figures in various incarnations populated science-fiction stories, comic books, movies and computer games. Superheroes have also inspired American military planners and researchers and their visions of a bioengineered supersoldier who mimics fictional mutant superpowers (Bickford 2020, pp. 65–74).

This chapter provides an overview of the prospects for neurotechnological human enhancement. Framed within John Boyd's concept of the OODA (Observe-Orient-Decide-Act) loop, it surveys advances in brain sciences and neuro-engineering for specific defence and national security applications. It focuses largely on US research and development as it is the most advanced. The tension between the expanding powers of AI-enabled military technologies and the evolutionarily limited human faculties is also discussed. Neuroenhancements are seen as an interim solution before cyborg techno-organic fusion becomes feasible.

Human enhancement, old and new

Enhancement is a contested notion, especially since the line between it and therapy, i.e., interventions to restore lost or deteriorated body function to normal, is increasingly blurred. The US military itself added to the conceptual ambiguity when, in an attempt to avoid ethical concerns, it switched instead to the term 'optimization' (Lin, Mehlman & Abney 2013, p. 16). Optimization, however, denotes the objective to maintain or improve peak performance relative to a pre-deteriorated level.

 DOI: 10.4324/9781003299011-36

Enhancement is more than that, and it is understood here as biotechnological interventions in the healthy body to boost a function above the statistically normal range of species-typical performance or above individual maximum capabilities, or to create novel attributes (Lin, Mehlman & Abney 2013, p. 11).

Although the term entered the popular lexicon in the 20th century, enhancements have a long history in the military. Through the ages, armies have attempted to invest their soldiers with extra powers. The stronger, fitter, more durable, alert and mentally resilient the troops, the greater their winning edge. Therefore, the military has developed various ways to muster courage, alleviate stress and fear, and improve cognitive and physical performance. The most popular have been rigorous training, drill and psychological conditioning; another, and remarkably widespread, approach has been the use of psychoactive substances (Kamieński 2016).

Stimulants taken to overcome fatigue, increase stamina, boost vigilance and raise fighting spirit have long accompanied combat. To stay awake on duty, the guards of the Great Wall of China used a plant that contained ephedrine. Inca warriors chewed coca leaves to endure long missions, particularly at high altitudes. Warriors of Siberian tribes, such as the Chukchi and Koriacs, consumed the *Amanita muscaria* toadstool for a combined stimulating and hallucinogenic effect. Warriors of some West African tribes strengthened themselves with cola nuts (Kamieński 2016, pp. 38–50, 87). During World War I, cocaine became a front-line upper, both self-prescribed by soldiers and supplied by the authorities (e.g., the British Army employed 'Forced March' tablets containing cocaine and cola nut extract) (Kamieński 2019). Wold War II brought about the large-scale use of synthetic amphetamine stimulants. German and Japanese forces distributed methamphetamine-based drugs, while British and American forces administered amphetamine tablets (Kamieński 2016, pp. 104–42; Ohler 2016, pp. 34–125). Later, the United States issued pep pills during the Korean War (1950–1953), and in the Vietnam War (1965–1973) the extent of their state-authorized use became widespread (Kamieński 2016, pp. 145–8, 189–91). The US government has continued to supply pilots with uppers (or *go pills*), although in a much more controlled manner. Under the fatigue management system reaffirmed in 2003, dextroamphetamine began to be supplemented and then in 2017 replaced by modafinil, a selective and safer attention-enhancing drug (Kamieński 2016, pp. 266–80).

Whereas regular forces abandoned or tightly restricted the use of psychopharmaceuticals, irregular fighters have employed them excessively. Consider a few examples. Since the 1990s, child soldiers involved in conflicts around the world (e.g., in Liberia, Sierra Leone and Iraq) have been drugged, mainly with amphetamines, to improve their performance and increase risk-taking behaviour (Kamieński 2016, pp. 243–62). Many insurgents who confronted US soldiers in Iraq in the aftermath of the 2003 invasion were intoxicated. From 2011 onward, combatants on both sides of the civil war in Syria and fighters of the Islamic State of Iraq and Syria have massively consumed the synthetic amphetamine-type stimulant Captagon, along with cocaine and methamphetamine (El Khoury 2020).

The states, however, have not said their last words. In 2011, the Chinese military unveiled 'Night Eagle', its own anti-sleep drug that was reported to sustain wakefulness for up to 72 hours (Moreno 2012). In 2019, US Marine Corps Major Emre Albayrak suggested microdosing lysergic acid diethylamide (LSD) to augment intelligence officers, given that instead of hallucinogenic effects, psychedelic microdosing produces cognitive enhancement (Albayrak 2019). Since 2018, the Special Operations Command has, for its part, supervised research on the anti-aging drug NAD+ and its strengthening effects, such as greater endurance and faster injury recovery (Philippidis 2021). However, as the soldier is increasingly considered a suboptimal component of the military system, the need for even more potent bio-high-tech enhancements has become pressing.

The weakest link

Over the millennia, the tools of war have steadily improved, while the ways in which armed forces could fortify their troops remained rather scant. With military hardware rapidly advancing, it is now the software, the soldier's body, that is seen as the weakest link, which requires upgrades to keep up with progressively sophisticated systems. Physically and psychologically, the human condition is the limiting factor that the US military wants to regulate and control. Indicative in this context is a recent shift in the US lexicon from 'soldier' to 'warfighter', which corresponds to the concept of 'army of one' in which enhanced operators are self-sufficient and have the capabilities, lethality and resilience of entire combat units (Bickford 2020, pp. 39, 249).

Since the early 2000s, remarkable progress in biotechnology, from genomics and genetic engineering to nanotechnology to bioelectronics to neuroscience, has opened up new opportunities for souping-up human performance. In its many programs, the Defence Advanced Research Projects Agency (DARPA) has explored novel ways of improving warfighters. For example, Continuous Assisted Performance investigated anti-fatigue measures to keep soldiers awake, alert and operative for up to seven days without deleterious mental or physical effects, Metabolic Dominance aimed at developing a nutritional pill for greater endurance, while Crystalline Cellulose Conversion to Glucose explored the use of bacteria to obtain energy from indigestible substances like grass (Moreno 2006, pp. 11, 121; Lin, Mehlman & Abney 2013, pp. 7, 25).

Today, neuroscience and neurotechnology (neuroS/T) seem to offer the most promising prospects for enhancements, with abundant military brain projects facilitated by fast-advancing techniques and devices, such as:

1 brain imaging to measure cerebral activity that enables the identification of individual neural profiles and the monitoring of cognitive, emotional and behavioural states, for example, electroencephalography (EEG) and functional magnetic resonance imaging (fMRI),
2 brain stimulation (neuromodulation) to regulate cognition by exciting or inhibiting neural activity in specific areas of the brain, which takes two forms: invasive or deep (DBS) and non-invasive or transcranial (TBS); the latter comes in several forms, including electric direct (tDCS), magnetic (TMS), focused ultrasound (FUS) and optogenetic (where selected, genetically modified neurons are managed by light),
3 neural interfaces to connect brain activity with machines (brain-computer interface, BCI) and with other brains (brain-brain interface, BBI).

Work on real-world applications of neuroS/T for defence and national security has been steered by the US BRAIN (Brain Research Through Advancing Innovative Neurotechnologies) initiative launched in 2013. One of its leading participants, DARPA, invests heavily in fostering the transition from neuroscience to neurotechnology. Research institutes of all service branches have also developed their neuro-programs. The Air Force Research Laboratory has run many neuro-projects and experiments. In 2010, the US Army, for its part, established its flagship innovation scheme: the Cognition and Neuroergonomics Collaborative Technology Alliance (CaN CTA), devoted to fast-tracking the application of advances in brain sciences to better understand soldier performance under different operational conditions. So, as overall there is growing interest in implementing cutting-edge laboratory research and neurotechnologies for practical battlefield use, most of the neurotech solutions covered in this chapter are being researched, in progress, or only partly developed, while many are still speculative.

What are the soldiering attributes that neuroS/T could help to create? Warfighters 2.0 are physically stronger and more durable, can stay awake and alert despite severe sleep deprivation, possess expanded cognitive abilities, such as quick processing of large amounts of data, are fast decision-makers, have augmented perception, are resistant to mental health problems, can control and master their emotions and display great courage. This catalogue of superhero powers can be summarized in six key qualities identified during the Unified Quest series, the US Army Capabilities Integration Centre's wargaming and experimentation program, as required by 2035–2050: operational fitness, resilience, adaptability, insight, character and self-discipline (Crane 2017).

Brain imaging can enable the military to select the most suitable candidates, allocate them to relevant branches and assign specific tasks to them. fMRI allows for the identification of fast learners, risk-takers or people resilient to mental distress. The ability to recognize individuals who perform quickly and effectively in close-quarter combat under high stress and time pressure is crucial, particularly for special operations forces. For example, experiments have revealed that subjects with a hypothalamic-pituitary system particularly sensitive to stress have a slim chance of completing Navy SEAL training (Taylor et al. 2006). Thus, brain scanning could be a useful personnel selection tool.

Offsetting humans with machines

The present-day US Third Offset strategy responds to the re-emergence of great power competition and aims to secure American strategic advantage until the mid-21st century. It assumes the accelerated development and large-scale deployment of autonomous systems for multiple tactical and operational purposes, including command, combat, communication and logistics (Ellman, Samp & Coll 2017). While the information revolution, the backbone of the Second Offset strategy, brought about digitalized systems, such as precision-guided munitions, unmanned vehicles (UVs) and Internet-based networks, artificial intelligence (AI) is promoting 'intelligentized' warfare. Soldiers must be able to closely partner with rapidly evolving machine learning algorithms and autonomous systems that will perform more tasks with greater speed and precision. In addition, emerging technologies, such as quantum computing, hypersonic weapons and high-kilowatt lasers, will further accelerate the conduct of war. Therefore, the main obstacle hindering the full implementation of the Third Offset is human-machine collaboration. To communicate effectively with high technology and keep up with algorithmic speed, soldiers must be made more compatible with progressively complex AI-based structures.

Existing and looming AI-enabled innovations promise to sharply accelerate all cycle stages of military operations, as famously identified by John Boyd (1986). His theory of OODA, standing for Observe–Orient–Decide–Act, captures the conduct of a combat operation. It is also known as the 'kill chain': from understanding what is happening to taking action. The ability to cycle the OODA loop (or close the kill chain) faster than an adversary and be ready to cycle again is essential for victory. Automatization and machine learning, the core features of the Third Offset, give technology an advantage over humans in the running of the loop. With AI allowing for the 'cognitization' of machines, individual platforms and battle networks emerge as their own self-contained kill chains. Intelligent algorithms give each phase of the loop greater speed, efficiency and flexibility. Thus, it is now the warfighter that hinders the execution of the OODA cycle. Michael Byrnes (2014, p. 57) explains:

Humans average 200 to 300 milliseconds to react to simple stimuli, but machines can select or synthesize and execute manoeuvres, making millions of corrections in that same quarter of a second. Every step in OODA that we can do, they will do better.

As militarized AI compresses the kill chain, keeping humans in the loop becomes even more problematic. The proposed solution to help servicemen match the technology is their augmentation. Thus, Boyd's concept is a useful framework for envisioning military applications of neuroS/T. Neuroscience research offers an explanation of how humans observe, orient, decide and act. Based on this growing understanding, neurotechnologies can provide the means to boost cognition and, in effect, enhance OODA performance. In that sense, the Boyd model and neuroS/T intersect in two ways: building into it up-to-date brain science findings about human cognitive functions and decision-making can further develop the concept, which itself serves as a useful tool for filtering the looming landscape of neuroenhancement techniques and devices. The following sections focus on the latter by discussing different neuroS/T solutions that can enable various human upgrades for all four steps of the OODA loop.

Observe

In 2019, an expert group commissioned by the Department of Defense (DoD) Biotechnologies for Health and Human Performance Council issued the *Cyborg Soldier 2050* report (Emanuel et al. 2019). Two of the four emerging cyborg technologies identified as most likely to become operational by the mid-century relate to expanded and reconfigured senses. The first is super-vision facilitated by ocular enhancements in imaging and sight. When an artificial retina is developed, it will provide greater-than-normal image resolution, empowering users to see more and in greater detail. Materials sensitive to wavelengths beyond the visible-light spectrum will enable perception in a wide range of electromagnetic bands normally inaccessible to humans (Jiang 2020). DoD experts anticipate that soldiers will see in the ultraviolet and infrared regions. Furthermore, since neural plasticity allows the brain to recalibrate itself to new sensory experiences, camera signals could ultimately be sent directly to the visual cortex (Emanuel et al. 2019, p. 4). This method, based on retinal implants for blind people, has already been explored. A team of Spanish bioengineers tested a breakthrough system in which machine learning software converts the camera signal into a neural code transmitted to the brain implant to stimulate neurons in the visual cortex and reconstruct a pictorial pattern. The resolution is still very poor, but it will certainly advance (Juskalian 2020).

Another cyborg solution is auditory enhancements for communication, perception and protection. Invasive reconfigurations, such as the modification or complete replacement with bionic equivalents of the inner ear bones and the cochlea, will develop from the current therapeutic technology of cochlear implants. Soldiers would then perceive sound waves at frequencies from very low to very high. Able to recognize infrared and ultrasound, operators would identify objects that emit or reflect acoustic waves. Capable of tracking the source direction of sound, warfighters will pinpoint targets precisely, gaining extended spatial orientation. Furthermore, when current external sound-modifying and corrective technologies, which attenuate noise and amplify specific wavebands, become implantable, the ability to distinguish sounds in loud battlefield environments will be radically improved. By filtering out harmful and potentially damaging noise, phonic neuroprostheses will also protect hearing (Emanuel et al. 2019, p. 7). The already existing apparatuses, such as the in-ear Tactical Communication and Protective System that monitors sounds and amplifies too-quiet sounds and suppresses too-loud ones, will likely be integrated into the nervous system.

The brain's ability to reprogram itself to perceive unexpected or unfamiliar stimuli allows sensory substitution: encoding information specific to one sense (e.g., sight) into signals recognized by another (e.g., touch). Researchers have already investigated whether sound waves detected by sonar or infrared light could provide diving commandos with orientation in deep murky water. Haptic interfaces have also been examined to test if vibrations felt by the skin could help soldiers navigate in the dark or give operators the perception of the location, speed and rotation of unmanned vehicles based on data sent from their onboard sensors. In the future, neurostimulator could project UV-generated images directly to the visual cortex, offering telepresence with a spherical view of the machine's surroundings.

In sum, sensory-boosted acuity and perceptual augmentation will expand the scope, type and pace of observation, while enhanced individuals will provide their unit with "intelligence data drawn from multiple sensory fusion inputs" (Emanuel et al. 2019, p. 4).

Orient

Situational awareness will be vastly expanded not only with AI-processed data from reconfigured senses, but also by actionable subconscious information that can be extracted from the brain. In 2012, as part of the DARPA Cognitive Technology Threat Warning System program, a neuro-wired device was developed based on retrieving P300, a wave occurring approximately 300 milliseconds after the brain records a specific image or sound. P300 enables the identification of a visual stimulus that, although recognized by the brain as important, is kept hidden from consciousness. The system uses EEG to monitor the brain activity of operators while they analyse images from a high-resolution panoramic camera for suspicious concealed objects, such as vehicles, crates, piles of stones or dead animals. If a potentially dangerous object triggers the P300 wave but is blocked from awareness, it is displayed on the screen for re-examination (Weinberger 2008). The device is highly effective, as it doubles threat detection capabilities. The perception of battlefield hazards can be further increased with TBS, as demonstrated in the 2010 experiment. Participants received tDCS and used an adapted version of the virtual military simulation software DARWARS Ambush!, originally designed to familiarize US troops with the realities of the Middle East. The results confirmed that neuromodulation accelerates learning and improves threat recognition ability with a prolonged effect of up to 24 hours (Clark et al. 2012).

The US military has for some time investigated the possibility of silently transmitting information crucial for orientation in a battlespace environment, such as reconnaissance and alerts. Already in 2002, DARPA initiated the Advanced Speech Encoding project to invent soundless methods of communication for acoustically challenging combat environments. A 'silent speech' option would be critical for special operations or reconnaissance units. Further research was sponsored by the Army Research Office of the US Army Research Laboratory (ARL), and in 2009 DARPA launched its Silent Talk program for creating 'thought helmets' to track neural signals with EEG, decode them and transmit them wirelessly to speech generators built into the helmets of unit members. The next step is to develop BBIs for the synthetic telepathic communication of words and images, something already proven possible by experiments in which the brains are merged into multi-person 'brain nets' (Jiang et al. 2019).

BCIs for instant connection with battle information networks will improve the quality of the intelligence received by soldiers and deepen their understanding in warfare. In the not-too-distant future, human cognitive abilities will be supplemented with algorithms: smart virtual decision assistants will allow "commanders to recall necessary information rapidly and right when they need it" (Brose 2020, p. 109) and to make better decisions on their recommendations. Additionally, continuous monitoring of warfighter brain processes will extend orientation to a new dimension: awareness of individual cognitive, emotional and physical states, which will facilitate more efficient micromanagement of troops. ARL has already explored 3-D printing to produce individualized brain monitoring helmets equipped with EEG (Binnendijk, Marler & Bartels 2020, p. 8).

To conclude, neuroS/T will help operationalize sensory stimuli and extensive data by innovatively contextualizing them. Enhanced situational awareness, in turn, will promote more informed, accurate and faster decision-making. Orientation is, after all, the most important part of the OODA loop as it shapes how humans observe, decide and act.

Decide

Although machines are becoming more and more autonomous, humans still remain 'in the loop' (in semi-autonomy when operators make decisions based on data provided by deep learning algorithms) or 'on the loop' (in supervised autonomy when machines analyse, decide and act but humans can intervene to stop or correct them). As ultra-fast 'intelligent' systems put personnel under increasing time pressure, neuroS/T can provide a way out.

Neuromodulation improves specific aspects of cognitive functioning that are key to decision-making, such as alertness, concentration and working memory. Studies have confirmed that tDCS helps retain complex decisional skills by maintaining vigilance and attention in subjects deprived of sleep (Opportunities 2009, pp. 52–3). TBS is therefore "a powerful fatigue countermeasure for combating performance-related attentional deficits" (McIntire, McKinley & Goodyear 2019). In 2010, under a DARPA-commissioned project, scientists developed a prototype helmet with an integrated FUS stimulation device aimed at enhancing the alertness and cognitive performance of soldiers (Drummond 2010). Working memory, which lasts up to a few dozen seconds, plays a key role in decision-making, such as whether to open fire. The ability to temporarily store and process information, which is crucial for effective action, deteriorates with fatigue, but it can be improved by up to 35% with tDCS (Fregni et al. 2005). Furthermore, a neurostimulation system designed in the DARPA Restoring Active Memory project revealed that TBS is effective in promoting long-term memory formation (Ezzyat 2018). In addition, cognitive enhancement programs managed by the US Army Futures Command have proven that executive control and creative problem solving are also amenable through neuromodulation, while studies by the Air Force Research Laboratory (AFRL) demonstrated that tDCS significantly improves "information processing capability" (Binnendijk, Marler & Bartels 2020, p. 13).

In battle, errors can be highly consequential. Brain sciences reveal that even before we become aware of our decision, it is possible to determine whether it is correct or not. This is limited to simple but often important choices, such as the identification of objects and people or whether to fight or flee in reaction to a sudden stimulus. Decisions are taken in the frontal lobe of the cortex and initially remain unconscious, for it takes around a second for the perceiver to become aware. A 'negative error wave' indicates that the brain registered having made a mistake. This specific neural activity occurs 50 to 80 milliseconds after an incorrect response and can be measured with EEG. Thus, the agenda for building a supersoldier will extend to in-helmet EEG brain scanning for life-and-death combat decisions and thereby alerting the wearer of their incoming erroneous choices (Cinel, Valeriani & Poli 2019, p. 8). The Army Research Laboratory has already explored 3-D printing to produce customized helmets equipped with EEG for brain monitoring.

In short, the military has explored neuro-techno-possibilities for strengthening various cognitive aspects of decision-making from the command and control level down to individual soldiers, such as working memory, information processing, problem solving, reaction time, and error detection and correction. The results are promising.

Act

Depending on the service branch, particular assignment or task specification, neuroenhancements could support action in various ways: either by empowering personnel physically or cognitively, or investing them with novel modes of human-machine interaction.

Our ability to perform quickly and effectively depends largely on learned and mastered skills. As automatic response is critical in combat, the US military has long pursued solutions for enabling shorter and more efficient training. By triggering neuronal plasticity and wiring, tDCS accelerates and improves new, especially motor, skill acquisition, such as athletic prowess and machine operating (Reis et al. 2009). In 2016, the DoD established a cooperation with Halo Neuroscience, the manufacturer of the Halo Sport tDCS device originally designed for athletes. After the headset was shown to speed up training and enhance performance, it was tested by Navy SEAL Team Six and AFRL. The results demonstrated that Halo improved physical skills, such as body balance and stability, approaching objects, targeting and reloading weapons, as well as cognitive abilities, mainly multitasking (Seck 2017).

tDCS is also effective in boosting motor strength, accelerating movement and increasing endurance, which are all key to maintaining peak performance. Subjects who underwent tDCS of the right primary motor cortex were found to be stronger compared to the control group, with an effect lasting more than an hour. By improving muscle endurance, neurostimulation also reduces the feeling of fatigue and increases pain tolerance (Feltman et al. 2020, pp. e53–e54). Furthermore, being potent in regulating mood and preventing depression, anxiety and other mental disorders, TBS can help warfighters stay fit for combat. In 2018, the DARPA Systems-Based Neurotechnology for Emerging Therapies project demonstrated that AI-assisted closed-loop brain scanning and stimulating interface allows for both continuous monitoring of user cognitive states and highly effective personalized interventions. A closed-loop system receives feedback from the brain and can self-correct. Once the adaptive algorithm detects the early signs of deterioration of certain mental functions, like mood, alertness or attention, it preventively activates focused neurostimulation to adjust certain parameters (Basu et al. 2021). Eventually, soldiers will not even know that their performance is improved.

Neural interfaces, which directly link-up humans and computers, can critically affect the final stage of the Boyd cycle. BCI consists of: (1) electrodes (either non-invasively positioned on the skull, semi-invasively placed on the surface of the cortex, or implanted in the brain) for recording neuronal activity; (2) a decoder and AI algorithm that analyse neural signals and convert them into digital codes used to operate; (3) a device or software to carry out relevant action. The ultimate goal is, as proclaimed by the former DARPA program manager Eric Eisenstadt, that "instead of acting on thoughts, warfighters have thoughts that act" (O'Connell 2017, p. 144) to, for instance, fluidly control an exoskeleton or unmanned vehicle, navigate in a simulator, run software or send instructions. In 2019, DARPA launched the Next-Generation Nonsurgical Neurotechnology (N3) program, aimed at developing "high-performance, bi-directional brain-machine interfaces for able-bodied service members" (DARPA 2019a). To reach its full potential, the interface must be truly cybernetic, with data being transferred both from and to the brain. The idea is that sensor signals from, say, drones are transmitted directly to the cortex through neuronal stimulation and are recognized by the user. Ultimately, such extended situational awareness will turbocharge the decide-act cycle.

N3 indicates the current trend in military BCI research towards non-invasive systems. Hybrid approaches that combine nanotechnology, genetic engineering, ultrasound, optics and magnetism promise opportunities for the soft installation of interfaces inside the skull. Such methods as genetic reprogramming of selected nerve cells, the use of viruses to carry light-sensitive nanosensors (optogenetics), and nanoprobes guided to specific locations with light or ultrasound are explored. For example, an N3 team is developing an acoustic-magnetic device to stimulate the brain with a local electrical voltage generated by the collision of ultrasound waves with a magnetic field. Another group works on a system that combines neuronal activity recording with light and ultrasound neurostimulation. Another promising method is the use of the bloodstream to deliver Stentrode, a stent equipped with a microelectrode, which nests above the cortex to detect and stimulate neural activity (DARPA 2019b).

Al Emondi, a former N3 manager, explained the rationale for military neural interfaces: "DARPA is preparing for a future in which a combination of unmanned systems, artificial intelligence, and cyber operations can cause conflicts to play out on timelines that are too short for humans to effectively manage with current technology alone" (DARPA 2019b). The goal is, in other words, to bridge the gap in the Third Offset strategy by reconfiguring the human link in the digitalized OODA. In this context, perhaps one of the most anticipated disruptive uses of BCI for fusing thought into action will be the operation of drone swarms. This application has already been proven feasible: in 2015, a paralysed patient managed to control an F-35 fighter jet in a flight simulator and in 2017, another subject succeeded in simultaneously operating three drones in a virtual environment (Axe 2019).

Neural interfaces are the final frontier of human enhancement. Doing things at great distances with thoughts will accelerate and vastly improve performance. Acting with an AI-assisted BCI will radically augment warfighters by revolutionizing their ability to collaborate and synchronize with machines. By boosting human cognitive processing, interfaces will streamline the OODA loop.

Conclusion: neuroS/T meets AI

Theoretically, the opportunities presented by neuroS/T are immense; however, the fundamental challenge is their translation into military applications. Although, as Jonathan Moreno and Jay Schilkin (2020, p. 4) remind us, "we shouldn't expect as much from brain interventions as we are often led to believe", the sought-after techniques are indicative of the US vision and venture to develop augmented supersoldiers.

AI will be critical for all neuro-reconfigurations. Machine learning benefits neuroscience, helping to further the understanding of the brain, and turbocharges a line-up of intelligentized neurotechnologies. These, in turn, profit AI as its progress hinges on neuromorphism: on a more complex mimicking of human neural systems in cognition (Hassabis et al. 2017). Simply put, AI has been in a co-productive marriage with neuroS/T. Theirs is a synergistic relationship of mutual inspiration and cross-fertilization. The future of neuroenhancement, then, rests upon this AI-neuro convergence, which is particularly pronounced when it comes to closed-loop and bi-directional BCIs. The Chinese have already also recognized the AI-neuro nexus as decisive for the transformation of warfare, a fact that adds yet another dimension to the ongoing US-Chinese strategic competition in emerging technologies (Kania 2020), as well as to future threats.

The capability-vulnerability paradox implies that new advantages bring new vulnerabilities. Since the brain has become a new battlespace, it will be imperative to protect personnel from attempts to out-enhance them. Grounded in bioelectronics and wireless communication, neuroenhancements are susceptible to enemy neuroattacks aimed at disarming augmentations, maliciously misusing them, or degrading performance through jamming, hacking, hostile manipulation of perception, cognitive state and behaviour. These can include incapacitating electromagnetic pulse attacks, sowing confusion, producing mental distress, sending false orders or inducing unintended action (Krishnam 2017; Evans 2021, pp. 48–58). Neurosecurity aside, because the human brain remains the least understood and most complex biological system and much of the mind is still an uncharted territory, brain-zapping generates an array of serious ethical questions concerning, in particular, consciousness, autonomy, free will, identity, responsibility and humanity (Evans 2021).

As AI-empowered technologies radically speed up the observation-action cycle, the temptation arises to remove humans, who are a sub-optimal element in machine systems, from decision-making roles. AI-neuroenhancements can, therefore, be seen as a way to keep humans in/on the decision-act loop, while exploiting to the full the benefits of machine learning for OODA superiority. Thus, the future belongs to operators sharing control over a task with algorithms. Following his defeat in 1997 by the Deep Blue supercomputer, chess grandmaster Garry Kasparov devised a 'centaur chess' competition, in which cooperation between a human player and a computer program brings a potent mix of human strategic imagination and computer tactical efficiency (Payne 2021, pp. 181–2). Similarly, hybrid cognitive teaming that combines the prowess of human intelligence (with its flexibility, robustness and ability to contextualize), intuition and creativity with ultra-powerful computational smart algorithms (with their precision, speed and automation) will bring about 'centaur warfare' (Rosenberg & Markoff 2016) waged by neuro-augmented 'centaur warfighters'. For centaurness, whether in chess or warfare, is, after all, about amplifying human capabilities and performance.

Note

1 The work is the result of the research project no. 2019/33/B/HS5/01297, "Neuroscience and Neurotechnologies in Warfare", funded by the Polish National Science Centre.

References

Albayrak, E 2019, 'Microdosing', *Marine Corps Gazette*, February, pp. WE1–WE5.

Axe, D 2019, 'The Pentagon's Wild Plan for Mind-Controlled Drones', *Daily Beast*, 30 April, <https://www.thedailybeast.com/the-pentagons-wild-plan-for-mind-controlled-drones> (accessed 21 July 2022).

Basu, I et al 2021, 'Closed-Loop Enhancement and Neural Decoding of Cognitive Control in Humans', *Nature Biomedical Engineering*, vol. 7, pp. 576–588, https://doi.org/1038/s41551-021-00804-y.

Bickford, A 2020, *Chemical Heroes: Pharmacological Supersoldiers in the US Military*, Duke University Press, Durham, NC.

Binnendijk, A, Marler T & Bartels, E M 2020, *Brain-Computer Interfaces. U.S. Military Applications and Implications. An Initial Assessment*, RAND Corporation, Santa Monica, CA.

Boyd, J 1986, *Patterns of Conflict*, <https://www.colonelboyd.com/s/Patterns-of-Conflict_Dec-1986-2n7k.pdf> (accessed 15 July 2022).

Brose, C 2020, *The Kill Chain. Defending America in the Future of High-Tech Warfare*, Hachette Books, New York.

Byrnes, M W 2014, 'Nightfall. Machine Autonomy in Air-To-Air Combat', *Air & Space Power Journal*, vol. 28, no. 3, pp. 48–75.

Cinel, C, Valeriani, D & Poli, R 2019, 'Neurotechnologies for Human Cognitive Augmentation. Current State of the Art and Future Prospects', *Frontiers in Human Neuroscience*, vol. 13, article no. 13, https://doi.org/10.3389/fnhum.2019.00013.

Clark, V P et al 2012, 'tDCS Guided Using fMRI Significantly Accelerates Learning to Identify Concealed Objects', *Neuroimage*, vol. 59, no. 1, pp. 117–28, https://doi.org/10.1016/j.neuroimage.2010.11.036.

Crane, C 2017, 'The Future Soldier: Alone in a Crowd', *War on the Rocks*, 19 January, <https://warontherocks.com/2017/01/the-future-soldier-alone-in-a-crowd> (accessed 28 June 2022).

DARPA 2019a, *Next-Generation Nonsurgical Neurotechnology*, DARPA, Arlington, VA, <https://www.darpa.mil/program/next-generation-nonsurgical-neurotechnology> (accessed 21 July 2022).

DARPA 2019b, *Six Paths to the Nonsurgical Future of Brain-Machine Interfaces*, DARPA, Arlington, VA, 20 May, <https://www.darpa.mil/news-events/2019-05-20> (accessed 21 July 2022).

Drummond, K 2010, 'DARPA Wants Remote Controls to Master Troop Minds', *Wired*, 9 September, <https://www.wired.com/2010/09/remote-control-minds> (accessed 19 July 2022).

El Khoury, J 2020, 'The Use of Stimulants in the Ranks of Islamic State: Myth or Reality of the Syrian Conflict', *Studies in Conflict and Terrorism*, vol. 43, no. 8, pp. 679–87, https://doi.org/10.1080/10576 10X.2018.1495291.

Ellman, J, Samp, L & Coll, G 2017, *Assessing the Third Offset Strategy*, Center for Strategic and International Studies, Washington, DC.

Emanuel, P et al 2019, *Cyborg Soldier 2050. Human/Machine Fusion and the Implications for the Future of the DOD*, U.S. Army Combat Capabilities Development Command Chemical Biological Center, Aberdeen Proving Ground, MD.

Evans, N G 2021, *The Ethics of Neuroscience and National Security*, Routledge, New York.

Ezzyat, Y et al 2018, 'Closed-Loop Stimulation of Temporal Cortex Rescues Functional Networks and Improves Memory', *Nature Communications*, vol. 9, article no. 365, https://doi.org/10.1038/s41467-017-02753-0.

Feltman, K A, Hayes, A M, Bernhardt, K A, Nwala, E & Kelley, A M 2020, 'Viability of tDCS in Military Environments for Performance Enhancement. A Systematic Review', *Military Medicine*, vol. 185, no. 1–2, pp. e53–e60, https://doi.org/10.1093/milmed/usz189.

Fregni, F. et al 2005, 'Anodal Transcranial Direct Current Stimulation of Prefrontal Cortex Enhances Working Memory', *Experimental Brain Research*, vol. 166, no. 1, pp. 23–30, https://doi.org/10.1007/s00221-005-2334-6.

Hassabis, D, Kumaran, D, Summerfield, C & Botvinicket, M 2017, 'Neuroscience-Inspired Artificial Intelligence', *Neuron*, vol. 95, no. 2, pp. 245–58, http://dx.doi.org/10.1016/j.neuron.2017.06.011

Jiang, H 2020, 'Artificial Eye Boosted by Hemispherical Retina', *Nature*, vol. 581, no. 7808, pp. 264–5, https://doi.org/10.1038/d41586-020-01420-7.

Jiang, L et al 2019, 'BrainNet. A Multi-Person Brain-to-Brain Interface for Direct Collaboration Between Brains', *Nature Scientific Reports*, vol. 9, no. 6115, https://doi.org/10.1038/s41598-019-41895-7.

Juskalian, R 2020, 'A New Implant for Blind People Jacks Directly into the Brain', *MIT Technology Review*, 6 February, <https://www.technologyreview.com/2020/02/06/844908> (accessed 16 July 2022).

Kamieński, Ł 2016, *Shooting Up. A Short History of Drugs and War*, Oxford University Press, New York.

Kamieński, Ł 2019, 'Drugs', in U Daniel et al (eds), *1914–1918-online. International Encyclopedia of the First World War*, Freie Universität Berlin, Berlin, <https://encyclopedia.1914-1918-online.net/article/drugs> (accessed 26 June 2022).

Kania, E B 2020, 'Minds at War. China's Pursuit of Military Advantage through Cognitive Science and Biotechnology', *PRISM*, vol. 8, no. 3, pp. 83–101.

Krishnam, A 2017, *Military Neuroscience and the Coming Age of Neurowarfare*, Routledge, London.

Lin, P, Mehlman, M & Abney, K 2013, 'Enhanced Warfighters: Risk, Ethics, and Policy', *Case Legal Studies Research Paper*, no. 2013–2, <https://ssrn.com/abstract=2202982> (accessed 29 July 2022).

McIntire, L, McKinley, A & Goodyear, C 2019, 'The Positive Effects of tDCS on Sustained Attention Performance Under Sleep Deprivation Conditions Are Consistent and Repeatable', *Brain Stimulation*, vol. 12, no. 2, p. 402, https://doi.org/10.1016/j.brs.2018.12.297.

Moreno, J D 2006, *Mind Wars: Brain Science and the Military in the 21st Century*, Dana Press, New York.

Moreno, J D 2012, 'Stay Awake, Comrades', *Psychology Today*, 12 April, <https://www.psychologytoday.com/us/blog/impromptu-man/201204/stay-awake-comrades> (accessed 6 July 2022).

Moreno, J D & Schilkin, J 2020, *The Brain in Context. A Pragmatic Guide to Neuroscience*, Columbia University Press, New York.

O'Connell, M 2017, *To Be a Machine. Adventures Among Cyborgs, Utopians, Hackers, and the Futurists Solving the Modest Problem of Death*, Granta, London.

Ohler, N 2016, *Blitzed: Drugs in Nazi Germany*, Allen Lane, London.

Opportunities 2009, *Opportunities in Neuroscience for Future Army Applications*, National Academy Press, Washington, DC.

Payne, K 2021, *I, Warbot. The Dawn of Artificially Intelligent Conflict*, Hurst & Company, London.

Philippidis, A 2021, 'U.S. Special Operations Command to Test Anti-Aging Pill', *Genetic Engineering & Biotechnology News*, 13 July, <https://www.genengnews.com/news/u-s-special-operations-command-to-test-anti-aging-pill> (accessed 22 July 2022).

Reis, J et al 2009, 'Noninvasive Cortical Stimulation Enhances Motor Skill Acquisition over Multiple Days Through an Effect on Consolidation', *Proceedings of the National Academy of Sciences of the United States of America*, vol. 106, no. 5, pp. 1590–95, https://doi.org/10.1073/pnas.0805413106.

Rosenberg, M & Markoff, J 2016, 'The Pentagon's 'Terminator Conundrum': Robots That Could Kill on Their Own', *The New York Times*, 26 October.

Seck, H H 2017, 'Super SEALs. Elite Units Pursue Brain-Stimulating Technologies', *Military.com*, 2 April, <https://www.military.com/daily-news/2017/04/02/super-seals-elite-units-pursue-brain-stimulating-technologies.html> (accessed 20 July 2022).

Taylor, M K et al. 2006, *Predictors of Success in Basic Underwater SEAL Training – Part I: What We Know and Where Do We Go from Here?*, National Technical Information Service, Springfield.

Toynbee, A 1964, 'Why I Dislike Western Civilization', *The New York Times*, 10 May.

Weinberger, S 2008, 'Northrop to Develop Mind-Reading Binoculars', *Wired*, 9 June, <http://www.wired.com/dangerroom/2008/06/northrop-to-dev/#previouspost> (accessed 18 July 2022).

31

HIGH-ENERGY LASER DIRECTED ENERGY WEAPONS

Military Doctrine and Implications for Warfare

Lauren J. Borja[1]

Introduction

Few weapon systems have had the promise and disappointment of directed energy weapons. Many countries have pursued these elusive weapons (Zarubin 2002; American Physical Society 2003), but few fielded systems exist. Yet the directed energy field has changed subtly since the later decades of the Cold War (Judd 1990). Today, the number of countries developing directed energy weapons has grown (Office of the U.S. Air Force's Chief Scientist for Directed Energy 2021). Applications for directed energy weapons extend beyond ballistic missile defence to other missiles and domains, such as counter unmanned aircraft systems and counterspace. Maturation of technology in the commercial areas, such as laser machining and telecommunications, has made these lower energy applications much more attainable. Instead of focusing solely on the most advanced, although potentially more strategically important, applications of directed energy, this chapter aims to present the broad range of potential uses of directed energy within various domains.

Directed energy refers to a class of weapons that uses a directed beam of electromagnetic radiation, supplied by particle beams, high-power microwaves or a high-energy laser (HEL), to achieve military effect of the three. High-power microwave and HEL directed energy weapons are more often considered for their potential strategic use (Sayler & Hoehn 2022). Because each type of directed energy weapon has its distinct mechanisms and consequently trade-offs, this chapter will mainly discuss HEL directed energy (DE) weapons; information on high-power microwave weapons (Ellis 2015; McGonegal 2020) and particle beams (Roberds 1984; Tucker 2019) can be found elsewhere.

To understand the scope of HEL DE weapons, this chapter takes a broad look at their application across different countries, doctrines and domains. First, the role of directed energy weapons within military doctrine is discussed, from official high-level statements to broader debates in military communities to national security goals motivating basic laser research. Second, this chapter presents several operational uses for HEL DE weapons at the tactical, counterspace and missile defence levels. Within each level, the capability, benefits and drawbacks and status of development. Finally, the conclusion presents the potential implications of HEL DE weapons within these operational levels and outlook for the future.

DOI: 10.4324/9781003299011-37

Military doctrines and directed energy weapon systems

Military doctrines and their associated discussions provide insight into a country's high-level goals that may motivate their directed energy (DE) research programs. The discussion, however, is far from uniform. Some countries choose to explicitly mention directed energy, whereas others leave the connection more implicit, especially in official documents. Furthermore, as the discussion shifts farther into basic laser research, these statements should be understood more as one of many motivating factors rather than a singular, explicit goal. This section illustrates these differences and concludes by offering key areas of difference between Russia, China, the United States and US allies.

Directed energy weapons are rarely mentioned by governments in their high-level national strategy and military doctrine documents, but such weapons can be a means by which countries achieve these strategic goals. DE weapons could deny adversaries the use of space assets or defend against missile threats, which are goals for many countries, but other potentially more mature technologies may prove more effective.

The United States most explicitly discusses DE capabilities in its military doctrine. For example, the United States mentioned DE weapons twice in the 2010 Ballistic Missile Defence Review (Gates 2010) and the 2019 Missile Defence Review (Shanahan 2019). The 2010 US Ballistic Missile Defence Review states that despite recent cancellations of high profile directed energy research efforts, the United States "will continue to research the potential of directed energy systems for missile defences, including the establishment of a directed energy research program inside MDA [the Missile Defence Agency]" (Gates 2010, p. 17). In the 2019 US Missile Defence Review, the United States states that: "Developing scalable, efficient, and compact high energy laser technology holds the potential to provide a future cost-effective capability to destroy boosting missiles in the early part of the trajectory" (Shanahan 2019, p. XIV). This document also mentions the DE capabilities being developed by other countries – "Russia is developing a diverse squire of ground-launched and directed-energy ASAT capabilities [...]" (Shanahan 2019, p. IV).

While not explicitly mentioned in Chinese or Russian official doctrine, DE weapons are found in the broader discussions of military doctrine in the strategic communities of both countries. Often, these capabilities are discussed as important towards establishing and maintaining control of the space domain. Topics of discussion include the role of DE weapons in warfare or within existing strategic frameworks. For example, *The Science of Military Strategy*, a white paper published by the Chinese People's Liberation Army (PLA) National Defence University in 2020, writes that:

> In terms of space offensive and defensive technology, the development focus of space weapons such as kinetic energy and directed energy will gradually develop from land-based, sea-based, and air-based to space-based, and mobile flexibility, rapid response, low cost, high reliability and strong penetration have become the main development directions and reached the combat level.
>
> (National Defence University 2020, p. 394)

According to a US analyst, DE weapons were among several key capabilities that would be key to achieving the "informatization" of warfare that is frequently discussed in Chinese military writing (Fisher 2017). Similarly, Russian authors have also published research papers on the role of DE weapons within the Russian ladder of strategic deterrence (Skrypnik 2012; Evsyukov & Hryapin 2020). The papers discuss using DE weapons to suppress space systems, air and missile defence radars, long-range radar and reconnaissance on aircraft, aerospace radio equipment, missile launch locations and control points on aircraft. On a strategic level, DE weapons could be used to contain a conflict at the conventional level, under the threshold of strategic conventional and/or nuclear weapon use (Skrypnik 2012).

Directed energy weapons are considered military-relevant emerging technologies. Governments or militaries use these documents to declare which technologies are of particular interest for research and development, and for what purposes. Within the United States, DE weapons, including HEL weapons, have been listed on the White House's "Critical and Emerging Technologies (CET) List" since 2018 (Trump 2020). As the overview in the updated 2020 CET list states, "not a strategy itself, this updated CET list will inform a forthcoming strategy on U.S. technological competitiveness and national security [...]. *This list should not be interpreted as a priority list for either policy development or funding*" (Trump 2020, p. 1, emphasis in original). The Japanese Ministry of Defence also included DE systems within their 2019 R&D Vision for the future of their military. Directed energy weapons, and specifically HEL weapons, are listed for future counter-drone and missile defence applications in the 2020s and beyond, respectively (ATLA 2019).

Directed energy is also one of the many applications, along with communications and fundamental scientific discovery, for research into lasers and optics. While much of basic science laser research is not relevant to HEL DE weapons, it is an important way for countries to maintain a strong talent base and industrial capability, which could impact the development and cost of more military-relevant systems. Academic reports on national goals for laser research from the United States (National Academies of Sciences, Engineering, and Medicine 2018) and China (Research Group of Strategic Research on China's Laser Technology and Its Application by 2035 2020) list DE as an important application for their laser research programs.

Russia and China see directed energy to accomplish their counterspace goals, whereas the United States and its allies place DE within broader capabilities for missile defence and counter-unmanned aircraft systems (c-UAS). This difference is largely due to the different advantages the different countries would seek in conflict, potentially against the other. China and Russia have long sought to deny the information advantage that enables the United States to project power at a distance or conduct precision strikes on valuable assets (Bronk 2020). Because China and Russia have fewer space assets (DIA 2022), the United States may stand to gain less by deploying a counterspace DE system. Instead, the United States is more likely to benefit in the near term from a c-UAS capability, especially in places like the Middle East. Different adversaries or conflicts may shift this trajectory. For example, in May 2022, Russia announced that it would deploy a c-UAS HEL DE system in Ukraine (Cheng 2022).

Operational roles of high-energy laser directed energy weapons

As illustrated in the past section, countries may pursue different uses for their HEL directed energy (DE) weapons. From least to most technically advanced, three main roles have been highlighted for HEL DE weapons: tactical, used against unmanned aircraft systems (c-UAS) or rockets, artilleries and mortars (c-RAM); counterspace; and missile defence. HEL DE systems have this broad potential for many different applications because they can have many potential effects on different targets. In addition to thermally damaging a system, laser filaments could charge, shock or erode the surface of various targets (Hambling 2021; Williams & Dahlgren 2022), which could degrade their operations. Electronic components on drones, satellites and missiles (Bronk 2020) could be particularly sensitive to these effects (Shepard 2021).

Regardless of application, there are several advantages these weapons could have over traditional kinetic weapons (O'Rourke 2022). First, the cost per shot could be significantly lower and have larger magazines than traditional kinetic interceptors. Of course, the exact ratio between costs is governed by the power and efficiency of current laser systems, which is a current focus of much research and development. Furthermore, heat dissipation or laser gain medium replacement could constrain the number of shots that a HEL DE system can fire. Second, HEL DE systems could engage targets much faster than traditional interceptors, which would be advantageous against more agile or manoeuvrable targets. Thirdly, HEL DE weapons could be more precise than traditional interceptors because the laser spot size could be only several inches in diameter. Lastly, the ability to tune the laser output could allow for a range of possible effects from one system.

HEL DE weapons also have several known disadvantages compared to other weapon systems (O'Rourke 2022). First, these weapons need line of sight to engage with targets, which could limit engagement distances. Secondly, HEL DE weapons are sensitive to atmospheric effects and thermal blooming that could cause the beam to lose energy, stability or quality of focus. While changing the wavelength or going to higher altitude platforms could reduce these effects, ultimately highly specialized adaptive optics systems, themselves a subject of much research and development, are needed to maintain the beam for the duration of the engagement. Third, lasers could cause unintended damage to the optical equipment or personnel of those using them, especially if they scatter onto sensors on friendly aircraft or humans in the area. Fourth, countermeasures could degrade the intended effect of the laser. Lastly, HEL DE weapons can only engage one target at a time, making them susceptible to suppression. More HEL DE weapon systems may be needed compared to traditional kinetic defences (Kershner 2022).

Further assessments on the utility of HEL directed energy weapons in warfare requires a discussion of the targets against which they would be used. For each of the three directed energy mission spaces—tactical, counterspace and missile defence—this section outlines the capability, more specific benefits and drawbacks and the current stage of development.

Tactical

The tactical mission space encompasses using HEL DE weapons against unmanned aircraft systems (c-UAS) or rockets, artilleries and mortars (c-RAM). Compared to other potential targets, such as satellites and missiles, these systems are slower and have less potential for hardening, which makes them relatively easy targets for thermal damage from HEL DE weapons. In addition to physically destroying the aircraft body of a UAS, HEL DE systems could be used to temporarily overwhelm, permanently blind any optical systems onboard which could interfere with the navigation or its ability to conduct intelligence, surveillance and reconnaissance (ISR).

There are few options beyond HEL or other DE weapons that could be used for c-UAS or c-RAM, but the defence may not be complete. Offensive UAS and RAM weapons challenge current defences because the cost of many of these offensive measures is much cheaper than defensive interceptors or hardening. This also increases proliferation of these systems, including to non-state actors. HEL DE weapons increase the options for defence because the cost per shot is much smaller than traditional measures and graduated effects could lead to many possible responses. However, technologically advanced actors may be able to harden these systems, particularly UAS, to limit the damage, although there might be a balance between hardening and performance. Furthermore, truly graduated response options require accurate information about the intended target – knowledge about the target's materials, onboard capabilities and operational role – to achieve precise effects. Defenders may not be able to confirm the effect or destroy the target before it has achieved mission success.

Several states have developed and deployed c-UAS HEL DE weapons as either ground- or ship-based systems. China has researched c-UAS DE systems for at least 20 years, with several major systems being unveiled in the mid- to late 2010s. Notably, the Silent Hunter c-UAS HEL DE system was unveiled for international sale at a 2017 defence technology show in Abu Dhabi (Nurkin 2018). Russia claimed to deploy the Zadira c-UAS system in 2022, several months into the war in Ukraine, ostensibly for tank protection (Defense News Staff 2022). Development on the c-UAS system was led by the All-Russian Scientific Research Institute of Experimental Physics (VNI-IEF), who is also developing the anti-satellite system that will be discussed in the following section, along with several Russian optics companies and defence contractors. Compared to the other c-UAS systems, which are based on solid-state lasers, Zadira appears to be a chemical-iodine laser mounted on a large truck (Hendrickx 2022). Similarly, the United States has also been working on c-UAS systems for at least the past ten years. The US Navy has several c-UAS systems in various stages of development, from several large defence contractors, such as Northrop-Grumman and Lockheed. According to press releases, these systems (called ODIN and HELIOS) could temporarily dazzle an ISR UAS (O'Rourke 2022). The United States is also developing other land-based systems as well (Sayler et al. 2021).

Other countries have also developed or deployed for c-UAS and c-RAM HEL DE weapons. Israel has developed the Iron Beam system, an upgrade to the Iron Dome to be used c-UAS and c-RAM. Israel expects to deploy the Iron Beam system within a year of the February 2022 test (Kellman 2022). In addition to the Israeli Ministry of Defence, the system was developed by Rafael Advanced Defence Systems and Elbit Systems (Egozi 2022). Elbit System also produces a directed infrared (IR) countermeasures system, which uses a laser to overwhelm heat-seeking ground-to-air missiles (Elbit Systems n.d.). In 2019, Turkey developed a drone system, called the Alka, which is made by the state-controlled Turkish company Roketsan (Bekdil 2021). A Belgium-based military news site reported that a Turkish-made HEL DE weapon destroyed a Chinese-made armed UAS during a conflict in the ongoing Libyan Civil War (Peck 2019).

Counterspace

Countries rely on the space domain, namely satellites, to conduct many aspects of civil society and military operations, such as communications; ISR; and position, navigation and timing (PNT). Many militaries, although some more than others, are increasing their presence in space (DIA 2022). The proliferation of space assets and actors with access to them has also increased the incentives for developing counterspace or anti-satellite capabilities as well (Bahney et al. 2019). Many countries are now including the aspects related to the space domain in their military doctrines. HEL DE weapons are one option for countries seeking to degrade or destroy satellite capabilities, usually from a ground-, air- or space-based platform.

There are many different types of counterspace attacks and countries could use HEL DE weapons for many of them. Counter space attacks can originate from the ground (earth-to-space) or be launched from an object already in orbit (space-to-space). The weapon itself can be kinetic, where the destructive force is caused by kinetic energy of the weapon, or non-kinetic, where another mechanism causes destruction. Damage can range from temporary or permanent (Weedon & Samson 2022). Furthermore, ground-based supporting equipment may also be vulnerable to certain attacks (DIA 2022). Ground-based HELs have been capable of blinding optical satellites in low earth orbit (below 2,000 km) since for the past three decades (Weedon & Samson 2022). More specifically, the infrared and charge coupled device (CCD) cameras on low-earth orbit satellites are particularly sensitive to infrared and visible light, respectively (Liu et al. 2020). It is significantly harder to reach higher orbits from the ground because their distances (GEO is about 40,000 km from the earth's surface); however, space-based HEL DE systems would increase the vulnerability of higher earth orbits (Hardesty 2018).

Comparing the relative benefits of various technologies remains challenging (Weedon & Samson 2022). There are different capabilities that could also offer similar counterspace options to directed energy, which include but are not limited to ground or space-based radiofrequency (RF) jamming, kinetic direct ascent or co-orbital weapons, or cyberattacks to satellite infrastructure. Like HEL DE capabilities, many of these topics are current areas of research and, because of their sensitive nature, countries have been hesitant to reveal the existence of such programs. Furthermore, much of the underlying technology for counterspace weapons could be used for other purposes, such as missile defence, satellite maintenance or space situational awareness. On a very basic level, HEL DE weapons have a wider range of possible effects, faster time to target once in range and create less space debris compared to kinetic interceptors; RF jammers and cyber weapons may offer many of these advantages as well. Air- or space-based HEL directed energy weapons may offer additional options for reaching higher orbits (Hardesty 2018), but these would likely require significant advances in laser technology.

Few countries beyond the United States, China and Russia have researched counterspace HEL DE weapons (Weedon & Samson 2022). Many countries have conducted tests of or fielded ground-based lasers capable of dazzling or blinding satellites in low earth orbit, but little is known about capabilities in higher orbits. Furthermore, it is hard to evaluate the evidence on counterspace weapons; many of the public tests occurred in the past and even countries, like Russia, who currently deploy systems for counterspace purposes have not released test data. In 1997, the United States conducted a series of tests with the Mid-Infrared Advanced Chemical Laser (MIRACL) system. These tests were declared a "partial success" according to the US Army, who was conducting the tests, because illumination interfered with satellite data transfer (Arms Control Association 1997). In 2006, the US National Reconnaissance Office confirmed that an American satellite had been illuminated by a Chinese ground-based laser (SpaceNews Editor 2006); this event was later referenced in a Chinese academic paper on laser weapons (Gao et al. 2013). In 2009, Russia illuminated a Japanese satellite with an airborne laser (Podvig 2011). Lastly, in 2018, Russia fielded several Peresvet systems, a truck-based HEL DE weapon, near its mobile intercontinental ballistic missile (ICBM) sites, potentially with the intent to blind optical satellite systems attempting to track the movements of the Russian ICBMs (Hendrickx 2020). Because of the miniaturization requirements, HEL DE laser tests on higher orbits are much more challenging and have not been reported; however, the airborne HEL DE systems developed by many countries for missile defence would be important steps along this path.

Missile defence

HEL DE weapons could be used to disrupt the trajectories of missiles within a broader missile defence architecture. HEL DE weapons could disrupt or destroy missiles by ablating or eroding missile surfaces and components (Williams & Dahlgren 2022). Certain areas of the missile might be particularly susceptible to laser interference, specifically sensing and guidance components; however, degrading or destroying these components alone may not be enough to annihilate the missile entirely, especially if the missile is close enough to target. Many of its supporters envision HEL DE systems as a component among many in a network of missile defence systems, particularly for regional bases (Gunzinger & Rehberg 2018). This is different from the discussion of DE missile defence in the late Cold War, which mostly focused on defence of a country's homeland (Lambakis 2014).

Many of the benefits mentioned earlier offer similar advantages for missile defence. These could be particularly useful in areas like boost phase missile defence, where few other options exist that offer the speed of HEL DE weapon systems. Compared to traditional terminal phase missile defence, many of the usual benefits apply – faster, cheaper cost per interceptor, deeper magazine if a stable power source is available. However, this could mean that HEL DE weapons have shorter engagement distances compared to traditional missile defences. Furthermore, the one-to-one engagement ratio could also mean that greater numbers of HEL DE systems would be needed to fend off a larger threat. While no one has deployed boost phase missile defences, the speed at which such defences would need to operate lends itself towards HEL DE weapons. Compared to traditional ballistic missile defence systems, HEL DE weapons could be less limited by geographic deployment, because a light-based defence could "catch-up" to a missile in a "tail-chase" scenario (Williams & Dahlgren 2022). However, this would mean that HEL DE weapons would be sufficiently miniaturized to be on either an air- or space-based platform.

More than any other nation, the United States discusses the goal of its HEL directed energy programs for missile defence. The Airbourne Laser (ABL), which used a chemical iodine laser, shot down a series of test objects simulating a boosted liquid-fuelled ballistic missile and a short-range solid-fuelled missile (Air Force 2010). The project, however, was cancelled shortly afterwards (D'Orazio 2012). Since then, the United States has focused on efforts to mature solid-state laser technology; many of these efforts were discussed in the tactical HEL DE subsection. Some of the next generation of systems the United States is trying to mature from these tactical demonstrators aim to be powerful enough to target cruise missiles. One such system recently shot down a drone simulating subsonic cruise missile flight (Duffie 2022). While not explicitly for missile defences, other countries have fielded ground-based solid-state laser systems with powers on the same order of magnitude as the United States. It is not unforeseeable that other countries could continue to mature these capabilities as well.

Implications

This chapter concludes by addressing the implications of the use of HEL DE weapons. These are important for two reasons: first, countries may choose to pursue or invest in capabilities that would give them previously unrealized advantages against adversaries; and second, countries want to understand which adversarial capabilities pose the greatest threat to their own assets. Implications of HEL DE weapons have been discussed before (Carter 1984; Wilkening & Watman 1986; Gouré 2003; Bronk 2020). To cover new ground, the discussion here focuses primarily on the recent developments in HEL DE weapons discussed in the previous section in the areas of tactical, counterspace and missile defence. One critique of this approach is that it limits the discussion to seemingly sort-sighted or tactical uses of these weapons; however, it is likely that these implications, which have been less of a focus in previous discussions, will also be impactful. The short-term tactical successes or failures of HEL DE are likely to shape the trajectory of more advanced systems by adding valuable operational data to their development. As has happened in the past, short-term failures of systems could also lead to a decrease in funding for the entire field.

Against unmanned aircraft systems (c-UAS) or rockets, artilleries and mortars (RAM) HEL directed energy systems could increase the options for response below the level of armed conflict and deterrence by denial. However, adversaries may choose to overwhelm defences by numbers, hardening or using more advanced capabilities. In the case of drones, the ability to scale from dazzling to complete destruction of an asset affords a range of options that offer various degrees of escalation, if it can be realized. Because many of these assets are cheaper than traditional kinetic interceptors, being able to target and incapacitate UAS or RAM using a system whose per-shot cost remains low is attractive to many countries. These costs may increase if more directed energy systems are needed during high-volume attacks. Furthermore, if DE maturation remains limited, adversaries may use a more advanced offensive system to overwhelm defences.

Many countries would find counterspace weapons, including directed energy weapons, destabilizing. That being said, failure to develop miniaturize HELs will limit most to mostly low earth orbits. Many countries consider space a warfighting domain and have identified the importance of space situational awareness and space control to their military success. Yet if HELs cannot be matured to the point where they could be deployed in space, it is unlikely that their effect would extend beyond affecting communications and ISR satellites in low earth orbit. Most secure military communications satellites, PNT and missile warning satellites spend most, if not all, of their time in much higher orbits which would offer a degree of protection.

There are many factors driving countries to improve missile defences. Among the two reasons most cited their US proponents are the proliferation of number and types of missile threats (Defense Intelligence Ballistic Missile Analysis Committee 2021) and the return to great power competition (Gunzinger & Rehberg 2018). Yet China and Russia claim that the United States wishes to use these systems to seek dominance by threatening their nuclear deterrents, despite technical analysis of US missile defences that find limited effect against strategic systems (Wilkening 2012). US missile defences may be more threatening to China, which has a smaller nuclear arsenal; however, much evidence points to a narrowing gap between the arsenal of the two (Office of the Secretary of Defense 2021). Ultimately, HEL DE missile defence systems are likely to be used by both sides to feed into these entrenched narratives rather than leading to movement or agreement from either side. Furthermore, using HEL DE weapons for tactical or counterspace purposes might make it harder to communicate intent and development trajectory than traditional missile defences.

From this broad view of HEL DE weapons, a more nuanced picture of HEL directed energy weapons can arise. First, it is rare for HEL DE to offer a capability that is entirely novel, except at the lowest and highest ends of their applications, such as against unmanned aircraft systems or boost phase ballistic missile defence, respectively. It is likely that many aspects of directed energy will be part of a suite of capabilities, rather than a singular solution. A second, related, point is that many of the areas where HEL DE could be of greatest strategic importance would require the most development and technical maturity. It is far from guaranteed that these levels can be attained. A more realistic, but still optimistic, picture of the use of HEL DE weapons in the future of warfare may be one that is modest in nature, where such weapons form part of a tactical, space or missile defence capability against some threats. This is not to say that such a role would not be consequential; it could shift the balance between offense and defence in some cases. But in this picture, HEL directed energy weapons are not a silver bullet that could predetermine the outcome of a conflict. Perhaps the key to avoiding disappointment with HEL DE weapons is keeping their promise bounded.

Note

1 The views and opinions of the author expressed herein do not necessarily state or reflect those of the United States government or Lawrence Livermore National Security, LLC, and shall not be used for advertising or product endorsement purposes This work was performed under the auspices of the U.S. Department of Energy by Lawrence Livermore National Laboratory under Contract DE-AC52–07NA27344; LLNL-MI-842713.

References

Air Force 2010, 'Airborne Laser Testbed Successful in Lethal Intercept Experiment', *Air Force*, https://www.af.mil/News/Article-Display/Article/117634/airborne-laser-testbed-successful-in-lethal-intercept-experiment/ (accessed 8 December 2022).

American Physical Society 2003, 'This Month in Physics History December 1958: Invention of the Laser' *APS News*, vol. 12, no. 11, https://www.aps.org/publications/apsnews/200312/history.cfm (accessed 8 December 2022).

Arms Control Association 1997, 'U.S. Test-Fires "MIRACL" at Satellite Reigniting ASAT Weapons Debate', *Arms Control Today*, https://www.armscontrol.org/act/1997-10/press-releases/us-test-fires-miracl-satellite-reigniting-asat-weapons-debate (accessed 8 December 2022).

ATLA 2019, *R&D Vision--Toward Realization of Multi-domain Defense Force and Beyond*, Aquisitions, Technology & Logistics Agency, Tokyo, https://www.mod.go.jp/atla/en/policy/policy_vision.html (accessed 8 December 2022).

Bahney, B, Pearl, J & Markey, M 2019, 'Antisatellite Weapons and the Growing Instability of Deterrence', in J Lindsay & E Gartzke (eds), *Cross-Domain Deterrence: Strategy in an Era of Complexity*. Oxford University Press, Oxford, https://doi.org/10.1093/oso/9780190908645.001.0001 (accessed 8 December 2022).

Bekdil, B 2021, 'Turkey Eyes Directed-Energy Weapons as Key Priority', *Defense News*, 21 March, https://www.defensenews.com/industry/techwatch/2021/03/15/turkey-eyes-directed-energy-weapons-as-key-priority/ (accessed 8 December 2022).

Bronk, J 2020, 'Disruptive Trends in Long-Range Precision Strike, ISR, and Defensive Systems', *The Nonproliferation Review*, vol. 27, pp. 39–47, https://doi.org/10.1080/10736700.2020.1783871 (accessed 8 December 2022).

Carter, A 1984, *Directed Energy Missile Defense in Space (No. OTA-BP-ISC-26)*, Office of Technology Assessment, Washington, DC, https://www.google.com/url?sa=t&rct=j&q=&esrc=s&source=web&cd=&cad=rja&uact=8&ved=2ahUKEwjrrJW75sT7AhUkIEQIHeg9DpIQFnoECAwQAQ&url=https%3A%2F%2Fwww.princeton.edu%2F~ota%2Fdisk3%2F1984%2F8410%2F8410.PDF&usg=AOvVaw1UM_JwCyrlSmMlyF9apX-y (accessed 8 December 2022).

Cheng, A 2022, 'Russia Touts New Laser Weapons, but Ukraine and U.S. are Skeptical', *Washington Post*, 19 May, https://www.washingtonpost.com/world/2022/05/19/russia-laser-weapon-zadira-peresvet-ukraine/ (accessed 8 December 2022).

Defense Intelligence Ballistic Missile Analysis Committee 2021, *2020 Ballistic and Cruise Missile Threat*, National Air and Space Intelligence Center, Wright-Patterson Air Force Base, OH <https://irp.fas.org/threat/missile/bm-2020.pdf> (accessed 8 December 2022).

Defense News Staff 2022, 'Russia Claims its Zadira Laser Weapon Destroyed a Drone in Ukraine', *Defense News*, 19 May <https://www.defensenews.com/global/europe/2022/05/19/russia-claims-its-zadira-laser-weapon-destroyed-a-drone-in-ukraine/> (accessed 8 December 2022).

DIA 2022, *Challenges to Security in Space*, Defense Intelligence Agency, Washington, DC <https://www.dia.mil/Portals/110/Documents/News/Military_Power_Publications/Challenges_Security_Space_2022.pdf> (accessed 8 December 2022).

D'Orazio, D 2012, 'Laser-Equipped 747 Missile-Buster Flies Last Flight, Claims its Spot in the Boneyard', *The Verge*, 21 February <https://www.theverge.com/2012/2/21/2814046/airborne-laser-testbed-canceled-boneyard> (accessed 8 December 2022).

Duffie, W 2022, 'Laser Trailblazer: Navy Conducts Historic Test of New Laser Weapon System', *Navy*, 13 April <https://www.navy.mil/Press-Office/News-Stories/Article/2998829/laser-trailblazer-navy-conducts-historic-test-of-new-laser-weapon-system/> (accessed 8 December 2022).

Egozi, A 2022, 'Iron Dome Laser-Based Option, Iron Beam, Takes Major Step Forward,' *Breaking Defense*, 22 March <https://breakingdefense.com/2022/03/iron-dome-laser-based-option-iron-beam-takes-major-step-forward/> (accessed 8 December 2022).

Elbit Systems n.d., 'Directed IR Countermeasures', *Elbit Systems* <https://elbitsystems.com/product/directed-ir-countermeasures-2/> (accessed 8 December 2022).

Ellis, J 2015, *Directed-Energy Weapons: Promise and Prospects*, Center for a New American Security, Washington, DC <https://www.cnas.org/publications/reports/directed-energy-weapons-promise-and-prospects> (accessed 8 December 2022).

Evsyukov, A & Hryapin, A 2020, ' Роль новых систем стратегических вооружений в обеспечении стратегического сдерживания' [The role of the new strategic armament systems in securing the strategic storage], Военная Мысль, no. 12, pp. 26–30. <https://cyberleninka.ru/article/n/rol-novyh-sistem-strategicheskih-vooruzheniy-v-obespechenii-strategicheskogo-sderzhivaniya.pdf> (accessed 8 December 2022).

Fisher, R 2017, 'China's Progress with Directed Energy Weapons', *Testimony Before the U.S.-China Economic Security Review Hearing,* Washington, DC, 23 February <https://www.uscc.gov/sites/default/files/Fisher_Combined.pdf> (accessed 8 December 2022).

Gao, M, Zheng, Y & Wang, Z 2013, 'Devlopment of Space-Based Laser Weapon Systems', *Chinese Optic*s, vol. 6, pp. 810–17, https://doi.org/10.3788/CO.20130606.810 (accessed 8 December 2022).

Gates, R 2010, *Ballistic Missile Defense Review*, Department of Defense, Washington, DC <https://dod.defense.gov/Portals/1/features/defenseReviews/BMDR/BMDR_as_of_26JAN10_0630_for_web.pdf> (accessed 8 December 2022).

Gouré, D 2003, *Directed Energy Weapons: Technologies, Applications and Implications.* Lexington Institute, Washington, DC <https://www.lexingtoninstitute.org/directed-energy-weapons-technologies-applications-and-implications/> (accessed 8 December 2022).

Gunzinger, M & Rehberg, C 2018, *Air and Missile Defense at a Crossroads: New Concepts and Technologies to Defend America's Overseas Bases,* Center for Strategic and Budgetary Assessments, Washington, DC <https://csbaonline.org/research/publications/air-and-missile-defense-at-a-crossroads-new-concepts-and-technologies-to-de/publication/1> (accessed 8 December 2022).

Hambling, D 2021, 'New U.S. Army Laser Machine Gun Fires 'Bullets' Of Light', *Forbes,* 11 March <https://www.forbes.com/sites/davidhambling/2021/03/11/us-army-develops-laser-machinegun-firing-light-bullets/?sh=4e8e29fb68a3> (accessed 8 December 2022).

Hardesty, D 2018, 'Space-Based Weapons—Long-Term Strategic Implications and Alternatives', *Naval War College Review*, vol. 58, no. 4 <https://digital-commons.usnwc.edu/nwc-review/vol58/iss2/4/> (accessed 8 December 2022).

Hendrickx, B 2020, 'Peresvet: A Russian Mobile Laser System To Dazzle Enemy Satellites', *The Space Review*, 15 June <https://www.thespacereview.com/article/3967/1> (accessed 8 December 2022).

Hendrickx, B 2022, 'Kalina: A Russian Ground-Based Laser to Dazzle Imaging Satellites', *The Space Review*, 5 July <https://www.thespacereview.com/article/4416/1> (accessed 8 December 2022).Judd, O 1990, 'Prospects for SDI Laser Research', *Optics & Photonics News*, vol. 1, pp. 7–16. https://doi.org/10.1364/OPN.1.4.000007.

Kellman, L 2022, 'Israel Successfully Tests New Laser Missile Defense System', *Defense News*, 15 April <https://www.defensenews.com/training-sim/2022/04/15/israel-successfully-tests-new-laser-missile-defense-system/> (accessed 8 December 2022).

Kershner, I 2022, 'Israel Builds a Laser Weapon to Zap Threats Out of the Sky', *The New York Times*, 3 June <https://www.nytimes.com/2022/06/03/world/middleeast/israel-laser-rockets.html> (accessed 8 December 2022).

Lambakis, S 2014, *The Future of Homeland Missile Defenses,* National Institute for Public Policy, Fairfax, VA <https://nipp.org/wp-content/uploads/2021/05/Future-of-Homeland-Missile-Defenses.pdf> (accessed 8 December 2022).

Liu, Z, Lin, C & Chen, G 2020, 'Space Attack Technology Overview', *Journal of Physics: Conference Series*, vol. 1544, pp. 012178, https://doi.org/10.1088/1742-6596/1544/1/012178.

McGonegal, J 2020, *High Power Microwave Weapons: Disruptive Technology for the Future (No. AD1107488),* Air Command and Staff Maxwell Air Force Base <https://apps.dtic.mil/sti/citations/AD1107488> (accessed 8 December 2022).

National Academies of Sciences, Engineering, and Medicine 2018, *Opportunities in Intense Ultrafast Lasers: Reaching for the Brightest Light,* National Academies Press, Washington, DC, https://doi.org/10.17226/24939.

National Defence University 2020, *Science of Military Strategy*, National Defence University, Beijing <https://www.airuniversity.af.edu/CASI/Display/Article/2913216/in-their-own-words-2020-science-of-military-strategy/> (accessed 8 December 2022).

Nurkin, T 2018, *China's Advanced Weapons Systems,* U.S.-China Economic and Security Review Commission, Washington, DC <https://www.uscc.gov/research/chinas-advanced-weapons-systems> (accessed 8 December 2022).

Office of the Secretary of Defense 2021, *Military and Security Developments Involving the People's Republic of China 2021*, Department of Defense, Washington, DC <https://media.defense.gov/2021/Nov/03/2002885874/-1/-1/0/2021-CMPR-FINAL.PDF> (accessed 8 December 2022).

Office of the U.S. Air Force's Chief Scientist for Directed Energy 2021, *Directed Energy Futures 2060: Visions for the Next 40 Years of U.S. Department of Defense Directed Energy Technologies*, Air Force Research Laboratory, Kirtland Air Force Base, NM <https://www.afrl.af.mil/Portals/90/Documents/RD/ Directed_Energy_Futures_2060_Final29June21_with_clearance_number.pdf?ver=EZ4QY5MG5UK2L DdwiuPc6Q%3D%3D> (accessed 8 December 2022).

O'Rourke, R 2022, *Navy Shipboard Lasers: Background and Issues for Congress (No. R44175)*. Congressional Research Service, Washington, DC <https://crsreports.congress.gov/product/details?prodcode=R44175> (accessed 8 December 2022).

Peck, M 2019, 'Did A Turkish Combat Laser Shoot Down A Chinese Drone? *The National Interest*, 1 September <https://nationalinterest.org/blog/buzz/did-turkish-combat-laser-shoot-down-chinese-drone-77286> (accessed 8 December 2022).

Podvig, P 2011, 'Russia Has Been Testing Laser ASAT', *Russian Strategic Nuclear Forces* <https://russian-forces.org/blog/2011/10/russia_has_been_testing_laser.shtml> (accessed 8 December 2022).

Research Group of Strategic Research on China's Laser Technology and Its Application by 2035 2020, 'Strategic Research on China's Laser Technology and Its Application by 2035', *Strategic Study of Chinese Academy of Engineering*, vol. 22, pp. 1–6, https://doi.org/10.15302/J-SSCAE-2020.03.00.

Roberds, R 1984, 'Introducing the Particle Beam Weapon', *Air University Review*, vol. 35, pp. 74–84 <https://www.airuniversity.af.edu/Portals/10/ASPJ/journals/1984_Vol35_No1-6/1984_Vol35_No5.pdf> (accessed 8 December 2022).

Sayler, K, Hoehn, J, Feickert, A & O'Rourke, R 2021, *Department of Defense Directed Energy Weapons: Background and Issues for Congress (No. R46925)*, Congressional Research Service, Washington, DC <https://crsreports.congress.gov/product/details?prodcode=R46925> (accessed 8 December 2022).

Sayler, K & Hoehn, J 2022, *Defense Primer: Directed-Energy Weapons (No. IF11882)*, Congressional Research Service, Washington, DC <https://crsreports.congress.gov/product/details?prodcode=IF11882> (accessed 8 December 2022).Shanahan, P 2019, *Missile Defense Review*, Department of Defense, Washington, DC <https://media.defense.gov/2019/Jan/17/2002080666/-1/-1/1/2019-MISSILE-DE-FENSE-REVIEW.PDF> (accessed 8 December 2022).

Shepard, J 2021, 'Rapid Pulse Laser Weapons Could Be The Pentagon's Future Edge', *Breaking Defense* <https://breakingdefense.com/2021/10/rapid-pulse-laser-weapons-could-be-the-pentagons-future-edge> (accessed 8 December 2022).

Skrypnik, A V 2012, 'О возможном подходе к определению роли и места оружия направленной электромагнитной энергии в механизме силового стратегического сдерживания' [On a possible approach to determining the role and place of directed energy weapons in the mechanism of strategic deterrence through the use of force], *Вооружение и экономика*, vol. 3, no. 19, pp. 42–9 <http://www.viek.ru/19/42-49.pdf> (accessed 8 December 2022).

SpaceNews Editor 2006, 'NRO Confirms Chinese Laser Test Illuminated U.S. Spacecraft', *SpaceNews* <https://spacenews.com/nro-confirms-chinese-laser-test-illuminated-us-spacecraft/> (accessed 8 December 2022).

Trump, D 2020, *National Strategy for Critical and Emerging Technologies*, White House, Washington, DC <https://nps.edu/web/slamr/-/2020-national-strategy-for-critical-emerging-technologies> (accessed 8 December 2022).

Tucker, P 2019, 'Pentagon Shelves Neutral Particle Beam Research', *Defense One* <https://www.defenseone.com/technology/2019/09/pentagon-shelves-neutral-particle-beam-research/159643/> (accessed 8 December 2022).

Weedon, B & Samson, V 2022, *Global Counterspace Capabilities: An Open Source Assessment*, Secure World Foundation, Washington, DC <https://swfound.org/counterspace/> (accessed 8 December 2022).

Wilkening, D A 2012, 'Does Missile Defence in Europe Threaten Russia?', *Survival*, vol. 54, pp. 31–52, https://doi.org/10.1080/00396338.2012.657531.

Wilkening, D & Watman, K 1986, 'Strategic Defenses and First-Strike Stability', *RAND Corporation* <https://www.rand.org/pubs/reports/R3412.html> (accessed 8 December 2022).

Williams, I & Dahlgren, M 2022, *Boost-Phase Missile Defense*, Center for Strategic and International Studies, Washington, DC <https://www.csis.org/analysis/boost-phase-missile-defense> (accessed 8 December 2022).

Zarubin, P V 2002, 'Academician Basov, High-Power Lasers and the Antimissile Defence Problem', *Quantum Electronics*, vol. 32, no. 12, p. 1048, https://doi.org/10.1070/QE2002v032n12ABEH002348.

32

SPACE-BASED SYSTEMS AND COUNTERSPACE WARFARE

Marek Czajkowski

Introduction

This chapter aims to explain how satellite systems contribute to modern warfare and how the means to negate their capabilities work. It also addresses current trends regarding the military use of outer space, which are likely to shape the future of combat and non-combat military operations in space.

Military-related activity in outer space is frequently called 'militarisation', meaning the use of the extra-terrestrial domain for military purposes. It entails three distinct but closely intertwined dimensions. The first involves activities directed from space to Earth using satellite systems to support or conduct combat on the ground (in the air and at sea). The second aspect refers to combating satellite systems with ground- or space-based assets – these activities are directed against space-borne targets from many directions. And finally, the third facet of militarisation of space entails the confrontation between ballistic missiles, which traverse this domain on the way to their targets, and missile defence systems designed to engage incoming projectiles in space, which involves space- and ground-based systems (Figure 32.1).

The chapter is organised into four sections. The first clarifies basic terms and definitions regarding space militarisation. The second explains how the use of space systems benefits military operations, including potential capabilities. The third section describes how space systems are and may be confronted with means of negating their capabilities. And the final section explores current trends in space systems development. Some issues pertaining to missile defence will be omitted as they do not necessarily involve the operation of space systems.

Military space – a backgrounder

As the first step to explaining how outer space is used for military purposes, it is necessary to present a short glossary of related terms and definitions. This is particularly important because patterns of human activity in the space domain and military operations therein are currently undergoing significant changes. Therefore terms and definitions present in the information/political sphere and academia are often conflicting and sometimes unclear. Furthermore, the laws of physics determining the opportunities for and limitations of space activity are not commonly understood,

DOI: 10.4324/9781003299011-38

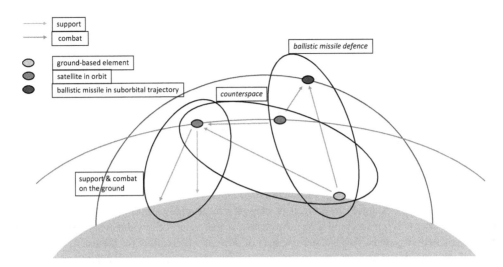

Figure 32.1   Space militarisation.

Source: Author's creation.

which hampers the understanding of space-related problems. Thus, it is essential to produce a backgrounder which will also outline the chapter's limits and scope in more detail.

To start with, it is necessary to delineate outer space as a domain in which the activities we are referring to occur. Usually, we think about space as something above the atmosphere, but in reality, there is no clear boundary between those two environments. Air density decreases with altitude, gradually turning into a near-vacuum of space some 10,000 km above the planet's surface.

Any object intended to remain in Earth's vicinity above the densest layers of the atmosphere must reach a velocity high enough to produce centrifugal force equal to the force of gravity at a given altitude. This is called **orbital velocity**, and once it is achieved, a spacecraft travels around Earth without propulsion along a circular or elliptical trajectory called an **orbit**. An object sent to space with an initial velocity smaller than an orbital one travels along a trajectory called **sub-orbital**; but this does not mean it cannot reach orbital altitudes, only that it is not fast enough to maintain orbit as defined above. Thus, in general terms, orbiting objects maintain inertial flight in low-density layers of the atmosphere or above it.

Bearing the above in mind, we define **outer space** as a domain which extends from the altitude at which the velocity needed to counteract gravity is achievable due to the ability of a craft to withstand the heat caused by atmospheric friction. It is widely accepted that spaceflight is possible up from 100–150 km above Earth's surface with the use of current and prospective technologies. Thus, for practical purposes, a 100-km limit is usually recognised as a boundary of outer space, though there is no universal legal definition and some nation-states adopt their own regulations in this regard.

An object in orbit is confronted with numerous factors slowing it down, which may result in its losing orbital speed and **deorbiting**. The atmospheric drag present at low orbits is the most important factor here; it is minimal, but its impact accumulates with time. Therefore, satellites must use their engines occasionally to maintain orbit. Furthermore, a change of orbit also requires extensive use of spacecraft engines (Wright, Grego & Gronlund 2005, pp. 49–76). This means that despite the inertial nature of orbital flight, most satellites are equipped with adequate means of propulsion for station-keeping and manoeuvring.

Outer space is enormously **hostile** to human beings and man-made objects. Extremely low air pressure or lack of it at all, a multi-spectral radiation environment, an abundance of charged particles and the presence of micrometeoroids, meteoroids and, occasionally, bigger bodies endanger both people and equipment. Means of mitigation of the destructive effects of depressurisation (when human flight is concerned), radiation induced-damage and physical damage require very sophisticated technologies. Additionally, low gravity is highly dangerous to human health.

Sending an object into space requires a tremendous amount of **energy** per mass of a payload, which has to reach orbital velocity to overcome the Earth's gravity pull. Relative to the properties of an orbit, the orbiter's mass may represent less than 1–5% of the total lift-off mass of the space vehicle. Note that the actual mission-related payload is even smaller since a great portion of the orbiter's mass is contained in its physical construction, power generation devices and station-keeping/manoeuvring engines with sufficient propellants.

Once a spacecraft is safely in orbit, it is supposed to provide certain services for the end users on Earth, but it is not working alone. An orbiter is just a part of a wider whole called a **space system** or satellite system. This is a complex set of devices which allow for the use of orbital craft for a selected mission. The main part is a **space element**, also called satellite, orbiter or spacecraft, which is permanently stationed in orbit around the Earth. A **ground element** involves communication and control stations connected with an orbiter by a radio or laser **link**, which forms the third part of a space system (Wright, Grego & Gronlund 2005, pp. 109–16). Space systems may perform various tasks, both civilian and military. In many instances, satellite systems are dubbed dual-use as they may be utilised for civilian and military purposes.

Every space activity requires large and sophisticated production facilities for satellites and launch vehicles. Furthermore, the ground infrastructure for conducting operations in space entails numerous fixed and mobile objects like launch pads (planes), maintenance facilities, control centres, and communication stations scattered throughout the world to enable constant links with satellites. And finally, the development of technologies needed in every stage of space activity requires enormous research&development effort. In effect, **massive spending** is necessary for conducting every space activity, including the military use of satellite systems.

Satellite missions may be adversely affected not only by natural phenomena but also by deliberate actions. Numerous techniques, technologies, devices and activities may be employed to hamper the operations of space systems. These are collectively called **counterspace measures (CSMs)**, and may be employed by various state- and non-state actors. Counterspace operations may affect satellite systems from space or the ground and affect every part of the system: satellites may be blinded, dazzled, damaged and destroyed, link jammed, spoofed or otherwise compromised, and ground infrastructure damaged, destroyed or otherwise jeopardised.

A specific counterspace device designed to damage or destroy satellites in orbit physically is called an **anti-satellite (ASAT) weapon**. ASAT weapons may employ explosive warheads, including nuclear devices, kinetic projectiles, ramming tactics and directed energy (DE) beams to destroy or damage satellites, or may physically grab orbiters and carry them away. Anti-satellite systems may be stationed in orbit (co-orbital weapons carriers or suicide craft) or ground-based (direct-ascent projectiles and DE weapons).

The development of weapons designed to operate in space invokes the term **space warfare**, understood as every kind of combat activity conducted in space. It involves attacks against satellites in orbit with space-based and ground-based assets. Additionally, combatting ballistic missiles frequently happens in space, and so it falls within the category of space warfare. This is because ballistic missiles with a range above 500 km usually cross into space as their apogee may exceed 100 km. In this way, they become suborbital vessels since they do not enter orbit, even though, in some cases, their apogee is higher than the orbits of many satellites. **Missile defence** entails all means and methods of defeating ballistic missiles. It may employ space-based sensors and interceptors or ground-based detectors and anti-ballistic weapons. Note that many anti-satellite weapons systems have an inherent capability to engage satellites in orbit.

Additionally, the term **space weapon** refers to any system which is designed to destroy or damage objects in or from space (Moltz 2019). This category also includes weapons which may conduct attacks on Earth from space; these, however, are not counted as a means of space warfare.

Military use of space systems

In the mid-1940s, the first analyses of the ways in which orbital craft may contribute to military activities depicted several features which have determined the usefulness of satellite systems to this day. First of all, while revolving around the world, a spacecraft can visit and view all the places on Earth. Furthermore, placed high above the ground, it is able to observe or attack great areas at the same time. Orbiting craft can also retransmit signals between distant places around the globe. And finally, a satellite in orbit is also relatively safe as it is difficult to reach from Earth. Since that moment in the 1940s, the desire to utilise the advantages of placing military objects in space has been the most important driving force behind the development of space technology (Burrows 1998). Satellites have proven over time that they are able to perform many tasks much better than any other platforms or technical means, generating previously unreachable abilities.

As of now, satellite systems routinely perform various missions for military purposes, which can be divided into three general categories. **Observation** refers to multi-spectral optical and radar intelligence gathering, electronic and signals intelligence and observation of natural conditions for military planning and operations. **Communication** means relaying radio and optical transmissions between ground stations. **Positioning, navigation & timing (PNT)** means the use of satellites to provide data for defining the geographic position and altitude of ships, planes, vehicles, individuals and weapons, plus extremely precise timing information.

These tasks may be labelled traditional because they have been performed since the onset of the military use of space. Thanks to the unique properties of orbital flight, space systems greatly enhance the effectiveness of military operations, providing more accurate and comprehensive information, allowing quicker and more effective communication and easy positioning. This does not mean, however, that the abovementioned tasks cannot be performed by other means, but space systems multiply the effectiveness of related activities many fold. Therefore, satellite systems are dubbed 'force multipliers' because, thanks to their use, militaries may perform their tasks with much less effort and much higher efficiency. Note that even though the role of satellites in military operations is of a supportive nature, this support is crucial for combat and non-combat mission effectiveness.

In theory, satellite systems may also be used to conduct combat missions against air/sea/ground targets. Orbiting weapons have access to all of an adversary's territory, and space bombardment has long been envisioned as an important role for space systems. Nevertheless, despite being technologically feasible, such missions have remained a theoretical possibility due to the many limitations described below.

In the future, satellite systems may also be able to combat other objects in space, like satellites or ballistic missiles traversing the space domain. In theory, satellites have advantages against other objects in space as they can control large areas of the Earth's surroundings. Thus, they may deploy intercepting craft or use DE weapons quicker and with greater effectiveness than ground-based systems. However, as of today, these missions also remain only a possibility, except for the use of space-based sensors to detect and track ballistic missiles. This mission is similar to the Earth observation mission; it only covers the area of space that is above the atmosphere.

There are important constraints which limit the use of satellite systems, of which the very high costs of producing, placing into orbit and operating sophisticated space systems are the most important. Technical and operational requirements pertaining to these systems are also very demanding, which necessitates using the most advanced, and thus expensive, components. Military systems must also be better protected and more robust than civilian ones. Even today, when miniaturisation and launch cost reduction generally favour the expansion of satellite use, military-grade systems remain very expensive. Furthermore, satellite systems usually consist of many orbiters forming constellations, which increases the overall price tag.

Due to the properties of space flight, orbiters are usually in constant motion relative to the Earth's surface, so an individual satellite can only see a part of it at a time. Consequently, if the satellite system's mission is supposed to be performed constantly over a certain area, at least several orbiters are needed for that purpose; the lower the orbit is, the more of them are required. If the mission is to be performed globally and on a permanent basis, the need for more craft is magnified manyfold. This is true not only of observation and positioning, but also of communication systems.

Satellites travel along precisely predictable paths and are extremely difficult to conceal once in-orbit, a fact which represents the key operational constraint. Moreover, the nature of individual satellites or constellations is also hard to hide, and an adversary usually knows the mission of the particular vessel. Therefore, it is relatively easy to organise counterspace activities, so the 'ultimate high ground' giving the best available observation and firing position against space and surface objects is, at the same time, the 'ultimate exposure' to observation and attack from Earth or space.

Satellites, once in orbit, are also vulnerable due to the usually limited available payload. That is why they do not have thick armour which could withstand attacks, so they are relatively soft targets. The fragility of orbiting craft is an increasingly important vulnerability of space systems, particularly in light of the maturing kinetic ASAT capabilities.

It has already been stated that besides the dedicated military satellites owned by nation-states, civilian space systems are operated by state-owned entities or commercial companies. This civilian infrastructure may also be employed for military purposes due to the supportive nature of space systems' missions. This is a particularly suitable method with regard to satellite communication. The difference between dedicated military and civilian craft may lay in the level of protection of the signal against jamming, spoofing or being tapped into, but not necessarily. The same goes for observation services, which are provided by many commercial entities offering optical and radar imagery in military-grade resolutions. Furthermore, existing space positioning systems used by militaries are the same as those used by civilian customers; the latter, however, cannot legally obtain military-grade receivers.

The commercial availability of space-derived services is very important from the military point of view, even though the quality of civilian services is usually lower than that of the best military ones. Still, they might be used for some military purposes, enhancing and supporting dedicated military infrastructure. Furthermore, entities other than the governments of the space-faring nations may use commercial services for military purposes. In this way, powers other than the rich ones can benefit from the satellite force multiplier. Other governments and non-state actors may obtain capabilities they cannot provide domestically for themselves and use them for military purposes. The dissemination of space-derived military-usable capabilities among non-space-faring nation-states and non-state actors is often dubbed the 'democratisation' of space and profoundly influences the global strategic landscape. This process does not necessarily diminish the preponderance of the strongest states, but it represents the wide distribution of abilities which were, until recently, exclusively reserved for them.

Counterspace

The rival powers during the Cold War possessed the technological abilities to destroy enemy satellites from the early 1960s, but they did not decide to deploy them in significant quantities. This was due to economic constraints and the passive nature of satellite systems, which did not pose an immediate and direct threat. Furthermore, the United States clearly declared that any attack on the nuclear early warning space infrastructure would be treated as if it were a nuclear strike against America, and that the United States would respond accordingly. Thus, the superpowers did not have good reasons to launch a costly and dangerous counterspace arms race.

In the 21st century, the situation in which military satellite capabilities were relatively secure has started to change. With the general advancement of space technologies and their dissemination among various actors, activities intended to adversely affect satellite capabilities increased in number, intensity and variety of means employed. The same factors, which for decades decided on the utility of space systems, have recently turned into vulnerabilities, for counterspace constantly evolves as a natural need to counter existing capabilities, much like an eternal sword vs shield competition. These vulnerabilities have been addressed above.

According to the authoritative "Space Threat Assessment 2022" (Harrison et al. 2022, pp. 3–7), there are four general types of counterspace weapons: kinetic physical, non-kinetic physical, electronic and cyber. Note that this report refers to all counterspace capabilities as 'weapons', but it is equal to our understanding of 'counterspace measures', as we reserve the word 'weapon' for the description of means of warfare which lead to physical damage or destruction.

The kinetic physical CSMs entail attacks on ground stations to hamper communication with orbiters by destroying or damaging the relevant equipment, as well as the satellites in orbit in an attack from the ground or using other space assets. If successful, this type of attack may produce debris from a damaged/destroyed spacecraft which remains in orbit. Kinetic physical attacks are relatively easy to attribute with proper means of detection.

Non-kinetic physical weapons do not have direct contact with targets but result in inflicting physical damage. This includes high-altitude nuclear detonations, which may render satellites inoperable due to an electromagnetic pulse destroying electronic circuits (note that nuclear warheads may also be used to destroy satellites physically, what falls into the category above). High-power lasers or microwave projectors may also damage satellites or otherwise make them inoperable by temporarily dazzling or permanently blinding them; the latter does not necessarily mean the destruction of the satellite. The distinction between weapons and non-weapons is slightly blurred at this point, as the same device, for example a laser, may be used to temporarily dazzle a satellite's optics or damage it permanently, relative to the beam's power and distance of attack. Non-kinetic physical attacks rarely result in the creation of debris as directed energy weapons do not necessarily fragment the target; however, it may be forced out of its orbit. The attribution of such attacks can also be established, even though it is more difficult than in the case of kinetic physical attacks.

Electronic interference targets an immaterial segment of space systems, the link between spacecraft and ground station. The most common is jamming, which involves generating a strong signal on the frequency used by a link to make it impossible to distinguish transmission, thus severing communication. Spoofing is the technique of transmitting false signals on the satellite frequency to disrupt the system's service and is particularly applicable to positioning signals. Electronic interference is relatively easy to perform and devices able to do so are commercially available. It is also much more difficult to attribute than the previously described techniques.

Attacks from cyberspace employ the tools used to corrupt data transmitted to or from satellites, intercepting this data for the adversary's benefit and, ultimately, taking control over orbiters through cyber intrusion. This type of attack can target satellites, ground-station or end users, and it is available to state and non-state actors with high IT skills. Clear attribution of such an attack is extremely difficult, although not impossible.

The most general observation concerning the character of modern counterspace activities is that non-destructive, easy-to-execute, and difficult-to-attribute modes of attack are more numerous than destructive physical ones. Thus, cyber and electronic anti-satellite attacks are quite frequent, as many nation-states and non-state actors use this technique when they deem it practicable. On the other side, ASAT weapons, potentially the most dangerous but easiest to attribute, have not been deployed in militarily significant quantities so far.

The following assessment referring to existing and prospective counterspace capabilities of international actors is based on the following representative reports: "Global Counterspace Capabilities 2022" (Weeden & Samson 2022), "Challenges to Security in Space 2022" (DIA 2022) and "Space Threat Assessment 2022" (Harrison et al. 2022).

As of August 2022, four countries have tested dedicated ASAT weapons: the United States, the Russian Federation, the People's Republic of China and India. These countries have conducted destructive tests involving ground-based interceptor missiles. This means that they are technically ready to deploy anti-satellite direct-ascent weapons. Additionally, the US, Russia and China have gained considerable experience in proximity/rendez-vous manoeuvres (PRM), which is an essential prerequisite for co-orbital ASAT development. However, despite these capabilities, none of these nations has decided to commence deployment of a significant number of ASAT systems to date. Also, none have officially stated such intent and none have revealed any doctrine of the use of such systems. This may indicate technical, operational or financial constraints which cast doubt on the cost-effectiveness of kinetic ASAT weapons, a reluctance to do so based on political considerations, or both.

Another kinetic capability concerns a ground segment of space systems which may be physically attacked. In theory, every country or sufficiently armed non-state actor may conduct this kind of activity against an opponent. This capability depends on an individual actor's military strength and the quality of its intelligence assets.

It is much more difficult to assess which country or non-state actor wields non-destructive counterspace measures. It is, however, safe to assume that every technologically advanced nation-state or even some well-organised and wealthy non-state actors can afford to develop and deploy laser devices capable of at least disrupting the operation of optical satellites. However, only one weapon of that sort has been revealed to date – the Russian *Peresvet* mobile laser. This is most probably a tactical satellite dazzler designed to be integrated into the combat structure of land forces to shield them from observation by overflying satellites. However, it is not known if it has been deployed, as of August 2022.

Electronic and cyber counterspace measures are even more prevalent, as components are easy to buy on the market. It is safe to say that every advanced country possesses at least a rudimentary capability to conduct such operations. Additionally, many non-state actors are also capable of conducting electronic and, especially, cyber counterspace operations.

Anti-satellite weapons systems, the most spectacular of counterspace measures, are widely discussed in the political sphere and academia. The persistent notion of a possible "space Pearl Harbour", envisioned over two decades ago (Rumsfeld Report 2001, p. viii), reflects on strategies directed to reduce vulnerabilities of space systems, even though the threat remains a potential. Therefore, it is important to shed some additional light on this issue.

ASAT weapons, even though they look very impressive, have many disadvantages of economic and operational nature. To start with, it is relatively easy to attribute the use of such weapons, which makes them highly escalatory and inflexible tools for influencing adversaries. Furthermore, it is necessary to deploy a significant number of sensors and effectors to achieve effective and significant anti-satellite capability. Firstly, to ensure the destruction of the enemy's satellite infrastructure, which may consist of a large number of vessels. Secondly, to ensure the operability of an ASAT component, which would be the first target of enemy forces in the case of conflict. ASAT systems therefore require a huge production and training infrastructure and the creation of dedicated military physical and organisational structures. Additionally, co-orbital anti-satellite systems are difficult to conceal once in orbit, so an adversary may destroy these assets before they are used. And finally, ASAT systems are, in a sense, similar to weapons of mass destruction because of the collateral damage they can inflict due to littering space with the debris of destroyed spacecraft.

Political constraints also hamper the development of anti-satellite weapons, which concerns chiefly the possible development of a space arms race with various negative consequences. First of all, ASAT weapons, if deployed in significant quantities, would endanger the existence of current space systems, thus limiting their value as supportive means used in peacetime or during a limited conflict. Furthermore, even though the United States does not have a dedicated ASAT system, it does possess the worldwide Ballistic Missile Defence System (BMDS), which is inherently able to destroy satellites. The US adamantly declares that it does not intend to use it as an anti-satellite weapon and is strongly committed to the idea of space as a sanctuary. But in the eventuality of an ASAT space race commencing, Washington would be well ahead of any adversary from its beginning by simply adding an anti-satellite mission to the list of tasks performed by the BMDS. And finally, there are numerous effective counterspace activities which do not involve risks associated with physical kinetic weapons, such as electronic and cyber capabilities. These are much cheaper, more difficult to attribute, and do not produce debris or otherwise endanger safety in space. DE weapons are also an interesting choice as they do not necessarily destroy or damage satellites, and therefore do not invoke the need for retaliation.

All the abovementioned constraints render kinetic ASAT systems an impractical instrument of deterrence and warfighting. Thus, destructive ASAT weapons will probably not be deployed in significant quantities in the foreseeable future, even if some countries conduct tests and other R&D activities. They will be treated as a technology demonstration and a hedge against unexpected future developments. The latter is important because some nation or nations may not necessarily use the logic described above and decide to deploy ASAT systems even though it would be against their own best interest.

To summarise the current state of military space, we first observe that access to satellite-derived services is paramount for every military combat and non-combat activity in peacetime and war alike. However, the rapid development of counterspace measures in recent decades has put into question this long-standing assessment, as counterspace weapons and tactics exploit the inherent vulnerabilities of space systems. Given this, it is widely feared that the significance of space systems will diminish in the future as their reliability decreases. Consequently, modern militaries relying greatly on satellite services are poised to lose the advantage or at least must be prepared for the decreased effectiveness of their space-borne intelligence-gathering, communication and positioning segment. However, that trajectory of military space development is far from inevitable due to the modern trends in space technology and new organisational concepts.

Trends in the development of space systems

The patterns of human activity in space are undergoing significant changes, which amount to a sort of revolution. This situation is marked mostly by the substantial decrease in the costs of space activities, which translates into a decreased cost of the space-derived services helping in their dissemination. In short, modern, more effective and cheaper launch systems lift smaller but increasingly more capable satellites which make up larger constellations. The ongoing commercialisation of space is also of great consequence, for it means that more and more entities unrelated to the interests of nation-states operate in the extra-terrestrial domain. In essence, outer space no longer belongs to governments; even though nation-states still regulate space activities, their expenditures amount only to slightly more than one-quarter of the space economy (SIA Report 2022).

The evolution of space launch and satellite technologies presents vast opportunities for the military use of space. The new technologies provide the military with the prospect of creating new capabilities and enhance existing ones by adopting new concepts of operating in space. Furthermore, cooperation with the mushrooming commercial sector opens up great opportunities to augment the military capabilities of space-faring nations and gives these capabilities to actors who are not in possession of internally generated space capabilities.

Thus, in more detail, and bearing in mind the practical applications of the abovementioned perspectives, we may point to two main trends that will shape the development of military space in the nearest future.

Firstly, and as has already been observed, counterspace measures have rendered space systems vulnerable to a degree not envisioned a decade ago and they are still in development. This trend, clearly visible in the last decade, will undoubtedly persist in the future. Electronic and cyber CSMs will evolve and disseminate quickly, and it is also likely that DE weapons will become more common. It is also possible, though unlikely, that kinetic ASAT weapons systems will be deployed in militarily significant quantities.

Secondly, and this is a trend that has emerged within the last decade, a huge effort has been made to begin addressing the vulnerabilities of space systems. In essence, this concerns the struggle to augment space systems' resilience, particularly against counterspace measures. This trend will greatly influence the future relationship between space assets and counterspace measures and will determine how effective space systems will remain and how robust space services will be.

The first of these trends has already been addressed above and does not need further description. Therefore, below we present the assessment of the second.

To begin with, let us observe that an obvious measure in the situation in which satellite systems may be compromised is to decrease the reliance on them and strengthen the alternative ways of providing missions performed by satellite systems. Much effort is being made with respect to that, as new hardware and technologies are being prepared to support and replace satellite services and militaries frequently train to operate in an environment with diminished access to spaceborne assets. This is, however, not within the scope of this chapter; we only note it for the sake of comprehensiveness.

The technologies and operational patterns designed to increase the resilience of space systems may refer to all of their three segments. A ground segment may be physically reinforced by various means, dispersed, concealed and better equipped against cyber intrusion; these means are somewhat obvious and are nothing new. The same goes with securing links that may be better coded and making working frequencies narrower and rotated to work better in conditions brought by heavy electronic warfare. What is rather new, and what amounts to the biggest change in the strategies set to strengthen the resilience of satellite systems, is the evolution of the space segment of military space architecture.

The current operational pattern of military systems rests on a relatively small number of expensive, difficult-to-replace satellites organised in specialised constellations. This means that military space systems are relatively easy targets for counterspace measures, mainly because planning and executing an operation against a limited number of fragile and exposed targets is a relatively easy task. Furthermore, rendering only one or two satellites of a small constellation ineffective may drastically hamper its overall effectiveness. Thus, making the space segment more resilient has become a focal point of the attention of governments, militaries and the military industry. As a result, offsetting the development of counterspace measures has become the main strategy, particularly in the United States.

An authoritative report, "Defending Against the Dark Arts in Space" (Harrison, Johnson & Young 2021), describes the following ways of protecting satellite systems against the CSMs.

Architectural measures for protecting space systems entail the construction of a new generation of space architecture which will be characterised by higher numbers of smaller and more universal satellites. This measure will create many more targets requiring a much larger counterspace structure of sensors, data-processing centres, launchers and interceptors. Proliferated constellations will also be able to suffer losses and remain operable, and their effectiveness will decrease gradually.

Technical means refer to the satellite segment of a space system and entail several measures like:

- increasing space operational awareness to warn of countermeasures being prepared and activated using ground- and satellite-based dedicated surveillance systems,
- the shielding of satellites' payloads against at least some of potential negative effects like EMP,
- creation of new optical devices able to filter light frequencies and equipped with shutters to protect lenses against lasing attacks, and
- enhancing the effectiveness of orbiters' transmission equipment to make it more resistant to jamming

Finally, operational defensive measures entail the ability to rapidly reconstruct or reconstitute satellite systems by placing pre-stored satellites in orbit after the attack or by quickly manufacturing new ones that are possibly more resistant to new CSMs. It may also entail increased manoeuvrability of individual satellites, stealth technologies and employing deceptive strategies or decoys. Additionally, military payloads may be hosted aboard commercial satellites, which would greatly complicate counterspace operations.

Active defence may also be used as a viable strategy against CSMs. It may entail jamming counterspace assets from Earth and attacking their supporting ground infrastructure. Furthermore, the new generations of satellites may be equipped with devices to jam or spoof enemy ASAT systems or dazzle/blind their sensors. They may also be equipped with weapons to fend off interceptor craft. Finally, enemy co-orbital ASAT systems may be pre-emptively destroyed or removed from orbit.

Implementing the abovementioned ideas will require great financial and organisational effort to perfect new technologies and create an expensive new architecture. But, particularly in the United States, this effort is well underway and generously funded by the government. Many aerospace companies are proposing already mature solutions and the military is about to deploy experimental systems based on new concepts and organisational patterns. This drive towards distributed and, therefore, much more resilient constellations will likely result in the advent of a new generation of military space systems. They will be more capable and, most importantly, much more resilient against counterspace measures. Thus, the most advanced space-faring nations will likely retain their space-derived advantages in the coming decades, despite the ongoing development of CSMs.

Conclusion

From the military point of view, the use of space systems is very important as it greatly enhances the overall effectiveness of military activities. That is why leading powers maintain and expand fleets of military satellites. But the space domain is not reserved for the strongest countries, as other international actors also deploy their own basic space capabilities or use commercial services for military purposes; this process is sometimes dubbed 'space democratisation'. Despite important limitations, the use of space systems for military purposes steadily increases in scope and relevance.

Of the limitations mentioned, the most important is the rapid development of counterspace measures over recent decades, which exploit the inherent vulnerabilities of space systems. Kinetic ASAT weapons will probably not be deployed in the foreseeable future because they are rather impractical. Given this, other CSMs like electronic and cyber capabilities or DE weapons, which are more versatile, difficult to attribute and less escalatory, will form the bulk of nation-states' and non-state actors' counterspace capabilities in the near future.

On the other hand, a huge effort has been set in motion, particularly in the United States, to address vulnerabilities of military space architecture. The drive to increase the resilience of space systems and make them provide services despite evolving countermeasures is a key trend in the development of military space. The future effectiveness of space systems will hinge on how well new technologies, operational concepts and organisational patterns will play out against evolving counterspace developments.

References

Burrows, W E 1998, *This New Ocean. The Story of the First Space Age*, Random House, New York.

DIA 2022, 'Challenges to Security in Space 2022', *US Defence Intelligence Agency*, <https://www.dia.mil/Portals/110/Documents/News/Military_Power_Publications/Challenges_Security_Space_2022.pdf> (accessed 20 August 2022).

Harrison, T, Johnson, K & Young, M 2021, 'Defending Against the Dark Arts in Space', *Center for Strategic & International Studies*, <https://www.csis.org/analysis/defense-against-dark-arts-space-protecting-space-systems-counterspace-weapons> (accessed 5 March 2021).

Harrison, T, Johnson, K, Young, M, Wood, N & Goeslsler, A 2022, 'Space Threat Assessment, 2022', *Center for Strategic & International Studies*, <https://www.csis.org/analysis/space-threat-assessment-2022> (accessed 5 May 2022).

Moltz, J C 2019, *The Politics of Space Security*, Stanford University Press, Stanford, CA.

Rumsfeld Report 2001, 'Report to the Commission to Assess United States National Security Space Management and Organization (Rumsfeld Report)', *Commission to Assess United States National Security Space Management and Organization*, <https://aerospace.csis.org/wp-content/uploads/2018/09/RumsfeldCommission.pdf> (accessed 10 May 2022).

SIA Report 2022, 'State of the Satellite Industry Report, Executive Summary (SIA Report)', *Satellite Industry Association*, <https://sia.org/news-resources/state-of-the-satellite-industry-report/> (accessed 12 August 2022).

Weeden, B & Samson, V 2022, 'Global Counterspace Capabilities 2022', *Secure World Foundation*, <https://swfound.org/counterspace/> (accessed 10 June 2022).

Wright, D, Grego, L & Gronlund, L 2005, *The Physics of Space Security*, American Academy of Arts and Sciences, Cambridge, <https://aerospace.csis.org/wp-content/uploads/2019/06/physics-space-security.pdf> (accessed 10 December 2018).

PART VI

Harbingers of Future Warfare

33

PROSPECTS OF GREAT POWER RIVALRY

Escaping the Tragedy?

Enrico Fels

Introduction

Making sense of contemporary and future international politics, of which the behaviour of its dominant members is perhaps the most often investigated feature, is no small endeavour. An enormous body of scholarship has evolved in International Relations (IR) for deciphering the actions of great powers as well as the interests, ideas, resources and roles that their key domestic actors hold. Before delving deeper into the complexities of future great power rivalries, it is necessary to first provide an ontological base for reading international realities and identifying core principles that heavily influence and structure states' actions in the international arena. Subsequently, a prognostic outlook can be made on what to expect for the foreseeable future with regards to contending great powers by closer discussing some of those variables that will likely shape their competition.

Deciphering international realities

The productivity of IR scholarship has led to a great variety of schools and provided IR with a "theoretical pluralism" (Walt 1998, p. 30) that makes the discipline both fruitful and challenging at the same time. These schools of thought are entangled in "a protracted competition between the realist, liberal and radical traditions" (Walt 1998, p. 30). Probably no other school in IR has had a more pronounced impact on the discipline and its schools as realism, which "has been the dominant discourse in the international arena for many centuries" (Mearsheimer 1995a, p. 42). Starting with the writings of Carr (2001 [1939]), who prominently challenged the idealistic thinking of his times by outlining a realist critique of international relations and delivering a "devastating rhetorical blow" (Barnett & Duvall 2005, p. 40) to the 'utopians', and Morgenthau (2005 [1948]), who combined realist thinking and scientific rigour into a consistent theoretical framework, realism as a *theory* entered the academic field of political science in the late 1930s.

One reason for the academic success of realist scholarship was the "practical and intellectual failures" (Buzan 2008, p. 48) of idealist policies and projects (e.g. League of Nations) during the inter-war years. In contrast to their idealist and radical counterparts, realist scholars argued that one has "to study the international system as it was, rather than as one might like it to be"

 DOI: 10.4324/9781003299011-40

(Buzan 2008, p. 48). By successfully presenting itself as a counterprogramme to the "utopian tendencies of liberalism" (Buzan 2010, p. 7), its emergence as "the dominant paradigm among international relations scholars" (Baldwin 1994, p. 12) was facilitated in light of the evident botches of idealist thinking in the real world. While realism held a fairly prominent discursive position in Western academia during the years of the Cold War, this considerably changed after the end of the Soviet Union and the subsequent unipolar moment of the United States during the 1990s, which led to a rise of constructivist, liberal and post-positivist thinking in Western universities. Subsequently, realist scholars increasingly had to challenge an idealist orthodoxy at universities by providing a sober take on international matters that differed paradigmatically from liberal and more radical normative approaches.

The re-emergence of China as a leading great power since the late 1990s, as well as Russia's hostilities against Ukraine since the Orange Revolution in 2004, gradually started to demonstrate the political necessity and intellectual importance of realist thinking both for a better understanding of international politics and a more appropriate reaction to key global developments in the post-Cold War era. Scholars increasingly began criticizing the lack of realist analysis of regional and global affairs and pointed to the gap between scholarly debates at Western universities and tangible realist policies pursued by regional states and great powers (Khoo 2014). Moreover, the argument was made that liberal idealism led many Western decision-makers to dismiss critical realist insights by pursuing foreign policies that invite strategic overstretch and threaten their states' international positions and future well-being (Cox 2013; Mearsheimer 2018).

Principles of international politics and competition

Realism is best understood as a plural tradition and eclectic approach towards international relations that seeks to avoid utopian, wishful thinking by trying to identify what international politics 'actually' are made of (Chiaruzzi 2012, p. 36). Accordingly, realists aim to "see the world as it is, not as we would like it to be" (Mearsheimer 2001, p. 4). Moreover, realism "is founded on a pessimism regarding moral progress and human possibilities" (Gilpin 1984, p. 290) and on the insight that "state behaviour is largely shaped by the *material structure* of the international system" (Mearsheimer 1995b, p. 91).

Realist scholarship has identified several key principles of international relations that are essential for shaping great power rivalry. Next to emphasizing "the continuities of the human condition" (Buzan 2008, p. 50) at the international level, realists hold that international politics are taking place in an anarchical world, which lacks an overarching, rule-enforcing entity. Thus, states are involved in a constant struggle for power in the international sphere. While this anarchy is "murky and difficult to read" (Rose 1998, p. 152), it is nevertheless the primary organizing principle of the international system. As international politics is defined by "the absence of a tribunal or police force, the right to resort to force, the plurality of autonomous centres of decision, the alternation and continual interplay between peace and war" (Aron 1967, p. 192), the world can be a dangerous place to interact although normative systems such as ethics, morals and legal procedures condemn, regulate and limit the competition for power not only within societies but also among states.

In such a world of a "recurring struggle for wealth and power among independent actors in a state of anarchy" (Gilpin 1981, p. 7), realists argue that for states "it is better to be Godzilla than Bambi" (Mearsheimer 2006, p. 162). Additionally, great powers usually seek to further expand their international footprint for gaining further power and security. Zakaria (1999, p. 185), for instance, observed that "the more powerful they become, the more influence they seek". In this regard, Deutsch (1968, p. 88) argued that

> *a nation's feeling of insecurity expands directly with its power.* The larger and more powerful a nation is, the more its leaders, elites, and often its population increase their level of aspirations in international affairs.

Under these conditions a *security dilemma* is created by the attempts of one state to improve its national security vis-à-vis others, which triggers a response by them, further accelerating and exacerbating a "vicious circle of security and power accumulation" (Herz 1950, p. 157). While war does not always have to be the result, security dilemmas can make violence among states more likely particularly due to uncertainty and miscalculation.

Another key principle of realism is that groups are "the building blocks and ultimate units of social and political life" (Gilpin 1984, p. 290) and that in the modern world, the nation-state receives the greatest loyalty of the people (after the family) and acts as the major (but not only) apparatus for intergroup conflicts. In a realist world, the most dominant international actors are states equipped with more power resources than their peers; they are called great powers (Fels 2017a, pp. 200–7). Related to this, realists hold that states usually possess some form of offensive weaponry that can be used to 'hurt' other states. Due to the persistence of anarchy, realists believe that states can never be sure about the intentions of other states as "[u]ncertainty is the dominant feature of international life" (Zakaria 1999, p. 184). Thus, the fear of cheating and the unknown intentions of other nations explain, why states "fail to cooperate even in the face of common interests" (Grieco 1988, p. 488). While realists assume international cooperation to be beneficial, they also argue that due to the fear of defection and subsequent danger to one's own position and interest, it is hard (though not impossible) to be established and maintained. States consequently pursue different foreign policies that reflect both their own capabilities and those of other actors, which lays the base for what is called balance-of-power-politics. Most important for the maintenance of a balance of power in a multi-state system are efforts to increasing one's power base and build alliances with other actors in order to add the power of other nations to one's own (Waltz 1979, pp. 125ff; Mearsheimer 2001, pp. 157–64). While forming and upholding alliances is difficult for instance due to internal strategic differences between allies and the preponderance of anarchy and uncertainty, alliances with other states are a key means for states to considerably alter the distribution of capabilities prior to as well as in a conflict (Snyder 1997).

Instead of balancing against a state whose power grows and upsets the existing balance of power, some states may prefer to align themselves to the rising state by following a *strategy of bandwagoning*, i.e. by forming an alliance or agreeing to other forms of international cooperation. They also might seek to avoid provoking the rising power and instead hope that another international player (the "buck-catcher" (Mearsheimer 2001, p. 158)) contains the increasingly powerful state. While *buck-passing* is essentially a defensive strategy of strong states aimed at deterring war, "bandwagoning is a strategy of the weak" (Mearsheimer 2001, p. 163), as states yield to the belief that a stronger power might take what it wants by force anyway, so aligning with them is seen as a better option. A middle-course strategy in the spectrum between balancing and bandwagoning is called *hedging*. The primary objective of hedging lies in "cultivat[ing] a middle position that forestalls or avoids having to choose one side at the obvious expense of another" (Goh 2005, p. 2). Importantly, the choice for one of these strategies is triggered not only by *power* considerations, but are also the result of how they perceive *threats* (Walt 1985, pp. 9–13).

The final key principle of realism is related to states' motivations: For one, states try to survive at all costs. Next, they seek to pursue this objective strategically. This means that realists see states as relatively rational agents (from a system-level perspective), which are sensitive to costs (i.e. seek relative gains and try to avoid losses), but are nevertheless prone to miscalculation, e.g. due to lack of information, poor judgement by their leadership, unsuitable cultural, political or religious beliefs, incorrect images of the other sides or ideological lust for power – which again raises the possibilities for war (Waltz 1979, pp. 173ff).

International relations therefore have one unique feature which distinguishes them from basically all other social relations: they take place within the shadow of war. Of course, this still allows for other ends to be pursued that are not related to national survival and security, but "all these more noble goals will be lost unless one makes provision for one's security in the power struggle among groups" (Gilpin 1984, pp. 290f). Accordingly, Waltz (1979, pp. 204ff) argued that powerful states can provide global commons, but will not refrain from using benevolent rhetoric to disguise their actual understanding of a 'necessary' global common (e.g. fighting a 'just' war in order to maintain a specific international order or a desired balance of power within a certain region). Indeed, very often non-security aims like economic prosperity or the spread of a particular ideology or religion are merely intermediate objectives for achieving this principal task of governments, as the underlying logic of the international realm gives primacy to power and security (Mearsheimer 2001, pp. 46ff). Despite having more resources at their disposal, great powers, just like other states, thus have to act cautiously in a harsh and quickly punishing international environment.

The continuation of great power rivalry

As the most capable actors in the international arena are especially filled with the desire to ensure security and gain more power both in terms of capabilities as well as in relational and structural influence (Fels 2017a, pp. 153–93), great powers continue to be trapped in strategic rivalries with peers (and lesser states) now and in the future. Given the anarchic conditions under which international relations take place, Mearsheimer (2001, pp. xiff) famously described international affairs consequently as a *tragedy* since

> hopes for peace will probably not be realized, because the great powers that shape the international order fear each other and compete for power as a result. Indeed, their ultimate aim is to gain a position of dominant power over others, because having dominant power is the best means to ensure one's own survival. Strength ensures safety, and the greatest strength is the greatest insurance of safety. States facing this incentive are fated to clash as each competes for advantage over the others. This is a tragic situation, but there is no escaping it unless the states that make up the system agree to form a world government.

Evidently, such a transformative development has not taken place yet, although the level of intergovernmental cooperation and global governance is much higher now compared to previous times as certain progress has been achieved in coordinating national policies, e.g. on economic, development or climate issues. Still, mankind is as far away as ever from a world government. Even the United Nations (UN), the world's most significant multilateral institution, evidently lacks both the means (its annual budget being less than that of the Maltese government) and the political and legal capacities (most states continue being protective about their national sovereignty) to perform such a function.

The lack of a profound transformation of the international realm's general logic is perhaps most apparent in the field of international security. Several great powers (and lesser states) have fought wars or intervened militarily in other UN members since the establishment of the organization. This was often done in violation of the UN Charter, the Geneva Convention and other segments of international law. Thus, while diplomatic agreements and legal texts have created a certain juridification of international affairs, placing too much hope on the pacifying effects of international law on great power rivalry is obviously ill-advised. In essence, international law has always been "a vital instrument of statecraft" (Armstrong, Farell & Lambert 2012, p. 311) of major powers as well as "an excellent tool for the pacification and stabilization of dominance" (Krisch 2005, p. 378). Setting the rules of the international game allows leading states "to project their vision of world order into the future" (Krisch 2005, p. 377). Realists have highlighted for a long time that "[m]ost international law is obeyed most of the time, but strong states bend or break the law when they choose to" (Waltz 2000, p. 27).

As great powers now and in the future have to operate under the shadow of war and anarchy, their quest for security, power and survival endures. Importantly, specific variables and trends in the economic, military and political realm alter to some extent the ways and means (as well as the theatres) great powers compete with each other in the 21st century. In order to better understand the trajectories and confinements of future great power rivalry, it is necessary to address some of the economic, military and geopolitical factors that influence this enduring competition between great powers.

Economic shifts foreshadow military ones

Realism holds that the material wealth of nations provides them with the necessary military and political tools to engage and succeed in international politics. States do therefore engage in fierce economic rivalry in order to ensure continuing access to resources, technologies and markets that provide them with the best possible capabilities in any international competition. If the distribution of wealth changes over time, this has enormous effects on the ability of great powers to maintain their international position and compete with old and new peers (Kennedy 1987). In short, economic shifts bear severe political consequences. Accordingly, as Zakaria (2008, p. 26) notes, "Britain was undone as a global power not because of bad politics but because of bad economics".

Economic globalization after the Cold War allowed some states to extent their relative share of global economic output more than other, which caused a dramatic change in the distribution of global wealth among great powers (Dalio 2021). The liberalization of global trade, largely facilitated by the United States to establish a liberal international order (as realism expected, Washington was trying to arrange the international system to the benefit of itself and its allies), permitted the Chinese economy to grow remarkably. In 2014, the latter eventually became even larger than the US economy in terms of Purchasing Power Parity (PPP)[1] – marking the first time in more than four generations (120 years) that Washington does not operate on the world's largest economy (Figure 33.1).

Due to globalization, the economic importance of world regions has shifted considerably: While the relative standing of Western Europe and North America was reduced over the last four decades, the regions of East and South Asia increased their position – a very significant trend which the International Monetary Fund (IMF) estimates to continue for the foreseeable future (see Figure 33.2). The economic decline of Western Europe is perhaps most drastic as the region's relative share is projected to be cut in half within less than 50 years (28% in 1980 vs 14% in 2027).

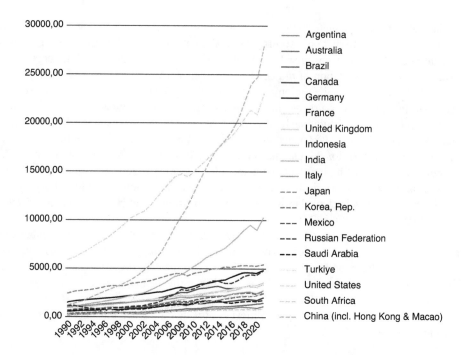

Figure 33.1 GDP (PPP) of G20 countries since 1990 in million current international $ (based on World Bank's World Development Indicators).

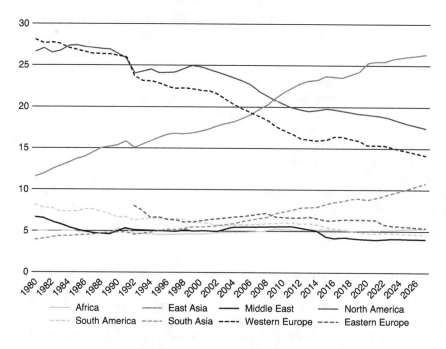

Figure 33.2 Percentage of global GDP (PPP) of selected world regions (based on IMF data; 2022–2027 estimates).

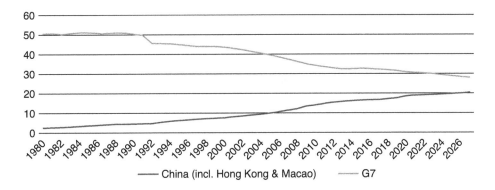

Figure 33.3 Percentage of global GDP (PPP) of China and the G7 (based on IMF data; 2022–2027 estimates).

In contrast, both East Asia and South Asia are expected to more than double their respective shares of global GDP (PPP) until 2027.

Beijing in particular has been benefitting from this key economic trend and strengthened its international position: The difference in shares of global GDP (PPP) between the G7 and China was more than 47% in 1980; it is estimated to be down to less than 8% by 2027. Taking a long-term strategic path in order to ensure that its re-emergence on the global stage is permanent, China has strategically embedded itself in many segments of the global economy and fared very well in its economic competition with other great powers. Having established an impressive ability to innovate as well as manufacture and distribute high technologies (Sapir 2022; Mayer & Lu 2023) or becoming *the* industrial leader for processing and refining strategic minerals (Fels 2022), China's economic rise will probably continue over the decades ahead, further fuelling rivalries with the United States and other great powers. It is, for instance, in this context particularly concerning that both Beijing and Washington face a high import dependency in 11 critical materials urgently needed to develop and manufacture the most modern high-technology. While this creates incentives to either increase own efforts to secure access to these materials or to ensure properly working global markets to satisfy the demand of all interested buyers, realism provides a rather pessimistic prognosis regarding the most like course taken by strategically competing great powers (Figure 33.3).

Thus, 30 years after the Cold War ended due to the implosion of the communist superpower, Washington is facing a strategic peer in the decades ahead that, unlike the Soviet Union, is also an economic powerhouse. Realists consequently warn that the competition between these two superpowers of the 21st century will most likely not be contained to the economic realm, but affect many aspects of international politics in the future (Bekkevold 2022). Next to the greater importance of Eurasia's Eastern regions as future theatres for strategic competition (reflecting the relative decline of Europe), this key economic trend of shifting wealth could not only trigger economic warfare via mutual sanctioning, technological blacklisting or logistical and infrastructural decoupling, but creates enormous military and geopolitical consequences now and in the future.

Military dynamics and strategic rivalry

Following realism's insights, changes in economic wealth have tangible impacts on the military capabilities of nations: Once taxable bases of national economies increase, governments tend to use the additional money to provide greater funding for their armed forces. Conversely, governments with shrinking economies and declining budgets (and limited options for creating more public debt) face a choice between spending on welfare *or* warfare: either fulfil important internal necessities, e.g. by public spending on education, social security or health issues to sustain internal stability, or maintain those military capabilities deemed necessary to prevail best externally. Given its impressive economic development, the Chinese government's choice has been very easy in this regard: Beijing became the world's second biggest military spender behind Washington in the early 2000s and has closed in on the US in military terms. Among other things, increased defence funding is allowing China to field a naval fleet *larger* by number than that of the United States – an indication of Beijing's growing maritime ambitions. The fact that China was able to considerably decrease the ratio between its own military spending and that of the United States within less than a generation stands in stark contrast to *all* other great powers. Measured in Market Exchange Rates (MER), Washington committed more than 20 times the amount of money on defence matters in 1992 compared to Beijing. The latter's rising wealth and subsequent rising military expenditures narrowed that quotient down to less than three times in 2021 (Figure 33.4).

Notably, data based on MER actually *underestimates* real military expenditures: Research shows that "China's budget in military-PPP terms is 1.62 times larger than the market exchange rate figure" (Robertson 2021) suggests. This means that in military-PPP exchange terms, the ratio between China and the United States was around 1:1.5 in 2017 (not 1:3 as suggested by MER data). Moreover, following military-PPP, the combined annual defence spending of China (US$393.58 bn) and Russia (US$206.54 bn) was already *on par* with that of the United States (US$605.8 bn) in 2017 (Robertson 2022, p. 805). This is indeed a very remarkable development.

To offset China's increasing defence spending and growing military capabilities, Washington has started – in alignment with realism – pursuing a balancing strategy by upholding and expanding its system of security alliances in Europe and Asia, while Beijing has been increasing own efforts to win international partners near and further abroad. For the future, this competition for allies will likely further intensify and growing pressure on other states to back only one of the rivalling contenders is to be expected. Next to the dangers of an arms race, history warns that such

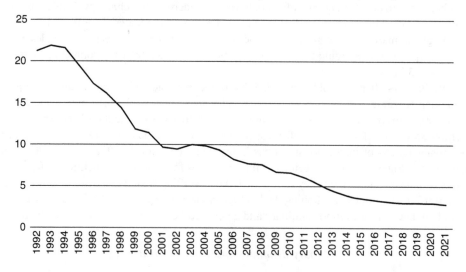

Figure 33.4 Ratio of military expenditures between the United States and China (based on SIPRI Military Expenditure Database; constant (2020) million US$, 1992–2021).

a constellation considerably increases the likelihood of both great powers entering into a military confrontation (Allison 2017; Dalio 2021).

Fortunately, one key variable in the military realm will likely limit chances for a *direct* military clash and might prevent a large-scale open war between antagonistic security alliances at all: nuclear weapons. Without entering the broad debates on the destructiveness of nuclear weapons and their usability in military conflict (Frühling & O'Neil 2012), the history of the Cold War shows that "[s]omewhat perversely, holding each other's civilian population hostage to nuclear annihilation can provide stability and peace between two adversaries" (Roy 2013, p. 76). Nuclear weapons are a strategic bargaining tool for 'nuclear blackmailing' and for preventing conventional military invasions. Today and in the future, nuclear arms constitute the 'ultimate deterrent' (Mearsheimer 2010, p. 396) and set significant limits for future great power rivalry: states with nuclear weapons will try to avoid direct military conflict with nuclear peers in order to avoid miscalculations that trigger nuclear war – and non-nuclear states will restrain themselves when competing militarily against a nuclear power.

With regards to the future of great power rivalry, this has four major effects: Firstly, the enormous destructiveness of nuclear weapons makes all great powers act very carefully when competing with nuclear-equipped peers in order to avoid any military escalation that might lead to the actual use of nuclear weapons. Importantly, next to nuclear armageddon following large-scale first- and second-strike waves, already a handful of electro-magnetic pulses (EMPs) generated by a few nuclear weapons' explosions 30–400 km, e.g. *above* the continental US or mainland China would create enormous consequences: depending on the altitude of the explosion and the weapon yield, wide areas of human settlements would be affected with electronic equipment being rendered unusable. Without microelectronics, most infrastructures in modern societies would cease to be working. The political, social and economic turmoil ensuing an EMP attack can hardly be overstated. States struck by an EMP would essentially drop out of *any* international competition for a very long time.

Secondly, once great power rivalry intensifies in the future, the number of states trying to get access to nuclear weapons might increase as non-nuclear states equipped with the technical know-how (like Japan or South Korea) face a great incentive to acquire nuclear weapons if the strategic situation requires it and the promises of allies to provide nuclear protection in times of need are deemed unreliable. Thirdly, due to the strategic consequences of nuclear proliferation, established nuclear powers have an incentive to collaborate so that the nuclear club remains as exclusive as possible as these weapons provide them with strategic leverage both over their allies and other states. Finally, as waging war with a nuclear-armed great power is exceptionally dangerous, great powers will tend to pursue hybrid engagements below the threshold of open warfare when rivalling with a nuclear peer. In addition to hard to attribute cyber-attacks or sabotage actions against infrastructures in space or in the maritime realm, this might also include the usage of private security contractors and the arming of different factions in proxy wars in order to bind and weaken strategic rivals.

Realpolitik's return

Geopolitically, the outlined trends and confinements will shape great power rivalry in several interconnected ways. With the end of the bipolar world of the Cold War and a brief moment of US unipolarity, the structure of the future international system is moving towards a new equilibrium with multiple poles. As China and – to a lesser degree – Russia, India, Brazil, as well as other members of the G20 are capable major powers, strategic rivalry between great powers will remain a key feature of the future international arena. Importantly, realist scholars hold that multipolar systems have a greater potential for instability due to the complex insecurities generated by multiple rivalling great powers. Despite the enormous wealth created by economic globalization and first steps towards a more capable system of global governance via the G20 format, further proliferation of multi- and minilateral regimes to limit the competitor's international access to resources, technologies and markets are to be expected as each great power tries to structurally bind allies and limit the reach of competing actors in the future.

Realism prognosticates that geopolitically this also includes closer strategic collaboration between great powers that feel threatened by a more powerful third: despite enduring strategic reservations, even more coordinated joint efforts by Moscow and Beijing are to be expected in order to strategically challenge Washington's dominant global position (Fels 2018). China's tacit support for Russia's war against Ukraine since February 2022 speaks volumes in this regard and suggests that the Chinese leadership pursues a bloodletting variant in its balancing strategy: ensure that the war in Ukraine is limited to Eastern Europe and sustain Russia's ability to fight a proxy war against the US and its Western allies in order to bind *both* sides' resources, which limits Washington's ability to strengthen its position in East Asia in order to challenge Beijing's regional hegemonic aspirations while making Russia more dependent on China both as a supplier of high-technology and a market for Russian raw materials.

Whereas respective regional political and economic integration efforts are not necessarily a bad thing, future strategies to exclude peer competitors will likely lead to pressure particularly on non-great powers, limiting their ability to hedge and manoeuvre. Rivalling great powers will likely seek to influence their contender's current and potential future allies in order to change their strategic behaviour from bandwagon to either hedging or balancing. In this regard, formats like the Belt and Road Initiative, the BRICS+ and the Shanghai Cooperation Organisation have to be seen as efforts for engaging in strategic rivalry with the United States by institutionally underpinning the different interests, norms and concepts of regional and global order held by decision makers in Beijing and Moscow and other non-Western powers (Fels 2017b).

Conclusion

Following Zakaria (1999, p. 34) "[t]he tragedy of international relations, as theorists from Thucydides to Rousseau to Waltz have understood, is that it does not take bad states to produce bad outcomes". As outlined, heighted geostrategic rivalry particularly between Washington and Beijing, the superpowers of the first half of the 21st century, is to be expected and might lead to an age of de-globalization and open political antagonism with severe consequence for all other international actors. Considering the insights gained from realism, the tragedy of great power politics will thus persist either until mankind has established a more widely shared, unifying vision of a single human civilization allowing for the formation of an international body of proper global government beyond the current global governance fora or until a hegemon can establish itself that is too powerful to be overcome even if all other states were to join forces against him.

While tensions between the world's different elites, cultures and civilizations will likely prohibit the first, the domination of the international system by a single state is very improbable in the nuclear age. Still, although no nation can gain *global* superiority, *regional* hegemony remains attainable and will very likely remain a key goal of rivalling great powers. Following realist logic, regional hegemons in one part of the world will moreover seek to prevent others from achieving the same by intervening in neighbouring regional affairs to prevent or delay the emergence of strategic peers.

Although the existence of nuclear weapons will render a direct clash between nuclear powers unlikely, realists are cautious due to the dangers of miscalculation between competing great powers caught in a security dilemma. Moreover, realists would not be surprised if strategic rivalry between great powers was increasingly taking place both in areas where attribution is difficult (cyber, outer space or in the maritime realm), via proxy wars (like in Ukraine since 2014 and perhaps over Taiwan in the future) or by excluding financial and trading regimes. The diplomatic failures, e.g. of the Budapest Memorandum and the Minsk Process, additionally highlight the inherent limitations of international treaties in an anarchic world, as well as the enduring importance of both military capabilities in major powers' strategic competition – something that will very likely drive national defence spending in the future if economic progress permits – and the perpetual uncertainty about the other side's true intentions.

Next to the dangers of a great power war due to the likely further militarization of international affairs, the predicted continuation of great power rivalries in the future is indeed tragic as it takes away indispensable funding and political will required for dealing with pressing global topics: The necessity to adapt to climate change, harvesting the economic and cultural benefits of globalization for lifting people out of poverty or fighting bad governance and extremism in its various forms in order to improve the livelihoods of humans all over the world.

Note

1 PPP is used in accounting in order to reflect the different relative costs of goods and services as well as incomes in comparative economic analysis. For a robust comparison of economies, the use of PPP holds several advantages, the most important being that it reflects the differing relative costs for goods and services and the differing purchasing value of money across several countries (Fels 2017a, p. 261; Sapir 2022)

References

Allison, G 2017, *Destined for War*, Houghton Mifflin Harcourt, Boston, MA & New York.

Armstrong, D, Farell, T & Lambert, H 2012, *International Law and International Relations*, Cambridge University Press, Cambridge.

Aron, R 1967, 'What Is a Theory of International Relations?' *Journal of International Affairs*, vol. 21, no. 2, pp. 185–206.

Baldwin, D A 1994, 'Neoliberalism, Neorealism, and World Politics', in D A Baldwin (ed), *Neorealism and Neoliberalism*, Columbia University Press, New York, pp. 3–25.

Barnett, M & Duvall, R 2005, 'Power in International Politics', *International Organization*, vol. 59, no. 1, pp. 39–75, https://doi.org/10.1017/S0020818305050010.

Buzan, B 2008, 'The Timeless Wisdom of Realism?', in S Smith, K Booth & M Zalewski (eds), *International Theory: Positivism and Beyond*, Cambridge University Press, Cambridge, pp. 47–65.

Buzan, B 2010, 'China in International Society: Is 'Peaceful Rise' Possible?', *The Chinese Journal of International Politics*, vol. 3, no. 1, pp. 5–36, https://doi.org/10.193/cjip/pop014.

Bekkevold, J I 2022, '5 Ways the US-China Cold War Will be Different from the Last One', *Foreign Policy*, 29 December, <https://foreignpolicy.com/2022/12/29/us-china-cold-war-bipolar-global-order-stability-biden-xi/> (accessed 17 January 2023).

Chiaruzzi, M 2012, 'Realism', in R Devetak, A Burke & J George (eds), *An Introduction to International Relations*, Cambridge University Press, New York, pp. 35–47.

Cox, D G 2013, 'The Age of Liberal Imperialism', *Orbis*, vol. 57, no. 4, pp. 643–52, https://doi.org/10.1016/j.orbis.2013.08.010.

Dalio, R 2021, *Principles for Dealing with the Changing World Order*, Avid Reader Press, New York.

Deutsch, K W 1968, *The Analysis of International Relations*, Prentice-Hall, Englewood-Cliffs, NJ.

Fels, E 2017a, *Shifting Power in Asia-Pacific?* Springer, Cham.

Fels, E 2017b, 'Beyond Military Interventions?', in C Neuhäuser & C Schuck (eds), *Military Interventions*, Nomos, Baden-Baden, pp. 149–91.

Fels, E 2018, 'The Geopolitical Significance of Sino-Russian Cooperation in Central Asia for the Belt and Road Initiative', in M Mayer (ed), *Rethinking the Silk Road*, Palgrave, London, pp. 247–67.

Fels, E 2022, 'Chinas Macht im Bereich der Kritischen Rohstoffe', in H Ohnesorge (ed), *Macht und Macht-verschiebung*, De Gruyter, Berlin, pp. 305–24.

Frühling, S & O'Neil, A 2012, 'Nuclear Weapons and Power in the 21st Century', in E Fels et al. (eds), *Power in the 21st Century*, Springer, Berlin, pp. 81–95.

Gilpin, R G 1981, *War and Change in World Politics*, Cambridge University Press, Cambridge.

Gilpin, R G 1984, 'The Richness of the Tradition of Political Realism', *International Organization*, vol. 38, no. 2, pp. 287–304, https://doi.org/10.1017/S0020818300026710.

Goh, E 2005, 'Meeting the China Challenge: The US in Southeast Asian Regional Strategies', *Policy Studies*, no. 16, <https://www.jstor.org/stable/resrep06541> (accessed 20 December 2022).

Grieco, J M 1988, 'Anarchy and the Limits of Cooperation', *International Organization*, vol. 42, no. 3, pp. 485–507, https://doi.org/10.1017/S0020818300027715.

Herz, J H 1950, 'Idealist Internationalism and the Security Dilemma', *World Politics*, vol. 2, no. 2, pp. 157–80.

Khoo, N 2014, 'Is Realism Dead? Academic Myths and Asia's International Politics', *Orbis*, vol. 58, no. 2, pp. 182–97, https://doi.org/10.1016/j.orbis.2014.02.007.

Kennedy, P 1987, *The Rise and Fall of the Great Powers*, Random House, New York.

Krisch, N 2005, 'International Law in Times of Hegemony', *The European Journal of International Law*, vol. 16, no. 3, pp. 369–408, https://doi.org/10.1093/ejil/chi123.

Mayer, M & Lu, Y-C 2023, 'Digital Autonomy? Measuring the Global Digital Dependence Structure', *SSNR*, viewed 15 April 2023, https://doi.org/10.2139/ssrn.4404826.

Mearsheimer, J J 1995a, 'The False Promise of International Institutions', *International Security*, vol. 19, no. 3, pp. 5–49, https://doi.org/10.2307/2539078.

Mearsheimer, J J 1995b, 'A Realist Reply', *International Security*, vol. 20, no. 1, pp. 82–93.

Mearsheimer, J J 2001, *The Tragedy of Great Power Politics*, W.W. Norton, New York.

Mearsheimer, J J 2006, 'China's Unpeaceful Rise', *Current History*, vol. 105, no. 690, pp. 160–62, https://doi.org/10.1525/curh.2006.105.690.160.

Mearsheimer, J J 2010, 'Why Is Europe Peaceful Today?', *European Political Science*, vol. 9, no. 3, pp. 387–97, https://doi.org/10.057/eps.2010.24.

Mearsheimer, J J 2018, *The Great Delusion*, Yale University Press, New Haven, CT & London.

Morgenthau, H 2005 [1948], *Politics Among Nations. The Struggle for Power and Peace*, McGraw-Hill, New York.

Robertson, P 2021, 'Debating Defence Budgets: Why Military Purchasing Power Parity Matters', *VoxEU Column*, CEPR, <https://cepr.org/voxeu/columns/debating-defence-budgets-why-military-purchasing-power-parity-matters> (accessed 20 December 2022).

Robertson, P 2022, 'The Real Military Balance: International Comparisons of Defence Spending', *Review of Income and Wealth*, vol. 68, no. 3, pp. 797–818, https://doi.org/10.1111/roiw.12536.

Rose, G 1998, 'Neoclassical Realism and Theories of Foreign Policy', *World Politics*, vol. 51, no. 1, pp. 144–72, https://doi.org/10.1017/S0043887100007814.

Roy, D 2013, *Return of the Dragon. Rising China and Regional Security*, Columbia University Press, New York.

Sapir, J 2022, 'Assessing the Russian and Chinese Economies Geostrategically', *American Affairs*, vol. 6, no. 4, pp. 81–6.

Snyder, G H 1997, *Alliance Politics*, Cornell University Press, Ithaca, NY & London.

Walt, S M 1985, 'Alliance Formation and the Balance of World Power', *International Security*, vol. 9, no. 4, pp. 3–43, https://doi.org/10.2307/2538540.

Walt, S M 1998, 'International Relations: One World, Many Theories', *Foreign Policy*, no. 110, pp. 29–46, https://doi.org/10.2307/114275.

Waltz, K 1979, *Theory of International Politics*, McGraw-Hill, Reading.

Waltz, K 2000, 'Structural Realism after the Cold War', *International Security*, vol. 25, no. 1, pp. 5–41, https://doi.org/10.1162/016228800560372.

Zakaria, F 1999, *From Wealth to Power*, Princeton University Press, Princeton, NJ.

Zakaria, F 2008, 'The Future of American Power', *Foreign Affairs*, vol. 87, no. 3, pp. 18–43.

34

INTERNATIONALIZED CIVIL WAR

Alex J. Bellamy

Introduction

Studies of war and peace tend to distinguish international from civil wars. This has yielded separate databases, different causal explanations and different ways of explaining their strategic direction. Resultantly, there is a tradition of enquiry into war's place and evolution in international society focused almost exclusively on war between states or state-like entities (e.g. Luard 1987) and a separate tradition focused on civil wars characterized by the assumption that their characteristics are primarily, if not exclusively, local in origin (e.g. Walter 2022). How international society regulates war is conditioned by these distinctions. Interstate wars are subjected to the United Nations' (UN) rules on armed aggression and principles of collective security, whereas intrastate wars are not. Legal obligations with respect to the conduct of war by states are more comprehensive and better codified than the obligations that inhere on non-state actors. Despite significant progress to better align them, interstate and intrastate wars continue to be governed by separate legal regimes. This bifurcation is becoming untenable, however, as civil wars are increasingly internationalized. What is more, since all combatants, state, non-state and hybrid alike must respond to common sets of incentives and constraints, there are few meaningful distinctions in the way these wars are prosecuted (Biddle 2021, p. xvi).

The risks and costs associated with war mean that major powers have always looked to local agents to prosecute them on their behalf. Meanwhile, war's escalatory logic means that local combatants have always looked to get the upper hand by recruiting external allies. What is new are the multiple ways in which local actors can draw in external parties and the relative ease with which external powers can engage in local conflicts. Technological advances allow major powers to employ kinetic force over great distances and at little material or moral risk to themselves. This has lowered their barriers to entry in even geographically distant wars and thus made engagement in other people's wars more attractive and less costly. But the pull of local allies and technological advances alone cannot explain the growing frequency of internationalized civil wars. The *want* to engage is driven also by geopolitical context, which today is one of increasingly militarized competition.

This chapter examines the phenomena of internationalized civil wars in three sections. First, it examines trends in the internationalization of war and categorizes different forms of external

                    DOI: 10.4324/9781003299011-41

engagement, demonstrating that internationalization is an epiphenomenon comprised of several elements. Second, it examines different explanations for the emergence internationalized civil wars and argues that whilst the underlying cause can be found in war's escalatory logics, proximate causes lay in the increase of civil war, changing technologies and heightened geopolitical competition. Third, the chapter examines how international society might respond to the challenge, which of these trends are likely to be sustained into the future and what might be their impact on the future of war.

Rise

There has been a sharp increase in the number and prevalence of internationalized civil war (UCDP 2021). For most of the period since 1946, internationalized civil war constituted no more than 15% of the total number of wars. From around 2011, that proportion increased to around 40% and was thus a function neither of the Cold War nor its end. However, this is only part of the picture since the Uppsala Conflict Data Program (UCDP) operates with a strict definition of internationalized civil war which requires that one or both sides of an intrastate conflict receive 'troop support from other governments that actively participate in the conflict'. This excludes the supply of mercenary soldiers by a state-related private military company (e.g. Wagner Group), the provision of real-time battlefield intelligence by remotely operated drones or aircraft (e.g. Turkish support to Azerbaijan in 2020) and the provision of support to local allies by non-state networks such as the Islamic State (IS). The War on Terror was a contributing factor, but there was a lag effect of a decade between 9/11 and the rise of internationalization. The increase of internationalized civil war was not exclusively, or even primarily, a result of increasing proxy wars between great powers since it postdates the Cold War's proxy killing fields (Chamberlin 2019). Finally, this picture addresses only internationalized intrastate war and not its twin interstate war (also termed 'domestically diffused' war (Bormann & Hammond 2016)): interstate wars that take on characteristics of intrastate war (e.g. Bosnia 1992–1995, Ukraine 2014).

Civil wars become internationalized in different ways. On the one hand, combatants have different reasons for internationalization guided by the different contexts in which they operate. On the other hand, the process of internationalization is relational not unidirectional in that they are rarely produced by simple patron-client relations wherein local clients exercise their patron's will. Clients invariably have their own political objectives and bargain with patrons and would-be patrons to persuade them to support their cause in part by aligning that cause to the interests and objectives of the patron. The process is therefore best understood as a two-way relationship between actors, each of whom is trying to influence the other except in the rarest of situations where their purposes align perfectly. Table 34.1 sets out the internationalized civil wars in 2021. It is based on UCDP (2022) data, modified it to take account of the points identified above. Since it is a snapshot, it does not capture every significant contemporary example of internationalized civil war.

From Table 34.1, we see that internationalization is not primarily about the imposition of an external power's will upon local actors whether for self-interested, humanitarian or other reasons. In all except one of the 16 cases (Russian support for separatists in Ukraine) internationalization involved the provision of military support to governments. More than two-thirds (11 of 16) of the cases are exclusively concerned with the provision of external support to governments. In large part, therefore, internationalization may not represent a challenge to international society but may instead be a mechanism for mutual aid. In the remaining four cases (Syria, Libya, DR Congo, Azerbaijan), foreign assistance by states to non-state armed groups was balanced by assistance provided by others to the government. Interestingly, three of those four cases centred around a

Table 34.1 Internationalized civil wars in 2021

Location	Party 1	P1 Supporters	Party 2	P2 Supporters
Afghanistan	Government	US	Taliban, Islamic State	[IS – various]
Azerbaijan	Government	[Turkey]	Artsekh Republic	Armenia
Burkina Faso	Government	Chad, France, Niger	Islamic State, UNIM	[IS Mali and Sahel]
Burundi	Government	DR Congo	RED-TABARA	
Cameroon	Government	Nigeria	Islamic State	[IS/ Boko Haram]
Central African Republic	Government	UN (MINURCAT), [Wagner Group]	CPC, UPC	
DR Congo	Government	Kenya, South Africa, Tanzania, Uganda, UN (MONUSCO)	Various, including M23, Islamic State	[Rwanda]
Iraq	Government	US, NATO allies	Islamic State	[IS – Syria]
Kenya	Government	US	Al-Shabaab	
Libya	Government (Tripoli)	Turkey, Qatar	Haftar (Benghazi)	Wagner Group
Mali	Government	UN (MINUSMA), France	Jama'at Nasr al-Islam wal Muslimin	[IS Sahel, Libya]
Niger	Government	Chad, France, US	Islamic State	[IS West Africa]
Nigeria	Government	Cameroon, Chad, Niger	Islamic State/Boko Haram/ Jama'atu Ahlis Sunna Lidda'awati wal-Jihad	[IS West Africa]
Ukraine	Government	–	Luhansk People's Republic, Donetsk People's Republic	Russia
[Somalia]	Transitional government	AU (AMISOM), Kenya	Al-Shabaab	[IS]
Syria	Government	Russia, Iran, Hezbollah	Islamic State, [HTS, various northern militia, Kurds]	[Turkey, US]

Source: Data based on UCDP (2022) modified by author ([denotes entries added by author]).

regional competition between two aspiring neo-imperial powers (Russia and Turkey). The internationalization of civil war is more commonly a demand-driven exercise than a supply-driven one, suggesting local actors have significant agency. Much of that demand stems from the rise of internationalized jihadism exemplified by the fact that almost every local jihadist insurgency draws upon an international network of ideological and material support. The second is that most cases revolve around one of two conflict matrices: jihadism and Russian revanchism. Thirteen of the 16 cases have something to do with one or both matrices. Given that international society has experienced a 'normal' rate of internationalized civil war of between 10% and 15% this would suggest that a substantial part of the rise can be attributed to these specific conflict groups.

From the perspective of the interveners, we can distinguish types of support based on their motivation/purpose and form (see Figure 34.1). With respect to the first, we can distinguish self-regarding interventions initiated by the intervener primarily for its own purposes (be they self-defence, self-interest or humanitarian) from other-regarding interventions that are primarily responding to local demands. Most interventions (around two-thirds of those listed in the table) are primarily other-regarding, their primary purpose to help the local actor achieve its goals, not to

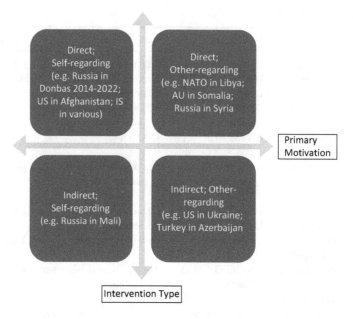

Figure 34.1   Types of internationalization: intervener's perspectives.

use the local actor to achieve the intervener's goals. There is an alignment of goals in some cases but even then, the initiation of intervention typically comes from the bottom-up (invited by actors seeking outside assistance) and local actors are far more invested in the outcome than foreign supporters. There is also a unique set of cases where self- and other-regarding intervention are fused, that of UN and African Union (AU) peacekeeping operations given combat functions. Whilst they are formally other-regarding, since peacekeeping operations are deployed with the consent of their host state, the process of negotiating their deployment involves interaction between local actors, international institutions and third-party states. Primarily, self-regarding interventions are rarer.

A second way of classifying intervention would be according to the form of assistance provided and whether it is direct military involvement or indirect assistance. More work is needed to specify which indirect forms of assistance should be included and I have limited myself to three: provision of mercenaries or armed groups, provision of real-time battlefield support and direct provision of arms and training (not more generalized transfers). Qualitative accounts of individual wars provide rich evidence of the breadth of ways in which foreign actors support local allies. Geographic proximity was central to this in the past, which explains why internationalization has sometimes been understood as a form of conflict contagion (Forsberg 2014), but the examples offered in Table 34.1 suggest two transformations might be overcoming geographical constraints. First, the capacity of major powers to move mercenaries and allied armed forces across regions increases their ability to intervene militarily in conflicts beyond their immediate neighbourhood without committing their own forces. The Russian air force, for example, delivered mercenaries to Libya, Central African Republic (CAR), Mali and Mozambique. Turkey engineered the deployment of several thousand Syrian combatants to Libya. Second, technological developments have widened the ways major powers can intervene in civil wars. Interconnected societies are societies with any number of strings that can be pulled to achieve influence or control (Galeotti 2022, p. 4).

Since internationalized civil war involves a relationship between local and foreign actors, we should also look at things from the client's point of view. In 2021, the recipients of military assistance were primarily states confronting armed challenges to their rule and jihadist insurgents connected to transnational networks, whereas during the Cold War, states commonly assisted and encouraged ideological brethren in foreign countries to violently unseat their own government. There is also evidence that states may sometimes shop around. For example, Mali turned to Moscow and the Wagner Group for assistance against Islamist insurgents when French and UN support proved ineffective and raised uncomfortable questions about human rights.

With the important exception of transnational jihadism, it is far less common for non-state actors to be the principal recipients of external aid. In 2021, there were just five such examples falling into two broad types. The first, which includes Syria and DR Congo, is assistance related to major protracted civil wars in which external states have either strong kinship interests (as in Rwanda and in DR Congo), national security concerns (as in Turkey and US in Syria) or strong humanitarian impulses (US/West in Syria is the sole case).

To understand the internationalization of civil war, we need also to think about the relationship between these supply- and demand-side factors. Internationalization tends to occur where patrons and clients have some common purpose or objective but in conditions where there is rarely a perfect match and where one tries to influence the other. Within that context, it is often true that for as long as they intend to pursue their common purpose, the two parties are mutually dependent, each capable of influencing the other. For example, since Russia and Syria needed each other, the weaker party (Assad) had leverage over the stronger (Putin) with which to shift Russian policy.

Explanations

That foreign powers influence the onset, escalation, duration and settlement of civil war is well established (see Gleditsch 2007, p. 294). What is less clear is *how* they influence civil wars and whether these forms of influence are general or specific. This section reviews three of the most common explanations: that internationalization is caused by proximity, by the pursuit of interests, and by humanitarian concern. It finds that whilst these theories have explanatory value, two additional factors need to be added: (1) the forms of political competition (including ideology) and (2) technological change.

The first and most common explanation is *geographic proximity*. This account holds that civil wars become internationalized when they impact upon the interests, preferences and expectations of neighbouring states (e.g. Wiener 1996). Several studies have found strong empirical evidence that civil wars have a contagion effect magnified by transboundary connections (Salehyan 2009, pp. 19–60). Others have demonstrated that by this mechanism civil wars can provoke interstate conflicts (Gleditsch, Salehyan & Schultz 2008) though one study found that states intervene in a neighbour's civil war to prevent diffusion (Kathmann 2010). An extension holds that kinship or ethnic ties are especially important (Fearon & Laitin 2003) whilst another suggests that contagion occurs because civil war increases mobilization opportunities for aggrieved groups in neighbouring states and lowers barriers to entry (for instance by reducing the price of arms and the power of normative restraint) (Collier & Hoeffler 2004). But whilst geographic proximity remains important, it appears to have declined in significance. Leaving aside the more complex question of transnational jihadism, at most, only half of the third-party interveners identified in Table 34.1 shared a border with the country into which they were intervening. Around a quarter of interventions did not originate even from the same continent. Nor was this exclusively a result of the US-led Global War on Terror. 'Remote warfare' is neither exclusively nor primarily an American innovation.

Other examples in Table 34.1 included France in Mali, Turkey, Qatar and Russia (Wagner) in Libya, and Russia in Syria. Going back a couple of years, Emirati and Iranian interventions in Yemen had elements of remote warfare too (Stoddard & Toltica 2021). Meanwhile, kinship/ethnic ties between intervener and intervened were relatively uncommon in 2021 (only a couple of clear cases, such as Rwanda in DR Congo) whilst most neighbouring state interventions involved mutual aid combatting jihadists insurgencies. Whilst we cannot read too much into a single year's snapshot, this does suggest that geographic proximity is less important than it once was.

A second common explanation is that states intervene in civil war to secure their *preferred outcome* or help their preferred party achieve the best-possible outcome (Gleditsch 2007, p. 295). States might do this through direct military intervention or, more commonly, by indirect means such as by supplying mercenaries, arms, training, finances or intelligence. Such interventions commonly decrease the amount of time it takes for the supported party to achieve victory (Balch-Lindsay, Enterline & Joyce 2008). However, when interventions tip the local balance in favour of one side, other states might conduct counter-interventions to restore the balance. Some accounts, for example, view Saudi Arabia's intervention in Yemen as a counter to Iran's support to Houthi rebels. Counter-interventions can nullify the imbalance created by the initial intervention and extend a civil war's duration (Balch-Lindsay, Enterline & Joyce 2008, p. 360). An extension of this theory views internationalized civil wars as delegated interstate wars, whereby it is the external interveners that shape the aims, strategies, and tactics of the principal conflict parties (Salehyan 2010, p. 500). This theory clarifies the strategic logic of intervention, since as Clausewitz explains, war is the use of force to make your opponent do your bidding – "you must either make him literally defenceless or at least put him in a position that makes his danger probable" (Clausewitz 2007, p. 15). It is the art of political decision by force of arms, a dynamic and interactive struggle between opposed forces that pushes inevitably to the extreme as each side martials its resources to inflict more violence on the enemy than it can inflict on the self to thereby achieve victory and dictate the terms of the political settlement.

However, since external actors have always had preferred outcomes in civil wars, this theory cannot by itself explain *increased* internationalization. It points us in the right direction by calling attention to the political objectives of intervener and local agent and the relationship between them. In the cases documented in Table 34.1, half are counter-insurgencies opposed to local jihadist armed groups, almost all of which receive external support from different branches of the Islamic State and its affiliates. In three other cases – Libya, Somalia and Syria – countering jihadism is one of the principal objectives shared by local actors and foreign interveners, but is not the sole objective. A significant portion of the increased internationalization of civil war can therefore be attributed to the global struggle against violent jihadism. In 2021, at least, this war on terror was far from an exclusively American affair, involving a wide range of local and regional as well as global powers. But the global reach of US military capability and the global vision of its war on terror helps explain the diminution of geographic proximity as a factor. Using air power, missiles and drones, the US is able to wage warfare almost anywhere on the planet at a relatively low risk to itself. Just as importantly, however, its global logistical and intelligence capabilities, and deployable special forces, allow the US to support local allies in a variety of ways.

The struggle for and against jihadism is by far the leading political cause of internationalization, but there is a second that features in around a quarter of cases identified in 2021: Russian imperialism. The Kremlin's intent to forcibly control neighbouring states is evident in Ukraine and in the 'frozen conflicts' of Georgia and Moldova not recorded in Table 34.1, where Russia controls territory without the consent of the state. The projection of Russian power well beyond its neighbourhood is a feature of direct intervention in Syria and mercenary interventions in Libya,

Mali, Central African Republic (as well as Burkina Faso, Sudan, Mozambique and Madagascar, not recorded in Table 34.1). But Russia is not the only imperial foreign policy internationalizing civil war. In Syria, Libya and Nagorno-Karabakh, Russian and Russian-backed forces have met resistance from Turkish and Turkish-backed forces. Just as Russia's President Putin claims to have inherited Peter the Great's imperial project, so has the government of Turkey's President Erdogan sometimes referred to its own foreign policy as 'neo-Ottoman'. Technology is important here, too. Both Russia and Turkey have developed remote fighting capabilities that allow them to project military force into areas where they have limited ground forces with minimal risk to themselves. But in so doing, they have also challenged fundamental norms such as the prohibition of mercenaries.

A third explanation focuses on the power of *humanitarian concern*. According to this theory, a rising tide of liberal humanitarianism provoked primarily Western states to intervene in civil wars to protect civilians from atrocities and extend the writ of human rights and democracy. For realists, such interventions undermined international security by escalating wars and extending their duration (e.g. Mearsheimer 2018) but other accounts suggest that interventions specifically aimed at diminishing anti-civilian violence or supporting peace processes can save lives, shorten the duration of civil war, and reduce the likelihood of recurrence (Seybolt 2008). Multilateral peacekeeping has also been found to limit conflict contagion (Beardsley 2011). Table 34.1 shows that whilst humanitarian concerns are a factor inspiring some interventions, the picture is not one of an aggressively liberal hegemony. In 2021, humanitarian impulses partly inspired three UN-led peacekeeping interventions that count the protection of civilians amongst their core objectives, an AU-led operation in Somalia primarily concerned with countering al-Shabaab but where humanitarian considerations are evident, and Western interventions in Syria which are primarily concerned with countering Islamic State, but which also had humanitarian components. These were primarily multilateral not Western interventions, primarily peacekeeping not warfighting, all except one was deployed with the consent of the government and all deployed into ongoing civil wars.

If the theory that liberal humanitarianism contributed to the overall internationalization of civil war was correct, we would expect an increasing number of Western interventions whose principal purpose was the extension of democracy and human rights. What we in fact find before 2021 is that while there was a small increase in such humanitarian interventions (six in total) after the Cold War, this effect was dwarfed by the war on terror. What is more, of these six interventions, five came in the 1990s and four of those in the first half of that decade. Since 1995, the US has conducted only two non-consensual humanitarian interventions – Kosovo in 1999 (with NATO) and Libya (NATO with UN authorization) in 2011. Intervention in Libya stands as the solitary example of humanitarian intervention in the first two decades of this century. Overall, humanitarian concern has inspired multilateral peacekeeping far more than it has inspired forcible intervention.

The internationalization of civil war can be understood in relation to three principal factors: contagion, interests and humanitarianism. By themselves, however, neither of these explains the increased internationalization observed in part 1 of the chapter. Instead, we need to understand that increase in terms of the emergence of two specific conflict matrices: (1) violent jihadism and its enemies and (2) Russian imperialism and its challengers, as well as the proliferation of technologies that allow major powers to contribute militarily to civil wars in geographically distant places with minimal risk to themselves. The conflict matrices provide motive, the technological developments provide the means and lower the costs associated with interference in a wider range of civil wars. It is important, however, to keep in mind the relational nature of internationalization described in the first part of the chapter. Whilst some internationalized civil wars involve delegation from major powers to local proxies, many are more complex and involve alignments between local struggles and global or regional fracture lines. For example, many civil wars involving jihadists are local in origin and involve localized actors either borrowing foreign ideologies and tailoring them to their needs or adopting alliances to win foreign supporters to help them with their cause. Likewise, the war for Nagorno-Karabakh is primarily a localized conflict between Armenians and Azeris into which Russia and Turkey have been drawn.

War has its own dynamic that changes how actors understand and pursue their objectives. In civil war especially, combatant objectives change because of the decisions and indecisions of battle (Kalyvas 2006). The relationship between outside powers and civil war combatants is dynamic too. They come together typically when there is some alignment between their political objectives and when each believes the other can help it achieve its objectives, both of which are suggestive of parallel local and international rivalries. There is rarely a perfect fit and the relationships themselves tend to change as the battle, the local context and the broader political picture change.

Management

Internationalized civil wars present a critical challenge to international peace and security for two principal reasons. First, internationalized civil wars tend to endure longer than non-internationalized civil wars and exact a higher toll of casualties (Balch-Lindsay & Enterline 2000; Balch-Lindsay, Enterline & Joyce 2008). All other things being equal, an international society in which more civil wars become internationalized is an international society with more armed conflict overall as the eruption of new conflicts outpaces the capacity of that society to resolve existing conflict. There are several reasons why internationalized civil wars endure longer. Most obviously, external support allows combatants to sustain warfare longer than they otherwise would by replacing lost soldiers, military material and other goods. As a result, it takes longer for wars to reach a condition of 'mutually hurting stalemate' thought necessary to move them from the battlefield to the negotiating table. This is an especially acute problem in situations where both parties enjoy external sources of backing. A second way that internationalization inhibits conflict resolution is through the multiplication of veto players. When outside actors involve themselves in civil wars, they are awarded an opportunity to inhibit conflict resolution since negotiated settlements require not just the assent of the local parties but the agreement of external players too. For example, negotiating ends to Islamic insurgencies in the Sahel is made more complicated by the need either to distance local jihadists from transnational jihadist networks or incorporate international jihadists into the peace process. In any peace process, the greater the number of potential veto players, the more difficult it will be to negotiate a peaceful resolution (Cunningham 2006, 2010).

The second challenge presented by internationalized civil war is to international society's capacity to manage and regulate armed conflict. Since the end of the Cold War, international society's toolkit for managing civil wars has tended to include multilateral peace processes overseen by the UN, regional arrangements or some combination of the two that prioritize local political solutions such as power-sharing, elections or some other settlement designed primarily to satisfy the internal parties but which are often overseen by peacekeeping operations (Pettersson, Hogbladh & Oberg 2019). The application of this multilateral toolkit depends upon a consensus among the major powers and its effectiveness in any given case is influenced significantly by the degree and depth of that consensus. Recent literature on peacebuilding emphasizes the central importance of local dimensions, arguing that even this standard approach involves too much outside imposition and too little internally driven local peacemaking (Mac Ginty 2021). The internationalization of civil war inhibits the capacity of this toolkit to manage and resolve conflict. Meanwhile, this model might over-emphasize the domestic at the expense of the international and thus fail to de-escalate or resolve civil wars with international dimensions (Jenne & Popovic 2017, p. 5). Internationalization limits the extent to which local initiatives themselves can alter conflict dynamics. But it also restricts the capacity of multilateral organizations to play a role in regulating, managing, guiding and overseeing peace processes, especially when one or more of the external parties hold institutional power in one or more of the relevant multilateral organizations. The Syrian civil war offers one of the clearest recent examples wherein one foreign backer (Russia) was able to utilize institutional power (UN Security Council veto) to foreclose any serious possibility of the UN managing conflict resolution. Russia has similarly inhibited the UN and the Organization for Security and Cooperation in Europe (OSCE) from playing roles in Ukraine and Nagorno-Karabkah (2020), multiple parties have inhibited the UN from more active engagement in Libya, and the US (among others) inhibited collective responses to the war in Yemen. This is not an exclusively 'global' problem though. Regional powers can also inhibit the involvement of regional arrangements.

International society is not well equipped to manage the problem of internationalized civil war. That is primarily because the principal means for managing and regulating armed conflict developed in the post-1945 UN order – Charter laws, peacekeeping and peacebuilding and human protection – are not well suited to this kind of warfare (Fearon 2017, p. 28). This problem is made more significant by liberal decline and the rise of geopolitical and ideational contestation. Such contestation makes it more difficult still for multilateral institutions to find the consensus needed to manage civil wars. To take just one example, China's increasing influence at the UN. China and the West have different values and these different values translate into different views about the proper role of the UN. Instead of the UN's current human-centred approach organized around the three pillars of human rights, development, and peace and security, China articulates what Foot calls a 'triadic model' of strong states, social stability and development (Foot 2020, p. 228). Over the past few decades, China's relative position has changed within the UN. Its increasing material power has translated into a more confident and assertive foreign policy. China exerts greater influence over key appointments, policies and decisions than ever before. It can offer its own vision of the UN as a viable alternative to the currently prevailing three pillars of security, development and human rights.

The effect of material change and ideological contestation has been to weaken the capacity of multilateral institutions to manage civil war and increase the role of unilateralism and great power management (Kane 2022, p. 179) – a shift from Turtle Bay (UN order) to Yalta – at precisely the same time as that order was being tested by the rise of internationalized civil war. We can see that transition very clearly in the way international society responded to protracted civil wars in Nagorno-Karabakh and Syria. The first Nagorno-Karabakh war was the first test for the new post-Cold War European order and its new multilateral security institution, the OSCE. Gradually, though, the OSCE's role was diminished as Western governments stepped back and Russia assumed the role of principal peacemaker. When the war resumed in 2020, Russia found its hegemonic status challenged by Turkey and the peace was worked out by great power diplomacy between Moscow and Ankara: multilateralism displaced by the great power management redolent of Yalta. Syria followed a similar trajectory. Regional efforts managed by the Arab League gave way to a UN initiative which in turn gave way to great power management, first through a series of Russia-US initiatives and then, when the US vacated the field, through a Moscow orchestrated troika of Russia, Iran and Turkey. The specifics of the two cases are quite different, but the direction in which mediation efforts travelled – from multilateralism to great power management – was similar.

If international society's approach to managing and resolving civil wars is to survive this period of transition, it must therefore take greater account of internationalization (Jenne & Popovic 2017,

p. 6). Indeed, Jenne (2015) argues that even well-designed fixes for the domestic sources of civil war are unlikely to produce peace in the absence of explicit regard for the interests and preferences of external actors. Jenne and Popovic suggest three possible approaches. First, paying greater political attention to the management of external interveners by treating external interveners as conflict parties (Cunningham 2010, p. 125). One avenue for doing this is to utilize multilateral institutions to tie major parties and external parties into the process (Kane 2022, p. 196) though this hits the roadblock of geopolitical contestation described earlier. Since decisions about whether and how to intervene are shaped by what other states decide to do, another approach may for like-minded states to coordinate their behaviours to pre-emptively influence the actions of others and shape conditions more amenable to multilateral approaches. Second, by doing more to manage and control international borders to inhibit the flow of arms, soldiers and other goods across them. This is an obvious and direct way of regulating transnational flows, but one dependent upon the very sort of international consensus so often found lacking. The third possible response is the 'regionalizing' of peace processes by bringing in external players as fully fledged conflict parties, ensuring that the process takes account of their interests and preferences and that institutional fixes address not only domestic problems but internationalized concerns too. Jenne and Popovic refer to the Dayton Peace Process for Bosnia as a good example, showing how international pressure was brought to bear on Serbia and Croatia to facilitate a peace deal within Bosnia (Jenne & Popovic 2017, p. 10). Again, though, this approach depends on there being a degree of international consensus and commitment to joint action often found wanting in the 21st century. More recent internationalized peace processes for Yemen, Syria and Libya have yielded less positive results.

Conclusion

There are several reasons why civil war has become more internationalized. The trend overall looks likely to continue since it is rooted not just in geopolitical transformation but in technological change too. Internationalization poses a significant challenge to an international order not well equipped to manage it. This suggests more fundamental reform may be needed to the norms, institutions, and practices international society utilizes to manage civil wars – the sort of reform that, historically, has tended to come only after moments of profound change in international order.

References

Balch-Lindsay, D & Enterline, A J 2000, 'Killing Time: The World Politics of Civil War Duration, 1820–1992', *International Studies Quarterly*, vol. 44, no. 4, pp. 615–42, https://doi.org/10.1111/0020-8833.00174.

Balch-Lindsay, A, Enterline, A J & Joyce, K A 2008, 'Third-Party Intervention and the Civil War Process', *Journal of Peace Research*, vol. 45, no. 3, pp, 345–63, https://doi.org/10.1177/0022343308088815.

Beardsley, K 2011, 'Peacekeeping and the Contagion of Armed Conflict', *The Journal of Politics*, vol. 73, no. 4, pp. 1051–64, https://doi.org/10.1017/S0022381611000764.

Biddle, S 2021, *Nonstate Warfare: The Military Methods of Guerillas, Warlords, and* Militias, Princeton University Press, Princeton.

Bormann, N-C & Hammond, J 2016, 'A Slippery Slope: The Domestic Diffusion of Ethnic Civil War', *International Studies Quarterly,* vol. 60, no. 4, pp. 587–98, https://doi.org/10.1093/isq/sqw031.

Chamberlin, P T 2019, *The Cold War's Killing Fields: Rethinking the Long Peace,* HarperCollins, New York.

Clausewitz, C. von 2007, *On War*, trans. P Paret, Oxford University Press, Oxford.

Collier, P & Hoeffler, A 2004, 'Greed and Grievance in Civil War', *Oxford Economic Papers,* vol. 56, no. 4, pp. 563–95, https://doi.org/10.1093/oep/gpf064.

Cunningham, D E 2006, 'Veto Players and Civil War Duration', *American Journal of Political Science*, vol. 50, no. 4, pp. 875–92, https://doi.org/10.1111/j.1540-5907.2006.00221.x.

Cunningham, D E 2010, 'Blocking Resolution: How External States Can Prolong Civil Wars', *Journal of Peace Research,* vol. 47, no. 2, pp. 115–27, https://doi.org/10.1177/0022343309353488.

Fearon, J D 2017, 'Civil War and the Current International System,' *Daedalus,* vol. 146, no. 4, pp. 18–31, https://doi.org/10.1162/DAED_a_00456.

Fearon, J D & Laitin, D D 2003, 'Ethnicity, Insurgency, and Civil War', *American Political Science Review,* vol. 97, no. 1, pp. 75–90, https://doi.org/10.1017/S0003055403000534.

Foot, R 2020, *China, The UN, and Human Protection: Beliefs, Power, Image,* Oxford University Press, Oxford.

Forsberg, E 2014, 'Transnational Transmitters: Ethnic Kinship Ties and Conflict Contagion, 1946–2009', *International Interactions,* vol. 40, no. 2, pp. 143–65, https://doi.org/10.1080/03050629.2014.880702.

Galeotti, M 2022, *The Weaponisation of Everything: A Field Guide to the New Way of War,* Yale University Press, New Haven, CT.

Gleditsch, K S 2007, 'Transnational Dimensions of Civil War', *Journal of Peace Research,* vol. 44, no. 3, pp. 293–309, https://doi.org/10.1177/0022343307076637.

Gleditsch, K S, Salehyan, I & Schultz, K 2008, 'Fighting at Home, Fighting Abroad: How Civil Wars Lead to International Disputes', *Journal of Conflict Resolution,* vol. 52, no. 4, pp. 479–506, https://doi.org/10.1177/0022002707313305.

Jenne, E K 2015, *Nested Security: Lessons in Conflict Management from the League of Nations and the European Union,* Cornell University Press, Ithaca, NY.

Jenne, E K & Popovic P 2017, 'Managing Internationalized Civil Wars', in W E Thompson (ed), *Oxford Research Encyclopedias: Politics,* Oxford University Press, Oxford, pp. 1–14, https://doi.org/10.1093/acrefore/9780190228637.013.573.

Kalyvas, S N 2006, *The Logic of Violence in Civil War,* Cambridge University Press, Cambridge.

Kane, S W 2022, 'Making Peace When the Whole World Has Come to Fight: The Mediation of Internationalized Civil War', *International Peacekeeping,* vol. 29, no. 2, pp. 177–203, https://doi.org/10.1080/13533312.2020.1760718.

Kathmann, J D 2010, 'Civil War Contagion and Neighboring Intervention', *International Studies Quarterly,* vol. 54, no. 4, pp. 989–1012, https://doi.org/10.1111/j.1468-2478.2010.00623.x.

Luard, E 1987, *War in International Society,* Yale University Press, New Haven, CT.

Mac Ginty, R 2021, *Everyday Peace: How So-Called Ordinary People can Disrupt Violent* Conflict, Oxford University Press, Oxford.

Mearsheimer, J J 2018, *The Great Delusion: Liberal Dreams and International Realities,* Yale University Press, New Haven, CT.

Pettersson, T, Hogbladh, S & Oberg, M 2019, 'Organized Violence, 1989–2018 and Peace Agreements', *Journal of Peace Research,* vol. 56, no. 2, pp. 589–603, https://doi.org/10.1177/0022343319856046.

Salehyan, I 2009, *Rebels Without Borders: Transnational Insurgencies in World Politics,* Cornell University Press, Ithaca, NY.

Salehyan, I 2010, 'The Delegation of War to Rebel Organizations', *Journal of Conflict Resolution,* vo. 54, no. 3, pp. 493–515, https://doi.org/10.1177/0022002709357890.

Seybolt, T B 2008, *Humanitarian Military Intervention: The Conditions for Success and Failure,* Oxford University Press, Oxford.

Stoddard, E & Toltica, S 2021, 'Practising Remote Warfare: Analysing the Remote Character of the Saudi/UAE Intervention in Yemen', *Defence Studies,* vol. 21, no. 4, pp. 447–67, https://doi.org/10.1080/14702436.2021.1994395.

UCDP 2021, *Armed Conflict by Type 1946–2021,* <https://ucdp.uu.se/downloads/charts/>, (accessed 23 November 2022).

Walter, B F 2022, *How Civil Wars Start: And How to Stop Them,* Penguin Viking, New York.

Wiener, M 1996, 'Bad Neighbors, Bad Neighborhoods: An Inquiry into the Causes of Refugee Flows', *International Security,* vol. 21, no. 1, pp. 5–42, https://doi.org/10.2307/2539107.

35

CHALLENGES TO THE NUCLEAR ORDER

Between Resilience and Contestation

Sanne Cornelia J. Verschuren

Introduction

In this moment of uncertainty and upheaval on the global stage, reaffirming our shared commitment to the grounding principles of the global nonproliferation regime has never been more crucial.

– President Joe Biden, 1 August 2022[1]

World politics today are characterized by "nuclear order anxiety" (Ritchie 2019, p. 440). Whether President Putin's nuclear threats in the context of the war in Ukraine, the continued nuclear weapons production and repeated missile tests by North Korea, the US and Russian withdrawal from various arms control treaties, the failure of the Joint Comprehensive Plan of Action to curtail Iran's nuclear ambitions, or the dangers posed by artificial intelligence and other emerging technologies, there is a sense that the global nuclear order is under continuous distress. At the same time, the global nuclear order has stood strong throughout the past six decades, overcoming massive changes in the security environment, technological shifts and moments of public opposition. Hence, this chapter explores the dynamics of resilience and contestation within the global nuclear order.

More specifically, I argue that the global nuclear order has always been fraught, whether through the tension between credibility and restraint in building up a nuclear arsenal, the countervailing pressures of antagonism and trust in the relationship between adversaries and the inequality between the nuclear 'haves' and 'have-nots' that underpins the nuclear order. Despite these contradictions, the global nuclear order has been marked by an incredible amount of resilience – a result of the deep embeddedness of the nuclear apparatus, the invisibility of states' nuclear pursuits, and the adaptability of the nuclear order to changing circumstances. Bearing in mind this stability, I then reflect on the major challenges that the nuclear order faces today: the unravelling of the arms control regime, the perceived threat from emerging technologies, the challenges posed by the disarmament movement and the overlooked implications of climate change for the nuclear order. This chapter concludes with some reflections on the role of future thinking about the world's nuclear order.

DOI: 10.4324/9781003299011-42

Defining the global nuclear order

The nuclear order refers to the institutions, norms and security practices that govern the development and use of nuclear technology worldwide (Walker 2012; Ritchie 2019; Egeland 2021, p. 208). Having emerged in the 1960s, the global nuclear order is the result of the quest for a 'third way', between unrestrained nuclear anarchy, on one hand, and world government to control nuclear weapons on the other hand. It rests on two key principles: the development of nuclear capabilities along the dictates of deterrence among a recognized set of states and the abstinence of nuclear weapons pursuits in return for economic, security and other benefits for all others (Walker 2000, p. 706).

Delving deeper into the first principle, a handful of states have been able to develop the nuclear hardware, delivery vehicles and related command and control infrastructures since the early 1950s (Narang 2014; Freedman & Michaels 2019; Holloway 2020). In doing so, these states have adopted a set of ideas and practices to govern these nuclear capabilities, called nuclear deterrence. At its core, deterrence revolves around a shared understanding that the threat of massive nuclear retaliation would induce stability in international politics. To cement this understanding, the United States and the Soviet Union/Russia adopted a number of arms control agreements. These agreements aimed to limit the number of nuclear weapons in the possession of the world's superpowers, outlaw investments in technologies or practices that could upset the strategic balance, and reduce other nuclear risks. The 1972 Anti-Ballistic Missile Treaty, for example, intended to limit the development of missile defence systems, contending that such a move would constitute "a substantial factor in curbing the race in strategic offensive arms" (ABM 1972).

The notion of abstinence, meanwhile, has been enshrined in the non-proliferation regime. This consists of the 1968 Treaty on the Non-Proliferation of Nuclear Weapons (NPT), a set of treaties to establish nuclear-weapons-free zones, and various export control agreements, such as the Nuclear Suppliers Group and the Missile Technology Control Regime.[2] Over time, the International Atomic Energy Agency has played an increasingly important role in monitoring states' non-proliferation commitments (Roehrlich 2018). Embedded within this regime are various tools for inducement and punishment, including a promise to disarm on the part of nuclear weapon states in return for other states' support for the NPT, the extension of nuclear umbrellas to allies to make them feel reasonably secure without having to acquire their own nuclear weapons, a guarantee not to target states that do not possess nuclear weapons through negative security assurances and nuclear-weapons-free zones and sanctions to punish those who do not abide by the rules of non-proliferation (Miller 2014; Budjeryn 2015; Gerzhoy 2015).

Since the beginning, the global nuclear order has been marked by deep contradictions, of which I will highlight three: (1) the tension between credibility and restraint in the build-up states' nuclear arsenals; (2) the countervailing pressures of antagonism and trust in the relationship between adversaries; and (3) the inequality between the nuclear 'haves' and 'have-nots' that underpins the nuclear order.

First, a deterrent strategy requires states to develop a significant nuclear arsenal that they can credibly threaten to use. This stands in contrast with another norm of the global nuclear order, namely the requirement to exercise restraint in the development and use of nuclear weapons (Tannenwald 2007; Walker 2012; Tannenwald 2018, pp. 11–20). Policymakers in nuclear weapons states, for example, have repeatedly declared that "nuclear war cannot be won and must never be fought".[3] In walking the line between establishing the credibility of a nuclear force and the nuclear order's demand for restraint, states have faced several difficulties. Throughout the nuclear age, there has been an intense debate about what a deterrent strategy is supposed to look like (Lieber &

Press 2020, pp. 33–41). In the early 1960s, for instance, there was disagreement between the leadership of the Navy and the Air Force about US nuclear force requirements (Rosenberg 1983). Notwithstanding these uncertainties, states have regularly pursued capabilities and strategies that were designed to engage in nuclear warfighting or to decrease one's vulnerability to an adversary's nuclear forces. Low-yield or tactical nuclear weapons, missile defences and counterforce strategies are great examples of this. However, by trying to escape the constraints of the 'deterrent principle' of the global nuclear order, states have provoked arms races, enabled risky nuclear conduct and undermined the stability that deterrence was supposed to induce. For instance, recent wargaming research has shown that tactical nuclear weapons increase the likelihood of nuclear use (Reddie & Goldblum 2022). In fact, states' choices regarding the development of their nuclear arsenals appear to be as much the product of individual beliefs, organizational and bureaucratic dynamics, and cultural traits as that they are driven by rational security objectives. At times, there has even been a disconnect between states' nuclear doctrine and the capabilities that they end up developing.

Second, nuclear weapons are often pursued in a context of deep antagonism (Jervis 1978).[4] States' nuclear pursuits are underpinned by the assumption that the only way to keep an adversary at bay is by threatening to annihilate it. Being willing to destroy an adversary in a nuclear exchange is thus a core tenant of the nuclear order. At the same time, such state of affairs requires a high level of trust between hostile opponents. States must sufficiently trust an adversary to use, and to only use, nuclear force when no other option remains.[5] To put it differently, leaders must deem an adversary rational enough to play by the rules of the deterrence game (Morgenthau 1964, p. 24). Even though trust could be nurtured – through dialogue, mutual agreements in the form of arms control, and various forms of cooperation (Wheeler, Baker & Considine 2016) – trust can be hard to come by in a context of deep antagonism. In essence, antagonism and trust are countervailing forces in the nuclear equation. Antagonism can quickly turn into hatred between adversaries and spur a quest for vengeance, which could have dangerous consequences (McDermott, Lopez & Hatemi 2017). To make this concrete, leaders have sometimes dismissed their adversaries as irrational, irredeemable even. Here, one could refer to President Ronald Reagan's portrayal of the Soviet Union as the 'evil empire' or President George W Bush's notion of the 'axis of evil'. In May 2001, for instance, President George W Bush stated: Unlike the Cold War, today's most urgent threat stems not from thousands of ballistic missiles in the Soviet hands, but from a small number of missiles in the hands of these states, states for whom terror and blackmail are a way of life. [...] They hate our friends, they hate our values, they hate democracy and freedom and individual liberty. Many care little for the lives of their own people. In such a world, Cold War deterrence is no longer enough (Bush 2001).

According to the Bush administration, the so-called 'rogue states' were irrational, willing to sacrifice their own populations to hurt their adversaries. They could not be trusted to abide by the rules of deterrence. Hence, the Bush administration sought a different solution to defend against these perceived threats: missile defence. Yet, the United States' unconstrained pursuit of missile defences since then has complicated the strategic relationship with Russia and China (Verschuren 2021).

Third, the nuclear order is marked by deep inequality between the nuclear 'haves' and 'have-nots'. Initially portrayed as a 'temporary trust', the nuclear hierarchy bestowed the right to access nuclear arms upon a handful of major powers, while restricting it to all others (Egeland 2021). And this distinction is not just military. The nuclear order also established clear rules regarding the import and export of nuclear weapons technology, nuclear energy trade, and the development of national nuclear energy production (Ritchie 2019). In doing so, the nuclear order cemented a strict social hierarchy, one that was rooted in colonial structures. Whereas the nuclear 'haves' were all former empires or major powers, the nuclear 'have-nots' were often former colonies and indigenous communities. Seen as 'subordinate' in the nuclear order, these states bore the brunt of the nuclear harms in terms of supplying uranium ore and suffering the consequences of nuclear testing (Hecht 2012; Mathur 2015 Egeland 2021). Finally, there has been little room for states to 'opt out' of the nuclear hierarchy. While some states have actively tried to push for change within these fixtures and others, like Israel, India and Pakistan, have been able to somewhat break out of them, many states have been less successful – with some having been designated as 'rogues' or 'pariahs', like North Korea and Iran (Gusterson 1999; Abraham 2018; Rodriguez & Mendenhall 2022).

The resilience of the nuclear order

Despite its deep contradictions – the tension between credibility and restraint, the countervailing pressures of antagonism and trust, and the inequality between the nuclear 'haves' and 'have-nots' – the nuclear order has endured throughout the last six decades. During that time, a handful of states have retained nuclear arsenals, some of them large enough to induce nuclear winter if used. Apart from China and India, the nuclear powers have also refused to adopt a 'no-first-use' policy. Contrary to expectations, the proliferation of nuclear weapons has remained limited – with only India, Pakistan and North Korea (and presumably Israel) becoming additional nuclear powers since the 1960s. In doing so, the NPT has continued to be one of the key aspects of global nuclear order. Policy innovation has also been minimal. The nuclear powers, for instance, still promote universalization of the Comprehensive Test Ban Treaty and negotiations for a Fissile Material Cut-off Treaty as major innovations – even though both proposals date back to the 1950s. To explain the resilience of the nuclear order, I point to three factors: (1) the deep embeddedness of the nuclear order; (2) the relative invisibility of the nuclear apparatus and (3) the adaptability that is built into the nuclear system.

Since the onset of the nuclear age, nuclear weapons have been deeply embedded within the international system – materially, ideationally and even as part of our imagination. They were seen as the material basis for security, not just for nuclear weapon states, but also for many others. Within the North Atlantic Treaty Organization (NATO), for instance, the political responsibility for nuclear defence has over time been transferred from the United States to the alliance as such, with NATO declaring itself a 'nuclear alliance' in 2010 (Egeland 2020). In addition to the institutions charged with managing the nuclear order at the international level, nuclear technology has also become deeply ingrained within the fabric of certain states, particularly among the nuclear powers. States' nuclear pursuits have produced an intricate structure of nuclear goals, actors and institutions at the domestic level, all geared towards protecting and promoting the nuclear apparatus (Masco 2006; Hecht 2009; Craig & Ruzicka 2013). Yet, the embeddedness of the nuclear order is not just a function of the material capabilities, it has also become part of the way that states see or want to see themselves. Indeed, nuclear weapons have had a profound impact on the social underpinning of the international systems. It has shaped states' identities, their ideas about defence and foreign policy, and what kind of state behaviour is deemed acceptable and what is not (Hymans 2006; Biswas 2014; Ritchie 2019). Taking it one step further, nuclear weapons have even taken up a prominent role in our imagination. It has become nearly impossible to envision a future without nuclear weapons (Pelopidas 2021).

Second, despite its deep embeddedness, the nuclear apparatus has remained largely invisible to the public and even to decision-makers themselves.[6] This plays out in multiple ways. From the early days of the nuclear age, nuclear weapons and their effects have been deemed to be 'unthinkable', 'unspeakable' and even 'unimaginable' (Masco 2006, p. 3; Considine 2017). For instance, Bernard Brodie – often seen as the original nuclear strategist – declared that total nuclear war was "unthinkable, too irrational to be born" (Brodie 1959, p. 313). In addition to these ideational constructs, states have shielded nuclear policy from the public's purview. Nuclear policy has been shrouded in secrecy, being debated and decided upon in institutions that are largely inaccessible to the broader public (Dahl 1985; Wellerstein 2021). Finally, the effects of nuclear weapons – uranium mining, nuclear testing and nuclear waste in particular – have taken place far away from the 'nuclear haves', among indigenous communities and in the Global South (Amudsen & Frain 2020; Philippe & Statius 2021; Jacobs 2022). All these mechanisms of invisibility have important political effects. They obscure both the ordinary and extraordinary effects of nuclear weapons in everyday life (Masco 2006), making it easier for the nuclear order to endure – despite its contradictions.

Third, a level of adaptability has been built into the nuclear order. Throughout its existence, the nuclear order has overcome massive changes, whether in terms of the security environment, technological developments or public opposition. To accommodate these shifts, the nuclear order has had to adapt. For example, the role that nuclear weapons are supposed to play has been reimagined multiple times, ranging from stabilizing the relationship between the superpowers, to deterring 'rogue states' and to even dealing with nuclear terrorists (Mutimer 2000; Masco 2015). Under the leadership of the Obama administration, for instance, the international community organized a series of world summits aimed at preventing nuclear terrorism. The ability to recraft the nuclear order, mostly on the part of the nuclear 'haves' (Gibbons 2022), makes it possible for the nuclear apparatus to remain relevant, even in times of radical change.

Contestation of the nuclear order

The resilience of the global nuclear order – which is a function of the deep entrenchment, invisibility and adaptability of the order – can shed light on the challenges that it faces today and will face in the future. I identify four such challenges, specifically the unravelling of the arms control regime, the perceived threat from emerging technologies, the challenges posed by the disarmament movement and the overlooked implications of climate change for the nuclear order.

First, the unravelling of the arms control regime is an often-heard worry in discussions about the nuclear order. Since the United States announced its intention to abrogate the ABM Treaty in December 2001, other bilateral agreements have ended up on the chopping block, including the Treaty on Conventional Armed Forces in Europe, the Intermediate-Range Nuclear Forces Treaty and the Open Skies Treaty. Multilateral institutions like the NPT have equally been under pressure. The 2022 Review Conference of the Parties to the NPT, for instance, ended without a final declaration. As a result, key fail-safes within the global nuclear order have been dissipating (Krepon 2021; Gibbons & Herzog 2022). Indeed, arms control has always played an important role in enhancing stability in the international system by outlawing disruptive technologies, avoiding costly arms races and creating tools to use during nuclear crises. As the competitive rhetoric between the United States, China and Russia increases, the absence of arms control mechanisms can prove problematic, particularly by not tackling the incentives for these states to engage in an offensive and defensive arms race, as well as the lack of mechanisms to communicate or to de-escalate tensions during a nuclear crisis.

Yet, the situation becomes even more dire when one examines why the arms control regime has been unravelling. The demise of the arms control agreements is a symptom of a deeper problem, namely a shift in thinking away from deterrence through mutually assured destruction among key policymakers in nuclear weapon states. Since the onset of the nuclear age, there has been a rift between those who believe that stability in the international system can be achieved through the sheer threat of nuclear annihilation and those who think that nuclear superiority and provocation would lead to stable relationships. Having abrogated the ABM Treaty in December 2001, the Bush administration fell into the latter category. Focused on the "rogue state threat", the Bush administration argued that: "Cold War deterrence is no longer enough. [...] We need new concepts of deterrence that rely on both offensive and defensive forces. Deterrence can no longer be based solely on the threat of nuclear retaliation" (Bush 2001). Since then, the shared understanding regarding the role of nuclear weapons in strategic stability has been crumbling among key insiders. And this is not just the case in the United States. In the context of the war in Ukraine, some Russian policymakers have argued in favour of nuclear use, particularly the possibility of using tactical nuclear weapons. In doing so, they have potentially moved beyond the nuclear sable rattling that is part of a regular deterrent strategy. All of this poses a real threat to the global nuclear order, especially as the major nuclear powers have a big role in promoting and upholding the system (Gibbons 2022).[7]

Second, the destabilizing effect of emerging technologies, such as artificial intelligence, cybersecurity, nanotechnology and hypersonic technology is another recurring theme in discussions about the global nuclear order (Acton 2018; Chyba 2020). These technologies are said to influence nuclear policy, whether in the form of a cyber-attack on nuclear command and control infrastructure, the integration of artificial intelligence into the nuclear decision-making process or the pursuit of hypersonic weapons that could evade defences. This is nothing new. The nuclear apparatus has always intersected with emerging conventional technologies. Throughout the Cold War, states faced many challenges of this nature, including the development of intercontinental ballistic missiles and other delivery vehicles, improvements in radar, stealth and electronic warfare, and the pursuit of precision munitions (Talmadge 2019). Still, the global nuclear order withstood and even incorporated these technological changes.

Yet, states' current investments in emerging technologies are part of a broader move among the nuclear powers to modernize their nuclear arsenals and add all sorts of new, potentially destabilizing capabilities to their military toolkits. For example, states are pursuing technologies that are designed to straddle the boundary between the nuclear and the conventional world, encouraged by the idea that rendering their nuclear arsenal more 'useable' would make deterrence more credible, particularly in the context of limited conflicts. This includes tactical nuclear weapons, missile defences and dual-use delivery vehicles. Yet, the global nuclear order rests on an assumption of nuclear exceptionalism – the idea that nuclear weapons are somehow different, separate, and thus exceptional. In 1965, Secretary of Defence Robert McNamara explained that: "While we may find very low yield weapons and enhanced radiation warheads to be of military utility, we should not acquire them simply for the purpose of breaking down the distinction between nuclear and nonnuclear warfare" (quoted in Tannenwald 2007, p. 277). Rather than the notion that emerging technologies will inevitably undermine the global nuclear order, the key is to examine the precise effects of these technologies on strategic stability. When states choose to adopt technologies that are designed to lower the threshold for nuclear use or that 'conventionalize' nuclear weapons, then those choices could prove to be a danger for stability in the international system going forward.

Third, born out of concern about the continued reliance on nuclear weapons and frustration with the lack of disarmament on the part of nuclear weapon states, 122 states adopted the Treaty on the Prohibition of Nuclear Weapons (TPNW) in September 2017. By December 2022, the Treaty had been ratified by 68 states. The TPNW is often presented as an important challenge to the global nuclear order, especially by nuclear weapon states and their supporters. The Treaty prohibits the development, testing, production, stockpiling, stationing, transfer and threat or use of nuclear weapons, as well as any support for prohibited activities. It has its roots in the humanitarian movement, which has been active since the 1990s. This movement promoted the idea that any use of nuclear weapons would have "catastrophic humanitarian consequences" and that nuclear weapon should therefore be banned (Hanson 2018; Ritchie 2019).

However, opposition to the nuclear order is certainly not new. The global nuclear order has always been contested by nuclear 'have-nots', whether they are states that do not possess nuclear weapons or citizens in nuclear weapons states that are excluded from the nuclear decision-making process (Intondi 2018). Concerns about the heightened possibility of nuclear war, for instance, triggered massive protests in the late 1970s and early 1980s across the United States and Europe (Santese 2017). These movements had some impact. They, for example, encouraged US and Soviet leaders to negotiate the Intermediate-Range Nuclear Forces Treaty. At the same time, these movements have not been able to undermine or transcend the nuclear order as such (Wittner 2022). Whether the TPNW will be able to do so, remains to be seen. Even though the Treaty has been praised for challenging the legitimacy of the nuclear order and building an alternative governance structure (Ritchie & Egeland 2018), others have critiqued it for not going far enough. For instance, the humanitarian movement perpetuated the idea that nuclear weapons were 'unthinkable' (Considine 2017) – one of the causes that I identified to explain the resilience of the global nuclear order.

Fourth, climate change will pose another major challenge to the global nuclear order. The effects of climate change range from increasing the risk of conflict, potentially even in a nuclear form, to undermining the effectiveness and safety of states' nuclear deterrent (Dupont 2008). Rising sea levels, for example, could pose a threat to key military bases, some of which host nuclear installations (Brown 2021). At the same time, states' nuclear pursuits also have an important impact on climate change. Even a limited nuclear exchange, for example, could radically alter the world's climate, through a so-called 'nuclear winter' (Witze 2020). Yet, this is not the only way for nuclear weapons influence the world's climate. Investments in nuclear and other classes of weapons produce greenhouse gas emissions, divert public investment away from measures to mitigate climate change, and lower incentives for states to engage in environmental cooperation at the international level (Egeland 2022). Taking a step back, nuclear weapons and climate change have always been intertwined – whether through the contested role of nuclear energy in addressing climate change or the fact that the study of nuclear explosions by nuclear weapons designers had a major impact on the modelling of climate change (Edwards 2012; Baron & Herzog 2020). Understanding the impact of climate change on the global nuclear order – not just today, but also in the future – will be important to predict the durability of the global nuclear order.

The way ahead?

Throughout the last six decades, the global nuclear order has been characterized by a remarkable amount of stability. The core principles, institutions and practices that underpin the nuclear order have remained in place. Hence, the nuclear order's resilience sheds a different light on the aforementioned 'nuclear order anxiety'. While some worries, like the threat from emerging technology as such, are relatively unwarranted, others are downplayed or overlooked. The latter includes the move away from deterrence through massive nuclear retaliation among 'nuclear insiders' or the interplay between nuclear weapons and climate change.

Still, the order's stability should not be mistaken for it being safe or adequate. While there have been no nuclear exchanges since the atomic bombings of Hiroshima and Nagasaki, the world's nuclear history contains many close calls (Lewis et al. 2014). In fact, the stability of the system might have been as much the result of sheer luck as it was caused by any careful planning on the part of the 'nuclear haves' (Pelopidas 2017). Continuing to envision different ways to manage nuclear weapons will therefore be crucial. This puts the imagination of the nuclear future front and centre.

Much of the debate around the global nuclear order is driven and will continue to be driven by actors' beliefs about what the nuclear order is or what it should be. Indeed, ideas about the future of the nuclear order are constitutive of the choices that are made in terms of nuclear policy today. At the same time, all of these visions are not equal. Some actors have more resources and opportunities to push through their ideas about the future. For instance, in contrast to the challenges that emerge from 'nuclear insiders', actors fighting for disarmament face a higher burden to address the inequities, injustices and dangers that are embedded within the global nuclear order.

Notes

1 Biden 2022.
2 A key point here is that the global non-proliferation regime consists of an entire 'ecosystem' of treaties and agreements that attempt to halt the proliferation of nuclear weapons. See, for example, Mallard 2014, p. 7.
3 For a recent statement, see White House 2002.
4 States can have motivations other than security concerns in their pursuit of nuclear weapons, such as prestige.
5 For a discussion of the concept of trust, see Ruzicka & Wheeler 2010. Per the authors' claim, trust is not just a necessity in the relationship between nuclear adversaries, but it also underpins the dynamics between the nuclear 'haves' and 'have-nots'.
6 Dahl (1985), for example, argues that the public contributes to this invisibility by delegating responsibilities to policymakers.
7 Tannenwald, for instance, envisions how nuclear risk could be reduced in a world without formal arms control agreements (Tannenwald 2020).

References

ABM 1972, 'Preamble', *Anti-Ballistic Missile Treaty*, 26 May 1972, <https://treaties.un.org/doc/Publication/UNTS/Volume%20944/volume-944-I-13446-English.pdf> (accessed 22 December 2022).

Abraham, I 2018, 'Decolonizing Arms Control: The Asian African Legal Consultative Committee and the Legality of Nuclear Testing, 1960–64', *Asian Journal of Political Science*, vol. 26, no. 3, pp. 314–30, doi:10.1080/02185377.2018.1485588.

Acton, J 2018, 'Escalation through Entanglement: How the Vulnerability of Command-and-Control Systems Raises the Risks of an Inadvertent Nuclear War', *International Security*, vol. 43, no. 1, pp. 56–99, doi:10.1162/isec_a_00320.

Amudsen, F & Frain, S 2020, 'The Politics of Invisibility: Visualizing Legacies of Nuclear Imperialisms', *Journal of Transnational American Studies*, vol. 11, no. 2, pp. 125–51, doi:10.5070/T8112049588.

Baron, J & Herzog, S 2020, 'Public Opinion on Nuclear Energy and Nuclear Weapons: The Attitudinal Nexus in the United States', *Energy Research & Social Science*, vol. 68, no. 101567, pp. 1–11, doi:10.1016/j.erss.2020.101567.

Biden, J 2022, 'President Biden Statement Ahead of the 10th Review Conference of the Treaty on the Non-Proliferation of Nuclear Weapons', The White House, *1 August 2022*, <https://www.whitehouse.gov/briefing-room/statements-releases/2022/08/01/president-biden-statement-ahead-of-the-10th-review-conference-of-the-treaty-on-the-non-proliferation-of-nuclear-weapons/> (accessed 22 December 2022).

Biswas, S 2014, *Nuclear Desire: Power and the Postcolonial Nuclear Order*, University of Minnesota Press, Minneapolis, MN.

Brodie, B 1959, *Strategy in the Missile Age*, Princeton University Press, Princeton.

Brown, P 2021, 'Weatherwatch: The Threat to Trident From Global Heating', *The Guardian*, 25 September, <https://www.theguardian.com/news/2021/sep/25/weatherwatch-the-threat-to-trident-from-global-heating> (accessed 22 December 2022).

Budjeryn, M 2015, 'The Power of the NPT: International Norms and Ukraine's Nuclear Disarmament', *The Nonproliferation Review*, vol. 22, no. 2, pp. 203–37, doi:10.1080/10736700.2015.1119968.

Bush, G W 2001, *Remarks by the President to Students and Faculty at National Defense University, 1 May*, <https://georgewbush-whitehouse.archives.gov/news/releases/2001/05/20010501-10.html> (accessed 22 December 2022).

Chyba, C 2020, 'New Technologies & Strategic Stability', *Daedalus*, vol. 149, no. 2, pp. 150–70, doi:10.1162/DAED_a_01795.

Considine, L 2017, 'The "Standardization of Catastrophe": Nuclear Disarmament, the Humanitarian Initiative and the Politics of the Unthinkable', *European Journal of International Relations*, vol. 23, no. 3, pp. 681–702, doi:10.1177/1354066116666332.

Craig, C & Ruzicka, J 2013, 'The Nonproliferation Complex', *Ethics & International Affairs* vol. 27, no. 3, pp. 329–48, doi:10.1017/S0892679413000257.

Dahl, R 1985, *Controlling Nuclear Weapons: Democracy versus Guardianship*, Syracuse University Press, Syracuse, NY.

Dupont, A 2008, 'The Strategic Implications of Climate Change', *Survival*, vol. 50, no, 3, pp. 29–54, doi:10.1080/00396330802173107.

Edwards, P 2012, 'Entangled Histories: Climate Science and Nuclear Weapons Research', *Bulletin of the Atomic Scientists*, vol. 68, no. 4, pp. 41–51, doi:10.1177/0096340212451574.

Egeland, K 2020, 'Spreading the Burden: How NATO Became a 'Nuclear Alliance', *Diplomacy & Statecraft*, vol. 31, no. 1, pp. 143–167, doi:10.1080/09592296.2020.1721086.

Egeland, K 2021, 'The Ideology of Nuclear Order', *New Political Science*, vol. 43, no. 2, pp. 208–30, doi:10.1080/07393148.2021.1886772.

Egeland, K 2022, 'Climate Security Reversed: The Implications of Alternative Security Policies for Global Warming,' *Environmental* Politics, [online first], doi:10.1080/09644016.2022.2146934.

Freedman, L & Michaels, J 2019, *The Evolution of Nuclear Strategy*, 4th ed, Palgrave Macmillan, London.

Gerzhoy, G 2015, 'Alliance Coercion and Nuclear Restraint: How the United States Thwarted West Germany's Nuclear Ambitions', *International Security*, vol. 39, no. 4, pp. 91–129, doi:1162/ISEC_a_00198.

Gibbons, R 2022, *The Hegemon's Tool Kit: US Leadership and the Politics of the Nuclear Nonproliferation Regime*, Cornell University Press, Ithaca, NY.

Gibbons, R & Herzog, S 2022, 'Durable Institution Under Fire? The NPT Confronts Emerging Multipolarity', *Contemporary Security Policy*, vol. 43, no. 1, pp. 50–79, doi:10.1080/13523260.2021.1998294.

Gusterson, H 1999, 'Nuclear Weapons and the Other in the Western Imagination', *Cultural Anthropology*, vol. 14, no. 1, pp. 111–43, doi:10.1525/can.1999.14.1.111.

Hanson, M 2018, 'Normalizing Zero Nuclear Weapons: The Humanitarian Road to the Prohibition Treaty', *Contemporary Security Policy*, vol. 39, no. 3, pp. 464–86, doi:10.1080/13523260.2017.1421344.

Hecht, G 2009, *The Radiance of France: Nuclear Power and National Identity after World War II*. MIT Press, Cambridge, MA.

Hecht, G 2012, *Being Nuclear: Africans and the Global Uranium Trade*, MIT Press, Cambridge, MA.

Holloway, D 2020, 'Racing Towards Armageddon? Soviet Views of Strategic Nuclear War, 1955–1972', in M Gordin & J Ikenberry (eds), *The Age of Hiroshima*, Princeton University Press, Princeton, pp. 71–88.

Hymans, J 2006, *The Psychology of Nuclear Proliferation: Identity, Emotions and Foreign Policy*, Cambridge University Press, Cambridge.

Intondi, V 2018, 'The Dream of Bandung and the UN Treaty on the Prohibition of Nuclear Weapons', *Critical Security Studies*, vol. 7, no. 1, pp. 83–86, doi:10.1080/21624887.2018.1468129.

Jacobs, R 2022, *Nuclear Bodies: The Global Hibakusha*, Yale University Press, New Haven, CT.

Jervis, R 1978, 'Cooperation under the Security Dilemma', *World Politics*, vol. 30, no. 2, pp. 167–214, doi:10.2307/2009958.

Krepon, M 2021, *Winning and Losing the Nuclear Peace: The Rise, Demise, and Revival of Arms Control*, Stanford University Press, Stanford, CA.

Lewis, P, Williams, H, Pelopidas B & Aghlani, S 2014, *Too Close for Comfort: Cases of Near Nuclear Use and Options for Policy*, Chatham House Report, London.

Lieber, K & Press, D 2020, *The Myth of the Nuclear Revolution: Power Politics in the Atomic Age*, Cornell University Press, Ithaca, NY.

Mallard, G 2014, *Fallout: Nuclear Diplomacy in an Age of Global Fracture*, University of Chicago Press, Chicago.

Masco, J 2006, *The Nuclear Borderlands: The Manhattan Project in Post-Cold War Mexico*, Princeton University Press, Princeton.

Masco, J 2015, 'Nuclear Pasts, Nuclear Future; Or, Disarming Through Rebuilding', *Critical Studies on Security*, vol. 3, no. 3, pp. 308–12, doi:10.1080/21624887.2015.1123960.

Mathur, R 2016, 'Sly Civility and the Paradox of Equality/Inequality in the Nuclear Order', *Critical Studies on Security*, vol. 4, no. 1, pp. 57–72, doi:10.1080/21624887.2015.1106428.

McDermott, R, Lopez, A & Hatemi, P 2017, '"Blunt Not the Heart, Enrage It": The Psychology of Revenge and Deterrence,' *Texas National Security Review*, vol. 1, no. 1, pp. 68–88.

Miller, N 2014, 'The Secret Success of Nonproliferation Sanctions', *International Organization*, vol. 68, no. 4, pp. 913–44, doi:10.1017/S0020818314000216.

Morgenthau, H 1964, 'The Four Paradoxes of Nuclear Strategy', *American Political Science Review*, vol. 58, no. 1, pp. 23–35, doi:10.2307/1952752.

Mutimer, D 2000, *The Weapon State: Proliferation and the Framing of Security*, Lynne Rienner Publisher, Boulder, CO.

Narang, V 2014, *Nuclear Strategy in the Modern Era: Regional Powers and International Conflict*, Princeton University Press, Princeton.

Pelopidas, B 2017, 'The Unbearable Lightness of Luck: Three Sources of Overconfidence in the Manageability of Nuclear Crises', *European Journal of International Security*, vol. 2, no. 2, pp. 240–62, doi: 10.1017/eis.2017.6.

Pelopidas, B 2021, 'The Birth of Nuclear Eternity', in S Kemp & J Andersson (eds), *Futures*, Oxford University Press, Oxford, pp. 484–500.

Philippe, S & Statius, T 2021, *Toxique: Enquête sur les Essais Nucléares Français en Polynésie*, Presses Universitaires de France, Paris.

Reddie, A & Goldblum, B 2022, 'Evidence of the Unthinkable: Experimental Wargaming at the Nuclear Threshold', *Journal of Peace Research*, doi: 10.1177/00223433221094734.

Ritchie, N 2019, 'A Hegemonic Nuclear Order: Understanding the Ban Treaty and the Power Politics of Nuclear Weapons', *Contemporary Security Policy*, vol. 40, no. 4, pp. 409–34, doi:10.1080/13523260.2019.1571852.

Ritchie, N & Egeland, K 2018, 'The Diplomacy of Resistance: Power, Hegemony, and Nuclear Disarmament', *Global Change, Peace & Security*, vol. 30, no. 2, pp. 121–41, doi:10.1080/14781158.2018.1467393.

Rodriguez, L & Mendenhall, E 2022, 'Nuclear Weapon-Free Zones and the Issue of Maritime Transit in Latin America', *International Affairs*, vol. 98, no. 3, pp. 819–36, doi:10.1093/ia/iiac055.

Roehrlich, E 2018, 'Negotiating Verification: International Diplomacy and the Evolution of Nuclear Safeguards, 1945–1972', *Diplomacy & Statecraft*, vol. 29, no.1, pp. 29–50, doi:10.1080/09592296.2017.1420520.

Rosenberg, D 1983, 'The Origins of Overkill: Nuclear Weapons and American Strategy', *International Security*, vol. 7, no. 4, pp. 3–71, doi:10.2307/2626731 10.2307/2626731.

Ruzicka, J & Wheeler, N 2010, 'Decisions to Trust', *RUSI Journal*, vol. 155, no. 2, pp. 20–5.

Santese, A 2017, 'Ronald Reagan, the Nuclear Weapons Freeze Campaign and the Nuclear Scare of the 1980s', *The International History Review*, vol. 39, no. 3, pp. 496–520, doi:10.1080/07075332.2016.1220403.

Talmadge, C 2019, 'Emerging Technology and Intra-War Escalation Risks: Evidence from the Cold War Implications for Today', *Journal of Strategic Studies*, vol. 42, no. 6, pp. 864–87, doi: 10.1080/01402390.2019.1631811.

Tannenwald, N 2007, *The Nuclear Taboo: The United States and the Non-Use of Nuclear Weapons Since 1945*, Cambridge University Press, Cambridge.

Tannenwald, N 2018. 'The Great Unraveling: The Future of the Nuclear Normative Order', in N Tannenwald, J Acton & J Vaynman (eds), *Meeting the Challenges of the New Nuclear Age: Emerging Risks and Declining Norms in the Age of Technological Innovation and Changing Nuclear Doctrines*, American Academy of Arts and Sciences, Cambridge, MA, pp. 6–31.

Tannenwald, N 2020, 'Life beyond Arms Control: Moving toward a Global Regime of Nuclear Restraint & Responsibility', *Daedalus*, vol. 149, no. 2, pp. 205–21, doi:10.1162/daed_a_01798.

Verschuren, S 2021, 'China's Hypersonic Weapons Tests Don't Have To Be A Sputnik Moment', *War on the Rocks*, 29 October, <https://warontherocks.com/2021/10/chinas-hypersonic-missile-tests-dont-have-to-be-a-sputnik-moment/> (accessed 22 December 2022)

Walker, W 2000, 'Nuclear Order and Disorder', *International Affairs*, vol. 76, no. 4, pp. 703–24, doi:10.1111/1468-2346.00160.

Walker, W 2012, *A Perpetual Menace: Nuclear Weapons and International Order*, Routledge, London – New York.

Wellerstein, A 2021, *Restricted Data: The History of Nuclear Secrecy in the United States*, University of Chicago Press, Chicago.

Wheeler, N, Baker, J & Considine, L 2016, 'Trust or Verification? Accepting Vulnerability in the making of the INF Treaty', in M Klimke, R Kreis & C Ostermann (eds), *'Trust, but Verify': The Politics of Uncertainty & the Transformation of the Cold War Order, 1969–1991*, Stanford University Press, Stanford, CA, pp. 121–142.

White House 2022, 'Joint Statement of the Leaders of the Five Nuclear-Weapon States on Preventing Nuclear War and Avoiding Arms Races', *The White House*, 3 January, <https://www.whitehouse.gov/briefing-room/statements-releases/2022/01/03/p5-statement-on-preventing-nuclear-war-and-avoiding-arms-races/> (accessed 22 December 2022).

Wittner, L S 2022, 'The Nuclear Freeze and Its Impact', *Arms Control Today*, <https://www.armscontrol.org/act/2010_12/LookingBack> (accessed 22 December 2022).

Witze, A 2020, 'How a Small Nuclear War Would Transform the Entire Planet', *Nature*, 16 March, <https://www.nature.com/articles/d41586-020-00794-y> (accessed 22 December 2022).

36

CONFLICT IN CYBERSPACE

Rain Ottis

Introduction

It would be easy to limit the discussion of conflict in cyberspace to the definition of armed conflict as understood by international law. However, this limitation would be artificial, since arguably there is no true 'cyber peace'. Regardless of the political situation or the *de jure* state of hostilities, there are regular and persistent cyber-attacks against critical infrastructure. Intelligence organizations, military cyber units, state-run advanced persistent threat (APT) groups and other actors with a range of motivations keep trying to establish a foothold in their adversaries' networks, in order to exfiltrate data or disrupt their current or future operations. Much of this activity will never see public scrutiny, even if it is detected by the victim. The public will only learn of this ongoing conflict when official reports are released or when the attackers make a mistake and their activities become widely exposed. For example, the case of Stuxnet (Langner 2011) became widely known only because the malware escaped the target environment and was detected and subsequently revealed by independent security researchers. One could argue that the victim of a truly successful cyber-attack of this nature is never aware of the attack, instead blaming their apparent misfortune on mistakes of their staff or accidental failure of their technology.

Western cybersecurity or cyber conflict discussions are often focusing on the technological side of cyber conflict: denial of service, malware, ransomware, APT groups, etc. However, in recent years, more attention has been placed on the content (data, information) of cyberspace and how its manipulation can be used for nefarious (or righteous) purposes. This emphasis on the content is really not new for the Western audience, as it has been previously discussed under the paradigms of a range of disciplines. These include Information Warfare, Psychological Operations (PSYOPS), Strategic Communications (StratCom) and Influence Operations (Info Ops). However, the relationship between the content focus (humanitarians) and the system infrastructure focus (technologists) has not fully benefited from a shared doctrinal view in the West. This is perhaps different in Russian (Thornton & Miron 2022) and Chinese (Kania & Costello 2018) doctrine, where there is more focus on cyber-enabled information warfare.

This chapter explores conflict in cyberspace in a broader scope, including armed conflict, as well as conflicts involving states that remain below the armed conflict threshold. Additionally, the chapter will explore some non-military aspects of conflicts that have a significant effect on the

 DOI: 10.4324/9781003299011-43

cyber capabilities, such as technological sanctions and supply chains. The chapter ends with a look at the future of cyber conflict, should some long-expected technological breakthroughs materialize in the coming years.

Conflict or war?

The idea of waging war in cyberspace gained traction in the 1990s and 2000s. For example, Clarke and Knake provide a fascinating insight into some of the thought processes behind early US cyber-security policy development (Clarke & Knake 2010). However, in the early 2020s, cyber war (or warfare) is still not a well-defined concept, even though over the years there have been numerous discussions about its nature. This discussion has covered a wide spectrum of ideas, ranging from the somewhat alarmist 'Cyber Pearl Harbour' warnings (Lawson & Middleton 2019) of a crippling first strike, to downplaying the utility or even the possibility of cyber war, as illustrated by Rid's *Cyber War Will Not Take Place* (Rid 2012). On the one hand, while the 'Cyber Pearl Harbour' narrative persists in literature, it has become less appealing as the complexities of setting up such an attack are becoming better understood. On the other hand, Rid's paper generated much needed debate over the nature of cyber war from the sceptical viewpoint. As an example, some of Rid's claims were countered in John Stone's reply *Cyber War Will Take Place!* (Stone 2013), which included a discussion on the vagueness of definitions used in the argument.

Rid (2012, p. 6) argued that "cyber war has never happened in the past, that cyber war does not take place in the present, and that it is unlikely that cyber war will occur in the future". He further argued that all relevant examples to date should be classified as sabotage, subversion or espionage. The context of such a claim is focusing on the definition of 'war' similar to the concept of 'armed attack', which might trigger the right to use (armed) force in self-defence according to Article 51 of the UN Charter (United Nations 1945). In that context, the argument may still stand, because to date there have been no cyber-attacks that have *de facto* sparked an armed conflict. However, there are other – more relevant – ways to approach cyber war.

The obvious contender for the extension of the 'cyber war' term is the use of cyber operations during an armed conflict, regardless of how this conflict started. In this context, 'cyber war' has taken, is taking and will (often) take place as part of modern warfare. The Russo-Georgian war of 2008, that is briefly covered in Rid's article, arguably fits into this category, even if its cyber component was justifiably overshadowed by ground and air operations.

Another interesting paper by Erik Gartzke (Gartzke 2013) echoes many of Rid's concerns. However, he also notes the potential value of "cyber war" emerges as an "adjunct" to conventional warfare, instead of seeing it "as an independent, or even alternative form of conflict". One of the points that Gartzke makes is that in order to be considered seriously in the context of cyber war, there must be at least the prospect of 'long-term damage'. Long-term damage in cyberspace usually does not mean physical destruction of hardware or permanent disabling of software, although it can happen. Rather, it should be viewed through the lens of loss of confidentiality or integrity of data. Once a secret is exposed, it is more or less impossible to make it truly secret again. Therefore, a single breach of confidentiality (e.g., list of undercover agents, contingency war plans against a neighbouring country, locations and contents of secure sites) could put national security at risk and undermine decades of diligent work on behalf of the people who collect, analyse and secure data. Similarly, a successful (unrecoverable) compromise of the integrity of a database may mean that the data is gone forever.

Gartzke (2013, p. 63) arrives to an unexpected conclusion that "cyberwar should be particularly appealing to capable states confronting weaker opponents". While offensive cyber operations require some level of technical sophistication, the barrier for entry is much lower than creating a submarine service or a convincing air defence capability. That barrier is virtually non-existent in cases where a nation has already created their offensive cyber capability in order to conduct sabotage, espionage or subversion operations in the context of 'not cyber war', which Rid's article focuses on. Therefore, the offensive cyber capability is actually more appealing for a country that is weaker and would prefer to engage their technologically advanced and technology-dependent adversary in a paradigm that is less than armed conflict.

It can be argued that the claim that cyber war is not real war encourages the use of cyber-attacks in order to 'solve' conflicts. 'Naming and shaming' – the strategy of publicly attributing state-sponsored cyber-attacks – does not carry much weight as a deterrent, if one is already considered a pariah in international circles. At the same time, one can be relatively secure in the knowledge that their 'not cyber war' operations are unlikely to provoke an armed response from the victim.

Military cyber operations

Much has been written about cyber operations within the context of armed conflict, as understood by the international relations and international law communities. Some of these discussions have been inspired by historical analogies, such as Rattray's *Strategic Warfare in Cyberspace*, which explored the same discussions from 20th-century development of US air power and showed their similarity to cyber power discussions a hundred years later (Rattray 2001). Others, such as the authors of the Tallinn Manual (Schmitt 2013) are applying existing laws, frameworks and doctrines, and adapting or reinterpreting them for cyber operations and conflict.

From the military perspective, cyberspace can be regarded as a 'new' domain of warfare, and is considered equal to land, sea, air and space. By the end of the 2000s, there were calls to establish a new branch to the US military – one that would be responsible for 'cyberwarfare' (Conti & Surdu 2009). In fact, various nations and organizations have made this decision by now and are incorporating cyberspace operations (among other terms) in their doctrine. For example, NATO included cyberspace as the fifth domain of warfare in 2016 (NATO 2016), thus showing broader acceptance of the concept on the international level.

Cyberspace operations doctrine is still developing, as it should be. The oldest domain of warfare – land – has been studied for thousands of years, yet it still evolves as new technologies are introduced. Most recently, the widespread use of cheap commercial drones for reconnaissance, artillery spotting and improvised kinetic strikes will require a doctrinal re-assessment for the land forces of today and tomorrow. The same is true for societal changes in the use of technology, such as using crowdfunding platforms to equip specific units or soldiers (of another state) fighting a war on the other side of the planet.

The continuous development of cyber conflict related doctrine is therefore expected and required for maintaining its relevance and effectiveness on the battlefield. It is also normal that the early years (decades) of this development have relied heavily on established doctrine and terminology from other domains, since these initial versions are mostly written by open-minded thinkers with a background in the other domains. This explains the re-use of terms such as 'key terrain' (Raymond et al. 2014), which is well established in land warfare, but requires a conceptual re-thinking and explanation in the context of cyberspace. However, in time we should expect more input from the 'natives' of the cyberspace domain. This is the generation that has grown up with computers, smartphones and ubiquitous internet access, and has been employed in cyberspace operations throughout their entire (military) career. This trend will not replace the lessons from history or from other domains, but it allows building on them to enable a deeper understanding of the full potential of cyberspace operations.

Broadly speaking, cyberspace operations can be divided into offensive and defensive activities. While both are important, it could be argued that an offensive cyber operations capability is optional, whereas defensive cyber operations capability is a critical requirement for all modern militaries and indeed society as a whole. An army may still be combat effective without any offensive cyber capabilities, since it probably has other ways to 'reach out and touch' the enemy. However, barbed wire, tanks and air defence missiles provide little or no protection against adversary cyber operations against command, control and logistics networks. Additionally, defensive cyber operations are continuously required, regardless of whether there is an ongoing conflict. Therefore, the basis for any credible (national) cyber power is an effective defensive cyber capability.

Once the security of own networks is covered, one can look to offensive cyber operations as a way to support warfighters of other domains, as well as achieving military effects solely in the cyber domain. In this first case, it is important that the supported command understands the capabilities that the cyber operators can provide. Perhaps more importantly, it is necessary to also understand their limitations. Hollywood notwithstanding, it is unrealistic to expect a 'hacker' to break into any system at short notice and achieve the desired effect. An offensive cyber operation more likely needs significant time to achieve several discrete stages. This includes reconnaissance of the target, researching potential vulnerabilities and mapping likely (collateral) effects before the target network is accessed. Once entry is gained, access and privileges are elevated and expanded until within reach of the target. It is only then that a payload can be delivered, while evading the adversary's cyber defenders. For some offensive cyber operations, the full cycle can be measured in years – something that may not work well within conventional operational planning cycles during a dynamic military campaign. Therefore, the options might be limited to targets of opportunity (possessing known vulnerabilities that one is able to exploit) and pre-determined targets that have already been scouted and researched, perhaps years in advance. However, these two categories are likely a minority of the pool of potential targets that may become available during the campaign.

Unlike the other domains of military operations, cyberspace is an artificial, man-made domain, and as such requires constant maintenance and monitoring. It is also in constant change, so there is no definitive map of this space – all we have are localized snapshots of the (at best – recent) past. In addition, many of the connected systems and their data are not held on the 'visible' networks, but hidden in the 'deep web' or 'dark web'. Deep web is a term for networks that are not indexed and require access credentials, whereas dark web refers to networks that require specialized software, knowledge or system configuration to access. All this makes the planning of offensive cyber operations more difficult, as there is never full certainty that the 'terrain' remains fixed until the plan is successfully executed. A routine software update or a minor configuration change in the target network may render months of preparation worthless. The obvious counter to this problem is to build redundancy and have multiple ways of accomplishing the set goals. However, achieving redundancy probably requires more scouting and it provides more opportunities for the adversary to detect an increased interest in the target system – trade-offs that the attacker must weigh at every step.

Although cyberspace is often discussed as an abstract, ephemeral or virtual 'space', it is physically constrained by the hardware (computers, network devices, sensors) or the transmission media (radio waves, photons) connecting them. Therefore, cyberspace can also be affected by conflict occurring in other domains. In air and space, this is likely to take the form of electromagnetic warfare – jamming signals or disabling devices with electromagnetic pulses. In the maritime domain, the most significant threat to cyberspace is the intentional or unintentional cutting of undersea cables, which carry the majority of global communications. Most of the hardware that 'contains' cyberspace is on land – servers, personal devices, communication infrastructure, etc. These can be physically captured (for example, seizing laptops and smartphones at a checkpoint) or destroyed by kinetic strikes (for example, artillery or missile fire against communication masts). As a result, cyberspace operations planning should take into account not only the 'cyber terrain', but also the physical location and status of the underlying infrastructure, if known.

Depending on the mission, it may be easier to achieve the set goals through other domains. For example, if the goal is to disrupt network connectivity of a city, perhaps the most economical approach would be to kinetically attack a key communication cable well. However, this requires accurate intelligence on the adversary infrastructure, their dependencies, as well as the capability to plan such cross-domain operations. Crucially, it is also important to realize the dependencies affecting friendly and neutral actors in the conflict zone. It was reported that in the spring of 2022, the Russians inflicted a self-denial of service on their ERA encrypted communication system by destroying the Ukrainian 3G/4G infrastructure that was required for these devices to operate (Atlamazoglou 2022).

An important point from Rid's article (Rid 2012) was the recognition of cyber operations or effects that fit better into the intelligence, than military, framework. Espionage, subversion and sabotage are conventionally the deniable responsibility of intelligence organizations. In 2009, the Ghostnet report shed light on Chinese cyber espionage operations (Information Warfare Monitor 2009). In 2010, Stuxnet – custom malware that seemed to target an Iranian nuclear facility – was discovered (Langner 2011) and is generally attributed to the United States and Israel. In 2013, Mandiant published a report about the threat actor APT1 and linked it to the Chinese military (Mandiant 2013). Russian intelligence has reportedly tried to tamper with the 2016 elections in the United States (Mueller 2019). Such publicly known examples are not rare and the above list is far from complete. Therefore, it should be safe to assume that the intelligence community has been, is and will remain an active participant in the cyber conflict paradigm.

Non-state actors in cyber conflict

One of the key considerations of conflict in cyberspace is that it is not really limited to military or government actors. Scholars like Dorothy Denning have explored this from the perspective of social networks and (patriotic) hacktivism (Denning 2011). There have been numerous examples where criminal groups or hacktivists also took sides and actively participated in various conflicts (van Niekerk 2018; Harašta & Bátrla 2022). For example, pro-Russian hacktivists and cybercrime groups targeting Estonia in 2007 (Ottis 2008) or the reported actions of Anonymous and the so-called IT Army of Ukraine hacktivists during the ongoing Russo-Ukrainian war. Typically, those involved will remain anonymous and do not attract the attention of law enforcement authorities, unless they operate from the country that they are attacking. In general, it is expected that such acts are motivated by ideology instead of personal gain, although exceptions may exist (such as a criminal group receiving payment for attacking someone).

It is not always clear if such actors operate independently or receive some support, encouragement or coordination from a state. For a cyber defender, this may not matter, as the tactics, techniques and procedures they encounter will be very similar. Cybercrime groups typically make use of relatively unsophisticated techniques. These include botnets to conduct politically motivated (vs financially motivated) distributed denial of service (DDoS) attacks to keep adversary systems offline, spreading malware (including ransomware) in order to disable systems, or harvesting data from compromised systems. Hacktivists might organize DDoS attacks, deface adversary systems (websites, notice boards, public broadcast systems) or steal data in order to publish it. These activities are by no means an exhaustive list, but they do display the variety of problems that defenders have to counter.

Since it may be difficult to demonstrate a clear attribution to a state, state-sponsored or curated non-state actors are ideal for causing confusion and performing deniable acts against the adversary. If a hacktivist group performs multiple different – but highly visible – attacks, it may distract the defenders from a more covert and more dangerous campaign by professional operators. These false flag operations can mask activity as regular cybercrime or hacktivism and so can make it even more difficult to gain true situational awareness and proper attribution of cyber-attacks.

Information warfare in cyberspace

In addition to technically focused cyber-attacks, cyberspace is also an ideal battleground for a range of information warfare techniques. Near ubiquitous internet availability allows people to access and share information like never before, but this does not mean that freedom of speech has improved everywhere. Government-imposed censorship exists and reflects what the government sees as harmful (Deibert et al. 2010). Some issues, such as violent extremism, are commonly censored, although the interpretation of an extremist can vary wildly across national borders and cultures. Similarly, the promotion of concepts, such as democracy, may also be considered 'harmful' by some governments. In both cases, the clash of cultures and accepted norms can increase the potential for conflict both internationally, as well as internally between the state and its citizens. The ability to control or manipulate the flow of information is therefore a key aspect of conflict in cyberspace. This may manifest itself in national initiatives to censor content within their jurisdiction, restrict citizens' access to foreign networks or services (for example, social media), blocking foreign access or mass surveillance of online activity. However, this may also encourage both grass roots and state initiatives to break through these various restrictions. These can include encouraging the use of virtual private networks (VPNs), encrypted communication apps, defacing adversary systems to spread information, or publishing hacked or leaked data.

Another layer of information warfare in cyber conflict is the use of technological communication platforms (forums, social media, chat channels) to shape the narrative of the conflict with true or manipulated content. Memes, deepfakes, citizen journalist blogs and publicly discussed open source intelligence are examples from the ongoing Russo-Ukrainian war (Global Conflict Tracker 2022). These have arguably contributed more to the public perception of the war than formal statements from governments or think tanks.

Economic aspects of conflict in cyberspace

Conflict in cyberspace can also be viewed through the lens of changes in 'terrain' that occur outside of the regular attacker-defender paradigm. Restricting (sanctioning) the sale of computing hardware or components, such as computer chips, can have a significant effect on the functionality and reliability of the economy and cyberspace capabilities of the sanctioned country (Hamblen 2022). Similarly, limiting availability of software or (cloud) services can force the sanctioned country to use outdated (vulnerable) versions or seek alternatives.

Arguably, there is no single nation on Earth that would be able to manufacture all of the hardware and software it needs, especially when considering the specialized information technology requirements of critical infrastructure. In practice, there are often only a limited number of companies that dominate their technological niche, such as desktop operating systems or central

416

processor units (CPU). This raises the stakes on technology sanctions as a punitive or coercive policy, if there are no national or otherwise 'friendly' alternative providers. Interestingly, it is also possible for a state to deprive itself of said technology by establishing sanctions on imports, in order to protect the (short-term) competitiveness of their own industry.

This reliance on a complex and often international supply chain also raises the prospect of supply chain attacks. Unauthorized adding, replacing or modifying of components or software at the factory or during transit is very difficult to detect or prevent. While it may be possible to reverse engineer a computer chip and check its integrity, it takes a lot of time and may damage the chip in the process – thus making wholesale testing of everything that is procured impractical. Similarly, the code base used in modern IT systems tends to grow in size and complexity. Code audits are expensive, time consuming and their results become obsolete after the first software update, configuration change or significant hardware upgrade – again reducing the practicality of preventive measures. This problem has been fundamental in the security discussions surrounding 5G and software defined systems, where what you buy as secure today can be potentially remotely re-programmed to work against you tomorrow.

The future of conflict in cyberspace

Cyberspace continues to develop as new technologies become available and people find new ways to use and abuse them. While it is possible to speculate on the development of future technologies and their potential effects, the results of such speculation should be considered as guesswork rather than a prognosis. Therefore, this final section that covers some potentially disruptive technologies should be taken with a large grain of salt as to its predictive quality.

One of the emerging technologies that could be discussed in the context of future conflict in cyberspace is quantum computing (see chapter by Der Derian and Rollo in this handbook). First, advances in quantum computing power could threaten the fundamental assumptions of the security of some cryptographic solutions that are widely used today. If the creation of a sufficiently powerful quantum computer were to be announced tomorrow, there would be a rush to replace these instantly obsolete solutions that are deeply embedded in our infrastructure. However, while such an event would cause opportunities for malicious actors, it is ultimately solvable by moving to post-quantum cryptography that is not vulnerable to currently known or theorized attacks leveraging quantum computing technology. More security-conscious actors have already started this process, so it is possible that this development will share the fate of the Y2K bug, which was widely discussed in advance and eventually did little real harm, because there was significant effort to prepare for it. Second, quantum computing can lead to (wider adoption of) new means of secure communication and cryptography. However, this does not automatically lead to significant changes in cyberspace or cybersecurity, as these would arguably be (costly?) 'quantum' alternatives to existing solutions instead of completely revolutionizing our understanding of cyberspace or its underlying infrastructure. A potential analogy would be the transition from copper cable to fibre optical cable, which significantly increases the throughput of a network connection, but is still used to transfer data in a computer network.

Another technological advance that has the potential to reshape conflict in cyberspace is artificial intelligence (AI). While specialized, narrow AI (focusing, e.g., on computer vision or playing chess) has made significant progress and is in use, the general AI (intelligent and creative, able to solve various problems) remains elusive, although research is ongoing (De Cosmo 2022). Perhaps this elusiveness is for the best, since it is difficult to see beyond the moment of singularity – when machines start to think for themselves. One would assume that it would have profound effects on conflict in cyberspace. Even with the narrow AI of today, it is somewhat difficult to distinguish human users from bots and real video from deepfakes. With general AI, this distinction might become practically impossible. A hostile AI could also be more effective on the offense, seeking out vulnerable systems and compromising them before the human defenders and their comparatively primitive technical defences can take any meaningful action. Obviously, such AI would also be able to access and manipulate cyber-physical systems in order to create effects outside of cyberspace. One would hope that the AI scholars and engineers find a way to infuse their creation with some form of ethics, as well as efficiency and adaptability.

Augmenting the human with more direct interfaces to computing technology is another area, which can lead to major upheavals. Human-computer interaction of today is still relatively clumsy – relying on buttons, screens, etc. However, even now there are first experiments with more seamless interface solutions (Scott-Morgan 2021). Moving a cursor around on the screen just by thinking about it would do wonders for someone who is paralyzed. 'Restoring vision' by converting optical sensor data to something that the brain can interpret as sight would also be a boon to a blind person. Basically, this is the positive case of hacking the human for his or her benefit by developing the read (to get cursor movement data or to move an artificial limb) and write (input optical or audio data) functionality of the 'biological computer' (human). However, the negative cases would surely follow as well, if the technology becomes more widely used and effective. Perfecting the read functionality would make interrogations a breeze, while perfecting the write functionality could raise the spectre of reprogramming a person in some way. The polarizing and radicalizing effects of the social media of today could be considered benign in comparison. Integrated smart medical enhancements would make the human also directly vulnerable to a cyber-attack, for example in the case of hacking a pacemaker, where the early attempts trace back at least to 2008 (Halperin et al. 2008). The human would go from someone who interacts with cyberspace to someone who is directly connected to (or part of) cyberspace, and therefore more exposed to conflict in cyberspace.

Another technology enabled by AI research is autonomous robots. Whether in the form of an automated machine gun turret, an autonomous loitering munition or a self-driving car, the line between cyberspace and physical space will become more blurred, expanding the potential target surface of cyber conflict. Today, the weapons industry is somewhat restricted in the use of autonomy, preferring or required to keep the human in the loop at least for the killing function, in order to reduce the legal and ethical problems that apply to autonomous weapon systems. However, this preference is not likely to hold in the face of a truly desperate struggle for survival against an otherwise overwhelming adversary. Equipping a cheap commercial drone with explosives has already been done on the battlefields of Ukraine. It will not be long until giving it autonomy and letting it loose in the general direction of the enemy will sound appealing to some, especially if they are struggling to overcome jamming and other anti-drone techniques. This would make conflict zones more dangerous both for combatants and non-combatants. As to cyber conflict, it becomes potentially easier to cause physical effects or to harm specific individuals. However, in most cases, it will probably still be easier and more cost effective to drop dumb munitions from Cold War era planes. The cyber option will likely be limited to high-value targets that are well protected from conventional effects.

Aside from the abovementioned major upheavals that may or may not take place as a result of technological progress in other areas, there is no reason to think that the future of cyber conflict will lack the currently existing arsenal of cyber weapons and tactics. Cybercriminals and hacktivists, whether state sponsored or self-organized, will continue to exploit old vulnerabilities (since there are always some systems that lack the required protection). States will continue to perfect their offensive and defensive cyber capabilities, and use them to secure their national security goals in the international setting. Besides international conflict, this can also affect the citizens, since it is likely that some states will also turn their cyber capabilities inward in an attempt to provide security for the ruling regime. This, in turn, will spark a counter from the hackers, technology entrepreneurs and human rights advocates, who will try to find solutions to protect the rights to privacy and freedom of speech. Conflict in cyberspace, as ill-defined as it is, will evolve and continue.

Conclusion

Conflict takes place in all domains of human endeavour, so it is not surprising to witness its various manifestations in cyberspace. Thanks to global connectivity and easy access to smart phones, few modern conflicts can be considered purely local affairs. Technological interdependence also means that conflict in cyberspace will rarely, if ever, remain a purely military matter. Over the last decade or two, much has been written on the intersection of armed conflict, cyber operations and the role of information in warfare. However, recent examples of (armed) conflict show that there are many other factors that have significant and relevant effects on or through cyberspace, even though they are generally not discussed in the context of armed conflict.

A multi-disciplinary approach is required in order to understand current and future conflicts in cyberspace. At its core is the engineering perspective of the technology that serves as the 'container' and 'enabler' of cyberspace, as well as the social sciences perspective of societies and people, including their perceptions and motivation for interacting with it. The topic should be further considered within the disciplines of international law, international relations, military studies and economics, in order to develop a holistic understanding of cyber conflict studies and to produce an operational view of how to achieve effects via or on cyberspace. Finally, cyberspace is the product of human imagination and the ongoing desire to invent and implement new technologies and concepts – both for good and bad – will be the one constant in this ever-changing environment.

References

Atlamazoglou, S 2022, 'Russian Troops' Struggle to Talk to Each Other in Ukraine Reflects a Problem That's Only Getting Tougher for All Militaries', *Business Insider*, 5 May, <https://www.businessinsider.com/russian-troops-in-ukraine-face-military-communications-challenges-2022-5> (accessed 22 December 2022).

Clarke, R & Knake, R 2010, *Cyber War: The Next Threat to National Security and What to Do about It*, Ecco, New York.

Conti, G & Surdu, J 2009, 'Army, Navy, Air Force, and Cyber - Is it Time for a Cyberwarfare Branch of Military?', *IA Newsletter*, vol. 12, no. 1, pp. 14–18.

De Cosmo, L 2022, 'Google Engineer Claims AI Chatbot Is Sentient: Why That Matters', *Scientific American*, 12 July, <https://www.scientificamerican.com/article/google-engineer-claims-ai-chatbot-is-sentient-why-that-matters/> (accessed 22 December 2022).

Deibert, R, Palfrey, J, Rohozinski, R & Zittrain, J 2010, *Access Controlled: The Shaping of Power, Rights, and Rule in Cyberspace*, MIT Press, Cambridge, MA.

Denning, D 2011, 'Cyber Conflict as an Emergent Social Phenomenon', in T Holt & B Schell (eds), *Corporate Hacking and Technology-Driven Crime: Social Dynamics and Implications*, Information Science Reference, Hershey, PA, pp. 170–86.

Gartzke, E 2013, 'The Myth of Cyberwar: Bringing War in Cyberspace Back Down to Earth', *International Security*, vol. 38, no. 2, pp. 41–73, doi:10.1162/ISEC_a_00136.

Global Conflict Tracker 2022, 'Conflict in Ukraine', *Global Conflict Tracker*, 12 September, <www.cfr.org: https://www.cfr.org/global-conflict-tracker/conflict/conflict-ukraine> (accessed 22 December 2022).

Halperin, D, Heydt-Benjamin, T, Ransford, B, Clark, S, Defend, B, Morgan, W & Maisel, W 2008, 'Pacemakers and Implantable Cardiac Defibrillators: Software Radio Attacks and Zero-Power Defenses', *2008 IEEE Symposium on Security and Privacy (Sp 2008)*, Oakland, CA, USA, pp. 129–42, doi:10.1109/SP.2008.31.

Hamblen, M 2022, 'Russia Faces Chip Shortage for Missiles, Parts in Ukraine Invasion', *Fierce Electronics*, 6 September, <https://www.fierceelectronics.com/sensors/russia-faces-chip-shortage-missiles-parts-ukraine-invasion> (accessed 22 December 2022).

Harašta, M & Bátrla, J 2022, 'Releasing the Hounds? Disruption of the Ransomware Ecosystem Through Offensive Cyber Operations', *14th International Conference on Cyber Conflict: Keep Moving! (CyCon)*, pp. 93–115, doi:10.23919/CyCon55549.2022.9811074.

Information Warfare Monitor 2009, 'Tracking GhostNet: Investigating a Cyber Espionage Network', *Information Warfare Monitor*, 29 March, <https://citizenlab.ca/wp-content/uploads/2017/05/ghostnet.pdf> (accessed 22 December 2022).

Kania, E & Costello, J 2018, 'The Strategic Support Force and the Future of Chinese Information Operations', *The Cyber Defense Review*, vol. 3, no. 1, pp. 105–22.

Langner, R 2011, 'Stuxnet: Dissecting a Cyberwarfare Weapon', *IEEE Security & Privacy*, vol. 9, no. 3, pp. 49–51, doi:10.1109/MSP.2011.67.

Lawson, S & Middleton, M K 2019, 'Cyber Pearl Harbor: Analogy, Fear, and the Framing of Cyber Security Threats in the United States, 1991–2016', *First Monday*, vol. 24, no. 3, doi: 10.5210/fm.v24i3.9623.

Mandiant 2013, *APT1 Exposing One of China's Cyber Espionage Units*, < https://www.mandiant.com/sites/default/files/2021-09/mandiant-apt1-report.pdf> (accessed 22 December 2022).

Mueller, R 2019, *Report On The Investigation Into Russian Interference In The 2016 Presidential Election*, US Department of Justice, Washington, DC, <https://www.justice.gov/archives/sco/file/1373816/download> (accessed 22 December 2022).

NATO 2016, '*Warsaw Summit Communiqué'*, North Atlantic Treaty Organization, 9 July, <https://www.nato.int/cps/en/natohq/official_texts_133169.htm> (accessed 22 December 2022).

Ottis, R 2008, 'Analysis of the 2007 Cyber Attacks Against Estonia from the Information Warfare Perspective', in D Remenyi (ed), *Proceedings of the 7th European Conference on Information Warfare and Security*, Academic Publishing, Reading, pp. 163–8.

Rattray, G 2001, *Strategic Warfare in Cyberspace*, MIT Press, Cambridge, MA.

Raymond, D, Conti, G, Cross, T & Nowatkowsky, M 2014, 'Key Terrain in Cyberspace: Seeking the High Ground', in *6th International Conference on Cyber Conflict*, NATO CCDCOE, Tallinn, pp. 287–300, doi:10.1109/CYCON.2014.6916409.

Rid, T 2012, 'Cyber War Will Not Take Place', *Journal of Strategic Studies*, vol. 35, no. 1, pp. 5–32, doi:10.1080/01402390.2011.608939.

Schmitt, M (ed) 2013, *Tallinn Manual on the International Law Applicable to Cyber Warfare*, Cambridge University Press, Cambridge.

Scott-Morgan, P 2021, *Peter 2.0: The Human Cyborg*, Penguin, London.

Stone, J 2013, 'Cyber War *Will* Take Place!', *Journal of Strategic Studies*, vol. 36, no. 1, pp. 101–8, doi:10.1080/01402390.2012.730485.

Thornton, R & Miron, M 2022, 'Winning Future Wars: Russian Offensive Cyber and Its Vital Importance in Moscow's Strategic Thinking', *The Cyber Defense Review*, vol. 7, no. 3, pp. 117–35.

United Nations 1945, *United Nations Charter*, <https://www.un.org/en/about-us/un-charter> (accessed 22 December 2022).

van Niekerk, B 2018, 'Information Warfare as a Continuation of Politics: An Analysis of Cyber Incidents', in *2018 Conference on Information Communications Technology and Society (ICTAS) Proceedings*, IEEE eXpress Conference Publishing / Curran Associates, Red Hook, NY, pp. 1–6, doi:10.1109/ICTAS.2018.8368758.

37

LARGE-SCALE CRIMINAL VIOLENCE IN THE 21ST CENTURY

Angélica Durán-Martínez

Introduction

Illicit activities, smuggling and illegal markets have a long history and are geographically wide-spread. Yet violence and conflict are not inherent to them, and the violence that occurs is generally seen as outside the realm of armed conflict because is perceived to not affect civilians and to be apolitical. Even in the case of drug trafficking, which can be more violent than other illicit activities, there is significant variation in the levels and types of violence it generates (Durán-Martínez 2018). For example, drug trafficking networks are more violent in Latin America than in East Asia, partially because of the types of drugs trafficked (cocaine vs heroin), the social and political contexts in which these networks operate and the internal organization of trafficking groups. This chapter discusses large-scale criminal violence as a phenomenon that affects state actors, civilians, and criminals alike, and involves non-state armed groups (with different levels of sophistication) engaged in illicit activities and with the potential to generate significant violence. The chapter reflects on whether this large-scale violence can be seen as a new form of warfare.

The chapter first summarizes the debate around defining criminal violence as war, briefly sketching recent trends. The second section analyzes the political dimensions of criminal violence connecting them with debates on the relation between illicit economies, crime and conflict. The third section describes the humanitarian consequences of criminal violence and argues that tracking and analyzing it as armed conflict can help address these consequences. The last section discusses how an uncritical use of war, insurgency and terrorism metaphors, and of war fighting techniques, even in extreme cases, carries risks. These terms can ignore differences among non-state armed actors and can contribute to escalate violence. I conclude suggesting future trends and arguing that despite the dangers of using war terminology to describe criminal violence, it is crucial to consider it as a threat to peace.

The geography and scale of criminal violence

According to the United Nations Office on Drugs and Crime's Global Homicide Report (UNODC 2019), between 2000 and 2017 nearly as many people were killed in armed conflict as in organized crime violence. Leaving aside methodological concerns in counting, classifying and

 DOI: 10.4324/9781003299011-44

comparing violence, these numbers indicate that a lot of organized lethal violence occurs outside of traditional interstate or intrastate wars. While these forms of organized violence are not new, they have grown in visibility and geographic scope, and gained notoriety since Mexico's violence skyrocketed after 2006.

Most large-scale criminal violence is geographically concentrated in Latin America and the Caribbean and therefore this chapter focuses on this region, although it also refers trends in other regions. In Latin America, homicide rates started to increase in the 1990s. This increase was paradoxical as it occurred when the region was democratizing and transitioning out of military dictatorships, and when most civil wars had ended with peace agreements (Arias & Goldstein 2010). In Colombia, the only country where a civil war remained active, drug-trafficking organizations carried out extreme acts of violence that resembled war contexts. For example, between 1984 and 1992, the Medellín Cartel, a powerful drug trafficking organization led by Pablo Escobar, engaged in a violent campaign opposing the extradition of Colombian nationals to the United States that claimed the lives of hundreds of civilians, police officers and politicians. Scholarly attention to such violence often got folded into the analysis of the civil war and was complicated due to the overlap between criminal and political motivations. Therefore, Colombia's experience did not spur the reflection about the nature of criminal violence that emerged a couple decades later.

While illicit drugs have a long history, drug flows in Latin America diversified geographically at the start of the 21st century making more locations vulnerable to violence (Durán-Martínez 2020). It is important to note that drug trafficking does not always generate large conflicts. In many countries experiencing organized criminal violence, as in El Salvador, the main actors of violence are not drug traffickers, but gangs primarily involved in extortion. Still in 2006, Mexico started to experience the most violent period of its recent history, as conflict among drug trafficking organizations, and between those organizations and the state, unfolded. Homicides increased exponentially – with some years of minor decline – from a rate of 8.5 homicides per 100,000 people in 2007 to 32 by 2021. Up to December 2021, this large-scale violence had left more than 320,000 victims of homicide, 93,000 victims of extortion, and 24,000 of kidnapping (SESNSP 2022). Militarization to combat organized crime, the transition away from the hegemony of the political party PRI and competition between criminal groups explained the explosion of violence. For decades, networks of collusion between criminal organizations and the state had maintained a relatively low violence equilibrium in illicit drug markets. This equilibrium became unstable as political competition grew, thus generating violence (Snyder & Durán-Martínez 2009; Durán-Martínez 2018).

Research institutions such as the Uppsala Data Conflict Programme and the International Institute for Strategic Studies have classified Mexico as a conflict zone and a one-sided armed conflict, prompting a debate on whether the situation in Mexico can be classified as a civil war. On one side of this debate, scholars argue that the level of organization and massive militancy in criminal groups and drug trafficking organizations is akin to that seen in civil wars. More importantly, the casualty counts far exceed the 1,000 deaths – the threshold used in the literature to distinguish armed conflicts from civil wars (Schedler 2014). On the other side, scholars argue that the lack of clear political agendas, or of territorial or governmental incompatibilities with the state, makes it difficult to label these conflicts as wars (Flanigan 2012; Kalyvas 2015; Uppsala 2022). Indeed, criminal organizations do not aim to topple the state (Lessing 2017), but as I discuss in the next section, the political connections and implications of criminals are numerous (Durán-Martínez 2018; Trejo & Ley 2020). While these connections are not a reason to classify criminal violence as war, they do indicate its complexity and the limitations of seeing it as completely apolitical.

One limitation of this debate is that it has overlooked other countries that according to metrics such as homicide rates are deadlier, as Brazil, El Salvador, Honduras or Venezuela (Phillips 2017). In these countries, violence is very high, and at times has been directly aimed at attacking state power or symbols of it. Yet, the organization and character of the groups involved varies greatly. For example, in Brazil, the prison-based gang Primeiro Comando da Capital has become a highly bureaucratic organization profiting from retail drug trafficking (Lessing & Denyer-Willis 2019). In El Salvador, the MS-13 and Barrio 18 gangs have evolved to be more hierarchical and complex (Cruz 2010; Farah & Babineau 2017) yet they do not display the organizational sophistication or access to high-grade arms of Mexican groups. In Venezuela, many criminal groups are connected to authoritarian, but fragmented state actors. As occurs in civil wars, organizational structures and micro dynamics of violence vary within the same country.

Outside of Latin America, significant criminal violence also occurs in parts of Africa. In South Africa, gangs and criminal syndicates engage in drug trade, extortion, environmental crime, and other semi-legal economies; they generate significant violence that makes the country one of the most violent in the world (GI-TOC 2022). These cases highlight the same dilemmas: on one hand, the scale of violence, the groups' organization, the tactics and the arms used by the armed groups and the states combatting them, resemble traditional conflicts. On the other, the lack of ideologies or clear political incompatibilities with the state seems to stretch the definition of war. Debates about new wars and the crime-conflict nexus have long recognized the blurry limits that separate criminal groups from traditional political armed groups, but often voiding criminal violence of political connotations. Even in recent efforts to characterize non-traditional conflicts, as in the Uppsala Data Program's non-state conflict dataset, it is assumed that the state is not part of criminal conflicts. Yet, the state is an active actor, both while combatting criminal groups, but also while engaging in relations with them, as I explore next.

The fuzzy limits between political and criminal violence

The violence of organized groups that lack clear political agendas concentrates in Latin America and the Caribbean, but the connection between illicit markets and organized violence is a widespread phenomenon, and illicit activities are prominent in many traditional conflicts. In the 1990s, the new wars, greed-grievance and the crime-conflict nexus literatures recognized the connection between traditional conflict and illicit markets (Kaldor 1999; Collier & Hoeffler 2004; Makarenko 2004). While this recognition was important, as stimulating debates on these literatures have emphasized, it had significant limitations. First, these literatures tend to ignore that the connection between illicit economies and crime could be traced back in time to many conflicts (Andreas 2019). They also overemphasize the prevalence of the links between insurgents, terrorists and illicit markets, confusing sporadic reliance on illicit activities, with systematic connections. Second, these arguments overlook the micro dynamics and foundations of individual participation in conflict and confuse strategic uses of illicit activities with motivations to engage in violence. Lastly, these literatures often overlook complex realities on the ground.

As Kaldor (2013) stated in a defense of her original argument, the advantage of the 'new war' concept was to recognize the blurry limits between motivations of conflict and between actors fighting wars. The analysis of large-scale criminal violence benefits from recognizing such blurry limits. Still, most existing discussions revolve around traditional conflicts or forms of violence like terrorism where illicit activities are present, and less around the violence generated by groups that emerge out of private economic motivations and outside of traditional conflicts. In analyzing these forms of violence, the tendency has been to depoliticize them or to minimize the role of the state, focusing on state weakness or failure as the root of crime-conflict connections (Makarenko 2004). While state weakness fosters crime and conflict, to understand large-scale criminal violence and the traditional conflict-crime connections, it is necessary to analyze their political dimensions.

There are at least three main political dimensions of criminal violence. First, criminal organizations perform multiple roles within societies and establish diverse relationships with politicians and civilians. Criminal groups can establish forms of governance akin to those seen in traditional civil wars, engaging in taxation (in the form of extortion), dispute resolution, regulation of individual behaviors and provision of social services. This has been documented extensively in countries such as Brazil, Colombia and Mexico (Arias 2017; Barnes 2017). Criminal governance may diverge from rebel governance because it often emerges embedded in state power (Lessing 2021), but it also resembles rebel governance in multiple ways. The forms of governance and the violence that emerges in illicit markets depend on changing relations among various non-state groups, and between those actors and the state.

Second, criminal actors have political engagements and politicians can use them to advance electoral interests (Albarracín 2018). The political engagement of criminal actors occurs in different ways and intensities. Politicians may use gangs and criminal groups to gain political support as occurs in countries such as Jamaica, Haiti and Colombia. Criminal groups in turn use corruption and violence to influence elections and extend territorial control and political influence. In Mexico, criminal actors increasingly engage in violence to shape the outcomes of elections; between 2018 and 2022 scholars identified 825 events of criminal-electoral violence against government authorities, candidates or personnel related to electoral campaigns (Trejo & Ley 2020; Datacivica 2022). Electoral rules and democratic transformations shape the interactions between politicians and criminals, which in turn further shape the prospects of democracy. In Guinea-Bissau, infighting between small elites that protect and increasingly directly engage in drug trafficking has led to high-level assassinations, political instability and military coups (Shaw 2015).

Third, the relation between state and criminal actors shapes the extent and nature of criminal violence. An important difference between traditional insurgencies and criminal groups is that the latter in principle benefit more from avoiding state attention or from colluding with state actors, to reduce attention on their activities (Lessing 2017; Durán-Martínez 2018). However, the interactions between states and non-state actors vary, both for insurgents (Staniland 2012) and criminal groups. Criminal groups sometimes collaborate with states, and sometimes confront them. These interactions are not just a function of group motivations but also of power relations within the state, bureaucratic dynamics and processes of democratization (Barnes 2017; Durán-Martínez 2018; Trejo & Ley 2020). Thus, the dynamics of criminal violence are not just determined by what states do, but also by how states are organized internally. And, as discussed later, the policies states enact against organized crime and drug trafficking also shape, and often increase, the violent capacity and organization of criminal actors.

A discussion of criminal violence thus requires acknowledging blurry limits between motivations and types of groups, while avoiding the depoliticization of criminality prevalent in debates on the connections between crime and conflict. Recognizing these political dimensions reveals that state actors play important roles even in contexts of limited state capacity. This understanding of criminal violence also adds nuance to the analysis of the impact of crime on conflicts.

Humanitarian implications of criminal violence

Large-scale violent conflicts generate enormous humanitarian consequences which resemble civil wars. Daily life profoundly changes in territories afflicted by criminal violence; yet given the nature of the groups inflicting the damage and the state's complicity or inaction, governments, and even international organizations have been slow in recognizing these humanitarian implications. This often means that responses to monitor and address these phenomena can be scarce and slow. Internal displacements and international refugee flows exemplify some of the most worrying consequences of criminal violence.

According to the Internal Displacement Monitoring Centre, in 2021 there were significant internal displacement flows caused by criminal violence, particularly in the Americas. The report identified 381,000 people displaced in the region mostly concentrated in Colombia and Central America, but also significant flows in Haiti, and for the first time a report of displacement due to criminal violence in Brazil (IDMC 2022). In Central America, for example, populations fleeing victimization from gangs and crime have grown exponentially since 2009 (Hiskey, Córdova, Malone & Orcés 2018). In El Salvador, a country of 11 million people, a survey estimated at least 175,000 internally displaced people. In Colombia, which concentrates the region's largest accumulated number of displaced people and one of the top 10 in the world, displacement is fueled by complex and fluid interactions between traditional armed conflict, criminal groups and illicit activities. In Mexico, between 2015 and 2020, 251,513 people were forced to move to a different state or city because of violence and insecurity (CMDPDH 2021). Outside of the Americas, in Papua New Guinea, there were at least 1,000 internally displaced people in urban areas, associated with growing criminality that increased during the Covid-19 pandemic (IDMC 2022).

Another example of humanitarian impacts is disappearance. In Mexico, over 100,000 people have disappeared since 2006. In El Salvador, the National Police received more than 12,000 reports of disappearance between 2014 and 2019 (FESPAD 2021). In Rio de Janeiro, Brazil, public prosecutors reported 7,937 disappeared people between 2013 and 2018. In São Paulo, 24,368 people were reported missing in 2018. Information about the causes and perpetrators of disappearance, as well as precise statistics, are hard to come by. Reporting is complicated by impunity, restrictive legal definitions or by the strictest interpretation of forced disappearance as only cases where the state is a direct perpetrator. Despite these difficulties, the research and statistics that exist point to criminal violence as one driver of this extreme human rights violation.

The humanitarian consequences also include high death tolls, insecurity, and constant police and military presence. These dynamics upend daily life for communities generating fear and trauma, forcing people to change routines and weakening political and social participation (Villarreal 2015; Ley 2018). Violence also complicates access to social services such as health and education. Yet, communities can also resist violence, and crime victimization can spur forms of activism (Bateson 2012; Moncada 2021). Whether communities and individuals disengage from social life or demand better responses from the state or resist violence depends in part on the state's ability to understand and address victims' needs. This requires expanding definitions of victims in need of support, which are often expansive in traditional conflicts, but not in the face of criminal violence. In Colombia, for instance, a system of recognition of victims has consolidated over the years as a result of different peace processes, including the latest one signed with the FARC guerrilla in 2016. Yet, the victims of criminal groups face difficulties to secure state recognition and victims' benefits. The binary distinction between war and crime has made it difficult for victims to have their voices heard creating hierarchies of victims. For instance, victims of the

Medellín Cartel were excluded from a Victim's Law promulgated in 2011. While one victim of an airplane bombing that caused 107 civilian deaths in 1989 eventually received recognition and reparation in the framework of the law, many others have not (Franko & Rodriguez 2023). This example illustrates how defining violence as criminal often closes avenues to protect those who suffer from it.

The idea of tracking large-scale criminal violence as armed conflict (for analytical purposes in current datasets tracking conflicts and threats to peace), relates to, but differs from, recognizing it for the application of international law. Legal scholars argue that motivations are not a defining criterion to determine whether International Humanitarian Law (IHL) applies to cases of criminal conflict. It is thus possible to argue that forms of violence like the ones described in this chapter can be classified as an armed conflict and that IHL should apply to them. But this classification still faces conceptual and legal dilemmas. Kalmanovitz (2022) argues persuasively against classifying criminal violence as an armed conflict based on three factors: (1) criminal groups, unlike insurgents, prefer to accommodate, rather than confront the state; (2) criminal groups, even those organized hierarchically, lack the motivations and organizational resources to enforce humanitarian law because they do not seek to gain legitimacy among populations. They also lack responsible command and capacity to comply with IHL principles; and (3) large-scale criminal violence is the exception rather than the rule of operation of criminal groups, and mass-scale criminal violence is uncommon. These factors highlight that it is important to maintain distinctions between criminal and political groups, yet these distinctions are often blurry in traditional conflicts. Some insurgent groups lack incentives or capacity to confront the state, or the discipline to enforce humanitarian principles within their rank and file, yet they are still subjects of international law. And while mass violence in criminal and illegal organizations is less common than situations of relatively quiet disputes, the former have become more common.

In sum, there is subjective judgment in deciding whether using the conflict terminology is appropriate for criminal violence. Considering large-scale criminal violence as conflict can help better address the needs of victims by going beyond law enforcement to include peace building principles, transitional justice, negotiation tools and principles of humanitarian law when confronting criminal violence. Yet the term 'armed conflict', especially when used to invoke IHL, can legitimize purely criminal motivations and facilitate militarization, escalation and extreme state responses. This is the challenge I discuss next.

Security responses

It is possible that characterizing criminal violence within the realm of humanitarian law as an armed conflict can militarize state responses by enabling the state to use force and target groups in a way that would not be otherwise available (Kalmanovitz 2022). Indeed, the use of terminology associated with war, insurgency or terrorism to characterize criminal violence has enabled militarization and extreme policies that have worsened violence.

While organized crime and illicit activities remain largely in the realm of criminal justice policies, many governments have militarized the policies aimed to combat crime. This is driven by the popularity of zero-tolerance anti-crime policies, and by the increasing use of militarized policing and of the military for domestic law enforcement, which has undermined the protection of human rights (Youngers & Rosin 2005, Flores-Macías & Zarkin 2021). Counter-drug efforts and military assistance for them, particularly in Latin America, have also been key contributors to the militarization of law enforcement.

Many studies have found that the militarization of the fight against organized crime and the removal of criminal leaders can fragment criminal groups and increase infighting, competition, and violence. In Mexico, a militarized campaign against drug trafficking organizations started during the government of President Vicente Fox (2000–2006) and was deepened with the declaration of war on drug trafficking organizations made by his successor Felipe Calderón in 2006. The militarization unleashed extreme fragmentation among and within criminal groups, which in turn heightened violence (Calderón et al. 2015; Lessing 2017). In 2008, the government recognized six criminal organizations operating; by 2012 there were at least 12, and by the early 2020s the number of organizations had grown exponentially: in the state of Guerrero alone at least 40 organizations exist (ICG 2020). Over the past 15 years, criminal groups in Mexico became more complex, engaging in widespread governance over their territories, actively intervening in elections and expanding illicit portfolios (Trejo & Ley 2020). In this sense, the conflict itself largely results from a disproportional, poorly targeted and inadequate militarization response by the state.

Repressive policies have often generated more sophistication within criminal groups. For instance, massive incarceration policies have been instrumental in the consolidation of groups like the prison gang Primeiro Comando Da Capital in Brazil, the MS-13 gang in El Salvador or prison gangs in the United States (Dias 2009; Cruz 2010; Skarbek 2014). Similarly, the militarization of smuggling policies in North Africa destabilized illicit activities that had social acceptance. As a result, the least powerful smugglers disappeared while the most organized ones became stronger and shifted to illicit markets that were more profitable and potentially violent, such as drug trafficking (Gallien & Herbert 2020).

There is thus enough evidence that militarization and counterinsurgency tactics that may work in reducing violence by rebel or terrorist organizations, such as targeting leaders that have enough control and symbolic influence, do not work with criminal groups (Philips 2015). Furthermore, even in traditional conflicts, the impact of military, counter-terrorist and counter-insurgency operations depends on the internal structure of armed groups, their relations with the population and the state (Felbab-Brown 2009; Shapiro 2013; Staniland 2014). Militarization alone has failed to create situations of sustainable peace in traditional conflicts. The characterization of an armed conflict under IHL could further militarize anti-crime policies and this is a strong argument against invoking armed conflict terminology (Kalmanovitz 2022). Yet the excessive militarization of anti-crime policies has occurred without invoking IHL or labeling armed conflicts, and the armed conflict language opens avenue to analyze and tackle the humanitarian consequences of criminal violence. Using labels of wars, insurgency or terrorism for situations of large-scale criminal violence does not bring clear analytical or policy payoffs and facilitates the introduction of highly militarized anti-crime policies. The challenge for scholarship and policy is thus to understand that criminal violence and criminal activities are more than law enforcement issues that affect only those involved in criminal activities, while avoiding simple characterizations about the nature of violence or its protagonists.

Future trends

In forecasting trends in criminal violence, a key challenge is that illicit activities are more widespread than cases of intense and organized criminal violence. The Global Initiative Against Organized Crime estimates that 80% of the world's population lives in territories with high levels of criminality, yet sophisticated criminal actors only appear to be pervasive in the Americas (GITOC 2022). There are also examples of sophisticated and organized criminal actors that engage in limited violence. In the Balkan region, for example, illicit activities and drug trafficking are widespread but homicide levels are low. With these caveats in mind, it is possible to argue that the risks of criminal violence have increased due to the geographic dispersion of illicit activities and the proliferation of illicit and semi-licit economies across the globe. The conditions of socio-economic marginalization that force populations to engage in illicit economies, and that make them more vulnerable to criminal groups, have also increased. Massive migration flows resulting from violence, crime and climate change have become more widespread. There are estimated 281 million migrants in the world today, and many end up stranded around borders and transit routes where multiple illicit economies and non-state actors interact. This makes more locations vulnerable to future criminal control and violence.

Still, extreme conflicts may remain geographically concentrated in the Americas due to the nature of the actors operating there. In the Americas, the risks of organized crime are high and criminal networks are more sophisticated although political institutions are stronger than in Africa, where high risks of armed conflict and illicit economies overlap. Countries that have not traditionally seen violence in the Americas are experiencing growing concentrated pockets of violence, as seems to be occurring in Argentina and Ecuador. This is a reason for concern in the medium to long run. Outside of the Americas, specific subregions such as West Africa, or specific areas within countries – even countries of the Global North – appear to be increasingly vulnerable to criminal violence. There are also multiple hybrid situations where illicit economies and conflict are widespread. The specific nature of the actors involved in these situations cannot be assumed *a priori*, so it is difficult to characterize them as purely criminal conflicts. Africa, Western Asia and the Middle East, and countries like Afghanistan, the Democratic Republic of Congo, Nigeria or Myanmar, concentrate many vulnerabilities of this type, as high levels of criminality, conflict and political instability overlap. The nature of criminal violence in these conflicts differs from that currently seen in the Americas and from the large-scale criminal violence discussed in this chapter. Yet as I have emphasized, lessons from the analysis of criminal violence outside of conflicts can help avoid simplistic generalizations about the impact of illicit activities in these hybrid situations which have become more widespread. To prevent situations of pervasive violence, it is crucial to monitor many areas where illicit economies exist while avoiding problematic generalizations or a-priori assumptions.

As this chapter has emphasized, illicit economies are not inevitably linked to violence, and it is often the policies and power relations within states that explain when does criminal violence emerge or increase. One of the major factors increasing the risk of large-scale criminal violence is political polarization and fragmentation across the globe, paired with a deterioration of democratic checks and balances. In the past decade, organizations like Freedom House have documented democratic backsliding, with more countries becoming authoritarian or hybrid regimes. Authoritarian regimes are more likely to generate networks of corruption and repression that can help organized crime flourish, but hybrid or transitional regimes may be more vulnerable in the short run to situations of high violence. Armed criminal groups colluding with state actors can impose social orders and control over communities while simultaneously reducing violence. Such cases, while not generating large scale lethal violence, may be particularly vulnerable to other forms of control and repression. The future trends of criminal violence thus will be significantly shaped by the strategies used by states, and not just by illicit markets trends. The militarization and sophistication of criminal actors has been driven in great part by the militarizing strategies of states against crime, and state policies often create more opportunities for criminal activities. For example, more restrictions on migration flows create more opportunities for human smuggling and trafficking. This does not mean that states are invariably corrupt or weak and cannot confront organized criminality, but that state actions can be more consequential than assumed in traditional discussions about organized crime and crime and conflict.

Conclusion

Over the past two decades academic debates on the relationship between crime, illegal activities and conflict have helped understand, on one side, the fuzzy limits that exist between traditional conflicts, terrorism and crime, and on the other, the risks of uncritically assuming the nature of these connections. Most of the discussion has tended to depoliticize criminal violence particularly when it emerges outside of traditional conflicts, as occurs in many areas of Latin America today. While debates on how to characterize this violence exist, they tend to focus on the nature of the actors involved and their behavior. By focusing on the humanitarian consequences, I argued that tracking large-scale criminal violence as an armed conflict is crucial to address these impacts, which have increased in scale and scope. However, using the war, insurgency or terrorism labels can strengthen the tendency to militarize and use indiscriminate repression in law enforcement. While large-scale attacks and violence may warrant responses that go beyond regular policing (such as when groups launch coordinated and simultaneous attacks), the militarization that often accompanies the use of war metaphors has already generated escalation and deterioration of security.

Adding precision and clarity to conceptual definitions of criminal violence is important for academic and policy purposes, yet labels that are necessary for analytical purposes can have negative policy and legal implications. The possibility of recognizing criminal violence as conflict, for example, can lead to granting political status to some groups that have not ever had political aspirations, thus generating moral hazards for governments and international organizations. However, from the perspective of the communities that suffer violence, rigid definitions have led to slow, ineffective or inexistent responses to humanitarian tragedies. Ultimately, as the literatures on greed and grievance, crime-conflict nexus and new wars emphasize, lack of attention to blurry areas can minimize important interconnections and overlaps. But as the many critics to these literatures emphasize too, uncritically assuming the nature of an actor or a situation can also have negative consequences. Even if situations where criminal actors resort to massive violence are less common than those where they do not (outside of traditional conflicts), these situations seem to have become more widespread geographically and persistent once they emerge. While the existence of a non-state armed group with capacity to engage in violence is not enough to characterize a situation as a conflict, the doors should be open to track and treat those situations as armed violence when they do emerge. Organized crime generates many other risks beyond homicidal violence, and thus its widespread nature is a concern on its own right. Ultimately, we need empirically grounded assessments; recent literature on criminal violence has shown that even if difficult, such analyses are possible.

References

Albarracín, J 2018, 'Criminalized Electoral Politics in Brazilian Urban Peripheries', *Crime, Law and Social Change*, vol. 69, no. 4, pp. 553–75, https://doi.org/10.1007/s10611-017-9761-8

Andreas, P 2019, *Killer High: A History of War in Six Drugs*, Oxford University Press, Oxford.

Arias, E D 2017, *Criminal Enterprises and Governance in Latin America and the Caribbean*, Cambridge University Press, Cambridge, https://doi.org/10.1017/9781316650073.

Arias, E & Goldstein, D M 2010, 'Violent Pluralism: Understanding the New Democracies of Latin America', in E Arias & D Goldstein (eds), *Violent Democracies in Latin America*, Duke University Press, Durham, NC, pp. 1–34, https://doi.org/10.1515/9780822392033-002

Barnes, N 2017, 'Criminal Politics: An Integrated Approach to the Study of Organized Crime, Politics, and Violence', *Perspectives on Politics*, vol. 15, no. 4, pp. 967–87, https://doi:10.1017/S1537592717002110.

Bateson, R 2012, 'Crime Victimization and Political Participation', *American Political Science Review*, vol. 106, no. 3, pp. 570–87, https://doi:10.1017/S0003055412000299.

Calderón, G, Robles, G, Díaz-Cayeros, A & Magaloni, B 2015, 'The Beheading of Criminal Organizations and the Dynamics of Violence in Mexico', *Journal of Conflict Resolution*, vol. 59, no. 8, pp. 1455–85, https://doi.org/10.1177/00220027155870.

CMDPDH 2021, *Newsletter on the Situation of Internal Displacement in Mexico January – June* 2021, Comisión Mexicana de la Defensa y Promoción de Derechos Humanos, <https://cmdpdh.org/temas/desplazamiento/wp-content/uploads/2021/08/newsletteridps2021-1.pdf> (accessed 19 August 2022).

Collier, P & Hoeffler, A 2004, 'Greed and Grievance in Civil War', *Oxford Economic Papers*, vol. 56, no. 4, pp. 563–95, https://doi.org/10.1093/oep/gpf064.

Cruz, J 2010, 'Central American Maras: From Youth Street Gangs to Transnational Protection Rackets', *Global Crime*, vol. 11, no. 4, pp. 379–98, https://doi.org/10.1080/17440572.2010.519518.

DataCivica 2022, *Votar Entre Balas: Entendiendo la Violencia Criminal-Electoral en Mexico*, <https://votar-entre-balas.datacivica.org/> (accessed 19 August 2022).

Dias, C 2009, 'Efeitos Simbólicos e Práticos do Regime Disciplinar Diferenciado (RDD) na Dinâmica Prisional', *Revista Brasileira de Segurança Pública*, vol. 3, no. 5, pp. 128–44.

Durán-Martínez, A 2018, *The Politics of Drug Violence: Criminals, Cops and Politicians in Colombia and Mexico*, Oxford University Press, Oxford.

Durán-Martínez, A 2020, 'Illicit Drugs and Organized Crime in Latin America: New Scholarship and the Future of Alternative Policies', in X Bada & L Rivera-Sánchez (eds), *The Oxford Handbook of the Sociology of Latin America*, Oxford University Press, Oxford, pp. 782–99, https://doi.org/10.1093/oxfordhb/9780190926557.013.43.

Farah, D & Babineau, K 2017, 'The Evolution of MS 13 in El Salvador and Honduras', *PRISM*, vol. 7, no. 1, pp. 59–73.

Felbab-Brown, V 2009, *Shooting Up: Counterinsurgency and the War on Drugs*, Brookings Institution Press, Washington, DC.

FESPAD 2021, *Desaparición de Personas en El Salvador*, FESPAD, San Salvador.

Flanigan, T 2012, 'Terrorists Next Door? A Comparison of Mexican Drug Cartels and Middle Eastern Terrorist Organizations', *Terrorism and Political Violence*, vol. 24, no. 2, pp. 279–94, http://www.tandfonline.com/doi/full/10.1080/09546553.2011.648351.

Flores-Macías, G & Zarkin, J 2021, 'The militarization of law enforcement: Evidence from Latin America' *Perspectives on Politics*, vol 19, no. 2, pp. 519–538, http://doi:10.1017/S1537592719003906.

Franko, K & Rodriguez, R 2023, 'Drug Violence, War-Crime Distinction, and Hierarchies of Victimhood', *Social & Legal Studies*, vol. 32, no. 1, pp. 75–95, https://doi.org/10.1177/09646639221091226.

GI-TOC 2022, 'Global Organized Crime Index 2021', *Global Initiative Against Transnational Organized Crime*, <https://globalinitiative.net/wp-content/uploads/2021/09/GITOC-Global-Organized-Crime-Index-2021.pdf> (accessed 19 August 2022).

Herbert, M & Gallien, M 2020, 'Divided they Fall: Frontiers, Borderlands and Stability in North Africa', *North Africa Report*, no. 6, <https://issafrica.s3.amazonaws.com/site/uploads/nar-6.pdf> (accessed 19 August 2022).

Hiskey, J T, Córdova, A, Malone, M F & Orcés, DM 2018, 'Leaving the Devil you Know: Crime victimization, US Deterrence Policy, and the Emigration Decision in Central America', *Latin American Research Review*, vol. 53, no. 3, pp. 429–47. https://doi.org/10.25222/larr.147

ICG 2020, 'La Guerra Cotidiana: Guerrero y los Retos a la Paz en Mexico', *Informe Sobre América Latina*, no. 80, International Crisis Group, <https://icg-prod.s3.amazonaws.com/080-mexicos-everyday-war-spanish_0.pdf> (accessed 19 August 2022).

IDMC 2022, *Children and Youth in Internal Displacement*, International Displacement Monitoring Centre, Geneva.

Kaldor, M 1999, *New and Old Wars: Organised Violence in a Global Era*, Stanford University Press, Stanford, CA.

Kaldor, M 2013, 'In Defence of New Wars', *Stability: International Journal of Security and Development*, vol. 2, no. 1, pp. 1–16, http://doi.org/10.5334/sta.at.

Kalmanovitz, P 2022, 'Can Organized Criminal Organizations Be Non-State Parties to Armed Conflict', *International Review of the Red Cross* [online first], https://doi:10.1017/S1816383122000510.

Kalyvas, S N 2015, 'How Civil Wars Help Explain Organized Crime—And How They Do Not', *Journal of Conflict Resolution*, vol. 59, no. 8, pp. 1517–40, https://doi.org/10.1177/0022002715587101.

Lessing, B 2017, *Making Peace in Drug Wars: Crackdowns and Cartels in Latin America*, Cambridge University Press, Cambridge, https://doi.org/10.1017/9781108185837.

Lessing, B 2021, 'Conceptualizing Criminal Governance', *Perspectives on Politics*, vol. 19, no. 3, pp. 854–73, https://doi.org/10.1017/S1537592720001243.

Lessing, B & Willis, G D 2019, 'Legitimacy in Criminal Governance: Managing a Drug Empire from Behind Bars', *American Political Science Review*, vol. 113, no. 2, pp. 584–606, https://doi.org/10.1017/S0003055418000928.

Ley, S 2018, 'To Vote or Not to Vote: How Criminal Violence Shapes Electoral Participation', *Journal of Conflict Resolution*, vol. 62, no. 9, pp.1963–90, https://doi.org/10.1177/0022002717708600.

Makarenko, T 2004, 'The Crime-Terror Continuum: Tracing the Interplay Between Transnational Organised Crime and Terrorism', *Global Crime*, vol. 6, no. 1, pp. 129–45, https://doi.org/10.1080/1744057042000297025.

Moncada, E 2021, *Resisting Extortion: Victims, Criminals, and States in Latin America*, Cambridge University Press, Cambridge, https://doi.org/10.1017/9781108915328.

Phillips, B J 2015, 'How Does Leadership Decapitation Affect Violence? The Case of Drug Trafficking Organizations in Mexico', *The Journal of Politics*, vol. 77, no. 2, pp. 324–36, https://doi.org/10.1086/680209.

Phillips, B J 2017, 'Is Mexico the Second-Deadliest 'Conflict Zone' in the World? Probably Not', *The Washington Post*, 18 May, <https://www.washingtonpost.com/news/monkey-cage/wp/2017/05/18/is-mexico-the-second-deadliest-conflict-zone-in-the-world-probably-not/> (accessed 19 August 2022).

Schedler, A 2014, 'The Criminal Subversion of Mexican Democracy' *Journal of Democracy*, vol. 25, no. 1, pp. 5–18.

SESNSP 2022, *Estadísticas de Incidencia Delictiva*, Secretariado Ejecutivo del Sistema Nacional de Seguridad Pública, <https://www.gob.mx/sesnsp/acciones-y-programas/victimas-nueva-metodologia?state=published> (accessed 13 September 2022).

Shapiro, J N 2013, *The Terrorist's Dilemma*, Princeton University Press, Princeton, NJ.

Shaw, M 2015, 'Drug Trafficking in Guinea-Bissau, 1998–2014: The Evolution of an Elite Protection Network', *The Journal of Modern African Studies*, vol. 53, no. 3, pp. 339–64, https://doi.org/10.1017/S0022278X15000361.

Skarbek, D 2014, *The Social Order of the Underworld: How Prison Gangs Govern the American Penal System*, Oxford University Press, Oxford, https://doi.org/10.1093/acprof:oso/9780199328499.001.0001.

Snyder, R & Durán-Martínez, A 2009, 'Does Illegality Breed Violence? Drug Trafficking and State-Sponsored Protection Rackets', *Crime, Law and Social Change*, vol. 52, no. 3, pp. 253–73, https://doi.org/10.1007/s10611-009-9195-z.

Staniland, P 2012, 'States, Insurgents, and Wartime Political Orders', *Perspectives on Politics*, vol. 10, no. 2, pp. 243–64, https://doi.org/10.1017/S1537592712000655.

Staniland, P 2014, *Networks of Rebellion*, Cornell University Press, Ithaca, NY.

Trejo, G & Ley, S 2020, *Votes, Drugs, and Violence: The Political Logic of Criminal Wars in Mexico*, Cambridge University Press, Cambridge.

UNODC 2019, *Global Study on Homicide*, United Nations Office on Drugs and Crime, Vienna.

Uppsala 2022, 'Mexico Profile', *Uppsala Conflict Data Program*, <https://ucdp.uu.se/country/70> (accessed 13 September 2022).

Villarreal, A 2015, 'Fear and Spectacular Drug Violence in Monterrey', in J Auyero, N Scheper-Hugues & P Bourgois (eds), *Violence at the Urban Margins*, Oxford University Press, Oxford, pp. 135–61.

Youngers, C & Rosin, E (eds) 2005, *Drugs and Democracy in Latin America: The Impact of US Policy*, Lynne Rienner, Boulder, CO.

38

STAGING THE CONFLICTS TO COME

Visions of the Future-Tracing Security Practices[1]

David Paulo Succi Junior, Helena Salim de Castro and Samuel Alves Soares

Introduction

Security, defence and military policies are structured around the future threats one expects to face and how the conflict is imagined to play out. Throughout the centuries, military commanders and policymakers have sought to possess some degree of predictability about the enemy's intentions and tactics, the characteristics of the terrain, the effects of strategic decisions, as well as its own armed forces' intentions as a way to decide how to proceed next (Bousquet 2009); that is, trying to bring order to a deeply uncertain realm so that one can know (or think to know) how to act. In this sense, the way in which both international security scholars and practitioners picture the future has direct implications for the legitimation and implementation of defence and security policies. Moments of great inflection in the security environment entail reshaping the expectations about the future, which involves identifying the threats one should prepare for, and which role one plays in this new arrangement. This was the case with the international system after the Cold War (Goldman 2001).

After the first moments of optimism and confidence, with the so-called end of history (Fukuyama 2006), more democracy and capitalism would mean a more peaceful world order (Freedman 2017). However, the increasing number of civil wars and unconventional dynamics of violence, although not unprecedented, raised questions about the security challenges to come, which can be illustrated by the development of two main agendas: new wars and new threats. The first is structured around the notion that the wars to come would be mainly intrastate, asymmetric, involving non-state violent actors, mainly in urban spaces. The second is focused on issues such as transnational organized crime, terrorism and migration flows, among other issues of different natures, which are deemed to be the main sources of threat to states' security. Both are characterized by the blurred lines between international and domestic security, as well as between the armed forces and the police.

These two agendas structured how the future of war and security issues was imagined right after the Cold War, exerting an impact on security and defence policies. Latin America's militarized response to public security issues since the 1990s is an emblematic illustration. The region that had historically been characterized by the prevalence of intrastate violence and domestic military deployment (Rouquié 1984) and that had recently experienced long periods of military dictatorships

(Linz & Stepan 1999) incorporated the trope of new wars and threats to sustaining and reframing state violence.

The chapter is structured as follows. First, we analyze how the ideas of new wars and threats dominated the imagination about the future of warfare and security as a response to the uncertainty posed by the dissolution of the Soviet Union and the restructuring of the international system. In the second part, we focus on how these agendas impacted security and defence policies in Latin America, underpinning practices of domestic violence. Finally, we explore recent trends in the images of the future of war and security issues and explore the potential implications of how it is imagined.

The new wars agenda

In the aftermath of the Cold War and the military tension between the superpowers that characterized it, there was a first impression that warfare was in decline and that a period of stability in terms of international security could be foreseen (Freedman 20179). Although it seemed to be true in terms of traditional interstate conflicts, this promising image of the future was shortly contrasted by blunt pessimism (Kaplan 2002), grounded on a growing number of intrastate wars and other forms of organized violence. Civil wars in post-Soviet countries, Africa and Asia, led scholars and policymakers to claim that a new kind of warfare was at play and would prevail in the years to come. In her broadly known definition, Kaldor (2012) characterized it as blurring the lines between crime and war, public and private, global and local, and foreign attack and domestic repression. It is fought by non-state armed groups, marked by the erosion of the state's monopoly on violence, and produced extensive human rights violations.

Guerrilla war, terrorism and other non-conventional tactics of combat were certainly not unprecedented. Kaldor (2012) tries to trace a distinction between her concept of new wars and low-intensity conflict, as this kind of asymmetric conflict used to be named during the Cold War. She argues that while the latter draws upon combat methods theorized by Mao Zedong and Che Guevara, it also incorporates the counterinsurgency tactics of fostering anger and fear. Regardless of the valid critiques about new wars' actual novelty, the fact is that these concepts permeated the scholars' and practitioners' imaginations about what future conflicts would predominantly be like.

By the same token, many works started to craft an image of the future in which the most pressing security issues would be associated with public disorder and private use of violence for both political and economic gains. Van Creveld's book (1991) illustrates how this image was built. He imagined future warfare to be waged: (a) by organizations other than the state, such as guerrillas, terrorists and bandits; (b) using low-technological weaponry that requires low scientific research, being cheap, easy to operate and manufacture; (c) without any legal restraints such as the distinction between civilians and soldiers, which is expected to fade away. Another common feature of this perception about future security issues is their geographical origin. Van Creveld sustains that the first places to be affected by this kind of conflict, which would be predominant in the 21st century, were Africa, Asia and Latin America. He also suggests that some of these features were already at play in these regions, claiming that "war and crime will break down much as is already the case today in places such as Lebanon, Sri Lanka, El Salvador, Peru, or Colombia" (Van Creveld 1991, p. 556). Consonantly, Kaplan (2002), in another influential book, sustained that civil wars and criminal activities in West Africa were a symbol of what should be expected to happen in underdeveloped countries in the following years. While in Africa future wars were deemed to take place in the form of tribal conflict, in Asia and Latin America its trigger was seen in organized crime.

The concerns about the future of warfare included the idea that the conflicts to come would play out predominantly in cities rather than in open fields. It is particularly the case within the United States military after they intervened in Somalia in the early 1990s (Hamlet 1998; Goulding Jr 2000). Since then, the American armed forces have been concerned about what they called military operations on urbanized terrain (MOUT), in which the technological advantages reached by the Revolution in Military Affairs (RMA) were not effective in urban combat (Graham 2011).

Much of this approach regards underdeveloped or peripherical countries as the loci of new forms of violence and the causes of the problems the world is expected to experience in the future. These areas are never conceived as a place from which innovative solutions could potentially emerge, for instance. Conversely, the developed states are framed as holders of more rational and civilized ways of war, ignoring the impact and brutality of colonial wars waged in these regions. In the way future urban wars are imagined, the Global South is the terrain where the military from central countries will have to operate. It is bluntly expressed in the title of a US intelligence officer's article: "our soldiers, their cities" (Peters 1996). Consequently, in the image of the future informing military technologies and training to deal with new wars in cities, the population of these marginalized areas are framed either as potential threats, i.e. combatants disguised as regular citizens, or, as Graham (2009, p. 40) puts it, "physical and technical noise" in the background of the urban battlefield, deprived of any right or humanity.

The 'new threats' agenda

The second set of images about the future of international security that permeated the international imaginary following the end of the Cold War is the 'new threats' agenda. It gave renewed prominence to old phenomena, such as organized crime, terrorism, migration, environmental degradation and poverty, by inserting them into security discourses and policies (Baldwin 1995).

The widening of the security agenda in the 1990s can be seen as a result of many processes, such as the effectiveness of nuclear deterrence between the West and the East, the perception of the high costs of the interstate war and the securitization of other themes, such as the international economy and the environment (Buzan 1997). In addition, international institutions shifted their attention towards the security of individuals rather than states.[2] Even though states are still important actors, they are not the only referent object that can be threatened.

Behind the concern for the security of individuals and the state was the prominence of transnational actors and threats, such as transnational organized crime (TOC). Its spillover across states' borders and the involvement of criminal organizations in many activities – drug and arms trafficking, contraband, human trafficking, etc. – put governments around the world on alert and made TOC an issue to be investigated in security studies and debated in international institutions (Williams 1994; Andreas & Price 2001; Edwards & Gill 2003; Cockayne 2007).

Globalization and political changes after the Cold War were identified as important elements to the emergence of TOC (Willians 1994; Shelley 1995). This spurred governments to outline collective strategies and policies to deal with it, such as those set out in the United Nations Convention against Transnational Organized Crime, adopted in November 2000. In addition to the emergence of TOC, the new century would see the globalization of practices to control such criminal activities (Andreas 2011).

Increased government attention to these security threats in the American continent has spurred (with US leadership) initiatives such as the implementation of the Declaration on Security in the Americas of 2003 and the adoption of the concept of 'multidimensional security' within the Organization of American States (OAS). The objective was to expand the security agenda in the continent to include themes presented as 'new threats'[3] by the United States (Donadelli 2018).

The expansion of this agenda would guide the security policies implemented by Latin American governments in the years that followed.

The concern with drug trafficking and the need to adopt a 'war on drugs' policy gained prominence. Academic and political debates focused on: (1) the centrality drugs had in the US security agenda concerning Latin America (Del Olmo 1991; Herz 2002); (2) how the prohibition and control of some drugs served the interests of transnational economic and political actors (Levine 2003; Paley 2014; Reis 2014); (3) the militarization of the fight against drugs and criminal organizations around the hemisphere (Salazar Ortuño 2008; Villa 2009; Rodrigues 2012); and (4) the impact of such policies on people's lives.

New wars and threats in Latin American security policies

Latin America is a particular region in terms of security issues. Although it has not been the scene of many interstate conflicts, its rates of homicide are among the highest in the world (UNODC 2019). Moreover, they are marked by non-state violent actors such as organized crime groups, paramilitaries and militias, precisely the set of phenomena at the core of future imagination in both new wars and new threats agenda. Even if the grim predictions that the theorists of future conflicts made about Latin America did not materialize, at least not in the highly catastrophic form it was foreseen, the new wars' vocabulary has been mobilized to legitimize old forms of state violence in the region. In Brazil, for instance, expressions such as civil war (Levy 1994), domestic war (Cantanhêde 2010) or postmodern war (Fernandes 2018) became pervasive in the media accounts and political discourses on the domestic military deployment against drug trafficking. Rates of homicides in Brazil were compared to the American casualties in the Vietnam War (Campos 1994), the number of deaths in the Syrian Civil War, and the United States occupation of Iraq (Brasil 2018a, 2018b).

Even though rates of criminality in Brazil are undoubtedly high, by characterizing criminal activities through the lexicon of the new wars, political actors justify and normalize lethal violence against criminals, as well as the resulting causalities. It is illustrative how the former Brazilian Minister of Justice, Torquato Jardim, while explaining a domestic military operation, argued that "we are living in an asymmetric warfare" in which "anyone can be the enemy, [they] are not uninformed [...]. You must be prepared for everything and everyone all the time". He concluded that "unfortunately [...] there is no war that is not lethal" (Dubeux, Rothenburg & Cavalcanti 2018). This trope is reaffirmed whenever this kind of military operation faces public pressure.

It is important to stress that this new vocabulary did not inaugurate a new pattern of military deployment in Brazil; instead, the domestic involvement of the armed forces has been pervasive in the country's history under the label of internal pacification. Examples of these practices can be pointed out in the colonial conquest, the repression of contesting movements in the 19th century, two military dictatorships in the 20th century and the contemporary fight against organized crime (Souza et al. 2017). However, the new wars' vocabulary helped to frame the armed forces' domestic deployment as acceptable and desirable, reshaping the discourses that legitimized it according to the notions about the future of war. It is illustrative that the Brazilian army's center for training on domestic operations was renamed the Urban Operations Instruction Centre, which was justified as a way to adopt "the most current terminology for land military doctrine used in the military doctrine of countries with high expertise in the subject such as the United States of America, Israel, and France" (Brasil 2021).

Internal deployment of the state's instrument of lethality – i.e. the armed forces – is depicted as a rational and pragmatic course of action, given the conflicts to come. Similarly, in Argentina, the new wars trope has been tapped into by actors attempting to defy the legal prohibition to deploy the armed forces against domestic criminal groups. While the National Defence Law from 1988 provides that the military must be exclusively trained and used to deal with external threats posed by states, a group of politicians and militaries have been attempting to frame terrorism and trans-national crime as external threats, blurring the line between crime and war (Sain 2018; Anzelini 2019; Battaglino 2019).

Considering South America, the policy of the war on drugs is a clear example of how the vocabulary of war has legitimated forms of state violence. To follow international conventions and US guidelines on drug control, South American governments have implemented strict and militarized anti-drug policies, at least since the late 1980s, which bring, on the one hand, economic and political benefits (such as free trade agreements) and, on the other hand, armed conflicts and violence. In countries such as Bolivia and Colombia, the state policy of forced eradication of coca leaf crops resulted, in the late 1990s and early 2000s, in an internal war between state security forces, violent non-state actors and the traditional population that survives from these plantations. The war on drugs policy also affects the peripheral areas of large cities in countries in the region, as is the case in Brazil. In the name of national security, and with the aim of confronting drug trafficking groups, the state intervenes militarily, through instruments of lethality, in people's daily lives, generating a scenario of armed confrontation and violence (Rodrigues 2012).

Those instruments and methods have functioned as a policy of controlling and pacifying society. As argued by Neocleous (2011, pp. 202–3): "the war [on drugs] has paved the way for the pacification of groups perceived as the least useful and most dangerous parts of the population, of regions regarded as 'ungovernable' and borders regarded as 'insecure'". This pacification serves the interests of political and economic actors in the expansion of capitalism, as well as promotes violence and the violation of the rights of certain social groups (Neocleous 2011; Paley 2014).

One of the most visible consequences of the war on drugs policy is the incarceration of women – especially poor, black, indigenous women (Salim de Castro 2020). The 2018 United Nations Drug Report pointed out that "an estimated 35 percent of women in prison had been convicted for drug-related offenses, while the figure for men was 19 percent" (UNODC 2018, p. 32). Considering that women often occupy the riskiest role in the drug supply chain (as 'mules'), they are more easily arrested by local law enforcement agencies that prefer to focus on those in the lower level of drug trafficking, which allows governments to achieve more immediate and visible results (UNODC 2018).

Furthermore, it is important to note that some women, or men, are more likely to be incarcerated under the drug law and to be victims of state violence. In Brazil, more than half of the incarcerated women (62%) are African descent (Santos 2018). In Bolivia, most incarcerated women are underprivileged and do not have access to education and formal jobs (Ledebur & Youngers 2018). Indigenous Bolivian women and Afro-Colombian women have their communities devastated and their bodies violated in the context of struggles between state security forces, non-state armed groups and organized criminal groups (Salim de Castro 2020).

To combat the new threats, these internal wars are structured by gender norms and a history of coloniality permeating the power relations between the actors involved. Some political rulers and economic groups reproduce a Eurocentric and masculinized logic on the domestic and international socioeconomic order. In this sense, territories are exploited, activities are criminalized and some bodies are discarded and violated. They need to be dominated and controlled in favor of the economic interests of transnational actors (such as large multinationals) who seek to expand their capital from time to time (Ballestrin 2021).

New images of the future of international security and warfare

Thus far, we have described how images of future warfare and security issues emerged in the early 1990s and how they found their way into Latin American security policies in the late 1990s and early 2000s, grounding militarized and violent state actions in the domestic realm. In this section, we aim to highlight current dominant images on the future of international security and reflect on their possible impacts on Latin America. Three main phenomena permeate current appraisals on the future of international conflict and warfare: (a) autonomous weapons, (b) the return of inter-state tensions and (c) environmental depletion.

At first, when the urban spaces in the Global South became the main battlefield for the American armed forces, such as in interventions in the Middle East, the promise of military dominance with reduced casualties under the RMA was challenged. It led to efforts to develop new technologies able to tackle the complexity of cities in these parts of the globe, as well as the problem of distinguishing combatants from non-combatants, which were characterized by the progressive automatization of weapons (Graham 2011). Lethal autonomous weapon systems (LAWS) are seen as unavoidable in the future of war. These instruments, driven by artificial intelligence (AI), are expected to autonomously identify targets and decide whether to engage or not without the interference of a human operator. Furthermore, advocates sustain that, as LAWS would supposedly provide a more precise assessment of combatants and non-combatants, it would allow for greater compliance with humanitarian and war regulations, resulting in a more ethical and humanized warfare (Arkin 2010).

While developed countries already use weapons with different degrees of autonomy, the Global South has assumed little prominence in the multilateral discussions on the legal, ethical and political implications of deploying these devices (Garcia 2019). However, this military and security technology transformation has deep implications for peripheral states and the international system's power relations broadly, of which we highlight three: (a) it could reinforce international hierarchies between those states that develop and detain these devices and those that do not; (b) as autonomous weapons are progressively framed as a more ethical way of waging wars, if they come to be deemed the most acceptable way of using violence in the international system, the unequal distribution of these instruments might lead to an unequal allocation of legitimacy to use coercive means (Beier 2020); (c) tracing acceptable and unacceptable forms of coercion based on these instruments might add to arguments that the violence coming from the North is more civilized and rational than violence from the South.

Moreover, LAWS promises to tackle tactic obstacles posed by the complexity of cities in the peripherical countries targeted by pivotal states, prominently the United States (Graham 2011). In Latin America, the advent of autonomous weapons may merely provide new instruments to old security dynamics, reinforcing the militarized response to criminality. In this sense, military equipment developed in the North to fight civil or asymmetric wars in the South is uncritically incorporated by Latin American militaries and deployed domestically. Moreover, artificial intelligence requires large amounts of data and experimentation. Peripherical regions, such as Latin America, may not only be the target of IA-guided military technologies but also serve as both a repository of data and a site for beta-testing, which can potentially reinforce biases and impose particular codes of conduct based on the kind of behavior that will be interpreted by IA as normal or threatening (Mohamed et al. 2020).

The second phenomenon observed is the return of interstate tensions. While in the early 1990s, the main debate was about the decrease in the number of wars between states as opposed to the intensification of intrastate conflicts, political researchers and analysts have recently turned their attention to the escalation of conflicts between countries. The conflict between Russia and Ukraine has shed light on old and new concerns about war, such as combat instruments, the involvement of extra-regional powers and the impacts on the global economy. The prolongation of the conflict is even a feature pointed out as a future trend of interstate disputes, especially when they involve the participation of great powers.

According to a report published by the Rand Corporation in 2022, conflicts between great powers could thus be protracted. Based on analyses of Western and Asian researchers, the report presents possible scenarios of a systemic conflict between the United States and China. One of the aspects raised is that the two powers would be involved in the form of conflict characterized by long duration and limited means and ends. In this scenario, other trends are listed, such as the change in international alliances and partners, the outbreak of economic and cyber wars, the increase in regional and global conflicts, the use of cyberspace as an environment of contestation, the competition for natural resources, among others (Heath, Gunness & Finazzo 2022).

The tension between great powers as a central concern for the future of international security might initially seem disconnected from the kind of violence and security issues circumscribed by the new wars and threats agendas. However, in past experiences, political pressures from great powers, specifically the United States, on Latin America to concentrate its military on domestic tasks, such as political dissidents, guerrilla groups and organized crime, have been associated with efforts to maintain the region as an area of influence, in the face of competing powers. For example, during the Cold War, there was a division of work, according to which the Latin American military was expected to quell domestic insurgencies, while the US was responsible for the global front. The new threats agenda is deemed to have perpetuated the same logic based on different security issues (Saint-Pierre 2011). Therefore, the current international tensions might similarly promote the continuous blurring between crime and war in the region, drawing upon non-state violence groups. Moreover, the great powers also transpose their disputes to the region, supporting opposing social and political groups, which might escalate intraregional rivalry and the risk of interstate conflicts.

Lastly, concerns about environmental depletion permeate future imaginaries about conflicts and their prevention possibilities, which were already present in the debate on new threats. For example, climate change is seen as a high-impact megatrend in escalating conflicts (Mustasilta 2021). Although its effects are global, some regions and countries are afflicted more sharply and/or do not obtain the instruments (economic and political) needed to address them. Increasing temperatures and the occurrence of prolonged droughts and floods are some of the effects already felt by humanity, which can lead to confrontations, whether between civil groups and state forces or between governments for the control of scarce natural resources.

The scarcity of natural resources generates a race for new energy sources, food, water and minerals, which involves governments, international extractive companies and transnational criminal groups. Both developing and underdeveloped countries are at the center stage for the action of those groups. Latin American countries, for example, are important routes for the international trafficking of animals and natural resources, which help finance other criminal activities, such as the production and smuggling of drugs and weapons and human trafficking. The exploitation of natural and mineral resources may also fuel conflicts between non-state armed groups, governments and indigenous peoples. The latter, as well as peasants, face violence from criminal and paramilitary groups who want to exploit their lands to achieve economic benefits (such as those groups that act to serve the interests of large mining companies and multinationals in the oil sector) (Svampa 2019). This violence, in turn, might reinforce patterns of state militarization of territories and, consequently, armed confrontations and insecurity.

Final remarks

Security studies and policies are permeated by attempts to identify future threats or developments in military technology. The process of constructing and disseminating images of the future is not only informed by interpretations of past and present events but also constitutive of identities, interests and behavior patterns. That was the case with the new wars and threats agenda, which were characterized by the division between where the future is imagined – at least the dominant images – and where the consequent policies took place, i.e. the Global North and the Global South, respectively, as well as who is entitled to address local or global security concerns.

In Latin America, by framing non-state armed groups as the pressing future to be tackled, this dynamic favored an acritical appropriation of concepts, tactics and military doctrines produced at and for other realities, which encouraged the blurred lines between public security and military defence, criminal and political violence, as well as reinforced a historical trend in the region: directing the states' instruments of lethality inwards (Succi Junior & Soares 2017). As a result, Latin American countries lead the world rankings for violence, incarceration and homicide. Moreover, the target groups of these policies continue to be poor young people, black men and women and indigenous populations, demonstrating the colonial, racist and gendered profile of such concepts and doctrines.

Recent appraisals of the future of security matters, highlighting autonomous weapons, renewed interstate tensions and environmental depletion, seem to reinforce the same logic, where the security issues to be addressed in the future are non-conventional uses of violence, and the suitable response is increasing state firepower directed to them. This requires Global South countries to imagine future threats and security policies based on their experiences and priorities.

Notes

1 We are grateful to Jonathan de Araujo de Assis, Kimberly Digolin, Lívia Milani, Luiza Elena Januário, Mariana Janot and Raquel Gontijo, members of the Group for Elaboration of Scenarios and Future Studies of São Paulo State University for the workshops.
2 It is important to point out that there was not a consensus about this change in the security studies. There was a fragmentation of the debate in three schools: "traditionalists, who want to retain a largely military focus; wideners, who want to extend the range of issues on the security agenda; and the […] Critical Security Studies, whose proponents want to cultivate a more questioning attitude to the whole framework in which security is conceptualized" (Buzan 1997, p. 5).
3 The themes were: "social and environmental vulnerabilities"; "organized delinquency and public insecurity"; "terrorism, weapons of mass destruction and cyber-attacks"; and "traditional threats, visualized from the military and defense scope" (Hamilton 2020, p. 122).

References

Andreas, P 2011, 'Illicit Globalization: Myths, Misconceptions, and Historical Lessons', *Political Science Quarterly*, vol. 126, no. 3. pp. 403–25, https://doi.org/10.1002/j.1538-165X.2011.tb00706.x.

Andreas, P & Price, R 2001, 'From War Fighting to Crime Fighting: Transforming the American National Security State', *International Studies Review*, vol. 3, no. 3, pp. 31–52, https://doi.org/10.1111/1521–9488.00243

Anzelini, L 2019, 'Between Discourse and Effective Action: The Contradictions of Macri's Defense Policy', *Revista Científica General José María Córdova*, vol. 17, no. 25, pp. 68–90, https://doi.org/10.21830/19006586.386.

Arkin, R C 2010, 'The Case for Ethical Autonomy in Unmanned Systems', *Journal of Military Ethics*, vol. 9, no. 4, pp. 332–41, https://doi.org/10.1080/15027570.2010.536402

Baldwin, D A 1995, 'Security Studies and the End of the Cold War', *World Politics*, vol. 48, no. 1, pp. 117–41, <https://www.jstor.org/stable/25053954> (accessed 2 May 2022).

Ballestrin, L M A 2021, 'Para uma Abordagem Feminista e Pós-Colonial das Relações Internacionais no Brasil', in A Toledo (ed), *Perspectivas Pós-Coloniais E Decoloniais em Relações Internacionais*, EDUFBA, Salvador, pp. 179–204.

Battaglino, J 2019, 'Threat Construction and Military Intervention in Internal Security: The Political Use of Terrorism and Drug Trafficking in Contemporary Argentina', *Latin American Perspectives*, vol. 46, no. 6, pp. 10–24, https://doi.org/10.1177/0094582X19858680

Beier, J M 2020, 'Short Circuit: Retracing the Political for the Age of 'Autonomous' Weapons', *Critical Military Studies*, vol. 6, no. 1, pp. 1–18, https://doi.org/10.1080/23337486.2017.1384978

Bousquet, A J 2009, *The Scientific Way of Warfare: Order and Chaos on the Battlefields of Modernity*, Oxford University Press, Oxford.

Brasil 2018a, 'Câmara dos Deputados, Ata Da 6a Sessão', *Diário Da Câmara Dos Deputados*.

Brasil 2018b, 'Senado Federal, Ata Da 11a Sessão', *Diário Do Senado Federal*, no. 10.

Brasil 2021, *Ministério da Defesa, Portaria* EME/C Ex nº 623, 24 December.

Buzan, B 1997, 'Rethinking Security After the Cold War', *Cooperation and Conflict*, vol. 32, no. 1, pp. 5–28, https://doi.org/10.1177/0010836797032001001

Campos, R 1994, 'Crime Sem Castigo', *O Globo*, 6 January.

Cantanhêde, E 2010, 'Cerco Ao Inimigo', *Folha de S. Paulo*, 26 November.

Cockayne, J 2007, *Transnational Organized Crime: Multilateral Responses to a Rising Threat*, Coping with Crisis – Working Paper Series, International Peace Academy, New York.

Del Olmo, R 1991, 'The Hidden Face of Drugs', *Social Justice*, vol. 18, no. 4, pp. 10–48.

Donadelli, L M 2018, 'Segurança Multidimensional', in H L Saint-Pierre & M G Vitelli (eds), *Dicionário de Segurança e Defesa*, Editora Unesp Digital, São Paulo, pp. 1071–9.

Dubeux, A, Rothenburg, D & Cavalcanti, L 2018, ' "Não Há Guerra Que Não Seja Letal", Diz Torquato Jardim Ao Correio', *Correio Braziliense*, 20 February.

Edwards, A & Gill, P (eds) 2003, *Transnational Organised Crime: Perspectives on Global Security*, Routledge, London.

Fernandes, R C 2018, 'Intervenção e Liberdade Nas Favelas', *O Globo*, 3 March.

Freedman, L 2017, *The Future of War: A History*, Public Affairs, New York.

Fukuyama, F 2006, *The End of History and the Last Man*, Simon and Schuster, New York.

Garcia, E V 2019, 'The Militarization of Artificial Intelligence: A Wake-Up Call for the Global South', *SSRN*, https://doi.org/10.2139/ssrn.3452323.

Goldman, E O 2001, 'New Threats, New Identities and New Ways of War: The Sources of Change in National Security Doctrine', *The Journal of Strategic Studies*, vol. 24, no. 2, pp. 43–76, https://doi.org/10.1080/01402390108565554.

Goulding Jr, V J 2000, 'Back to the Future with Asymmetric Warfare', *Parameters*, vol. 30, no. 4, pp. 21–30, https://doi.org/10.55540/0031-1723.2005.

Graham, S 2011, *Cities Under Siege: The New Military Urbanism*, Verso Books, New York.

Graham, S 2009, 'The Urban "Battlespace"', *Theory, Culture & Society*, vol. 26, no. 7–8, pp. 278–88, https://doi.org/10.1177/0263276409349280.

Hamilton, M 2020, 'Relaciones Cívico-Militares: Reflexiones Críticas y Multidimensionales Para el Hemisferio', *Seguridad, Ciencia & Defensa*, vol. 6, no. 6, pp. 118–30, <http://35.190.156.69/index.php/rscd/article/view/79> (accessed 29 April 2022).

Hamlet, M E 1998, *Military Operations on Urban Terrain (MOUT), The Key to Training Combat Forces for the Twenty-First Century*, Army Command and General Staff College, Fort Leavenworth, KS.

Heath, T R, Gunness, K & Finazzo, T 2022, *The Return of Great Power War: Scenarios of Systemic Conflict Between the United States and China*, RAND Corporation, Santa Monica, CA.

Herz, M 2002, 'Política de Segurança dos EUA Para a América Latina Após o Final da Guerra Fria', *Estudos Avançados*, vol. 16, no. 46, pp. 85–104, https://doi.org/10.1590/S0103-40142002000300007.

Kaldor, M 2012, *New and Old Wars: Organised Violence in a Global Era*, 3rd edn, Polity, Cambridge, MA.

Kaplan, R D 2002, *The Coming Anarchy: Shattering the Dreams of the Post Cold War*, Vintage, New York.

Ledebur, K & Youngers, C A 2018, *Promoviendo Políticas de Drogas con Enfoque de Género en Bolivia*, Washington Office on Latin America, Washington, DC.

Levine, H G 2003, 'Global Drug Prohibition: Its Uses and Crises', *International Journal of Drug Policy*, vol. 14, pp. 145–53, https://doi:10.1016/S0955-3959(03)00003-3.

Levy, R 1994, 'Intervenção Já', *Folha de S. Paulo*, 1 November.

Linz, J & Stepan, A 1999, *Transição e Consolidação da Democracia: A Experiência do sul da Europa e da América do Sul*, Paz e Terra, São Paulo.

Mohamed, S, Png, M T & Isaac, W 2020, 'Decolonial AI: Decolonial Theory as Sociotechnical Foresight in Artificial Intelligence', *Philosophy & Technology*, vol. 33, no. 4, pp. 659–84, https://doi.org/10.1007/s13347-020-00405-8.

Mustasilta, K 2021, *The Future of Conflict Prevention: Preparing for a Hotter, Increasingly Digital and Fragmented 2030*, EU Institute for Security Studies, Paris.

Neocleous, M 2011, 'A Brighter and Nicer New Life: Security as Pacification', *Social & Legal Studies*, vol. 20, no. 2, p. 191–208, https://doi.org/10.1177/0964663910395816.

Paley, D 2014, *Drug War Capitalism*, AK Press, Chico, CA.

Peters, R 1996, 'Our Soldiers, Their Cities', *Parameters*, vol. 26, no. 1, pp. 43–50, https://doi.org/10.55540/0031-1723.1768.

Rodrigues, T 2012, 'Narcotráfico e Militarização nas Américas: Vício de Guerra', *Contexto Internacional*, vol. 34, no. 1, pp. 9–41, https://doi.org/10.1590/S0102-85292012000100001.

Rouquié, A 1984, *O Estado Militar na América Latina*, Editora Alfa Omega, São Paulo.

Sain, M F 2018, '¿Los Militares Como Policías?: Cambios en la Seguridad en Argentina, 2013–2018', *Nueva Sociedad*, vol. 278, pp. 36–47.

Saint-Pierre, H L 2011, '"Defesa" ou "Segurança"?: Reflexões em Torno de Conceitos e Ideologias', *Contexto Internacional*, vol. 33, no. 2, pp. 407–33, https://doi.org/10.1590/S0102-85292011000200006.

Salazar Ortuño, F B 2008, *De la Coca al Poder: Políticas Públicas de Sustitución de la Economía de la Coca y Pobreza en Bolivia, 1975–2004*, CLACSO, Buenos Aires.

Salim de Castro, H 2020, 'The Drug Policy in the Americas From a Gender Perspective', in H E Vanden & G Prevost (eds), *The Oxford Encyclopedia of Latin American Politics*, Oxford University Press, Oxford, https://doi.org/10.1093/acrefore/9780190228637.013.1738.

Santos, T 2018, *Levantamento Nacional de Informações Penitenciárias*, 2nd edn, Ministério da Justiça e Segurança Pública, Brasilia.

Shelley, L 1995, 'Transnational Organized Crime: An Imminent Threat to the Nation-State?', *Journal of International Affairs*, vol. 48, no. 2, pp. 463–89, <https://www.jstor.org/stable/24357599?seq=1> (accessed 6 May 2022).

Souza, A B, Silva, A M D, Moraes, L E S & Chirio, M (eds) 2017, *Pacificar o Brasil: Das Guerras Justas Às UPPs*, Alameda Casa Editorial, São Paulo.

Succi Junior, D P & Soares, S A 2017, 'A Hibridização das Forças Armadas no Brasil: As Missões Policializadas e as Debilidades Democráticas e Estratégicas', in M Gaspardo (ed), *Globalização e os Fundamentos da Cidadania*, Alameda, São Paulo, pp. 201–31.

Svampa, M 2019, *As Fronteiras do Neoextrativismo na América Latina: Conflitos Socioambientais, Giro Ecoterritorial e Novas Dependências*, trans. L. Azevedo, Elefantes, São Paulo.

UNODC 2018, *World Drug Report 2018. Women and Drugs: Drug Use, Drug Supply, and Their Consequences*, United Nations Office on Drugs and Crime, Vienna.

UNODC 2019. *Global Study on Homicide 2019*, United Nations Office on Drugs and Crime, Vienna.

Van Creveld, M 1991, *Transformation of War*, The Free Press, New York.

Villa, R 2009, 'A Securitização, o Overlapping das Guerras às Drogas e ao Terror, na Agenda de Segurança dos Estados Unidos: caso Colômbia', in R M Nasser (ed), *Os Conflitos Internacionais em Múltiplas Dimensões*, Unesp, São Paulo, pp. 191–201.

Williams, P 1994, 'Transnational Criminal Organisations and International Security', *Survival*, vol. 36, no. 1, pp. 315–35, https://doi.org/10.1080/00396339408442726.

39

SAVAGE WARS AND CONFLICT DEHUMANIZATION

Paweł Ścigaj

Introduction

This chapter explores the idea that dehumanization plays a key role in justifying violence and mobilizing violent acts in regular and irregular conflicts. Moreover, in irregular conflicts, dehumanization is especially significant because of its role in forming a specific type of conflict awareness that impedes potential strategies for achieving resolution and reconciliation. The importance of conflict dehumanization will increase in the future with reference to the emerging transformations of international and regional security. The key to further efforts to reduce the degree of dehumanization effects in 'savage wars' is to understand and implement mechanisms of rehumanization.

On 'savage wars'

120 years ago, Rudyard Kipling, in the poem *The White Man's Burden,* encouraged the colonization and enlightening of the Philippines through 'savage wars of peace'. His words expressed the then-common racist conviction that there was a qualitative difference between a white and non-white man, and subsequently between 'civilized wars' – waged by the countries that follow the rules, are moral, lawful and have a mission to civilize the world – and 'savage wars' in which the backward, uncivilized parties are unable to harness cruelty and have an inclination towards violence (Slotkin 1998). Such 'savage wars' were sometimes referred to as 'small wars', for they were different to conventional conflicts of the time as it was difficult to pinpoint the strategical and tactical moves of the combatants. Massive armed clashes were absent or rare, and the strength of an enemy's armed forces was frequently unknown.

Civilizing 'the savage' or 'half-civilized races' has deep roots (Bowden 2010); however, in the 19th and at the beginning of the 20th century, this was usually presented as a form of mutiny and guerrilla suppression, colonial conquest or colonial punitive expedition (Gray 1999, p. 275). Later on, the 'savage war' category was used in the descriptions of military operations carried out without war principles and atrocities related to this, which took place especially during civil wars – including the American Civil War (Murray & Hsieh 2016) – or conflicts and liberation wars in colonies (Horne 2006), to present their atypicality when it came to military operations both at the level of the actors involved and the measures undertaken. The concept of 'savage wars' also

DOI: 10.4324/9781003299011-46

pictured harmful stereotypes and clichés, with the actors perceived and presented as savage and brutal (McDougall 2005) – often based on the belief of white supremacy and colonial discrimination (Shor 2019, pp. 9–21).

In the 20th century and the post-Cold War period, small wars and savage wars changed – as did conventional wars. Apart from the unambiguously negative (as well as dehumanizing) overtone of the notion of 'savage wars' and the normative premises of 'small wars', today these conflicts would be called 'asymmetric', as well as 'wars of the flea', 'guerrilla wars' or 'low-intensity conflicts'. Obviously, these are not synonyms, and their semantic relationships are complex and ambiguous. However, it may be said that they are related – as understood by Wittgenstein. Eventually, all of them refer to actions often carried out by enemies of asymmetric strength, and there are usually no typical military operations involving a clash between trained and organized soldiers. These conflicts differ from conventional wars because of the nature of the fighting and the forces involved, but not because of the scale of destruction, atrocities, consequences for the civilians, etc. – for these may be enormous (Gray 1999, p. 273).

'Savage wars of peace' may literally last a few days or decades and may involve better or worse organized small or quite large groups of armed forces, usually comprised of illegitimate and internationally unrecognized political and military actors. It is often unclear what their battlefield is, who participates in fighting, who is an ally and who is an adversary, and there are no clearly indicated winners. These include punitive, protective, pacification and profiteering conflicts (Boot 2002), most often aimed (by international legitimized actors who intervene) at conflict reduction, creating the conditions for population development and supporting and maintaining peace, as well as promoting the rule of law and democracy (Fishel 1998a). Hence, 'savage wars of peace' should be fought according to three pragmatic rules: to do no harm, to achieve political legitimacy and to promote democracy (Fishel 1998b), thereby making them a mirror of a peacekeeping operation to maintain international security. As a result, in these kinds of operations aimed at combating 'savage wars' the real adversary is a violent conflict in itself, not an enemy army or population (Last 1998), and accidental civilian casualties do not result from the warfare but from peace efforts (Brewster 2011).

Bearing in mind the above, I mean by 'savage wars' conflicts in which the fighting is waged by irregular armed forces of non-state actors, there are no conventional military operations, and military, strategic and tactical goals are often undefined. Moreover, in savage wars, it is difficult to indicate a clear difference between service members and civilians, and international law covering armed conflicts and international humanitarian law are not respected. Instead, there is acquiescence to, and even a cult of, violence, atrocity, rape, torture and murder. Savage wars defined in this manner lead, like small wars, to many important ethical and legal questions related to the definition of an enemy soldier, the possibility of separating armed forces from civilians, the application of the law on conventional armed conflicts or holding war criminals accountable. The problem is that irregular armed forces of non-state actors in small wars do not respect the law of armed conflicts and international humanitarian law (Sitaraman 2013). This is what makes them savage wars.

On dehumanization

What distinguishes savage wars from conventional wars is not so much the scale of total combat losses, but civilian casualties and various manifestations of violence, atrocities and mass killing. In recent decades, this has been observed in numerous conflicts around the world, e.g. Rwanda, Somalia, Sierra Leone, Mali, Afghanistan, Syria, Libya and many others. A significant problem here concerns the question of mobilization for violence and its legitimization. Dave Grossman explicitly specified this problem in a reflection on the mechanisms that enable soldiers to commit acts that are (in his opinion) unusual and contradictory to 'human nature', but necessary for the effectiveness of military operations (i.e. instrumental killing) (Grossman 1996). And even if Grossman's argument about the 'unnatural' nature of killing is problematic – only because of the results of research on the evolutionary foundations of violence and war – the question of the factors that facilitate coping with the burden of killing is crucial. Among them, dehumanization has a very important place, and it is worth looking at it briefly before presenting examples of its presence in savage wars.

For several decades, dehumanization studies have flourished in many fields of scholarship, including security studies, social psychology, sociology, economics, pedagogy, feminist studies, postcolonial studies, communication studies, psychiatry and many others. In this broad scope of research, dehumanization mainly appears in four basic contexts. First, as a phenomenon of group perception, dehumanization is defined as the perception of others as being less human or inhuman. Second, these images of others are found in the discourse, in dehumanizing language that takes away human characteristics from others through metaphors and in comparison to animals (e.g. cockroaches, pigs), mechanical figures (e.g. robots, automatons), objects, monsters (e.g. beasts), demons (e.g. evil, Satan), medical or sanitary issues (e.g. cancer, disease, dirt, rot, poison) and others. Such metaphors may also refer to glorification (i.e. to deprive someone of humanity leading to apparent exaltation) or superhumanization (e.g. becoming angelic). Third, certain harmful behaviours are also considered to be a form of dehumanization (e.g. torture). And fourth, certain living conditions, features of social phenomena, structures and institutions within which life becomes inhumane (e.g., slavery, work in an industrial society, psychiatric hospitals or the modern battlefield) (Smith 2011; Kronfeldner 2021).

The commonness of dehumanization in conflicts with direct violence is widely, though not uncritically, accepted (Over 2021). However, apart from that, it also appears in conflicts characterized by structural and cultural violence (Galtung 1996, pp. 196–208). Thus, dehumanization enables the use of physical force, including killing, permanent exclusion of a group of people from various sorts of possibilities and the acceptance of a vision of a social order in which some people are permanently perceived as inferior. What connects all uses of dehumanization as a justification for violence is the context in which power is being wielded or, more precisely, the fact that it is always associated with the possibility of using another person instrumentally, deciding upon their fate, disregarding their opinion, etc. This is regardless of whether dehumanization is explicit or subtle, whether it is intended to lower or elevate one's position, whether it is serious or ironic, or whether is intended to be either an insult or not.

Crucial theoretical frameworks for dehumanization research derive from social psychology (Smith 2016, pp. 419). Some theories are focused on dehumanization functions in justifying violence – mainly through the removal of others from the community or moral exclusion (Kelman 1973; Opotow 1990), their delegitimization (Bar-Tal 1989, p. 170), and the use of dehumanizing labels and metaphors (Bandura, Underwood & Fromson 1975). Moreover, the pioneering research of Jacques-Philippe Leyens et al. allowed for the automatic phenomenon of *infrahumanization* to be described as a decrease of the humanity of out-groups by associating primary emotions with them but denying them secondary ones (Leyens et al. 2000). A few years later, Nick Haslam noticed that infrahumanization was a form of animalistic dehumanization in which others were denied uniquely human features, such as civility, moral sensibility or rationality. The second form of dehumanization is mechanistic, when others are perceived as lacking human nature (e.g., responsiveness, interpersonal warmth, cognitive openness). On an emotional level, the first relates to disgust and contempt, the latter to disregard and indifference (Haslam 2006). Numerous studies based on Haslam's theory have shown that dehumanization may lead to a decrease in prosocial be-haviour (e.g. refusal to help, decreased level of empathy) and an increase in anti-social behaviour (e.g. aggression, willingness to impose severe punishments). This changes the moral assessment of the dehumanized people and may be functional in medicine (e.g. dehumanization of patients). Dehumanization also correlates positively with right-wing authoritarianism and the social domi-nance orientation (Haslam & Loughnan 2014).

Dehumanization is of great importance to military operations and appears in three key areas. First, dehumanization occurs in the context of mobilizing for and legitimizing violence and covers research on: (a) images of enemies that enable the overcoming of moral resistance to violence and killing, including research on the language that allows an effective transition from military action to post-conflict activities, as well as bringing peace. Mechanistic or 'neutral' categories, such as 'target', or 'object' allow for avoiding the negative and long-term effects of using animalistic categories in the form of contempt and disgust (French & Jack 2015; Wingrove-Haugland 2015, pp. 207–8; Kooistra & Mahoney 2016); (b) images of others in propaganda and ideologies that support and legitimize violence against the dehumanized victims of mass killing and enemies (Dower 1986; Hagan & Rymond-Richmond 2008; Tirrell 2012; Savage 2013); (c) mechanisms of self-dehumanization and their negative effects, for instance the occurrence of dissociative symp-toms, depersonalization, derealization, amnesia, loss of identity and the PTSD that is related to it (Group for the Advancement of Psychiatry 1964, pp. 235–8; Herzog et al. 2020), as well as some positive effects, for instance, group-building and mobilizing use of animalistic symbols (e.g. nu-merous birds, mammals or insects as the symbols of military units). It is also worth stressing that a certain level of self-dehumanization, like de-individualization or group thinking, seems necessary in military training, regardless of whether we are talking about regular or irregular armed forces (Moskalenko 2010).

Second, dehumanization refers to changes caused mainly by technological advancements in warfare, including the possibility of using unmanned military vehicles and the 'disappearance' of the soldier from the battlefield (Heintschel von Heinegg, Frau & Singer 2018), the moral and legal responsibility of drone operators and the right to use violence without being in mortal danger (Asaro 2012; Chamayou 2015). The problem of dehumanization also appears *à rebours* in research on the superhumanization of soldiers and their strengthening through pharmacology and technol-ogy (Kamieński 2017; Caron 2018). Third and finally, dehumanization is present in harmful be-haviour, especially acute direct violence, rape, bullying or torture, that emphasizes the inhumane nature of such actions, as well as the need to dehumanize both parties – those who are harmed and those who harm.

Dehumanizing the 'other' in savage wars

There are too many examples of dehumanizing metaphors in savage conflicts. In Rwanda, Tutsi were commonly referred to as 'cockroaches', but other animalistic categories (e.g. 'hyenas', 'go-rillas') were also used with reference to Hutu. Sanitary and gardening metaphors calling for clean-ing, pulling out weeds and cutting shrubs were commonplace too (Higiro 2007). In Sierra Leone, rebels were called 'wicked animals' and 'devils' (Mitton 2012, p. 110). In Darfur, the dehumaniza-tion of the native population was racially motivated by assigning labels such as 'nuba', 'slaves', 'dogs', and 'monkeys'. (Hagan & Rymond-Richmond 2008, p. 882). Most often, dehumanization was not only instrumentally induced, but also deeply rooted in cultures and the history of the conflict, and sometimes supported by stimulants, drugs and other means that facilitate murder (Mitton 2015).

Many similar examples of dehumanization may be found in the politics and discourses of states involved in savage conflicts. After all, there is no doubt that regardless of ethical reasons – compliance with international law, civilian involvement, the type of actor and the degree of their legitimation, etc. – dehumanization is mutual in every conflict. The aim of such propaganda is usually the delegitimization of claims of the others. The outcome represents a double stigma for the victims of being inferior and without any rights (Merom 2003, p. 78). The lexicon of dehumanizing terms is similar as before and it has been observed in many conflicts (e.g. in Egypt, Vietnam, Somalia and others) where the enemies were, for instance, 'wog', 'gook' or 'skinny' (Butt, Lukin & Matthiessen 2004, p. 287; French 2012, p. 747); Chechens were called 'cockroaches' or 'bedbugs' by the Russian propaganda (Winslow, Moelker & Companjen 2013, p. 130), Rhodesian guerrillas were 'primitive *magandanga*' (Evans 2007, p. 186). It is also interesting and depressing that sometimes dehumanizing metaphors are disseminated by the media in highly developed countries. For instance, Rwandan refugees have been described in some American magazines as being little better than animals, as 'swarm people' who are like 'a tide', a 'flood' and are helpless or even pathetic (Wall 2007, pp. 267–8). Again, this is not an isolated situation, especially regarding metaphors associated with refugees. It is worth recalling that the term 'savage wars' may be treated as dehumanizing itself. More precisely, barbarism and savagery in infrahumanization theory are a sort of animalization and, as such, evoke persistent feelings of distance and disgust. In this sense, 'savage war' may be understood as an expression of the feeling of superiority, domination and power of 'the civilized' over 'the savage'.

Dehumanizing metaphors are a key element in the mobilization of violence. Many researchers indicate that they are a necessary, though insufficient, condition for mass murder (Savage 2013); however, the discussion continues (see Lang 2010). Nevertheless, no one disputes the fact that dehumanizing, derogatory terms are at the core of the language of the eliminationist ideologies that divide the world into 'ours' and 'theirs' (Tirrell 2012, pp. 190–3) – by justifying violence, especially killing, by redefining norms, so that acts of wrongdoing were not immoral, or by showing violence as just and necessary in the struggle for the survival of the in-group (Savage 2013, pp. 144–54). Using the example of the genocide in Rwanda and the Holocaust, Maria Armoudian says that murders are always preceded by hateful communication. At their source lies the language of social division, with harm and hostility resulting in the creation of the circumstances necessary for mass killing. Therefore, frames composed of themes of demarcation like 'us-them', stereotypes of 'the others', perceived guilt, dehumanization and demonization of others are important, along with the necessity to kill out of self-defence and noble purposes (Armoudian 2020, pp. 145–6). On a collective level, dehumanizing language and propaganda legitimize internalized hatred of group members (and the legitimacy and perceived justice of mass killing); they are the result of the activity of political leaders and dehumanizing discourse and narratives that enable the transition from individual to collective intentions. This was also clearly seen in the conflict in Darfur, where dehumanizing language, amplified by the perception of Arabian supremacy, resulted in mass murder (Hagan & Rymond-Richmond 2008).

It is worth adding that an important element that distinguishes savage wars from conventional armed conflicts is also the situation of the civilians, especially women and children, who are often subject to harmful and dehumanizing activities sometimes designed and implemented institutionally. An instance of this is the activities of the Dinka tribe in South Sudan, where – at the training stage for members of the Sudan People's Liberation Army (SPLA) – soldiers were prepared for ethnic discrimination and the use of violence against civilians, including burning people in their homes, beating them to death, forcing victims to eat the flesh of their relatives thrown into the fire, to drink the blood of the deceased and to sexually abuse women from other ethnic groups

– including rape, forced marriage and trafficking (Pinaud 2021). In Somalia, there are also examples of persecution and kidnapping of civilians that result from the perception of others as sinful, inhuman and inferior. The oppression of the civilians taken by Mohamed Farrah Aidid's combatants resulted also in the dehumanizing of the conflict (e.g., Kaempf 2012, pp. 395–6).

A special place among dehumanizing behaviours is sexual violence, including rape, sexual slavery, forced prostitution, impregnation, abortion, sterilization, forced marriage and more. Sexual violence is even treated as a deliberate genocidal activity (such as that in Rwanda) and is certainly common and accepted by non-state actors in savage wars. Examples may be found in the history of conflicts in the DRC, South Sudan, Darfur and Uganda (see Fredrick Fredrick & The AWARE Committee of Rape 2001; Brown 2012; Pinaud 2021, pp. 205–8). Sexual violence also leads to further discrimination and social exclusion by communities that perceive raped women and their children born of rape as unclean or cursed (Totten 2014, p. 171). The dehumanization of children and the abuse of them while in the military are also characteristic of some savage wars. Child soldiers in conflicts in Africa are portrayed as innocent, naive and forced to serve, but also as 'demons', 'bandits', 'monsters' or 'vermin' (Drumbl 2012, pp. 6–8).

Dehumanization in savage wars most often affects close, neighbouring, coexisting groups that have usually lived together for many centuries. Just like in cases of genocide, bystanders and perpetrators of mass killings are generally 'ordinary' citizens (Dutton 2007). This is perhaps most clearly demonstrated by the research on mass murder in Rwanda, where the proximity of victims and executioners – defined in terms of social distance – was closer and correlated more strongly with dehumanization than in the case of Central and Eastern Europe during World War II (Haagensen & Croes 2012).

From dehumanization to rehumanization?

The brutality and cruelty of savage wars often lead to deep social divisions and widespread hostility, which are then reproduced in successive generations. Dehumanization is even less conducive to reconciliation and hinders post-conflict actions undertaken in the aftermath of small wars and peacekeeping operations. This opens up a space for rehumanization activities. The fight against the negative social consequences of a conflict may take two main forms: the first consists of attempts to restore the elements that make up the social order, including the normative order and values in existence before the conflict and prior to the emergence of the violence justified by dehumanization. Such actions are rather ineffective – they usually restore a social order that is still characterized by all the same divisions and issues that originated the conflict, which might therefore reopen the space for new conflict.

The second approach is to take active steps to change the perceptions of hostile groups and support reconciliation through judicial and extrajudicial tools such as the organization of special tribunals and the prosecution of perpetrators, thereby enabling the investigation of the truth, reparations, institutional and legal initiatives, amnesty, as well as unusual cultural activities (e.g., literature, music, comics). These must always take into account the experiences of the suffering of others and be based on empathy and high 'conflict sensitivity' rooted in cultural, historical and socio-political conditions (Halpern & Weinstein 2004; Haider 2017). On the psychological level, most rehumanization activities use (not always directly) or are inspired by the 'contact hypothesis' or Intergroup Contact Theory. They are undertaken to reduce inter-group hostility through face-to-face, interpersonal contact under planned and specific conditions, especially in terms of equality of status, common goals, the support of authorities and inter-group cooperation (e.g., Gobodo-Madikizela 2002; Cameron 2007). Rehumanization can also be achieved by using techniques based on theories developed in the Social Identity Approach framework (especially the Common Identity In-Group Model), which is targeted at building inclusive identities. Interventions undertaken in Rwanda are a good example; here, in order to stress the intragroup character of the conflict and reduce hostility, the opposed categories of Hutu and Tutsi were replaced by the common category of Rwandan or 'human' (Aoki & Jonas 2016).

Forecasts and predictions

Looking at the geopolitical situation in the year 2022 and the potential hotspots and possible conflicts at the global, regional and local levels, the future of savage wars seems to be complex and involves the presence of both existing and new phenomena. There is no indication that their number or the role of dehumanization in them will decrease. Undoubtedly, dehumanization will continue to play a mobilizing and legitimizing role in violence, while the violence itself will continue to take the most radical forms, including rape, slavery, torture, the use of child soldiers, massacres of civilians and many more. In other words, there is no hope that savage wars will disappear, just as there is no hope that they will stop being 'savage'.

What seems new, and what may be significant for the future of savage wars, are the following issues. First, the war in Ukraine opens up new possibilities for the barbarization of conventional wars. The conflict widely recognized as a conventional war is perceived otherwise by one of the parties, in this case Russia, which refuses to abide by the international code of conduct for armed conflicts, including the rights of soldiers and the protection of civilians. A similar move by China against Taiwan, North Korea against South Korea or various other territorial conflicts in the world may start a new era in the barbarization of war and threaten the global security system. Paradoxically, the barbarization of war may become a way of increasing the effectiveness of actions and may avoid the limitations imposed on the states. States may instrumentally exploit this new type of savage war where one of the combating sides or both of them refuse to recognize a conflict as a war, limited by the laws governing armed conflict and international humanitarian law. The purposes may be various: to unilaterally 'resolve' territorial disputes, to 'deal' with political, ethnic, religious or other 'opponents', to 'prepare' the ground for negotiations, to 'persuade' international actors to acknowledge the new status quo as if it had been achieved as a result of 'internal' decisions as if no war was ever waged. In this way, it is possible to achieve useful goals for the 'ghost aggressor', including those which are military (e.g. destruction of the enemy's forces, demobilization), social (e.g. disintegration, erosion of social norms, radicalization of attitudes, exacerbation of social divisions), political (e.g. authorities delegitimization, political leaders' creation), economic (e.g. destroying infrastructure, lowering GDP) or other types. A clear example here is once again the war in Ukraine and Russia's efforts to present it as an inside problem of the 'Russian world'.

Second, while there is no indication that future savage wars will be less brutal and that there will be less dehumanization involved in them, the means of expression and representation are likely to change. The pornography of violence and dehumanization, which is characteristic of such conflicts nowadays, will most likely develop in two ways (i.e., the further and more effective use of new forms of communication – including social media and other communication platforms – and the search for universal symbolic means to gain support and legitimacy among non-involved actors and their societies). An instance of the latter may be the use of a metaphor related to mythology and the popular fantasy world about the Russians and, therefore, to call them Orcs. This is an interculturally understandable category, especially in the Western civilization, and facilitates the understanding of and identifications made in a conflict.

Third, the application of new technologies to the warfare also has consequences for dehumanization in savage wars, and this is taking place on several levels. In this kind of conflict, combat strategies that exclude direct human participation are used. In this case, we are dealing with the same problems as in the broader discussion on the dehumanization of the warfare (i.e. the issue of accepting killing via unmanned military vehicles or the moral and legal abilities of drone operators). Moreover, what ought to be of concern is the possibility of the illegal and increasing use of new technologies in savage wars by non-state actors, especially for purposes beyond international law, such as terrorist attacks, fighting attacking civilians, and harassing and killing discriminated groups. In other words, there is a significant risk that in the future, as a result of the introduction of new technologies into the warfare, we will have to face new 'savage technologies'.

And finally, the number of savage wars as well as their long-lasting dramatic and traumatic effects like inter-group hostility, strong prejudices and negative emotions – especially disgust and contempt, leading to or reinforcing existing unsolvable conflicts as well as creating favourable conditions for people trafficking, uncontrolled arms trafficking, drug smuggling, terrorism and more – will continue to force initiatives for the improvement of existing mechanisms of reconciliation and propose new ones. Undoubtedly, an important place must be taken by techniques and tools for the rehumanization of the parties in savage wars, and this applies to both state and other actors.

References

Aoki, E & Jonas, K M 2016, 'Collective Memory and Sacred Space in Post-Genocide Rwanda: Reconciliation and Rehumanization Processes in Mureithi's ICYIZERE', *Journal of International and Intercultural Communication*, vol. 9, no. 3, pp. 240–58, https://doi.org/10.1080/17513057.2016.1195007.

Armoudian, M 2020, 'In Search of a Genocidal Frame: Preliminary Evidence from the Holocaust and the Rwandan Genocide', *Media, War & Conflict*, vol. 13, no. 2, pp. 133–52, https://doi.org/10.1177/1750635218810927.

Asaro, P 2012, 'On Banning Autonomous Weapon Systems: Human Rights, Automation, and the Dehumanization of Lethal Decision-Making', *International Review of the Red Cross*, vol. 94, no. 687–709, https://doi.org/10.1017/S1816383112000768.

Bandura, A, Underwood, B & Fromson, M E 1975, 'Disinhibition of Aggression Through Diffusion of Responsibility and Dehumanization of Victims', *Journal of Research in Personality, vol. 9*, no. 4, pp. 253–69, https://doi.org/10.1016/0092-6566(75)90001-X.

Bar-Tal, D 1989, 'Delegitimation. The Extreme Case of Stereotyping', in D Bar-Tal, C F Grauman, D Kruglanski & W Stroebe (eds), *Stereotyping and Prejudice: Changing Conceptions*, Springer-Verlag, New York, pp. 169–82.

Boot, M 2002, *The Savage Wars of Peace. Small Wars and the Rise of American Power*, Basic Books, New York.

Bowden, B 2010, 'Civilization and Savagery' in G Kassimeris & J Buckley (eds), *The Ashgate Research Companion to Modern Warfare*, Ashgate, Farnham – Burlington, VT, pp. 271–87.

Brewster, M 2011, *The Savage War: The Untold Battles of Afghanistan*, John Wiley & Sons, Mississauga.

Brown, C 2012, 'Rape as a Weapon of War in the Democratic Republic of the Congo', *Torture*, vol. 22, no. 1, pp. 24–37.

Butt, D G, Lukin, A & Matthiessen, C M I M 2004, 'Grammar – the First Covert Operation of War', *Discourse & Society*, vol. 15, no. 2–3, pp. 267–90, https://doi.org/10.1177/0957926504041020.

Cameron, L J 2007, 'Patterns of Metaphor Use in Reconciliation Talk', *Discourse & Society*, vol. 18, no. 2, pp. 197–222, https://doi.org/10.1177/0957926507073376.

Caron, J F 2018, *A Theory of the Super Soldier: The Morality of Capacity-Increasing Technologies in the Military*, Manchester University Press, Manchester.

Chamayou, G 2015, *A Theory of the Drone*, The New Press, New York-London.

Dower, J W 1986, *War Without Mercy. Race and Power in the Pacific War*, Pantheon Books, New York.

Drumbl, M A 2012, *Reimagining Child Soldiers in International Law and Policy*, Oxford University Press, Oxford & New York.

Dutton, D G 2007, *The Psychology of Genocide, Massacres, and Extreme Violence: Why 'Normal' People Come to Commit Atrocities*, Praeger Security International, Westport, CT.

Evans, M 2007, 'The Wretched of the Empire: Politics, Ideology and Counterinsurgency in Rhodesia, 1965–80', *Small Wars & Insurgencies*, vol. 18, no. 2, pp. 175–95, https://doi.org/10.1080/09574040701400601.

Fishel J T 1998a, 'War By Other Means? The Paradigm and its Applications to Peace Operations', in J T Fishel (ed), *"The Savage Wars of Peace": Toward a New Paradigm of Peace Operations*, Westview Press, Boulder, CO, pp. 21–39.

Fishel J T 1998b, 'Normative Implications of "The Savage Wars of Peace"', *Small Wars Insurgencies*, vol. 9, no. 1, pp. 102–13, https://doi.org/10.1080/09592319808423198.

Fredrick, S & The AWARE Committee of Rape 2001, *Rape: Weapon of Terror*, Global Publishing, River Edge, NJ.

French, D 2012, 'Nasty Not Nice: British Counter-Insurgency Doctrine and Practice, 1945–1967', *Small Wars & Insurgencies*, vol. 23, no. 4–5, pp. 744–61, https://doi.org/10.1080/09592318.2012.709763.

French S E & Jack, A I 2015, 'Dehumanizing the Enemy: The Intersection of Neuroethics and Military Ethics', in D Whetham & B J Strawser (eds), *Responsibilities to Protect. Perspectives in Theory and Practice*, Brill Nijhoff, Leiden & Boston, MA, pp. 169–95.

Galtung, J 1996, *Peace by Peaceful Means: Peace and Conflict, Development and Civilization*, Sage, London.

Gobodo-Madikizela, P 2002, 'Remorse, Forgiveness, and Rehumanization: Stories from South Africa', *Journal of Humanistic Psychology*, vol. 42, no. 1, pp. 7–32, https://doi.org/10.1177/0022167802421002.

Gray, C 1999, *Modern Strategy*, Oxford University Press, Oxford & New York.

Grossman, D 1996, *On Killing. The Psychological Cost of Learning to Kill in War and Society*, Back Bay Books / Little, Brown and Company, New York & Boston, MA.

Haagensen, L & Croes, M 2012, 'Thy Brother's Keeper? The Relationship between Social Distance and Intensity of Dehumanization during Genocide', *Genocide Studies and Prevention*, vol. 7, no. 2–3, pp. 223–50, https://doi.org/10.3138/gsp.7.2/3.223.

Hagan, J & Rymond-Richmond, W 2008, 'The Collective Dynamics of Racial Dehumanization and Genocidal Victimization in Darfur', *American Sociological Review, vol. 73, no.* 6, pp. 875–902, https://doi.org/10.1177/000312240807300601.

Haider, H 2017, 'Breaking the Cycle of Violence: Applying Conflict Sensitivity to Transitional Justice', *Conflict, Security & Development*, vol. 17, no. 4, pp. 335–60, https://doi.org/10.1080/14678802.2017.1337420.

Halpern, J & Weinstein, H M 2004, 'Rehumanizing the Other: Empathy and Reconciliation', *Human Rights Quarterly*, vol. 26, no. 3, pp. 561–83, https://doi.org/10.1353/hrq.2004.0036.

Haslam, N 2006, 'Dehumanization: An Integrative Review', *Personality and Social Psychology Review, vol. no. 3*, pp. 252–64, https://doi.org/10.1207/s15327957pspr1003_4.

Haslam, N & Loughnan, S 2014, 'Dehumanization and Infrahumanization', *Annual Review of Psychology*, vol. 65, pp. 399–423, https://doi.org/10.1146/annurev-psych-010213-115045.

Heintschel von Heinegg, W, Frau, R & Singer, T (eds) 2018, *Dehumanization of Warfare: Legal Implications of New Weapon Technologies*, Palgrave Macmillan, Cham.

Herzog, S, Fogle, B M, Harpaz-Rotem, I, Tsai, J & Pietrzak, R 2020, 'Dissociative Symptoms in a Nationally Representative Sample of Trauma-Exposed U.S. Military Veterans: Prevalence, Comorbidities, and Suicidality', *Journal of Affective Disorders*, vol. 272, pp. 138–45, https://doi.org/10.1016/j.jad.2020.03.177.

Higiro, J M V 2007, 'Rwandan Private Print Media on the Eve of the Genocide', in A Thompson (ed), *The Media and The Rwanda Genocide*, Pluto Press, London, pp. 73–89.

Horne, A 2006, *A Savage War of Peace: Algeria 1954–1962*, New York Review Book, New York.

Kaempf, S 2012, 'US warfare in Somalia and the Trade-Off between Casualty-Aversion and Civilian Protection', *Small Wars & Insurgencies*, vol. 23, no. 3, pp. 388–413, https://doi.org/10.1080/09592318.2012.661608.

Kamieński, Ł 2017, *Shooting Up: A History of Drugs in Warfare*, Hurst & Company, London.

Kelman, H C 1973, 'Violence Without Moral Restraint: Reflections on the Dehumanization of Victims and Victimizers', *Journal of Social Issues*, vol. 29, no. 4, pp. 25–61, https://doi.org/10.1111/j.1540-4560.1973.tb00102.x.

Kooistra, P G & Mahoney, J S 2016, 'The Road to Hell: Neutralization of Killing in War', *Deviant Behavior*, vol. 37, no. 7, pp. 761–83, https://doi.org/10.1080/01639625.2016.1140993.

Kronfeldner, M 2021, 'Introduction: Mapping Dehumanization Studies', in M Kronfeldner (ed), *The Routledge Handbook of Dehumanization*, Routledge, London & New York, pp. 1–36.

Lang, J 2010, 'Questioning Dehumanization: Intersubjective Dimensions of Violence in the Nazi Concentration and Death Camps', *Holocaust and Genocide Studies*, vol. 24, no. 2, pp. 225–46, https://doi.org/10.1093/hgs/dcq026.

Last, D M 1998, 'Winning the Savage Wars of Peace: What Manwaring Paradigm Tells Us', in J T Fishel (ed), *"The Savage Wars of Peace": Toward a New Paradigm of Peace Operations*, Westview Press, Boulder, CO, pp. 211–40.

Leyens, J-P, Paladino, M P, Rodriguez-Torres, R, Vaes, J, Demoulin, S, Rodriguez-Perez, A & Gaunt, R 2000, 'The Emotional Side of Prejudice: The Attribution of Secondary Emotions to Ingroups and Outgroups', *Personality and Social Psychology Review*, vol. 4, no. 2, pp. 186–97, https://doi.org/10.1207/S15327957PSPR0402_06.

Merom, G 2003, *How Democracies Lose Small Wars: State, Society, and the Failures of France in Algeria, Israel in Lebanon, and the United States in Vietnam*, Cambridge University Press, Cambridge.

McDougall, J 2005, 'Savage Wars? Codes of Violence in Algeria, 1830s–1990s', *Third World Quarterly*, vol. 26, no. 1, pp. 117–31, https://doi.org/10.1080/0143659042000322946.

Mitton, K 2012, 'Irrational Actors and the Process of Brutalisation: Understanding Atrocity in the Sierra Leonean Conflict (1991–2002)', *Civil Wars*, vol. 14, no. 1, pp. 104–22, https://doi.org/10.1080/13698249.2012.654691.

Mitton, K 2015, *Rebels in a Rotten State: Understanding Atrocity in the Sierra Leone Civil War*, Oxford University Press, Oxford & New York.

Moskalenko, S 2010, 'Civilians into Warriors: Mechanisms of Mobilization in US Army Recruitment and Training', *Dynamics of Asymmetric Conflict*, vol. 3, no. 3, pp. 248–68, https://doi.org/10.1080/17467586.2010.532562.

Murray, W & Hsieh, W 2016, *A Savage War: A Military History of the Civil War*, Princeton University Press, Princeton, NJ, https://doi.org/10.1515/9781400882908.

Opotow, S 1990, 'Moral Exclusion and Injustice: An Introduction', *Journal of Social Issues,* vol. 46, no. 1, pp. 1–20, https://doi.org/10.1111/j.1540-4560.1990.tb00268.x.

Over, H 2021, 'Seven Challenges for the Dehumanization Hypothesis', *Perspectives on Psychological Science*, vol. 16, no. 1, pp. 3–13, https://doi.org/10.1177/1745691620902133.

Pinaud, C 2021, *War and Genocide in South Sudan*, Cornell University Press, Ithaca, NY & London.

Group for the Advancement of Psychiatry 1964, *Psychiatric Aspects of the Prevention of Nuclear War. Formulated by the Committee on Social* Issues, vol. V, no. 57, <https://ourgap.org/Past-Reports> (accessed 2 September 2022).

Savage, R 2013, 'Modern Genocidal Dehumanization: A New Model', *Patterns of Prejudice*, vol. 47, no. 2, pp. 139–61, https://doi.org/10.1080/0031322X.2012.754575.

Shor, F 2019, *Weaponized Whiteness: The Constructions and Deconstructions of White Identity Politics*, Brill, Leiden & Boston, MA.

Sitaraman, G 2013, *The Counterinsurgent's Constitution: Law in the Age of Small Wars*, Oxford University Press, Oxford & New York.

Slotkin, R 1998, *The Fatal Environment: The Myth of the Frontier in the Age of Industrialization 1800–1890*, University of Oklahoma Press, Norman, OK.

Smith, D L 2011, *Less Than Human. Why We Demean, Enslave, and Exterminate Others*, St. Martin's Griffin, New York.

Smith, D L 2016, 'Paradoxes of Dehumanization', *Social Theory and Practice*, vol. 42, no. 2, pp. 416–43, https://doi.org/10.5840/soctheorpract201642222.

Tirrell, L 2012, 'Genocidal Language Games', in I Maitra & M K McGowan (eds), *Speech and Harm: Controversies over Free Speech*, Oxford University Press, Oxford, pp. 174–221.

Totten, S 2014, 'The Darfur Genocide: The Plight and Fate of the Black African Children', in S Totten (ed), *Plight and Fate of Children During and Following Genocide*, Routledge, Abingdon & New York, pp. 167–93.

Wall, M 2007, 'An Analysis of News Magazine Coverage of the Rwanda Crisis in the United States', in A Thompson (ed), *The Media and The Rwanda Genocide*, Pluto Press, London, pp. 261–73.

Wingrove-Haugland, E 2015, 'Moral Sensitivity and Dehumanization in the Military', in D Mower, W L Robison & P Vandenberg (eds), *Developing Moral Sensitivity*, Routledge, London & New York.

Winslow, D, Moelker, R & Companjen, F 2013, 'Glocal Chechnya from Russian sovereignty to pan-Islamic autonomy', *Small Wars & Insurgencies*, vol. 24, no. 1, pp. 129–51, https://doi.org/10.1080/09592318.2013.763655.

INDEX

Note: Page numbers followed by "n" denote endnotes.

Technology 322; National Intelligence
Strategy 274; National Reconnaissance
Office 327, 358; National Security Agency
324; Naval Institute 81; Navy 18, 32, 81,
125, 300, 312, 324, 357, 402; Navy SEAL
231, 344, 348; Office of Naval Research 79,
311; White House 125, 207, 355
universal jurisdiction 115–16
University of Amsterdam 162
University of Tübingen 34
unpredictability 12, 17, 212, 232
UN *see* United Nations
unpeace 3
Uppsala Data Conflict Program 422
urban: battlefield 434; battlespace 25, 167;
environment 54, 156, 173, 300, 314; guerilla
104; operations 337; spaces 104, 432, 437
UrbanSim 81
US *see* United States
USSR *see* Soviet Union
Uzbekistan 289

Van Creveld, M. 39, 215, 433
Venezuela 78
victimization *see* victims
victims 115, 257, 422, 425–6, 436, 445–7
Vietnam 91–4, 121, 158, 186, 203, 446; Tet
Offensive 146; Viet Cong 184; Vietnam War
215, 229, 349, 435
violence 1–3, 5, 6–7, 41, 44–5, 57, 59, 63–71, 74, 82,
88, 91, 93, 99–102, 121–2, 124, 126, 132–3,
135–6, 140, 156–7, 163, 171, 180, 190–8,
205, 208, 212, 214–16, 219, 247, 252,
254–5, 257, 262, 264–5, 274, 277, 284–5,
287–92, 326–7, 379, 394–5, 421–9, 432–9,
442–8; armed 2; autonomous 195; criminal
41, 50, 284, 421–9; cultural 444; lethal
88, 422, 428; military 221; mimetic 326;
organised 44, 64, 216, 218, 220, 326, 423,
433; political 14, 47, 63–4, 66, 68–71, 92,
136, 178, 198n2, 439; sexual 44, 49, 88, 447
violence ecologies 64, 70
violence ecology *see* Violence ecologies
violent networks *see* networks
Virilio, P. 24
virtual cultural awareness training 313
virtual reality 25, 220, 308, 310, 312
Visions of Warfare 2036 76
volunteer 120–1, 204–5, 246; volunteering 96n10;
volunteerism 145
Von Neuman, J. 297
vulnerability 3, 17, 21, 25, 49, 93, 100, 102–3, 125,
131, 133, 135, 139, 158, 170, 193, 195, 204,
232, 239, 275–7, 280–1, 285, 302, 315, 349,
358, 368–9, 371–2, 374, 402, 414, 418, 428,
439n3

Wagner Group 120, 123, 186, 208, 390–1, 393–4
Walker, R. G. 164
Walt, S. 23, 213, 238
Waltz, K. 380, 386
Walzer, M. 251, 255–6, 258
Wanted 79
war: asymmetric 191, 437; barbarization of 448;
civilized 390, 434, 442; conventional 76,
88, 143, 214, 240, 254–5, 258–9, 443, 448;
on drugs 435–6; of the flea 443; forever
197, 205, 326; laws of 116, 195, 304, 331;
liberal democratic 196; liberation 442;
major 52, 202–3, 326; nature of 2–4, 38–9,
235; posthuman 325; postindustrial 325;
post-modern 214, 216, 325, 435; riskless
191; risk-transfer 191; savage 442–9;
small 144, 442–3, 447; technophilic 215;
technoscientific 215; on terror 33, 80, 169,
191, 194, 202–3, 217, 227, 229–31, 234,
390, 393–5; total 64, 228, 253; unnecessary
23; urban 434; vicarious 201–3, 206–7, 209
War in the age of intelligent machines 68
War in the Gulf (1990–91) 215
warfare: asymmetric 5, 76, 132, 142–3, 274, 435;
chaoplexic 1, 227, 229, 231, 233–4, 236;
compound 1, 156; conventional 167, 197,
277, 412; decision-centric 227, 232–3;
hybrid 105, 155–60, 163, 172, 218–19,
278–9, 315, 319, 327, 333; irregular 166,
169–74, 284, 291–2, 327; liminal 3, 29;
mosaic 1, 219, 221, 227, 232, 234; net-
centric (*see* network-centric); network-
centric 2, 53–4, 60, 78, 216, 227, 229, 232,
315; post-heroic 191, 215, 267; post-modern
1, 212–15, 218–19, 221; remote 6, 124, 126,
190–8, 393–4; riskless 216–17, 220; space
172, 174, 366; surrogate 1, 58, 191, 202;
three-block 1, 325; unconventional 166–7,
169, 174, 209, 274; unrestricted 1, 29, 156,
169; urban 104, 106, 312; vicarious 1, 191,
208; western 190, 202
wargaming 15, 344, 402
War in Ukraine *see* Russo-Ukrainian war
warlords 99, 216
warrior ethos 193, 198n5
War Stories From the Future 76
war studies 5, 21–2, 28–9, 179, 213
Washington 386
weaponisation 3, 29, 48, 214, 219, 321
weapons 4, 31, 39, 45, 47, 49, 54, 79, 82, 96n11,
113, 122, 125, 127, 133, 136, 146, 168–9,
179, 186, 191, 214–15, 217, 220–1, 230,
246, 251, 264, 289, 319, 334, 338n2, 348,
366–7, 369, 373, 437–9; anti-ballistic
367; anti-satellite 366, 370–2, 374,
418; atomic (*see* nuclear); autonomous

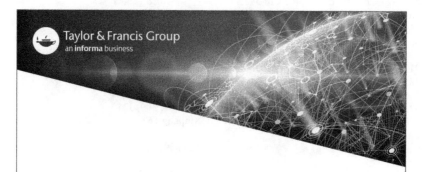